Groupware
**Collaborative Strategies for
Corporate LANs and Intranets**

Groupware
Collaborative Strategies for
Corporate LANs and Intranets

David Coleman

To join a Prentice Hall PTR Internet mailing list, point to:
http://www.prenhall.com/mail_lists

Prentice Hall PTR
Upper Saddle River, NJ 07458
http://www.prenhall.com

Library of Congress Cataloging-in-Publication Data
Groupware: collaborative strategies for corporate LANs and intranets
  / David Coleman, editor.
       p.   cm.
     Includes bibliographical references and index.
     ISBN 0-13-727728-8
     1. Groupware (Computer software)   2. Intranets (Computer networks)
   I. Coleman, David, 1954-
   HD66.2.G763   1997
   651.7'9--dc21   97-6066
                                                          CIP

Editorial/production supervision: *Craig Little*
Cover design: *Bruce Kenselaar*
Acquisitions editor: *Mary Franz*
Editorial assistant: *Noreen Regina*
Manufacturing manager: *Alexis R. Heydt*
Marketing Manager: *Dan Rush*
Page layout/formatting: *Bear Mountain Type*

© 1997 by Prentice Hall PTR
Prentice-Hall, Inc.
A Simon & Schuster Company
Upper Saddle River, NJ 07458

The publisher offers discounts on this book when ordered in bulk quantities. For more information, contact Corporate Sales Department, Phone: 800-382-3419   FAX: 201-236-7141 E-mail: corpsales@prenhall.com or write:

> Corporate Sales Department
> Prentice Hall PTR
> One Lake Street
> Upper Saddle River, NJ 07458

Prentice Hall books are widely used by corporations and government agencies for training, marketing, and resale.

Trademarks
A number of entered words in which we have reason to believe trademark, service mark, or other proprietary rights may exist have been designated as such by initial capitalization. However, no attempt has been made to designate as trademarks or service marks all personal computer words or terms in which proprietary rights might exist. The inclusion, exclusion, or definition of a word or term in not intended to affect, or to express any judgment on, the validity or legal status of any proprietary right that may be claimed in that word or term.
All product names mentioned herein are the trademarks of their respective owners.

Printed in the United States of America

10 9 8 7 6 5 4 3 2 1

ISBN: 0-13-727728-8

Prentice-Hall International (UK) Limited, *London*
Prentice-Hall of Australia Pty. Limited, *Sydney*
Prentice-Hall Canada Inc., *Toronto*
Prentice-Hall Hispanoamericana, S.A., *Mexico*
Prentice-Hall of India Private Limited, *New Delhi*
Prentice-Hall of Japan, Inc., *Tokyo*
Simon & Schuster Asia Pte. Ltd., *Singapore*
Editora Prentice-Hall do Brasil, Ltda., *Rio de Janeiro*

Table of Contents

6. Workflow: Applying Automation to Group Processes

7A. Electronic Meetings as Today's Presentations *David Coleman* 183

17. Groupware & Reengineering: The Human Side of Change

18. Applying Groupware to the Architectural Design and Construction Industry: PRC's Genesis Strategy *Frank A. Lancione*

19. Groupware in Hardware and Software Development Environments

Foreword

by Eric Hahn

Like most human endeavors, the pursuit of technological advancement requires a passion, a faith, an unwavering belief that the unanticipated is not unachievable, that the unlikely is not unfeasible, that the unproved is not unattainable. Throughout the sibling fields of science and engineering, those laboring in the study of computer supported cooperative work, more popularly known as "groupware," have drawn considerably upon their reserves of faith, passion, and technical acumen in their quest for something at once simple and hugely complex: technology that helps people work together in new and productive ways.

Like moths to the light, the quest for groupware products has attracted a wealth of intellectuals, researchers from academia, engineers from industry, students of organizational behavior, and business people the world over. For the better part of three decades, these individuals and the organizations that sponsor their work have invested mightily in the pursuit of groupware theory, practice, and infrastructure. Entire careers and entire companies have been dedicated to one unwavering belief—that the computer can make new modes of cooperation between humans more realizable and existing modes more efficient.

One can hardly think of a more noble goal than this. What manner of worldly ills would be expunged by limitless collaboration and cooperation? Crossing the vastness of space to land on the moon, spanning land and sea to terra firma continents, decoding the complexities of nature to conquer the ravages of disease, and revealing the inner secrets of matter and energy and their role in the essence of existence itself—the most durable of our species' achievements are in largest measure due to the cooperative efforts of individuals, organizations, and nations. Surely, the application of computer technology towards these endeavors must rank among the most worthwhile campaigns imaginable. The benefits of increased collaboration and cooperation scream out to each of us as members of the human collective.

But closer scrutiny of collaborative science yields a complex and murky landscape. In Chapter 17, *Groupware & Reengineering: The Human Side of Change*, critical behavioral issues are addressed. On the path toward great commercial or national achievement, what does the role of individuality play? What is the social value of information itself and how does it flow throughout an orga-

nization of workers? In the discharge of individual duty, do the needs of the many
outweigh the needs of the few, or of the one? What truth is there in the oft-quoted
adage "knowledge is power"?

The commercial pursuit of groupware products has presided over its reasonable share of perplexing challenges, as well. How can cost and benefit be
quantified for groupware products? What challenges of commercial enterprise
are benefited by groupware? How are technological "innovations" assimilated by
the organization without disruption? What technologies will be accepted most
readily by market influencers and by customers? *Groupware—The Changing
Environment* (Chapter 1) gives an excellent taxonomy of groupware technologies
that help to explain the categories that have become most popular.

More fundamentally, does groupware exist? An industry that has in turn
promised incalculably profound benefits from "artificial intelligence," "mas-
sively-parallel processing," or "pen-based computing," must at least occasionally
audit new claims of productivity gains when extolling the merits of the technology of the latest and greatest arrival. After all, the much ballyhooed "year of the
LAN" continued for nearly a decade. Are phenomenal gains in groupware-
induced collaboration visible today, just around the corner, or merely a *folie a
deux*—a tragic conspiracy between well-meaning technologists and corporate
"early adopters" in search of any conceivable competitive advantage?

The quest for quantifiable groupware success is haunted by a dark secret, a
quiet whisper, a notion against which customers and vendors alike amass
mighty weapons of rationalization and denial. That notion is this: the pursuit of
commercially successful groupware has consumed more wealth than it has generated. While many of the endeavors the reader will encounter herein have generated phenomenal industry notoriety and some considerable revenues, they
have done so on the backs of immense capital and intellectual investment.

It is therefore against a canvas of seemingly plentiful obstacles and discour-
aging historical economic performance that the intrepid groupware evangelist
must paint his dream, putting bright strokes of technical and financial optimism
to a darker backdrop of doubt and uncertainty.

But throughout this collage of approaches, behaviors, markets, and technologies lies a common calling. A tether back, always back, to the fundamental ideal
that drives this pursuit; that surely the application of computer technology
towards the betterment of human cooperation and collaboration must rank
among the most worthwhile campaigns imaginable, whether for the realization
of commercial or social goals. In the end, it cannot be a question of whether
groupware exists. To the contrary: Increased communication and collaboration is
one of the greatest harvests Man can reap from the application of this wondrous
device—the computer. The pivotal question is how to free this collaborative diamond from the rough myriad of complexity. The reader will likely find Chapters
18 and 19 exciting as they detail how specific organizations have reaped these
benefits through successful deployment of groupware.

There are as many views on this topic as there are independent groupware
thinkers. Much of the art's best reasoning awaits the reader in these pages. Vendors such as Lotus, Novell, TeamWare, and Oracle present compelling, yet differ-

ent, perspectives on their unique approaches to designing and delivering groupware products. Of late, astounding progress has been made in the uses of global messaging, information sharing, and collaborative technologies born of the Internet and Intranet phenomena—*Collaborating on the Internet and Intranets* (Chapter 2) provides an excellent introduction to the subject and these approaches show tremendous promise. Electronic mail (outlined in Chapter 4) and electronic group discussion tools, possibly the most mature forms of groupware, are in use now by nearly 100 million people. Surely, this serves as testament to the fact that viable groupware technology can prosper and prosper on a planetary, let alone corporate, scale. There are ever-increasing signs of a "bull market" for groupware offerings. Maybe the year of groupware will be sooner in coming than the year of the LAN. Many would say it is upon us now.

But we cannot linger here on the comfortable laurels of the current state-of-the-art. The opportunities are too great, the social and commercial rewards too lucrative to settle for the present. As a federation of researchers, vendors, and end-users, we must all rededicate ourselves to the search for better and better groupware tools. Imagine the wonder of it: businesses that communicate more effectively than ever thought possible, organizations that collaborate to achieve goals beyond the means of each individually. Imagine a world whose differences and conflicts are melted away, dissolved into a great sea of shared hopes and dreams, empowered by access to information that knows not the trivial boundaries of state or race. Imagine the future, the bright future made possible by the technologies of collaborative computing.

Eric Hahn
Senior Vice President
Enterprise Technologies
Netscape Communications Corporation

Preface

Groupware: Technology and Applications was released only 15 months ago. That book covered the groupware industry, before Lotus was bought by IBM, before Collabra was bought by Netscape and before the word *intranet* was part of the common vernacular. In fact, the book was almost obsolete as soon as it was released. In part, that is characteristic of paper publishing, however, it is also due to the increasingly frantic pace of technologic change in our world. In order to release information in a more timely manner, I often publish the results of my work as a Hot Tip of the Month on my firm's web page at www.collaborate.com. Even so, traditional book publishing gives us the opportunity to collect the thoughts of industry leaders and quantify them in a form that is not dependent on being connected to a computer. Therefore, when Prentice Hall suggested an update to *Groupware: Technology and Applications,* the opportunity to report on the changes in collaborative products and technologies was not to be missed.

There are two other reasons why a new edition is valuable at this time. First, the increased velocity of change presents new challenges to organizations, and there are no established procedures for dealing with these changes. Change comes so fast and so often that when technology is introduced and updated, people hardly have a chance to get used to one new way of working before they are confronted with another new way to work. One of the side effects of working in this dynamic environment is that people have increased their resistance to these changes, effectively undermining the project. Almost every chapter in this book addresses the issue of change management in one form or another. Our goal was to provide business readers with the benefit of other's experiences, in a risk-free manner.

The second reason for a new book is the new reality of doing business on the Internet and intranets. When the first book was written, the Internet was just emerging as being a curiosity for hackers and geeks. Some companies had posted web pages as marketing tools, but most of those companies were hi-tech organizations. The Internet had still not hit the mainstream. Today, having Web presence is essential to doing business and almost all major corporations have well developed web sites. Additionally, intranets have become the infrastructure of choice for intra-enterprise collaboration. Groupware, which was initially LAN-based, has rapidly moved its functionality onto these IP networks. The result is that technologies that were counter-intuitive, expensive, and difficult to learn, administer, and maintain, have now become more visual, easier to use and very inexpensive. Consequently, groupware on the Internet and intranets has become one of the hottest trends in computing today.

The first section of this book provides an introduction to groupware and some of the major issues businesses face when adopting collaborative technologies, either on a LAN or Web-based infrastructure. Additionally, a full chapter is devoted to the results of research performed by Collaborative Strategies. In this study, we spoke with CIOs and other MIS executives about how they are currently using the Internet and intranets to support electronic collaboration, and how they want to in the future.

The second section focuses on specific collaborative technologies, such as e-mail, workflow, group calendaring and scheduling, electronic meeting systems, and video conferencing. These chapters provide significant detail about how the products were developed, what business issues they address, and where they are going in the future.

The third section contains chapters contributed by major groupware vendors who discuss their design philosophy, current product offerings, and their plans for the future. Vendors discuss both their web-based functionality as well as their tried and true LAN-based functionality.

The fourth section focuses on user case studies and user stories. Many of these case studies are about Notes, because Notes is the most mature collaborative product in the market. However, the purpose of this section is to show how many different collaborative technologies are used. Also, many of the ideas about the organizational aspects of groupware which I introduce in the opening chapter are explored more fully in these case studies.

Finally, the fifth section provides a comprehensive reference source for information on groupware, collaboration, organizational development, management consulting, intellectual property, re-engineering, BPR, workflow and many other things.

The primary goal of this book is to provide timely information on all aspects of electronic collaboration. The trend toward distributed workforces, project teams, and collaborative strategies will increase well into the next century. We find collaboration is different in each culture, each corporate culture, and with each technology. This makes for a very interesting mix, an interesting field of study, and a formidable challenge to the vendors in this area.

Questions, comments and feedback on this volume are welcome, via e-mail, at davidc@collaborate.com

Acknowledgments

Preparing a manuscript of this magnitude requires the effort of many people. In this case, 29 authors, representing almost as many organizations, contributed their time, knowledge, and expertise to the body of knowledge for emerging technologies. In many cases, they gave their non-business time and resources as well as their expertise and creativity. Their contributions cannot be applauded enough and I extend my personal thanks to each one.

But there were many others who contributed to this volume. Abby Kutner, my associate, was tireless in orchestrating the endless logistics of preparing the manuscript and working with contributors. She called and cajoled authors, reviewed drafts, critiqued content, played confessor, and dealt with egos and publisher's deadlines—all with great diplomacy and tenacity.

Additional thanks go to Mary Franz, my editor at Prentice Hall, who suggested the project and her assistant, Noreen Regina, who worked diligently with Abby. Rebecca Ballard handled the chaos of our office so that Abby and I could work on this volume. My partners, Ellen Hongo and Gordon Stone, allowed me the time to work on the book and supported the effort by contributing the chapter on knowledge management. And thank you Deb Furey for shouldering the work load in my absence.

We are privileged to have contributions from some of the best people in their respective fields. From academics to vendors, from students preparing theses to veteran freelance writers, from consultants to analysts—you all put a tremendous amount of work into your contributions. This volume would not exist without your mighty contributions.

Saving the best for last, I would like to thank my wife Nancy, who has put up with a workaholic husband for all these years. Her quest for knowledge, insight, and profound love of books provided great impetus for me to create this second volume.

I thank you all for your contributions, your conversations, and mostly your willingness to collaborate on this large project.

David Coleman
October 15, 1996

Groupware—The Changing Environment

David Coleman
Collaborative Strategies™

AN INTRODUCTION TO GROUPWARE

Groupware is an umbrella term describing the electronic technologies that support person-to-person collaboration. Groupware includes e-mail, electronic meeting systems (EMS), and desktop video conferencing (DVC) as well as systems for workflow and business process re-engineering (BPR). Technologies that support collaboration are in greater demand today than ever before, and, in recognition of that fact, vendors are integrating collaboration technologies into their products. Distributed workforces, information overload, and getting products to market as quickly as possible are just a few of the motivations pushing collaboration technology development. In this chapter, we will discuss many of the issues fundamental to groupware strategy and success.

1.1 WHAT DOES GROUPWARE REALLY DO?

First and foremost, groupware supports the efforts of teams and other paradigms that require people to work together, even though they may not actually be together, in either time or space. Groupware maximizes human interaction while minimizing technology interference. The following graphic (Fig. 1.1) provides a view from both the technology and human interaction perspectives.

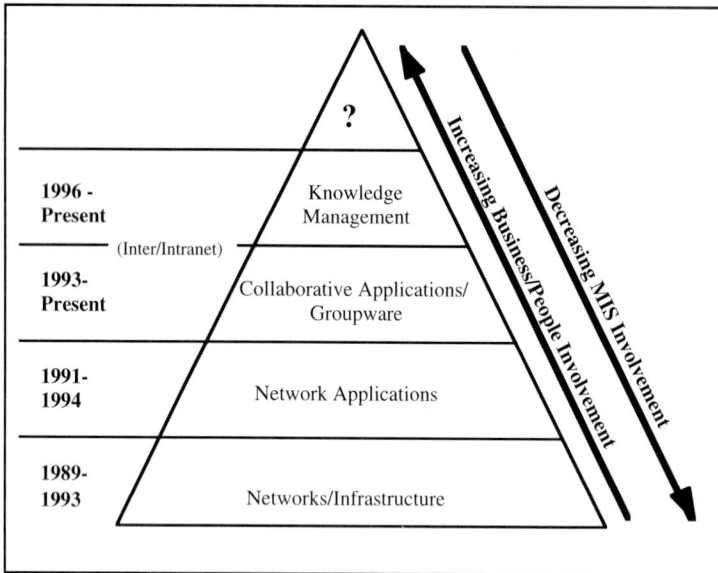

Fig. 1.1 Increasing Levels of Human Involvement

The organization of this chapter follows this diagram. It starts with the technology issues (networks and infrastructure) and builds to the discussion of collaborative products and taxonomy, which classifies this rapidly expanding industry. We then move to the application of these products, supported with case studies, and finally discuss how groupware can support organizations in the future through de-engineering and/or knowledge management. This chapter is intended to provide readers with a broad base of information regarding groupware technologies and strategies.

1.2 DEFINITIONS OF GROUPWARE

Groupware is a relatively new term, first coined in 1978. The following definitions, the most commonly used, are presented by industry leaders:

☞ *Intentional group processes plus software to support them.* Peter and Trudy Johnson-Lenz, 1978

☞ *A co-evolving human-tool system.* Doug Englebart, 1988

☞ *Computer-mediated collaboration that increases the productivity or functionality of person-to-person processes.* David Coleman, 1992

1.2.1 Groupware Taxonomy

The twelve functional categories listed below form a logical taxonomy, which includes a separate category for groupware services, a new category for groupware applications, and a special category for the emerging Internet-based collaborative applications and products.

☞ Electronic Mail and Messaging

☞ Group Calendaring and Scheduling

☞ Electronic Meeting Systems

☞ Desktop Video and Real-time Data Conferencing (Synchronous)

☞ Non Real-time Data Conferencing (Asynchronous)

☞ Workflow

☞ Group Document Handling

☞ Workgroup Utilities and Development Tools

☞ Groupware Frameworks

☞ Groupware Services

☞ Groupware Applications

☞ Collaborative—Internet-based Applications and Products

Following is a partial list of products associated with each category and a sampling of outstanding issues. These issues direct attention to some of the technical, organizational, and cultural challenges associated with each category and often present questions one might ask if considering the use of this product category in a specific organization. It is important to realize that many products fit into more than one category. For example, Lotus Notes fits into many categories because of its broad range of functions.

1.2.1.1 Electronic Mail and Messaging:
Includes messaging infrastructures and e-mail systems

Sample Products:

cc:mail—Lotus	Eudora—Qualcomm
Microsoft Mail/Exchange	QuickMail—CE Software
Banyan Intelligent Mail—Banyan	OracleMail—Oracle

Issues:
➤ Standards, XAPI, MAPI, X.400, X.500 (directory services)
➤ How to integrate multiple mail systems in one enterprise
➤ Security, and who owns my e-mail?
➤ Etiquette and the efficient use of e-mail
➤ Filters, agents and the ability to deal with 100s of messages a day

1.2.1.2 Group Calendaring and Scheduling
Products for calendar, meeting, and resource coordination

Sample Products:

Lotus Organizer—IBM/Lotus	OnTime—FTP Software
Synchronize—CrossWind Technology	Meeting Maker—On Technologies
Microsoft Schedule +	Network Scheduler—CE Software
Pencil Me In—Sarrus Software	CaLANdar—Microsystems Software

Issues:
➤ Proliferation of meetings because they are now easier to schedule.
➤ Privacy for personal calendars (big brother is watching!).
➤ Having enough users in the company to make it worthwhile.
➤ Scheduling across multiple time zones.

1.2.1.3 Electronic Meeting Systems (EMS)
Real-time conferencing systems (local and remote) as well as collaborative presentation systems

Sample Products:

Group Systems—Ventana	Meeting Works 2—Enterprise Solutions
Council Services—CoVision	Option Finder—Option Technologies
Facilitate.com—McCall Szerdy Assoc.	TeamTalk—Trax SoftWorks

Issues:
➤ Integration with calendaring/scheduling systems
➤ Post-meeting follow through; action items, goals, commitments
➤ Affordability of desktop videoconferencing
➤ Availability of multi-point conferencing
➤ Lack of standards is limiting the application of this technology
➤ Acceptance within the corporate culture

1.2.1.4 Desktop and Real-Time Data Conferencing:
The focus is on real-time, rather than BBS or Notes. All products in this category store documents and / or allow others to see and work on the same document simultaneously, whether on each others' screens or on a shared whiteboard.

Sample Products:

ShowMe—Sun Solutions	RoundTable—ForeFront Group
Aspects—Group Logic, Inc.	Being There—Intelligence at Large
NetMeeting—Microsoft	PictureTalk—Picture Talk
CoolTalk—Netscape	FarSight—Databeam

Issues:
- Control of the cursor on the screen?
- Number of people who can conference efficiently?
- Role of the facilitator. Is a facilitator needed?
- Interaction/baud rates, equipment compatibility
- Internet and intranet availability
- Post-meeting follow through; action items, goals, commitments

1.2.1.5 Non-Real Time Conferencing

Synchronous conferencing is most like a bulletin board, where you carry on a conversation over time, leave a message for someone and they answer it, and you can respond back to them later. These messages can be public (as in a BBS) or private (as in a Notes discussion database).

Sample Products:

TeamTalk—Trax SoftWorks	WebBoard—O'Reilly
Pacer Forum—NetManage	WebShare—RadNet
Lotus Notes—IBM/Lotus	FirstClass—SoftArc Inc.
InterOffice—Oracle	News Server—Netscape

Issues:
- Number of people who can conference efficiently?
- Role of the facilitator. Is a facilitator needed?
- Maximizing the benefits of conferences/discussion databases; ROI
- Replication, network topologies, scalability
- Transaction-based vs. store and forward databases
- Support for worldwide locations
- Integration with legacy systems
- Integrating with electronic calendaring and scheduling systems
- Post-meeting follow through; action items, goals, commitments

1.2.1.6 Group Document Handling:

Group editing, shared screen editing work, group document/image manage-ment, and document databases

Sample Products:

Face-to-Face—Crosswise	Documentum—Documentum, Inc.
MarkUp—Mainstay Software	OnGo Document Management— Uniplex

Issues:
- Page markup standards such as SGML, HTML, and CALs?
- Support for word processors and page layout programs
- Version control and document security
- Integration with enterprise document/image databases or repositories
- Where does group document management stop and multimedia begin?
- Data integrity and integration with other documents and repositories
- Compression issues

1.2.1.7 Workflow

Workflow process diagramming and analysis tools, workflow enactment engines, electronic forms routing products

Sample Products:

Workflow Analyst—Action Technology	JetForm—JetForm Corp.
Staffware for Windows— Staffware	Formflow—Symantec
Open Workflow—Wang	Flowmark—IBM
Metro—Action Technologies	Workflow BPR—Holosofx

Issues:
- Workflow coalition standards
- Passing documents and information between products
- Automating poor processes
- Integration with EDI and other customer services

1.2.1.8 Workgroup Utilities and Groupware Development Tools:

Utilities to support, group working, remote access to someone else's computer, and specific tools for workgroup applications development.

Sample Products:

Windows for Workgroups— Microsoft	CoEX—Twin Sun
Lotus Notes—Lotus	Replication Reporter—Ernst & Young
InterOffice—Oracle	ReplicAction—Cassal

Issues:
- ➤ What functionality should be part of the OS and what functionality should be part of the application?
- ➤ What are the decision-making issues when deciding whether to develop for the OS, GUI, or network?
- ➤ How to insure issuer compatibility; standards; object-oriented (reusable) code; licensing (network, multimedia, intellectual property rights).

1.2.1.9 Groupware Services:
Services to support collaboration.

Sample:

Planning and Implementation	Business Process Re-Engineering
Application Development	Knowledge Management
Training and Maintenance	Electronic Meeting Facilitation
Change Management	Consulting

Issues:
- ➤ Expertise is a most valuable commodity in the groupware market. It is highly unusual to find all the necessary expertise in-house. Additionally, no single vendor offers a complete groupware solution and re-engineering often requires multiple products and service vendors in order to collaborate. How do you identify and pull together the resources best suited to your organization?
- ➤ How are meetings facilitated successfully?
- ➤ What tools are best suited for re-engineering?
- ➤ How do users identify the problems with the greatest potential for turnaround from groupware?
- ➤ How are consultants best used? What do they know that people in your organization don't?
- ➤ It is imperative that top management and all stakeholders support any process change. How do you enlist and sustain their support.
- ➤ How to evaluate the return on investment of your groupware?

1.2.1.10 Groupware Frameworks

This meta-category focuses on products that help integrate "islands of collaboration" to realize seamless integration across computer platforms, operating systems, e-mail systems, and network architectures.

Sample Products:

GroupWise—Novell	Lotus Notes—Lotus/IBM
TeamOffice—ICL/Fujitsu	OpenDoc—Apple/IBM
GoldMetal Workgroup—Decathlon	OpenMind—Attachmate

Issues:
- Integrating the desktop while supporting collaborative efforts
- Security
- Can frameworks-products help collaboration outside of the organization?
- Will establishing groupware standards make frameworks less attractive?

1.2.1.11 Groupware Applications

Vertical applications that use collaborative technologies to either enhance processes or support collaboration in a specific work environment.

Sample Products:

BAI-5000 Distribution Management System—Business Automation	HelpDesk—Trellis
Patient Tracking System—Management Directions	ProTEAM—Scopus
CustomerFirst—Repository Technologies	CenterPoint—Bank of Montreal

Issues:
- Customizing applications; infrastructure and cost issues
- Vertical market competition
- Does application solve specific collaborative business need?
- Integration with existing legacy systems

1.2.1.12 Collaborative Internet-Based Applications:

Many collaborative functions are moving to the WWW and use the Internet as the input and output while still using traditional groupware on the LAN.

Sample Products:

InterNotes Publisher—IBM/Lotus   PCS 50—PictureTel

RoundTable—The ForeFront Group   Metro—Action Technologies

SamePage—WebFlow

Issues:
- Application customization for seamless collaboration on the WWW
- Costs of publishing to/from the Web
- Data/information storage
- Balance between security and collaboration
- Limitations of traditional groupware relative to Web applications
- Limitations of Web applications relative to traditional groupware
- Integration with existing legacy systems

Although a taxonomy is useful for classification, do not get trapped into believing your product or the product you have selected will fit neatly into one category. The Web has changed everything for collaboration; vendors of traditional groupware are moving their products onto the Web and adding functionality that lets them support multiple categories.

1.3 THE CHALLENGES OF GROUPWARE

Groupware supports this new way to work by providing tools to solve "collaboration oriented" problems. However, groupware functions in a sauce-technical environment, so focusing exclusively on technical issues is a sure way to a very expensive failure. The most important lesson to learn when working with groupware is that while the technologies and infrastructure are new and interesting, they are only one part of the picture. Focusing on the people issues, the "sauce" part of the system, dramatically increases the potential for success. Remember, people systems are much more complex than technical systems.

When addressing technical challenges, a technical solution must be found. However, even if technology solves the problem, works well, and is rolled out efficiently, support from the corporate culture is essential to the implementation's success. Further, even if the culture supports the groupware success, but there is no economic justification for a groupware solution, the implementation will fail. Finally, even if technology, culture, and economics combine to support groupware, the success of a project can be destroyed by politics.

Taking these issues into consideration, we have developed the following formula for success with groupware.

Groupware Success = Technology + Culture + Economics + Politics

The further to the right a factor is in this equation, the greater its potential impact on the success of the project. It is important to address each of these factors in any groupware implementation.

1.3.1 Take the Groupware Challenge

Using these criteria, we have developed the following table to objectively calculate your organization's potential for success with groupware. For example, if your organization has a full client-server architecture and all the enabling technologies for groupware, then give yourself a 10 on a scale of 1–10. Organizations with very limited infrastructure or only a few computers would get a much lower score, perhaps a 1 or 2. In the following example (Fig. 1.2), XYZ Company, their technology usage is fairly mature, so their technology score is 8.

XYZ Company's Potential Success with Groupware				
Technology	**Culture**	**Economics**	**Politics**	
Score = 8	Score = 2	Score = 5	Score = 3	
Weight = 1	Weight = 2	Weight = 3	Weight = 4	
Subtotal = 8	Subtotal = 4	Subtotal = 15	Subtotal = 12	**Total** = 39

Fig. 1.2 Sample Company's Potential for Success with Groupware

In the example above, XYZ Company is a manufacturing organization of the old school.

Culture: XYZ uses technology for solutions and the people are only there to implement the technologies. Thus, their culture does not focus on solutions for human issues and XYZ Company gets a 2 for Culture.

Economics: XYZ is the dominant player in their market niche, therefore, there is no real economic need to use groupware. It's the *if it ain't broke, don't fix it* school of thought. But executives are aware that groupware has enabled a competitive advantage at some of their competitors, so XYZ gets an Economics score of 5.

Politics: XYZ is a snake pit filled with backstabbing, power-hungry executives, any of whom might shoot down a groupware project on a whim. XYZ gets a Politics score of 3.

Scores below 60 are poor; scores between 61–80 are fair; scores above 80 are good and indicate a greater likelihood of groupware success.

XYZ Company ends up with an overall weighted score of 39 points out of a potential 100; not very good. Groupware will not succeed in this organization unless some drastic changes are made. Insofar as change is constant, changes will certainly occur. The question for XYZ is, if the changes that do occur are the ones that support groupware. Again, returning to the table above, XYZ is quickly able to identify the most problematic areas in order to address the right issues.

Another way to look at this score is as a snapshot in time. At this time, XYZ has a score of 39 and is not ready for groupware. But changes in their market niche could jeopardize their position as market leader, causing their Economics score to zoom to 10. This kind of market shift would impact the other criteria as well, perhaps bringing Politics to an 8 and Culture to a 6. Now, XYZ's total point count is 82, a much better score reflecting an environment where groupware has an excellent chance for success.

Now use Fig. 1.3 below to compute your company's potential for success with groupware.

Your Company's Potential Success with Groupware				
Technology	**Culture**	**Economics**	**Politics**	
Score =	Score =	Score =	Score =	
Weight = 1	Weight = 2	Weight = 3	Weight = 4	
Subtotal =	Subtotal =	Subtotal =	Subtotal =	**Total =**

Fig. 1.3 Your Company's Potential Success with Groupware

Let's take a look at a company that did it right. The Oticon A/S case study (see page 24 for a detailed account of Oticon's experience), which Tom Peters also talks about in his books, shows how a company can implement large scale changes successfully. I filled out the chart for Oticon, based on company conditions in 1992, to see how ready they were for groupware and how to rate their chance of success.

Given the fact that Oticon was faced with a change-or-die situation, they get a 9 for economic incentive. Because this was a political decision and the Oticon CEO was able to convince his executive committee to get behind him, I gave the political factor a 10. This gives Oticon a score of 67 between politics and economics alone, which means that on our scale, they already have a fair chance of success with groupware. Oticon's culture, just like most others, is resistive to change. However, they are getting a good strong push from management because of the urgency of their situation. Therefore, I gave them a 6 for culture. Because they moved to a new building, which was built to support this technology, and have implemented a new computing and network architecture to support their new processes, I gave them a 9 for technology. The result, a score of 88, reflects an organization with a very good chance of success with groupware (see Fig. 1.4).

Oticon's Potential Success with Groupware				
Technology	**Culture**	**Economics**	**Politics**	
Weight = 1	Weight = 2	Weight = 3	Weight = 4	
Score = 9	Score = 6	Score = 9	Score = 10	
Subtotal = 9	Subtotal =12	Subtotal = 27	Subtotal = 40	**Total = 88**

Fig. 1.4 Oticon's Potential for Success with Groupware

A score of 88 is a very high score. Working with the people in my classes, we have found scores in the 90s but rarely. My own organization, Collaborative Strategies, got a score of 82, 6 points below Oticon! I guess we did not have the same *do or die* situation.

1.3.2 Twenty Rules for Success with Groupware

The following list of 20 commonsense rules to ensure success in deploying groupware in your organization is based on the author's experience with groupware:

1. Find a groupware champion! The higher in hierarchy, the better. Get management's hands on the keyboard. By getting top management involved, they see the benefits, and you get a lot more support!
2. Groupware changes the corporate culture. Plan for it!
3. Pick a pilot project rather than trying to roll groupware out to the whole organization.
4. Pick a bounded project with a group that is supportive of both technology and innovation.
5. Pick a project with visibility and financial impact.
6. Realize that training, maintenance, and support will be the majority of the cost, rather than the initial cost of the software.
7. Measure productivity factors before and after the project has started. This is a good way to cost-justify groupware!
8. Pick groupware software based on a specific business problem that needs to be solved and has not been solved successfully using traditional methods. Corollary: Don't pick the groupware first and then find a problem.
9. Make sure you have adequate planning, support, training, and maintenance for your project.
10. No single groupware product can do it all. Don't expect it to!
11. Don't expect software vendors to offer you all the services you need for groupware. You may need to use internal people or consultants to ensure your project's success.
12. Groupware is not a quick fix! As part of a re-engineering effort, it may take 2–4 years to see the results.
13. Listen to the people involved in the pilot project. They are experts on what needs to be done and can often suggest ways to better the process.
14. Don't be afraid to make changes! A pilot project is an experiment. Learn as you go.
15. Make sure the software you pick fits with existing systems. Try to amortize your LAN investment by connecting to your mainframe or other legacy systems.
16. You can't change people overnight. Be prepared for resistance!
17. People take time to change. Organizations take even longer!
18. It takes courage to change a corporate culture! Applaud those who are willing to change.

19. Be careful about paving the cow path. There is no point in automating a very inefficient process. There are no big productivity wins here!

20. Groupware can be very political. Make sure it is a big win!

1.4 FOUR TRENDS FOR COLLABORATION

The trend toward collaboration is a strong one, fueled from two sides, technology and culture. Technology includes the increased proliferation of networks and startling growth of the Internet. Network growth has been explosive, 30 percent on average, for the last eight years. This trend will probably continue over the next decade, as less than 60 percent of the computers in the U.S. are networked, only 45 percent of the computers in Europe are networked, and less than 20 percent of Japan's computers are on a network (these figures are approximate and derived from a conversation with Karl Wong of Dataquest, San Jose, CA). Network growth is fueled by economic and organizational pressures such as increased global competition and a worldwide recession, which was felt first in the U.S., Europe, and most recently, Asia.

Cultural changes are the second driver for collaboration. As our world becomes more like a global village, we have greater involvement in other cultures. Whereas, just a few years ago, we traveled thousands of miles, taking days out of our regular routines to meet with people in other countries, today, desktop video and data conferencing provides an immediate, inexpensive, and minimally disruptive method to conduct the same meeting. This interaction with other cultures drives changes in our own organizations. In addition, cross-cultural issues implementing any new technology or program force changes in the organization, many of which are characterized by teams and other collaborative paradigms.

The third driver for collaboration is the "net." Even though the Internet and WWW are not fully interactive or collaborative, vendors are incorporating collaborative functionality into new versions of Web-based products. The acquisition of Collabra by Netscape is a good example. Netscape bought Collabra in order to integrate CollabraShare's collaborative functionality into its product line. Additionally, HTML 3.0 can now support forms, and companies like JetForm are developing products to route these forms in both simple and complex workflows. Research performed by Collaborative Strategies showed that most collaborative functions were migrating onto intranets (the network inside a firewall) and would not move out to support inter-organizational collaboration until the 1998 timeframe.

Other examples that highlight the movement toward collaborative functions on the Internet include Lotus' InterNotes Publisher 4.0, which allows bi-directional information flows between the Web and Notes. Also, InterNotes now includes a browser. There are five functional differences between traditional groupware and WWW collaboration, which will be discussed later in this chapter.

The fourth driver for collaboration is our ongoing effort to realize greater efficiency. Collaborative technologies support our efforts to create new relationships and new ways to work. These efficiencies challenge the old hierarchical organizational structures, which are often not flexible enough to meet today's demands; especially the increasing velocity of information and an environment where "right" decisions must be made quickly. Many businesses are reinventing or re-engineering themselves using groupware tools to meet these challenges.

1.5 THE MAIN MESSAGE—COLEMAN'S LAW

If you get only one message from this chapter, it is that groupware is not just technology, it is also social. Groupware is collaborative technology. That means it impacts the way people communicate with each other. Impacting communications results in impacting the way people work and eventually the structure of the organization. In other words, groupware is people as much as it is a tool that people use. Most organizations are able to handle the technology obstacles because there are many technical alternatives available. The difficulty lies with the relationship between technology and the people who have to use it. Quantifying this reality results in Coleman's Law:

> *People resist change and organizations resist change to an exponentially greater degree!*

A corollary to this law is:

> *The larger the organization, the greater the change, or the more complex the project, the greater the exponent for the resistance to change.*

This resistance to change is not unique to groupware. It is true of any new technology or change in business process. The upside and downside of groupware is that these technologies have such a great impact on the way people work and communicate that it magnifies the degree of change and can engender strong opinions either for or against the technology. Planning for change drastically improves the probability of success. Change Management is a group of practices and technologies that evolved out of the field of Organizational Development (OD). Change Management is critical with groupware.

1.6 WHY GROUPWARE?

Downsizing and organizational restructuring or redesign and other trends of the 90s are targeted toward increasing productivity, i.e., fewer people doing more with less. These are not the only challenges for business in the 90s. Increased quality, better customer service, lower cost of sales, greater employee autonomy, and more flexible and responsive organizations are all challenges for the current business climate.

Still, many of today's businesses are coping, even thriving, in this dynamic environment of diverse pressures and changing technologies. How do they do it? How do they stay competitive? How do they maintain a focus on increasing customer satisfaction, retaining high quality, and decreasing time to market while reducing costs? What technologies are being introduced to reshape the organization to achieve these goals? The answer to these questions is groupware.

If, as industry analysts claim, groupware will be a multi-billion dollar market in a few years, who will be the customers? Why are businesses the world over so interested in groupware? What is driving the growth of the groupware "market?" The answers are provided in part by the businesses already invested in groupware. The following list represents the primary motivations for making the move to groupware:

☞ Better cost control

☞ Increased productivity

☞ Better customer service

☞ Support for TQM

☞ Fewer meetings

☞ Automating routine processes

☞ Extending the organization to include both the customer and the supplier

☞ Integration of geographically disparate teams

☞ Increased competitiveness through faster time to market

☞ Better coordination globally

☞ Providing a new service that differentiates the organization

☞ Leveraging professional expertise

As you can see, groupware uses technology to provide solutions to business processes. Looking more closely, we see seven major forces that provide the initial propulsion toward groupware:

1. A network infrastructure capable of supporting groupware is now available.
2. Improved price/performance of groupware hardware and software has made it more available to a larger population.
3. The worldwide recession and downsizing is forcing increased white-collar productivity.
4. Well known vendors such as Microsoft, WordPerfect, IBM/Lotus, and Digital Equipment Corporation (DEC) are promoting groupware products, thereby increasing awareness in the marketplace.
5. Increased competition imposes change on organizations, making them flatter and more flexible, often requiring groupware for this transformation.
6. Increased complexity in today's products and business procedures is driving the use of ad hoc teams supported by groupware.
7. Articles in the trade and business press have increased awareness of groupware and aroused the curiosity of business leaders.

The laws of physics can be applied to markets and technologies. The groupware market is driven by three forces: an initial force used to overcome inertia, followed by momentum, and finally a reaction that is equal and opposite to the initial force.

There are also equal and opposing forces that inhibit the growth of groupware including:

1. Low level of education in the business community about groupware.
2. Confusion in the marketplace as to the nature of groupware. Much of the conflicting/competing information distributed by groupware vendors has increased this confusion.
3. Economic recession is decreasing budgets, and many firms perceive that they cannot afford the investment in groupware.
4. Distribution channels for groupware are new and not fully implemented.
5. MIS shops worry that they will become dependent on a groupware vendor.
6. Organizations are resistant to change.
7. There are few standards in the groupware market to foster rapid growth.

Additionally, when 500 groupware users were surveyed at previous GroupWare conferences about their success and/or failure with groupware, those who were not successful noted the greatest problems with groupware were not technological but social. Problems stemmed from the lack of support from top management or lack of a well defined business problem, rather than infrastructure or application issues.

Since this is such a critical issue, in a 1996 survey we asked "What is stopping groupware (on the Internet or intranets) in your organization today?" Overwhelmingly, people responded that although new infrastructures were a challenge, it was the people issues that were inhibiting the adoption of groupware (see Fig. 1.5).

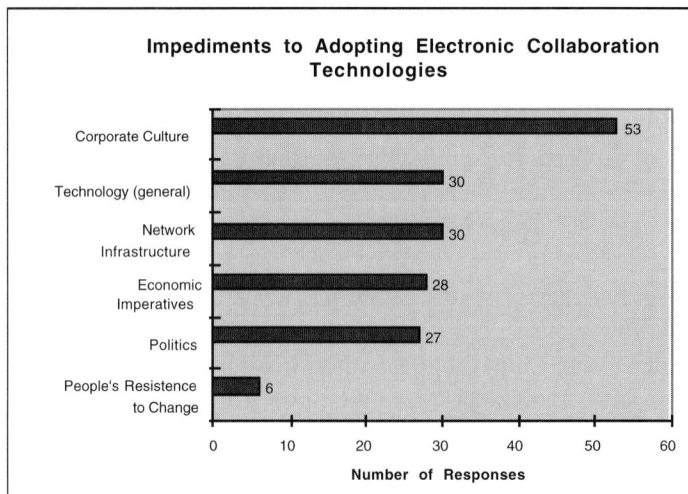

Impediments to Adopting Electronic Collaboration Technologies

Category	Number of Responses
Corporate Culture	53
Technology (general)	30
Network Infrastructure	30
Economic Imperatives	28
Politics	27
People's Resistence to Change	6

Fig. 1.5 Study Participant's Overwhelmingly Reported that their Company's Corporate Culture Interfered with Adopting Groupware

The current trend toward flatter organizations, decentralization, and outsourcing is reflected in the information technologies that businesses employ. The rapid growth of networks and the decline of legacy systems has managers searching for ways to amortize their LANs as well as discover a use for old mainframes that have been paid for and are still functional. The move toward linking companies to their suppliers and/or customers has led to the extension of the organization to include these two groups as well as project-oriented ad-hoc teams that may cross corporate boundaries.

Many organizations realize that they cannot be all things to all people. They have discovered the best way to stay competitive is to focus on their primary business and deliver it as efficiently as possible. This specialization means that in order to provide a complete groupware or business solution, many organizations need partners and must enter into new alliances to meet these demands.

The structure of these alliances is often awkward, and the integration of two very different organizations can be painful. There is no set form to follow. However, groupware, because it promotes communication, can often provide a solution.

In essence, groupware is the competitive glue of the '90s. Groupware provides a vehicle for organizations to remain flexible, yet fast on their feet, a way to stay focused on the customer, yet support the external salesperson, and a way to provide all employees with greater information and autonomy to be more productive.

1.7 WHY PEOPLE BUY GROUPWARE

Collaborative Strategies performed two studies in 1995, which identified the major reasons people buy groupware. Supporting cross platform communication and collaborating at a greater level than merely using e-mail was the top reason for buying groupware.

Criteria Used in Purchase Decision (choose 3)	%
Ability to support communications across multiple hardware systems and operating systems	65%
Technical superiority of product	51%
Ability to send e-mail messages to a colleague	38%
Compatible with in-place software	38%
Price of the software	37%
Ability to support conferences with threaded topic	22%
Software already in place in the organization	17%
Relationship with the groupware vendor	16%
Product availability	27%

Criteria Used in Purchase Decision (choose 3) (cont.) %

Groupware brought in as part of TQM or re-engineering	15%
Leverage internal expertise	12%
Ease of use	18%
Functionality: Fit with business need	12%
Vendor name recognition	10%
Scalability	5%

The three most popular business applications for groupware were office automation and productivity, group project management, and publications coordination and routing.

Application (choose 3)	Responses
Office Productivity	101
Group Project Management	86
BPR	80
Customer Service	74
Publications Coordination and Routing	73
Electronic Meeting Facilitation	70
Change Management	62
Integrate Compound Documents & Multimedia	61
Distribute/Restructure Organization	50
Sales Force Automation	40
Downsizing Support	32
Move from mainframe to LAN	31

1.8 GROUPWARE VERSUS THE INTERNET

There is a popular argument, especially as the Internet and intranets become more commonplace, that the Internet and WWW will make "traditional" groupware obsolete. However, until IP (internet protocol) networks mature and vendors provide the same level of product functionality and reliability as is available on LANs and WANs, collaborative technologies will still require a hybrid network. Organizations that we surveyed are using an "and" rather than an "or" philosophy for collaboration, i.e., today they are supporting both infrastructures for collaboration.

However, to fully leverage each infrastructure, it is important to know what collaborative functions work best on what infrastructure. There are five primary functional differences between groupware and the WWW that demonstrate the superiority or added benefit of using groupware.

Security and Collaboration: Notes today provides better security than the Web (witness the offer from Netscape of a free T-shirt to those helping patch the holes found in Netscape's supposedly secure server technology). All collaboration calls for some trade off between security and communication. Different technologies are appropriate in different circumstances.

Sharing objects: Notes version 4.0 is OLE 2 compliant. Passing objects on the Web is not so easy.

Replication: Notes works well in a connected and disconnected mode, i.e., you can replicate with your Notes server and the Notes application enables you to do work while mobile and in a disconnected manner. This is not true of the Web, which supports a continuously connected model of interaction.

Threaded Discussions: While some Internet news groups support threaded discussions, they are not as powerful as Notes, Collabra, TeamTalk, or Conference Plus. Not only do the latter products allow the user to track the threads of conversations, they have additional functionality that allows users to summarize discussions by topic and to scan topics. This functionality is probably one of the strongest reasons Netscape bought Collabra—to integrate this type of collaborative technology into Navigator 3.0 in the second half of 1996.

Workflow: IP networks are not inherently process oriented and they are just starting to be used for this function. Notes, today, easily supports workflow, and has an API to which many workflow vendors write. Vendors, such as Action Technology, are more tightly integrated, to the extent that they can generate code for Notes applications and databases directly from the workflow diagram. On the other hand, the Web supports only the most rudimentary workflow, i.e., e-mail messaging is available on someone's Web page by simply clicking a button. These functions and the growing trend towards "Web-enabled" collaborative or process oriented applications had Action Technologies releasing a Web-based workflow product called "Metro" in 1996. Action is one of the first, but almost every workflow vendor is porting their software over to the Web, and some are rewriting their software to take advantage of this infrastructure.

Since collaborative technologies are rapidly converging with the Web, we believe that by late 1997 many of these differences will have disappeared. Does that mean Lotus and other groupware vendors probably will be outdone or squeezed out of the market? Not likely!

We might compare this situation with that of the U.S. Postal Service and Fed Ex. Both will deliver mail or a package, but Fed Ex is more secure, offers a tracking system, and assures arrival the next day. The Postal Service now offers some of the same high quality delivery services at a lower cost, but they have not put Fed Ex out of business. Why? Fed Ex continually pushes the edge of technology to offer better services, maintaining their competitive advantage and leaving the Postal Service to play catch up. This analogy holds true for the competitive nature of groupware.

1.9 GROUPWARE TECHNOLOGY AND THE IT ARCHITECTURE

Where does groupware sit in today's enterprise IT architecture? As demonstrated in Fig. 1.5, it lies on a network infrastructure that includes PCs, cabling, network operating systems, and administration utilities or phone lines for a wide area network (WAN). Although groupware is part of the networked applications environment, not all networked applications constitute groupware. For example, access to a corporate database through a network is not necessarily groupware.

Interactive or discussion databases may be part of a groupware application (see Fig. 1.6). Often groupware applications are workgroup-oriented and not enterprise-oriented. The issues involved in scaling up these applications for a multinational corporation are not trivial and often require the cooperation of competitive vendors, establishing standards, and a mature supporting infrastructure. Many of the requirements for "enterprise-ware" are not yet available. The advent of IP networks, especially the intranet, is driving this new collaborative infrastructure at a frantic pace.

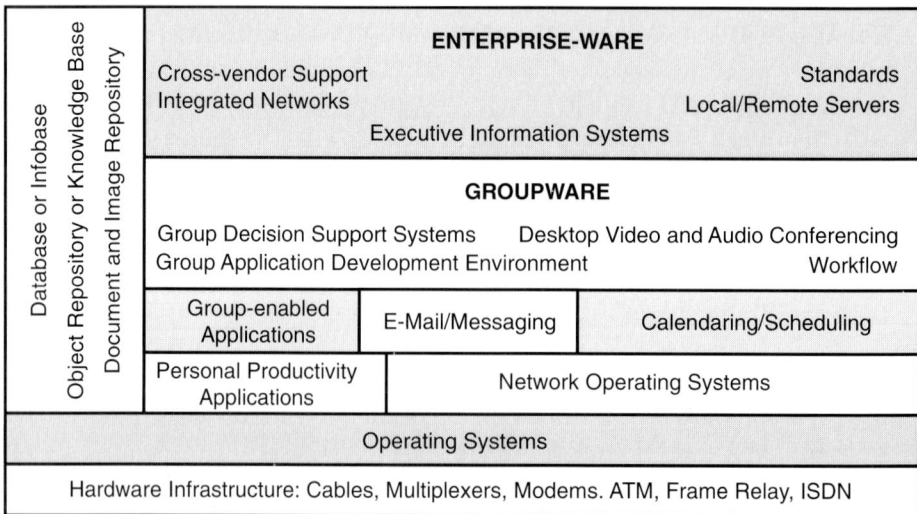

Fig. 1.6 Groupware Gives Substance to Technology to Accomplish Enterprise Goals

1.10 Some Case Studies in Collaboration

Different companies have different uses and goals for implementing groupware. The following case studies have been chosen to illustrate some of the principles we see in evolving organizations today. We have case studies from several areas of business including manufacturing and service organizations. Each case study has a common thread—collaboration—and how it enabled a critical evolution within the organization, which was necessary for success.

1.10.1 Re-engineering for the Virtual Organization

Leveraging knowledge is one of the most critical functions in a consulting organization. After all, knowledge and experience is all they have to sell. This case study shows the "right" way to self re-engineer. Decathlon Systems is a 30-employee, UNIX-based groupware vendor in Colorado. In order to reduce overhead and provide better client service, they re-engineered their own organization with groupware. Decathlon's solution was to use groupware to create a "virtual organization." Decathlon products are run in-house on a SCO UNIX server and consist of e-mail, group calendaring and scheduling, group resource management, cooperative document editing, and personal information management tools.

Before the re-engineering, all Decathlon employees worked in one 6000 sq. ft. office. After deploying groupware, the entire Decathlon staff telecommutes. They maintain a 500 sq. ft. office for staff meetings, get-togethers, and customer demonstrations. The office is used to house the central groupware servers for the company. For Decathlon, this was an inexpensive and trouble-free process. All the employees were enrolled in the transition process and provided input during a six-month period prior to the rollout.

Decathlon's primary advantage was that employees were already familiar with the software, and only new hires required training. The only reorganization related expenses related to network and telephone infrastructure upgrading, which amounted to a few thousand dollars. "The transition cost us less than one month's rent would have been," noted Bob Williams, Decathlon CEO.

Bob goes on to say, "There have been many advantages to distributing our organization: People are more productive, morale is better overall, and we have saved on overhead and commute time for employees. Even though we have only been doing this for a short time, my estimate is that we are saving 30 percent on our overhead. We found this works especially well for our technical people who often work at night. We have assigned people to be available at certain hours so there is always coverage."

Decathlon is still structured with departments, but they are moving to a team structure, coordinating through e-mail and their software's conferencing facility. Each team works with a prime government contractor. However, the requirements are often multi-disciplinary. To deal with the issues of cross platform support, training, and complex customer issues, all account management is done by teams.

All aspects of implementation for the client are accomplished electronically. All account knowledge is in a repository. Other team members can review the account activity and status if, and when, the prime sales person is not physically available. Additionally, problems of lost or unacknowledged mail and other client-related information are eliminated because the groupware's forwarding functions resend the mail to another team member if the lead account representative does not respond within a specified time.

Williams admits that although security has not been an issue so far, it could be problematic in the future. Therefore, Decathlon maintains two parallel servers—an internal server and an external server in a firewall configuration.

What is unusual about Decathlon is that it is a small company. Most studies about companies adopting groupware indicate that groupware is being used by larger organizations, usually having over 1000 employees and that it has not yet been embraced by smaller organizations employing fewer than 100 unless the smaller organization is required to do so by a large enterprise partner.

1.10.2 Doing Groupware Right

A good example of an organization that successfully overcame the organizational challenges of using groupware is General Foods. This project was successful because General Foods was able to learn from a prior failure. The systems manager, Bob Sickles, was successful because he was aware of these challenges and worked both with the technology and the organization to overcome them.

General Foods has 4000 people at its headquarters in White Plains, NY. Trying to schedule meetings can not only be frustrating but a waste of time. It got so bad that Bob Sickles, Systems Manager for Dinners and Enhancers Division (110 people), created a video called "Nightmare on North Street: The Scheduling Monster." This 20-minute video detailed the frustration and inefficiency of scheduling a meeting at General Foods in a humorous way. It was just one of the things Bob did right in integrating groupware into General Foods successfully.

Success often grows out of failure. Five years ago, General Foods tried to implement an electronic scheduling program with PC clients and a VAX server. It failed miserably. "It was too much of a behavioral change," said Sickles. "People were not used to having their PC on and running the whole day. Now with e-mail so prevalent, keeping the PC on is standard. If you are not on e-mail, you can't do your job."

Bob first found a champion in top management, Jim Cook, who is responsible for both TQM and Information Systems at General Foods. Next, Bob went one step further and got buy-in at both the staff and at the secretarial levels, so the middle managers who would use the scheduling software heard good things about it from both above and below. Taking both a top-down and a bottom-up approach proved to be a successful strategy for General Foods.

After hearing about the initial failure to introduce electronic scheduling systems, Bob realized he would have to change people's behaviors, overcome their fears, and competently train them to use the system in order to have a successful rollout. A decree from the division president stating that everyone must attend the two-hour training session for the scheduler was also helpful.

To tackle the specter of fear, Bob asked the staff about their anxieties. The most common concerns were loss of control of personal calendars and a fear that they would be inundated by meetings because they were now easier to schedule. Bob finessed these fears with a two-pronged strategy. First, he rolled the product out in a phased manner and only gave it to specific functional groups to start. These were groups that had considerable contact with everyone else in the division, so the word spread that these fears were unfounded. The second prong of the attack was to publicize the success of the project. He wrote articles for the company's Total Quality Management (TQM) newsletter about how much time the scheduler saved in the initial pilot tests and how easy it was to use. The word got out, and the fears evaporated.

Finally, Bob made sure it was fun. He used the video to poke fun at the current process and get buy-in from the whole division, so that when rollout occurred he was only fighting technical battles, not organizational ones. Bob realized that he was dealing with not only a technology but behavioral changes on the part of the division. They had successfully rolled out Microsoft Mail a year before and it had become the predominant way to communicate in the division. Bob was part of the company-wide TQM effort, and in the spirit of TQM he did a survey before and after electronic scheduling. He found that the time needed to schedule a meeting was reduced by 74 percent from 5.1 hours to 1.4 hours by using Network Scheduler 3.0. Average actual time to schedule a meeting (the actual number of work minutes needed to schedule a meeting) was reduced 71 percent from 19.5 minutes to 5.6 minutes.

General Foods has had a LAN for two years, and Bob's division is one of the first to be up and running on a LAN. There is a 386 or 486 PC running Microsoft Windows on every desktop of this 110-node LAN Manager/Token Ring network. The current groupware products in use at General Foods are Microsoft Mail and Network Scheduler 3.0. They are evaluating the use of Lotus Notes and other bulletin board systems to access market reports and the on-line clipping service.

When asked about his secret to success, Sickles stated, "The TQM focus on measurement and the customer, as well as thorough planning, helped us in the long run." Sickles was not looking for a quick fix and was willing to invest the time up-front to deal with the users of the technology. He had the support of his management and was able to train managers and administrative staff to adapt to their new roles. He used the lines of communication within the organization to allay the fears of the users and publicized the project widely within the company, both to help spread information and to focus the division's and the TQM's program on the project.

In our view, Bob learned from General Foods' prior mistakes and was rewarded with success in the form of a dramatic productivity increase. For those of you considering similar projects, learn from Bob's success. Plan well and reap some groupware successes of your own!

1.10.3 Groupware for Competitive Advantage

Bullivant, Houser, Bailey, Pendergrass & Hoffman, a Portland law firm, uses groupware not only to save their clients legal fees but to extend their organization to include their clients. "Clients often want reports at periodic intervals. This is an expensive process for the clients and time consuming for our lawyers," noted Don Evans, COO at Bullivant. "Rather than reporting to clients on a regular basis, we can change the process and bring the client into our organization. Using groupware, the client can examine documents in the working file or database, so the reporting time goes away. This can save the client up to 20 percent of their cost."

Although the major goal of Bullivant's program was not cost savings, they have received some return on their investment. Bullivant invested $250,000 to purchase Lotus Notes software and build a suite of custom applications to support their lawyers and clients. Training costs were low due to the design of the application, but maintenance and support costs ran up to $100,000 per year. Including these expenditures, actual cost savings include $50,000 in redundant data entry in 1993 alone. Another $75,000 in savings was expected in 1994.

"The biggest benefit we have seen from this system is the intangibles," explains Evans. This application differentiates Bullivant in the mind of the client. "We can now measure how long it takes to resolve a matter, which has raised the level of consciousness on the client side of how much it costs to work with Bullivant. From the client's perspective, they want their problem resolved quickly and inexpensively. This system lets them track that and see how well we are doing."

The next case study profiled, Oticon, is a good example of how teamwork and the groupware tools to support it helped a company turn itself around and become very profitable in a short time. What made Oticon's effort successful were three things: they were ready for change; they had clear direction and support from top management; and they used good tools to help proliferate and leverage knowledge while building a knowledge architecture for the organization.

1.10.4 Oticon: Reorganizing for Better Customer Service

Oticon A/S of Copenhagen had a customer service problem. Their customers were elderly and not receiving the kind of service they needed. Oticon was taking too long to get new products to market, morale was low, and profits were down. Oticon wanted to use groupware to not only enhance the quality of their products but to reorganize in order to better meet the needs of their elderly patients.

Oticon's goal was to improve responsiveness to customers by decreasing the amount of time it took to process paperwork. They set a goal of a 30 percent productivity increase over three years.

To accomplish this rate of return, Oticon re-engineered their IT systems and organization simultaneously. Oticon's reorganization was focused around greater customer contact and greater contact between employees. Oticon examined a variety of groupware technologies like electronic mail and video conferencing but decided to use a group document and image management system tied to workflow software, all from Recognition Technologies, as their solution. Cultural changes, such as a customer focusing on the abolishing departments, assigning all employees to multiple projects, and decreasing the layers of management, all contributed to turning Oticon around.

To show their commitment to the new technology and organizational structure, dramatic changes were made at the first point of contact—the mail room. All incoming mail, except critical documents, was scanned and the originals were then shredded and employees could view the shredding process through a transparent tube installed in the employee cafeteria. The immense volume of paper provided a visual and continuous reminder of Oticon's commitment to greater efficiency through less paper.

Oticon estimates that the paperless system and new workflow methods allowed them to bring products to market in half the time (relative to their experiences during the previous two and a half years). Paper storage was decreased by 70 percent. Oticon easily reached their goal of 30 percent productivity efficiency. This is not the radical re-engineering proposed by Dr. Mike Hammer and Jim Champy, authors of *Re-Engineering the Corporation*, which looks for a 70-100 percent change after re-engineering a business. Expense reduction directly attributed to the system and organizational change is 10–15 percent. They have decreased employee turnover and cut costs by 15 percent, and sales have increased by 20 percent. All of these changes have impacted the bottom line positively, resulting in increased earnings of 500 percent from 1992–93.

1.11 GROUPWARE AND RE-ENGINEERING

As stated earlier in the chapter, groupware is a technology often used to support the process of re-engineering. Unfortunately, many who have taken the path to re-engineering have failed. Michael Hammer, the prophet of re-engineering, predicted that American companies will spend $32 billion this year in re-engineering efforts and that two thirds of those efforts will fail!

When the roadblocks to re-engineering were examined by a 1993 Delloite-Touche survey, it turned out that re-engineering (like the technology it uses—groupware) has two major obstacles: people and technology.

Re-engineering, *per se*, is a misnomer, as many processes were not engineered in the first place. Business processes tend to develop under the pressure of finding a way to get something done—quickly. Often, these processes are not well thought out, but are invented by the person responsible for the task. Their ingenuity becomes policy and is implemented on paper. A bureaucracy grows up around these processes and people get jobs based upon the inefficiencies of the processes. So, of course, when a re-engineering program comes along, they are resistant.

By nature, people are resistant to change, and even more resistant to being told what to do and how to do it (at least in our culture). This resistance becomes the greatest organizational problem in re-engineering. The second problem, technological, can be defined in terms of the limitations of existing systems. Without solving both problems simultaneously, your enterprise may not be successful in re-engineering or with groupware.

1.12 GROUPWARE AND DE-ENGINEERING

Collaborative technologies often support the concept of self organizing systems in our consulting activities. The underlying premise comes from the chaos theory—it leads us to believe that perturbing such systems at a critical time can cause the systems to reorganize into a higher order (less chaos). We believe that since most human systems have some degree of chaos, human systems (organizations, people, processes) also have the ability to self organize, instead of being re-engineered.

The idea of self organizing and reorganizing systems is fundamentally different from re-engineering in that re-engineering attempts to exert control over chaos, by imposing a new system template and a new semblance of order. Self organizing systems are always seen in process (like a learning organization). In this self organizing model, the system has to redesign itself. This means that no outside control is exerted or imposed upon the system, just a perturbation to get the process started. However, it helps if the people who are reorganizing themselves know where the organization or business wants to go.

The process of reorganizing to a less chaotic system hopefully follows the informational goals of the organization. These goals can be stated in a Knowledge Architecture (KA), an overarching view of where knowledge is in the organization, where it flows, and where it is best used. When this KA is combined with the right groupware tools, it enables people and organizations to self reorganize, resulting in a qualitatively superior organization, relative to the organization that results from traditional re-engineering.

People, and the processes they work with, are dynamic. My view is that given the right tools and environment, people will re-engineer themselves and be much more successful. But successful self re-engineering requires that the people involved understand knowledge creation, knowledge flow (which is process oriented and related to workflow), and knowledge management. Additionally, the project champion must be prepared to work with the people, culture, and organization as well as the technology infrastructure and software applications.

1.12.1 Self Re-engineered Systems

Margaret Wheatley, an organizational development professional at the Berkana Institute, is working with the issues of increased velocity of change, increased velocity of information (brought on by technology), and new and more flexible organizational structures. All of this happens while trying to make order out of a chaotic and paradoxical universe (or business climate).

Wheatley is not so different from the rest of us, except in her approach, turning to new science for answers to organizational questions. She moved from an investigation of organizations to some of the new discoveries in hard science: quantum physics, self organizing systems, and chaos theory. Her belief is that metaphors from all of these disciplines can help organizations deal with many issues facing them today.

Wheatley is looking for a simpler way to manage organizations, or for ways that organizations can manage themselves in this complex, chaotic, and ever-changing environment. Interestingly, BPR is a methodology many have used, or tried to use, to impose order over chaos, especially in business processes.

This is where groupware and knowledge architectures come in. Groupware, which supports communication, collaboration, and coordination, is the informational glue that ties together today's and tomorrow's organizations. A knowledge architecture is a framework that looks at the flows of information in a corporation, organization, or enterprise, and helps structure this information so it has meaning and becomes knowledge. Information becomes knowledge when it is actionable, when it is incorporated by people and they use it, believe it, or do it! But more importantly, this knowledge becomes a corporate resource with quantifiable value, and that resource can then be applied where it is most needed for competitive advantage.

1.12.2 Groupware and Organizational Change

Dr. Wheatley is of the learning organizations school, much like Peter Senge. This school of management science believes that in order to survive, organizations, just like the people that compose them, must continuously change or die! Flexibility, the ability to deal with continual change, is the earmark of a "learning organization." The traditional hierarchies that worked well for command and control organizations from feudal times on (see Fig. 1.7) are giving way to *fishnet*, *spaghetti*, and other types of organizations that Tom Malone of MIT and Alvin Toffler (the futurist) call "adhocracies."

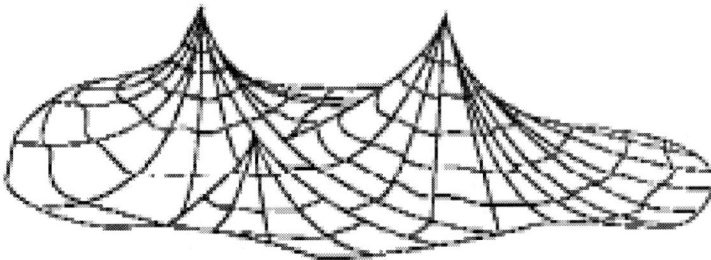

Fig. 1.7 The Fishnet Organization. © Dr. Robert Johansen, Institute for the Future, Menlo Park, CA, (415) 854-6322.

Wheatley notes that our view of natural and social structures comes from 17th century Newtonian physics, a view that is drawn from the world of the natural sciences. But as our view of science changes, so does our view of organizations.

Wheatley feels that case studies, which various management consultants have written up about famous organizations, can give us little more than a road map of where others have gone, not a good map for where we are going. Insofar as the transfer of knowledge about organizational change involves some general principles, they will be abstracted from these case studies. However, the specifics of change within a particular organization are not always transferable between organizations, generally because corporate cultures tend to be distinctive, and different companies operate in different organizational circumstances.

1.12.3 The Subjective Universe

Quantum physicists have noted that the universe is subjective; our interactions and perceptions affect the real world. This was most adroitly put in Heisenberg's uncertainty principle, which states that the observer has an effect on the observed, and that it is impossible to objectively observe a particle without affecting some aspect of that subatomic particles physics. In the world of quantum physics, RELATIONSHIP is the key determiner of what is observed and how particles manifest themselves. Particles come into being and are observed only in relation to something else, they do not exist as independent "things." It is the unseen connections between what we thought of as separate entities that define them and are the elements of creation. Why should this not be true also for organizations? Think of the relationships between people in an organization; they define both the person and the organization.

Illya Prigogine, the Novel prize-winning chemist who worked with crystal structures, noted that when he disturbed these structures/systems at a specific time they reorganized themselves into a higher level of order. He postulated that dissipated structures or living systems have the ability to respond to disorder with renewed life and move to a higher plane of organization.

In management science, these new ideas have been used to examine the roles of leadership, relationship, and motivation. Organizations are looking at what the whole person brings rather than just traditional views of the person as a machine or a cog on the wheel of a big machine (a Taylorist and mechanistic view). Vision today can be seen as such a force or field for change. Organizations are seen as living, dynamic entities with as many properties as the people who make them up.

Today, the BPR philosophy focuses on control and structures rather than on purpose and direction. We no longer let the structure emerge the way a stream finds its course down a hill. Instead, we try to structure a process or an outcome. The fact that BPR has not met with great success leads us to believe that we may be taking the wrong approach; rather than imposing a structure (re-engineering) on a business or process, it might be better to provide a direction (like the stream) and some tools to help the organization move in that direction and then let the people re-engineer themselves.

We believe "the direction" is provided by a knowledge architecture, and the tools for self re-engineering systems are found in the groupware arena. Many of our clients have come to understand that the changes they are looking for are available through self reorganization, rather than imposed upon them by re-engineering. As capable, intelligent people who work with these processes on a day-to-day basis, they can make the appropriate improvements—IF they are given the right tools and a clear corporate direction.

1.13 Defining Knowledge Architectures

Today, we hear more and more about the Knowledge Economy and the belief that the future of business success will be based on the ability to manage and leverage an organization's intellectual capital. What does this mean? And how do you create a framework to manage enterprise knowledge?

Companies are realizing that the ability to better manage the knowledge of the firm will have tremendous benefit to all levels of the organization. For example, the ability to stop reinventing the wheel every time a new project starts because the knowledge learned from past projects is available and accessible by all; to collaborate and work with team members around the world—applying the best ideas and experts to problems regardless of where they're located; to coordinate and organize information so that the appropriate knowledge is shared with the appropriate people to avoid information overload and redundancy of information. These are just a few examples of how organizations are benefiting from using groupware technology in support of knowledge management.

Many of these initiatives started as grass roots implementations with initial applications supporting discrete problems such as issues or document tracking. The problem comes as the organization begins to see the benefit of these applications and desires to ramp up the implementation to higher strategic levels to solve broader sets of knowledge management issues. Because the initial projects were discrete in nature and only focused on single processes or issues, the ability to scale the applications to encompass multiple processes or groups becomes extremely difficult.

Furthermore, they haven't taken the time to create a framework or knowledge architecture under which to map the knowledge of the firm. The relationships between groups, divisions, and teams are not clear and therefore, when it comes to creating seamless connectivity throughout the firm, they are unable to "see" the big picture.

When an organization takes the time up front to create a knowledge architecture or framework, they create a high level blueprint. A knowledge architecture is not a detailed map of all the knowledge of the firm but rather, a representation of the knowledge—a set of mental models or frameworks.

1.13.1 Building a Knowledge Architecture

The first step in building a knowledge architecture is to gain an understanding of the organization's overall strategy and understand what role knowledge plays. (See Chapter 20 for more information on Knowledge Management.) Many times, we find that organizations have not built any thoughts around knowledge and the leveraging of intellectual capital into their current strategy. Therefore, the first step is to gain a clear vision from leadership on where they see knowledge playing a key role and how they would like to communicate the value of knowledge to the organization.

The role of leadership is to create "intention" or vision so that the organization understands the direction it should be moving. The goal is to create order not control, and therefore intention creates the direction that the organization should be moving toward.

This strategic piece is critical because it drives many other steps in the process of creating knowledge architectures. Without it, assembling multiple cross-organizational teams to map integrated processes is virtually impossible. Without guidance from leadership, groups have no opportunity to understand how they connect and link with other groups in the organization.

We are currently working with a consulting firm to design their knowledge architecture and implement groupware systems to support collaboration and knowledge sharing. The project is designed in three phases; building a knowledge architecture, developing the underlying knowledge infrastructure, and the groupware implementation.

The initial phase of the project established leadership's vision of knowledge management and potential benefit for the organization. By helping the client gain a better understanding of their business processes—how knowledge is used in their organization today—and what the potential benefits could be, we were able to help articulate a clear strategy for the project.

Once the vision and direction were established, joint teams began defining the knowledge architecture and its underlying domains. Leadership has played a strong role throughout the project and further articulating the knowledge strategy has created a whole new set of questions to be explored by the organization.

1.13.2 Aligning with Work

Now that the organization has created a vision and strategy for knowledge management, the next step is to understand how knowledge currently exists within the organization and how it is used today. It is also critically important to understand how information and knowledge interplay with the work of the organization.

When thinking about how information flows through an organization, imagine how water flows down a hill. It finds its own path and the water pools naturally in different locations along the journey. This is very similar to how knowledge flows through an organization. The difference is that knowledge is tied directly to the work of the organization. Work defines the paths that knowledge takes and the "pools" of knowledge are formed where groups of people have a need to gather and share knowledge. Changing the flow of knowledge in the organization requires changing the path of work.

Many companies will attempt to capture the learning and knowledge of the firm by building groupware applications to hold the knowledge. Thinking they have implemented a excellent solution, they stop. Then they can't understand why no one is using them. Building the groupware application is a critical first step, but not the last. Consider that most employees regard their most important tasks to be the ones that directly contribute to getting their jobs done. If capturing knowledge is viewed as extra work, or something "nice" but not essential to have, they have no incentive to capture the knowledge. Providing specific rewards for sharing provides incentive for them to invest the time and energy to use knowledge management tools effectively.

Any knowledge management or learning system must also play a role in helping users to get their work done easier, faster, etc.... This is the trade-off to get users to share their knowledge. If their efforts contribute to making their job easier (or their perception of their job), it will help to change the behaviors within the organization. Remember, you must answer both "What's in it for me?" and "What's in it for the organization?"

The concept of knowledge architectures will continue to evolve as more and more companies attempt to manage their intellectual capital. It's important to remember that knowledge architectures are not data architectures—rather, they are frameworks and mental models for mapping knowledge from a strategic business perspective.

1.13.3 Groupware and the Preservation of Intellectual Capital

Intellectual capital is information about the organizations' operations, customers, history, policy, databases, and records. Intellectual capital takes two forms, explicit and tacit. It is the tacit knowledge that never gets quantified into a manual or other accessible form, but resides in the minds of the people who have worked with and developed that information. The problem is that when someone leaves, either to a different assignment within the company or out of the company, this intellectual capital in his/her mind leaves also. As you may have surmised from the above discussion, nothing is more important in today's competitive market than preserving and leveraging intellectual capital.

Two Japanese management consultants, Ikujiro Nonaka and Hirotaka Takeuchi, talk about knowledge creation in their book *The Knowledge Creating Company* (Oxford University Press). They draw the distinction between tacit and explicit knowledge: Tacit knowledge is in your mind, but not quantified through either spoken or written communication. Explicit knowledge is spoken and/or written knowledge. The Japanese function very well with tacit knowledge because of their high context culture. In other words, the intentionality of their communication is influenced by the context in which it is presented. In Western cultures, we are good with explicit knowledge. We like to write things down. My point is that organizations must capture both kinds of knowledge. In order to remain competitive, organizations cannot continue to squander this type of intellectual capital.

1.13.4 Keeping the Corporate Assets

Maintaining confidentiality and ownership of intellectual assets presents a significant challenge to corporations. Jeff Conklin, CEO of Corporate Memory Systems notes, "Storing corporate knowledge and experience is becoming more critical as more and more companies become distributed across the globe, and both the products and the organizations become more complex."

For example, John, a hypothetical manager, has worked for XYZ Company for 40 years. When he retired, his knowledge about specific clients, products, organizational systems, etc. left with him. But if John had shared his knowledge over time, through an electronic conferencing system, that knowledge would now be part of a collective, corporate memory or learning, which could be leveraged across the organization. In this way, John's knowledge becomes an asset, intellectual property, of the organization as he develops it. His co-workers have access to the information while he's still at XYZ. His successor has the benefit of John's understanding the history, needs, and preferences of his customers as well as a better understanding of the corporate operation.

Products like Lotus Notes, QuestMap from Corporate Memory Systems, CollabraShare from Netscape, DCA's OpenMind, Team Talk from TRAX, Pacer Share from Pacer Software, and ICL's TeamWare can all support the effort to preserve the corporation's most valuable asset—people's experience.

1.14 USING GROUPWARE TO LEARN ABOUT GROUPWARE: THE BUSINESS TRANSFORMATION GAME

As we can see, groupware provides a number of technologies that support collaboration, communication, and coordination in the enterprise, department, or work group. But how can companies evaluate whether groupware can solve their particular business needs? Much of the business community's education about groupware has come from vendors like IBM/Lotus, Microsoft, and Novell. They believe, and wisely so, that an informed customer is more likely to buy than an uninformed one. However, vendor-developed education is often limited to the vendor's product, and the potential groupware user must look at what product(s) will best solve their business problem(s) in an unbiased manner.

Consulting firms and integrators, like Collaborative Strategies, GroupWorX, Strategic Decisions Group, and PRC, provide one-stop-shopping groupware services where customers can evaluate the offerings of many vendors and determine what will work best in their organization. However, choosing the right business process and the right product is really the easy part of the much larger goal; improving the bottom line. The hard part is teaching the behaviors that are necessary for these products and processes to be effective. To that end, Collaborative Strategies and PRC jointly developed a groupware business simulation, The

Business Transformation Game (BTG), which uses groupware to teach about group behavior and collaboration. The goal of the *game* is twofold. First, to introduce collaborative technologies in a non-threatening situation where experimentation and making mistakes will not compromise careers. Second, to teach collaborative behaviors.

Again, the easy part is working through the "how do I get this thing to work" process. The game is fully facilitated. Participants work with leading collaborative products to experience the business processes of prioritizing issues, group decision making, assigning and following through on action items, and, ultimately, resolution of the project. These are processes with which we are familiar in traditional business settings and transferring them to an electronic environment is not particularly difficult.

The hard part is the "how do I get us to work together" part. Realistically speaking, this should not be a surprise, since our educational and professional experiences rarely encourage collaboration. That's not to say that teams aren't the newest hot organizational theory or that we didn't participate in group projects in school. Rather, recognizing these attempts at creating collaborative environments, the reality is that when it comes time to recognize one's achievement, whether in an academic or business setting, the emphasis is put on the individual's contribution. For example, remember the science projects we did in high school and college? These projects were presented to us as "team efforts" where we were instructed to "work together" and "share ideas." However, when it came time for assigning grades, each participant was graded on at least two criteria and one of them was certainly his/her individual contribution to the project. It certainly seems peculiar to grant each member of the group the same grade when the instructor and participants are aware that some people contributed more and better material than others. In fact, we would object at the "unfairness" of such a grading system. The problem this example illustrates, which I believe can be applied in form to many business and academic situations, is the mixed message. First we're told to work together, but ultimately, our reward is based on our individual contribution.

Recognizing that we really don't have adequate training in collaborative behaviors, the Business Transformation Game expressly teaches participants how to collaborate while providing the opportunity to experience the benefits of working this way. In the BTG, professionals work with groupware technology and go through the process of solving a particular business problem—COLLABORATIVELY. This experience allows them to see, first hand, how groupware products and the collaborative behaviors they foster will help their organization.

Unfortunately, traditional training about groupware does not address the unique nature of using groupware and, therefore, fails to demonstrate in any meaningful manner the powerful impact collaborative behaviors and products can have on an organization. For example, what's wrong with the following scenario?

> Nancy needs a new car. She does her homework, checking out Web sites and calling car dealers to get an idea of product features, availability, and pricing. Next, she goes to her favorite automobile dealership, which has a well

deserved reputation for top quality inventory and service. She walks into the showroom where the salesperson engages her in a discussion about what kind of car she wants, what her driving habits are, how many miles she puts on a car each year, whether she wants all the bells and whistles, and a long list of other issues designed to identify which product in his inventory will best suit her needs. Next, Nancy is shown a video all about the car, including segments on its design and construction as well as how it handles on the road. The video even includes testimonials from established customers, all expressing their initial satisfaction with the product or explanations about how the dealership solved any problems which did surface. The salesperson answers all her questions and finally, based on this information, Nancy makes a well thought out decision to purchase the car and negotiates her deal.

What's missing? The test drive. When was the last time you bought a car without taking it on the road to experience for yourself the feel of its drive, its acceleration, its handling on a tight curve, the atmosphere inside the car, the leg and roof room, how cramped the back seats will be when carpools involve growing teenagers, whether the radio buttons are easy to access without distracting you from the road, and most importantly, whether this car will hold the entire family, pets, and camping gear for those long-weekend, summer camping trips?

The point is this, the more *experience* we have with a product, the better prepared we are to understand how it will fit into and impact our lives. We take cars for test drives to experience these things without risking our time, money and mental energy. The same is true for groupware and collaborative behaviors. Participating in the BTG provides direct, hands-on experience of the collaborative environment and behaviors without consuming time and money resources or disrupting day-to-day business operations.

1.14.1 The Business Transformation Game

In general, people resist changes to how they work. In order to overcome this resistance we had to make it fun! Following the Murder Mystery game format, each person in the BTG is assigned a role, usually a business role such as VP of Sales, CEO, CFO, etc. and the only thing murdered is a business process.

Each BTG participant has a laptop computer connected to a network. We identify a broken business process to be fixed with groupware. First, everyone reviews the public and private information about his/her role. Then we begin to repair the process without groupware. As usual, pandemonium ensues. After we discuss the shortcomings of traditional approaches to solving the problem, we move on to a facilitated electronic meeting. Using an EMS application such as GroupSystems for Windows by Ventana, or McCall-Szerdy's Facilitate.com, the problem is discussed in a facilitated manner. Brainstorming generates viable solutions and anonymous voting takes place. When a solution is reached, we proceed to the next phase.

The next step uses Lotus Notes to create a variety of discussion databases. The participants enter ideas about requests for more information, the impact of the decision, and other issues, essentially creating a virtual forum or discussion around this problem. The discussion is available to all meeting participants and can be accessed locally or remotely.

Finally, we move into the solution phase where the broken process is fixed using Workflow Analyst and Workflow Builder, both workflow tools from Action Technologies, Inc. (Alameda, CA). Participants cooperate in an interactive process demonstration, adding information as needed in the workflow. Discussion continues throughout the exercise until the participants are familiar with how it feels to collaborate using groupware, what business problems groupware can be applied to, and what an "automated" vs. "re-engineered" solution will look like.

1.14.1.2 Benefits of Experience Over Information

Learning about collaborative behavior gives facts and figures, but actually learning collaborative behavior only results when one adds the experience of collaboration to the information. The Business Transformation Game combines both; participants get to work with several groupware products in a group environment while they are practicing the collaborative behaviors that these products support. What follows is a real understanding of the contribution this style of working can make to their organization. In this way, we not only teach about collaboration, we *teach* collaboration.

1.15 THE FUTURE: AN ARCHITECTURE FOR THE CONNECTED ORGANIZATION

Many clients and organizations we have studied have implemented groupware in pieces; e-mail in this department, calendaring and scheduling in another department, Notes over in finance. To make matters worse, the technical/MIS people don't believe in groupware at all.

We ask these clients what they are trying to accomplish. Why groupware? Yes, it's neat technology, but what is the collaborative problem you are trying to solve? And, is the chosen problem critical to the organization?

1.15.1 An Integrated Collaborative Project Management System

The ideal is an integrated collaborative project management system would use the best-of-breed collaborative products, all linked together to provide an almost seamless integration of information, process flow, and accountability.

For example, after using an electronic meeting system to facilitate a specific discussion, meeting notes are exported into a Notes-like or Collabra-like database that provides an organized forum for ongoing discussion and decision making for the project. Additional benefit would be derived if those decisions were exported directly to a project management tool, like products from Digital Tools (Santa Clara, CA) or Project Gateway (Sausalito, CA). Ideally, tasks or assignments could then be imported into a workflow tool that would not only help map the project process, but enable "What if" analyses in moving around project resources. The workflow tool would also track and route tasks and assignments, with time and date stamps. Such a system would finally insure that when someone in a meeting volunteered or was assigned a task, it could be tracked through to completion and integrated into the project plan and resource management. The project would be completed and then the cycle would begin again (see Fig. 1.8).

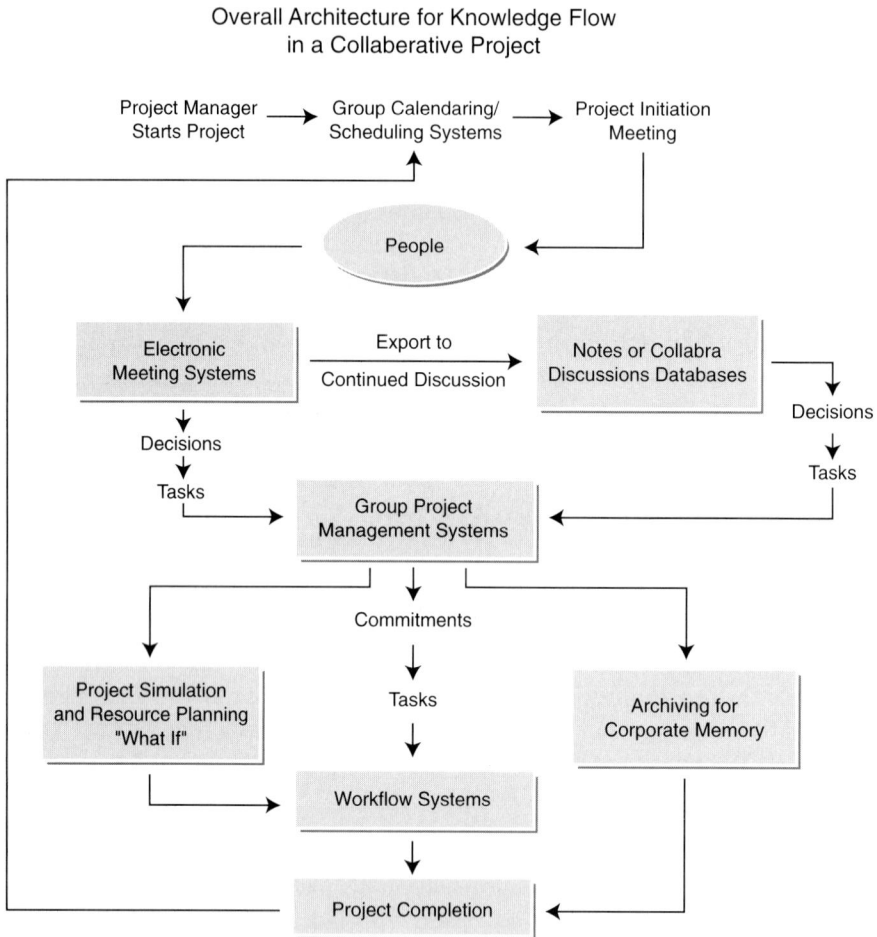

Fig. 1.8 How Knowledge Flows through People and Collaborative Technologies in a Collaborative Project

1.16 SUMMARY

This chapter covers a lot of ground on groupware and organizations. It covers definitions and a framework for groupware. It looks at the business reasons for using groupware, the size of the groupware market, and justifications for groupware.

It also looks at some of the current findings in new sciences and tries to apply them to organizational evolution with groupware. A tall order. It shows that there are circumstances where imposing control on a chaotic system doesn't always work. Rather, defining a knowledge architecture and giving your people the right tools can help them engineer themselves and become a self organizing system. Groupware is an important and valuable component in a company's overall competitive strategy.

BIBLIOGRAPHY

1. *The Corporation of the 1990s,* Michael S. Scott Morton, Oxford University Press, 1991
2. Is Information Systems Spending Productive? New Evidence and New Results, Paper #143, MIT Center for Coordination Sciences, June , 1993
3. GroupWare '92 Conference Proceedings, Robert Johansen, Page 210, San Francisco, CA 1992
4. *Re-engineering the Corporation,* Michael Hammer Harper Business, New York, NY, 1993
5. *The Re-engineering Revolution,* Michael Hammer, Harper Business, New York, NY, 1994
6. *The Knowledge-Creating Company: How Japanese Companies Create the Dynamics of Innovation* by Ikujiro Nonaka and Hirotaka Takeuchi, Oxford Press, 1995
7. *The Monster Under the Bed: How Business Is Mastering the Opportunity of Knowledge for Profit,* Stan Davis and Jim Botkin, Simon & Schuster, 1994
8. *Shifting Gears: Thriving in the New Economy* by Nuala Beck, Harper Collins Publishers Ltd., 1992

BIOGRAPHY

David Coleman, founder and Managing Director of Collaborative Strategies, has been involved with groupware and collaborative technologies since 1990 as an industry analyst, author of books and magazine articles on collaborative computing, conference chairman, and consultant to vendor and user organizations.

As the principal consultant with Collaborative Strategies, David works with clients to ensure the best outcome from groupware. He has led several organizations through the process of determining their readiness for collaboration practices, the appropriate business processes to apply groupware to, and the best tools to use in each case. He has facilitated meetings, using electronic collaboration tools, to determine success factors for collaborative projects. His facilitation has enabled organizations like NASA and PacifiCare to determine their internal groupware strategy.

Additionally, David advises vendor clients, such as NEC, ICL/Fujitsu, Apple, The Forefront Group, Hewlett-Packard, and others, on product strategy and positioning. Often, product positioning comes from market input. Mr. Coleman has lead market research studies for Merrill Lynch, and many of the vendors listed above to help determine product features, pricing, and competitive differentiators. His unique perspective on the collaborative technologies market allows him to see the critical issues facing users of collaboration technologies. David often writes marketing white papers explaining product positioning in relation to market issues and concerns (see www.collaborate.com).

As founder of the GroupWare '9X conferences, David has watched over 10,000 people from Western cultures cope with collaboration in a competitive culture. From this experience, he developed "The Business Transformation Game" a role-playing game that exposes users to a variety of groupware products while teaching them about personal and computer-based collaboration. David is known for his creative solutions to marketing, analytical, and collaborative problems. He has run an independent management consulting firm for eight years and is a seasoned leader and project manager.

Prior to establishing Collaborative Strategies, David held positions of Director of Marketing (Natural Language) and Product Line Marketing Manager (UNIX Products Group, Oracle Corporation).

David's entrepreneurial spirit and commitment to electronic collaboration led him to found the GroupWare '9X conference in 1992 (held annually in San Jose, Boston, and London). He is the author/editor of *Groupware Technologies and Applications* (Prentice Hall, 1995) and *Groupware: Collaborative Strategies for Corporate LANs and Intranets* (Prentice Hall, 1997). He was the editor and publisher of GroupTalk, the newsletter of workgroup computing. He is the founding editor of *Virtual Workgroups* magazine and still contributes a monthly column. Additionally, David writes monthly columns on groupware for *Computer Reseller News* and *MainSpring* (an on-line resource for intranet and Web developers). David has written for many trade and business publications such as *Network World*, *Datamation*, *Fortune*, and is a frequent speaker at conferences and tradeshows worldwide.

David holds a bachelors degree from Connecticut College and masters degrees from San Jose State University and Standford University. He can be contacted directly at 415-282-9197, or at davidc@collaborate.com. More information on Collaborative Strategies can be found at www.collaborate.com.

Collaborating on the Internet and Intranets

David Coleman
Abby Hyman Kutner
Collaborative Strategies™

The global marketplace is no longer an abstract—it is in full swing today—and realizing its benefits requires that companies develop new ways to conduct business. As the need for managing multiple sites and geographically dispersed teams becomes more prevalent, collaboration for individuals and teams is becoming a critical issue. The challenge for organizations is how to effectively deploy collaborative applications in order to realize their benefits.

Electronic collaboration products, usually known as groupware, allow people to work together without having to actually *be* together. Today, e-mail, the most popular groupware product, is ubiquitous in most organizations. Other groupware applications, such as group calendaring and scheduling, group document management and editing, and data, voice, and video conferencing are becoming increasingly important as people look for more tools to support electronic collaboration. Until recently, these applications have run exclusively on a LAN/WAN client/server architecture, however, that infrastructure is no longer sufficient for the tremendous quantity of work being performed with electronic collaboration tools. The Internet and intranets are emerging in conjunction with collaborative software products to provide the means to support the ideal of a highly interactive, collaborative workforce with the appropriate infrastructure.

This chapter reports on research performed by Collaborative Strategies, which looked at how large companies are using IP networks (internet protocol, i.e., Internet and intranet) to support electronic collaboration. The primary questions to be resolved in the research were:

☞ How do firms collaborate using Internet and intranet tools?

☞ What tools and applications are companies using today and what do they expect to use in the future?

☞ What infrastructure supports these tools today and what do users expect in the future?

☞ How important do companies feel the Internet and intranets are to their computing strategy?

☞ How does the advent of Internet and intranets impact traditional groupware, such as Lotus Notes?

☞ What major issues do organizations face as they attempt to work more collaboratively?

2.1 RESEARCH METHODOLOGY

Collaborative Strategies contacted over 400 companies in order to conduct 100 interviews. Approximately 20 percent of these companies were not yet implementing Internet and intranet applications on an enterprise-wide scale and, therefore, were not qualified for this study. Another challenge was identifying the person most knowledgeable about a company's intranet strategy. In many cases, several people from a single company were interviewed in order to develop a comprehensive picture. Qualified people were interviewed by telephone and each interview took between one and two hours. Approximately 10 percent of the people participated via e-mail. Interviewers were qualified to ensure sufficient business and technical knowledge. Participating companies were guaranteed complete anonymity in order to encourage open dialogue. Figure 2.1 depicts the breakdown of participants.

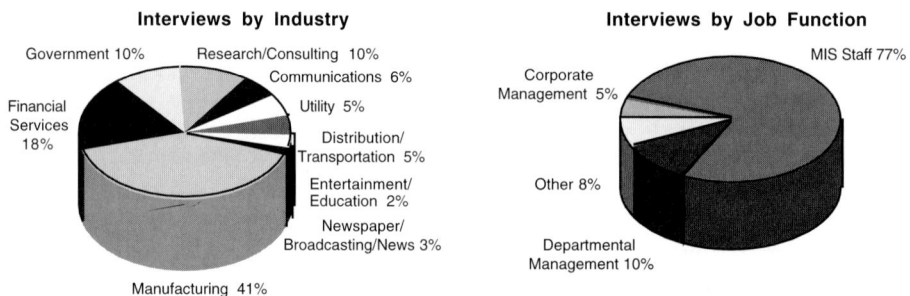

Interviews by Industry

Government 10%   Research/Consulting 10%
                 Communications 6%
Financial   Utility 5%
Services
18%   Distribution/
                 Transportation 5%
                 Entertainment/
                 Education 2%
                 Newspaper/
                 Broadcasting/News 3%

Manufacturing 41%

Interviews by Job Function

                                    MIS Staff 77%
Corporate
Management 5%

Other 8%

Departmental
Management 10%

Fig. 2.1 One hundred companies, representing multiple industries, excluding computer hardware and software development, were interviewed. Participants were high level MIS personnel—77 percent were in MIS and technical management positions.

2.2 KEY FINDINGS FROM THE SURVEY

Intranets are growing at a very rapid rate because users *perceive* that they offer better security, are cheaper to implement, and are easier to use than most proprietary software. Intranets are being used to support a wide range of collaborative functions, and interviewees reported that they expect to expand their use of intranets. In spite of this anticipated growth, participants reported that they do not expect to replace LAN/WAN networks. In fact, they expect selected collaborative functions to remain on existing LAN/WAN networks. Ultimately, IP and proprietary infrastructures will be integrated, resulting in hybrid environments.

The companies interviewed for this study expect to double their IP network size by 1997 and again by 1998. The average IP network today has about 5,300 seats. Interviewees reported that they expect an average of 11,200 seats by 1998. By the year 2000, these companies expect to have an average of 21,400 seats, almost four times the number of seats in today's IP networks.

In April 1996, the editors at *Network World* magazine interviewed 500 leading users of network technology by mail survey. Some of their findings were interesting enough to note in this report.

- ☞ 54% worry about security
- ☞ 78% use the Internet for research and to access electronic information
- ☞ 89% have or will implement an IP network strategy in the next 12 months
- ☞ 85% already have Web servers for Internet applications and 73% have intranet Web servers
- ☞ 28% use IP networks for EDI/electronic commerce, and 48% plan to use do this over the next year
- ☞ 88% said ISPs and RBOCs will become more important to their enterprise network strategy as these carriers begin to offer new services

Lou Gerstner, CEO of IBM states, "In the long run, closed, proprietary architectures are a losing strategy.... Every day, the Internet grows, in size, in reach, and in importance. Every day, people add more function, more security, and capability to the Net" (*Internet World*, March 1996).

The 1999 worldwide Internet software market will exceed $8 billion, according to a Forrester Research, Inc. study. Senior analyst Eric Brown says, "The Internet is now the center of innovation in the software industry—everyone from garage based start-ups to entrenched players like Microsoft and Oracle is bringing out new products in this space. Internet software spending will overtake client/server spending in many accounts. Server software will be the major component, expected to sell $4.4 billion worth in 1999. At the same time, Net software authoring tools will be worth $1.2 billion."

2.3 HOW FIRMS COLLABORATE USING INTERNET AND INTRANET TOOLS

2.3.1 Is Collaboration Critical to the Function of Your Business?

Eighty-three percent of those interviewed replied "yes!" The reasons they gave were:

☞ Collaboration is necessary to support a distributed workforce by increasing communication, coordination, facilitation, and planning. Sales force automation and distributed project management were two key functions where collaboration was identified as critical

☞ Collaboration strategies reduce cycle times in product development, thereby realizing an increase in competitive advantage

☞ Collaboration technologies increase productivity and coordinate or facilitate complex processes

When participants said that collaboration was not a *critical* function in their company today, the primary reason given was that the network and collaboration products were not yet mature, or stable enough.

2.3.2 What Kinds of Work Are Being Supported by the Internet and Intranets?

Insofar as collaboration is more prevalent within a company than it is between companies, we found that most collaborative functions were supported by intranets. The basic functions that firms are currently supporting fall into five main categories:

☞ **Document Management**: document publication coordination and routing, broadcast publishing, document editing

☞ **Group Calendaring/Scheduling**: staff and facilities calendar updates, meeting management support, including meeting facilitation, and support for virtual, remote, or distributed meetings

☞ **Project Management**: workforce management and project coordination, including distributed project management, support for mobile working, sales force automation

☞ **Communication**: information sharing and threaded discussion forums, including video-conferencing, collaborative working around a common "table," accessing remote and distributed applications, conducting key functions on business processes such as product development

☞ **Knowledge Management:** sharing corporate knowledge, creating a corporate memory, preserving and recycling intellectual capital

The following graphs show what functions businesses are performing on the Internet and intranets. Only the most popular functions are listed on each graph. At least 50 company responses were required to be listed on the intranet graph, but since Internet usage was less overall, functions being used by 30 or more companies are listed on the Internet graph.

Business activities most frequently supported by intranets include: Internal broadcast publishing of human resources, corporate policy, and marketing materials; sharing corporate knowledge; and accessing data and information from internal sources, such as mainframe legacy systems (see Fig. 2.2).

Collaborative Functions on Intranets

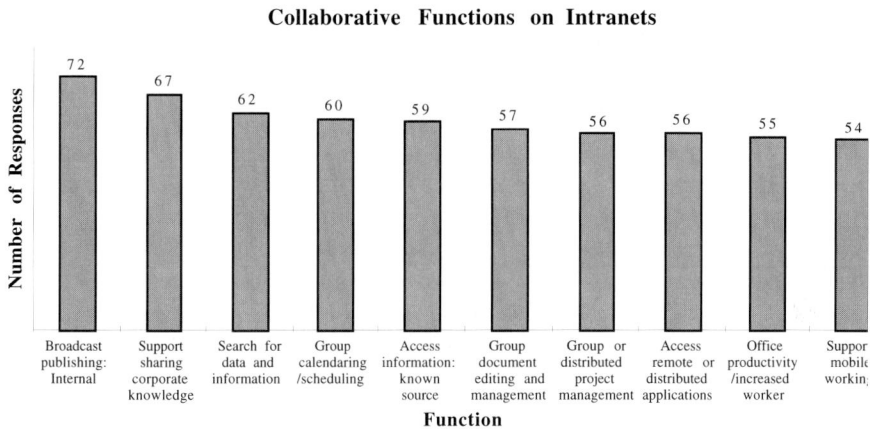

Fig. 2.2 Companies Reported Many More Collaborative Functions on Intranets

Business activities most frequently supported by the Internet include: Searching for data and information, threaded electronic discussions, customer service, and support for mobile working (see Fig. 2.3).

Companies are searching for data and information (i.e., surfing), supporting mobile working, accessing information from a known source, and accessing remote or distributed applications on both the Internet and intranets. Several other functions, such as coordinating financial transactions, are far more infrequent on these networks, although they are quite frequent on LAN/WAN architectures.

Collaborative Functions on the Internet

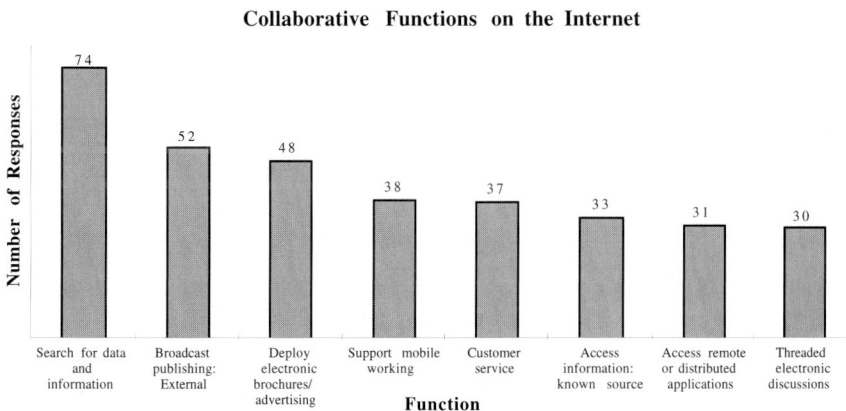

Fig. 2.3 Companies Reported Fewer and Less Collaborative Functions on the Internet

Most of the participating companies are not using either the Internet or intranets to support "mission critical" functions. However, they are using them for applications that are important to the business, i.e., increasing sales through the Internet channel, or customer service, but they are not using IP networks for the traditional mission critical applications, such as finance and human resources. These functions still reside on proprietary LANs and WANs, we believe, primarily because of the lack of absolute security. Still, an indication that companies are anxious to leverage IP network infrastructures is that 86% said they considered integrating legacy data with their intranet implementation to be critical. Given that intranets are only two years old, this is a tremendous endorsement (see Fig. 2.4).

How Critical is Integrating Legacy Data in Your Intranet Deployment?

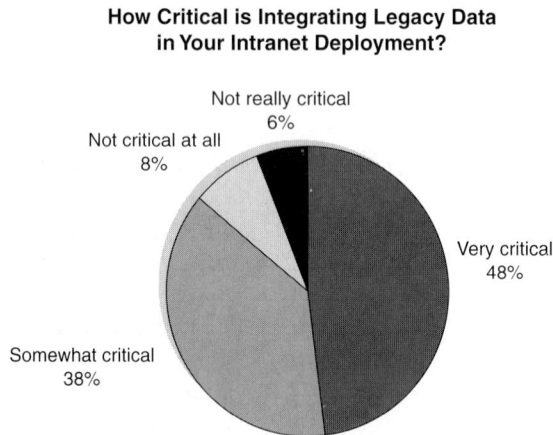

Fig. 2.4 Study Participants Felt that Integrating Legacy Data was Critical

2.3.3 The Infrastructure to Support Collaboration tools

In 1996, most organizations have almost twice the number of intranet servers as Internet servers (an average of 6.4 compared to 3.6). The most popular choices for server hardware and operating systems are Pentium PCs and Multiprocessor UNIX servers for rapidly growing IP networks (see Figs 2.5 and 2.6).

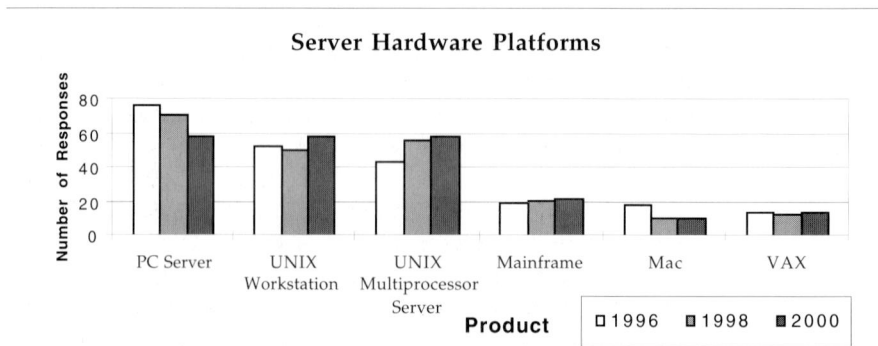

Fig. 2.5 P.C. and UNIX Servers Will Dominate through the Century

We believe that more companies will migrate mission critical applications to their intranets as the technology becomes more secure, more features and functions are added, standards are ratified and strengthened, and the infrastructure improves.

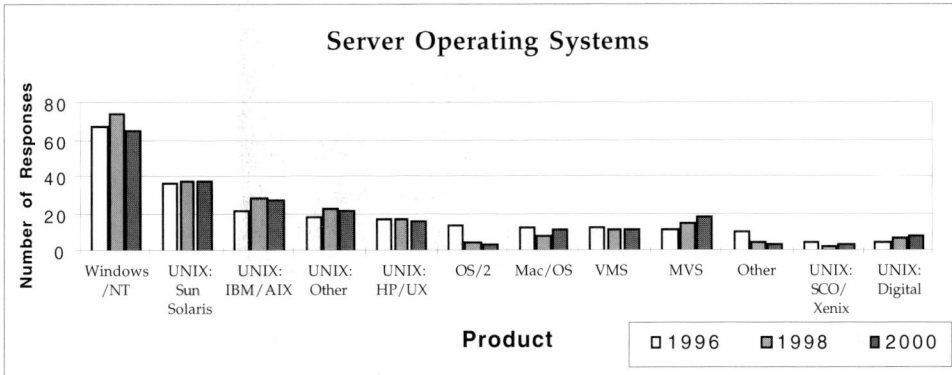

Server Operating Systems

Fig. 2.6 Windows NT and UNIX Sun Solaris Will Dominate through the Century

Windows 3.1/NT on a Pentium PC is the most popular client hardware/ operating system configuration (see Figs 2.7 and 2.8).

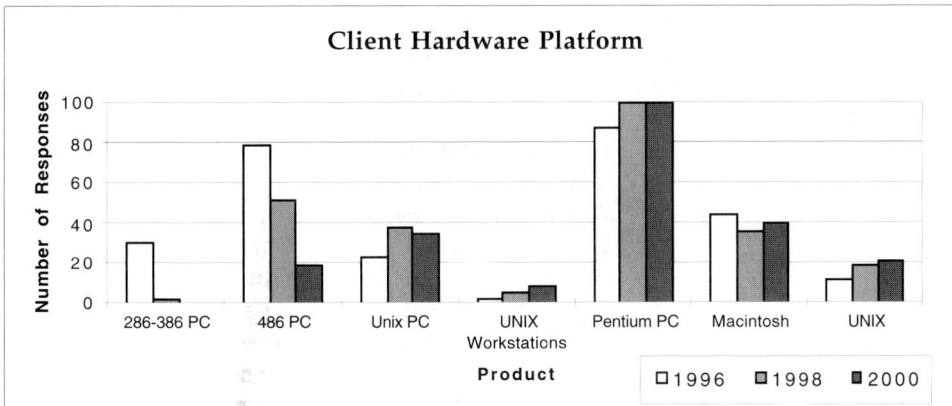

Client Hardware Platform

Fig. 2.7 PCs Will Dominate the Market through the Century

Client Operating Systems

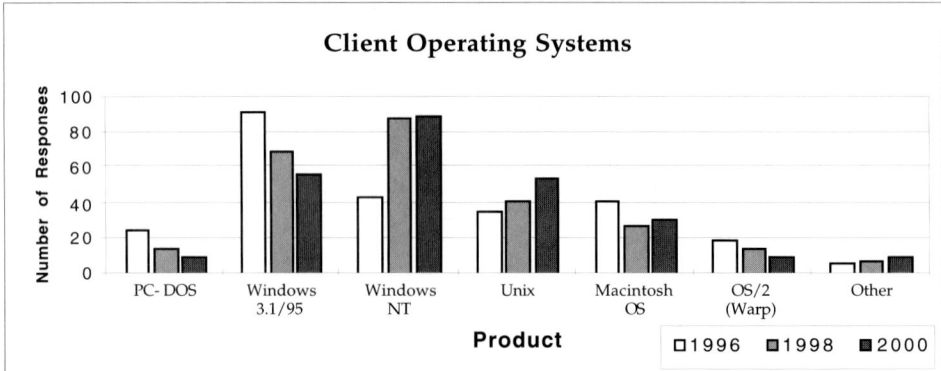

Fig. 2.8 Windows 3.1, 95, and NT Continue To Dominate the Market

2.3.4 Tools and Applications on IP Networks

2.3.4.1 Browsers

Respondents were hesitant to predict which browser software they would be using in the future. However, today Netscape Navigator is the most popular browser software and Microsoft Internet Explorer is gaining in popularity.

2.3.4.2 Programming and Scripting:

C and C++ are most frequently used for Web application development. However, participants report that by 1998 they will be ready for Java, or, if not Java *per se,* a more Java-like tool. Respondents were not as enthusiastic about adopting Java as we expected, frequently noting security and reliability problems. We found that Visual Basic was considered a stable, reliable product, although its use will drop off significantly by the year 2000.

2.4 APPLICATIONS FOR WEB-BASED COLLABORATION

Most groupware products are being developed and enhanced for IP networks. Group calendaring/scheduling, data conferencing, video conferencing, group document editing, workflow, and most other applications are now available in Web-based versions and more enter the market on a daily basis. Still, it is not the case that Web-based applications will eliminate the need for traditional LAN/WAN applications, a fact borne out in this study. People reported that they see IP and LAN/WAN networks as complimentary not competitive. Therefore, they are using a mix of products, and reported that they expect to continue in a hybrid environment for the foreseeable future.

In this study, the most popular product for electronic collaboration was Lotus Notes. Even so, it's not that these companies use Notes *instead* of Web-based applications, rather *with* Web-based applications. Most of the companies using Lotus Notes reported that they are also using Netscape products. Microsoft's Exchange was just being rolled out at the time this study was performed, yet 33 percent of our respondents said that they were either using Exchange currently or planned to in the near future. Fewer than 10 percent of the respondents are using Novell's GroupWise. Again, most of those companies are also using Netscape Navigator and other Web-based products.

A recent report by the US consultancy Input stated "Lotus Notes has only two years left as the dominant groupware system. After that, it will face fierce competition from Internet-based groupware such as Radnet's WebShare and Action Technologies' ActionWorkflow Metro." However, study participants reported healthy growth in Notes seats for the next four years. Although the rate of growth is more rapid from 1996 to 1998 (269 percent), there is still significant growth from 1998–2000 (74 percent) and, we believe, beyond.

2.4.1 Costs of Web-Based Applications and Infrastructures vs. Proprietary Applications and Infrastructures.

Study participants reported that they perceived the cost to build a Web infrastructure was dramatically less than the cost to build the infrastructure for a proprietary product such as Lotus Notes. They perceive a Notes infrastructure averages just over $1M whereas their perception of a Web site was just less than $200,000 (including sites with thousands of pages). The average cost of a Web page was $320. This study looked at people's perceptions—we made no attempt to construct actual costs (see Table 2.1).

This is significant because people's perception of cost influences their decision making. In this case, the reality does not bear out the perception. Intranets are only less expensive at the beginning. For example, Microsoft offers the Internet Information Server and Web client at no cost, but the Notes client is $69 per seat and servers are $495. Netscape seats are around $40. However, the initial purchase is only the beginning and comparing Notes to an intranet is not a one-to-one comparison. Web applications lack specific functionality that is still only available on proprietary LAN/WAN products, so it's not a one-to-one comparison. Recent reports indicate that in the long run, assuming the same functionality, the costs for proprietary applications are comparable to Web applications.

Only 32 percent of the companies who are currently using Notes are planning to move their Notes seats to the Web, and even then, they do not plan to move all their seats. This finding reflects the understanding that Web-based applications are not a replacement for Notes-type applications and that both will coexist in most organizations.

Table 2.1 Perceived Cost to Deploy Lotus Notes vs. Web Site

Perceived Cost of Lotus Notes	Number of Responses	Percent
<$500,000	11	23%
$500,000–$999,999	10	21%
$1–5M	8	17%
Expensive/Too much	14	29%
Unknown	5	10%

Perceived Cost WWW	Number of Responses	Percent
$10,000–$49,999	5	19%
$50,000–$99,999	8	31%
$100,000–$499,999	6	23%
$500,000–$999,999	4	15%
$1–$3M	2	8%
> $3M	1	4%

2.5 WHY ARE COMPANIES USING INTRANETS AS WELL AS LAN-BASED GROUPWARE?

2.5.1 Limitations of IP Networks

1. **Security:** The perception is that intranets are more secure than the Internet (which is vulnerable to hackers and other attacks). However, the fact is that the same 64-bit public key encryption security is used in both Notes and Netscape. It's just that inside the firewall, there is less chance of an attack.
2. **Hypertext Transfer Protocol (http):** the Internet protocol, is inadequate for the demands of some of today's intranet and Internet applications. HTTP has been used by the World Wide Web global information initiative since 1990. HTTP is an application-level protocol with the lightness and speed necessary for distributed, collaborative, hypermedia information systems. It is a generic, stateless, object-oriented protocol that can be used for many tasks, such as name servers and distrib-

uted object management systems, through extension of its request methods (commands). A feature of HTTP is the typing and negotiation of data representation, allowing systems to be built independently of the data being transferred. The problem is that HTTP, as originally conceived, is not able to support the many uses people are doing on the Internet and intranets.

3. **Replication:** Lotus is rumored to be unbundling these replication functions and will be offering them to enterprise INTRAnet clients.

2.6 ISSUES AND IMPLICATIONS

This research uncovered many important problems, some of which are to be expected given the rapid rate of application and infrastructure development. They are the typical problems of early adoption. The most commonly cited concerns and their implications for business are as follows:

☞ *Security of Information on the Network:* For collaboration to be successful, information must be easy to access—but ease of access compromises security. Without exception, every company we interviewed reported that network security was an important consideration. Intranets provide greater security than the Internet through the use of firewalls—servers that control access to the networks. Still, no network is absolutely secure, so companies judiciously select functions to move to their intranets.

☞ *It's All Evolving Too Quick!* A full third of the firms interviewed were uncomfortable with the rapid pace of software product evolution. The frequency with which new products and new versions of established products are released creates disruption to normal business processes. Companies would rather see a minimum of six months between version introductions, allowing them to more effectively manage the changes they bring.

☞ *Hindrances to the Adoption of the Technology:* Implementing any new system challenges the established patterns of people's working. Introducing collaborative technologies, especially on a broad scale, requires new behaviors as well as expectations. For example, our experience in consulting engagements shows that when collaborative technologies are introduced, one of the most noticeable changes occurs around the ownership of knowledge and, therefore, the dissemination of power. Patterns of access to information change immediately, concurrently changing people's roles and expectations. Not only is this disruptive to the flow of work in the organization, people perceive that their jobs are vulnerable. Consequently, they do not work to ensure the success of the new system. The single greatest hindrance to the adoption of these technologies is people's resistance to change.

Most businesses are going to require outside expertise to help in two primary areas. First, they will need help facilitating the traditional change management and technology transfer that occurs when large scale changes are implemented, and, second, to re-architect the flow and management of knowledge within their business processes and employees' minds.

2.7 THE FUTURE STATE

In discussing the future state of both type and capability of collaborative technologies with interviewees, it became apparent that predicting with any certainty is reliable only over a small window of time. For many respondents, there was some vision of likely events over the next 1–2 years, but a lack of confidence in extending those thoughts beyond 1998. Interviewees reported that the technologies are simply developing too quickly for them to feel confident in predicting product usage beyond a year or two. Most businesses are unwilling or unable to commit to any product for the long term—they don't want to be locked into fixed solutions, hardware, operating systems, types of databases, or browsers because they believe that by the year 2000 products and services will be available to them that do not even exist today.

This research has identified several opportunities for vendors of collaborative technology. Users reported that the following items were on their "radar screen" as criteria for future product selection.

☞ Import and export functions, minimal on most browsers, are seen as key to integrating legacy data. Users expect this functionality to be enhanced in the future

☞ Cross-platform environments will continue to be the norm. Vendors are required to develop for diverse operating system environments

☞ Users expect to increase their Web server usage. Therefore, vendors offering more powerful, better optimized servers will be best positioned to realize larger market share. Several participants are already outsourcing the maintenance of the Internet servers, however, intranet servers will continue to be maintained internally

☞ IP network growth will be explosive between 1998–2000. This is a significant market opportunity for suppliers of hardware and software for IP networks

☞ Introducing intranets, and all collaborative technologies, necessitates significant change management. Consultants and systems integrators are best positioned to offer objective and effective solutions to maximize this investment

2.7.1 Interviewees Reported the Following Technology Trends

☞ Intranet server growth is anticipated to be over 200 percent by 1998 and over 500 percent by the year 2000

☞ The average number of seats per IP network will increase from the current 11,065 to 14,239 in 1998, and to 39,216 by the year 2000

☞ Demand for intranet collaboration applications will be greater than for Internet applications

☞ Making predictions regarding software products and operating system usage for the long term is very difficult. Users have a wait-and-see-what's-new-on-the-market attitude regarding future purchases

☞ Pentium PCs will continue to lead the market for client hardware

☞ Mission critical activities will continue to migrate to Internet and intranet applications as the technology becomes more secure, robust, and when standards are ratified and strengthened.

2.8 CONCLUSION

Intranets are quickly evolving to be the infrastructure of choice for electronic collaboration. Using an intranet results in benefits that are realized quickly and visibly to the organization. For example, connecting to groupware applications from remote locations means that information is more available, holistic, and timely. Easy connectivity to the Internet provides an array of data, allowing companies to gather and disseminate dynamic internal and external information across the organization via their intranet and internal networks. A good example of the benefits of this kind of connectivity is the trend toward integrating customers, suppliers, and vendors via IP network applications.

Just as the technology is evolving, so businesses are pursuing the benefits of collaboration. The new set of challenges for business leaders includes identifying the best organization for the new working environment, leading management teams in reforming habits and behaviors and beginning to practice the new working style. And this is only one small step to the ultimate goal of creating a living corporate memory.

In 1996, the technologies that provided the benefits of working collaboratively via the Internet and intranet were in flux, limiting our ability to examine their benefits. This was the consequence of the evolution of technical capability and the emerging needs and challenges of the host businesses themselves. However, it is clear that this is a viable proposition today and endowed with latent capability for the future in helping businesses to be more effective.

2.9 DEFINITIONS USED IN THE RESEARCH

A number of words and terms appear in this report that are defined here for the purpose of full and common comprehension

Collaboration: The ability of two or more people or groups to transfer data and information with the capability of on-line interaction. The distinguishing feature is the ability for many-to-many interactions and information sharing, unlike e-mail where the interaction is one-to-one or one-to-many.

Groupware: Applications that allow two or more people to work together or as a group. The application can be scaled up to support departments, total processes, or the entire enterprise. Examples of groupware applications are synchronous and asynchronous conferencing, e-mail, group calendaring and scheduling, and group document editing and management.

Intranet: An IP-based network that resides behind a firewall, thus affording greater security for the business.

Internet: An IP-based network that resides outside the firewall.

BIOGRAPHIES

David Coleman is the founder and Managing Director of Collaborative Strategies. He has been involved with groupware and collaborative technologies since 1990 and is the author/editor of *Groupware Technologies and Applications* (Prentice Hall, 1995). He also was the founder and conference chairman for the GroupWare '92–95 conferences that were held in San Jose, Boston, and London on an annual basis. Mr. Coleman was the editor and publisher of *GroupTalk*, the newsletter of workgroup computing. He is the founding editor of *Virtual Workgroups* magazine, and currently a columnist. He also writes a monthly column on groupware for *Computer Reseller News* and for *MainSpring* (an on-line resource for intranet and Web developers). Mr. Coleman has written for many trade and business publications such as *Network World*, *Datamation*, *Fortune*, and is a frequent public speaker worldwide. He has consulted to groupware vendors on product marketing, positioning, market research and competitive analysis, and for groupware users in assessing their organization's groupware readiness as well as tool selection and the human factors involved in a successful groupware project. Mr. Coleman can be contacted directly at 415-282-9197, or at davidc@collaborate.com. More information on Collaborative Strategies can be found at www.collaborate.com.

Abby Kutner is a Project Manager with Collaborative Strategies, responsible for several areas of company operation. She has managed client research into how companies are using the Internet and intranets to support electronic collaboration, how companies are using, and expect to use Web servers, how companies are integrating Lotus Notes with their legacy systems, and several specific Web-based collaborative technologies. Abby has led focus groups and managed other marketing activities including commercialization plans. She was responsible for editing the *GroupTalk* newsletter, developed and reviewed articles for *Virtual Workgroups* magazine, and worked with Mr. Coleman in the compilation of both of his books on collaborative technologies. Before joining Collaborative Strategies in 1994, Abby was responsible for introducing collaborative technology to executives and utility members of the Electric Power Research Institute. Abby holds a bachelors degree from the University of California at Berkeley.

The Evolution of Web-Based Conferencing and Workflow

David Coleman
Collaborative Strategies™

In the prior two chapters, we have introduced the trend that vendors of LAN-based collaborative products are rapidly moving their products to the Web. In this chapter, we will examine two functional areas that are evolving their collaborative functions in a new and less expensive way, on the Web. I believe that over this year (1997), the focus for collaboration will shift away from the LAN: It's not that LANs will go away, but collaboration inside and outside of an organization is easier with a common graphic standard platform (like a browser) and this is found on the Web. The other trend I see, and one which is encouraging these functions onto the Web, is the acknowledgment that collaboration is not just technology, and that focusing on the people, culture, economics, and politics are all as critical as the technology.

This chapter focuses on the rapid evolution of workflow from LAN-based workflows to Web-based workflows. We also present a functional analysis of Web-based workflows. (See Chapter 6 for a detailed review of the workflow industry, its evolution, maturity, and products, as well as discussion of the business motivation for using workflow technology and how to implement workflow for maximum benefit.) The second technology covered in this chapter is Web-based conferencing. Again, we have included a functional analysis of this area. These two collaborative functions have made significant progress in Web migration and, therefore, offer insight into how other technologies can successfully migrate from LAN to Web-based architectures.

Much of the data displayed today on the Web is static data, i.e, the calendar for the month, or policies and procedures for an organization. Vendors developing these applications have had many of the same problems moving them from LANs to IP networks. But collaborative data is often dynamic, such as a chat session, or status tracking in a workflow process. The problem for vendors of collaborative technology comes in response time. What is real time? In some industries, a computer takes only a fraction of a second to respond and that is called real time. In the collaboration arena, real time is usually defined by the patience of the person using the program. In general, a second or two for response time is allowable for human-to-human interactions mediated by the computer. The current language to build Web-based development (for real-time and non real-time collaborative products) is Java, but Java is slow. Although vendors like Sun Microsystems and HP are now releasing compilers for Java that will compile on the fly, speed is still the fly in the ointment! Since this is a ubiquitous problem, my assumption is that there will be an equally ubiquitous solution developed and promulgated over the next year to deal with this interactivity issue.

3.1 LAN AND WEB-BASED WORKFLOW

The fact is that there was no real market for Web-based workflow products until late in 1995, and that most entrants to this market have announced over the last six months. However, the LAN-based workflow market has many vendors (150 at last count) and is very competitive.

In a 1995 report on Workflow, Ovum estimate the world-wide workflow market alone for 1996 was about $2.35 billion. However, with rapid growth, this market will reach $5.5 billion in the workflow product and services market by the year 2000. Even though this annual growth rate is rapid, and higher than I would expect for this technology, it is a smaller number than the growth rate of the WWW. For this reason, I feel that Ovum's numbers are low. This is unusual, as most market research firms estimate high (it makes their clients happier). But Ovum did not see this trend developing when this report was being developed. At the rapid rate workflow vendors are moving to this new infrastructure, I believe that the 5.5 billion mark will be passed by 1998 and that it will almost double that by the year 2000. Also, when this report was done, the Web was not really considered as a new and alternative corporate infrastructure for electronic collaboration. This report focuses on LAN-based groupware, but we are now in a situation where hybrid products are very useful

As we see it, there are three types of workflow: Web-initiated workflows, hybrid workflow products, and Web-native workflow products. The Web initiated workflows (WIW) are the easiest to do and many have already been implemented. These workflows simply involve Web access to a LAN-based workflow process. For example, a Web page on your intranet is an expense form you fill out. The workflow routes the form over a LAN to your boss for signature and then to finance to get a check cut.

The second form of Web-based workflow is exemplified by the hybrid products. In a recent study by Collaborative Strategies, we were able to determine that companies have no plans to discard their LAN networks in favor of IP networks (as the pundits were predicting six months ago). Instead, they are adding the intranet to those LANs. In this case, hybrid products that support multiple functions on either architecture will provide a low cost, low risk way to implement

Web-based workflows for the next few years. A good example of such a hybrid product is NEC's Star Enterprise Workflow, marketed in the U.S. by OneWave.

The third type of product is the Web-native workflow product. These are the most difficult to do and require the vendor to redesign the product to be optimally functional on the Web. The good thing about these products is that they take full advantage of the strengths of the Web and Java. The down side is that they often don't have all the functions a LAN-based products might have. This is because both the products and the infrastructure for this are very young. Another down side is that these products often only run on the Web.

3.1.1 The Market for Workflow

According to the Yankee Group, workflow revenues are growing rapidly. The Yankee Group breaks workflow out into four categories: Production, Administrative, Ad-hoc, and Collaborative. Production-based workflows are transaction oriented and a good example would be the process to generate a life insurance policy. Administrative workflows are just that, the automation of mundane processes such as expense reports. Ad-hoc workflows are the most difficult and are most often found in the front office rather than the back office, they have the quality of being changed on the fly, and can easily be re-configured. Collaborative workflows are those that are starting to pop up on the WWW, which require the interaction of two or more people in the process. Products like ATI's Metro and JetForm's WebLink are good examples of this class of product.

The Yankee Group reports the overall revenues for Workflow Worldwide in 1995 to have been $768 million, with the majority of this being production workflows. By 1998 this figure will have jumped to $2.2 billion with the greatest increase being in collaborative workflows (114 percent) (see Fig. 3.1).

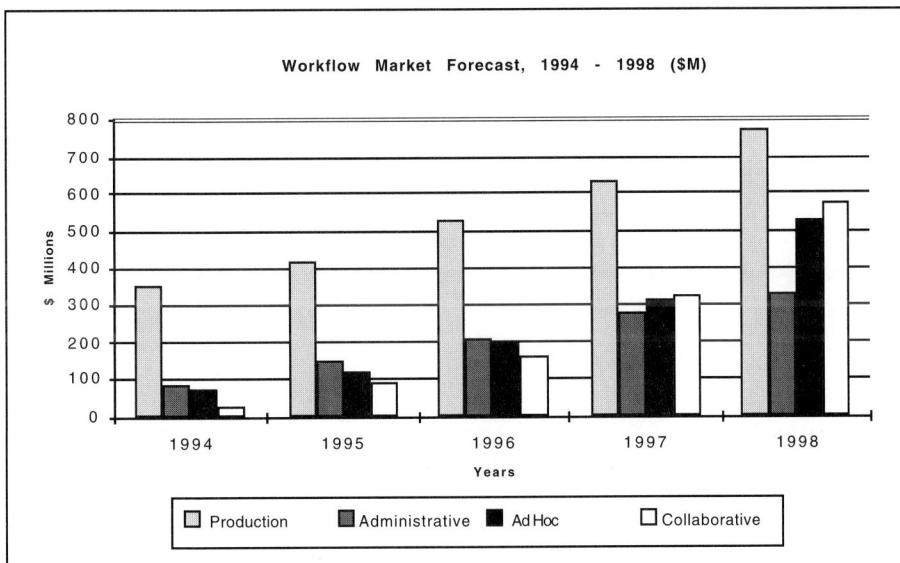

Fig. 3.1 Anticipated Growth in Workflow Market (Courtesy of Yankee Group)

It is important to look at some of the tools and functions of workflow products. Figure 3.2 shows a detailed examination of several workflow products, both low and high-end.

	Production and/or ad hoc Workflows	Price per seat	Graphic process depiction	E-mail routing/ notification	Electronic forms routing	UI customization	Hooks to C, C++, Visual Basic, or 4GLs	Supports rulebased workflow
FileNet WorkFlo and Ensemble	Both	Ensemble $295/user	Yes	Yes	Yes	some	Yes	Yes
Ultimus WebFlow	Production	$590/user (Kit w/ 5 clients $2,950)	Yes	Notification	Yes	Yes	No	unknown
IBM FlowMark	Production	$695/user; quantity discounts available	Yes	Yes	Yes	unknown	Yes	unknown
Action Technologies Metro	Both	$40.00	Yes, for development	Yes	Yes	Yes	Yes	Yes
Delrina FormFlow 2.0	Ad hoc	$90.00	No	Yes	Yes	Yes	Yes	Yes
OpenText/ Odesta LiveLink	Both	$65/user (estimated cost)	Yes	Yes	via 'inbox'	Some	Scripting language (OpenText's)	Yes
ViewStar ViewStar	Production	$80/user (estimated cost)	Yes	Yes, must be programmed	Yes, must be programmed	Yes	Yes, plus Power-Builder, Delphi	Yes, must be programmed
WebFlow SamePage	Both	$315/user (20 users, volume discounts)	Yes	Yes	Yes	Yes	No	Yes
Wang Open Workflow	Both	unknown	Yes	Yes	Yes	Yes	Yes, plus COBOL, Power-Builder	unknown
NEC Star Enterprise Workflow	Yes	$125/user ($1200/ server—100 users)	Yes	Yes	Yes	Yes	VB compatible	Yes
STATUS TRACKING	Whole workflow	Personal action items	Time/ date stamping	Digital signatures	Client (browser or other)	Technological Infrastructure: WWW native or ported from LAN	Distribution channels	Workflow Management Coalition Standards
FileNet Workflo and Ensemble	Yes	Yes	Yes		Visual WorkFlo/Performer	WorkFlo Web server, OLE controls, and browser plug-ins	Self; ValueNet Business Partners	Yes
Ultimus WebFlow	Yes	Yes	Yes	Yes	Ultimus Client	WWW native	Self; VAR program	No
IBM FlowMark	Yes	Yes	Audit Trail	With Lotus Notes	FlowMark	WWW/ FlowMark Process Initiation	Self; IBM Business Enterprise Solutions Team, Resellers & VARs	Yes

Fig. 3.2 Tools and Functions of Workflow Products

Action Technologies Metro	Yes	Yes	Yes		Browser	HTML forms based on MS SQL and NT Back Office	Self; Netscape, Healthdyne Information Ststems, Productive Data	Founder
Delrina FormFlow 2.0	Forms route and status	Yes	Yes	Yes	E-mail	Standard e-mail packages, Internet FTP site for forms	Self; Alliances with PC DOCs, Amex, VARs and consultants	No
OpenText/ OdestaYes LiveLink	Yes	Yes	Yes	No	Browser	WWW native and LAN	Self; Informix relationship	Yes
ViewStar ViewStar	Yes	Yes	Yes	Yes	Browser	Initially a LAN product	Partners and Direct Sales	Yes
WebFlow SamePage	Yes	Yes	Yes	Yes	Browser	Web Native with Java applets	Direct Sales, VARs, OEMs	No
Wang Open Workflow	Yes		Yes		Document Management; High Performance & Remote Workstations	LAN based, unknown WWW strategy	Self; Alliance with Microsoft	Yes
NEC Star Enterprise Workflow	Yes	Yes	Yes	Authentication only	Star Enterprise Workflow Client	Lan-Based and WWW intent	OneWave in the US, NEC in Japan	Yes

Compliance	CORBA	ODBC	Java	Other
FileNet Workflo and Ensemble		RDBMs		
Ultimus WebFlow		Yes		
IBM FlowMark				
Action Technologies Metro		Yes	Yes	
Delrina FormFlow 2.0		Yes	No	Forms by fax, Notes and MS Exchange OLE compliant
OpenText/ OdestaYes LiveLink		RDBMs	Yes	ActiveX, PDF, SGML
ViewStar ViewStar	No	No	Yes	ActiveX, OLE, Notes
WebFlow SamePage	Yes	Yes	Yes	OLE
Wang Open Workflow		Yes		
NEC Star Enterprise Workflow	No	Yes		

Fig. 3.2 Tools and Functions of Workflow Products (Continued)

3.1.2 Strategic Alliances

In 1995 there was a great deal of consolidation of the workflow market. Many companies were acquired by the large groupware/software vendors, and other alliances were made. Two of the best known were Novell's alliance with FileNet and Microsoft's alliance with Wang. Since then, Watermark has been acquired, HP has new an alliance with FileNet, and Recognition was purchased by BancTech. For a more detailed analysis of the alliances and the market for Workflow, see Chapter 6 by Ronni Marshak.

3.1.3 Web-based Workflow and Other Collaborative Functions

In recent Collaborative Strategies research (see Chapter 2), we found that collaborative functions, in general, were more popular on the intranet than the Internet. Workflow was also one of these collaborative functions. We found double the number of companies implementing workflow on an intranet than an Internet. It is our belief that once these functions are implemented inside companies, they will move outside, on the Internet, to foster electronic commerce between companies or to work with customers and suppliers. Figure 3.3 shows the relationship of various collaborative functions to workflow.

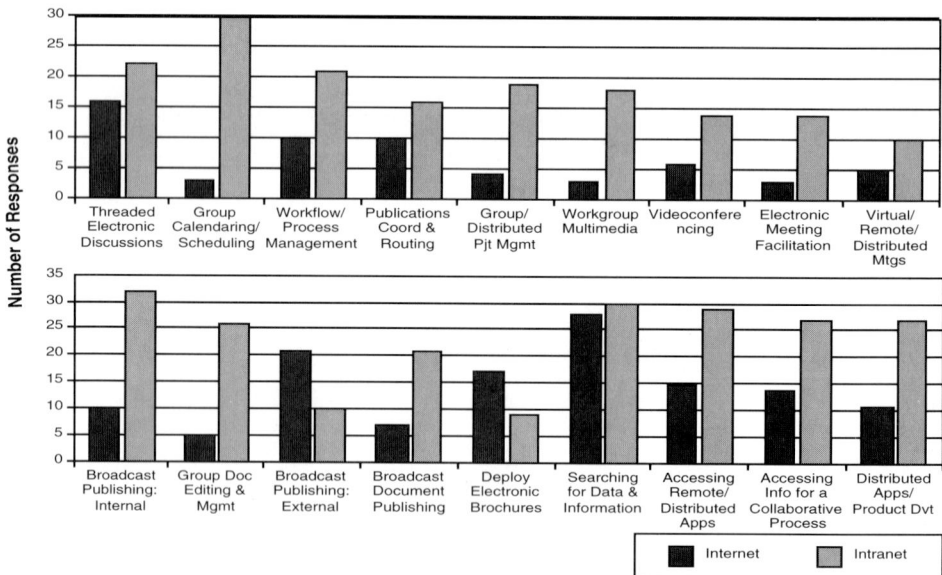

Fig. 3.3 Workflow and Other Collaborative Functions on the Internet and Intranets

3.2 BACKGROUND: WORKFLOW REPORTS

While there seems to be some argument on where the workflow market is going, there is no argument that all of the workflow vendors are beginning to provide Web-based solutions. The remainder of this section is focused on a functional comparison of 10 different Web-based workflow products.

3.2.1 The Delphi Workflow Study

The Delphi Consulting Group of Boston performed a study of the workflow market in 1996, analyzing detailed information from 60 suppliers of workflow today. What they found was that overall market revenue growth will have reached a plateau in 1995 compared to the market performance from the prior five years. 82 percent of those working on workflow are not yet in the implementation phase, but rather are in the planning, strategy, pilot project, or evaluation phases. Delphi sees this as an explanation to the plateau in growth for the workflow market, as well as good news for rapid growth in the next few years after the early adopter phase is completed.

Delphi has identified a number of factors that have slowed workflow growth:

☞ BPR has not been a success in the U.S.

☞ New corporate communications and computing infrastructures are now in place to support workflows

☞ The WWW and Electronic Commerce will focus more attention on workflow and makes workflow solutions available to a wide range of new problems

☞ The workflow market is a broad and diverse market. Today, the market leader is FileNet with 14 percent, however, Delphi expects to see this leadership broaden to other players over the next few years.

3.2.1.1 Workflow Market Growth

From 1990–1994, the compound annual growth rate for workflow software was 34 percent. From 1994–1995 this rate was only 13 percent, slowing almost two-thirds rather abruptly (see Fig. 3.4). The market for workflow in 1995 was calculated at $816M, and is estimated for 1996 to have been $970M. This slowdown is explained as the lag between the first and second workflow waves (see Fig. 3.5).

Workflow Market Growth

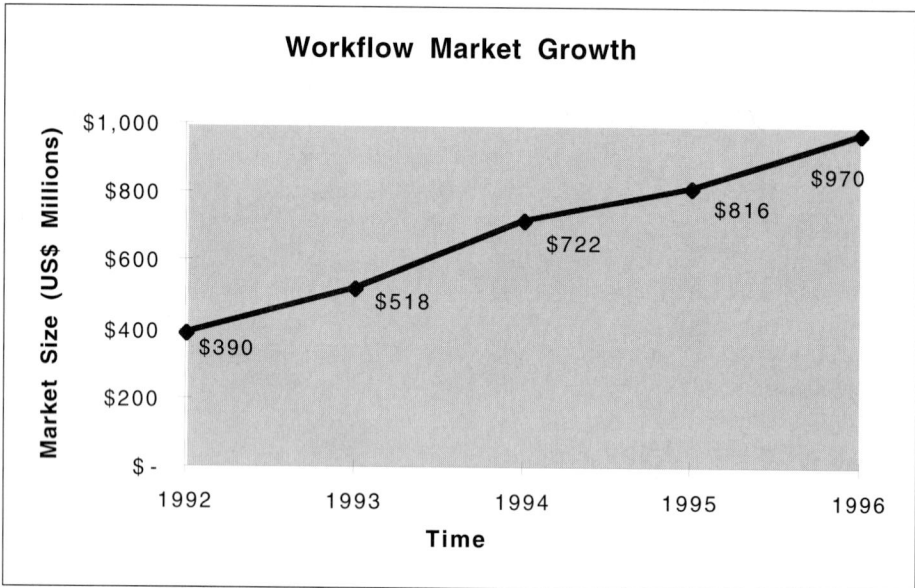

Fig. 3.4 Workflow Market Growth (Courtesy of Delphi Consulting Group, 1996)

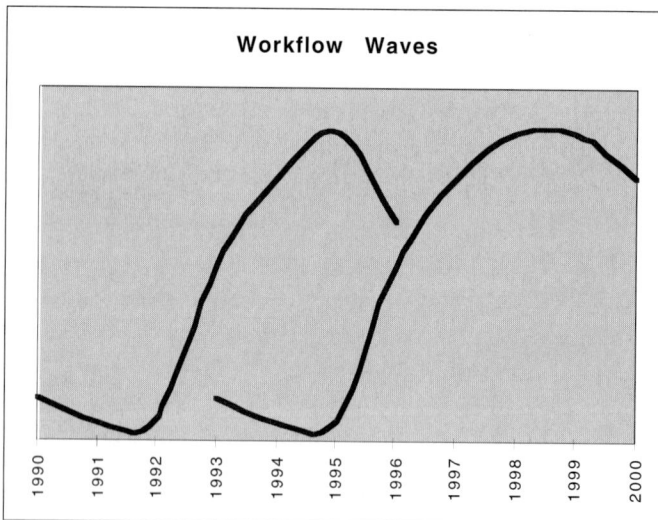

Fig. 3.5 Workflow Waves

Specifically, 1990–1994 was the time workflow was chosen by the early adopters. In 1995, most of the early adopters had bought their workflow software and were busily applying it to pilot projects, and so consequently not much software was bought. Delphi believes that this early adopter phase will have concluded (either successfully or not) in 1996 and that companies that had successful pilots will go into the implementation phase, where many more licenses for workflow software will be bought. Obviously, the big winner in this analysis is FileNet, as they are the current market leader and most probably have the largest number of trials and pilot projects occurring. FileNet has increased its lead in this industry from 14 percent in 1994 to almost 20 percent today. Other vendors with some market share are: IBM with 5.5 percent, Wang with 4.3 percent, ViewStar with 3.1 percent. It is important to note that over 55 percent of the workflow industry revenues are made by companies that have less than 3 percent of market share (i.e., Action Technologies, JetForm, Symantec/Delrina, etc.)

This has led to a great deal of consolidation of vendors. FileNet is aligned with Novell, Wang with Microsoft, others with Netscape, and many smaller workflow and imaging companies (i.e., Watermark Software, Saros, etc.) have been bought up by larger firms for their technology. The fact that 1995 was not a good year for workflow sales accelerated this consolidation phase in market maturity.

Another way to look at this data is to use Geoffrey Moore's technology adoption model (see Fig. 3.6) from his book *Crossing the Chasm* (Harper Business 1991).

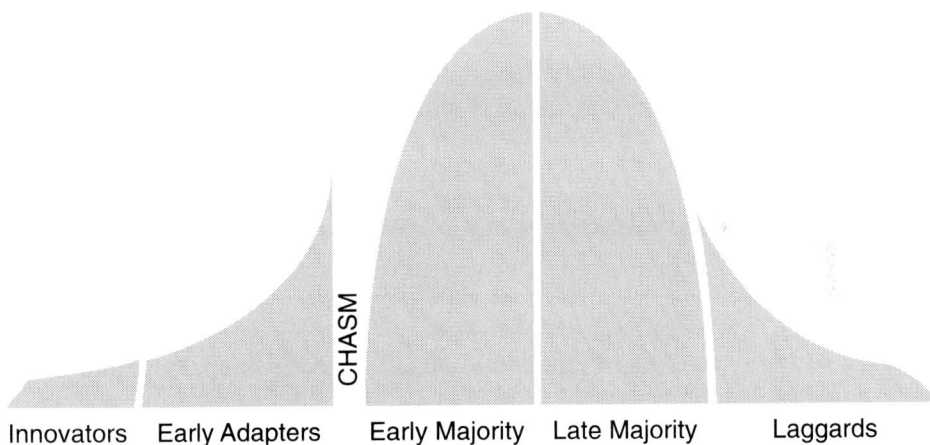

CHASM

Innovators   Early Adapters   Early Majority   Late Majority   Laggards

Fig. 3.6 Moving Your Product from the Early Adopters to the Early Majority Is the Most Difficult Phase in Market Penetration (Geoffrey Moore, *Crossing the Chasm*, p. 17). Copyright © 1991 by Geoffrey A. Moore. Reprinted by permission of HarperCollins Publishers, Inc.

Applying this model, 1990–94 can be seen as the early adopter phase. In 1995 workflow reached the brink of the chasm. Will workflow as a technology be able to cross this chasm to the land of riches promised in the "early majority" phase of this model? If so, what compelling reason will pull workflow across? Delphi believes that electronic commerce is this compelling reason and that EDI has already made a beachhead with the early majority. Boosted by Web-based transaction systems, on-line malls, and intercompany supply chains supported by the Web or intranets, Delphi believes that this application is what helped move workflow into the mainstream in 1996. Delphi estimated a 20 percent growth for 1996, up from the 13 percent in 1995, but not as robust as the 24 percent from 1990–1994. Furthermore, Delphi believes that FileNet, will move workflow across the chasm, much as Lotus moved groupware across the chasm.

Delphi believes that the second workflow wave will have companies expanding their definition of workflow. In the first wave, many of the applications were production or administrative applications where there was good customer contact, good payback, and the workflow was used every day in a production manner. These workflows, once established and optimized, become routine. The same is true for administrative workflows, except that there may be a greater degree of flexibility in these applications as administrative procedures may change more often.

Delphi and Collaborative Strategies look at how to carve up the workflow market. If you look at it from an applications/technology perspective, there are:

☞ Mail/message centric: Leading vendors—JetForm, Delrina, Banyan

☞ Document/image centric: leading vendors—USI, NIC

☞ Process centric: leading vendors—FileNet, IBM

If you look at workflows from a development environment perspective:

☞ Ad-hoc

☞ Transaction-based

☞ Object-oriented

☞ Knowledge-based

The drivers for the second wave of workflow software are:

☞ the implementation of networks throughout corporations

☞ the advent of the World Wide Web

☞ BPR, while not successful itself, has caused companies to take a new look at organizational analysis

☞ EDI and electronic commerce will support the rapid growth of network based workflows

On the other hand, factors that are limiting growth are:

☞ Uncertainty of what the open computing environment will be

☞ What the desktop environment will be

☞ No workflow standards (WfMC not ratified yet)

Revenues for workflow vendors are mostly generated by product sales (66 percent) with the other 34 percent generated by consulting and services. What this means is that most workflow vendors are partnering with professional services firms to deliver the necessary services while they deliver the software. FileNet is the leader in both product and service offerings today.

3.2.1.2 Industry Focus

The industry that is adopting workflow most rapidly is Finance/Banking. This is no surprise as they are adopting all networked technologies very rapidly. Whether it's because of the intense competition between banks, brokerage houses, and insurance firms for the same customers, or the deregulation of these industries (including insurance), they are adopting workflow solutions rapidly. These are also the same firms that are putting these workflow applications up on their internal and external Web pages.

Medical/pharmaceutical, manufacturing, and telecommunications are the other industries adopting workflow.

3.2.1.3 Geographic Focus

North America, with its leading network infrastructure accounts for over two-thirds (68 percent) of workflow revenues. Europe accounts for 25 percent, Japan 2 percent and the rest of Asia 4 percent. Obviously, there will be tremendous growth in workflow applications in Europe over the next few years and Japan following later, as network infrastructures become more available.

3.2.2 AIIM Study on Workflow

Interestingly, an AIIM study of workflow that claims to have interviewed the same vendor population shows a growth rate of over 50 percent for 1995, and expects that growth rate to continue through the year 2000. They claim that the average revenues for workflow software and service providers was $10 million. Both studies agree that new implementations will fuel future growth and that there are a lot of pilot projects that will turn into full fledged implementations in the 1996–1998 time frame. Another interesting observation noted in this report is that 21 percent of those currently using workflow are dissatisfied with the systems they are using. This is not surprising, as most of these systems are new and not perfected. However, most of those complaining about these systems have noted that their workflow systems are undergoing rapid change.

AIIM also interviewed end-users to validate some of these findings. Many of the users interviewed (55 percent) across all industries were investigating workflow. AIIM projects 50 percent growth per year (based on $1.25 billion in 1994) for the next 3–4 years and they expect the workflow market to have reached $2.8 billion in 1996. If the market grows at a 50 percent rate through the end of the century, the workflow market (software and services) will be $4.2 billion in 1997, $6.3 billion in 1998, $9.5 billion in 1999, and almost $14 billion by the year 2000.

3.3 WEB-BASED WORKFLOW PRODUCTS

Although the number in the AIIM study may be close to the truth, I think the reason for it is the Web. As the Internet/intranet makes collaborative technologies less expensive and more accessible, more and more firms will begin to use these technologies. I see this happening especially in Europe and Asia, and ultimately in Africa and South America as their infrastructures start to come on line. Usually, the first collaborative technology to be used is e-mail, and then workflow is next. It is probably because both of these functions are easy to understand and implement. Also, production workflows are the "low hanging fruit," i.e. they are low risk with high return.

On the negative side, even though the move toward the Web is a major trend, the prices for client software on the Web tend to be lower than LAN/WAN software. Additionally, if workflow continues to be associated with BPR (which is currently moving out of favor due to its high failure rate of over 70 percent), this may inhibit the growth of the workflow market.

At the time of this survey, over 70 percent of the users surveyed planned to use workflow software or services in the future, however, only 43 percent were actually using or implementing workflow. Interestingly, only 15 percent of those companies surveyed implemented workflow outside the U.S.

AIIM estimates there are currently 150 workflow vendors. However, I think that number has dropped over the last year due to consolidation of the market (many companies have been bought or have merged). Although, to some degree, this consolidation in the LAN workflow market is compensated for by the emergence of many new companies (like WebFlow) appearing on an IP network infrastructure.

Workflow users have focused on the easiest challenges with the biggest paybacks first.

- 75% are using workflow for production processes
- 35% use it for groupware or collaborative purposes
- 35% for company-wide forms and e-mail
- 22% for document management

This corresponds well with how the vendors see their products

- 71% production
- 41% collaborative
- 25% publishing and project management
- 17% e-mail applications

The most critical factors found for choosing a workflow system were:

- cost (27%)
- compatibility with legacy systems (21%)
- good product support (14%)
- and the reputation of the vendor (12%).

Those that use workflow most highly are the insurance industry (31%) followed by banking and finance, manufacturing, and government.

Interestingly, this report notes that the key trend affecting the workflow industry will be imaging technologies. I feel this is a biased answer for two reasons. First, many of those surveyed are part of AIIM, an association that is focused on imaging. Second, this survey must have been done early in 1995 when the use of the Web was not as prevalent as it is today. I came to this conclusion because using workflow on the Web was not discussed in this survey. Twenty-two percent said that they felt groupware and network technologies will have a major effect on workflow over the next five years. I agree. Twenty-nine percent saw improved software having a major affect on usage. If "improved software" is translated into "it will run on the Web," I can agree with those numbers. One of the reasons I feel so strongly about the move of workflow functionality to the Web is because the Web provides a low cost, cross system platform architecture that is easy to use. Forty-five percent of those interviewed stated that ease of use was one of the highest criteria in selecting workflow software. Couple this with their demand for lower cost, and it is easy to imagine many workflow systems on the Web, or at least having the workflows initiated from the Web.

All users want lower cost and better performance from their workflow systems, and many (23 percent) believe that emerging technologies will make both integration with other software and the implementation of workflow easier.

The previous section of this chapter focused on LAN-based workflow. However, the growth in the workflow market will be from Web-based workflow. To this end, we have done functional research to survey some of the top products. This section focuses on the transition of both workflow functions and the use of workflow products from the LAN to the Web.

3.3.1 Research Methodology

A list of workflow functions was developed and research was performed to determine which products had which functions. Direct interviews with vendors and researching product literature published on their Web-sites provided most of the raw data. No in-depth technical analysis was performed.

3.3.2 Results

After examining 10 vendors and their products, it is clear that many of the workflow products available on the Web today were created for a LAN and then ported over to the WWW to allow an additional interface to the LAN-based workflow product. Some of the products we looked at were created on the Web and are Web-only products, i.e., Ultimus WebFlow and WebFlow. Both of these products are somewhat different in architecture than the LAN-based products that were ported.

Another factor to examine is whether the workflow product is messaging-based, database-based, or both. Messaging-based products are better at routing and connecting a process by e-mail, enhancing communication between people and tasks. However, with such products, the usual drawbacks are the ability to easily add ad-hoc workflows or support sophisticated process branching. These functions usually require a sophisticated database that not only deals with task state, but process branching, authorization, etc. Some of the products examined have the advantages of a hybrid messaging-database architecture, which combines the best of both architectures and that allows all of the above functions.

Currently, with intranets being the hot trend, some of the Web-based products are getting some play on these new corporate infrastructures. Interestingly, in talking to the product manager at WebFlow, SamePage (which is focused towards the software development process) is being used by JavaSoft to deal with the licensing of Java over the Web. To license Java, you log onto their Web page, and get a SamePage form that you fill out. SamePage routes your form to legal for an NDA, then to an account representative to determine the level of licensing and support. SamePage also routes the form to other buckets for payments, licensing terms, etc. This five part multi-form workflow is an excellent example of how Web-based processes are being used today.

However, we feel that intranet-only workflow applications are limiting. Corporate LANs will not disappear anytime soon. Although they may also become IP networks, most companies now testing workflow software are testing it on a LAN rather than an intranet. This means that most of the workflow software to be bought over the next few years will work on a LAN. Since the new trend is toward the less expensive and more intuitive infrastructure of the intranet, it is important for a workflow product of today and the next few years to support both infrastructures.

Additionally, because many of the Web-based workflow products are so new, they only support a few standards, mostly Web-based standards like HTML or HTTP. None of the Web-based workflow solutions we examined support the Workflow Management Coalition standard (version 1 or 2). This standard, while not yet accepted industry wide, is emerging as the most likely candidate for the transfer of information between processes or different workflow products. We can see a scenario in the near future where different products are used for LAN-based workflow and Web-based workflows, and that the task data and the meta data about the process itself will both have to transparently pass between products on these two different infrastructures. Although the workflow management coalition standard will support this transfer of data, a more elegant solution is to use a product that allows this to happen transparently, while supporting the most critical features for workflow in both infrastructures.

3.3.3. Ad hoc vs. Production

One of the strengths of many of the LAN-based products is the ability to not only support robust production based workflows, but also to support ad hoc workflows. In today's chaotic office environment, often workflows are created for a process that may be critical, but used only once. For example, in an advertising agency, the creative department has decided to build a sample video to show their ideas for advertising to one of their clients. They create a one time process for the building of this video, so each of the creative people can attach a video clip, story board, or idea outline to a mail message from the head of the team who will be developing the script for the video. With an ad hoc workflow product, not only is this possible, but when the client calls and wants to see the progress of the creative team, he too can be added to the workflow on the fly, to monitor their progress.

We found that many of the products reviewed were production oriented and do not support ad hoc workflow or the ability to add people and processes without having to redo much of the application and process logic. Of the Web-based products, Ultimus' WebFlo is production oriented and falls into this category, while Webflow's SamePage product is just the opposite, it is ad hoc oriented and requires consulting to develop a Web-based production process. There were a few LAN based systems that do support both; FileNet, Odesta, Wang, and Action Technology all support both, and ATI's Metro looks like a strong contender for one of the best Web implementations.

3.3.4 Partners and Focus

ATI has also implemented support for HTML forms, MS SQL, and MS Back Office, and we believe they will support Microsoft's drive from the desktop to the Web. Office '97 and Outlook, announced by Microsoft, will integrate desktop applications directly into the Microsoft Explorer Web browser, making this browser the actual desktop environment. We believe that because of strong ties with Wang, they will integrate Wang's workflow product into this Office Suite. Since Office and Outlook will have been made available to developers in late '96, we expect ATI to hook Metro to these products as soon as they can, since this seems to be their strategic direction.

Many of the vendors we examined seem to be focused on the Microsoft platform. FileNet, the market leader, is fairly neutral, IBM, with the purchase of Lotus, is more focused on FlowMark and the integration with Notes than it is on Microsoft, ViewStar's strength is imaging, and Odesta's strength is document management.

3.3.5 Pricing/Value

In terms of cost, ATI's metro has the lowest cost per user at $40 and the highest that we were able to verify was IBM at $695/user. Products like Delrina's, or even JetForm's, are more forms routing products that can be initiated from the Web. However, JetForm has recently added a full blown workflow engine to their product as well as offering the ability to do Web-initiated workflows.

NEC's Star Enterprise Workflow (SEW) is about mid range in terms of per user pricing. However, it is high in terms of value. Some of the lower priced products, like ATI's Metro and Delrina's products, are limited in function or are single function products and therefore do not provide as high a value as SEW. Along with running on both LANs and the Web, it is one of the few products that allows you to graphically depict your workflow in a workflow editor while on the Web. Although it only has development hooks to a Visual Basic-like language, it does support rule based workflows, forms routing, and electronic mail notification. It also does all of the standard workflow functions such as: escalation, time and date stamping, and authentication.

3.4 CONCLUSIONS

In the year 1995 there was a year of vendor consolidation. The growth of the Internet and intranets in 1995 has spurred many LAN-based workflow vendors to migrate to IP networks and a more graphic Web browser interface. Many LAN-based functions are not yet available on the Web and this is also true for workflow products. Those products that are solely Web-oriented seem to focus their functions in one specific direction, i.e., on sales force automation, or document management, or imaging. Having this focus will require these products to take and defend specific market segments.

The current distinction NEC has is its ability to span both infrastructures, LAN and IP networks. SEW is the ultimate hybrid product gracefully bridging the LAN and intranet infrastructures as well as production and ad hoc applications, and messaging and database architectures. It is focused toward an office environment and supports processes as easily in the front office as the back office. It supports the Workflow Management Coalition Standard as well as Java (by year end). It is these abilities and the fact that NEC has moved away from a proprietary messaging systems that makes it the best choice for today's hybrid infrastructure environments that will have to support both production and ad hoc workflows. Additionally, SEW supports a collaborative model and is well positioned to support collaborative workflows.

Whether the workflow market was stagnant or growing rapidly in 1995, it is clear that many of the companies currently examining workflow solutions will begin to implement them as their pilot studies are successful in the next few years.

What is unclear is who will be the winner in this market. Those with the best technology or those with the best partners and distribution channels. What we have seen time and again is that the best technology does not often win, but rather the best sales and distribution wins, even if the workflow product is not as good technically.

Our initial analysis of workflow shows a market in turmoil. Also, a market that is in transition and in the process of consolidation. At least in the U.S., the LAN-based workflow market is overcrowded. Many of these vendors have chosen to retrofit their products to meet the needs of the intranet. However, consolidation of these vendors is still taking place and moving to the intranet is not a solution because there are many new Web-based vendors popping up forcing the competition into new arenas. We see the workflow market starting to fragment, splitting into industry specific solutions (i.e., workflow for publishing), as well as horizontal niche markets (ad hoc, production, collaborative, administrative) for workflow over the rest of this year. We also see continual consolidation and an integration of imaging and forms routing technologies into the workflow market.

Just as workflow and process oriented functions are moving to the Web, so are other collaborative functions. One of the functions that has always been part of the Internet is newsgroups and mailing lists. But these functions are limited in their ability to support collaboration. Rather, another class of products are emerging on the Internet/intranet to support collaboration—real-time conferencing products.

3.5 DATA CONFERENCING FOR THE INTERNET AND INTRANETS

What is electronic conferencing? Why is it suddenly hot and what are the new technologies and infrastructures that now support it? These are some of the questions answered in this section. Although this section narrowly focuses on Web-based conferencing, this topic in itself is quite large. We have broken the conferencing function into two major areas: real-time conferencing and non-real-time conferencing. This paper will not focus on non-real-time conferencing solutions, although many of them are now available on the Web.

3.5.1 Conferencing Software:

There are currently four classes of conferencing software on the Web today which are mature enough for general business application. They are real-time chat, data conferencing and whiteboard/shared screen, discussion forums, group document editing, and full audio and video conferencing with full whiteboard and group editing capabilities (see Fig. 3.7). A fifth class of conferencing software is available today, however, it is not yet mature enough for general business use. This class includes LiveWorld (LiveWorld™ Productions, Inc.) and LivingWorlds (America Online) which provide a virtual content studio using avatars. This is a popular venue of the Web-based gaming industry, so I would expect innovation to come from that community.

The Four Levels of Realtime Conferencing

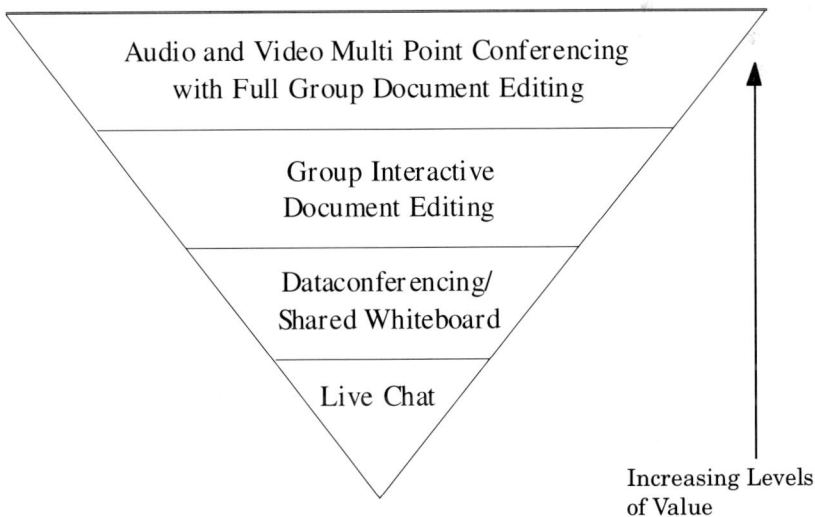

Fig. 3.7 Value Increases with Level of Interaction

This chapter focuses on real-time conferencing so we will not discuss support for discussion databases and forums as they are usually a non-real-time function.

There are many products that support this function currently available on the Web, for example Netscape's incorporation of the Collabra functions into their News Server has now enabled this capability. Lotus Notes also offers this capability, although not on the Web. For those who want Web-based discussions, Web-Board by O'Reilly and Associates and WebShare by RadNet offer this function.

Of the tools for real time available on the Web today, we will also not discuss videoconferencing in great detail, as that is a whole chapter in itself (see Chapter 9 by Christine Perey). Instead, our analysis focuses on data conferencing and live chat functions. We will also discuss some of the standards that are required for these collaborative functions.

3.5.2 Data Conferencing

Although data conferencing on a LAN has been available for many years, this function is relatively new on the Web. It is less expensive and easier to load, maintain, and use than videoconferencing software, and is often the most appropriate technology. Much of what we discuss in a meeting or conference does not require that we see the other person to get their reaction, as many times the addition of audio and video is not necessary, can be done with other technologies (i.e., the telephone), and often slows down the application.

Data conferencing software usually provides a whiteboard, which is a shared space where a document, a diagram, or picture can be placed for viewing by all parties. There is also a "chat" window for real-time chatting and discussion about whatever is on the whiteboard. Although, if you want to make a remark or announcement to the whole group, you can often just type it on the whiteboard. Many products use a separate window for chatting and often have a "whisper" function that allows you to make a private comment to just one person.

The advantages of these systems is the ability to collaborate and share a common document, talk about it in real time, and hopefully make changes and decisions about the document. Having a picture of the person or people you are talking to on the screen is not always necessary. Although humans are social animals, it is not always necessary to take it this far, but it is usually necessary that the document, diagram, or picture be available for discussion.

One of the functions we have found to be useful for real-time conferencing or chatting is the ability of the person who calls the meeting to facilitate or moderate the meeting. Some conferencing tools support this function (Microsoft Net-Meeting, Collabra Share and RoundTable), and others provide a more democratic open forum (PictureTalk).

3.5.3 Audio Support

Audio support for a dataconferencing tool is an option. Some tools have it, others don't. The ones that do not can be supplemented by an audio conference on the telephone. This is particularly effective if you have more than one phone line available. If you only have one phone line available for conferencing, then the ability to talk (voice) allows for a faster transfer of information. The downside to this function is that if you use the "chat" function, the whole discussion, while slower, is recorded for posterity, archives, or CYA functions. Although some of the data conferencing tools like RoundTable do not currently support audio and video conferencing, they are T.120 compatible and will support emerging standards for these technologies like H.323.

3.5.4 Multipoint Multimedia Conferencing

Multipoint multimedia teleconferencing offers the required solution. As defined here, it involves a user-specified mix of traditional voice, motion video, and still-image information in the same session. Participants in multimedia teleconferences can hear and see each other, as well as create, manipulate, edit, and annotate still images, all in real time. The images can be documents, spreadsheets, simple handwritten drawings, highly-detailed color schematics, or photographs. Participants see the same image at the same time, including any changes or comments on that image that are entered by other participants. Actually, these functions do not differ that much from traditional data or document conferencing, as most of these products support the T.120 or H.320 standards. The only thing not shared is the voice and video channels. Many of these standards and the role of voice and video in collaboration are more eloquently explained in Christine Perey's chapter on videoconferencing (Chapter 9).

3.5.5 What is the Role of Electronic Conferencing

Everyone goes to meetings. After all, humans are social animals. However, as organizations become more and more distributed, and the global competition heats up, the need for high quality meetings is magnified. One solution to this is to support more efficient and often distributed meetings through the technologies of electronic conferencing.

Electronic conferencing is one aspect of groupware or collaboration technologies that has caught fire in the last few years. But what is electronic conferencing and why is it so hot? What are some of the technologies involved and how can they benefit you?

Since electronic conferencing is a part of groupware, let's first define groupware. Groupware is a catch phrase for a group of technologies that mediate interpersonal collaboration through the computer such as; e-mail, electronic meeting systems (EMS), and desktop videoconferencing (DVC), as well as systems for workflow and business process re-engineering (BPR). More and more new areas of technology are looking at collaboration as an integral part of their growth. The Internet and World Wide Web (WWW), which has only been in existence a short time, appear to be the most active growth areas for collaborative technologies in the late 1990s.

Electronic conferencing systems, when classified in the groupware taxonomy available in the first chapter of this book, can be put into three different categories: real time conferencing, non-real-time conferencing, and Internet-based collaborative applications.

For the purposes of this chapter, we will leave the non-real-time conferencing functions to products like Lotus Notes, Bulletin Board Systems, and threaded discussion databases, and focus on Web-based real-time conferencing. For more information on non-real-time conferencing systems, see Chapter 10 on Lotus Notes by Jeff Papows.

It is also important to point out that another category, electronic meeting systems (EMS), has some of the same collaborative functions as real-time conferencing systems. However, these products tend to focus more on specific meeting functions such as anonymous voting, brainstorming, and categorization of ideas. These products are often used on a LAN and are run by a meeting facilitator, whose goal is to work the meeting agenda and bring the meeting to a successful completion. The EMS functionality supports the facilitator in reaching this goal.

Although most EMS are LAN-based, these systems are moving to the Internet very quickly. One system, McCall-Szerdy's Facilitate.com, is already available on the Internet, Ventana's GroupSystems is in Alpha testing and Meeting Works will release their Web-based product in the fall. For a complete overview of EMS, see Chapter 7A–E.

The costs for text-based conferencing are very low, as there is usually only software required and no additional hardware (which is usually required for videoconferencing). We have developed a table (Table 3.1) that shows the value of each of these collaborative functions. Specific products and product categories are placed in this matrix based on the level of collaboration they support versus what they cost.

3.5.6 Value Positioning

If we look at value as the number of features and functions per dollar of price, it is clear that Web-based conferencing products like RoundTable and Microsoft NetMeeting provide the best value for money right now. Figure 3.8 depicts those relationships in a matrix.

	High Value	Low Value
High Collaboration	RoundTable = Web based conferencing Microsoft NetMeeting	Group Document Editing Videoconferencing EMS
Low Collaboration	E-mail On-line chat	Whiteboard only Web phone Document sharing

Fig. 3.8

Once you move away from text-based interactions, the costs increase steeply. Although DVC software and hardware pricing has dropped dramatically from several thousand dollars per user to a bit over $1000/user in 1995, the price still remains much higher than text-based conferencing software. However, we expect the price will continue to drop even more with the advent of the P6 from Intel and Windows '97. The new Intel P6 should have audio and video capabilities built in. We expect future versions of the Windows OS and GUI to have the ability to communicate over audio and video and T.120 compatibility built in.

If this comes to pass, the only cost of DVC will be a camera, although many multimedia machines, like the high-end Apple computers, are building the camera right into the computer. Connectix offers the QuickCam for about $85, providing a low cost option for those who need to purchase a camera. This digital camera reduces the cost of entry to this market significantly, and with free video-conferencing software like Cu-SeeMe, the costs to get started are now minimal. By 1998, the additional functionality provided by software will be the main focus of the DVC market. Although hardware will be critical, it will start to become a commodity item by then and the prices will fall even further.

There are videoconferencing rooms (found today in many corporations) where you can see and hear a group at another site. These rooms tend to be highly utilized, which shows that there is an identifiable demand for a remote, but visual, meeting function. However, these rooms are expensive, generally between $40,000–$100,000 for a room, so the drive today is to support DVC or desktop conferencing.

Finally, an EMS can be the most expensive technology because they actually augment a face-to-face meeting in real time. In this case, you have the costs of the meeting (travel costs, etc.) plus the costs of the computer technology to augment that meeting, as well as the cost of a trained meeting facilitator.

As we look toward the future, we will have "virtual" meetings where the barriers of space and time disappear. In reality, the technologies for many of these virtual meetings are now in place. What often stops the use of these technologies is the resistance of people to change the way they work or interact.

3.5.7 Internet Spurs Conferencing Growth

Because it is expensive, in both time and money, to travel to meetings travel, virtual conferencing has not only an immediate payback in terms of travel costs, but also offers the convenience of meeting from your desktop, where you have all your resources at your fingertips.

Because of the rapid advance of the Internet and the technologies to support it, that future is here today. A new category of software, Web conferencing, supports virtual, data, and document conferencing (and will soon support audio and video conferencing) is quickly evolving to meet the demand for virtual conferencing.

With the rapid growth of the Internet over the last year (see Fig. 3.9), many products that were formerly LAN-based have been moved to the Web. Many companies are now using IP networks or intranets as their infrastructure for collaboration, although recent Collaborative Strategies research shows that intranet implementations do not necessarily replace LAN networks. Instead, many companies are exploiting both to get the functionality they need.

Growth of the Internet

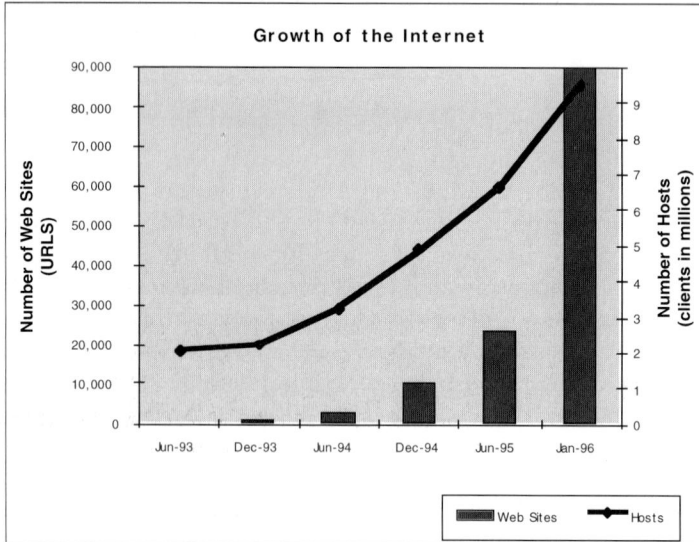

Fig. 3.9 Data Courtesy of Network Wizards (http:www.nw.com) and Matthew Gray of net.Genesis

3.6 BUILDING THE BUSINESS CASE (STRATEGIES)

As the technology and infrastructure of the Web advances, and compression algorithms help deal with some of the bandwidth problems, more and more people will learn how to use these conferencing technologies. This does not mean that the introduction of these new technologies will be easy. Generally, our survey work shows that the biggest impediment to the use of these technologies is not the technology itself, but rather the resistance of people to change the way they work.

Web-based conferencing can cause a shift in work processing. Although this shift will make work more productive (see case studies and examples section), often people have to be helped over their resistance to anything new. Here are some strategies that we have found successful.

"Show the person the technology while stressing the benefits to them! Show them how they can do something with this technology that they were not able to do previously. For example, with RoundTable Web-based conferencing, you can get online with our office in New York and work on the brochure together. I did this the other day and we were able to complete all changes to the brochure with the designer, printer, production manager, and client in under an hour. Normally, this process would have taken over a week and involved both fax and Federal Express, and we would have had to pay late charges. Working this way took less of everyone's time, allowed us to coordinate in real time, got the project done, and changed the relationships from adversarial to collaborative."

Focus on supporting the people involved in the process not the technology! For example, an organization that successfully overcame the organizational challenges of using groupware is General Foods. This project was a success because General Foods was able to learn from a prior failure and the technical manager focused on people problems not just technical problems.

3.7 PRODUCT STANDARDS, FUNCTIONS, AND FEATURES

Now that we have positioned Web-based conferencing as part of groupware, and have been able to determine some categories of functionality, we need to examine some of the standards for data and video conferencing.

3.7.1 Standards

A summary of the current technical standards for videoconferencing or multimedia teleconferencing focuses on two umbrella standards, T.120 and H.320. These are standards developed by the United Nations-sanctioned ITU's Telecommunications Standardization Sector. T.120 comprises the audiographics standards and the H.320 videotelephony standards.

Ratification of the core T.120 series of standards is complete and happened in April of 1995. These recommendations specify how to use a set of infrastructure protocols to efficiently and reliably distribute files and graphical information in a multipoint multimedia meeting. The T.120 series consists of two major components. The first addresses interoperability at the application level, and includes T.126 and T.127. The second component includes three infrastructure components: T.122/T.125, T.124, and T.123.

Graphical Representation of the T.120 Stack

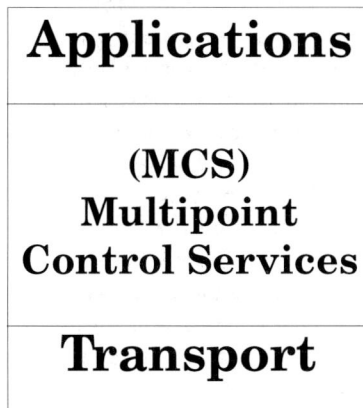

Applications
(MCS) Multipoint Control Services
Transport

Fig. 3.10

Figure 3.10 shows the T.120 stack in graphic form. The first layer in the T.120 stack is the transport layer on the bottom. This layer looks at the networks T.120 works on, PSTN POTs, ISDN, ATM, or Frame Relay. The second layer is the MCS or multipoint control services layer, which allows multiple networks and sites to participate in a conference call with documents (this is the same MCS facility that is used by the video conferencing vendors to enable multipoint conferencing as well). The top layer, the applications layer, defines how the users at remote sites interact with each other, i.e. who controls the pen or cursor, color choice, line thickness, etc. This layer is designed to be simple and supports the lowest level of commonality.

The H.320 standards were ratified in 1990, but work continues to encompass connectivity across LAN-WAN gateways. The existing H.320 umbrella covers several general types of standards that govern video, audio, control, and system components. With many businesses using LANs to connect their PCs, the pressure is on to add videoconferencing to those networks. Since the H.320 standards currently address interoperability of video conferencing equipment across digital WANs, it is a logical and necessary step to expand the standards to address LAN connectivity issues. As the work to expand H.320 continues, it remains the accepted standard. Again, because of the interoperability it facilitates, continued compliance with the H.320 standards across the videoconferencing industry contributes to falling equipment prices and rising sales, as well as an overall increase in the market.

Both the T.120 and the H.320 series of standards will be improved upon and extended to cover networks and provide new functionality. This work will maintain interoperability with the existing standards.

Over the last year, many software and equipment suppliers and service providers alike are starting to support these standards. These standards represent the most effective and rational market-making mechanism available. For example, ISDN, fax, X.25, and X.400 are a few obvious examples of standards-based technologies. Without internationally-accepted standards and the corresponding ability to interoperate, the services based on these technologies would go the way of the buggy whip.

Interoperability is particularly important in multipoint operation, where more than two sites communicate. A proprietary solution might suffice if two end-users want to communicate only with each other; however, this limited type of communication is rare in today's business world. In typical business communications, multiple sites, multiple networks, and multiple users have communications equipment from multiple manufacturers, requiring the support of industry standards to be able to work together.

Standards have a second level of significance in multimedia communications. Teleconferencing equipment must work not only with similar systems, but also with systems of lesser functionality. For example, a conference call might include two parties with fully-functional audio, video, data, and graphics sharing, two parties with only audio and video, and two parties with audio only. Compliance with new and existing telephony standards will ensure that all of these parties are able to communicate with each other. In short, adopting a common set of standards will allow multipoint, multimedia equipment makers to integrate into the existing communications world and insure the interoperability of their products into the future.

Perhaps the most important effect of standards is that they protect the end users' investments. A customer purchasing a standards-based system can rely on not only the current interoperability of his equipment but also the prospect of future upgrades. In the end, standards foster the growth of the market by encouraging consumer purchases. They also encourage multiple manufacturers and service providers to develop competing and complementary solutions and services.

3.7.2 The Snake in the Garden of Eden

When is a standard not a standard? When vendors develop enhancements to the T.120 Standard (called "Standards +" by this industry segment), much like they did to UNIX. In the UNIX world, the POSIX standard was developed to bring (at that time) almost 60 different versions of UNIX into a common standard. Most of the vendors complied with the POSIX standard but developed additional functions or enhancements.

For T.120, such "enhancements" are usable only between devices that support these enhancements, i.e., similar hardware and software. A good example of this is the US Robotics Courier HST modem. For a while, this was the fastest modem on the market because of a proprietary compression algorithm, but you had to have another HST modem at the other end to take advantage of the high speed. The modem works with other Hayes compatible modems at regular speeds, but not at the high speed. This same situation is true of T.120 vendors. Why would vendors pursue such a strategy? The reason vendors do this is it creates a captive market, i.e., if you have an HST modem, they can then sell you more for the other end, pushing the enhanced speed and additional functionality. It also provides room for product differentiation and creativity on the vendors side. The risk with T.120 is that some key vendors are only implementing the bottom two layers of this standard. However, even with only two-thirds of this stack implemented, you can still do a multipoint call. I believe we are in Phase II (see Fig. 3.11) and that we are just in the midst of transitioning to a full T.120 standard by all of the vendors. At that point, T.120 will act like a standard and be ubiquitous and transparent.

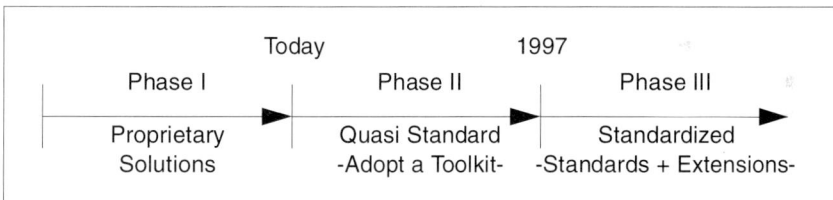

Fig. 3.11

3.7.3 Integration with Legacy Data

In a recent study of Fortune 1000 companies, when asked how critical it was to integrate legacy data with the Internet or intranet, most companies answered it was a highly critical feature (48 percent) and another (38 percent) felt it was somewhat critical, so 86 percent overall felt integration of the Web and legacy data is a critical feature (see Fig. 2.4 Chapter 2).

Although this chapter has set a background for Web-based collaboration, and has touched on a few of the technical and organizational issues, there is nothing like first-hand experience. We invite you to download a copy of any of these Web-based conferencing products. For example, The ForeFront Group has a free demo of RoundTable that allows you to join a conference on their Web site at www.ffg.com.

Now that we have looked at the market for Web-based conferencing tools, the critical standards and some of the functionality involved, lets compare a variety of these product functions (Fig. 3.12).

	NetMeeting Microsoft	PictureTalk PictureTalk	CollabraShare Netscape	CoolTalk Netscape	FarSight Databeam	RoundTable ForeFront Group
Discussion DB	No	No	Yes		No	No
• Moderated?	N/A	N/A	Can be		N/A	N/A
Live Chat	Yes	Yes	Yes	Yes	No	Yes
• Moderated?	???	No	Yes		N/A	Yes
Audio	Yes	No	No	Yes	By regular telephone	N/A
Video-conferencing	Yes with CamWiz	Can share images via camera	No	Yes	No	In development
Data conferencing	Yes				Yes	Yes
Whiteboard	Yes	No	Composition window supports OLE 2.0 and file attachments	Yes	Yes	Yes
Realtime Group Editing	Yes	No			Yes	Yes
File Sharing	Yes	Yes	Yes		Yes	Yes
Application Sharing	Yes, across LANs, Internet, or telephone network	No	No		Yes, across LANs, WANs, and dial-up connections	Yes
File Transfer	Yes	No	Works with the existing e-mail		Yes	Yes
Client Software	Microsoft NetMeeting	Picture Talk Communicator	CollabraShare		FarSight Client	RoundTable client
Integration with browser	Element of Internet Explorer version 3.0 beta	Plug-in for the browser	Part of Netscape	With Netscape Navigator Gold	Unsure	Plug-in for browser
Platforms	Mac, PC	Mac, PC, working on UNIX	Windows and Mac	Windows, Mac	Windows 3.x and 95 only	Windows and Mac
Compliance						
• T.120	Yes	No		Yes	Yes	Yes
• H.320	Yes	No		Yes	Yes	Yes
• ActiveX	Yes	No				
• Java	Yes	Working on Java client				
Price	Free	Server is $100/ per user min. 100 users	10-user License $490	$39	Corporate $199/ Standard $99	

Fig. 3.12 Comparison of Web-Based Conferencing Products

3.8 SUMMARY AND CONCLUSIONS

Two products standout in this analysis of Web-based conferencing: Microsoft's NetMeeting with CamWiz and the ForeFront Group's RoundTable. For simple data conferencing, with a usable interface and a well-tested Web-conferencing engine, RoundTable stands out.

Both NetMeeting and RoundTable provide good, inexpensive platforms for Web-based conferencing that are standards compliant (T.120 and H.320). This compliance allows these products to integrate well with other applications to provide full multimedia capabilities.

Microsoft's NetMeeting provides a tight integration with Microsoft Explorer 3.0, but not with Netscape Navigator. However, RoundTable supports both browsers and is non-combatant in the browser wars. Microsoft NetMeeting along with many of the other conferencing products all are built on top of Databeam's T.120 kit (the list of vendors that use this kit includes Apple Computer, AT&T GIS [now called NCR], AT&T Conf. Systems, British Telecom, Canon, Cisco Systems, Creative Labs, ConferTech, Incite, Intel, LiveWorks, Lucent, MCI, Microsoft, Mitsubishi, Motorola, MultiLink, Netscape, PictureTel, PolyCom, Sony, Sun Microsystems, Vivo Software, and many others). Because all of these vendors use the same T.120 product, applications sharing between them should work.

BIOGRAPHIES

David Coleman is the founder and Managing Director of Collaborative Strategies. He has been involved with groupware and collaborative technologies since 1990 and is the author/editor of *Groupware Technologies and Applications* (Prentice Hall, 1995). He also was the founder and conference chairman for the GroupWare '92-95 conferences that were held in San Jose, Boston, and London on an annual basis. Mr. Coleman was the editor and publisher of *GroupTalk*, the newsletter of workgroup computing. He is the founding editor of *Virtual Workgroups* magazine, and currently a columnist. He also writes a monthly column on groupware for *Computer Reseller News*, and for *MainSpring* (an on-line resource for intranet and Web developers). Mr. Coleman has written for many trade and business publications such as *Network World*, *Datamation*, *Fortune*, and is a frequent public speaker worldwide. He has consulted to groupware vendors on product marketing, positioning, market research and competitive analysis, and for groupware users in assessing their organization groupware readiness as well as tool selection and the human factors involved in a successful groupware project. Mr. Coleman can be contacted directly at 415-282-9197, or at davidc@collaborate.com. More information on Collaborative Strategies can be found at www.collaborate.com.

Introduction to Chapter 4

Electronic mail and messaging are enabling technologies for collaboration. Looking at Fig. 1.1, you will see that e-mail is the most common example of a networked application.

To date, there are an estimated 30 million people on e-mail worldwide, and the number is growing daily. We're all familiar with using e-mail to keep in touch with family and friends, as well as business associates. In addition to the simple communication e-mail enables, it is also a common medium for collaboration.

In this ever-shrinking electronic global village, the advent of conducting business via e-mail is one of the most interesting trends. For example, since the time difference between San Francisco and Japan makes talking between normal business hours impossible, my Japanese clients and I exchange reports and assignments via e-mail. In this case, e-mail not only expedites the process of delivering the client's product, it allows us to do so without the expense and delays of international Fed Exes. We find ourselves "working" with people we have never met or even spoken to on the phone.

Another illustration of how electronic messaging is becoming ubiquitous in business is exemplified in how people from all over the world use our web page. After seeing an article or report we have posted, users initiate "conversations" via e-mail—either to ask a clarifying question or otherwise gain additional information. These "conversations" can result in many different outcomes—from new clients to helping a student with his/her thesis or dissertation (Chapter 16 was just such a collaboration). Whatever the outcome, the benefit of e-mail is that it makes possible collaborations that could not exist without it.

Chuck Stegman is the messaging analyst for Dataquest (recently acquired by the Gartner Group) and one of the most knowledgeable people in the industry. His contribution reflects his tremendous body of knowledge about messaging and e-mail. Chuck begins his chapter with the claim that collaborative technologies, whatever they are, can be peeled back like an onion to reveal other technologies and functions. Messaging is one of the layers, although, it is a different layer on different onions. The next section provides an overview of terminology and definitions for e-mail and messaging. Chuck goes beyond the boundaries of collaboration and adds paging and faxing, which are tools used in collaboration. Next, he looks at the various functional components of these systems, how they are put together, and how different architectures influence functionality.

Chuck gives an overview of messaging standards and looks at how different systems can be hooked together (or not) and how they can work together through APIs, gateways, or other interconnections. Finally, he looks at issues: Why is e-mail not enough for full collaboration? Where is e-mail going? How will we support the millions of people yet to use this function?

Chuck uses product examples to identify each category and function. His chapter talks about components of the technology rather than anecdotes of how technology is used today and will be used in the future.

As an e-mail user, here are some of the questions you may want to think about: Why do organizations like the Electronic Messaging Association see collaboration as the future of e-mail? What new standards will emerge around e-mail as browsers add e-mail functionality, and include the ability to mail URLs and Web pages as attachments? What are some of the organizational ramifications of e-mail? How do organizations deal with flaming e-mails and are there legal ramifications to them. What about e-mails that send copyrighted material?

Electronic Mail and Messaging

Chuck Stegman
Dataquest Consulting

It is often hard to imagine the impact of a new form of communications. In 1876, Sir William Preece, chief engineer of the British Post Office, said "The Americans have need of the telephone, but we do not. We have plenty of messenger boys." As the Internet ties together the islands of corporate and proprietary public electronic mail systems together, this means of communication assumes an entirely new importance.

4.1 INTRODUCTION AND OVERVIEW

As workgroup software and groupware continue to be buzzwords in the software industry, less emphasis has been placed on their foundation: electronic messaging. It is less flashy. Most of us use it and at least think we understand it.

But this infrastructure can be quite complex. It is like the proverbial onion. Each time vendors think they have thought of everything, a new problem arises that must be addressed. And, complex or not, when it doesn't work, people get unhappy.

For the purposes of this chapter, we will draw a distinction between *electronic mail (e-mail)* and *messaging*. For the most part, you will find that vendors and the press use these terms to mean two different things.

E-mail is an application that allows end-users to interact. At its most basic level, e-mail allows end-users to create, send, and read messages.

Messaging is the infrastructure upon which e-mail operates. Historically, e-mail and messaging were tightly integrated proprietary products bought from the same vendor.

This chapter will cover:

☞ Terminology—We define some relevant terms before diving into the details.

☞ Components—A description of the different elements of electronic messaging.

☞ Environments—There are several different environments where e-mail is found. First came the host systems and proprietary public systems, then the LAN-based systems, and today, of course, the Internet has entered the picture.

☞ Architectures—Most of the LAN-based mail installed today uses an architecture called shared file-based. For the most part, newer releases of these products, as well as new competitors, are using a client/server architecture.

☞ Standards—As in many other areas of technology, the nice thing about e-mail standards is that there are so many to choose from. And some of them are even important!

☞ APIs—Application Programming Interfaces (APIs) have played an important part in the development of uses for messaging beyond simple e-mail.

☞ Issues—There are challenges in messaging that have yet to be solved satisfactorily.

☞ Mobile—Not everyone works at a desk! In this section we discuss the issues around those who need access from their laptops or home.

☞ Products—An overview of Microsoft, Lotus, and Novell product offerings.

☞ Messaging—There is more to messaging than simply e-mail. In this section, we discuss some of the other uses that can be made of a messaging infrastructure.

☞ Future—What is likely to change over the next several years?

4.2 TERMINOLOGY

4.2.1 Introduction

As the name indicates, e-mail has roots as an electronic version of paper mail. A letter and an e-mail message have much in common. There is an indication of who it is from (the return address on the envelope), who it is to be delivered to, and, inside, away from prying eyes, there is one or more documents. Most e-mails consist of only a text message, but many do have other items, typically files, enclosed as well. These files might be a budget spreadsheet, a graphic showing sales results or even an image representing a fax that has been received. Although less common, the enclosures could even be an audio file or a video file.

Think back to the early telegraph days to see the origins of e-mail. It isn't as new as you might think! But what has changed over the past decade or so is that far more of us have direct access to e-mail as computers have become standard on most corporate desktops and even common in many homes. Add to that the impact of the Internet interconnecting the islands of e-mail and the situation has changed dramatically.

4.2.2 E-Mail versus Messaging

The terms *e-mail* and messaging can cause confusion. In the beginning, e-mail often referred to the entire system of people exchanging messages on monolithic host systems. As e-mail began to evolve to do more and more tasks, the concept of e-mail began to change. Continuing our analogy with paper mail, e-mail is what creates the letter, messaging is the postal service that makes sure it gets delivered to the right person.

Or, to put it in computer terms, just think of e-mail as an application. It performs the task of creating and reading electronic mail messages. Messaging is the electronic infrastructure upon which e-mail and other applications can reside. E-mail, along with scheduling, workflow, voice, and fax, among others, uses the messaging infrastructure for delivery. The distinction between e-mail and messaging is often gray, indeed many people use the two terms interchangeably. The important thing to remember is the context in which the terms are being used.

4.3 Components

Electronic messaging in its basic form is composed of two components: the user agent and the messaging services. As Fig. 4.1 illustrates, the basic architecture of a messaging system is divided into these two components.

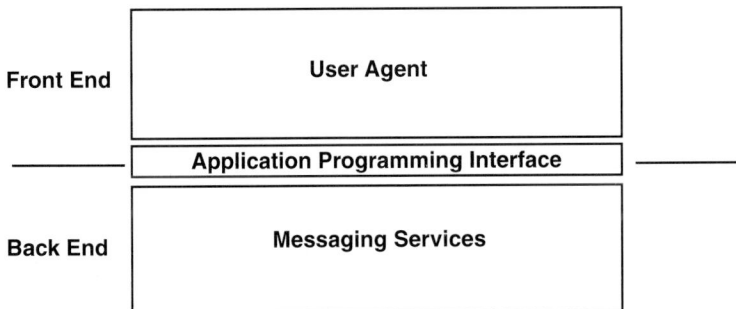

Fig. 4.1 Basic Elements of Messaging

The middle component, the application programming interface (API), is a very thin but important layer residing between the front end and the back end of a messaging system. Additional information on messaging APIs is provided later in this chapter. Let's break down these two basic components a bit further and explain them and their functions.

4.3.1 The Front End—User Agents (UA)

The user agent (UA), sometimes referred to as the "front end," is the client or the mail agent of an electronic messaging system and is what most people see or think of when the term e-mail is used. The UA is the part of the email package that users see and interact with. Within the UA, users create, edit, send, and read email messages. In addition, the UA may provide some form of notification of incoming mail. While the user interface (UI) may be radically different from one package to the next, all UAs have a common set of basic features for the creation and reading of messages. The UA is probably one of the most significant elements that differentiates one email package from another. Because users will be spending a considerable amount of time within the UA, often the successful implementation of a messaging system is based on how users interact with the UA user interface. If users don't feel comfortable with the UI of the email package, they will be less inclined to use it and see the benefits of email as a tool.

4.3.2 The Back End—The Messaging Services

The messaging services component of an email system, sometimes referred to as the "back end," is the infrastructure responsible for moving electronic messages. The back end of a messaging system is further subdivided into three components:

☞ The message transport agent (MTA)
☞ The message store
☞ The directory store

Figure 4.2 illustrates where these components fit into the overall messaging back end.

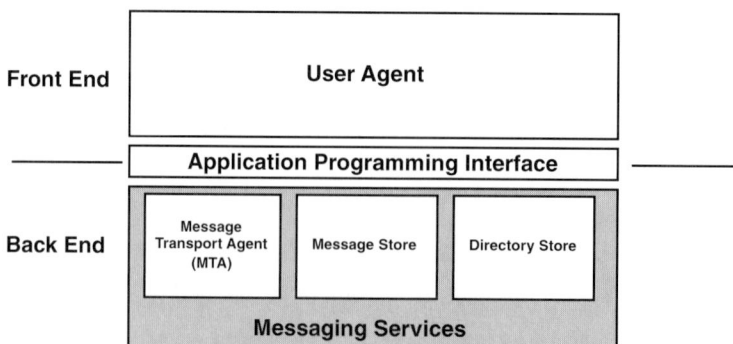

Fig. 4.2 Components of the Back End

4.3.2.1 Message Transport Agents

The message transport agent or message transfer agent (MTA) is the software responsible for collecting, sorting, and delivering the email from one computer, or mailbox, to another. Depending upon the type of electronic messaging system, the MTA will move or copy the mail message from the sender's mailbox to the recipient's mailbox or to a type of database from which it is read by the recipient. The MTA is the portion of the electronic messaging system that the typical user does not see or has little knowledge of. The MTA also defines the overall connectivity possibilities and limitations of an email system. MTAs are broken into two separate camps: open, or standards-based, and proprietary. X.400 and SMTP are open or standards-based examples. The MTAs used today within popular electronic messaging systems such as Microsoft Mail or Lotus' cc:Mail are closed or proprietary. These proprietary MTAs can communicate with any other MTAs of the same type, but they must interact with a gateway (see below) to exchange messages if the MTAs are of different types.

4.3.2.2 Message Store

The message store is where electronic messages are stored. The message store, usually found on the hard drive of a file server or messaging server, is often referred to as the "post office." As with the paper mail analogy, the post office contains the mailbox of each user on the mail system. The sender of a message creates and sends an email message to another user. The MTA will direct the message to the appropriate recipient's mailbox, where it is stored until the recipient picks it up. If a user is not on that particular post office, then the message is forwarded to the post office where that user's mailbox resides. Hence, the mail message is "stored" and "forwarded" to the recipient. The term "store and forward" is often referred to when describing an electronic messaging system.

4.3.2.3 Directory Store

The directory store, sometimes referred to as "directory services," provides the address book from which users can address email messages. The directory store usually provides each user's name and also maps those users' names to specific email addresses. Users access the directory and address messages from within the user agent transparently much like a regular address book. The directory can contain more than just users' names and email addresses. Often the directory store will contain additional information on the users such as their positions or titles, physical locations, or telephone extensions. Often the directory store is a subset or superset of an existing LAN directory. Basically, the directory store of an electronic messaging system is a flat-file database containing records, or users, and the information about them. In fact, many organizations map existing human resource or other personnel databases to their electronic messaging directory to tie this information in with their email.

4.3.3 Accessories—Expanding the Basic System

Although not always an essential part of an electronic messaging system, certain accessories are needed to expand beyond the basic electronic messaging system. Some of these include:

☞ **Gateways**—Gateways act as translators between dissimilar electronic messaging systems. In essence, a gateway will translate an email message from one MTA, such as cc:Mail, to another MTA, such as Microsoft Mail. Unfortunately, because most email UAs provide additional functionality beyond simple text messages, most gateways are forced to the lowest common denominator, usually text. Any added elements of a message a certain UA may add, such as rich text or sound, may be lost during the conversation, depending on the gateway.

☞ **Switches**—There is often confusion between the terms gateway and switch. In short, the difference between a gateway and a switch is that one switch can do the work of many gateways. As an example, Fig. 4.3 shows an organization that needs to connect four different messaging systems, which would need six gateways. A messaging switch provides a many-to-many solution. In essence, the switch may include the necessary MTAs of the four messaging systems in order to do the translation between systems. One of the most obvious benefits of a switching system is reduced management. There are also fewer points of failure than a complex gateway solution.

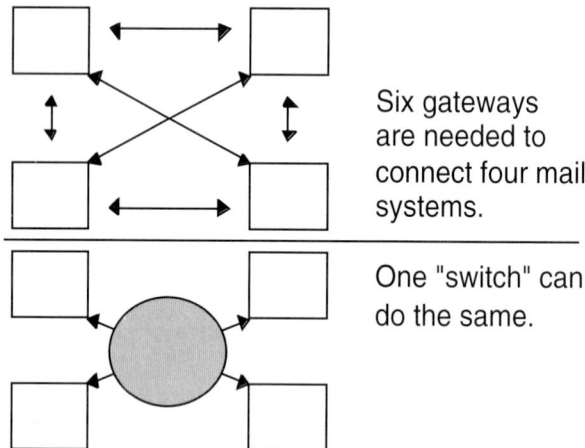

Fig. 4.3 Gateway versus Switch

☞ **Message management**—The tracking and routing of messages can be a daunting task. Message management tools help facilitate the management of electronic messaging systems by providing useful tools such as troubleshooting capabilities for bottlenecks in an electronic messaging system, notification of MTA failures, remote management of post offices, disk usage of the message store, and so on.

☞ **Directory management**—Management and synchronization of electronic messaging directories can be one of the biggest nightmares of novice mail administrators and seasoned veterans alike. Directory management applications aid in the management of messaging directories by providing tools and systems to facilitate directory synchronization, duplication of directory entries, directory synchronization across disparate electronic messaging systems, and network operating system directory interoperability.

☞ **Agents and filters**—As the popularity of email expands, so does the number of messages. Agent and filtering technologies provide a mechanism for users to cut through the flood of both inbound and outbound messages. One form of messaging agent is "rules," found in many email systems today. An example of a rule would be the classic "I'm on vacation." In this example, a user could implement a rule stating that all inbound messages from a certain date would return or "auto-reply" back to the sender a message stating that he/she is on vacation. Other examples include auto-forwarding, auto-delete, and auto-printing. Agents can reside at the UA and/or the message services level.

4.4 ENVIRONMENTS

E-mail, like everything else, comes in all shapes and sizes. In the past, e-mail was found mainly on large mainframe, or host, systems in which users logged in via a terminal or terminal-emulation program. If this host was primarily used by the employees of a single company, it was referred to as a "host system." If the host was owned by a company who sold the services to anyone who was willing to pay, it was called a "public e-mail system." Eventually, of course, the LAN arrived on the scene and added an alternative to the host as an e-mail platform.

Today, e-mail systems can be found on any of four environments:

☞ Host-based—Examples include IBM PROFS, OfficeVision/VM, and Digital ALL-IN-1/VMSMail

☞ LAN-based—Examples include Lotus cc:Mail, Microsoft Mail, and Novell GroupWise

☞ Public service-based—Examples include the MCIMail, AT&T Mail, Sprint-Mail, CompuServe, and America Online

☞ Internet

Each of these systems can be used independently or in conjunction with one another; today, most e-mail systems are connected to the Internet.

4.4.1 Host-Based

The birth of e-mail came on a host system. While some consider the mainframe and mini-computer relics of the past, many corporations still depend on existing infrastructures of IBM's PROFS and Digital's ALL-IN-1 for their day-to-day e-mail business.

Although host-based messaging systems are on a definite downturn, a 1993 Dataquest survey found that 39 percent of all corporations are still host-based-only sites. Another 34 percent of the surveyed sites used host-based messaging systems in conjunction with newer LAN-based electronic messaging systems.

The key thing to remember with host-based systems is not that mainframes and minicomputer systems are being used, but that the software running on them is important. While these electronic messaging systems are in a state of transition as many organizations move toward LAN-based electronic messaging systems, the hardware itself may find a new life.

Many corporations and public messaging services are increasingly finding that well-established host system disk and backup management services can provide yet another option to growing messaging storage demands.

4.4.2 LAN-Based

The majority of electronic messaging systems installed today are LAN-based. Growth of LAN-based electronic messaging systems have exploded in the last five to seven years. When the "Year of the LAN" finally did occur in about 1985, companies ended up with systems on many more desktops then could share server storage and printers and began looking around for other applications that leveraged this infrastructure. As these individual LANs were interconnected within an establishment, LAN-based e-mail emerged as an important application. In fact, it often was the incentive to get everyone on a LAN.

This growth accelerated as corporations downsized both staff and systems in the late 1980s and early 1990s.

Companies leading the charge in the advancement of LAN-based messaging include Lotus Development (cc:Mail) and Microsoft (Microsoft Mail, or MS Mail). Products such as cc:Mail and MS Mail, along with Novell's GroupWise, provide a friendly user interface and relatively simple administration when compared to host-based systems. Also, the LAN-based systems provide a much lower cost-of-entry solution than other types of messaging systems.

4.4.3 Public/Online Services-Based Systems

Depending on a company's needs, a public or online messaging service provider may provide a cost-effective messaging solution. For individuals such as free-lance consultants (and even consumers), they are often the only solution available.

Online services have been around for several years, but competition has increased considerably in the last few years. The type of online service depends on the groupware needs of the individual situation. Almost all of these services provide access or gateways to other messaging systems, including the Internet.

There are two ways to look at an online messaging service provider. The first way is for only e-mail needs. A user on one of these systems, such as MCI-Mail or AT&T Mail, can let the service provider handle all of the infrastructure requirements. The user and the user's company would be defined as a user account or accounts. All messages would go through the service provider.

This type of arrangement has many benefits. Little or no hardware is required on-site other than a PC and a modem, and a user can often access a mail account in other cities while traveling on business. The downside is that a user has little control over the host system and that all these benefits come at a cost. Most of these services charge by the message or byte count. Depending on messaging traffic, this cost could be large.

The second way to use these online service providers is as messaging hubs, or gateways, to other messaging systems such as the Internet.

CompuServe, for example, provides a hub service for most of the popular message transport agents (MTAs) such as cc:Mail and MHS. With this capability, companies would use the service provider in addition to their internal messaging systems. By linking with the service provider in a hub fashion, companies can link disparate sites or vendors and customers to the service provider's vast network. Once again, cost may be an issue if messaging traffic is high. The costs of building and maintaining the enterprise's wide-area messaging network must be weighed against the costs of using a messaging service provider.

As more and more companies installed proprietary "islands" of e-mail, often LAN-based, within their companies, this backbone usage seemed poised to explode. But then the Internet exploded instead.

4.4.4 The Internet

The Internet could be combined with public/online services, but for this chapter we will handle it separately. While there are some similarities, there are some important differences. One obvious difference is that the Internet isn't owned by a single company. But the most important difference is the momentum behind the Internet.

The Internet is much more than just e-mail, as seen by the recent explosion in usage of the World Wide Web (or simply "the Web"). Still, many people realize that e-mail and messaging is an important component of the Internet.

Much like the options of a public messaging service provider such as CompuServe, the Internet can be used as a standalone messaging option, perhaps by an individual, or as a backbone or hub.

Many popular Internet service providers such as Netcom and Performance Systems International (PSI) provide both individual and corporate Internet accounts. Increasingly, the players in the public/online services-based world are also offering "pure" Internet access as a service. Basic Internet e-mail and Web access can be had for as little as (U.S.) $20 a month. Whether through an Internet shell account or through one of the Internet browsers such as Netscape Navigator, the Internet and its services may provide enough messaging services for a given user's groupware needs.

A July 1996 Dataquest study found that an impressive 66 percent of U.S. organizations reported that they were using Netscape Navigator. This ubiquity will drive e-mail vendors to enhance their support for Internet integration, the most obvious need being an easy way to point at a World Wide Web address in an e-mail message and have the browser go directly to that Web site.

Today, it is fair to say that the Internet is the de facto worldwide backbone for messaging, a role many companies in the public and online services-based world targeted only a few short years ago. It is used by individuals, small and large corporations, educational institutions, and governments alike as a messaging backbone or common gateway to vendors, partners, customers, and other users.

4.5 ARCHITECTURES

There are two basic architectures in the LAN-based e-mail market today. One is shared file-based; the other is client/server.

A shared file-based e-mail system is like the open mail room on the floor of an office building. Each person with mail puts it in the inboxes of others on that floor. For recipients on other floors, there is a box that is sorted and delivered by someone else. A mail system like this relies on users not to tamper with the mail of other people. In general, systems like this have been the mainstay of the LAN-based e-mail market. Products like Lotus cc:Mail and Microsoft Mail operate this way. Concerns with security and desire for additional functionality and performance that are not easily achieved in this environment have led to plans by most major vendors to introduce another style of LAN-based e-mail.

A client/server-based e-mail system is more like the mail at your home. The postman picks up what you want to send and drops what has been sent to you through a slot in your door. There is far less security risk and some new functionality is possible. In addition, well architected client/server systems provide enhanced performance. Products like Lotus Notes and Microsoft Exchange are client/server-based.

4.6 STANDARDS

Someone once said that the nice thing about standards is that there are so many to choose from.

Messaging is no different. A standard, or specification, as defined by a standards organization, enables programmers, engineers, and information technology professionals to create and work on interoperating products. Some of the standards organizations involved within messaging are also involved in other areas of software and information technologies. They include the American National Standards Institute (ANSI), the Consultative Committee for International Telephony & Telegraphy (CCITT), the Institute of Electrical and Electronics Engineers (IEEE), and the International Standards Organization (ISO).

Although standards cover a broad area, the focus within messaging revolves around the core messaging services portion, or back end. Within the messaging category, the following standards are important to anyone interested in messaging:

☞ X.400—A CCITT standard method for the exchange of electronic messages between computer systems. Traditionally thought of as only existing at the MTA level, the X.400 specification includes information at the user agent (UA) and message store levels. X.400 is found almost exclusively within large, global corporations. As the messaging industry continues to move toward open standards, messaging standards have become more important. X.400 is rapidly losing ground to the SMTP/MIME standard (see later bullets), and this has been accellerated with the increasing importance of the Internet.

☞ X.500—A CCITT standard method for the exchange of messaging directories. The X.500 standard is designed to provide directory information in a global setting, or at least that is the goal. Critics argue that X.500 is over-engineered and too complex. Unlike the case of X.400, the crucial directory function is not one where the Internet has an established strong solution to offer as an alternative. Recently, however, Netscape and others have been discussing the Lightweight Directory Access Protocol (LDAP), which might help to bridge Internet standards into other directories, including X.500.

Although this general directory has many advantages, including a hierarchical tree structure, the standard is in a state of continuing maturation. Unlike the X.400 standards, which were defined as early as 1984, certain X.500 standards were not defined until 1992. As a result, a variety of X.500-like services were developed. Also, many corporations have been reluctant to exchange sensitive directory information (including personnel information) in any global directory exchange within a public directory. The developments in directory standards are one of the most interesting aspects of messaging in the late 1990s.

☞ SMTP—Simple Mail Transport Protocol. This messaging protocol is used in TCP/IP networks for exchange of electronic messages between computer systems. Originally widely used primarily within government and universities, SMTP now has widespread usage in corporations. Today, this is often in order to connect with other enterprises (and to connect in the UNIX-oriented workstations within their enterprise). In the future, it seems more companies will use this standard within their enterprise, the "intranet" phenomenon referred to above. (A July 1995 Dataquest study found more than 30 percent of leading edge companies using intranets.) In any case, SMTP will continue to gain momentum as the importance of the Internet continues to grow. This growth is at the expense of X.400 and proprietary offerings.

☞ MIME—Multipurpose Internet Mail Extensions. This is a standard used in conjunction with SMTP. MIME is used for the standardization of exchanging files such as spreadsheets, word processing documents, graphics, audio files, videos, and so forth via Internet mail. Without MIME, SMTP would not be nearly as successful as it is. With the inclusion of MIME, it appears SMTP will increase its dominance.

☞ MHS—Message Handling System. MHS usually refers to Novell's MHS. Novell MHS, through its one-time inclusion within the NetWare network operating system, had become a popular MTA on many LANs. Although it still maintains an installed base, MHS as a standard has seen better days. Today, it is found mainly on smaller messaging networks or is used as a backbone bridge between messaging systems—and even that role is being replaced by SMTP/MIME-based solutions. There are other less prevalent usages of the term distinct from Novell.

4.7 APIs

Writing applications for electronic messaging systems, whether for e-mail clients (front ends) or for message-reliant add-ons, relies on one thing to work with the messaging service's back end: application programming interfaces (APIs). An API is a tool (usually a set of documentation and some software) used by a programmer to simplify the task of writing software.

An API is prewritten code with "hooks" that enable a programmer to integrate one portion of code with another. A person writing an application for a messaging system would need to write new code for each electronic messaging system he or she was developing. However, common messaging APIs allow the programmer to write to one set of APIs instead of to multiple ones.

Although there are other messaging APIs, as we will discuss, developments have made Microsoft MAPI the clear winner in the heated messaging wars of years past. Many believe that standards associated with Internet-based mail (POP3 and IMAP4) will give MAPI's dominance a challenge.

Important messaging APIs of interest:

☞ MAPI—Messaging Applications Programming Interface. Developed by Microsoft for the Windows operating environment, MAPI comprises two separate versions: Simple and Extended.

Although it does not have all the cross-platform advantages Vendor Independent Messaging (VIM) did, the MAPI architecture of client and server interface levels is well designed for open messaging. In 1994, Lotus and WordPerfect, both supporters of the competing VIM API standard, announced support for MAPI for inclusion within cc:Mail (Lotus), Notes (Lotus), and GroupWise (Novell). With this announced support for MAPI, the messaging industry can move more rapidly toward the goal of ubiquitous mail enabling of applications.

☞ POP3 and IMAP4—These standards, originating in the Internet community, have recently started to attract interest as messaging APIs. In the Dataquest study published in July 1996, about one and a half times as many people agreed with the statement "We plan to migrate to messaging within our organization that is based upon Internet standards such as IMAP/POP" as disagreed. That is not an overwhelming endorsement, but it does indicate growing interest.

☞ VIM—Vendor Independent Messaging API. Originally developed by Lotus, the VIM API was adopted by a consortium of companies including Lotus, WordPerfect, IBM, Apple, and Oracle. A benefit of VIM touted over MAPI was its cross-platform support (MAPI is Windows-only).

Much debate within the messaging industry during 1992 and 1993 came over which messaging API should be supported. As Microsoft and the rest of the industry fought this issue out, the customer was caught in the middle. The result was a lack of progress. In any case, this debate is largely history now. VIM is not going to be further enhanced.

☞ CMC—Common Messaging Calls API. As mentioned, the 1992/1993 messaging API war that erupted between Microsoft and the rest of the industry caused much confusion. As a possible soothing of the tensions, the X.400 Application Programming Interface Association (XAPIA) developed the CMC API. With XAPIA, members from most of the major messaging companies, including Microsoft and Lotus, were able to establish a set of specifications for basic messaging interface calls.

☞ AOCE—Apple Open Collaboration Environment. Apple's AOCE includes mail and messaging, catalog services, and various levels of security. The PowerTalk messaging system found within Apple System 7.5 is an example of a messaging application using AOCE. At present, AOCE is only for the Macintosh operating system. Apple's attempt to establish a messaging foundation built around the Macintosh operating system seems to have failed in the market. AOCE may be of interest to those in a strictly Macintosh environment who use the core messaging services from Apple.

☞ SMF—Standard Message Format API. The SMF API was supported in Novell MHS systems. SMF-71 is the most current version. Novell, after its acquisition of WordPerfect and its GroupWise product, moved away from SMF and toward the MAPI API. As part of its migration plan to move existing MHS customers to GroupWise, Novell has announced support for the SMF-71 API in the GroupWise environment. The support allows existing SMF applications written for MHS to move to GroupWise as the preferred Novell messaging platform.

4.8 ISSUES

As messaging continues to gain momentum as a groupware tool, it faces the issues and problems that surround any expanding technology.

This section examines some of these issues and the trends toward their solutions.

4.8.1 Privacy and Security

Millions of users are beginning to rely on e-mail for a variety of purposes, including personal letters, business correspondence, information, and messages. Many of these messages are sensitive, and users want their privacy protected.

Yet, after pressing the "send" button, a message can pass through a handful of mail forwarders and dozens of packet-switching nodes. A system administrator, or someone who has gained privileged access to any of these transfer points, may read those messages, depending on the e-mail system used. More users are becoming aware of such risks as e-mail use grows.

The challenges for e-mail security breaks down into two issues:

☞ Message confidentiality—The contents of a message can be encrypted using a conventional encryption scheme such as the Data Encryption Standard (DES). The most difficult technical challenge for such schemes is the secure exchange of encryption keys between pairs of correspondents. The goal is to prevent anyone but the intended recipient from reading the message.

☞ Message authentication—Message authentication is often referred to as "digital signature" security. A digital signature, implemented using public-key encryption, makes use of two keys: a private key known only to its owner, and a public key that is disseminated to all users. If a block of data is encrypted with the sender's private key, any recipient may decrypt that block with the sender's public key. The recipient is assured that the block must have come from the alleged sender, because only the sender knows the private key.

Another development that may help in messaging security is the adoption by e-mail vendors of the Privacy Enhanced Mail (PEM) standard, which describes a common way of encapsulating encrypted messages and defines when software should decrypt a message. The standard, approved recently by the Internet Engineering Task Force, should help bring standard, secure e-mail to market more quickly.

4.8.2 Scalability and Manageability

As mentioned earlier, LAN-based messaging systems have evolved beyond simple mail for small workgroups. Now, they must be able to support "information sharing," messaging-enabled applications such as group scheduling, and workflow.

As the move toward distributed LAN-based messaging systems continues and organizations turn away from mainframe and minicomputer systems, some of the luxuries these centralized systems provide have disappeared or are missing.

Traditional mainframe and minicomputer systems often supported an entire enterprise using one computer system. Such systems are clearly incapable of handling the kinds of applications needed for doing business in a distributed fashion.

However, LAN-based messaging systems do not have the scalability and manageability of the old host systems, and that is creating major problems for information systems (IS) managers. LAN-based messaging systems are strong on application functionality but do not yet include the robust services and management features that customers desperately need.

One approach toward placing some solutions in distributed messaging includes a three-tiered architecture:

☞ User agents level—The e-mail UAs and mail-enabled applications provide the basic layer at which the typical end user sees the messaging system.

☞ Workgroup and departmental server level—At this level, messaging servers are placed to handle the workload where many of the communications happen.

☞ Messaging backbone—This is the highest level. The backbone is used to connect different systems, both inside and outside the company. The backbone exists solely to enable interoperability between systems and make that interoperability manageable.

Lotus is one messaging provider that has embraced this idea. Lotus acquired SoftSwitch, the leading supplier of messaging backbone switches (Soft-Switch EMX, renamed Lotus Messaging Switch, or LMS). This important development signals a maturity of the LAN-based messaging business, and that is good news for system administrators of enterprise messaging systems. LMS products manage directory synchronization between connected systems, and over time, that synchronization will include externally connected public and private directories.

We will begin to see some relief for managers of enterprise messaging systems over the next several years. As these systems continue to mature, we will see tools and products to enhance LAN-based messaging systems.

With all of this information sharing, some serious improvements in directory support will be necessary. The manual synchronizing of internal mail directories, often done today, is difficult at best, but wait until synchronization with the rest of the world is tried with standards such as X.500 becoming more prevalent.

In the end, the most important trend today will be management tools. As messaging vendors begin to offer integrated products capable of providing a backbone in a three-tier architecture, such management issues will be easier to answer, and a user will be more capable of managing the messaging network as a whole.

A messaging standard gaining support is MADMAN, a standard for managing e-mail via SNMP. Mail and Directory Management Information Base (MIB) is the first step toward alleviating problems associated with e-mail.

MADMAN administers e-mail systems by monitoring the flow of messages, a time-consuming task for messaging administrators. The MIB is designed to work with SNMP management platforms.

To date, more than 20 vendors in the Technical Subcommittee (TSC) of the Electronic Messaging Association's (EMA) Messaging Management Committee are supporting MADMAN by working to adopt a specific implementation schedule. Lotus, Microsoft, Novell, AT&T, Banyan, and Intel are among the companies already in full-fledged implementation development.

4.8.3 Bandwidth

It is reasonable to ask about the impact of the explosive growth on bandwidth availability. If a user sends an e-mail to someone and the message does not arrive within a certain amount of time, the next time they will go back to using the phone or a fax. Most estimates put the delay that will be tolerated for e-mail messages at between 15 minutes and 4 hours. Typically, the more experienced user has less tolerance!

The most likely scenario is that, with occasional minor problems, the infrastructure will continue to evolve to stay under the delivery delay tolerance. Messaging service providers that cannot do so will lose subscribers to those who can.

Another scenario, considerably less likely in the near to mid-term, is that new standards will be developed for many different classes of service and be widely adopted. The situation is not analogous to the overnight delivery of packages where one provider takes the package all the way from the sender to the recipient. In messaging, the "package" will typically need to pass from the sender's service, perhaps through a backbone service, to the recipient's service.

4.8.4 Interoperability

The issue of interoperability transcends messaging. The integration and interoperability of different hardware platforms, networking protocols—such as TCP/IP, SNA, NetBIOS, and IPX/SPX—and messaging protocols—such as X.400 and SMTP—are difficult at best.

Networking managers and messaging administrators must deal with the issues of interconnecting not only PC LAN-based systems but also messaging among host-based systems, external systems such as the Internet, and emerging messaging-enabling technologies like faxing, paging, and telephony.

4.8.5 Mailbox Proliferation

For some users, one of the challenges of the 1990s is numerous e-mail accounts. There is a tough trade-off to balance here. On the one hand, it would be nice if all of the mail came together in one single mailbox. On the other hand, that would imply that certain "value-added" (also known as "proprietary") functions would not be supported in this "universal inbox" client.

As the market evolves, standards such as MAPI and IMAP/POP will enable a single client to do this if the user wishes. But not all users will opt for this, preferring instead to maintain the full functionality of the front-end, optimized for the system they are using.

For the most part, the technology is now available to have a "universal inbox" if one is willing to deal with a very basic set of features.

Essentially, all major e-mail vendors have some method of supporting other data types (such as fax and voicemail messages) in their inbox. The fax support is considered quite useful by some, but not all users. The voicemail support makes for good demonstrations, but has yet to catch on in a big way.

4.8.6 Rules and Filters

Thanks to pioneering work based upon research at the Massachusetts Institute of Technology by a company called Beyond Mail (later bought by Banyan Systems), a set of techniques have been developed that are marketed under names such as rules and filters.

The objective is to allow a user to deal with the ever increasing flow of e-mail messages.

For example, all messages from a user's boss might be automatically filed in a folder for urgent attention. Messages about the corporate menu or the ubiquitous Internet jokes might be automatically stored in a low priority folder.

There are major challenges remaining in this area. There are rules that should run at the server. The classic example is one that returns a message about the user being on vacation. There are, however, also rules that are best run on the client. Most vendors support only one of these two necessary configurations today.

At the high-end of the market, most of the heavy users would like to see additional functionality. At the low-end, additional ease-of-use is needed.

That said, even today's simplistic rules can be a major help in dealing with the growing problem of junk e-mail.

4.8.7 Collaboration

E-mail can be used for collaboration, but it requires fairly well organized people to be at both ends. For this reason, a variety of vendors have offered products that automate more of the process of collaborating.

It is too much to ask of busy users to remember to follow-up on each work request they have e-mailed. Software can and should do that for them.

4.9 MOBILE

Mobile computers have revolutionized the way we work. Packing the power of desktop systems, mobile computers are small enough and lightweight enough to carry in a briefcase. They have also become portable communications devices. This holds true as we move forward into wireless messaging. What was once a luxury is now often a growing necessity. Wireless communication is becoming an effective mechanism for enhancing the enterprisewide messaging system.

Mobile computers have already freed users from the restrictions of power cords and the desktop. The next step going forward is complete wirelessness by breaking mobile computers' other tether: the telephone cord. Wireless computing is possible today because of the convergence of several enabling technologies. For one, wireless radio modems, like mobile computers, have become relatively small and inexpensive. Also, communications companies are offering services for wireless computer users in urban areas and major transportation corridors. Leading software companies are enhancing their applications to take advantage of these wireless networks.

4.9.1 Circuit Switching

Circuit switching is the technology behind all cellular telephone communications, both voice and data. When used in wireless data communication, circuit switching establishes a dedicated, end-to-end connection between two computers. The connection begins with the initiation of the call and ends when the computers disconnect. Users pay for the entire time this circuit is in use.

Because the typical e-mail message is fairly short, operators of the major cellular networks have announced a new technology to make their existing systems more cost-effective for wireless e-mail. The proposed new system, called Cellular Digital Packet Data (CDPD), would intersperse packets of data with voice conversations. This technology could give users both the cost-efficiency of circuit switching for sending long messages and the lower cost of sending short messages as packets.

4.9.2 PCS Narrowband (Two-Way Paging)

Paging has become so commonplace that high school students are giving pagers to their girlfriends or boyfriends. The new generation of two-way paging became a reality in the second half of 1995. Several big-name companies began building nationwide, two-way paging networks since the Narrowband PCS auctions. Messages sent from the network are high bandwidth (24,000 bps), cheap, and effective. Acknowledgment of a page via the return channel assures receipt of the message. The return channel allows for as much as a page of text. The nationwide aspect not only allows anytime, anywhere wireless messaging, but will also lend itself to nationwide distribution and support.

4.9.3 Packet Switching

Unlike existing cellular networks, wireless packet-switched networks are specifically designed for data communication. Packet switching breaks messages into packets and sends these packets individually over the network. There are two major providers of packet radio networks: RAM Mobile Data Wireless Networks and Ardis.

Packet radio is particularly cost-effective for wireless messaging because most e-mail messages are short enough to fit easily into the packet structure. Users pay for only the data they send, as measured by the number of packets. Packet radio also offers some security advantages over today's cellular technology. Transmissions are digitally encoded, so listening in is not as simple as it is with cellular voice communications.

Packet radio networks provide wireless messaging services in major urban areas, including airports and transportation corridors. The RAM network, for instance, divides metropolitan areas into geographic zones called "cells." Servicing each cell is a base station that sends and receives data packets from a mobile computer. When a message is sent, the base station receives it and can route it either to other mobile users in the same cell or to the local switch for transport to another cell or wired connection, such as a LAN.

Other key issues in mobile and wireless messaging to think about include bandwidth, data compression, security, filtering methods, and coverage.

4.10 PRODUCTS

Although there are several vendors providing electronic messaging product, the e-mail market is dominated by three primary vendors: Microsoft, Lotus, and Novell. In a survey of US-based respondents published in July 1996, these were also the first three companies that came to the minds of those involved in decision-making for their organization. This is very consistent with previous studies. This section briefly describes the existing products of these three companies and provides a glimpse at what the future holds for these messaging systems.

4.10.1 Lotus cc:Mail

With millions of users, cc:Mail is one of the most popular LAN-based e-mail systems on the market today. A Dataquest study, published in July 1996, found that 23 percent of U.S. organizations were using cc:Mail.

Based on a shared file architecture, cc:Mail is a cross-platform e-mail system. On the UA or workstation level, cc:Mail is available on Windows, DOS, Macintosh, OS/2, and UNIX operating systems. The Windows UA provides rules for message management and message searching. By using a simple, unified directory, messages can be addressed to recipients on local networks or distant LANs, as well as to recipients who receive mail through fax machines. cc:Mail provides rich and complete administration for network directory synchronization and management.

Also provided is the ability for the posting of messages and viewing of messages in company-wide bulletin boards. cc:Mail provides message transfer software enabling server-to-server communication and remote user access. cc:Mail also includes single-copy message-store technology, global directory services, and store-and-forward design. The server platform supports a rich set of networking protocols, including TCP/IP, SNA, and X.25.

cc:Mail enhancements are planned, including an enhanced UA to take advantage of Windows 95, and hierarchical folder and bulletin boards. MAPI will be supported as well, at both the UA and the service provider levels.

4.10.2 Lotus Notes

Lotus Notes is by far the leader in the groupware category. In the same Dataquest study, 23 percent of the organizations also reported they were using Notes. One big difference was that the median organizations using cc:Mail reported that 80 percent of their users were using cc:Mail as compared with 18 percent for Notes.

Lotus Notes is best described as a platform. This client/server platform supports multiple network and desktop operating systems in order to connect heterogeneous workgroups, and it includes an integral messaging system, a distributed document database, and a robust development environment. The Notes applications that reside on this groupware platform represent group-enabled software. Far beyond simple support for e-mail, Lotus Notes applications improve the business performance of people working together by enabling them to access, route, track, share, and organize the information they use in their everyday business processes.

Developers can build Lotus Notes applications using the platform's tools or by using traditional programming languages such as C or Visual Basic through a set of open interfaces.

Lotus recently released a new version of Lotus Notes, version 4.0, that contains an enhanced scripting language, LotusScript, for applications development in addition to the existing macro language. Also included is an improved user interface, additional server platforms, and increased scalability. MAPI will also be supported.

4.10.3 Microsoft

MS Mail

MS Mail is sold alone and also included as part several other Microsoft products. Microsoft Mail has an installed base of millions of users. In the July 1996 Dataquest study, 27 percent of organizations reported that they were using Microsoft Mail.

Microsoft Mail is available for the Windows, DOS, and Macintosh operating systems. Microsoft Mail's strength is found primarily in the Windows environment. With a rich user interface, strong editing, and OLE support, the Microsoft Mail UA is very approachable. Also included are nested public folders. The back-end services provide communications and file distribution services over the LAN.

Message transfer software enables server-to-server communication and remote user access. Microsoft Mail also includes global directory services, and store-and-forward design; it permits communication with a variety of e-mail systems including PROFS, X.400, FAX, MHS, SMTP, MCI Mail, and SNADS.

Microsoft Exchange

The future of Microsoft's messaging strategy lies with the Microsoft Exchange server product. The same July 1996 study found 17 percent of the organizations using Exchange.

This client/server messaging system provides NT server-based e-mail, fax, and voice mail integration capabilities.

Exchange also integrates group scheduling, electronic forms, and business productivity applications under one unified user interface.

With a backend running on the Microsoft Windows NT operating system, Exchange provides centralized system monitoring and administration. It supports Internet SMTP/MIME mail transfer, agents, X.400 protocols, and X.500 directory services. Clients run on DOS, UNIX, Macintosh, Windows 3.1, and Windows 95. A simple version of the full Exchange client is included with Windows 95.

4.10.4 Novell

GroupWise

Novell GroupWise is more of an integrated groupware application than strictly an e-mail package. Formerly called WordPerfect Office (acquired in the Novell merger with WordPerfect), Novell GroupWise includes e-mail, an integrated personal calendar, an integrated group scheduler, rules-based message management that allows users to assign action to incoming and outgoing e-mail messages, and task management.

Sixteen percent of the organizations surveyed in the July 1996 Dataquest study reported that they were using GroupWise.

GroupWise allows users to monitor a message's progress through the system. Novell integrated Collabora's collaborative discussions software within the GroupWise product.

At the time of this writing, Novell was testing a new, greatly enhanced version of GroupWise 5.0, code-named GroupWise XTD, that includes a complete rewrite of much of the code of a variety of products to produce a very modular and sophisticated offering that goes far beyond simple e-mail.

4.11 MESSAGING

E-mail as a form of communication is equal in function and utility to the telephone, fax, and paper mail, but as we have noted, e-mail is much more than sending memos or attaching files. Messaging is a transport for delivering information, and the next generation of messaging software will provide the underpinnings for applications that will deliver new productivity gains to information workers.

Workgroup software is designed for a group of users, but it is also suitable for the core business applications, such as accounting, inventory control, and database management. Group scheduling, forms, and workflow are a few of the applications built on the messaging infrastructure one installs for simple e-mail.

4.12 GROUP SCHEDULING

Calendaring and scheduling, often referred to as group scheduling, are typically the first applications to be added to a messaging backbone.

Because of the relatively low barrier and number of customizations required, users can relatively quickly employ electronic calendars within their e-mail to set appointments for themselves and others. Group scheduling products are usually provided in one of two ways: as a standalone scheduling product designed either to work with an existing messaging system or to be integrated within a unified messaging architecture (like that of GroupWise).

The more tightly integrated applications use APIs such as MAPI. Group scheduling products like CE Software's Network Scheduler or Microsystems' CaLANder work with messaging systems such as MS Mail or cc:Mail in providing group scheduling capabilities on top of the existing e-mail UA.

An important development by the XAPIA association is the approval of a common group scheduling API. A calendaring and scheduling API (CSA) is designed as a common method or procedure for group scheduling programs and nongroup scheduling products to obtain access to the underlying group scheduling system.

In theory, with CSA, one group scheduling UA should be able to access the database of another scheduling system. Likewise, a program such as a project management program will be able to poll and post times and tasks through the CSA API. Like CMC, this opens new opportunities for exciting groupware applications using group scheduling.

At the time of this writing, Netscape has proposed some new standards in this area.

4.13 FORMS AND WORKFLOW

Electronic forms, or e-forms, can also take advantage of a messaging infrastructure transport system.

Companies typically venture into workflow with e-forms because they are looking for ways to reduce their use of paper and because the routing paths and interfaces for forms are straightforward. Many companies start with e-forms and workflow routing for expense reports or purchase order requisitions. Companies such as JetForm have led the way, but Lotus, Microsoft, and WordPerfect have entered the market with Lotus Forms, MS E-Forms, and InForms, respectively.

To successfully implement an e-forms solution, security and authorization issues must be hurdled. An e-form cannot be authorized by typing a name because anyone could type that name, and it would look the same. There must be a secure form of digital signature. Companies such as RSA Data Security are attempting to tackle this issue with some of the encrypting techniques mentioned earlier. Electronic forms can also handle the results of database queries. With e-forms for data access, query results can be turned into an e-mail message.

Workflow's future lies not in simple tasks, such as routing expense reports, but in real large-scale corporate applications. Workflow software can automate business processes—it can routinely decide where to send documents. For workflow to be effective for core business applications, the system must be scalable and robust. It must be usable in a wide area network (WAN) as well as with mobile or remote employees. To achieve this, messaging and database systems must adopt some of each other's characteristics, such as the standardization of SQL within the e-mail UA and messaging API support on the database systems.

4.14 FAXING

Besides e-mail, probably the most common text-based form of communication is faxing technology.

With the boom in faxing technologies of the 1980s and the advent of cheap faxing units, it would seem that the integration of faxing technologies and electronic messaging would be a natural fit. Many vendors have just those solutions in place.

There are two basic ways to use faxing technology within an e-mail system: outbound and inbound use. Each has benefits and disadvantages compared to a more traditional faxing solution. Outbound faxing allows a user to fax directly from within the e-mail UA, either through a fax server on the LAN or directly through a local modem.

With an e-mail faxing solution, the user does not need to worry whether the receiving location's fax machine is busy or on. Fax messages are queued until the line is available. Also, outbound faxing eliminates the need to print the message before transmission.

Inbound faxing, either through a fax server connected to the LAN or directly to the desktop using direct inward dialing (DID) or dual-tone multifrequency (DTMF), enables users to receive faxes in digital form. Once within this digital format, users are free to import the messages into a word processing document or spreadsheet. Often an optical character reader (OCR) is used by fax messaging solutions to transform the digital fax into standard ASCII characters.

4.15 PAGING

Once used only by professionals such as doctors, paging technology today is a ubiquitous tool used by a wide cross section of people. Some even use it as a social statement—the ultimate in being "wired." As such, many people now believe that the lowly pager will lead us into a promised land of carefree wireless communication. But this is not an ordinary beeper. Instead, a new generation of display pagers and enhanced paging services, coupled with future two-way services and pagerlike communicators, is refashioning the beeper business into a far more attractive wireless option.

A wide variety of new paging services have been introduced in the past three years or so. In particular, nationwide networks such as MobileComm, PageNet, and SkyTel have extended their services to include e-mail messages, news briefs, stock quotes, and other information. They can even notify a user of faxes and voice mail messages and arrange to have them forwarded.

SkyTel's pagers, for instance, can receive e-mail from public networks such as AT&T Mail, the Internet, and MCI Mail; from private networks such as cc:Mail, Microsoft Mail, and WordPerfect GroupWise; or from any other mail service using the X.400 protocol. Lotus and SkyTel recently introduced a Pager Gateway for Lotus' Notes workgroup software, and SkyTel also supports Microsoft's Exchange.

Paging wireless communication has some unique advantages. Instead of depending on users to initiate connections, paging systems simultaneously broadcast, or simulcast, data to all parts of their covered areas as they receive it, using radio towers linked by phone lines and, in some cases, by satellites. Simulcasting ensures that users get messages instantly and automatically wherever they happen to be. A paging system's redundant and overlapping radio coverage also makes it extraordinarily reliable and able to reach spots that other wireless systems often cannot, such as inside office buildings or tunnels.

However, there are also disadvantages to paging. Primary among them is that phone numbers in numeric paging or messages in alphanumeric paging are sent to the user, but the user cannot respond. Instead, the user must reach for a phone or a portable PC. Moreover, many paging services can transmit only short messages.

This could be changing soon, however. Two-way paging is on the horizon. Some paging networks already are experimenting with what is known as "acknowledgment paging," in which the sender receives an automatic response indicating that the message was received. Future pagers will also be able to send canned responses, such as "yes," "no," or "call me."

However, more robust two-way messaging will require vastly updated paging networks and a new generation of personal communicators. One such effort is already under way. Microsoft and SkyTel's parent company, Mtel, are building a $150 million system called Destineer that uses pagerlike signals to let a user receive and send messages (see section 4.9.2 "PCS Narrowband (Two-Way Paging)").

4.16 TELEPHONY

One social stumbling block to the use of e-mail comes from the widespread use of telephony and voice mail. Voice mail has gained wide acceptance based on its approachable format of the telephone. It often seems that users are dedicated to either voice mail or e-mail. The differences in the two technologies transcend the average user. The conflicting use of either of the technologies is the subject of hot debate between voice mail and e-mail vendors. However, there is a growing trend toward products that merge the worlds of PCs and telephones.

Our workday lives involve the mundane routing of calls to appropriate people, answering a seemingly endless number of voice mail messages, and trying to tie all these different points of information (voice, fax, and e-mail) into one cohesive mental and digital database. Electronic messaging and telephone integration offers one way out of telephone turmoil.

The integration of the telephone and the computer is nothing new. Anyone who has had a meal interrupted by a computerized telephone sales system can attest to this. And with this new generation of integration come new standards, or APIs, competing to become the next standard.

At the center of the telephony battle stand two big camps: the Microsoft/Intel alliance with its Telephony API (TAPI), and the AT&T/Novell alliance with its Telephony Services API (TSAPI). Their respective APIs specify how to integrate computers to control dialing, answering, routing, and conferencing of phone calls:

☞ TAPI—Microsoft and Intel, as might be expected, have a PC-centric vision of telephone integration. Their viewpoint is that TAPI is to telephone enabling what Microsoft's MAPI is to message enabling. With various TAPI-enabled products, a user will be able to do such things as control a phone from a computer, screen calls (with Caller ID), and have the information about that caller pop-up on the computer screen, create a personal interactive voice-response system, and place calls directly from word processors or applications. The TAPI specification does not require a network connection. It focuses on what are called first-party features. This means that the call that comes in on a personal phone and is under the user's control; once the user routes or forwards the call, that control is gone.

☞ TSAPI—AT&T and Novell's TSAPI handles first-party features, but it extends to third-party call features. These make it a better solution for the large-scale office. The fundamental architectural difference between the two is that TAPI specifies a physical link between the PC and the phone, while TSAPI's links can be logical—a map between the server and the phone address. Third-party features include the ability to maintain and track a call as it is routed throughout the system. TSAPI requires that the private branch exchange (PBX) be linked to a server. Because the server is linked to the PBX directly, it has greater and more far-reaching control of the call.

There are pros and cons to each API. TSAPI is available as an add-on module to versions of Novell's NetWare 4.01 and above. TAPI is an integral part of Windows 95. Only time and the market's reception of these competing APIs will decide how, with whom, and when the convergence of messaging and telephony takes off.

4.17 ELECTRONIC DATA INTERCHANGE (EDI)

The merging of EDI and e-mail promises to produce new opportunities for companies interested in integrating their messaging systems with existing transaction-based systems. EDI involves the exchange of business transactions in a computerized format. EDI's integration with messaging opens up another avenue of this exchange. Many organizations are placing EDI on top of existing e-mail or messaging hierarchies as the X.435 specification for EDI/e-mail merging becomes more prevalent. This one will take some time to unfold, partly because the success of the Internet was not foreseen, so IS organizations have time to orient and establish themselves as contenders in this emerging marketplace.

4.18 THE FUTURE AND CONCLUSIONS

The messaging market of 1996 and beyond can at best be described as controlled chaos. The future of the market is pretty much dominated and determined by the three large players: Microsoft, Lotus, and Novell. But some feel that dominance is threatened by the success of the Internet and products such as Eudora (in use in 18 percent of U.S. organizations according to a July 1996 Dataquest survey) or Netscape's browser with built-in e-mail. Although other players such as Banyan, On Technology, and CE Software will continue to profit in the continuing e-mail expansion, the "big three" software vendors and developments on the Internet will drive the market.

   However, even for these dominant players, many issues remain undefined or need to be further refined, and each of these vendors faces big challenges ahead. Lotus continues to formulate a strategy of integration of its cc:Mail and Notes products.

   Microsoft needs to get users to migrate to its Exchange Server and provide the rich set of tools and applications already found within the Lotus Notes environment. And Novell, must ship GroupWise 5.0 and clearly articulate (and deliver) a vision of the future.

   The future remains bright for organizations planning or maintaining an electronic messaging system. Increased competition and continued expansion of e-mail will only enhance the number of options and tools available for messaging environments and their administrators.

   Ask any moderate to heavy e-mail user if they are completely satisfied with their product and you'll hear that there is still room for innovation in this market.

BIOGRAPHY

Chuck Stegman is a Vice President in the consulting practice at Dataquest. He is responsible for managing and executing marketing strategy, positioning and researching projects primarily in the areas of Internet/online, multimedia, and software. Currently, he is serving Gartner Group as the Managing Vice President of Asia/Pacific Consulting. Before recently joining the

Dataquest Consulting team, Mr. Stegman was the Vice President and Worldwide Group Director for the Online, Multimedia, and Software analyst group.

Prior to joining Dataquest, Mr. Stegman was Enterprise Marketing Manager with Lotus Development Corporation. In this position he held worldwide strategic and product management and marketing responsibility for several product lines in the Lotus cc:Mail family. At the Lotus cc:Mail office in Silicon Valley, Mr. Stegman created a product management department and established standard product management procedures. He managed product marketing programs targeting enterprises that involved extensive travel and high-level interaction with technology professionals of large corporations throughout the world. He developed and delivered high-level training to Lotus and IBM sales forces targeting the enterprise market. Mr. Stegman also created and managed a successful program for third-party software vendors integrating with cc:Mail.

Mr. Stegman holds a degree in Electrical Engineering and Computer Science from the University of Colorado at Boulder where he was a member of several honorary societies.

Introduction to Chapter 5

Group Calendaring and Scheduling systems have come a long way. If you thought they were just an adjunct to e-mail, you were wrong. If you thought they were only LAN-based, you were wrong. This type of collaborative software has emerged as a class all its own, dealing with a critical, non-renewable resource...time.

Not only can calendaring and scheduling software be used to track and schedule events, it can be used to allocate all kinds of resources, such as equipment, facilities, personnel and technology. Increasingly, group calendaring and scheduling programs are being used to provide a one stop information center for resource availability.

This chapter covers the evolution of calendaring and scheduling technology from the LAN to intranets and looks to the future of these collaborative functions.

A major stumbling block for calendaring and scheduling technology has been the lack of standards—or conversely, the abundance of different standards. In response, Netscape called a meeting of the calendaring and scheduling vendors to work out standards for this class of software. These emerging standards are also discussed in this chapter by Chris Knudsen and David Wellington. Even though they are with a Calendaring and Scheduling vendor, CrossWind Technologies, they have objectively presented data about group calendaring and scheduling technologies, the market place and the evolution of these products from e-mail add-ons and PIMs to full blown web-based enterprise resource scheduling tools.

Many of the technologies in this section of the book deal with overcoming the problems associated with distributed working from the perspective of distance issues. This chapter deals with time...an individual's time and the group's time.

More and more calendaring and scheduling products will soon be web-enabled and will have to interact with each other inside of an organization. Even though there are still 5 million users on mainframe e-mail/C&S programs like PROFS, the trend towards a new corporate IP infrastructure seems unstoppable. With inexpensive desktop PC's, laptop PC's, client software and powerful servers this move will be accomplished in a fraction of the time it took for these technologies to spread across LANs. The vendors only have one target to port to (well two, if you count Microsoft Explorer), and the users now have an easy-to-use, more graphical interface to this data.

In this chapter, products are categorized according to the size group they serve, showing how certain products are workgroup-oriented, others are department-oriented and still others are enterprise-oriented. The real difference is in scalability. Scalability is not something you can add on; it is a feature that has to be built into the product's architecture.

This chapter serves as a tutorial for both sides of the equation—technology and people issues. After contrasting file-based, client/server-based and Web-

based architectures, Knudsen and Wellington take on the issue of interoperability. Most large organizations have more then one calendaring and scheduling system, just like they have multiple e-mail systems. It is just as critical to get calendars working across systems as it is to delivering mail messages. As a matter of fact, the two processes are very similar. Attempts have been made at interoperability standards in the past through XAPIA. Although this standard API has been available for two years it is not widely adopted. The role of the IETF working group for calendaring and scheduling seeks to develop a standard that is very focused and near term. Membership is informal and meetings are held electronically (I wonder who's scheduling program they use for that?). Such an informal group is able to act more quickly than a formal consortium. In July 1996, the first of these meetings occurred and a charter was written focusing on the representation and transfer of calendaring objects across the net. It is believed that a standard will be available by this summer (1997).

How else are calendaring and scheduling products moving on to the Web? Group calendars are never static, and so need to utilize the dynamic and interactive functions of the Web. This means that the browser front end must access a calendar database server. Right now CGI scripts are being used because they are the easiest solution and they can be used with any browser. But as the Web becomes more dynamic and interactive, CGI will lose its desirability as it can only represent static data, i.e. a display of a monthly calendar. Java and ActiveX components offer the best avenues for more interactive calendaring and scheduling products. Java brings true platform independence, but because Java interprets and compiles code to machine independent instructions, Java currently carries with it a performance penalty. OLE modified for the Web is called ActiveX and allows Windows developers to leverage all their work onto the Web. Since this is not an interpretive language, speed is not an issue. However, portability is, and UNIX and Macintosh machines are not supported.

This thoughtful and objective chapter is not only well written and well thought out, but shows a great deal of insight into the technical issues vendors and users alike will be facing in moving these critical collaborative functions onto the intranet and then the Internet.

Calendaring and Scheduling: Managing the Enterprise's Most Valuable, Non-Renewable Resource—Time

Chris Knudsen
David Wellington
CrossWind Technologies, Inc.

The Internet has made available many new technologies that will enable the corporate intranet, if done well, to become an organization's competitive advantage. The utility and success of the intranet implementation will depend on the accessibility of information and the quality of the applications that will manage data.

Supporting Web technologies is no longer a product differentiator for applications providers such as Calendaring and Scheduling vendors—it is a requirement. The overwhelming support for these technologies will eventually cause the cachet of the Web to diminish, like all *de facto* standards, and the technology focus will return to the feature/functionality questions like "does it do the job?"

5.1 THE CALENDARING AND SCHEDULING MARKET

If you can ignore, for just a moment, the rigidity of a mainframe environment from the user's perspective, you would have to admit that it provides a very efficient model for datasharing and administration. These two ingredients are key in the optimal implementation of a corporate-wide group scheduling solution, and that explains why the mainframe scheduling solutions worked so well. But, as the PC revolution of the 80s made abundantly clear, individual needs for personal productivity and resource access must also be met.

While the PC revolution led the way to sophisticated technologies, it also created a culture of individualistic end users who were no longer willing to wait for the ordained corporate solution. In the time it took for a committee to decide, the PC user could acquire whatever software was wanted (and probably pay through petty cash). In keeping with this situation, successful Calendaring and Scheduling products were designed with the end user in mind; they focused on manipulation of personal calendar data and information.

Unfortunately, this PC-oriented culture frustrated the growth of workgroup applications because it caused networking and operating environment support to become very problematic. Calendaring and Scheduling tools in particular were demoted from a corporate communication system to the role of a secondary personal desktop accessory. Without the ability to easily share information, the utility of scheduling was diminished.

During the past five years, networked and client/server architectures have woven the PC back into the organization's computing infrastructure—evolving scheduling from a desktop accessory back to a departmental and enterprise necessity. In the late 80s, corporations began to realize the productivity benefits of an e-mail communication system. In the 90s, corporations began to embrace the groupware ideals of "communication, coordination, and collaboration." Today, corporations are seeing the "coordination" benefits of electronically exchanging calendar and resource information among departmental workgroups and across the enterprise. The Internet has created some important data sharing standards that will enrich these Calendaring and Scheduling solutions.

The following is IDC Corporation's projections of the Calendaring and Scheduling market for the next five years (see Fig. 5.1). These figures do not include Calendaring and Scheduling users contained within integrated product suites such as Exchange, Notes, or GroupWise.

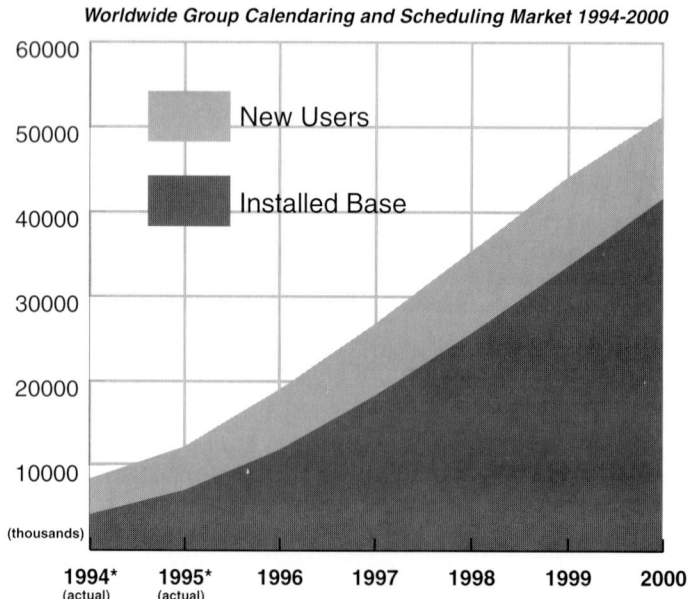

Fig. 5.1 Calendaring and Scheduling Market 1994-2000. © 1996 International Data Corporation

5.2 HOW CALENDARING AND SCHEDULING CONTRIBUTES TO GROUPWARE STRATEGY

In the complex and sometimes confusing world of groupware, the simplicity of electronic Calendaring and Scheduling is appealing: It automates specific processes with which everyone is familiar and it does not require arcane vocabulary to describe its workings or benefits. So, from a pragmatic viewpoint, scheduling is a straightforward groupware investment with a fairly predictable return—and it's available right out of the box.

Calendaring and Scheduling Products are among the easiest of all groupware products to cost/justify:

Costs of Scheduling a Meeting by Traditional Methods:

The time spent scheduling a meeting can often take longer than the meeting itself. The net time spent contacting participants and resolving time conflicts can easily add up to an hour. Assuming an employee's annual compensation of $31,000 and two meetings a week:

*$15 per meeting x 2 meetings x 50 weeks = **$1,500 per year for one employee***

Creating a meeting using a Calendaring and Scheduling tool shouldn't take more than two minutes, the RSVP process is also typically automated.

Costs of Attending a Traditional, Synchronous Meeting:

Assume that the $31,000/yr employee attends three one-hour meetings a week (this is actually conservative, since higher compensated employees typically attend more meetings):

*$15 per meeting x 3 meetings x 50 weeks = **$2,250 per year for one employee***

The availability of electronic discussion forums in Calendaring and Scheduling products support asynchronous discussions and consensus building processes that are associated with times and dates (supporting the time-relevant Meeting paradigm).

Although e-mail and Calendaring and Scheduling are very complementary products, attempts to simplify the groupware market by lumping Calendaring and Scheduling products in with e-mail systems as "communication" tools is not a useful exercise. Calendaring and Scheduling provide a unique perspective to the desktop that e-mail does not—a sense of time. This time domain aspect affects the entire technical design from the user interface down to the underlying architecture. The newer standalone (those independent of integrated suites) applications, have optimized their server engines to manage those unique issues associated with synchronous, real-time coordination as well as to support other time-relevant, but asynchronous, collaboration processes. Calendaring and Scheduling products built on top of more generalized platforms such as e-mail or other file based designs typically don't completely address these basic time management paradigms.

Time is an essential element of any organization's productivity management plans. From the corporate viewpoint, time is a basic component in determining the ROI on any project. Now, with the data collection and sharing capabilities provided via Web technologies, the utility of Calendaring and Scheduling tools goes beyond the mechanics of time management and coordination and is beginning to include the wealth of information, the corporate memory, they collect as a by-product of these time management activities. This trend will continue as corporations make data from Calendaring and Scheduling an integral part of their data warehousing efforts.

From the end user perspective, the impact of a Calendaring and Scheduling tool's sense of time is more immediate. Everyone manages time dependent commitments, tasks and appointments. Calendaring and Scheduling software becomes the primary tool in this management and is often the "command" center of the user's desktop (or PDA, as the case may be). With many standards-based Calendaring and Scheduling applications, the scheduling tool can be integrated with other time independent processes, such as reporting tools, to provide these processes a sense of time. For example, a user could execute an agent through the scheduling tool to automatically generate a report at a specific time or back-up their hard drive, or schedule network intensive processes at non-peak hours. Another important area of integration will be with Web-based information access and publishing tools to facilitate time-relevant information sharing (e.g., information distribution as a preparation for or replacement of a traditional meeting). From the user's perspective, almost all activities have time relevance and the more a Calendaring and Scheduling solution can help manage activities the more valuable that product is.

5.3 AN OVERVIEW OF CALENDARING AND SCHEDULING PRODUCT CLASSES

The terms "Calendaring" and "Scheduling" are not synonymous. Calendaring involves the placement and manipulation of data on a calendar, while Scheduling involves the communication and negotiation between calendars for such data placement. The Calendaring and Scheduling products available today can be classified by their architecture and platform support, which in large part is determined by their emphasis upon Calendaring vs. Scheduling (see Fig. 5.2).

SCHEDULING

CLASS: Workgroup	CLASS: Departmental	CLASS: Enterprise
ARCHITECTURE: File-based	ARCHITECTURE: Peer-to-peer Store & Forward	ARCHITECTURE: Client/Server
FOCUS: Calendar Data Manipulation	FOCUS: Calendar and Scheduling Management	FOCUS: Scheduling Data Communication

CALENDARING

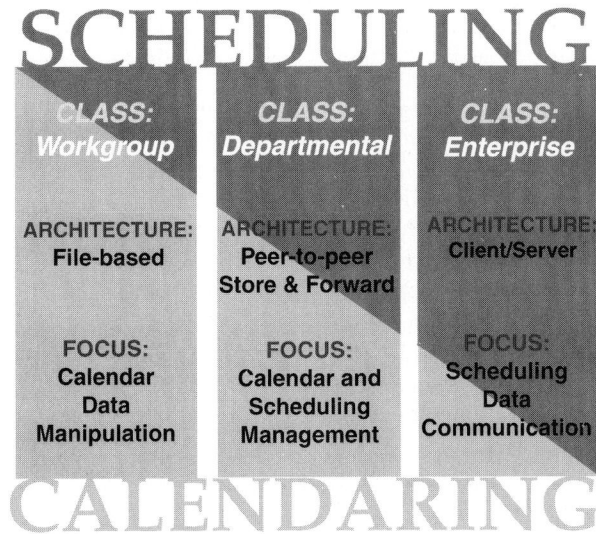

Fig. 5.2 Calendaring vs. Scheduling Technology Focus

5.3.1 Workgroup Calendaring and Scheduling

The products that serve the Workgroup Calendaring and Scheduling market include network-aware Personal Information Managers, "PIMs." The calendaring-oriented feature set in products of this category is much richer in depth and variety than those of departmental and enterprise solutions. The majority of these features, however, are not solely concerned with time management *per se.* Instead, they offer a variety of personal productivity tools from databases to contact management. Their feature sets are focused on personal rather than group productivity and this generally comes at the expense of networking or other information sharing performance.

This focus on personal productivity is an acceptable trade-off for environments where people work independently, need to manage unique sets of data, and only occasionally wish to share information. Another advantage of products in this category is that they require significantly less administration resources than larger-scale scheduling products. However, although some workgroup products are being deployed at sites with more than 100 users, latency and scalability have not been adequately addressed in this class of scheduling product. So, if you are in a quickly growing group or plan to deploy the product across a larger organization, these products may not be a suitable long-term solution.

Characteristics of Workgroup Calendaring and Scheduling Products:

☞ Excellent personal productivity features

☞ Simple Administration

☞ Limited scalability

☞ Latency issues

5.3.2 Departmental Calendaring and Scheduling

The products that serve the Departmental Calendaring and Scheduling market include those using e-mail or store-and-forward architecture. This category includes many of the popular scheduling tools that helped develop the Calendaring and Scheduling market as we know it. These products were initially designed to serve LAN-based workgroups. Many of these products have since been retrofitted to address larger user populations. These products typically have a solid feature set oriented towards group productivity, good-to-excellent user interfaces, and reasonable network throughput for up to 500 users and above (depending upon the product and configuration).

While they have been enjoying the marketshare advantages of established players, they are now in the unenviable "middle market" position. New scheduling users in the smaller LAN workgroups are finding the Web-enabled PIM products very appealing, but existing users in larger workgroups are often frustrated in their attempts to deploy these tools at the enterprise level. Some vendors are now in the process of re-architecting their products to a client/server design to address this situation and to stave off competition from higher-end products.

Characteristics of Departmental Calendaring and Scheduling Products:

☞ Some scalability (varies by vendor)

☞ LAN Administration resources required for large sites

☞ Latency issues

5.3.3 Enterprise Calendaring and Scheduling

The principal design effort in Enterprise-wide Calendaring and Scheduling products is focused on the architecture required to support scalable, real-time information sharing for thousands of users across local and wide area networks. Although the goal of real-time information sharing may not be a requirement for other types of groupware applications, it is essential for effective group and enterprise coordination. This is especially true for the larger scale implementations.

The feature set in this class of Calendaring and Scheduling products tends to be more focused on time services and is very group-oriented at the expense of the variety of personal productivity features that can be found in a PIM. Older products in this class employ a host-based design (e.g., mainframe), while newer applications are client/server based. Newer enterprise scheduling architectures support transparent scaling across the enterprise, which is a significant benefit for large or quickly growing organizations. The disadvantage of this class of scheduling application is that it requires system administration resources for all sites. For large sites, the administration resources required per user are quite low, but with a small number of users, it is just not as cost-effective.

Characteristics of Enterprise Calendaring and Scheduling Products:

☞ Excellent Scalability

☞ Real-time

☞ More limited personal productivity features

☞ System Administration resources typically required for all sites

For many organizations, the Calendaring and Scheduling component is a cornerstone of their groupware solution. As such, the selection of the product that best meets the unique business and cultural needs of the organization requires careful consideration. The following is a product comparison checklist developed by Creative Network, Inc., to assist organizations looking to implement or upgrade their current Calendaring and Scheduling system. This checklist is useful for planning the implementation of a Calendaring and Scheduling system as well as side-by-side comparison of products under evaluation.

General Feature Set	User interface look and feel, Uses same DB for all O/S environments, IN/OUT of the office "pegboard", Name and address database, Message center, On-line user-to-user chat, On-line help, Context-sensitive help, Bubble help, Animated icons, Graphical shortcuts (toolbar icons), Forms overlays for descriptions, Drag-and-drop capabilities, Search capabilities, Data entry method, Automatic time zone adjustment, User-specified work days/hours, Comma delimited ASCII import/export, Multiple account notification and access, Appt. time notification with description, Quick reminder facility, Multimedia sound support, Customizability, Add/subtract sections, Move sections, Rename sections, Include sections from other users, Change section appearance, Change display (view) of information, Customizable time slots
Group Scheduling Features	Group appointments, System-wide groups, Personal groups, Groups that span multiple databases, Displays group's free/busy time, Real-time display of group free/busy time, Find free (available) time, Automatically sends cancellation notices, Invite attendee not using C&S application, Multi-write access to shared file, Process meetings for another person, Recurring group meetings, Allow conflicting appointments, RSVP, Accept, Accept with note, Decline, Decline with note, Tentatively accept, Tentatively accept with note, Delegate, Delegate with note, Defer, Presumptive scheduling, Counterpropose alternative meeting, etc., Auto-update of meeting status, Auto-update of attendee status, Option by chairperson: update attendee status, At-a-glance view of attendee status, Recipients attach notes to appt. request, FYI participants, Resource tracking, Administered, Unadministered

Personal Calendar	View by day, week, month, Year, Alarms (Audible Visual) Schedule recurring appointments, Automatic conflict checking, Mark appointments confidential, Show appointment duration, Show ToDo's, events, anniversaries, Events span multiple days, Launch applications at specified time
Task Management	Group ToDo's, ToDo Lists, Assign tasks to others, Priorities assigned to Tasks, Categorized ToDo's, Recurring ToDo's, Indicate status by color, Automatic roll-over, Hide completed ToDo's, Show start and end date, Show ToDo's in calendar
Reports and Printing	Daily, weekly, monthly reports, Planner formats: manual organizer (Franklin, DayTimer, etc.), Print additional formats (labels, rolodex, envelopes, letter, legal, etc.), Print schedule by day, week, month, Report generation, Customizable page formats, "Filtered text" reports, Group reports, Color reports, Tri-fold reports
Address Book	Find individual record, Filter for display customized record sets, Sort contacts by name, company, zip code, type, Auto-dial, Phone log, Export for mail merge, E-mail requirements,
E-mail and Export Features	E-mail support, Import/Export, ASCII, dBASE, Cardfile, Visual field mapping, Other import/export
Migration Tools	Special tools for migrating "legacy" (m/f, mini) systems, Special tools for migrating LAN systems, Migration support for legacy calendars (specify)
Development Environment	Programming language used, Programmatic, GUI or rules-based, How it integrates w/other applications, Proprietary or standard,
Pricing and Packaging	Overall pricing policy, Client pricing, Server pricing, Site license pricing, Client packaging model, Server packaging model, Site packaging model
Cost of Ownership	Hardware, Software, Annual maintenance, Upgrades and updates, Training, Support and service, Consulting, Design, Implementation, Growth
Client/server Features • Supported Server Platforms • Supported Client Platforms	Server hardware supported, Server operating systems supported: Banyan VINES, Windows 3.x, Windows 95, Windows NT, Novell NetWare (specify 3.x and/or 4.x), OS/2, Unix/version(?), VMS, Others, Clients Supported: Browser (e.g.

- Supported Protocols

  Navigator, Explorer, etc., Windows, Macintosh, UNIX/Motif, ASCII, Protocols supported: Banyan VINES, IPX, OSI, SNA, TCP/IP, Administrative/management interface, DOS, Windows 3.x, Windows NT client, Windows 95 client, OS/2, Macintosh/PowerMac, UNIX, Other

E-mail System Supported

Mail, Microsoft Mail, Lotus cc:Mail, Lotus Notes, HP OpenMail, OfficeVision/PROFS, Novell MHS, Novell GroupWise, Da Vinci E-Mail, DEC All-in-1, Other

Minimum System
Requirements

Client system (CPU, RAM, disk space), Windows 95, Windows 3.x, Windows NT client, DOS, Macintosh/PowerMac, OS/2, Server system (CPU, RAM, disk space): Windows NT, OS/2, NetWare 3.x, NetWare 4.x, NetWare NLM, Other[1]

For a resource list on Calendaring and Scheduling products, please refer to the Product and Vendor listing at the end of this chapter.

5.4 ARCHITECTURAL EVOLUTION OF SCHEDULING PRODUCTS

"The attention recently lavished on the browser has obscured the fact that the Web is a client/server paradigm where the server plays an equally important, if not more important, role in delivering Web content. If we choose to move beyond simple static Web pages, the underlying foundation to integrate multiple live components becomes a critical concern. This architecture determines how components of Web pages interact with one another as well as back office resources and legacy applications."[2]

5.4.1 File-based

In the late 80s, PC-based Calendaring and Scheduling vendors developed their products for LAN environments. Many of these Calendaring and Scheduling products used e-mail as a transport mechanism, while others simply accessed calendar files directly over the network, usually within NetWare NOS (Novell's proprietary Networking Operating System) environments.

Despite the fact that tens of thousands of users at single sites were served by mainframe e-mail and scheduling applications, the general feeling in the PC world was that Calendaring and Scheduling was a peripheral application and usage would most likely be limited to workgroup, or at most, departmental levels. By the mid-90s the popularity and subsequent adoption of group scheduling

---

[1] © 1996 Creative Networks, Inc. www.cnilive.com

[2] From the July 29, 1996, Flashnote "The Battle for the Foundation" by Clay Rider, © 1996 Zona Research Inc. www.zonaresearch.com

products began to outstrip the scalability potential of the PC-based Calendaring and Scheduling products. This caused a significant technical shift by these PC-based vendors, towards the adoption of a client/server model. The vendors unable to make this transition have been squeezed between the overcrowded, low-margin PIM market and the enterprise client/server market.

5.4.2 Client/Server Based

According to many industry pundits, the Web isn't a successor to client/server computing—it is an example of client/server computing "done right." Since it took time for PCs to be effectively networked together, non-PC based (e.g., UNIX and VMS) Calendaring and Scheduling tools tended to have client/server scheduling capabilities before PC-based tools. For example, CrossWind Technologies introduced the first client/server based Calendaring and Scheduling product in 1992. This first implementation was on UNIX. By 1994/1995, when the ability to scale became paramount and NT became viable, most vendors of Calendaring and Scheduling tools announced or implemented plans for client/server based architectures.

In light of the explosive growth of the Internet, the move to client/server and support for TCP/IP was a critical move for those vendors. The ability to operate within a client/server, TCP/IP environment provides the foundation for Internet/intranet capable products.

5.4.3 Web-based

Now, many vendors are announcing limited read-only and read/write versions of their products that make Calendaring and Scheduling information accessible via the Internet using technologies such as CGI. These limited Web products are only stop-gap offerings from most vendors until more advanced development environments become available. But regardless of what advanced technology is driving your browser-based client, you need to look at how the back-end technology is going to make it all work for you.

5.5 INTEROPERABILITY

"The cultural issues surrounding successful groupware deployment is growing in importance. Although these issues have been discussed in theory for the past few years, corporations are only now recognizing the practical importance of: (a) matching the tools to the work process and; (b) addressing the human barriers to collaboration. In many cases, multiple solutions can coexist, but the fact that each solution addresses different organizational needs will provide the path to the highest ROI. For the CIO, it is important to recognize that standardization is no longer the Holy Grail—ROI is."[1]

---

[1] Ian Campbell, Director, Collaborative Computing, International Data Corporation.

The notion that Calendaring and Scheduling only works when "everyone is using it" or when everyone is using the same system, is apparently not true. In fact, there are very few Fortune 500 firms that have successfully implemented a comprehensive, homogeneous Calendaring and Scheduling system for every desktop in their organization, yet the Calendaring and Scheduling market has flourished for years.

One-hundred percent organization-wide adoption is not necessary to reap benefits from a Calendaring and Scheduling system. With respect to scheduling alone, the addition of each user to a group Calendaring and Scheduling system potentially decreases the complexity of the manual coordination process correspondingly. However, to get the full benefit of scheduling and sharing of time-revelant information across the enterprise, user compliance and interoperability are certainly important. Total participation in any groupware roll-out is an ideal, but for the sake of those brave souls directly responsible for implementing it, we should acknowledge that the very strong user preferences (as evidenced by maverick departmental IS decisions, PIM diehards, and pocket calendar loyalists) have and will continue to outmaneuver this ideal.

To make a corporate Calendaring and Scheduling system work well, it is important that scheduling information be somehow shared across the enterprise. The obvious solution would be to have a single, homogeneous solution—if this is a viable option for your organization, by all means do it. However, as noted above, this is not always a likely scenario, particularly with the plethora of legacy applications found in larger enterprises. By the time most large enterprises had made the decision to select and implement a corporate-wide scheduling solution, they already had a significant installed base of disparate calendaring and scheduling solutions.

The selection process of a single, enterprise-wide scheduling solution is a very politically intense and protracted process (this process took six years by committee for one Fortune 500 high-tech company, resulting in the selection of not one, but two Calendaring and Scheduling products as "standards"). One benefit of this lengthy process is it gave the deliberating companies the opportunity to see which of their legacy applications could actually scale to meet their needs and which could not. The downside of this is of course that these burgeoning installed bases were getting more and more entrenched users.

So, for the enterprise-wide Calendaring and Scheduling system here are some options:

1. The first choice is a single-vendor solution that meets the needs of your entire organization and that your organization will adopt—a very tall order!
2. The second choice is a dominant-vendor solution that meets the majority of the IS and user requirements and with a small, manageable number of alternative solutions for the most vocal user groups. The idea here is that eventually, through attrition, the dominant solution will be the only solution.
3. The third choice is the *laissez faire* approach that allows users and departments to chose whatever solution best meets their needs.

This last option has historically been the most popular approach in practice, but is falling out of favor (in principle at least) because of the increased complexity and cost associated with this model in terms of support and opportunity loss associated with the limited information sharing potential.

The number of users that can usefully share information and coordinate activities decreases with each option. Since the second and third options comprise the majority of the corporate market, the ability to share information between different Calendaring and Scheduling products has become a serious IS issue at most large organizations and has given rise to serious Calendaring and Scheduling standards efforts on the part of the vendor community.

5.5.1 Scheduling Standards

"A standards development process must perform a difficult juggling act. It must select among a range of technical alternatives, and it must do so in a manner that attends to the political concerns of its members. A process which attends only to technical excellence may produce a solution which is applicable only in a very narrow context. . . However, if the process places too much emphasis upon polite accommodation of the desires of each and all its members, the well-known problems of 'design by committee' are guaranteed to sabotage the results."[1]

Currently there is no *de facto* Calendaring and Scheduling standard that allows scheduling information to be usefully exchanged between third-party Calendaring and Scheduling products. However, a recent spate of activity by the Calendaring and Scheduling vendor community may change that. The combination of heightened industry demand and the past experience of failed standard attempts have inspired both a sense of urgency and openness that will help fuel the new standards effort currently underway.

As mentioned earlier, the terms "Calendaring" and "Scheduling" are not synonymous. *Calendaring* involves the placement and manipulation of data on a calendar, while *Scheduling* involves the communication and negotiation between calendars for such data placement. This distinction takes on special meaning in the area of standards. The main focus of current Calendaring and Scheduling standards effort will be upon the representation and transfer of calendar objects across the net. The set of information to be exchanged will be, by necessity, limited to the basics. This means that the richness and variety of scheduling-related information exchanged within a multi-vendor Calendaring and Scheduling environment will likely be limited to what is covered in the standards specifications.

5.5.1.1 Past Standards Efforts
Calendaring and Scheduling vendors have made several unsuccessful attempts toward the goal of creating a standard that would enable different products to dynamically share information. The difficulty in such an undertaking lies

---

[1] ©1993 "Making Standards the IETF Way" by Dave Crocker, principal at Brandenburg Consulting, www.brandenburg.com, and co-founder of the Internet Mail Consortium (IMC)

in the heterogeneous architectures and feature sets of the different Calendaring and Scheduling products involved. Using the democratic process adopted by most consortia, vendors try to negotiate the inclusion of the technologies that form the substance of their product implementation. With many vendors involved in this process, the resultant specification may be too unwieldy for any of the individual participants to adopt—much less the non-participant vendors who didn't have the opportunity to share their unique views on product architecture.

The XAPIA Calendaring and Scheduling API (CSA), was the latest example of this approach. The XAPIA Association (X.400 Application Program Interface Association), formed in 1989, was created initially to provide assistance to developers of applications running on X.400 networks. The XAPIA charter had been expanded to include guidance in API development for mail systems as well as mail-enabled applications (which includes a subset of the Calendaring and Scheduling products on the market).

In late 1994, the proposed XAPIA Calendaring and Scheduling API was made generally available to all scheduling vendors and was adopted by very few. In hindsight, this may have been the result of an overly ambitious technical scope, or perhaps Calendaring and Scheduling vendors just weren't ready to "bite the bullet." Some of the specifications from the XAPIA Calendaring and Scheduling API, however, are being brought forward within the vCalendar proposal from the Versit Consortium for review within the current standards creation effort.

5.5.1.2 Current Standards Efforts

A group of Calendaring and Scheduling vendors along with other interested parties met in July 1996 with the intent of creating a new standards effort through a process very different from past standards efforts—the creation of an IETF (Internet Engineering Task Force) Working Group for Calendaring and Scheduling. The decision to develop a standards specification via the IETF Working Group process may prove to be instrumental in the resultant specification's market success.

There are many key differences between the standardization efforts via the IETF vs. the traditional consortium process, as noted below:

IETF Working Group process:	Traditional consortium process:
narrow technical focus	general design approach
addresses only near-term goals	addresses long-term goals
meetings held electronically	meetings held face-to-face
membership is informal	formal membership

For more information on the IETF standards process, read "Making Standards the IETF Way" by Dave Crocker at http://www.brandenburg.com. Besides providing information on a standards process, the IETF overview presents a very successful model of open, electronic collaboration.

The IETF Working Group's development time is usually much faster than standards development via consortium. One reason for this is that the process doesn't wait for face-to-face meetings—collaboration continues literally around the clock and around the globe. To reduce barriers to participation and to maintain a level playing field, decisions can only be made electronically via the Working Group's e-mail list. This is how the typical IETF process manages to move from formation of a Working Group to submission of the specification as a Proposed Standard within nine to eighteen months. The success rates for industry adoption of standards created via the IETF process are quite good.

The goal of the initial face-to-face Calendaring and Scheduling meeting in July 1996 was to achieve consensus that a IETF Calendaring and Scheduling Working Group be formed. That done, the next step is that a charter be written and approved. The charter, essentially a statement of work, describes the focus and scope of the Working Group. The scope of this particular effort will be narrowed to perhaps 2-3 of the most elemental specifications concerning the representation and transfer of calendar objects across the net. This IETF effort will not attempt to model the attributes of the actual calendar on the other end of such a transfer—a pitfall of past standards efforts.

Assuming all goes according to plan, the specifications should reach "Proposed Standard" status after the Summer IETF Meeting in June 1997.

Vendors participating in the July 1996 meeting included:	
Amplitude Software Corp.	Automatrix, Inc.
Banyan Systems, Inc.	Clear Blue Network Systems, Inc.
CrossWind Technologies, Inc.	Corporate Software & Technology
Goldmine Software	Hewlett-Packard
IBM Corporation	IET Intelligent Electronics
Lotus Development Corp.	Microsoft Corp.
Microsystems Software, Inc.	NetManage, Inc.
Netmosphere, Inc.	Netscape Communications Corp.
Nokia	Novell
Now Software	ON Technology Corp.
OnTime Software, a division of FTP Software, Inc.	Phase2 Software Corp.
Puma Technology	Sarrus Software
Software.Com, Inc.	Starfish Software, Inc.
TeamWare	Versit Project Office

Of these participants, several presented individually developed technical drafts:

☞ *Internet Calendar Access Protocol (ICAP)* presented by Clear Blue Network Systems and Lotus

☞ *MIME-based Application/Properties* profile presented by Microsoft Corporation

☞ *Calendaring and Scheduling Interoperability Protocol (CSIP)* presented by OnTime/FTP Software

☞ *Simple Scheduling Transport Protocol (SSTP)* presented by On Technology

☞ *Scheduling Wide-area Transport Protocol (SWTP)* presented by Phase2 Software

☞ *"Calendar"* presented by the Versit Consortium

The multiple technical drafts were representative of the diverse architectures and technical philosophies within the Calendaring and Scheduling products currently on the market. The Versit Consortium, a consortium working to propose personal data interchange standards for interoperable Electronic Business Cards (vCard) and personal calendaring objects (vCalendar) contributed its vCalendar specification as a proposal. The vCalendar specification includes X/Open-based calendar semantics from the XAPIA effort.

5.5.1.3 General Information Sharing Standards that Will Affect Calendaring and Scheduling

While no scheduling specific standards currently exist, a number of other more generalized standards will assist in the information sharing and communications direction of Calendaring and Scheduling products. Most scheduling vendors support TCP/IP (Transport Control Protocol/Internet Protocol) as their communications protocol, which provides a level of commonality between scheduling vendors that didn't exist two years ago. Other important standards are HTML (HyperText Markup Language) and HTTP (HyperText Transfer Protocol), which establish standard formats for data presentation and transfer.

5.6 HOW THE CALENDARING AND SCHEDULING MARKETPLACE IS JOINING THE WEB REVOLUTION

The emergence of the World Wide Web, HTTP, and HTML have created an environment where information sharing is happening (and happening very quickly) on a scale never before possible. This revolution was originally limited to static HTML pages. It is now quickly gaining the capability to generate information specific to the needs of the requester. Calendaring information (especially group calendaring information) tends not to be static and certainly is specific to the requester of that information. As a result, calendaring systems need to utilize the more dynamic capabilities that the Web offers in order to be useful within such an environment. That is, the information typically needs to be extracted from a calendaring database and then mapped "on the fly" into a format that can be delivered to the user. It is also important to keep in mind that some kind of database mechanism needs to lie behind any Web-based approach to Calendaring and Scheduling. No matter how easily implemented and accessible Web solutions may be, such solutions applied to Calendaring and Scheduling need to provide real-time information in order to adequately serve this part of a useful Web solution.

5.6.1 Web/browser Clients

Information needs to be extracted from a calendar database of some sort, which necessitates a well-designed engine behind such efforts. There are also performance issues involved with the front-end, data delivery. The three main methods for delivering such information to the user are currently the following:

1. the CGI (Common Gateway Interface)
2. Java
3. ActiveX

5.6.1.1 The Common Gateway Interface

CGI typically offers the easiest mechanism for enabling access to scheduling information over the Web. Through the CGI mechanism, Web servers can be instructed to execute external programs (CGI scripts) that can do the type of formatting necessary to display calendar information to the user. From a development viewpoint, it is fairly simple to generate a monthly calendar using the TABLE construct of HTML. Given an HTML reference that stipulates the month and year, the CGI script can be instructed to generate an HTML page that constructs a calendar for that month and year. This HTML page is then transferred by the Web server back to the user's browser (see Figs. 5.3, 5.4, and 5.5).

There are a number of advantages of the CGI approach to calendaring on the Web. The first, and most important, point about the CGI approach is that CGI is available and it works. Other technologies, as of this writing, are being feverishly developed, and, as such, are currently not "ready for prime time." Another advantage of CGI is the relative ease with which a developer can generate HTML code, either within the CGI script, or within an agent with which the CGI script communicates. As a result, one can create a CGI-based calendaring solution fairly quickly. Finally, if the developer is judicious about the HTML constructs utilized, one can use just about any browser to access calendaring information provided through CGI scripting.

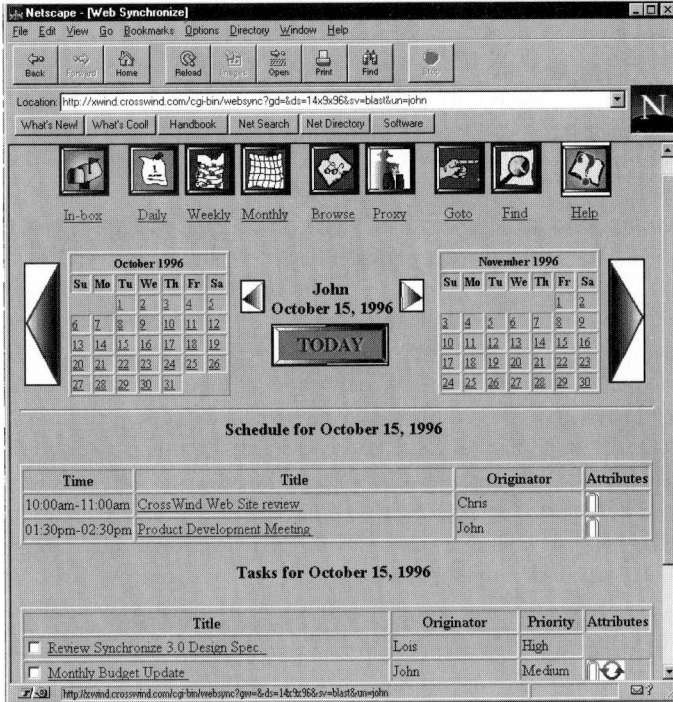

Fig. 5.3 Example of a CGI-based Web client for Synchronize (Daily view), from Cross-Wind Technologies

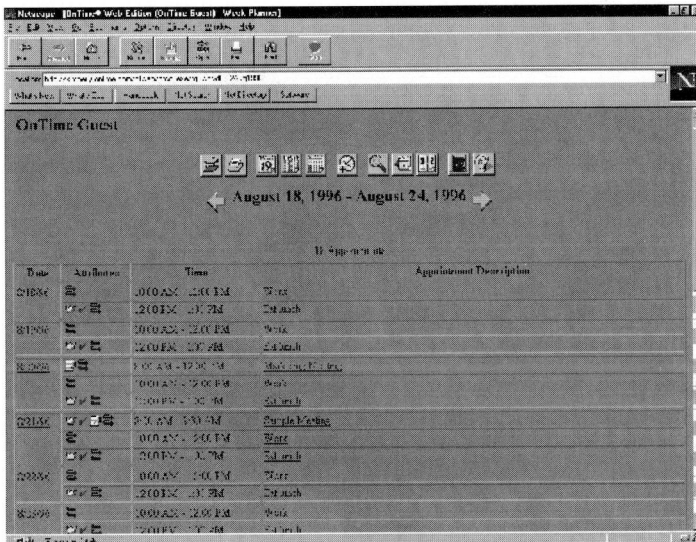

Fig. 5.4 Example of a CGI-based Web client for OnTime (Weekly view), from FTP Software

Web Module 2
(NLM, UNIX, NT, OS/2)

Web Module 1
(NLM, OS/2)

| NGWINTER.NLM |
| Or |
| INTERSRV.EXE |

TCP-IP

GWWEB.EXE

HTTP Server

CGI
Common Gateway Interface

CGI 1.0 Compliant

GroupWise Engine

Firewall

HTML 1.0

.HTM Files

HTML 2.0
HTML 3.0

Internet Cloud

UNC Path   Or   Drive Map

GroupWise PO   GroupWise PO

Internet Browser

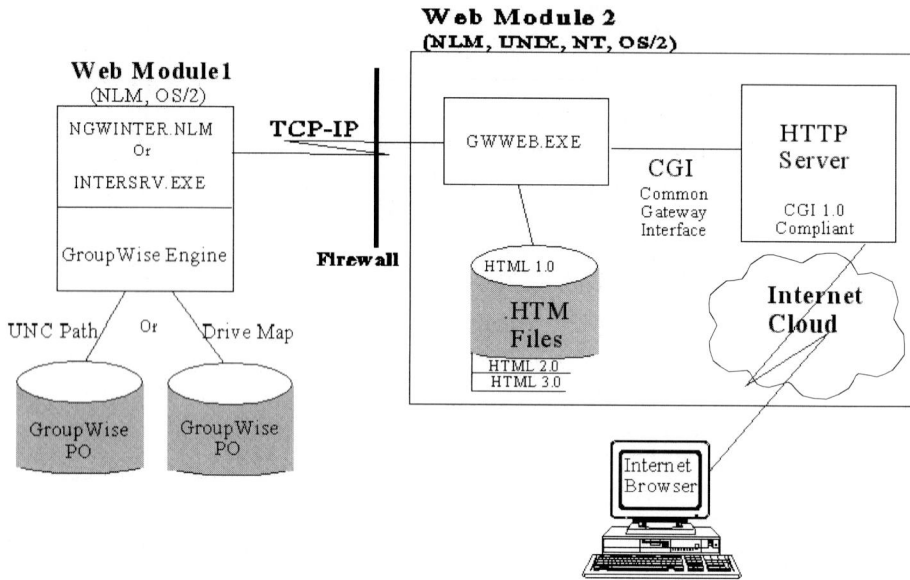

WebAccess Architecture

Fig. 5.5 The "WebAccess" architectural diagram for GroupWise, from Novell

Given these advantages, a CGI-based approach to calendaring may be a good decision, for the near-term at least, if time is of the essence in implementing a Web-based calendaring solution. However, there are a number of disadvantages with using CGI. The most important of these is the relatively static nature of CGI and HTML. While it is easy to generate HTML code to display a calendar, for example, any minor change to that calendar necessitates that an entirely new HTML page be downloaded to the browser and re-drawn (see Fig. 5-6). In addition, the number of GUI objects supported by HTML is very limited, and not nearly as visually appealing as those supported by Java or ActiveX. These constraints tend to enforce the development of Web based applications that are not as visually appealing or as fully functioned as their more traditional client counterparts. As a result, vendors are moving, over time, to other approaches that will require a much more significant R&D investment, but which promise much better results than CGI. Currently, the most popular of these technologies are Java from JavaSoft, a division of Sun Microsystems, and ActiveX from Microsoft. Figure 5.6 shows the implementation differences between CGI and ActiveX.

CGI Approach   ## Active X/Java Approach

CLIENT

User Display

Graphics code

data transfer

User Display & Graphics Code

network bandwidth

data transfer

SERVER

Web server

Calendaring & Scheduling Database Server

Web server

Calendaring & Scheduling Database Server

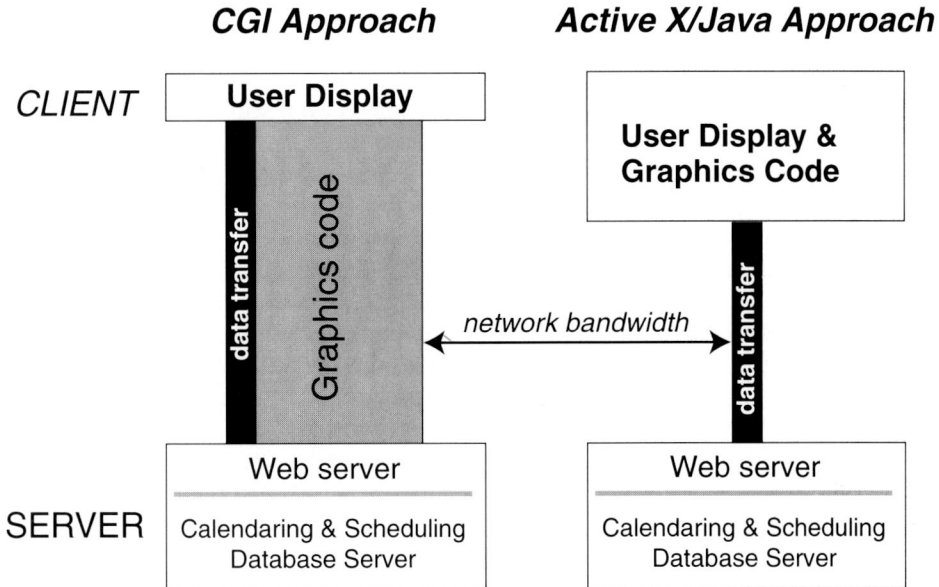

Fig. 5.6 Implementation differences for Calendaring and Scheduling between CGI and Java/ActiveX

5.6.1.2 Java

Java is a programming language that was originally developed by Sun Microsystems to control set-top boxes on televisions. As such, it was designed to be portable and work in embedded environments. With the advent of the Web, Sun repositioned (and redesigned) Java so that it could be used to "bring life" to the rather static world of HTML. Because it is a programming language, Java allows the developer to control everything that is drawn within the browser frame allocated to the application. As a result, the output can be visually appealing, changes to the output can be limited to only those portions that need to be redrawn (with the accompanying improvements in performance), and network bandwidth can be used for data only, as opposed to data and code, as in the case of CGI scripts.

Perhaps the greatest advantage of Java is the platform independence it would bring to Calendaring and Scheduling. Java compiles to "byte-codes," machine independent instructions that are interpreted by a Java Virtual Machine that resides within a browser. Since it is highly desirable that all user populations participate equally in corporate time management and coordination, availability of these tools across the three major platforms (Windows, Macintosh, and Unix) has become extremely important at many major corporations. A Java-based Calendaring and Scheduling tool would bring the cross-platform benefits of such portability to users.

There are, of course, disadvantages to a Java approach. The current Java development environments are not as well developed as more traditional ones (e.g., the Microsoft Foundation Classes, MFC). In addition, the interpretive nature of Java makes for slower performance, although this problem is being addressed with the emergence of just-in-time compilation techniques. As a result, the emergence of full-featured Java applications has been slower than expected. Over time, this will change, but there are other choices available.

5.6.1.3 ActiveX

Microsoft has modified their networked OLE technology to provide Web-enabling capability for Windows based applications. The result, called ActiveX, is a component framework that allows developers to use their Windows expertise and current Windows applications to create applications that can utilize the Web. The advantages of this approach are appealing: The vast body of Windows capability and technology can be leveraged to be used with a Web framework. Speed is not an issue, since the code is not interpreted. However, the trade-off is that portability is not possible with the current technology, since the ActiveX components are compiled for a particular machine architecture (almost always the x86 architecture). As a result, the important minority segments of the market (Macintosh and Unix) are not served by an ActiveX solution.

While progress is being made by vendors to deal with these portability issues, the simple solution that Java brings to the portability problem is not readily available with ActiveX at this time. If a choice is to be made between Java and ActiveX, then Java is the better choice when portability is paramount, while ActiveX should be chosen if one wants to utilize current Windows technologies.

5.6.2 Other Methods

Other candidates besides CGI, Java, and ActiveX are being used for Web development by innovative developers who cannot wait for Java and ActiveX. For example, TCL (Tool Command Language) is an integral part of a development environment being provided by a Web development tool vendor. Since it is a scripting language, TCL provides for rapid development and is an ideal candidate for work in the fast-paced Web world. This product uses the Netscape plug-in API with TCL to render dynamic views in a browser window that would not be possible with CGI, and which may be easier than Java or ActiveX.

Netscape plug-in techniques, in general, have been used successfully by developers such as Macromedia, publishers of Shockwave. However, these plug-ins are transient in that, when the URL reference goes away, the plug-in goes away also; this is all due to HTML's statelessness. Reloading calendar clients each time one wants to check one's schedule and restoring the user's state may be too slow to make plug-ins viable (as they are currently implemented).

Given the ever evolving state of development technologies for the Web, there is no clear cut answer to the question of what technology to use for Calendaring and Scheduling integration with the Web. In general, if an immediate solution is required, CGI is the best approach. If portability is necessary and the solution can wait, Java wins the race. If leveraging a Windows code base and Windows expertise is important, then ActiveX should be the choice. In general, however, things are changing so rapidly that one needs to pay close attention to on-going developments. The correct decision for today may not be the correct decision for tomorrow, and both developers and users need to keep that in mind.

5.7 IMPLEMENTATION FOR THE INTRANET

5.7.1 Scalability/Performance

"Organizations reviewing scheduling products will be asking the hard questions of will it scale, can we selectively secure calendar information, and is the time database open to other information processes?"[1]

It is quite a challenge to find a corporate Calendaring and Scheduling solution that meets current needs and has the potential to address future needs as an organization grows and changes. As user demand for Calendaring and Scheduling capabilities has increased, many system administrators are discovering that their legacy solutions will not scale to address their current needs. For companies with an entrenched user population, the challenge of switching to a more capable Calendaring and Scheduling tool can represent a significant cultural challenge. Because of the difficulties in switching a user population and the long time-frame between initial investment and the return on that investment, the pressure to select the "right" solution the first time is very real. To ensure that the investment will be in a long-term solution, the underlying architecture of candidate products must be considered—it is essential that the solution is truly cross-platform and has the ability to transparently scale across the enterprise.

5.7.2 Using the Web as a "Framework Platform"

What is a "framework"? Current framework products ostensibly provide a generalizable infrastructure for data sharing and management. Another way to look at framework offerings is as integrated product suites that have the ability to extend the platform to include other products. The upside of this approach is that the data sharing and data management within the core product suite is usually excellent. The downside is that the framework platform was optimized for its core products and as users extend it to support other types of applications, (like real-time scheduling), performance and flexibility may become issues. Although one-stop-shopping is appealing from an implementation viewpoint, the

---

[1] Robert Rustici, analyst and principal at Zero-In Technologies, Inc.

resultant solution may not provide the competitive edge expected from the IS investment. The three major "framework" platforms in the groupware arena—Lotus Notes, Microsoft Exchange, and Novell's GroupWise—all have calendaring and scheduling capabilities of differing performance and technical emphasis.

One of the attractions of implementing a corporate intranet is the option of not being tied to any one proprietary "framework" platform, and the ability, or at least the promise, of selecting the best-of-breed applications to meet specific business and cultural requirements. This approach is not necessarily instead of framework products; many companies are finding that implementing a corporate intranet allows them to tune their framework solutions to meet specific corporate needs.

In a recent example of this hybrid approach, a company divided the functionality of their calendaring and scheduling requirements between an intranet-based scheduling product and their current messaging-based framework product, based upon the relative strengths of each. The end result was that the framework product (which has a Calendaring and Scheduling component) was selected to communicate the company events calendar and business forms, and the intranet-based scheduling product was selected as the medium for group Calendaring and Scheduling for the user base (see Fig. 5.7).

A Hybrid Implementation

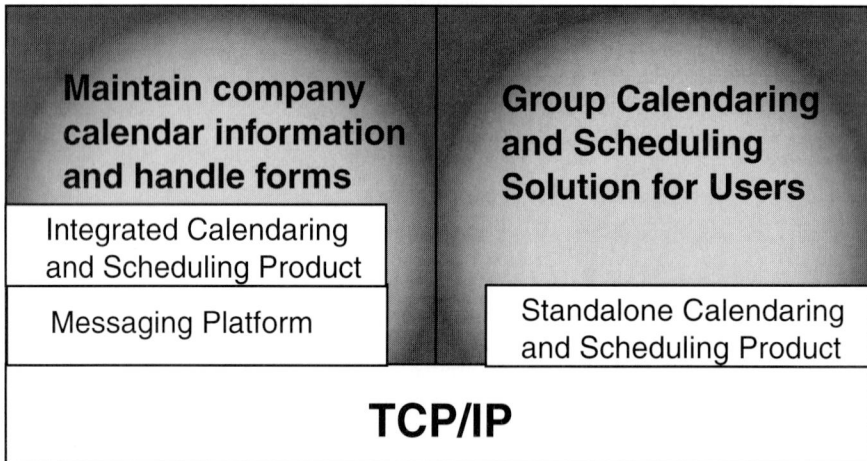

Maintain company calendar information and handle forms

Integrated Calendaring and Scheduling Product

Messaging Platform

Group Calendaring and Scheduling Solution for Users

Standalone Calendaring and Scheduling Product

TCP/IP

Fig. 5.7 A Framework/intranet Hybrid Approach

One of the performance issues in a situation like this is the ability to schedule in real-time. Although messaging implementations are providing "near" real-time performance, this is not sufficient for scheduling time and resources with large groups of users. Near real-time scheduling is about as useful as near real-time telephone service in a fast-paced corporate environment.

5.7.2.1 Incorporation of Calendaring and Scheduling within a Web Framework

There are two contexts within which users will be seeing traditional Calendaring and Scheduling appearing on the corporate intranet. The first of these will be fairly straightforward "ports" of those applications to the Web, while the second will be characterized by a higher level of integration of Calendaring and Scheduling tools with other, relevant Web-based applications.

Stand-alone Calendaring and Scheduling applications running within the Web are beginning to appear, mostly based upon CGI, with Java or ActiveX implementations to follow. The basic server architecture will be the same, but will sport a new Web front-end, allowing access from any machine within an intranet, or even access from the Internet, assuming that security issues are worked out. The speed with which these applications can be delivered will depend, in large part, on the strength of the "engines" behind them. If access to those engines is simple and well defined and the engines provide good performance, then providing standalone Web-based Calendaring and Scheduling solutions will be a straightforward task for vendors.

A second, more interesting type of application of Calendaring and Scheduling technology to the Web will manifest itself in the integration of that technology to other Web-based applications. There are a large number of applications that have a very high degree of time awareness, including work-flow tools, project managers, contact managers, etc. As they move to the Web, integration of Calendaring and Scheduling capability will become a given over time.

The older framework technologies in use today (Notes, Exchange, Group-Wise) were necessary in order to provide "backbones" over which applications written to those frameworks can communicate. However, integration of tools within those frameworks has proved to be a fair amount of work for customers and third-party vendors alike.

With the advent of the Web, a number of advantages over the more traditional approach present themselves. First, the point and click connectivity provided by browsers lends itself very well to easy and seamless integration of independent front-ends. Secondly, the standard methods of CGI and HTML lend themselves to a simple communication mechanism that can be utilized by those independent front-ends and independent back-ends to complete the integration of the whole, without much of the pain involved in such efforts when using older frameworks.

5.7.2.2. Adding Scheduling to Existing Intranet Infrastructure

One of the reasons for the explosive growth of the Web has been its foundation upon open, and in some cases simple, standards like TCP/IP, HTML, and HTTP. Such simplicity and openness helped allow a wide variety of distributed applications and applets to be developed quickly by the average developer (as opposed to the more complex and arcane world of CORBA and DCE). In addition, the Web provides, through its hypertext capability and through the CGI interface, the semblance of seamless integration of otherwise disparate applications— regardless of whether those applications are really integrated or not.

This appearance of seamless integration has raised user expectations for all applications, including Calendaring and Scheduling. If Calendaring and Scheduling is to be integrated well with a company's intranet, it will have to work with those standards mentioned above, with standard browsers (e.g., Navigator and Internet Explorer), and with standards-based Web servers. In addition, true integration will necessitate adoption of additional emerging standards, like the IETF interoperability specification and directory services like LDAP (Lightweight Directory Access Protocol).

5.8 WHAT'S NEXT—EXTENDING TO THE INTERNET

After Calendaring and Scheduling tools become well integrated parts of corporate intranets, the next step is the Internet. People will want to schedule outside the corporate firewall with individuals outside the company. Many meetings today are with individuals and groups outside a corporation (e.g., with customers, vendors, prospects, etc.). In fact, as vendor/customer relationships become closer, the need to share tasks across companies also arises. An ideal situation will have Calendaring and Scheduling work as well across corporate boundaries as it does within, as does electronic mail. The World Wide Web is certainly poised to make such an ideal situation a reality.

However, while the path to Calendaring and Scheduling integration with intranets is fairly clear, such is not the case for the Internet. There are security issues to be worked out, as well as the less well-defined concerns of what kind of information should be protected behind a corporate firewall and what should be made available. In addition, such a scenario will only be viable if some level of Calendaring and Scheduling interoperability is achieved.

The issue of protecting valuable corporate data once it travels outside a firewall is simply part of the more general security issues of secure transports (addressed by the Secure Sockets Layer) and bullet-proof user authentication schemes (the same issues being dealt with currently in the context of such areas as Internet commerce). These are relatively easy problems to deal with, since other people have either solved them or are in the process of solving them. The more difficult issues that each corporate entity must decide for itself, include:

☞ What calendaring data, if any, should be made available outside the firewall?

☞ Should schedules be made available to "trusted" outsiders?

☞ Should only free/busy information be made available?

☞ What are the rights of outsiders?

☞ Should they be allowed to insert meetings onto insiders' schedules, or should they just be capable of proposing meetings that an insider can choose to view or not?

☞ Should outsiders be capable of delegating tasks to insiders, or should these be advisory tasks that can be viewed or not?

From a cultural viewpoint, the answers to these questions are not simple. Some corporations will choose to put nothing outside the firewall, at the expense of continuing to live with the lack of inter-corporate scheduling capability. Others may try to get a competitive advantage by making hard choices and using the available Calendaring and Scheduling standards.

In general, calendaring data is considered to be very proprietary and is not lightly released outside a corporation. In addition, users guard their schedules fiercely, since it is their time upon which others are impinging when a meeting is scheduled or a task is delegated. Care needs to be taken that Calendaring and Scheduling does not fall into the e-mail trap, where countless meetings, tasks, and reminders are deposited on people's schedules daily, to the point where they need filters to ignore all but a select few or just ignore them entirely. Since inter-company scheduling will provide a significant competitive advantage and a means to make companies work more closely together, these issues will be addressed by Calendaring and Scheduling vendors together with their customers.

The day may even come when you will be able to schedule a haircut or a dentist appointment with your computer, instead of juggling with your phone in one hand and your appointment book in another. All of this depends on standards being developed and accepted by the vendors and customers of Calendaring and Scheduling solutions. Once those standards and their subsequent implementations are in place, Calendaring and Scheduling will indeed be as ubiquitous as e-mail on the Internet.

5.9 CONCLUSION

As information and intellectual property become the new business currency, companies are turning to groupware technologies to remain competitive. The investment in technology and training should provide a means by which an enterprise can effectively convert the tidal wave of information into a competitive advantage.

Groupware may be the key to increasing productivity in spite of fewer available resources. Time management services are often at the top of the groupware implementation list because they help optimize the most expensive, non-renewable resource a company has—employees' time.

CALENDARING AND SCHEDULING PRODUCTS RESOURCE LIST

The following is a sampling of products that fall into the different class categories. Most of these vendors have either announced plans or introduced products to provide Internet/intranet access for scheduling information. To get the up-to-the-minute product information on all of these, URL addresses are provided. To get information on new vendors, set your Internet search engine request to: "Calendaring and Scheduling." If they don't have an Internet presence—it isn't a good sign.

WORKGROUP Calendaring and Scheduling Applications

Day-Timer Organizer
Day-Timers, Inc.
URL: http://www.daytimer.com

ECCO Pro
NetManage Inc.
URL: http://www.netmanage.com

Lotus Organizer
IBM/Lotus Development Corporation
URL: http://www.lotus.com

Pencil Me In
Sarrus Software, Inc.
URL: http://www.sarrus.com

DEPARTMENTAL Calendaring and Scheduling Applications

CaLANdar
Microsystems Software, Inc.
URL: http://www.microsys.com

ClockWise
Phase2 Software Corporation
URL: http://www.p2software.com

Microsoft Outlook 97
Microsoft Corporation
URL: http://www.microsoft.com/msoffice/

Meeting Maker XP
On Technology Corporation
URL: http://www.on.com

Now Up-to-Date
Now Software, Inc.
URL: http://www.nowsoft.com

OnTime Enterprise for Novell NetWare and Banyan VINES
FTP Software, Inc.
URL: http://www.ftp.com

TimeVision Network Scheduler
CE Software, Inc.
URL: http://www.cesoft.com

ENTERPRISE Calendaring and Scheduling Applications

Calendar Manager
Russell Information Sciences
URL: http://www.russellinfo.com

GroupWise
Novell, Inc.
URL: http://www.novell.com

OpenTime
Hewlett-Packard Company
URL:http://www.openmail.external.hp.com/
Corporate Software & Technologies
URL: http://www.cst.ca

Oracle InterOffice
Oracle
URL: http://www.oracle.com

Synchronize
CrossWind Technologies, Inc.
URL: http://www.crosswind.com

BIOGRAPHIES

Chris L. Knudsen is the Vice President of Marketing for CrossWind Technologies, Inc., the provider of enterprise collaboration software for the cooperative workplace. Knudsen is responsible for marketing CrossWind's premier product, Synchronize, the leading cross-platform Calendaring and Scheduling solution for the enterprise intranet.

Before co-founding CrossWind Technologies, Inc. in 1989, Knudsen was the Product Marketing Analyst for Integrated Solutions, Inc., where she managed and contributed to the corporate strategic planning process and served as Product Manager for peripheral devices and an entry-level system. Before joining Integrated Solutions, Knudsen consulted for Stevens-Arnold (a subsidiary of Computer Products, Inc.) where she created a new product development process; and for Zambon Farmaceutici, SpA, Milan, where she worked on pre-launch and early promotional phases of a key new product introduction. Knudsen holds a B.A. in Creative Arts/ Computer Art Applications from San Francisco State University and an M.B.A. from Babson College, Wellesly, MA.

David Wellington is the President and CEO of CrossWind Technologies. Wellington co-founded CrossWind Technologies in 1989, where he is a pioneer in collaborative computing for the cooperative workplace. At CrossWind, he brought the first client/server groupware application to market in 1992, years before competitive products. Prior to founding CrossWind, he served as Vice President of Engineering for Integrated Solutions, Inc., where his group was responsible for bringing the first commercially available RISC workstation to market. Prior to joining Integrated Solutions in 1984, he served as the Languages Manager at Zilog Systems Division, where he was responsible for the compiler group, including development and maintenance for C, F77, assemblers, and linkers. Wellington's areas of expertise include client/ server architectures, collaborative computing, and real-time software.

Wellington holds a B.S. in Mathematics from Stanford University and an M.S. in Statistics from the University of California, Berkeley.

URL: http://www.crosswind.com
CrossWind Technologies, Inc.
1505 Ocean Street
Suite 1
Santa Cruz, CA 95060 VOX: (408) 454-1852
Voice: (408) 469-1780   Fax: (408) 469-1750   e-mail: chris@xwind.com

Introduction to Chapter 6

Workflow deals with process. Einstein is reputed to have said "God is in the details," to which someone else replied, "No, God is in both the details and the process." The modern day corollary is "The job's not done until the paperwork is done." These ideas give insight into how today's businesses have begun to focus on work and business processes. When this chapter was first written for Groupware: Technology and Applications *almost 2 years ago, we were in the midst of a re-engineering revolution, just coming out of a recession, and investing in workflow applications was just taking off.*

Because Ronni Marshak is one of the top analysts on groupware worldwide, I asked her to update her earlier chapter in light of the trend toward business process automation, i.e., electronic workflow. Ronni does an exemplary job of evaluating the more important issues, such as, what is workflow? What is process? How does workflow deal with the automation of paper processes? How do these technologies help the redesign processes? What is the ROI of workflow, and how is it determined?

Ronni also presents a taxonomy of workflow: Ad-hoc, collaborative, administrative, and production. Anecdotes, case studies, and examples make these differences clear, however, it is also important to remember that workflows are not of discrete types, rather they are in a continuum. The next section examines BPR (business process re-engineering or redesign) and the stages of process automation. Ronni's classification and examination of workflow tool types (with plenty of examples) leads to a thorough discussion of the most important issues facing workflow, such as interoperability standards. There is an additional discussion of how workflow is applied, where it is implemented, and what functions are being used for/with workflow, such as image processing, document management, forms routing and processing, e-mail, transaction-based applications, etc. It is here we first encounter the Workflow Management Coalition (WfMC), a body of vendors developing a number of standards that will allow data to be moved between workflow products and applications. This is very similar to the T.120 standard in the videoconferencing world, or the ODBC standard in the database world. Standards help everyone. The vendors have specifications to build to, the users are not trapped in expensive proprietary systems, and the market for workflow expands dramatically. Ronni gives a good overview of the Wfmc standard, its direction, and its implications.

In the final section of this chapter, Ronni broaches the difficult technical questions for workflow developers, such as, should workflow applications be messaging-based or database-based, or both? What de facto standards must be supported? What are the barriers to entry in workflow, and what are some of the benefits you can derive from the application of workflow? Finally, Ronni closes with a detailed analysis of workflow products and vendors.

Ronni's chapter is one of the most cogent summaries of workflow technologies, functions, products, and issues I have ever seen, and if you only read a few chapters in this volume, this will be one of the most valuable.

Workflow: Applying Automation to Group Processes

Ronni T. Marshak
Patricia Seybold Group

6.1 WHERE WORKFLOW FITS IN GROUPWARE

If you look at technology through sports-colored glasses, then groupware is the basketball team, passing and rebounding to score team points—or its the crew team, rowing together to speed past the competition—or its the cheerleading squad, standing on each others' shoulders and jumping into each others' arms to whip the crowd into a frenzy of support—well, you get the picture. In this sporty world of groupware, workflow is the relay race, where only one team member at a time is actually running, but the hand-off of the baton spells the difference between success and failure.

There is a basic difference between other sports and a relay race, and that difference has to do with teamwork—or collaboration. Typically, you think of collaboration as an active explicit joining of minds, working together to achieve a certain goal—brainstorming, co-authoring, etc. This is the sports team model, where the football team huddles together to plan the next play. But workflow is more focused on process—combining individual achievements into a sequence of actions that achieve a goal.

6.2 THE ROLE OF WORKFLOW TECHNOLOGY

Often, the difference between corporate success and failure is determined not by the vagaries of the business you are in but by how you conduct business—the processes your organization has developed that allow you to do things just a bit better . . . faster . . . more easily . . . more effectively . . . than the competition.

For the past few years, technical toolsets have been available to help you automate these business processes. These sets of tools are called *workflow*.

6.2.1 Letting the Computer Handle Paper-Pushing

Workflow technology is justified on the assumption that there are some things that a computer does more effectively than a person. We humans are very good at making decisions, being innovative, identifying unexpected exceptions to rules (not to mention making up the rules that these processes follow). But we are not usually as efficient at things like finding documents (from among thousands of files), keeping track of deadlines (and noting reminders of them in a timely fashion), and making sure that completed work gets from one desk to the next in the proper sequence. An automated system for pushing the (electronic) paper sure comes in handy.

6.2.2 Holding the Big Picture

In addition, although each of us has a role as a participant in a process, maintaining an overview of how the process is running is not typically within the scope of our individual roles. An automated workflow system can manage and coordinate the execution of even the most complex system, maintaining all the information on who did what, what decision was made, when things were completed, and so forth. Oh, sure, a manager is assigned to keep track of all this information, but he or she is dependent on timely communications from all participants. And let's face it—consolidating all that information from all the participants is extremely difficult to do manually.

6.2.3 Debunking the Workflow Myth

There has been a lot of mystique surrounding workflow automation, but let me assure you that workflow is not mysterious. It is, very simply, the automation of business processes.

6.3 REDESIGNING PROCESSES FOR COMPETITIVE ADVANTAGE

In the face of the increasing pressures of global competitiveness, organizations are reexamining the ways they do business. All of the processes that make up an organization have fallen under scrutiny. It is no longer enough to simply streamline your manufacturing operation or upgrade your customer service operation. Now the pressure is on to improve the competitiveness of organizations by examining entire business processes, from the conception to the consumption of the products and services being offered.

The widespread use of manufacturing automation and information technology within organizations in the developed economies of the world has amplified the sense of urgency that companies feel. They can clearly see that the organizations that redesign, streamline, and automate their business processes with workflow technology are able to leapfrog their competition.

6.4 THE GROWING SCOPE OF WORKFLOW APPLICATIONS

6.4.1 Inter-enterprise Workflow via the Internet

Although we currently see workflow applications that operate within a single enterprise, in the next few years, we will start to expand our processes to encompass our customers and suppliers, creating truly inter-enterprise workflows. These inter-organizational processes are now realistic as a result of the flurry of activity in the Internet market. Almost all workflow vendors are developing (or have already developed) Web browser-based client access into the workflow engines. These are primarily targeted at intranet solutions (within a multi-location, but single enterprise). But very soon, as the security and management capabilities of the Web improve, they will grow beyond single organizational boundaries.

6.4.2 Managing Multiple Organizational Domains

A workflow application has to reflect the policies and practices of an organization. Roles are based on organizational hierarchies and relationships. And the routing of information is determined by enterprise directories. When a single process spans organizations, you have to take into account different cultures, rules, and organizational charts. Thus, workflow products will have to be enhanced to handle multiple organizational domains, where the specifics of each company are maintained. This also leads to the issues of ownership—which company owns the process? In the next few years, we will witness a breaking down of organizational boundaries regarding business processes. While this is a good thing—conceptually—it is vital that we understand all the management issues involved in routing strategic information back and forth.

6.4.3 Identifying the Process to Automate

Many people ask, "What is the best workflow product on the market?" This is, however, the wrong question. What you should be asking is, "What is the most appropriate product to address my unique business process?" You should always start from your organization's point of view. You need to identify existing processes (or areas where a process *should be* developed) that are a source of both great pain and great potential. Pain can be measured in wasted effort, redundancies, dissatisfied employees, slow turnaround time, and poor quality. Potential is measured in terms of new opportunities, improved quality, faster time to market, happy employees, and satisfied customers.

Automating business processes is not, however, a panacea that will automatically ensure global success. You must give serious thought to which processes you are going to automate. Here are some guidelines to help you determine the most effective areas for implementing workflow technology.

6.4.3.1 Mission-Critical Processes

Mission-critical production processes, such as loan processing and insurance claims, are very visible targets for automation. By automating these workflows, your organization can both save money—reduce staffing expenses, reduce paper expenses, and others—and become more productive—process more applications, process more claims, and do similar tasks.

6.4.3.2 Departmental Business Processes

Similarly, the departmental business processes, such as purchase order requests and travel reimbursement, are naturals for workflow automation. These types of processes have the additional attraction of being much simpler and less expensive to automate. And, as an added bonus, they are often easier to introduce to the corporate culture by virtue of being smaller by nature and requiring less behavioral modification. Typically, the advantages of automating these types of processes are significant time-savings, improved management, and better tracking of process-related information.

6.4.3.3 Look beyond the Obvious

However, when selecting a business process to automate, you sometimes have to look beyond the obvious.

In the keynote address at Workflow '94 Boston, Ellen Knapp of Coopers & Lybrand gave an excellent presentation stressing that the key to workflow is not just getting the process right, but getting the right process right. This means automating those processes that are directly tied into the identity and goals of the organization. For example, payroll is often a process that gets a lot of attention when processes are selected to automate. Yet the payroll process is not high on the list of company goals—unless, of course, your company is ADP, whose main business is handling the payroll process for its many clients. She also pointed to a bank that streamlined loan processing from two weeks to four hours but neglected to develop a strategy for increasing the number of loan applications that came in; the bank eventually filed for bankruptcy.

6.4.3.4 Find the Differentiators

To most effectively take advantage of workflow technologies and methodologies, you should look beyond automating production and administrative processes and try to identify *differentiating* processes. These are processes that are visible to the market—the ones that make your company different and better. As a result, customers and potential customers should become attracted to your organization because of the efficient and effective way you handle your business.

6.4.3.5 Support Business Goals

Look for business processes that are closely tied into your business goals, such as quality of products, excellence in customer service, revenue per employee, etc. If you are running a process that doesn't meet some goal, you are wasting valuable time, effort, and money.

6.4.3.6 Focus Outward on Customers and Stakeholders

One area where payoffs have proven to be particularly fruitful is redesigning and focusing on customer-related processes. Too often, companies get mired in the exhausting detail of internal processes, such as travel reimbursement and vacation requests. While automating these processes might save some clerical time, they are not particularly meaningful to your business. All organizations have customers and/or stakeholders—people or companies to whom the organization must deliver some product or service. Organizations are successful when they deliver products and services that satisfy the customer in terms of quality, timeliness, appropriateness, and appeal. When you spend too much time looking inward, you get a closed view of what your business is, making assumptions about what customers want and what competitors offer. Thus, I recommend designing and automating processes that capture information from the outside—such as customer service, customer outreach, and similar processes. Typically, the results are more satisfied customers and an improved bottom line.

6.4.3.7 Nonfinancial Goals

Of course, business goals do not necessarily need to be financial. A business goal can be to have a great Christmas party or to improve communications between the marketing and development departments. One of the business goals of the Patricia Seybold Group is high quality of life for employees. This goal has no bottom-line price tag but is a very valid business goal; ironically, it is also a goal that usually leads to happier and more productive and innovative employees, which inevitably results in increases to the bottom line.

☞ Determining Return on Investment (ROI)

☞ The promise of increased productivity as a result of redesigning processes and implementing automated workflow is twofold: cost savings and increased revenue.

6.4.3.8 Cost Savings

Innumerable clerical improvements can be implemented with well-designed workflow systems. Thus, fewer people can handle the same amount of work, freeing people to undertake other assignments. In addition, by automating processes, you often lower supply costs by reducing the amount of paper used or eliminating reliance on overnight delivery services.

6.4.3.9 Increased Revenue

Automated workflows also allow more cases to be handled, more loans approved, more purchase orders authorized, more customer requests filled. Further, by freeing people from routine tasks, they can create new products that can then be delivered in a more timely fashion, resulting in increased sales.

In both these cases, the increased numbers are measurable and, as such, traditional proof of ROI.

6.4.3.10 Unmeasurable Results

Justifying the pain and expense of implementing workflow applications based on clerical improvements may not be enough in itself.

I propose that, in addition to measuring the *amount* of work that can be done, we also measure the *quality* of the work that gets done. By automating our processes, which ensures that the right information gets to the right people in the right order with the right tools to process that information, we are freed from the mundane and annoying acts of *finding* information and *tracking* who has already seen it. We therefore have more time to think about the decisions we have to make, and we are less stressed when we make those decisions. Productivity and return on investment should not only measure whether more work is being done, but whether the results of the work are better. So, as you look to putting a workflow solution into your organization, take a moment to consider the unmeasurable—the increases in qualitative decisions that could result from information being routed to the right person at the right time, making it available when the decision must be made.

6.5 CATEGORIES OF WORKFLOW: USEFUL GUIDELINES

Because workflow can be a difficult area to understand, many have attempted to separate types of workflow applications into categories. Common practice divides workflow applications into four categories:

6.5.1 Ad Hoc

Ad hoc workflow is a one-time only process that emerges from your daily work. It is typically electronic-mail-based and can be thought of as an intelligent routing slip, where, once one person is done with the information, it knows to route itself to the next person on the list.

> ***Example: A New Service:*** *A fax comes in from a customer requesting a new type of service that you currently don't offer. The customer service representative can scan (or attach, if the fax is received electronically) the document and route it to someone in product planning to determine if the service is appropriate for a new product area. After product planning adds comments, it is routed to someone in marketing, then to someone in sales, and so on. The fax finally returns to the customer service department with all the comments and a determination of whether, indeed, you plan to offer this service so that the customer can be informed.* The advantage of using a workflow application for this type of routing is that you can predetermine the route and you can maintain the status of the fax (knowing who is working on it). With some products, you could also assign deadlines by which each person must comment on the fax and send it along its route.

6.5.2 Collaborative

Actually, the workflow product doesn't build an application where collaboration takes place. Rather, collaborative workflow *coordinates* the collaborative process where people work together to achieve a goal, providing a management layer to processes that are used regularly in your organization. Collaborative workflow is usually supported via e-mail or document management-based workflow products.

> ***Example: Approving a Marketing Brochure:*** *The process actually begins in the marketing department, where the elements that need to be addressed in the brochure are specified. These specifications are then routed to copy-editing. The completed copy is returned to the marketing manager for approval. If rejected, it goes back to copy-editing. If approved, the copy and specifications move to the art department. Once the brochure layout has been designed, the brochure returns to marketing for approval. The tools allow you to specify the routing flow as well as the conditions (business rules—in this case, approve or reject) that determine the sequence in which the information passes from person to person.*

6.5.3 Administrative

Internal administrative processes, such as expense reimbursement and purchase order requests, are usually addressed with forms-based workflow products. The intelligent forms can front-end data from underlying corporate databases (such as personnel databases), which are then delivered from person to person (or department to department) using your organization's e-mail infrastructure.

Example: A Purchase Order Request Application: *Any employee may fill out a purchase order request, including the name of the vendor, product, price, and amount. A list of preferred vendors may even be electronically available as a dropdown list in the appropriate field on the form. The completed form calculates the total amount of the request. If the amount is over \$50, the request goes to the supervisor of the initiator (the person who is making the request). If the amount is over \$500, it goes to the departmental manager. If the request is \$50 or less, it goes directly to the purchasing agent. In order for the request to be approved by the supervisor or manager, it must be compared to available budget. This can be automatically calculated in the form by accessing the budget spreadsheet and doing the comparison. If the request is over budget, or if the supervisor or manager choose to reject the order for any reason, the request form is routed back to the initiator. If approved, it moves to the purchasing agent. The process continues through the receipt of the order and the accounts payable process. The workflow tools support the definition of the routing rules, the integration with underlying data (such as determining who the appropriate manager is, based on who initiated the process), and the comparison with the budget spreadsheet.*

6.5.4 Production

Most workflow applications implemented to date are high-end, mission-critical, strategic, transaction-oriented processes. Often, these applications include image processing requiring specialized hardware and software. They may also include the use of intelligent forms, database access, and ad hoc capabilities. However, in production workflow applications, the database transaction is key. A good way to think about transaction-based workflow is that, in these cases, the business process *is* the business—consider the strategic nature of claims processing to insurance companies and loan processing to banks.

Although these categories are very useful and have helped customers get their minds around a very complex and diverse set of products and methodologies, they should be looked at as guidelines rather than gospel—general category buckets where people can look at the processes used in their businesses and figure out where to start looking at technology solutions to automate them. It is important to remember that processes often span categories of applications, and that when you are defining your process and selecting workflow tools, you need to consider the entire process cycle. It can then be broken down into smaller applications that are often addressed with different tools.

> *Example: Claims Adjustment:* As mentioned earlier, claims adjusting could be considered the archetypal workflow application. When the receptionist at the insurance company takes your claim information, he or she accesses your record from the customer database, which automatically launches a subprocess (a smaller process within the scope of the complete business process) whereby a letter and claim form are mailed to your home. When you return the completed form, it is scanned into the system, and a data entry clerk enters the relevant information into a form that will be routed through the process along with the image of your claim report. Depending on the nature of the claim (theft or accident) and the amount of the claim (over $1,000 or not), the information is routed to the correct-level person in the appropriate department, who determines if and how much of the claim is to be paid. If the claim is approved, another subprocess is launched to cut and send a check. If it is rejected or more information is needed, the appropriate letter is sent or a customer service agent is given the information in order to follow up by phone. After the claim is paid, if the claimant has been determined to be at fault, an underwriting process is initiated, whereby the underwriter determines if coverage should be continued or if a surcharge should be applied. Note that in these mission-critical workflow applications, the process is often made up of a series of interconnected subprocesses.

6.6 WORKFLOW APPLICATIONS AS A CONTINUUM

The ad hoc/collaborative/administrative/production categories should not be considered different countries with impenetrable boundaries. Workflow applications are better viewed as a continuum of automated processes, not mutually exclusive arenas. Workflow solutions often start at the ad hoc level, are developed by business users without a lot of preliminary planning, and are very flexible within predefined rules and structure. But these self-same ad hoc workflows quickly grow into more well-defined administrative or collaborative workflows. And once administrative workflows—such as purchase order requests and expense reporting—are used extensively and have the bugs worked out, they often identify areas that can and should be rigorously structured and automated, thus becoming production workflows. (See Fig. 6.1)

Determining whether a process is a one (or few)-time-only operation can be a good starting point. Is it ad hoc, such as a task force decision-making process for designing a new corporate logo? Is it a departmental administrative procedure, such as travel requests or expense reimbursement? Is it a full-time, heads-down, mission-critical production application, such as insurance claims? But understand that these applications need to be scalable up and down, and that often two or more processes might be combined. When evaluating workflow builder software, be sure to check how well the resulting applications scale.

Many of the new generation of workflow products on the market take their lead from object-oriented technology, separating basic components of the workflow definition into objects, which can then be reused and modified. (See Fig. 6.2) Newer workflow products separate the routing of the information—or the sequence of the tasks—from the information/data/documents being routed—the work packets. A third component is the applications for processing the information for each task. For example, in a workflow application, the information or documents being routed include an imaged application for credit, a form front-ending a customer database, and a credit rating sheet. The route the information takes goes from the application clerk to the supervisor, to the manager, to the approval clerk. The tools for processing the information are an image management system, a forms processor, a database management system, terminal emulation software for accessing credit ratings, and a word processor for sending out the approval or denial letter.

Keeping these components separate makes them interchangeable. For example, you can easily swap in a new routing using the same information packets and processing tools. Or you could change the productivity tools without affecting the information or the route.

The Workflow Continuum

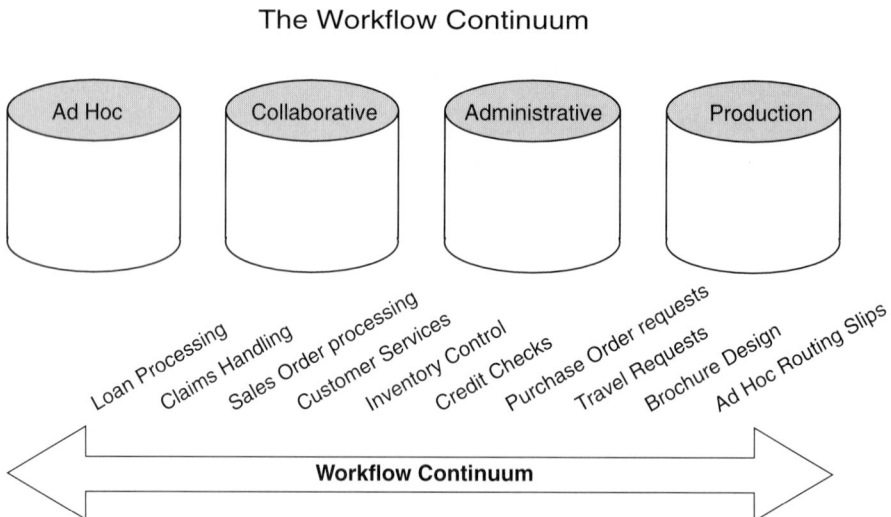

Fig. 6.1 Buckets are convenient places to put application types, but a continuum is a better metaphor for viewing workflow categories.

Adopting an object approach to designing workflows also offers advantages when it comes to building new workflow applications. In some workflow systems (and the number is increasing daily), once you define an activity, rules, or routing sequence, it can be named, saved, and reused.

6.7 A BASIC TAXONOMY OF WORKFLOW APPLICATIONS

A workflow application is made up of different elements. (See Fig. 6.2) These elements are:

Activities
An automated workflow application is made up of the different activities (a.k.a. tasks or steps) that must be completed to achieve a business goal.

People
These activities are performed in a specific order by specific people—or automated agents taking the roles of people—based on business conditions or rules.

Tools
The actual work—processing of the information within each activity, such as performing a credit check or writing a letter—is not really handled by the workflow application. Usually, these tasks are performed in personal productivity applications and line-of-business applications (such as an accounting system).

Data
The data are the documents, files, images, database records, and others used as information to complete the work. The tools must access multiple shared data sources.

A Taxonomy of Workflow

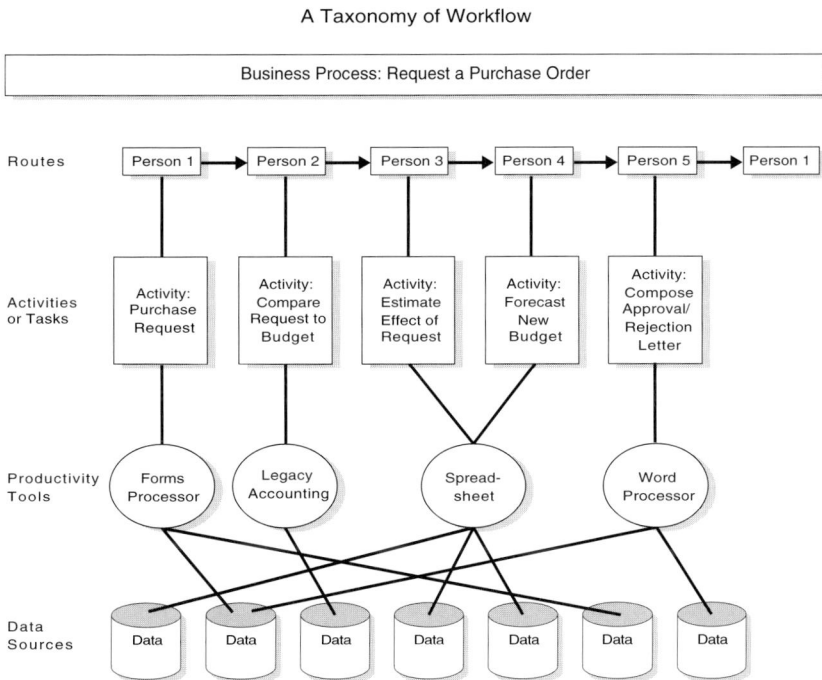

Fig. 6.2 This is a simple workflow, where a single person performs a single activity and then forwards the work along its preassigned route. Notice, however, that, even in this simple process, the same productivity tool is used for two separate tasks performed by different people. Note also that a variety of data sources are accessed at each activity.

6.8 PRODUCT CONSIDERATIONS

6.8.1 Support for Multiple Clients

Currently, most workflow is being developed for Windows clients; servers vary from PC LANs to Unix, OS/2, or NT environments. Several workflow solutions are built on SQL database underpinnings. A major factor in the success of workflow applications is the ability for all members of the workgroup to be able to participate in the solution. Vendors cannot expect the Macintoshes and Unix workstations already installed in an organization to go away. It is not vital that workflow development tools or the execution engine be multiplatform, but it is important that the deployment environment span the platforms you use in your organization.

The need to support multiple server platforms and underlying databases become increasingly important when the scope of the workflow application spans organizations. And, in this era of mergers and acquisitions, the systems used in your organization can increase significantly as the result of a business deal.

6.8.2 Support for Remote Users

The ability to include the occasionally connected user—the traveler who works primarily on airplanes and in hotel rooms, the field representative who works out of his or her car, and the telecommuting user who works in a home or field office—is vital in ensuring successful workflow implementations. Automated processes depend on activities being handled in sequence and in a timely fashion. If a process cannot move from one step to another because the next person in line is on the road, the process is brought to its knees.

Yet, the ability to access work remotely is only the tip of the iceberg. You also have to ensure that security and status-tracking are in effect, to consider whether other people need access to the information while it is "checked out" to the remote user, and many other related matters.

Obviously, the new generation of Internet clients that will come out in 1997 and 1998 will help support nomadic users who are part of strategic business processes within single or multiple organizations.

6.8.3 Leveraging Existing Systems

In general, you should not have to put in a completely new technical infrastructure in order to implement workflow. Products are available that run on virtually every server platform, from Windows to OS/2, to Unix, to NT, to NextStep. And the same goes for client platforms, with the newest emerging client for workflow being the World Wide Web and standard Web browsers.

6.8.4 Support for de facto Standards

Be sure that the workflow system you purchase takes advantage of de facto industry standards, such as OLE, MAPI, SQL, and ODBC. It is important that all your existing applications and data be able to be accessed by the work-flow tools. You should not have to keep entering and exiting your workflow environment to find documents or data. The workflow engine should manage the process while you work in your standard line-of-business and personal pro-ductivity tools.

6.8.5 Using the Database of Choice

Most workflow systems use a relational database as the repository for pro-cess-related data. Check to see if the system you are interested in can leverage your installed RDBMS, such as Oracle or Sybase. If it cannot, can it integrate with your corporate databases for accessing data? And how much database maintenance and administration must be done on the new database? If you are, for example, an Informix shop, you do not want to train a database administrator on Sybase.

6.8.6 Leveraging Directory Services

Because workflow is often based on sending sensitive information to people using underlying messaging transports or over the network, directory services becomes a major issue in workflow administration. You need to maintain a data-base of users that goes beyond just a role table. You have to maintain access information and location information, as well as other types. Many workflow sys-tems maintain their own directories, independently from either the messaging infrastructure, the underlying database, or the network operating system. This results in duplication of effort when changes must be made. If, for example, a new person is brought on board, he or she must be added to multiple directories. Some workflow systems leverage the directory of the messaging system or data-base. This allows changes made in one directory to be reflected in the other.

6.8.7 Cost of Ownership

When considering a workflow solution, there are a lot of hidden costs—as there are in all areas of technology. The cost of the software is often just the beginning. Often, individual workstations must be upgraded in order to sup-port reasonable performance of the workflow applications. Besides factoring in the cost of consulting—BPR consulting, integration consulting, and implemen-tation consulting—there is the cost of training and administration. Finally, understand that one of the promises of workflow automation is that processes can be modified to reflect all the changes in how you do business that keep pop-ping up. Someone has to make these modifications. This could be outsourced, sent to MIS, or be done by a business user, but updating processes involve time and cost. The benefits to keeping processes current, however, should offset these expenses.

Ask the workflow vendors that you are considering to supply estimates on these costs and ask for user references so that you can verify these estimates.

6.9 APPROACH TO WORKFLOW

Another consideration when choosing a workflow product is the technology approach the product takes to automating processes.

Some products could be considered souped-up e-mail systems, where message routing is the primary consideration.

Other products approach workflow from the imaging point of view, and are optimized for building applications that process scanned-in images.

There are products that focus on the routing and management of electronically generated documents, typically used in editorial and publishing types of applications.

Forms processing is typically the preferred approach to administrative types of processes.

A database approach is used when transactions are the key to the process.

Understand that the same process can be automated using a variety of approaches. The key is to find a product that approaches the workflow application in a way that makes sense to you and your organization. You should not have to force fit your processes into, say, an imaging approach simply because a popular vendor offers an imaging workflow product.

6.9.1 Determining the Design Center

Popular sentiment—and logic—seems to be dictating that workflow application development be done by the person most familiar with the process—typically, a line-of-business manager. After all, this is the person who understands the ins and outs of the process and who knows the rules and the exceptions. However, the typical business user cannot, alone, make all the technical connections to underlying data, leveraging directory services, ensuring data integrity and security, etc. For this reason, many workflow builders on the market tend to separate what is specified by the business user from what is developed by the professional programmer. Products such as IBM's FlowMark, XSoft's InConcert, and FileNet's Visual WorkFlo provide graphical environments for specifying the basic flow of data, defining straightforward (usually boolean if/then/else) rules, and assigning people to the roles that are used to execute the tasks. Professional developers are responsible for things like integrating with data sources and scripting the actual programs that will run during the steps of the process.

The trend, however, is to try to put as much development capability in the hands of the non-technologist. Builders, such as ViewStar, Staffware, and ActionWorkflow, can generate reasonably sophisticated workflow applications developed entirely by point-and-click methods where no scripting or technical expertise is required.

Some products, however, such as the WorkPoint system, put workflow development into the hands of MIS, believing that, to build truly complex, flexible, and scalable systems, you should define all the rules, routes, and roles for a workflow in code.

As you investigate workflow products, you need to consider your organization and determine where the design center for process applications should be— with the user, with MIS, or with some combination of the two.

6.9.2 Imaging Systems Too Limited in Scope

Increasingly, an imaging-specific focus is becoming inappropriate for the types of business applications being automated with workflow tools. Thus, image processing vendors who offer workflow as part of the package are not making the short lists of many potential customers. Although most of these vendors are financially sound, their technology is limited in scope and, I believe, will not be viable as a discrete industry (except within a very small niche market) within the next two to three years.

6.9.3 Products from StartUps Are Risky

Companies are reluctant to invest a great deal of money and time in products from vendors who might disappear within a few years. They have been burned in the past. And many workflow companies are so new that they have few customers to point at.

6.9.4 Systems Vendors Need to Refocus both Technology and Sales

In the past few years, a number of formerly successful, but lagging, systems vendors are looking to workflow as the way to regain a market that has abandoned them. Companies such as IBM and Wang are focusing on groupware in general and workflow in particular to put themselves back on the map. This can be a difficult adjustment for sales and support forces that have traditionally sold hardware and complete enterprise systems.

6.9.5 Vendor Viability

It is important to consider the viability of the vendor who is selling a workflow solution to you. We are in a very fickle industry, where technical excellence does not guarantee success. So you do need to determine if your workflow vendor will still be around a year from now. Thus, it is important to investigate the partnerships the vendor has made with other technology suppliers. Look at the reseller relationships with systems integrators and value-added resellers. Determine what other customers the vendor has and how satisfied these customers are.

New workflow products are coming to market almost every day. And many are from start-ups. They don't have a track record to point to. Does this mean you should strike them off your short list of vendors? Not necessarily. There are two advantages to being one of the first customers for a new company:

6.9.6 Technical Excellence

New products don't carry old baggage and can take advantage of the latest and greatest enabling technologies on the market. Existing product lines have to consider backwards compatibility, which often means that enhancements are slow in coming.

6.9.7 Influence

As one of the first to use a new product, your input has the rapt attention of the vendor. Your input, requests, and demands are paramount because this vendor needs you to be a reference for future accounts.

Thus, there is a trade-off here. New companies are a risk, but the solutions may be a better fit for your needs. You have to make that determination. One safeguard is to ensure that even the newest product is built on de facto standards and that all data can be migrated to other systems down the road.

6.10 DESIGNING BUSINESS PROCESSES: BPR

Business process reengineering (BPR) is the exercise of planning and analyzing processes prior to, or independent of, automating them as workflow applications.

6.10.1 Process Design Sessions

Obviously, there is a close relationship between designing your processes and automating them (see Fig. 6.3). Enterprise-wide, strategic workflow applications are often preceded by business process design sessions where an organization, often in conjunction with an outside consultancy, evaluates its current processes and redesigns them for efficiency and effectiveness. The redesigned applications are then automated. (I tend to prefer the term business process design rather than business process reengineering, because the latter implies that the process was, at one time, engineered). Frequently, little thought was given to the engineering of a process; processes typically evolve based on habits and spur-of-the-moment decisions. The industry, however, has standardized on the BPR term.

Stages of Process Animation

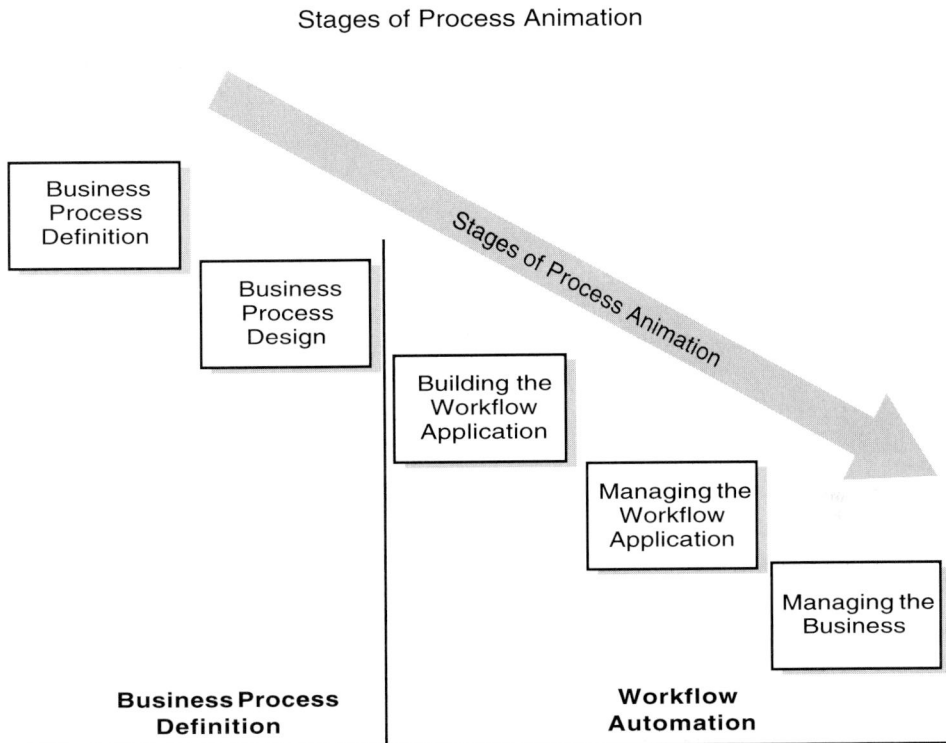

Fig. 6.3 The Workflow Management Coalition separates workflow into two sections: business process definition and workflow automation. I further segment the sections.

There are disadvantages to undertaking process design sessions. They are time-consuming and, if you use a consultant to facilitate the redesign effort, they are expensive. BPR does not offer any "instant gratification." Rather, it is an investment where the payoff doesn't come until the process is implemented.

6.10.2 Automate Existing Business Processes.

It is not always necessary, however, to go through a complete process-reengineering session in order to define a workflow application. Workflow applications can mirror existing non-automated processes—what is often called "paving the cow paths." This is not necessarily a bad thing to do. Often, by quickly prototyping and piloting an automated procedure, you can evaluate its effectiveness and efficiency sooner and more easily than if you try to figure it out beforehand.

Obviously, the scope and strategic nature of the business process to be automated plays a large part in determining the amount of up-front business process design that should be undertaken. But there are general guidelines to follow if you plan to automate without "reengineering."

1. Pick a process that is clearly defined already. Many processes have clear steps and the rules that govern the behavior are well understood.

2. Do not pick a process that is broken. Automating a bad process simply means that you are doing it wrong faster! If a process isn't working, do not assume that adding technology will fix it. Technology should be used to enable an effective process.

It is also important to understand the role of human nature and business reality in this situation. Although you may assume that, by automating a working process that could use improvement, you will make the incremental adjustments to move the process forward, this rarely happens. Inertia sets in. It is human nature to leave alone something that is working rather than improve it so that it works better. So many things are broken that those things that are "less than perfect" are deemed "good enough." Remember, improving processes takes time and attention. In the fast-paced business climate we all work in, there never is enough time. Our attention is always divided among our dozens of number one priorities. Working processes quickly jump down to lower priority.

6.11 STAGES OF PROCESS AUTOMATION: BUSINESS PROCESS DEFINITION

6.11.1 Process Definition Methodology

One of the challenges of defining the process is ensuring consistency of the definition. One of the most effective ways to do this is by using a Business Process Reengineering (BPR) methodology. Such a methodology provides the structure and guidelines to help you identify all the elements of the process as well as gives you models and methods to ensure that you are providing the necessary depth of detail consistently for all components. Typically, the person or team of people charged with defining a new (or analyzing an existing) business process understands certain aspects of the process very well but has sketchy information on others. For example, these people know exactly how loan applications are completed and entered into the system. They understand how the database is organized. But they may not know what criteria the loan officer uses to make a decision. As a result, more details are captured about the application processing than the decision-making process. Without some sort of methodology, you may find that certain tasks are defined in granular detail while others are painted with a very broad brush. When it comes time to develop the workflow application, these ill-defined tasks are impossible to build. Using a methodology requires time, effort, and, often, expense, but it can significantly facilitate the workflow building and implementation process.

6.11.2 Separating Process Design from Workflow Automation

The Workflow Management Coalition is an international organization of vendors, users, and consultants chartered with developing software specifications that will allow different workflow products to interoperate. One of the first tasks undertaken by the coalition was to come up with a common definition of workflow and business process design.

The coalition has agreed that a process is specified in a process definition, which is composed of either a manual process definition or a workflow process definition. Thus, workflow is the automation of a business process. (See Fig. 6.4)

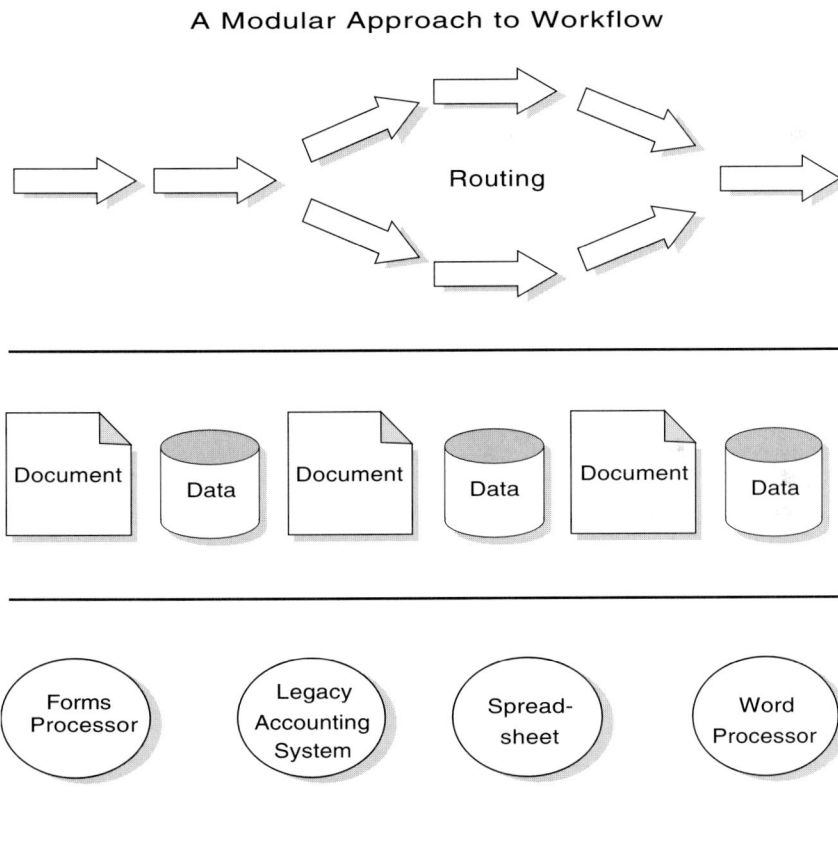

A Modular Approach to Workflow

Routing

Document Data Document Data Document Data

Forms Processor   Legacy Accounting System   Spread-sheet   Word Processor

Fig. 6.4 Many of the newer workflow products on the market take a modular approach: The routing sequence is separate from the documents and/or data that are being sent, and both are separate from the productivity tools that process the information. Keeping the three components separate makes changing the applications much easier.

6.11.3 Business Process Definition and Business Process Design

Building on this separation of process definition from workflow automation, I further segment the two categories.

☞ Process Definition; identifying the details of how the process works

☞ Process Design; graphically mapping the flow of the process

In many ways, defining the business process is the most difficult challenge you will face. In the definition process, you must determine how the process works (or should work), specifying the sequence of activities or tasks that must be completed, the responsibilities of the people who do the activities, and the conditions under which the sequence of activities might change—the rules of the process.

Many options are available for taking advantage of a process definition methodology.

6.12 STAGES OF PROCESS AUTOMATION

6.12.1 Using an Automated Definition Methodology Tool

Workflow applications can also be defined by members of your organization. Ideally, the process definition is done by a group of stakeholders including the actual participants in the application, the management team, and the executive or high-level "champion" for the project. Some commercial tools are available to help define the process, such as project planning tools and methodology tools. Often, these tools are also used by consultants, ranging from systems integrators to small vertical-industry VARs.

6.12.2 "Do It Yourself" Designing

Designing a business process can be done in a more unstructured, ad hoc fashion—a "low-tech" approach—using a whiteboard and a marker, and soliciting input from your team. Though "do it yourself" may appear to be the least expensive method of process reengineering, unless the redesign team is experienced, there is also the greatest chance of missing important steps and making incorrect assumptions, thus resulting in an inefficient or ineffective process. Also, your people are pulled away from other work during reengineering. However, there is extreme value to using any methodology, even when not supported by technology, and that is to ensure that you are capturing the same amount of detail for each step in a process—that you have asked and answered all the relevant questions. This usually leads to a more usable—and realistic—result.

It is important to note that process definition and analysis does not necessarily lead to workflow automation. Indeed, there are great benefits to be achieved by the act of analyzing and mapping out even your manual processes. One of the often unheralded advantages to analyzing processes is that it gives you the opportunity to surface the business rules and assumptions under which you have been conducting business. The act of capturing this information and examining it is extremely valuable. The decision to automate the process with workflow technology can actually be considered a separate decision from the choice to do a BPR exercise.

6.12.3 Buying BPR Services

It has been said that the only people making money on workflow are the consultants. And this may be true. BPR consulting is a lucrative business that is offered by all the big six consulting firms as well as hundreds of midsize and small consultants, systems integrators, and industry-specific VARs. As just stated, BPR can be extremely valuable. But it can also be expensive (good consultants don't come cheap), time-consuming (a major reengineering project can take months just for the process analysis), and, too often, frustrating. The frustrations can result from a number of reasons:

☞ By the time you have finished analyzing the process, you no longer do business that way—the rules have changed.

☞ Corporate sponsorship and/or funding disappears mid-project.

☞ Exquisite process plans are developed, but the organization is too overloaded running the current processes to even begin working on the new plans.

☞ Before you go into a BPR consulting relationship, you need to determine the scope of the project, the time frame, which includes both the consultant's time commitment as well as the amount of time that your internal process team can realistically devote to the project, and the commitment of dollars and support from upper management. Only when all are in place will a BPR exercise prove fruitful.

6.12.4 Business Process Design

Once the criteria and specifications for a business process have been identified, you actually map out or design the process by creating a graphical representation of the flow of activities and information as it is affected by business rules. This can be done on paper or online, using a flow-charting tool or one of the many workflow-mapping tools available. The result of this design stage is a map of the process—a process that can be manual or that can be automated, i.e., turned into a workflow definition. This process map is not only used as the blueprint for actually building an automated workflow application but also as a reference tool for planning for improvements and modifications. In addition, it is very useful to offer a picture of the entire process as specified for training and reference purposes.

Most, if not all, of the BPR methodology software tools include graphical mapping capabilities to visually capture the process design. Similarly, most workflow builders (see below) include a process mapping environment. Standard flow-charting tools are often used to lay out the flow of a workflow process.

6.13 THE RS AND PS OF WORKFLOW

The Rs and Ps of Workflow represent the primary features that the application must include. The three Rs of workflow are:

☞ Routes

☞ Rules

☞ Roles

6.13.1 Routes

Routing is probably the first area of the business process that was automated. In the imaging world, the first workflow products allowed vendors or resellers (and, later, customers) to define the order in which images were to flow. In today's world, you need to be able to specify the flow of any sort of object. These objects should be able to be routed sequentially (one after another) or in parallel routes with rendezvous points (an object can go off on any number of different sequential routes and then reconcile into a single route at a specified point) and should be able to be sent in a broadcast mode (the e-mail model, where everyone gets the object at once) or in any ad hoc order (as described by the user at the time of processing).

The ability to route tasks to remote or occasionally connected users is vital in workflow applications. In order to ensure the successful flow of information and decisions, every member of the team needs to be able to take part in the process. As more and more users operate primarily away from their offices, workflow tasks need to be handled offline and then be put back on the network to move to the next step.

Routing needs to take into account more than just the person (or process) to whom the work is routed. It must also include what objects—document, forms, data, applications—are to be routed. (See Fig. 6.5)

Workflow Routing

Serial Routing

Start → Activity 1 → Activity 2 → Activity 3 → Activity 4 → Activity 5 → Activity 6 → End

Parallel Routing

Start → Activity 1 → Activity 2 → (Activity 3 → Activity 5) and (Activity 4 → Activity 6) → Activity 7 → Activity 8 → End

Conditional Routing

Start → Activity 1 → Activity 2 → Yes: Activity 3A → Activity 4A → Activity 5A → Yes: Activity 6A → End; Activity 5A → No: Activity 5B; No: Activity 3B → Activity 4B

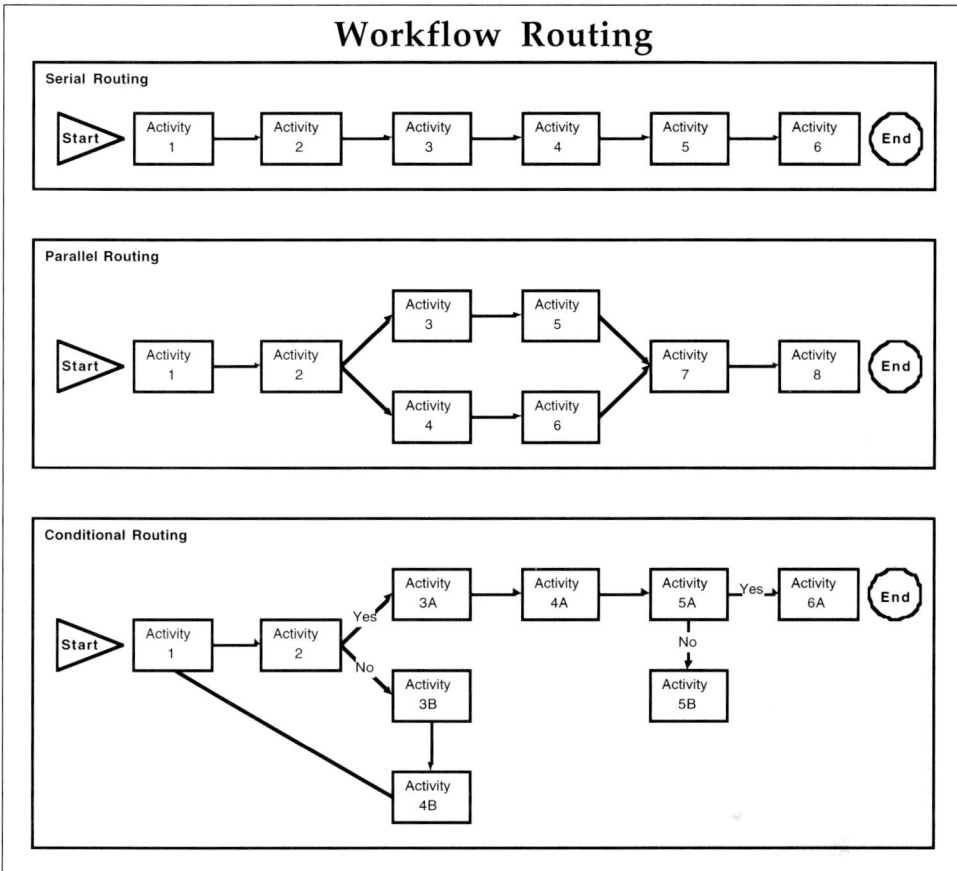

Fig. 6.5 Routing models for workflow processes.

6.13.2 Rules

A more advanced feature of workflow automation is in its defining of rules that determine what information is to be routed and to whom. This is sometimes called *conditional routing* or *exception-handling*. Most workflow builders have mechanisms for defining rules.

Defining the rules of workflow can be very difficult, and rules can be very complex and convoluted, with multiple options, variations, and exceptions. Trained programmers and application developers, who can be sure to think through the entire set of possibilities that can result from a single rule, are necessary for sophisticated, multipath, exception-laden processes. However, business users can think through the more obvious (and more commonly used) rules, such as "if an amount is greater than $5,000, send it to the supervisor; otherwise, send it to Purchasing."

The method of specifying rules varies from workflow builder to workflow builder. Some provide a simple point-and-click front-end for defining Boolean-based and other if/then/else conditions. Others require rudimentary scripting (e.g., if employee_number < 500 then route to human_resources). Some require programming in SQL, a 4GL, or a lower-level language.

6.13.3 Roles

This leads us to roles. In the example above, the request was not routed to Sue or to Max, but rather to a supervisor or to Purchasing. The ability to define roles independent of the specific people—or processes—that happen to fill that role is very important to ensure flexibility of a workflow application. For example, if the system did route the "amount greater than $5,000" to Sue and if Sue left the company, the application developer would have to re-specify the recipient under the new conditions. If the request is sent to the role, the administrator (not the developer) will simply add the new person's name to the role of supervisor. Now, agreed, it takes the same amount of work to add a name to a role as to change the name in a single workflow step. But consider what happens if Sue is involved in multiple steps in dozens of workflows. The change could be indicated once—in a role table, typically a table or database where a person is related to a role—and any workflow that needed to route something to supervisor (Sue) would now route the information to her replacement.

Roles are also vital when a number of different people have the authorization to do the same work, such as claims adjusters. It doesn't really matter which of these people handle the task as long as someone with that role does.

6.14 WORKFLOW ROUTING

The three Ps of workflow are:

☞ Processes

☞ Policies

☞ Practices

6.14.1 Processes

The processes (a.k.a. procedures) that we have established to run our businesses are as varied and as personal to our companies as the people who take part in them. Often, processes aren't "designed" but are identified after the fact, extracted from common usage. "We've always done it this way" is a common cry when people try to examine and evaluate processes. One of the biggest areas of pain and potential is redesigning existing processes, eliminating the redundancies, identifying the bottlenecks, and understanding why it is you do what you do. Business Process Design tools and methodologies are often employed to help define the process.

You should also keep in mind that processes often span *applications*. For example, a sales process includes an order entry application, a credit check application, and a billing application. Each of these applications can also be considered a process—each requires a sequence of activities to be performed based on business conditions. Sometimes, an application, such as a credit check, can be part of several processes (loan application, credit card approval, and similar processes).

6.14.2 Policies

Policies are the formal written statements of how certain processes are handled. For example, every company has a vacation policy and a benefits policy, and it should have a policy for how to handle each automated business process.

6.14.3 Practices

Practices go beyond the formal written policies of how certain processes are handled; they are the actual reasons for doing the work—the guidelines that explain how the decision was made to do things a certain way. Formal policies rarely capture this information. Most of it is anecdotal at best. "Oh, the reason that everything must go through Charlotte in quality control is that we want to deliver a working product. Before Charlotte came on board, Henry in packaging did the final check, and he missed so much!" And, even more, practices are the "breaking of the rules" of the process that make the process really work. For example, "Everything must go through Charlotte, unless it is product type X, in which case, we usually send it right to Henry because he understands this type of product much better than Charlotte." Or, "Everything goes through Charlotte unless we're running more than two days late, in which case, we skip Charlotte altogether and yell at Henry to make sure he does a check at his end."

Too often, when designing a workflow application, we consider only the routes, rules, and roles. We take into account the processes (of all types) and automate them based on their policies, and then we wonder why they don't really work. Perhaps it is because we have ignored the real-life practice of how the process has evolved. Only when we capture the practices will we truly automate how we run our businesses.

6.15 WHERE THE DATA FIT: ENACTING THE PROCESS

The final elements of a workflow system are the data being acted upon and routed in the application, and the tools with which the users perform the activities in the tasks of the workflow. Typically, the individual tasks are performed in personal productivity tools, such as spreadsheets and word processors. When building a workflow application, you must consider what data or documents need to be accessible for each activity and what tools need to be available to process that data.

Translating the business process map into a workflow application is called *enacting* the process. I see three different phases in workflow enactment:

6.15.1 Building the Application

There are many tools on the market that allow you to enact the process design based on the process definition map. These tools range from standard programming languages, such as C, to higher-level tools, such as Visual Basic, to dedicated workflow *builders*.

6.15.2 Managing the Application

Once the workflow application is built, you monitor the status of the process as each individual instance or case (such as John Mackie's loan application or Susan Sutton's insurance claim) goes on its way. The workflow management *engine* alerts the administrator of any bottlenecks or problems and provides workflow-specific metrics for evaluating the business process.

6.15.3 Managing the Business

One of the advantages to automating a process is that it gives you the opportunity to capture and analyze information about your business that you may never had available before. For example, by capturing the details of a loan application process, you can discover if a specific age group has been a good risk for auto loans. You can then target this demographic group for increased marketing of car loans.

6.16 WORKFLOW AUTOMATION TOOLS: DEVELOPMENT TOOLS AND RESULTING APPLICATIONS

Workflow tools fall into multiple categories, shown in Fig. 6.6 below

☞ The Business Process Definition Methodology (discussed earlier)

☞ The Process Design Mapping Tool (discussed earlier)

☞ The Workflow Builder

☞ The Workflow Management Engine

☞ The Workflow Deployment Environment

Types of Workflow Tools

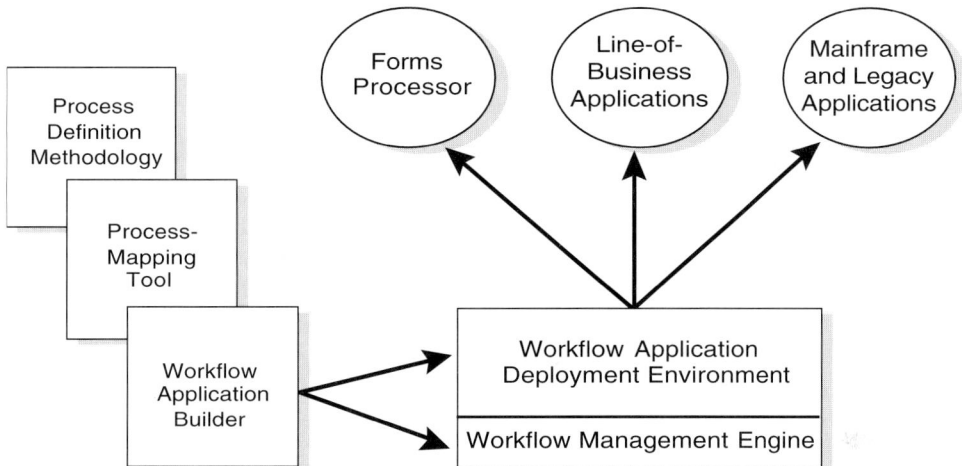

Fig. 6.6 Although the different functions of workflow tools are separated in this diagram, most commercial workflow products address more than one function. Indeed, some products handle the complete spectrum of workflow automation tools. Often, the tools that build and manage the workflow integrate with a separate deployment environment, such as Lotus Notes or a document management application. Workflow can be integrated directly into line-of-business or legacy applications, as well as with desktop productivity tools, by programming to the API's. Further, developers can use popular front-end development tools, such as Visual Basic and PowerBuilder, to build workflow-specific application front ends.

6.16.1 Builder

Builders, which are tools used to actually code the workflow applications, come in a variety of flavors, from complex scripting languages to very accessible graphical mapping and flow-charting tools. Correspondingly, they are aimed at a variety of developer skill-levels, from professional programmers to average business users. Builders often include a graphical process-mapping component.

6.16.2 Management Engine

The engine manages the actual running of the process. Every workflow application must have an underlying engine that ensures that the data are being flowed to the right person (or process) in the right order, depending on business conditions. The engine also tracks where each instance is in the process. Workflow engines are rarely available separate from the builder environment.

6.16.3 Deployment Environment

The deployment environment is where users access their workflow assignments and often where administrators track the status of instances of workflow applications. Most workflow products offer their own task list interface, but, more and more, workflow vendors are allowing customers to decide how and where users can access their workflow assignments. Integration is commonly requested with the users' standard e-mail inboxes or their to-do lists in Personal Information Managers or group calendaring systems.

An excellent example of a workflow deployment environment that is separate from a workflow builder or engine is Lotus Notes. Many workflow products are available that use Notes as the user environment, providing the builder and the engine separately.

Some workflow implementations don't use a single deployment environment but instead track the work as it flows among desktop applications. Basically, they workflow-enable your word processor, spreadsheet, e-mail, and other applications. Increasingly, workflow products support building alternate front-end screens and applications using such tools as Visual Basic or Power-Builder.

6.17 WORKFLOW INTEROPERABILITY STANDARDS

Most workflow tools interoperate only at the most basic level today. However, the WorkFlow Management Coalition (WFMC), a standards body made up of software vendors, user organizations, as well as consultants, has just released three interoperability interface standards:

Interface 1, with its initial working draft specified in February 1996, specifies standards for analyzing, modeling, and describing business process workflows, thus allowing conforming BPR software tools to integrate with compliant workflow engines.

Interface 2, which was announced in 1995, specifies how any client (desktop) application written to the interface can interact transparently with any workflow engine that supports the standard.

Interface 4, announced in February of 1996, specifies how two or more workflow engines can exchange and process work. The first implementation of Interface 4 is Microsoft's MAPI Workflow Framework. The MAPI Workflow Framework is a set of guidelines for creating workflow-specific MAPI properties, such as Route_Type, Status_Type, Next_Recipient, Workflow_Script, and Current_Role_Guide. The Framework is a combination of highly structured property definitions and some pretty loose definitions. Workflow vendors can write to the MAPI Workflow Framework guidelines and be assured that any MAPI-compliant front end application can interoperate with the workflow engine. This means that workflow users can get work assignments or check status from within their MAPI applications. Further, work packages can be sent from one location to another via MAPI messaging.

These standards, especially Interface 4, promise that customers will be able to mix and match workflow systems as needed. This will become increasingly important as inter-enterprise workflow applications become more common.

6.18 WHERE IS WORKFLOW BEING IMPLEMENTED?

Today, workflow is being implemented in five primary types of applications:

6.18.1 Image Processing

Workflow gained visibility as part of production imaging applications, where images were scanned, collected into folders, and routed in a specific order for approval or comments. FileNet, a leading imaging vendor, claims to have coined the term "Workflow" in its first implementation of this functionality, called "WorkFlo." The original workflow components of the image processors were difficult to use, requiring coding at the programmer level and allowing little, if any, flexibility in routing. The newer generation of tools are much more flexible, supporting graphical development, object-oriented designs, and user-level definition of business rules. Within the next few years, discrete imaging-based workflow systems will probably go away as image processing, itself, is assimilated into more standard computing environments. The costs of image-based hardware, viewing, and storage devices are going down rapidly. Also, few applications deal exclusively with bitmapped images. One of the promises of workflow is to manage applications that span technology areas. In the new generation of image-oriented workflow tools, other media types, such as electronic documents, are also managed. Soon, the distinction between image processing and document processing will go away.

6.18.2 Document Management

Within the last year, we've seen integration of workflow into standard document management products that organize and manage electronic files in an organization. These document management systems range from simple systems, which manage word processing files (using workflow for routing documents through the organization), to high-end systems managing engineering specifications, and the like (using workflow to ensure that the documents go through the proper approval and revision cycles).

6.18.3 Forms Processing

A forms environment is comfortable and familiar to most users. Thus, it is an excellent front-end deployment vehicle for routing information in a workflow application based on the value in form fields. In the past two years, the most popular forms designer vendors have added workflow routing to their traditional form products, which have already been mail-enabled to the most popular LAN-based mail products. Thus, users can specify conditional routing of these forms via your company's e-mail system. In addition, many workflow builder products provide forms builders or integrate with third-party forms builders.

6.18.4 Mail Rules and Filtering

In addition to simply using e-mail to route forms or other information, most mail systems today provide serial routing as well as event-based rules. These rules can range from the filtering of incoming mail to launching external applications and macros, thus creating full workflow applications based on the mail rules.

6.18.5 Transaction-Based Applications

Transaction workflow stores the information, rules, role tables, and other elements, on server-based relational databases, executing the workflow on GUI clients—typically, MS Windows. These applications typically include a large data-entry component, such as sales order processing. Often, transaction systems are integrated with imaging capabilities.

6.19 ORGANIZATIONAL AND BUSINESS FACTORS OF WORKFLOW

6.19.1 Defining the Process Problem

In real life, processes are rarely explicitly "engineered," but rather evolve as we continue to use them and refine them. A byproduct of this is great loyalty to our familiar ways of doing things. The rewards of streamlining your way of doing business can be monumental. But be forewarned: The cultural shock that accompanies change can also bring a process to its knees. Here are several recommendations that will help you ease the pain associated with change:

6.19.1.1 Involve the Users

Your people are your greatest asset and, in some ways, your greatest obstacle. I cannot stress too much the importance of soliciting input from the actual users of the process. These are the people who truly understand what needs to be done in order to successfully achieve the business goal. These are the people who can identify the practices and help determine what works and what doesn't. An added benefit of involving users while designing the workflow is that you build in user support and ownership of the application from the start. This can go a long way toward overcoming the resistance that always comes when new systems are implemented.

6.19.1.2 Human Factors Are Vital

Workflow is very visible to the individual workers in an organization. These are applications that affect the way they do their jobs. While you are trying to improve productivity and quality of work life by implementing workflow applications, you are also imposing new models and methods on people who are much more comfortable with the way things have always been done. Thus, in order to improve the chances of a successful implementation, you must spend time and money on preparing your people for the workflow solutions.

Set expectations. At those sites where the solution is introduced without specific expectations being set, there is a greater likelihood that users will initially reject the new solution. However, if realistic expectations have been set, workflow implementations have a better chance of succeeding.

Expectations must be set in two areas: (1) how the workflow applications will be used or what problems they are being implemented to solve, and (2) how productivity will be affected during the initial stages of roll-out.

☞ **Reasons for Use:** One factor that explains why group solutions in general, such as Lotus Notes, are taking so long to catch on in many organizations is that the people were given the tool without any good reason to use it. They were encouraged to "play with it . . . figure out what you can use this for." But people don't have time to play. It is important that specific applications with specific purposes—and perceived value—be introduced even at the pilot stage. Otherwise, no expectations at all are set, and people simply will not use the new tools.

☞ **Potential Benefits:** Once you have set expectations about how the solution works and what it is intended to do, you need to set realistic expectations about the potential benefits. Invariably, the first few weeks of any new implementation will lower productivity as people figure out how to change their work habits to take advantage of the new solutions. People resist change; it will take a while before they get used to the new way of doing things. It is in this period that you get the greatest number of complaints. If people expect an instant panacea, they will jump ship as soon as the pain of change sets in. If expectations have been set that there will be problems initially, but that, over the course of a few weeks, it will get easier, and if the potential benefits are clearly explained, people may still complain, but they are more likely to stay on track to get over the hurdles.

☞ **Education and Training:** Training on workflow is not optional! Unlike personal productivity tools, where each user approaches the software with his or her own set of understanding, willingness to learn, and ways of doing things, these are group solutions and rely heavily on group members knowing exactly how the application works and what is expected of them. If one person doesn't play by the rules, the application can fail.

An important way of preparing users is by providing training specific to the workflow implementation that is being piloted. Time and time again, I have seen companies offer generic courses on the base technology that makes up the workflow strategy. But users don't take any ownership of generic applications. With specific courses designed to teach how their organization is going to manage and route their documents for their application requirements, users take a greater interest and have more to relate to.

One caveat, though. When a specific solution is being deployed in an environment such as Lotus Notes, some organizations have found it much easier to train first on the Notes platform and its behavior and then introduce the business-specific workflow application. Otherwise, users tended to blame the idiosyncrasies of the Notes environment on the customized application. One user organization found that, if the staff spent about three hours training on Notes, a new Notes workflow could be taught in under a half-hour. However, even in the case of generic environment training, the success came by following it up with organization-specific training.

Just as important as specific training, however, is general education about the whats and whys of the process. You need to foster an environment where learning is encouraged and rewarded. In a true learning environment, the participants in the process will feel free to suggest modifications to the process, often resulting in significant improvements that can be noticed only by those who are part of the workflow.

☞ **The Pilot Project:** Because of the many human and organizational implications of workflow applications, it is important that you start small, identifying potential usage problems as well as technical glitches. Try to select a representative group as your pilot so that you can surface the issues most likely to affect the organization at large. Solicit feedback and encourage ideas from all members of the pilot team about how to most effectively use the software. Avoid rolling out to others prematurely. Often, others will start to envy the pilot group and will demand that they, too, get to use the new workflow immediately. Problems can arise because the pilot group has been specifically prepared for the introduction of the new solution, whereas the other users are reacting only to what they perceive to be preferential treatment or imagined benefits for the pilot team. Roll out on a predetermined schedule, which takes into account setting expectations and training.

On the other hand, don't view the results of the initial pilot as the final solution. As the use of the applications gets past the bounds of the pilot team, the need for additional functionality and new ways of working with the software will occur to other users as they become more proficient. Keep the users focused on identifying those opportunities and communicating them back to the development team for consideration.

☞ **Building Buy-in at All Levels:** In order for strategic workflow applications to succeed, you need buy-in at the top; you need a high-level champion. This champion will assure the funding and support to get the project from the planning stage to roll-out. Further, buy-in at the executive level will show the participants in the workflow solution that the company is serious about the application. This type of high-level champion may not be required for smaller-scale, less strategic departmental solutions, where the support of the manager is sufficient to see the project through.

Buy-in at the management level is equally important. The manager is the person who will actually be monitoring the workflow and making sure it is being used effectively. If managers resent the intrusion of software to do what they believe they have been doing all along, progress will be difficult.

Finally, you absolutely must have buy-in at the user level. This buy-in will probably not be universal from the beginning. Initially, users will take part in the process simply because the high-level champion has made it clear that they are expected to. But, once the project is underway, user buy-in can be solicited. This is accomplished by actively involving the users of the workflow when defining the process to be automated, providing input into the piloting process, and encouraging and rewarding constructive feedback on the actual implementation of the workflow application. In fact, soliciting user input during the workflow definition stage is vital. The users are the ones who truly understand the practices being implemented in the processes to be automated. Not only does involving users during planning help speed the buy-in process, but it also ensures a more detailed and realistic definition of the workflow application.

☞ **Rewarding Usage:** Not only must feedback be rewarded, but so must usage of the workflow application. Users must perceive an added value to using the new application. Invariably, there is extra effort involved in using a group tool—at least initially. Users must get something out of making that extra effort. A reward can be as simple as praise from the boss for participating. But the best reward is one that the application itself gives. When you design workflow applications, it is important to consider what added benefit the application gives the users. If there is no benefit to the users, only one to the "organization," it will be more difficult to enforce usage of the application.

☞ **Providing Support—The Guru Factor:** It is vital that every workgroup have someone who is responsible for supporting the users of workflow applications. Your company must plan for this from the beginning. If a "workflow guru" is not designated and trained, then whoever happens to learn the application quickest or to understand it best will be constantly interrupted in his or her own work to help others with theirs. Though the de facto expert may be very happy to help out, his or her own productivity will plummet as he or she spends time training others on the workflow. By planning for this type of mentorship, the time this guru spends with others becomes part of the job description rather than time pulled away from the main job. Be aware that supporting workflow, like supporting a network, is an interrupt-driven job. While it may not be a full-time position, it is an "anytime" responsibility.

☞ **Addressing Cultural Changes:** Sometimes, implementing workflow applications results in a change in corporate culture. After all, what you are doing is imposing rules and structure on processes that may have been very free-form in the past. For example, when *TV Guide* implemented a structured editorial and publishing process to automate the layout and publishing of 119 editions of the weekly magazine, many of the participants in the process felt that they had lost some freedom. In the past, those staff members dealing with advertisers could "fudge" a little on ad size or deadlines to please a customer. With the new system in place, there was no fudge factor.

When planning processes, you must look at this trade-off. In some cases, you want to enforce stringent structure to optimize performance improvements. However, there are many cases where the strict adherence to policy should give way in the face of practice. If, for example, major advertisers got angry at *TV Guide* and pulled their ads because of the rigidity of the new rules, the process would have failed. These determinations must be made in partnership among the people who do the work, the people who define the application, and the people who manage the business.

6.20 BARRIERS TO IMPLEMENTING WORKFLOW: CUSTOMERS AREN'T BUYING WORKFLOW

Despite the recognized imperative for automating business processes and the advances in workflow technology that have been coming out left and right, sales of workflow systems have been disappointing. It seems that the only people making money on workflow right now are the major reengineering consultancies, which use the tools as part of their stable of system development solutions.

I believe that there are several reasons why workflow has not taken off in a major way. They are:

☞ Workflow is intimidating.

☞ Workflow solutions might not work.

☞ Workflow vendors are not mainstream or financially viable.

☞ The workflow market is new in the industry.

6.20.1 Customers Find Workflow Intimidating

Even though workflow can be approached from the bottom—small, tactical, departmental automation of standard procedures—as well as the top—enterprise-wide strategic reengineering of processes—it is the latter view that most customers envision when thinking about implementing workflow in their organizations. This can be very intimidating from both a cost and a time commitment standpoint. Customers working with the major consultancies often spend so much time in the planning stages that, once the time comes to implement, the vendor landscape has changed significantly from when the project began, and new plans need to be made.

6.20.2 Workflow Might Not Work

When customers attempt to develop workflow applications, they encounter a lot of barriers.

6.20.3 Workflow Vendors Are Not Mainstream

In general, there are three categories of workflow vendors:

☞ Vendors of imaging systems known only in their niche market

☞ Small startups without a proven track record

☞ Formerly powerful systems vendors trying to "reinvent" themselves and return to profitability

6.20.4 Technology and Design

Technology: Too often, new systems, especially group or enterprise systems that depend on networked communication, actually bring the network to its knees. Sudden increased traffic, incompatible commands, unexpected glitches—all these happen when new systems are put into place. Heck, they happen when you load a new word processor!

Design: Work processes change—sometimes overnight. Workflow applications, especially those with long planning cycles, are often so complex and so difficult to modify that they are out of date before they have a chance to work. Another classic workflow design problem is that of efficiently automating an inefficient process. Even long and painful business design sessions sometimes yield poorly designed processes.

If a workgroup isn't properly prepared or motivated to use a new workflow application, the application won't succeed. Too many good applications have failed because they were basically sabotaged by users who liked the way things were done before automation.

6.21 EVALUATING WORKFLOW PRODUCTS: THE BUYER'S GUIDE

6.21.1 Categories of Workflow Tools

Workflow technology comes in a variety of tools, addressing different aspects of analyzing and automating business processes. In general, these tool categories include:

☞ **The Business Process Reengineering or Definition Methodology:** A relatively new category of software tools has emerged over that past two years that provide automated BPR methodologies, available with and without consultants attached. These tools provide the consistent framework for process analysis in graphical environments for mapping out all the components of a business process. These tools range in price from about $500 to over $30,000 and provide a variety of capabilities, including features such as generating development code for workflow systems and providing relevant business metrics and measurements on costing and resource usage. Figure 6.7 lists a number of vendors and products offering BPR software. (This table is separate from the listing of other workflow tools because BPR is, as mentioned, often a separate endeavor that does not necessarily result in building automated workflow applications.)

Company	Product	Price	Contact Info.	Platforms
Action Technologies	Workflow Analyst	$495	1-800-workflow www.actiontech.com	Windows
Business Transformation Design	Business Transformation Management	Part of Consulting	Albert Linder 203-968-8670	Windows
Delphi Consulting Group	Workflow Factory	$595	Nathaniel Palmer 617-247-1511 www.delphigroup.com	Windows
HOLOSOFX	Workflow∂BPR	$2,500	Scott Dixon Smith 310-798-2425 E-mail: support@holosofx.com	Windows
IBM	The Business Process Modeling Tool	TBD	Karl Van Leuven 919-543-9587	OS/2 /Windows
IDS Prof. Sheer	ARIS	$8,000 base module $7,000 server	610-558-7600 www.ids-scheer.com	Client: Windows 3.1 or Win95 Server: NT or Novell
Interfacing Technologies	FirstSTEP	$4,000 to $6,250 including all software and simulation engine	514-856-9097 Email: firststep@interfacing.com www.interfacing.com	Windows, Mac, Unix
Knowledge Based Systems, Inc.	ProSim (process modeling and simulation) ProSim Workbench (process modeling, data modeling, and function modeling with simulation)	$5,995 $10,000	Pete Courtois 409-260-5274 products@kbsi.com www.kbsi.com	Windows 3.x & NT
Meta Software	Workflow Analyzer	$14,995 includes both Modeler and Simulator	Patty Kostusiak 617-576-6920 x35 patty@metasoft.com www.metasoftware.com	Windows, Mac, Sun

Fig. 6.7 Product and Contact Information for Major Workflow Vendors

☞ **The Process Design Mapping Tool:** Once the criteria and specifications for a business process have been identified, you actually map out or design the process by creating a graphical representation of the flow of activities and information as it is affected by business rules. This process map is not only used as the blueprint for actually building an automated workflow application, but also as a reference tool for planning for improvements and modifications. Most, if not all, of the BPR methodology software tools include graphical mapping capabilities to visually capture the process design. Similarly, most workflow builders (see below) include a process mapping environment. Finally, standard flow-charting tools are often used to lay out the flow of a workflow process.

☞ **The Workflow Deployment Environment:** The deployment environment is where users access their workflow assignments and often where administrators track the status of instances of workflow applications. Most workflow products offer their own task list interface, but, more and more, workflow vendors are allowing customers to decide how and where users can access their workflow assignments. Commonly requested is integration with the users' standard e-mail inboxes or their To-Do lists in Personal Information Managers or group calendaring systems. An excellent example of a workflow deployment environment that is separate from a workflow builder or engine is Lotus Notes. Many workflow products—such as Action Technologies WorkflowBuilder for Notes (Alameda, CA), flowMaker from Workflow Incorporated (Pennsylvania), and ViewStar (Alameda, CA)—are available that use Notes as the user environment, providing the builder and the engine separately. There are also products, such as GroupFlow from Pavone (Paderborn, Germany) that not only deploy in Lotus Notes, but which use the Notes engine to manage the workflow. In addition, some workflow implementations don't use a single deployment environment but instead track the work as it flows among desktop applications. Basically, they workflow-enable your word processor, spreadsheet, e-mail, etc. More and more products support building alternate front-ends with tools such as Visual Basic or PowerBuilder.

☞ **The Workflow Builder:** Builders, which are tools used to actually code the workflow applications, come in a variety of flavors, from complex scripting languages up to very accessible *graphical mapping and flow-charting tools*. Correspondingly, they are aimed at a variety of developer skill levels, from professional programmers to average business users. When you use both a BPR tool with graphical mapping and a workflow builder with graphical capabilities, the output of the BPR tool can often feed information into the builder, generating the basic process map used to generate the application.

☞ **The Workflow Management Engine:** Every workflow application must have an underlying engine that runs the process, ensuring that the data are being flowed to the right person in the right order at the right time depending on business conditions. The engine also tracks where each instance is in the process. Workflow engines are rarely available separate from the builder environment.

Typically, an offering from a single vendor includes a combination of mapper/builder/engine, along with some sort of deployment environment, ranging from simple worklist interfaces to customized front-end application builders.

6.22 WORKFLOW MARKET NEW IN THE INDUSTRY

For an industry that gets as much publicity as workflow, there are surprisingly few success stories. Much as Lotus Notes was on everyone's lips before it was in anyone's company, workflow has gathered mindshare rather than market share.

But workflow implementation is bound to increase as the products improve and as the industry becomes more educated about business process design and workflow automation. Many vendors are betting the farm on workflow. They will be willing to put a lot of information, time, and money on the line to get customers to buy into their vision.

And the vision is a valid one—intelligently automating your business processes will help you become more competitive by removing administrative burdens from your staff, by guaranteeing that work is done according to the policies and practices of your company, by ensuring that the information being processed can be found, and by providing timely management and feedback on what is being done.

But, in order to succeed, implementing workflow is going to have to become easier. The tools need to be more straightforward and the technology must be able to support workflow applications without breaking down.

Ultimately, however, it should not be "workflow" that customers buy. Customers are looking for solutions to very real business problems. In many cases, workflow technology can be part of the solution to a problem, but the check is being written for a solution—not for a hot new technology.

6.23 THE FUTURE OF WORKFLOW: LIKELY CHANGES IN CURRENT TRENDS

6.23.1 Alliances Among Vendors

Workflow vendors are joining forces with vendors of other types of software, such as forms processors and document managers. The vendors, or, more commonly, the VARs and system integrators, are using a combination of groupware tools to develop more vertical or application-specific workflow solutions.

6.23.2 Workflow Enablement

As currently defined, workflow is the umbrella application under which sit services such as document management, time management, and messaging. Customers use workflow application builders as they design new applications. And, while the workflow tools you use must interoperate with and leverage existing installed software, the workflow software is viewed as the development and execution environment.

An alternative view of workflow, which is equally valid, is modeled on Microsoft's view of groupware: Group-enable all software by providing group functionality in the operating system rather than in specialized products. I envision workflow-enabled software. Take, for example, a document management application. Your users are familiar with their document manager, using it to save and locate documents, to check in and out of documents, and for version control. Now, you want to start routing these documents based on certain rules and/or conditions. Rather than building a workflow application in a new paradigm, you want to be able to add these workflow capabilities to the existing document management application. This vision is already a reality in the leading client/server applications, including SAP and PeopleSoft products, both of which have announced their own workflow enablement.

6.23.3 Is Workflow Enablement Enough?

Because complete process reengineering is intimidating and expensive, customers might choose to go the workflow enablement route for all but the most strategic, mission-critical applications. This would significantly limit the types of applications that could be developed, but the ease of building those workflow-enabled document management, time management, document creation, spreadsheet, and project management applications might outweigh the more process oriented, but painful to develop, workflow umbrella applications. If the ISVs workflow-enable their applications intelligently and in a timely fashion, workflow builders could become extinct.

6.23.4 Mix-and-Match Workflow

Currently, each vendor offers what are basically proprietary workflow solutions—though they run on standard platforms and integrate with other productivity applications. You cannot combine applications written with different workflow products without writing customized computer routines (new programs) to get them to interoperate.

The work of the Workflow Management Coalition could change that by providing standard workflow APIs. This would be a definite boon for the workflow industry, not only providing interoperability among applications created with different products but also allowing customers to mix and match business process methodologies and mapping tools with different development tools and different execution environments.

6.23.5 Is Workflow Worth It?

So, I have just told you that workflow is expensive, time-consuming, and risky. But is it worth the effort? I firmly believe it is. We don't work in a vacuum performing discrete tasks. We do our jobs as part of a process with a much greater goal than just doing our little piece of the puzzle. We need to coordinate our efforts and manage the big picture. We need to gather information about how we do things and how successful we are at doing them. We need to free our people from the drudgery of finding files and passing papers and let them use their minds and talents to make creative decisions and achieve unexpected results. Workflow technology can help us do that.

Introduction to Chapter 7

Electronic Meeting Systems (EMS)

This chapter focuses on the technologies that support meetings. Each author examines the technology of the product being discussed as well as how those products have evolved from LANs to the Internet and intranets. Additionally, readers will find a number of case studies which provide insight into other's past mistakes and successes.

After general introduction to electronic meeting systems, we begin looking at specific technologies. The first technology doesn't even use a computer! Bill Flexner and Kimbal Wheatley of Option Technologies talk about how keypad technology supports group decision making and can be coupled with a computer to support collaboration in meetings.

The first traditional electronic meeting system technology is discussed by Julia Szerdey and Mike McCall who look at how meetings will move into a more distributed environment. Next, Jay Nunamaker and his team at the University of Arizona examine how several EMS products are migrating from LANs to the Web. They have included some case studies of their product usage over the last few years. In addition to focusing on the technology, they also examine the power shifts in organizations that these technologies catalyze.

The last section of this chapter is contributed by Jana Markowitz, who has a tremendous amount of experience using electronic meeting systems. She also shares several case studies, addressing many of the common questions about EMS, for example: How many people should be in an electronic meeting? How much time will it save? What are the advantages and disadvantages of using these technologies? Is it possible to do EMS from a desktop? and How do you do an EMS across time zones?

You should notice that the major point in the overview section (7A) is that although the technology is available, and increasingly more affordable, it is still not commonly used. Why? Human factors have limited the adoption of electronic meeting technology. I have never run into a Vice President of Meeting Quality in any organization: no one is charged with the responsibility of ensuring the effectiveness of meetings. Considering how much time we spend in meetings, how ineffective they can be, it would seem that finding someone to champion these technologies would be welcomed.

Electronic Meetings as Today's Presentations

David Coleman
Collaborative Strategies

It has been said that between one half and two thirds of every manager's time is spent in meetings. Unfortunately, these meetings tend to be grossly inefficient. A few of the major "effectiveness culprits" include irrelevant discussion, limited use of the management resources in the meeting, posturing because of public vote taking, and failure to follow through on action items. But these time wasters are only part of the story. Consider the cost, in time and hard money, of travel, hotels, and administrative support when people from different locations are included in a meeting. Real and substantial savings can be achieved from using new technologies to support meetings, making them more efficient and effective.

7A.1 WHAT IS AN ELECTRONIC MEETING?

An electronic meeting is just that; a way people meet, exchange information, and talk, either face-to-face or from disparate sites, using a computer or keypad for information access and transmittal. Electronic meetings fall along a continuum from electronic bulletin boards and Internet news groups to the face-to-face Electronic Meeting Systems (EMS) described in this article. The greater the level of interaction and data transferred, the greater the cost (see Fig. 7A.1).

Estimated
Cost

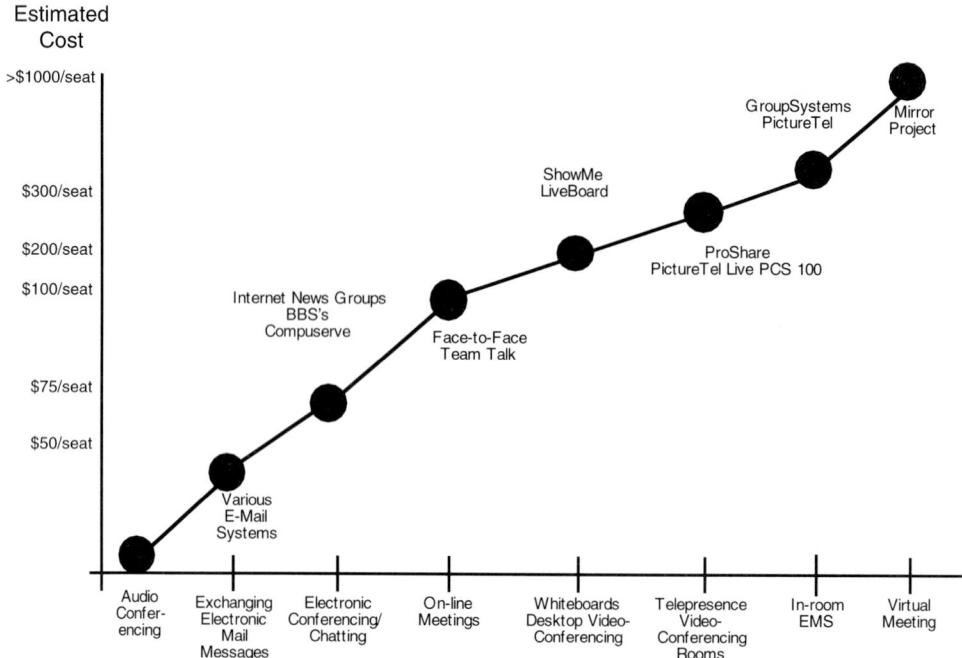

Fig. 7A.1 Amounts of Presence
            Continuum of Electronic Meetings

Bulletin Boards (BBS) allow people to leave messages and reply to messages, but the discussion is not in real time. Some on-line services like CompuServe, The Well, and America Online allow you to have meetings in chat or forum rooms, where there is interaction. Other groupware products offer more focused interaction such as CollabraShare, which is like a BBS but allows you to follow the thread of a conversation, and allows someone to moderate the discussion.

Once you move away from text-based interactions the costs go way up. Desktop videoconferencing software and hardware pricing has dropped dramatically from several thousand dollars per user to a bit over $1000/user. The price should drop even more over the next few years until it is in the $400-500 range. Desktop video conferencing allows you to see a picture of the other person on your screen as well as the document you will be working on together. This can work with one person or several people if your system supports multi-point conferencing.

There are also videoconferencing rooms (found in many corporations) where you can see and hear a group at another site. An electronic meeting system can be the most expensive because it allows a face-to-face meeting in real time (without incurring travel and other expenses) augmented by computers and a facilitator. Finally, as we look toward the future, we will have "virtual" meetings where the barriers of space and time disappear and there will be both audio and visual contact, but there may also be virtual "physical" contact and interaction.

Most electronic meetings are facilitated by a trained facilitator. Additionally, a "scribe" or technographer will record what is being said and/or "write" things on the computer so everyone can see the same information. Electronic meetings and regular meetings are motivated by the same issues, but electronic meetings have some big advantages:

☞ People can fully participate in the meeting even though they are geographically remote;

☞ People can vote anonymously, so more "truth" is available;

☞ Data can be entered and viewed by all participants simultaneously. This results in fewer misunderstandings and greater productivity; and

☞ All decisions and action items from the meeting are recorded electronically and can be distributed electronically.

Most electronic meetings take place in a special electronic meeting room where computers are networked and each client runs an EMS application. In addition to Ventana's GroupSystems, the best known EMS application, Team Focus from IBM, VisionQuest from Collaborative Technologies, Council from CoVision, and C.A. Facilitator from McCall-Szerdy and Associates offer a variety of functions at a broad range of price points.

7A.2 HOW AND WHEN ARE EMSS USED?

Anytime a group gathers and their mission can be put in the form of a question, there may be an opportunity to use meetingware to facilitate the gathering, and prioritize and analyze the information. Here are some successful applications of meetingware.

1. Strategic & Tactical Planning
2. Business Process Redesign
3. FOCUS groups with employees, clients, suppliers, experts
4. TQM—cause and effect/fishboning/affinity diagramming/Quality Improvement Teams
5. Joint Application Development (JAD)
6. Conflict Resolution/Impasse/Team Building
7. Selection Committee Awards—grants, recognition, performance
8. Training—Diversity, Change Management, et al.
9. Resource Allocation/Budgeting/Distribution of dollars, FTE, points
10. Process Flow and Sequencing
11. Needs Analysis/Job/Training/et al.
12. On-Line Document & Policy Edit/Review/Development
13. Questionnaires/Surveys/Suggestion Systems

14. Americans with Disabilities Compliance (Essential Functions/ Accommodations)
15. Marketing Research
16. Organizational Effectiveness & Development

7A.3 HOW ARE EMSS CLASSIFIED AS PART OF GROUPWARE?

Electronic meeting systems can be put into two different groupware categories: Group Decision Systems or Conferencing products. Products are assigned to either category based on their primary function. Below we have listed the categories, the technologies, and sample products.

7A.3.1 Group Decision Systems

Functionality includes audio and video conferencing, desktop conferencing, group decision systems, and shared screen products. These technologies can also be used for meetings as well as EMS products.

AVD Desktop Conferencing—InVision	C.A.Facilitator—McCall, Szerdy & Associates
TeamTalk—Trax Softworks	Council—CoVision
GroupSystems for UNIX—GlobalWare	CM/1—Corporate Memory Systems
VisThink—Vidya Technology	GroupSystems—Ventana

7A.3.2 Conferencing Products

Functionality includes a focus on sharing information through shared databases or the ability to interactively converse with another via the computer. Electronic meetings in this category are usually done by remote contributors, maybe a facilitator and the messages are synchronous (i.e., like e-mail not like talking on the phone, which is asynchronous).

7A.3.3 Shared Databases:

Notes—Lotus	Open Mind—DCA
Oracle Office—Oracle	OfficeVision—IBM
TeamOFFICE—ICL	

7A.3.4 Shared Screen

Face-to-Face—Crosswise	Teamworker Solution—Teamworker L.C
CollabraShare—Netscape	Virtual Notebook—The ForeFront Group
Team Expert Choice—Expert Choice	grapeVINE—Quest Technologies
Conference Plus—MESA	

7A.4 CASE STUDY: THE REAL BENEFITS OF ELECTRONIC MEETING SYSTEMS

Carl DePietro introduced meetingware into Marriott Corporation's international headquarters in 1991. The technology, which was used by thousands of employees from Marriott and other organizations, was installed in a meeting room called the Marriott Group Decision Center (MGDC). The MGDC was a traditional meeting room in every respect except that it was equipped with computer workstations on a LAN.

When appropriate, the meeting leader would instruct participants to use computers to "anonymously" contribute their ideas. Those contributions were then prioritized according to the order of importance, profitability, or any other standard selected. Among the benefits to Marriott, participants reported that using the computers to contribute anonymously to the meeting provided more truthful responses to issues, a higher quality and quantity of useful ideas, creative synergism, and immediate printed feedback for the participants and the leader. At the time the MGDC was opened, Marriott was an $8 billion service organization with 200,000 employees worldwide. Three thousand employees worked in the vicinity of the MGDC, Bethesda, Maryland.

7A.4.1 What Happened at MGDC?

The performance of the MGDC and its effectiveness were measured from the opening day. After nine months of operation, over 3,000 participants from Marriott and other companies had used the MGDC. Approximately 60 percent of the meetings were facilitated by a person trained in the use of the software. Using a standardized meeting template of exercises, 40 percent of the meetings were managed by the meeting owner without outside technical or facilitation assistance. These types of meetings continue to grow in popularity.

The MGDC was booked over 85 percent of the time and users generated over 30,000 ideas. Most (over 90 percent) of the ideas were judged by users to be valuable and useful. In user surveys, users estimated that, if it would have been possible to accomplish similar results using traditional meeting techniques, it would have been about 10 times longer. Annualized, an estimated 35,000 man-hours ($1,000,000) are saved using the MGDC.

7A.4.2 Lessons Learned

Mr. DiPietro has facilitated meetings for over 6,000 people and been privy to countless "moments of truth." In fact, something about human relations, group interaction, or the technology is learned at just about every meeting. Although almost all the groups reacted favorably to the technology, groups of disabled people had the strongest positive reaction because of the empowerment they gained from the technology.

Some of the lessons Marriott learned included things that, on the surface, may seem to be common sense, but often only come to light in a facilitated group situation. One example is to anticipate the political issues and power focus as part of the meeting planning process. Sharing power is not always well received by those who have it and also feel they have the "right" answers. Marriott discovered that when the facilitator reviewed the first day's meeting with the boss, reviewing the areas that might be improved and working out a strategy for the second and subsequent days, things went much better.

Realize that group behavior is not the same as one-on-one behavior. For example, one company president, who had excellent relationship with his executive group, was surprised to hear that issues, important to his executive team, were not being discussed at their meetings. Erroneously, the president believed that his good relationship with his leadership team supported openness at executive meetings. Apparently, issues were being discussed in one-on-one meetings but executives failed to bring up them up in group meetings because (1) they did not know these issues were important to others in the room and (2) they didn't want to be the one to bring it up.

In another example, staff was hurriedly going down the wrong track. Bringing in meetingware clarified and amplified client priorities. The meeting lasted no more than thirty minutes and accomplished the right goals.

The EMS facilitator is in a unique position to observe meeting attendees' behavior. In this case, the lesson to learn is to not judge what people believe by observing their behaviors ("game face"), regardless of how enthusiastically and unanimously the behavior supports an idea or course of action. For example, in a meeting of bilingual, Spanish speaking people, the group verbally indicated that English was their preferred language. Why would Spanish speakers choose to conduct a meeting in English? There were several reasons. First, the facilitator, as the leader, suggested English, which biased the group even though participants felt more comfortable thinking, reading, and/or typing in Spanish. Second, participants felt their future promotions might be influenced in some way by their perceived command of English.

Another lesson learned was "Divide and Conquer." When a group is faced with a large or complex problem, it is often better to divide the group into small teams, thereby allowing each person or smaller group to focus on a piece of the project. Using a computer, each participant has access to work done by other groups and can contribute his/her ideas. This technique explodes productivity, minimizes duplication of effort, yet allows total group involvement on every issue. Division of labor can be a very powerful technique when using meetingware.

"Men are judged more by their appearance than reality."—Machievelli. Rank, gender, knowledge, etc. have little to do with the contributions a participant can make to the decision process. For this reason, inviting those with a different perspective and placing them in a "risk free" environment can greatly enhance the quality input. The phenomena mentioned here is a common occurrence when using meetingware. Excellent ideas/solutions often come from participants who otherwise do not have a great deal of influence in the group. Most of the time, owners of highly rated ideas do not identify themselves. Only rarely will a meeting leader persist in knowing who owns which ideas. Some meeting participants have reported that identifying themselves after an idea has been implemented and is working well was vastly preferred over taking credit for an idea too early.

The less groups work together, the more difficulty they may have establishing rapport and understanding (Norm & Storm). Even with a critical decision hanging over the heads of those in the meeting, people often don't collaborate, as they have their own agendas. This is a tough lesson for a facilitator to swallow, but one that proves true time after time! Sometimes the technology can help the meeting move forward and decisions get made. In one session, a large group was able to sort through a lengthy list of issues reaching consensus quickly and easily. Having a printed copy of prior meeting decisions was seen as another major advantage of the meetingware and improved chances of implementation of results after the meeting.

This lesson brings up another issue. Where do the decisions, assigned tasks, and information go after the meeting? Often meetingware does no more than print out a report that can be distributed to everyone who attended. But this negates some of the effectiveness of the meetingware. Products like Ventana's GroupSystems allow you to export the text into a Notes database or project tracking software. However, this is usually not an easy or elegant process. Better links between meetingware software and group project management software are needed and we certainly expect to see this function from a variety of vendors in the near future.

The ability to vote anonymously using meetingware should not be underestimated. In one case, certain key individuals had serious concerns about the viability of the group. For political reasons, they continued to attend meetings, dutifully making contributions, but did not talk to each other about their concerns. The anonymity of meetingware helped this group open up, become much more effective, and complete their mission. They continued to use meetingware in subsequent meetings.

A corollary to this lesson is that of the double standard. Meetingware, as currently formatted, offers users the tempting opportunity to "tell the truth" from their perspective. But the political reality often entails truth being defined as what leadership says it wants. We know that management's perspective and the perspective of those in the trenches is often quite different. Until leadership becomes more accepting of the way things really are and becomes willing to hear diverse views, the anonymous features of meetingware may make its acceptance difficult.

7A.5 PERCEIVED RISKS AND EMS

A major lesson to learn for EMS facilitators is that often progress on business issues can not be processed successfully until underlying issues of greater importance are explored and resolved. Routinely, groups with sensitive issues have no problem discussing them, using the anonymity provided by meetingware. However, it is important for the facilitator to be sensitive to such issues and try to expedite the discussion.

Additionally, facilitators may not understand what is going on in an EMS meeting. In this case, go to the people if you want to know what is happening. Place them in a "risk free" environment for candid feedback. Interviews, even if conducted by outside consultants, are not usually seen as "risk free." Paper and pencil surveys take a long time to complete, don't allow for adequate evaluation of open ended responses, and can disrupt the organization. Using focus groups can be very effective but care must be taken when evaluating results in relation to sample size.

One of the greatest problems with collaborative technologies is convincing people that sharing knowledge will increase effectiveness for all and not necessarily at the expense of their personal power. If knowledge is power, sharing knowledge is often seen as a sure way to lose power. Meetingware is still seen by some as a threat to power. Losing control and having contradictory views expressed are seen as risks. With the sharing of knowledge and possible loss of power can come the loss of job security. The concept of self-directed teams and flatter organization are already contemporary threats to the leaders sensitive to the knowledge and power issue. When meetingware is widely seen by all as a tool to gain power and knowledge and not lose it, meetingware will flourish.

Information Management is becoming a more critical lesson. In some cases, especially with EMS, "less is more." Technology has provided an avalanche of information at work and at home—database management, computer on-line services, 500 channels of TV, telecommunication innovation, etc. There is more information readily available now than most people want or can handle. How to manage and use information effectively is the challenge. When groups gather to use meetingware, sorting through the amount of information that can be generated can be a detractor to its use. As mentioned, facilitation techniques can help manage this concern but meetingware technology will have to build in software solutions for information overload.

7A.6 CONCLUSION

EMS technology is designed to foster collaboration and enable higher quality, more productive meetings. But meetingware is not something you simply load on your computer and use that moment. Most of the systems mentioned here require some type of projection device and technical infrastructure.

BIBLIOGRAPHY

1. Carlson, P. "The Awful Truth About Meetings," *Washington Post,* December 20, 1992, Coleman, David D. and Khanna, R. in *Groupware: Technology and Applications,* Prentice-Hall, New York, 1995.
2. Doyle, M. and Straus, D. *How to Make Meetings Work*, Jove, New York, 1982.
3. Kirkpatrick, D. "Here Comes the Payoff from PC's," *Fortune* Magazine, March 23, 1992.
4. Opper, S. and Fersko-Weiss, H. *Technology for Teams - Enhancing Productivity in Networked Organizations,* Van Nostrand Reinhold, New York, 1992.
5. Patterson, J. and Kim, P. *The Day America Told the Truth*, Plume, New York, 1992.

BIOGRAPHY

David Coleman is the founder and Managing Director of Collaborative Strategies. He has been involved with groupware and collaborative technologies since 1990 and is the author/editor of *Groupware Technologies and Applications* (Prentice-Hall, 1995). He also was the founder and conference chairman for the GroupWare '92-95 conferences that were held in San Jose, Boston, and London on an annual basis. Mr. Coleman was the editor and publisher of *GroupTalk*, the newsletter of workgroup computing. He is the founding editor of *Virtual Workgroups* Magazine, and currently a columnist. He also writes a monthly column on groupware for Computer Reseller News, and for MainSpring (an on-line resource for intranet and Web developers). Mr. Coleman has written for many trade and business publications such as *Network World*, *Datamation*, *Fortune*, and is a frequent public speaker worldwide. He has consulted to groupware vendors on product marketing, positioning, market research and competitive analysis, and for groupware users in assessing their organization groupware readiness as well as tool selection and the human factors involved in a successful groupware project. Mr. Coleman can be contacted directly at 415-282-9197, or at davidc@collaborate.com. More information on Collaborative Strategies can be found at www.collaborate.com.

When You Really Must Have Them: Face-to-Face Meetings Using Keypad Electronic Meeting Systems

William A. Flexner
Kimbal L. Wheatley
Option Technologies, Inc.

Nine senior executives of a $2.5 billion transportation leasing company took less than four hours to brainstorm 52 risks to the corporation and then identify the 10 that represented the greatest risk to achieving the company's strategic objectives and the 10 that should receive the highest priority from internal audit. After 6 months, the results of this four hour meeting were still guiding the focus of both the senior executives and the internal audit staff.

The technical analysis was complete. All 300 projects, spread across 10 program areas, had been given priority rankings. It was now time for the nine members of the Research Advisory Council (RAC) to make the political decisions regarding which projects would be included in the $200 million budget for 1996. The meeting began promptly at 9 AM. Six hours later, all but $20 million had been allocated. The last hour was spent determining which of the "tabled" projects would be funded. At the conclusion of the meeting, it was clear that the RAC members were comfortable with the amount of discussion and the quality of decisions they had made throughout the day.

The customers came into the room ready for the usual approach. Here was Big Blue asking their typical survey questions about customer needs. Wait a minute!! What is this? They want to know what issues we want to talk about? They want us to brainstorm the ideal solutions to the problems we identified? They want us to tell them which solutions should have the highest priority? And, they want to know why we hold these opinions so they can feed this information directly into the strategic product planning process of the division? Is this really Big Blue?[1]

The task was to get senior management's strategic perspective concerning which of 14 business processes should receive the most immediate focus of the Business Process Re-engineering Task Force. The senior executives were certain that it would take more than the four hours allotted to the discussion. They were concerned that the alternatives would be discussed to death without making the necessary decisions. However, precisely at the end of the four hours, agreement was reached that three of the processes should receive the immediate attention of the task force.

The members of the congregation filed into the church sanctuary filling every seat in every pew. The top ten priorities of each of the five church task forces were projected on five screens along the side wall. The task of the 467 people in the sanctuary was to choose which, among all 50 priorities, were the ones that the church should spend their limited time and budget addressing. Three hours later they were singing the praises of the process. They had reached agreement on the 13 priorities that the congregation should focus on during the next year. Was this divine intervention, effective facilitation, or just the technology that was employed?

7B.1 WHY KEYPAD TECHNOLOGY?

All of these processes, except, possibly, the last one, could have been accomplished by most of the *keyboard*-based LANs or intranet technologies identified previously in this chapter and elsewhere in this book. Yet, each of the processes was in fact completed in a face-to-face meeting using a *keypad*-based technology called OptionFinder® from Option Technologies, Inc.[2]

As much as many of us would like to use LANs and intranets to eliminate face-to-face meetings such as these, it is highly unlikely that this will ever be accomplished, nor do we think this goal is even desirable. Face-to-face meetings serve several useful purposes.

7B.1.1 Build Social Bridges

Face-to-face meetings help to build understanding, trust, and emotional bonds that sustain the work of a group when its members are working across time and space. They help to establish a belief among the members that "we are all in this boat together."

---

[1] This experience is described in an article entitled "Customer feedback the old-fashioned way—listening" by Scott Carson, that appeared in the *IBM Rochester News,* Second Quarter 1993, pp.4-7

[2] According to Fleetwood Inc., the manufacturer of wireless keypads, Option Technologies, Inc. in Ogden, Utah, is the largest purchaser of keypads among the dozen or so developers of keypad EMS products. Each of these products varies in its ability to adapt to specific meeting facilitation requirements. Readers are urged to "kick the tires" (e.g., perform an effective due diligence) to be certain the product they are getting will best meet their needs.

7B.1.2 Respond to the Human Need for Social Intercourse

The more electronic technology (e-mail, fax, voice mail, telephone, net-worked meetingware) is used to bridge time and space, the more empty people will feel emotionally. The innate human need for social interaction does not go away just because we have electronics that can replace the need for face-to-face meetings.

7B.1.3 Help Create the Political Environment Necessary for Making and Implementing Decisions

There is a political reality that electronic technology scattered across time and space cannot successfully address. That is, it is extremely difficult to create the political environment required for bold moves without getting people together face-to-face—the political environment that says "We are one, we are behind this, and we did this together."

Thus, here is the story of how a lower-cost, completely portable technology can be used to successfully accomplish a wide range of meeting tasks previously left either to traditional paper and pencil facilitation techniques or the emerging keyboard-based LAN or intranet technologies.

7B.2 WHAT IS A KEYPAD EMS?

Fig. 7B.1 OptionFinder Wireless Keypad

A keypad EMS is a combination of hand-held numeric keypads (See Fig. 7B.1), computer software, and a projection system. The keypads are handed out to the participants in a face-to-face meeting. During the course of the meeting, the facilitator, or meeting leader, uses the software to pose a question or a statement to the participants, along with a set of response choices, which is projected on a large screen. The participants press the keypad number of the response that matches their opinion. The software takes the keypad responses and instantly produces a graph of the results. The graph is then projected before the group for all to see.

A simple example of a keypad EMS event is measuring the comfort level of the participants. The projection system displays the keypad EMS polling screen illustrated in Fig. 7B.2. The participants respond with their keypads. The system then displays the graph in Fig. 7B.3, showing the responses.

How comfortable are you including this project in the budget?

1. Comfortable
2. Indifferent
3. Uncomfortable
4. ...
5. Very uncomfortable

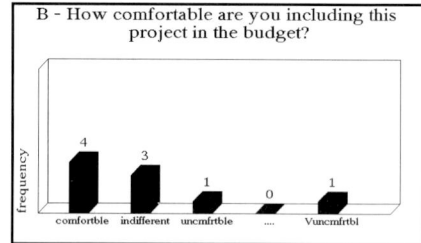

B - How comfortable are you including this project in the budget?

Fig. 7B.2 Question Format Used to Measure Participants' Comfort with Decision

Fig. 7B.3 Graphic Showing Participants' Comfort with Decision

This example is drawn from the $200 million budget allocation process described above. In the actual meeting, three projection screens were used. On one was projected an elaborate spreadsheet showing the members of the Research Advisory Council (RAC) the impact on the budget of their allocation decisions. On the second screen was an explanation of the project under discussion. On the third screen was the keypad EMS question posed to the members of the RAC: "How comfortable are you including this project in the budget?" A decision rule was agreed to from the outset: If two or more people were "uncomfortable" or one person was "very uncomfortable," the group would table the project for later consideration.

7B.3 WHAT ARE THE BENEFITS OF A KEYPAD EMS?

For a straightforward question like the "comfort" one above, what's the advantage of keypads over raising hands? One advantage is **anonymity**. The keypad EMS allows participants to respond anonymously, thereby encouraging more honest and accurate responses. The members of the RAC, above, immediately saw the impact of this compared to previous years when the politics of hand-raising and the dominating voice of a senior member of the organization's executive team played a much larger role in the process.

Another advantage—one available to all computer-based systems—is that **you get more, faster**. Users of keypad EMS routinely report achieving a 20 percent to 40 percent productivity gain when compared to non-technology assisted meetings. The Business Process Re-engineering Task Force meeting described above is one example of this. A second example comes from IBM. In 1987, reducing time was the key reason for adding a keypad EMS to an education program for customer executives in IBM's Asia/Pacific region. The designers of the program found that they were more likely to get a time commitment from the executives for a 2 day event than the 3 days that were required without the technology.

Improved understanding is a third benefit from this technology. Look back to our sample question. With the keypad EMS, you are not just finding out who's comfortable with the decision, but the *degree* of comfort. There is a difference between people answering that they are "uncomfortable" and "very uncomfortable." The former response may mean the group needs to iron out a few wrinkles before it proceeds. The latter response instantly shows that the group has some serious work to do, either in coming up with another decision, or in winning support to back the current decision. A simple raising of hands is unlikely to give the group as clear a picture of the true range of opinion as quickly as the keypad EMS can.

This example demonstrates a fourth benefit of the keypad EMS: *democracy of input*. Every participant gets a keypad, every participant gets to register his or her opinion—not just the participants who talk the most or have the most "power." Even if some participants don't speak up later, they have expressed their opinions and have had them acknowledged. By using the keypads early in a process, the group can quickly find out *what* everyone thinks, so that it can spend most of the time discussing *why* they think this way and *what to do about it*. As a result, a facilitator will find building alignment easier because participants know they were heard. With the keypad EMS, they feel the decision-making process is fairer and the decision more legitimate. They will be more willing to support the decision, even if they don't agree with it.

A fifth benefit of a keypad EMS arises from the *public display screen*. The facilitator can use the graphs of results to focus the group and keep the discussion on track, or as a means of stimulating creative thought by directing attention to the responses that weren't chosen. The graph also helps participants feel less emotionally attached to their own opinions. Participants begin to see themselves as part of a group with a range of ideas, rather than isolated individuals with independent thoughts. Furthermore, participants can see quickly how they fit into the group as a whole. The facilitator can use the public display of responses to get the group to explain what is going on (instead of telling the group), to take ownership of the range of opinions present, and to focus on the outcomes that are critical to the success of the group.

A sixth benefit focuses on the *portability of the technology* when compared to keyboard-based EMS. All of the equipment required to support a meeting of up to 20 people (including a notebook computer with the EMS software, an LCD projection panel, 20 keypads, and the transmitter/receiver for the keypad responses) fits into a soft carrying case—a small enough package to fit easily into the overhead compartment of an airplane. This means that you can go anywhere (e.g, the factory floor, on a sailboat, to whichever conference room is available, or into the corporate boardroom) and complete the physical setup for the meeting in less than 5 minutes. With the small package also comes *low intimidation*. Eleven buttons on a keypad (from "0" to "10") is as easy as using a push-button telephone. An 82 or 110 button keyboard, on the other hand, is quite intimidating for some people (often including more senior people in an organization).

A final benefit is the ***cost of rental or purchase***. A one-time, one or two day rental of a 20 keypad EMS including all of the above equipment ranges from $2,000 to $3,000, not including an operator of the system. Renting a system is often an effective way to introduce this technology and to show how it can enhance a face-to-face meeting. However, for an organization that plans to make more extensive use of a keypad EMS, the purchase price of $14,000 to $20,000 (depending on the brand of EMS and number of keypads purchased), amortized over a one or two year period, will clearly reduce the per meeting cost considerably below the per meeting rental cost.

7B.4 DESIGNING THE KEYPAD EMS INTO A MEETING PROCESS

Since face-to-face meetings are unlikely to go away, how do users add value to them with a keypad EMS. Based on more than 20 years combined experience designing and facilitating meetings using this technology, having conversations with users over the telephone helpline, and listening to users present meeting methodologies at five customer conferences, we have identified seven meeting components in which keypad EMS can be used to help the group achieve its objectives:

Warm-up: It is always important to engage the participants from the start of a meeting. We use keypads early in a meeting to break the verbal ice, to indicate that this meeting is going to be different than ones they have previously attended, and to have a bit of fun. For example, we have developed a set of questions that we often use for people we assume are first time keypad users:

- ☞ *"Have you ever used an anonymous opinion gathering device such as this?"*...(Yes/No)

- ☞ *"Have you ever driven more than 30 MPH over the speed limit?"*...(Yes/No)

- ☞ *"Did you lie to Mom?"*...(Yes/No/Well...it was not exactly a lie!!!)

In using these questions, we teach the participants how to use the keypad at the same time that they have the opportunity to "feel" anonymity. The participants almost always laugh at both the questions and the answers. For those who answer yes to the first question, we might ask "Who has been on *Love Connection* or *America's Funniest Home Videos*?" For the latter two questions, the participants get engaged as a group by pointing accusing fingers at each other to identify the people who say "no." And, possibly most important, they begin to both relax and get serious at the same time. In other words, they see possibilities in the polling-feedback loop provided by the keypads that they can take advantage of during the meeting.

Lay of the Land: A "lay of the land" exercise is used in a meeting to set the frame for an exercise that immediately follows or as a way to set the framework for a whole meeting. The purpose of this type of exercise is to get the participants (and the facilitator) to understand what the group believes about the agenda topic. A good example of this occurred in a meeting designed to re-engineer the process of market communications in a large multi-national corporation. In order to get the group thinking about what changes needed to be made, a series of statements were posed to the group. A balanced 6-point agree/disagree scale (*clearly disagree, pretty sure I disagree, tend to disagree, tend to agree, pretty sure I agree, clearly agree*) was used to force participants to commit to a positive or negative response. Statements presented to the group represented real material that focused their attention on tough and sensitive issues. Examples of the statements were:

☞ *"Market communications is currently used as a key vehicle to achieve sales and productivity growth in our company."* (A follow-up discussion question to generate ideas would be: What do we need to do to make it such a vehicle?)

☞ *"The way market communications is managed in our company provides a clear competitive advantage."* (A follow-up discussion question to generate ideas would be: How should we manage market communications differently in order to create competitive advantage?)

☞ *"The WISDOM exists in this room to identify what WE should do to make the biggest difference."* (A follow-up discussion question would be: How do we harness that wisdom to make an impact?)

When lay of the land is used early in a process, it can create a "let's get down to business" or "why beat around the bush" atmosphere, leading the participants to realize that this meeting is different, that what we are looking for are straight answers to tough questions. The group quickly realizes that the results are their results, not those of the facilitator or some outside consultant. As a result, it produces a very thorough airing of the issues, identification of the direction that may need to be taken to resolve those issues, and, possibly most important, it helps stimulate the group to take ownership of the problem and work more seriously to finding the solutions.

As facilitators, we seldom go into a meeting without using a series of "lay of the land" statements to get key beliefs out in the open and to get the creative juices flowing.

Valuing Perspectives: Used in conjunction with lay of the land exercises, as well as many of the other meeting components described in this section, this step asks the members of the group to identify themselves through their key-

pads. A series of questions will be posed early on, which focus on their characteristics (traditional demographics such as position in the organization, time in
company, functional area), as well as their beliefs (whether you believe a competitor's product is a serious threat or not, may affect your thinking far more than
whether you come from the marketing department). By using the same keypad
throughout the meeting and linking the responses to the characteristics questions to all other questions answered with the keypads, we can then slice any of
the results by the characteristics and use the resulting graphs to stimulate
focused discussions.

We have found that participants are fascinated to see where the group they
belong to differs, and by how much, from a group not like them. They look for the
differences, but the facilitator can also help them find similarities. By looking for
differences in perspective head on, and setting it up as a process for benefiting
from and appreciating diversity in viewpoint, we can create an atmosphere
where being open about differences builds teamness. Other benefits include:
having a feeling of ownership, alignment, and a willingness to address differences; using the differences to stimulate discussion and brainstorming; and
vicariously participating when someone else from the same characteristic group
talks.

Self-Assessment: When the Malcolm Baldrige National Quality Award
was introduced, companies began using the "Baldrige Criteria" for assessing
their own performance on quality. While integrating our keypad EMS into the
process, we learned that the act of assessing one's self helps participants understand and internalize the values and desired outcomes inherent in the model.
Participants simply couldn't assess themselves on the 3 areas of leadership
unless they understood what is expected of an award-winning leader. Once
understood, the assessor/assessee (same people) could make rational decisions
about whether or not the criteria applied to them.

The process of self-assessment accomplishes several things at one time:
It helps build an in depth understanding of the area being assessed; it helps
show the gap between what is and what the group feels it wants to be; it
serves as a motive for change; and since the results are clearly based on the
knowledge, experience, and beliefs of the participants in the room, they are
more likely to take ownership and initiate actions that help make the changes
happen.

An excellent example of an effective self-assessment process occurred several years ago with the 18 members of a self-managed team responsible for all of
the "back-office" operations of one of the largest financial services companies in
the United States. Using a keypad EMS, nine statements focusing on different
dimensions of teamwork were posed to the 18 participants. Figures 7B.4 and
7B.5 show an example of one of the statements and the results that can be produced by using it:

Fig. 7B.4 Questions Used in Teamwork Process

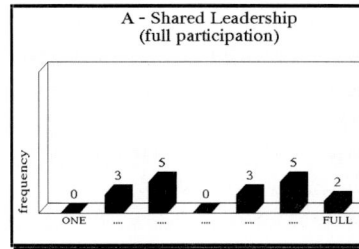

Fig. 7B.5 Participants' Perceptions of Approach to Shared Leadership

All nine statements were posed and responded to within three minutes. The resulting 4 1/2 hour facilitated discussion was lively, at times heated, and enormously useful for the team on several levels: It helped the participants see and understand the range of opinions held by the group; it helped to surface the critical issues that the group would have to address collectively if they were to succeed as a team; it helped them learn about "teamness" and its implications for their future behavior; and it helped to set the agenda for the rest of the meeting and the efforts back at the office for the next six months.

The process of Control Self-Assessment (CSA) that is sweeping the internal audit field in North America and Europe is another example of a self-assessment process that is taking advantage of a keypad EMS. MAPCO, an energy company located in Tulsa, Oklahoma, is one of the strongest proponents of the CSA process. Their experience, as reported by Larry Baker and Rodger Graham at the 1995 CSA Conference, was that the integration of a keypad EMS was a critical component in their success within the company. They explained that the portability of the technology allowed them to go anywhere in their far-flung organization to conduct their workshops. In the workshop process, the technology itself allowed them to quickly help members of a business unit see the gap between actual performance and their desired level of performance and as a result to find opportunities to compete more effectively in the marketplace.

Brainstorming: The keyboard LAN and intranet technologies, described previously in this chapter, initially get attention because of the power and efficiency that they bring to the brainstorming process in meetings. The ability to capture anonymous ideas in digital form and then transfer those ideas to other meeting processes with the "click of a mouse" is very attractive. So, how do facilitators using keypad EMS technologies manage the brainstorming process? Not surprisingly, since most brainstorming techniques were developed before we had rooms filled with networked computer technology, facilitators usually employ one or more of these brainstorming techniques to generate the ideas and then either the facilitator or a "technographer" enters the resulting ideas into the computer that is used to run the keypad EMS.

The nine executives of the transportation leasing company used the Nominal Group Technique (NGT) to identify 52 risks facing the company. The facilitator began the process by leading the executives in a discussion of the factors critically important to the success of the company. Then the facilitator asked each of the executives to take ten minutes to silently brainstorm (on paper) the things that could happen that would prevent the company from achieving its success. After the ten minutes, the facilitator asked each of the executives in turn to identify one of their risks, using traditional NGT ground rules: Read out one item at a time with no repetition of items already placed on the list. Without the keypad EMS, the facilitator would normally write each of the identified items on a flipchart. However, since the computer was already present, the facilitator simply asked the technographer to capture all of the ideas in "real-time" in front of the group and project the computer screen through an LCD projection system to a large public screen for all to see. The resulting list was reviewed on the screen by the executives and the facilitator made certain that all of the items belonged on the list and that there were none missing. Once this review was completed, the assessment using the keypads was initiated with a "click of a mouse."

In planning sessions where brainstorming is particularly useful, facilitators often divide the participants into "buzz groups" of 4 to 8 people, give instructions for the groups to brainstorm ideas that respond to a particular challenge facing them and then capture the ideas in one of several ways: on flipcharts, on Post-it™ Notes, or on 4 x 6 index cards to be placed on a sticky wall.[1] At a recent session of a Big Six accounting firm, 70 participants were divided into four breakout groups and asked to identify as fast as possible all of the things that needed to be done to achieve the division's Year 2000 objectives. Within each breakout group, the participants were divided into three buzz groups. Using Post-It Notes, each of the buzz groups generated over 50 ideas in less than ten minutes. They then spent 15 minutes looking at their ideas and clustering them into 6 to 8 key success factors, of which their 3 most important were reported out to the entire breakout group.

Focus (or List Reduction): The challenge with any brainstorming process (whether manual or electronic, and whether completed prior to the meeting or during the meeting) is what to do with the lengthy list that is produced. Finite resources dictate that we focus our attention and energies on only those things that must be acted upon. And this in turn requires that we develop and use one or more criteria for the selection/deselection process.

☞ The executives in the transportation leasing company used one criterion to reduce their brainstormed list to 10 risks.

☞ The Business Process Re-engineering Task Force brought 14 processes to the attention of senior management, who then used four criteria to reduce the list to the three processes that should receive immediate attention.

☞ The members of the congregation used only one criterion to select the 13 priorities to assign to the church task forces.

---

[1] A sticky wall is made by taping 4 to 8 sheets of flip chart paper on a wall with the edges overlapping and then spraying the paper with a spray adhesive such as 3M's Spray Mount™ Artist's Adhesive (Catalog No. 6065). The adhesive allows the participants to place the 4 x 6 index cards on the sprayed paper and then move them around as they are organized into families of ideas.

When the participants from the Big Six accounting firm reconvened into a plenary session, they reported out the top four critical success factors for each group. Each factor was entered into the keypad EMS software projected on the public screen and then through a facilitated discussion with the entire group, the list of 16 was reduced to 10 to eliminate duplications from the different groups. Finally, the keypads were used to assess the list using two criteria: importance to achieving the Year 2000 objectives and likelihood of achieving it without change in the way of doing business.

Users of a keypad EMS have found that its application to reduce a list and focus the energies of the group is one of the most powerful ways to employ this type of technology. They report that when a group trims the list down to a chosen few, their choices represent the collective wisdom of the group, not the wisdom of a vocally dominant few. In fact, most have found that the short list *is* the best bet based on the wisdom of the participants. The quality of the information displayed on the public screen rivals that of any other as a reason to choose one option over another.

This is the outcome that was achieved by participants in the Big Six accounting firm meeting. The results of their assessment (presented in Fig. 7B.6 as a Pareto chart of importance and in Fig. 7B.7 with the likelihood criterion also reviewed) indicate that four critical success factors (I, C, E, and H) were more important than the remaining six. The ensuing discussion verified this outcome and led the group to conclude that, while factors I and C might be slightly more likely to occur, specific plans needed to be developed for all four or these critical success factors.

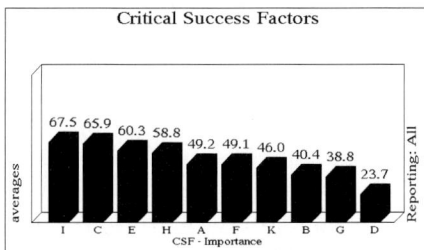

Fig. 7B.6 Pareto Chart Showing Critical Success Factors in Priority Order

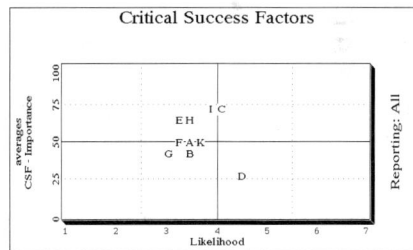

Fig. 7B.7 Display of Results on Two Dimensions: Importance and Likelihood of Achievement

Action Planning: Nothing seems to make things happen like accountability.

"Kim, will you see to it that the IS task force gets the resources they need?"
"Yes."
"When?"
"By next Friday."
"How will we know when you have succeeded, Kim?"
"They are processing POs."

With a word processing package built into the keypad EMS software or loaded on the same computer, all of this can be logged onto the public screen with Kim's peers looking on. There is an old adage, "Never take oaths," which reminds us that it's hard to back out of something committed to publicly. Therefore, we modify the adage to "Make them take oaths."

Users of a keypad EMS routinely create a memo right in front of the group that summarizes the conclusions of the meeting and assigns responsibilities and timeframes to each of the action steps that are required. And, different from a memo received a day or week or month later from the meeting's scribe, this one is the *group's* memo. Prior to building this memo, the keypads are often used to get the group's opinion regarding how soon an action should be taken and the extent to which the group in fact has sufficient control to successfully implement the action. In England, this is known as a Swamp Analysis because only those things that are most immediate in time and clearly under control of the group are on *firm ground*. The rest are in the *swamp*, that soft, squishy, uneven terrain that is either too far in the future or outside the group's control. We are reminded of a session in England reported by a keypad EMS user where the participants didn't get truly excited about the task in front of them until they completed the swamp analysis and were able to see on the public screen those things which really did have a high probability of success.

Organizational inertia is an awesome thing. Unless something is better because of the meeting (better information, better team, better accountability, better *something*), the meeting is a waste of resources. Releasing the clutch on the machinery and resources of an organization is as amazing as its inertia. Things start to happen, people get reassigned, budgets get released, technology and know-how get ramped up, etc. The place to start releasing the clutch is in the meeting itself.

CONCLUSION: A GROWING MARKET ACCEPTANCE

Keypad EMS products were first introduced in the late 70s and early 80s. For example, we first used the OptionFinder System with a group of physicians in the summer of 1985. Since then, the number of users around the world of keypad EMS products has grown into the thousands, and there are a dozen or so developers and vendors located in North America, Europe, Asia, and Australia supporting these users.

With this growth, the market is saying two things: Face-to-face meetings are still important and keypad EMS technology clearly adds value to the face-to-face meeting processes. The size, cost, and portability of wireless keypads mean that the facilitator can take a keypad EMS anywhere it is needed within the organization. The flexibility and robustness of some of the keypad EMS software products currently on the market mean that the facilitator can accomplish a wide range of tasks not previously available through technology.

If an organization's objective is to involve more people in their own context and at their own site, then keypad EMS products represent a critical alternative solution for face-to-face meetings, ranging from boardrooms filled with executives through conference rooms filled with members of cross functional teams to factory floors filled with workers on the production line.

We challenge those of you who are focused on using technologies to keep people out of meetings to spend at least some time determining how you can also use technologies to re-engineer those face-to-face meetings that are still critical to organizational success.

BIOGRAPHIES

William A. Flexner is co-founder and CEO of Option Technologies, Inc. He has more than 30 years experience as a manager, researcher, teacher, consultant, and facilitator. In the early 1970s, he was one of the first people in the United States to focus on marketing as it applies to the health care field. He is recognized internationally for creativity, challenging of conventional wisdom, and his ability to facilitate diverse groups of people to work together to achieve common strategic purposes. The development of the OptionFinder System was a direct result of Mr. Flexner's need for tools that would help executive teams work more effectively together.

Kimbal L. Wheatley is co-founder and General Manager of Option Technologies, Inc. He is directly responsible for the conceptual development of OTI's keypad EMS—OptionFinder. Mr. Wheatley has been a scientist, college professor, academic administrator, hospital administrator, consultant, marketer, and computer person. His ability to switch from concentrated detailed analysis to highly creative brainstorming has permitted him to work effectively with many different kinds of people in many different settings.

Information about the OptionFinder System can be obtained from Option Technologies, Inc., 389 West Second Street, Suite B, Ogden, Utah 84404 Tel: 801-621-2500; Fax: 801-621-4677; e-mail: info@optionfinder.com

How To Facilitate Distributed Meetings Using EMS Tools

Julia Szerdy and Michael R. McCall
Facilitate.com

The power of technology, from high speed desktop computers and networks that interconnect locations around the globe to simple user interfaces that enable any novice to get started, has opened up a whole new world of opportunity for work group collaboration. In this chapter, we will explore the things that a facilitator or team leader *should know and think about how to make the most of* Electronic Meeting Systems (EMS) in a distributed environment. The promise of distributed meetings is for greater participation, innovation and problem solving capability. The skill of the facilitator is to enable groups to realize this promise by paying attention to the design and substance of the collaboration, managing the people issues, and selecting the right technology tools.

7C.1 COLLABORATION FROM YOUR DESKTOP AND ACROSS THE WORLD

To begin, we will discuss what we mean by distributed meetings and how EMS tools offer organizations and teams some distinct capabilities and benefits. We will also consider the challenges a facilitator faces in making the most of these capabilities to create highly effective and productive meetings. Later sections address the roles of people and technology in successful meetings and what participants in EMS meetings will see on their computer screens. In Section 7C.4 we provide detailed tables and lists for preparing and facilitating distributed meetings. We will wrap up with application examples and answers to frequently asked questions.

7C.1.1 What Is a Distributed Meeting?

A distributed meeting, also know as an asynchronous or virtual meeting, is one in which participants can join in from any location and at any time. They work from their desktop computer or in small groups, in the same office or in remote locations, at a scheduled time or at their convenience. Technology, as well as the skills of a good facilitator or meeting organizer, is what enables people to join the meeting in this way, seeing and contributing to the work and results of the whole group. The key characteristic of a distributed meeting environment is that participants are no longer constrained by distance and time zones. As a result, distributed meetings tend to run over several hours, days, or even weeks. Over that time, participants move through a series of agenda items and activities controlled and directed by a facilitator.

7C.1.2 Electronic Meeting Systems Distinct from E-mail and News Groups

There are several technology tools discussed throughout this book that enable people from across an organization to communicate and collaborate from their desktop. These include e-mail, news groups, listservs, and document sharing products. EMS tools have some distinct characteristics from these other technologies (see Fig. 7C.1).

It is helpful to think of EMS tools from the model of a traditional facilitated meeting, an event where a group of people come together to solve a problem, exchange information on an issue, or make a decision. In this kind of meeting the facilitator defines the objectives of the event, prepares an agenda, develops a process to guide the group through their deliberations, and leads the group to the desired results in the time available. The facilitator may write ideas up on a flip chart, give everyone sticky pads to post their ideas themselves, help the group organize, and prioritize their thoughts. All this is very similar in a meeting using EMS tools in both a synchronous or asynchronous environment.

In an EMS event, distinct from an exchange with e-mail or a discussion group, meeting participants are brought together in a structured and organized fashion around defined topics, problem statements, and objectives. The goal of the group's work is more clearly defined and the collaboration is steered by the facilitator, not to restrict innovation and creativity, but to guide the group's energy through a series of steps to meet some specific objectives.

E-Mail

- *Model: postal service*
- *Mail sent and delivered to individual mail boxes.*
- *Functions include forwarding, carbon copying, attaching documents.*
- *One to many collaboration.*

News Groups, Listservs, Bulletin Boards

- *Model: free flowing group conversation*
- *Documentation of threaded discussions with string of items to read through.*
- *Many conversations at once.*
- *Gatekeeper option.*
- *Mail delivered to individual mail boxes or posted on server.*

Electronic Meeting Systems

- *Model: facilitated meeting, group decision making and problem solving.*
- *Facilitator guides group through agenda.*
- *Ideas and issues can be organized by topics, sub-topics, categories, priorities.*
- *Evaluate options generated by group. Create action plans.*
- *Links to documents, web-sites, E-mail.*
- *Many to many collaboration.*

Shared Documents, White Boards

- *Model: group authoring*
- *Build a common product, text or graphics.*
- *Maintain different versions.*
- *Many to many collaboration.*

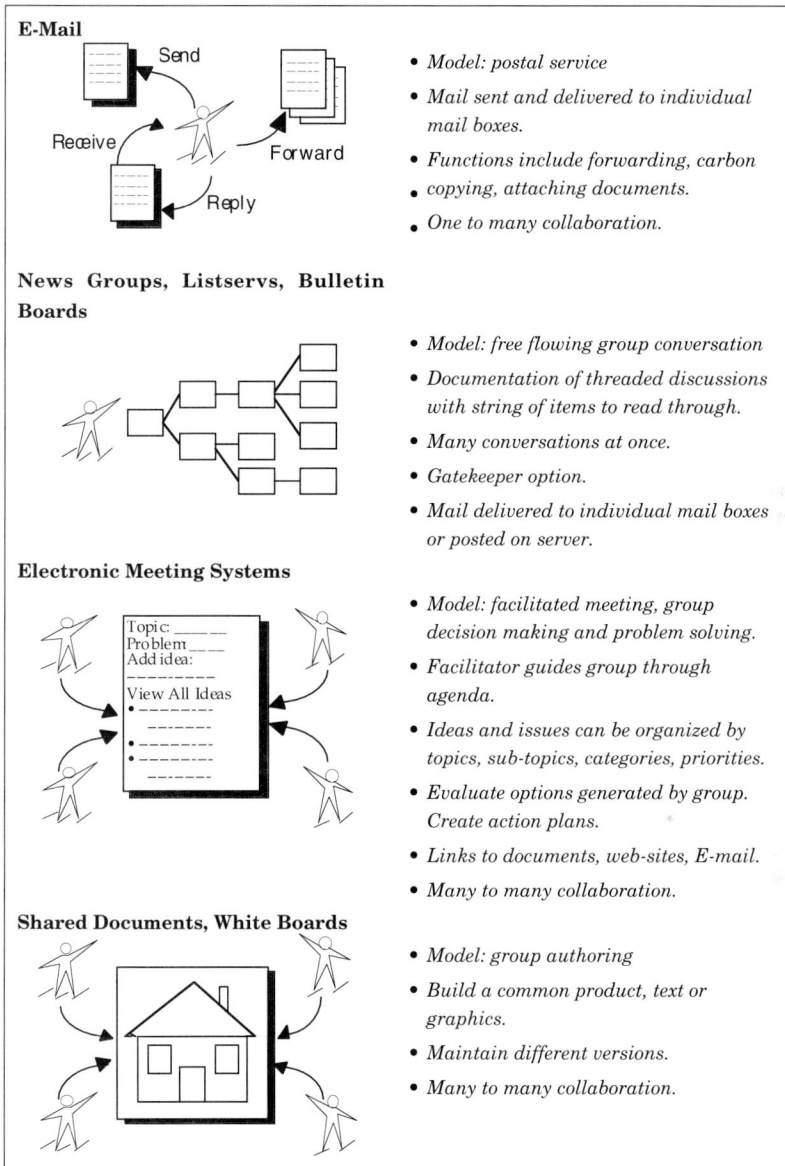

Fig. 7C.1 Distinguishing EMS Meetings from Other Distributed Forms of Collaboration

7C.1.3 What to Expect—Benefits and Challenges

So what do EMS distributed meetings enable us to do that we can't do already? Simply speaking, they allow us to combine the benefits of facilitated meetings without having to coordinate everyone's schedules and pay for their travel costs to get to the same place. Table 7C.1 lists some of the benefits and results we should expect to see as well as some of the challenges that the facilitator needs to be able to address.

Table 7C.1 Benefits and Challenges of Distributed Meetings Using EMS Tools

Benefits and Challenges

Potential Benefits of EMS	Special Challenges for Facilitators
• More people able to participate.	• Making sure everyone has access to tools and ability to use them.
• Flexibility to match schedules and time zones.	• Making sure that participants take the time, greater reliance on self-management by team members.
• Parallel processing, allowing participants to all work on the same topic at once.	• Keeping the discussion and ideas on track, guiding the conversation towards meeting objectives and desired results.
• More data and ideas collected, broader perspectives.	• Coping with the quantity of items generated, keeping them organized and filling in any gaps
• Innovation and creativity, new ideas and possibilities.	• Recognizing "baby ideas" and helping the grow into well formed concepts and solutions that can be implemented.
• Focused participation, addressing specific topics and problem statements.	• Changing the agenda midstream when the topics presented are not working.
• Level playing field, anonymous contributions (if desired), removal of political overtones and presumptions.	• Asking follow-on questions and seeking to understand where perspectives are coming from.
• Everyone can see everyone else's contributions and build upon them.	• Funneling ideas and discussion to reach an end point.
• Group satisfaction with level of participation and increased buy-in to results.	• Identifying and dealing with resistance.

7C.1.4 Special Challenges for a Facilitator

The challenge for the facilitator or moderator of a distributed meeting is to coordinate, inspire, persuade, or cajole the contributors to participate in a timely and organized manner so that the output of the collaboration meets the desired results. Unlike a traditional meeting where all the participants are in the same room and the facilitator controls the agenda, here, group members participate when they have time or when they remember, follow the agenda at their own pace and can stray off the topic without immediate redirection. The facilitator must find new ways to ensure that problems are solved, deadlines are met, perspectives are heard, and objectives are accomplished.

Facilitators must pay attention to three areas for a successful distributed meeting with groupware: the substance of the meeting, the participants and the technology (see Fig. 7C.2). We will discuss specific facilitation techniques in detail in section 7C.4.

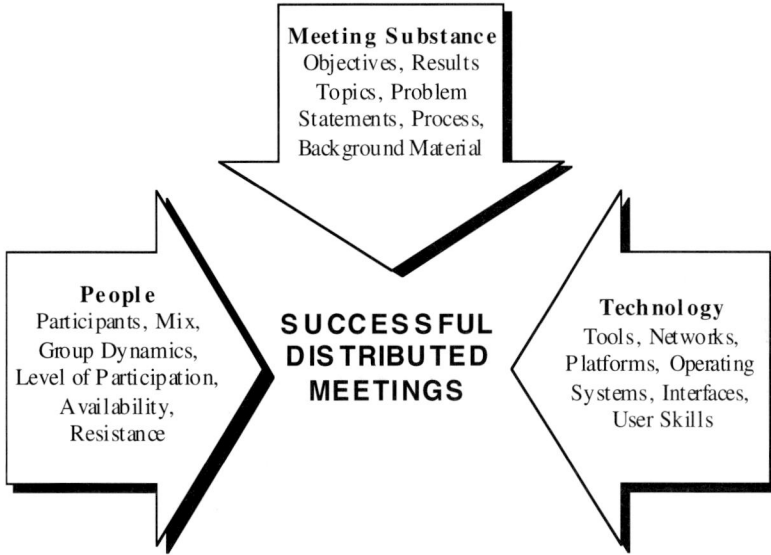

Meeting Substance
Objectives, Results
Topics, Problem
Statements, Process,
Background Material

People
Participants, Mix,
Group Dynamics,
Level of Participation,
Availability,
Resistance

SUCCESSFUL DISTRIBUTED MEETINGS

Technology
Tools, Networks,
Platforms, Operating
Systems, Interfaces,
User Skills

Fig. 7C.2 Three Areas of Focus for Facilitator

7C.2 ROLES AND RESPONSIBILITIES IN A DISTRIBUTED MEETING

To get a better understanding of how make a distributed meeting work, it is useful to identify the roles and responsibilities of the people and technology involved (see Table 7C.2).

As with conventional meetings, there are distinct roles that people can play in a distributed meeting. There is usually an owner or client for the meeting, someone who initiated the event and who owns the results. The person assuming the facilitator role designs and directs the meeting. Then there are the participants who provide contributions navigated by the owner's objectives and the facilitator's road map. It is also important to consider the role of technology, what it can do to support the group process and results, and its limitations. It is useful to have technical support resources available to help manage the technology and inevitable hitches that will occur until the team gains experience in using these tools.

Clearly, there can be overlaps in roles: The owner and the facilitator may be the same person; different participants may lead different parts of a group's work. EMS tools allow the owner and facilitator to participate in discussions in a way that are not always feasible in traditional face-to-face meetings. Their contributions can be anonymous and can be considered for their quality and insight without compromising their additional roles.

Table 7C.2   Roles and Responsibilities in Distributed Meetings

Role and Responsibilities

Owner or Client	Participants
• Define meeting objectives and desired results or outcomes	• Be prepared for involvement in the meeting
• Determine who should participate and why the contributions are valuable	• Provide input openly and honestly
• Provide background information	• Speak out
• Work with facilitator to design and conduct distributed meeting	• Listen to and consider the ideas of others
• Keep an eye on meeting products, confirm group is on track	• Seek to understand before seeking to be understood
• Make decisions, responsible for meeting outcomes	• Make suggestions, make decisions
• Ensure next steps are completed	• Take responsibility for next steps and implementation

Facilitator	Technology
• Understand desired results in terms of business outcomes and group process	• Enable the group to do things it couldn't otherwise accomplish
• Design meeting process and agenda	• Make work groups and individual team members more productive
• Communicate process and schedule	• Enable people to contribute at convenient times and places
• Match tools and technology to agenda and desired results	• Let people know where they are the process and what's expected of them
• Ensure technology tools are ready to go, set-up and test	• Enable everyone to speak at once
• Check technology continues to work during the meeting	• Keep track of information, make it accessible
• Confirm the group is on track, redirect as needed and adjust agenda	• Allow people to contribute anonymously
• Keep the group focused, move through the agenda	• Support, not drive, the agenda and outcomes
• Get whole group engaged, seeking participation and commitment to collective results	• Get out of the way when not needed or inappropriate
• Identify and remove obstacles, resolve conflict	
• Summarize discussions, accelerate decision-making	
• Review meeting effectiveness and adjust process for future events	

7C.3 THE TECHNOLOGY—EMS TOOLS FOR DISTRIBUTED MEETINGS

As David Coleman has outlined in Chapter 7A, there are a number of different EMS tools on the market, many of which can be used in both a meeting room and a distributed environment. Although each of these tools has a different interface and a slightly different way of leading participants through a meeting agenda, there are many similarities. To give you an idea of what a participant in a distributed meeting will see on their computer screen and what they will be asked to do, we will use one computer aided facilitation tool called Facilitate.com 4.0 (see Chapter 7A for more details about this particular product).

7C.3.1 A Participant's Perspective: Facilitate.com 4.0 as an Example

To join a distributed meeting, participants first select an icon on their computer desktop. This will open up the EMS application running over a network that links each participant's computer to a central machine containing the meeting database with details of the agenda, topics, background information, names of participants, and so on. The network can be established on your corporate LAN, intranet, or Internet. For Web-based EMS products, participants access the meeting home page via their Web-browser on the World Wide Web or local intranet.

Once inside the EMS application (see Fig. 7C.3), a participant will be presented with a number of meetings or conferences that are open and available to join. Facilitators can use group membership and security tools to control participation as necessary. Information included on this main screen shows participants the name, purpose, and objectives of the meeting, its status and owner, as well as the number of ideas or contributions collected so far. The participant decides which meeting to join and moves on to see the topics available for discussion.

To manage an agenda or discussion flow within each meeting or conference, the facilitator uses a series of topics and sub-topics. These contain descriptions of the topics or issues to be addressed by the participants, the questions that are being posed, and any background information to focus the discussion. Participants choose which topic or sub-topic they want to work on and arrive at the meeting space (see Fig. 7C.4). If a meeting is already underway, participants will see the work produced so far and add their contributions, which become immediately made available to others. A participant may choose to join a topic several times over the course of distributed meeting to see new contributions and the progress of the discussion. Voting and survey options (see Fig. 7C.5) allow participants to evaluate items generated by the group against one or more defined criteria.

The facilitator controls how long a particular topic stays open and the process, such as brainstorming, data gathering, prioritizing, or voting which participants will use at a certain time. Since participants may be joining the meeting over an extended period of time, the facilitator needs to keep track of the information gathered and decide when to move on to another topic or activity.

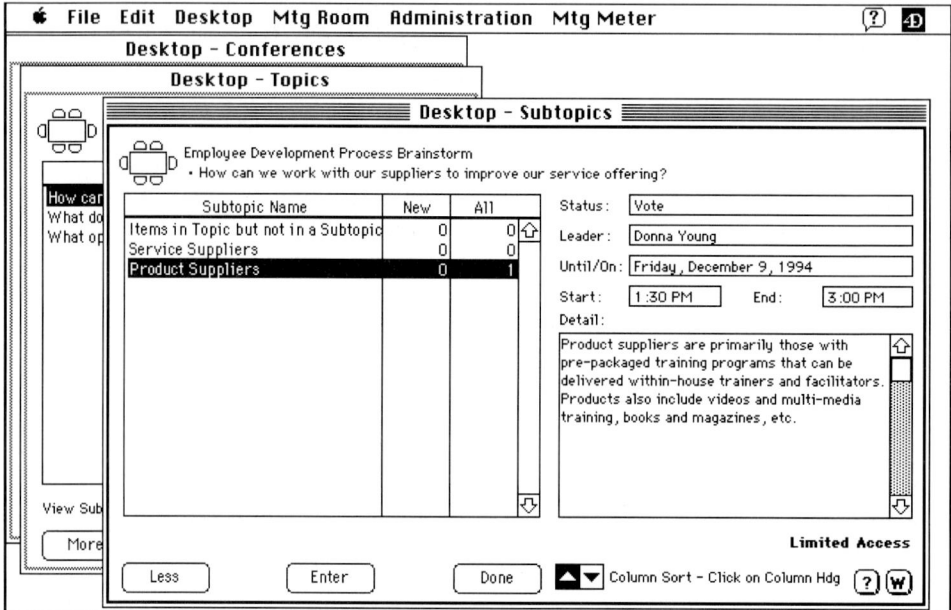

Fig. 7C.3 Participants View and Select from a Series of Conferences and Topics

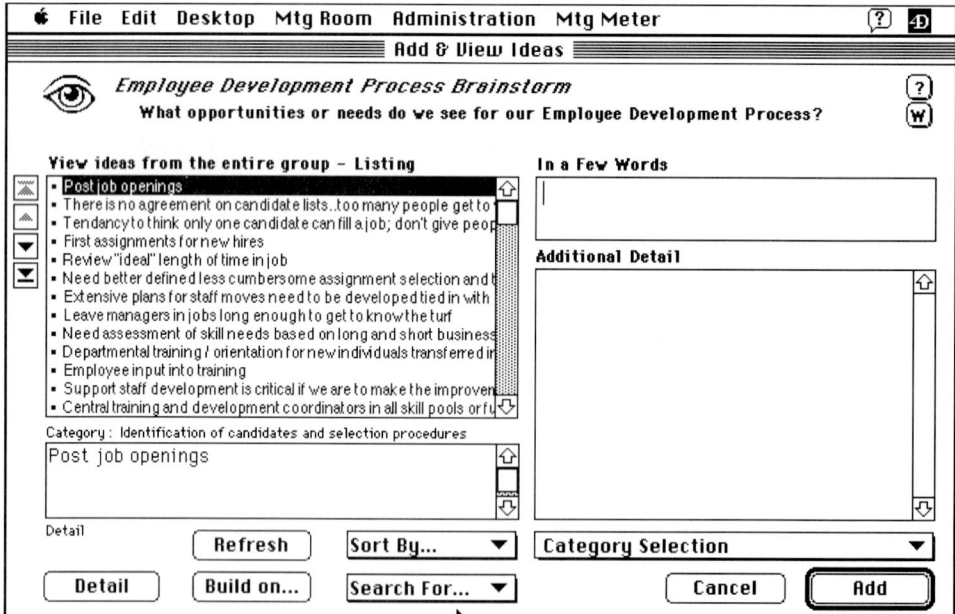

Fig. 7C.4 Brainstorming—Adding Ideas to a Topic While Viewing the Ideas of Others

 File   Edit   Desktop   Mtg Room   Administration   Mtg Meter   (?)

Vote

✓ *Employee Development Process Brainstorm*

What opportunities or needs do we see for the Employee Development Process?

Select	Priority	ID) In a Few Words	Urgency	Impact
☒	2	1) Update training and skills for more senior staff :skills get rusty need renewal	5	2
☐	2	2) Central training and development coordinators in all skill pools or functions.	5	8
☐	8	4) Motivation and training.	7	1
☒	6	5) View training expenditures as an investment and not a cost.	1	2
☐	4	7) Employee input into training	9	1
☐	4	8) Training courses need to be evaluated for value added	8	9
☐	2	9) Review inside v. outside training	5	6
☒	1	10) Develop policies, procedures and training manuals for new supervisors	1	1
☒	2	11) Training and development of staff need to be built into our mgmt reward syst(	1	8

| 0 | 0 | ▲▼ Column Sort – Click on Column Hdg | Sort By ▼ |

Totals   View Detail   Vote Rules   Done

Fig. 7C.5 Voting—Evaluating a List of Items Against Defined Criteria

7C.3.2 Web-Based EMS Tools for Internet and Intranet

Electronic meeting tools are now available for use over the World Wide Web. This is a new area of development for EMS tools and the future direction for this type of groupware. These tools combine the benefits of focused discussions and problem-solving capabilities provided by EMS applications with the added advantage of ready access to anyone with Internet or intranet access via a Web-browser. Software distribution is elilminated and meeting setup is significantly easier. Speed and performance are increased, and software prices will come down significantly.

Participants will see slightly different screen configurations from a client-server version (see Fig. 7C.6), but the functions of adding ideas, viewing, and building upon others' ideas, categorization, voting, etc. are very similar.

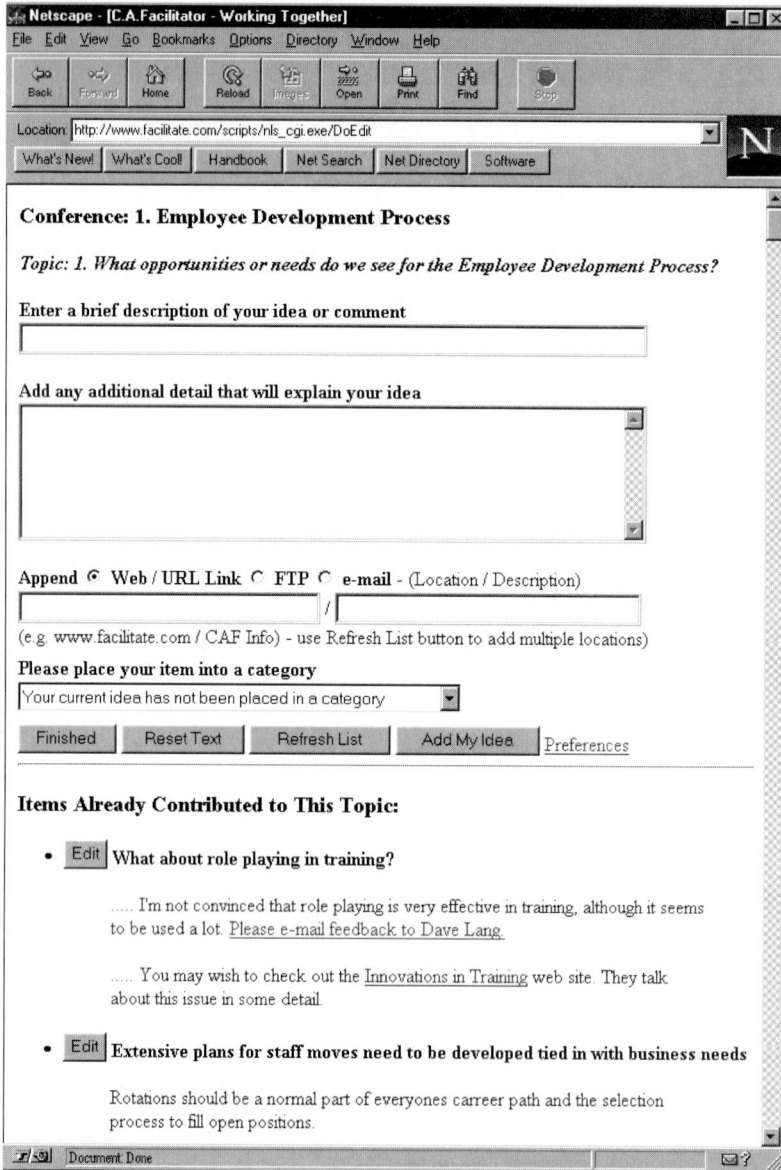

Fig. 7C.6 Web-Based EMS Tool Example: Brainstorming—Adding Ideas to a Topic While Viewing the Ideas of Others

7C.3.3 Meeting Output and Products

The output of a meeting will take several forms, depending on the work conducted. Figures 7C.7 and 7C.8 provide examples from an idea generation activity and a voting exercise respectively. These meeting products can be exported from the EMS tool and distributed as documents to participants. This is an example where e-mail or document management tools can assist the group process, providing the means to share final products with a wide audience, perhaps beyond the meeting participants, and maintain archives of meeting results. While EMS tools can be used to make available the output of past meetings, as they do while meetings that are still in progress, other groupware tools are often better suited to document management and message broadcasting.

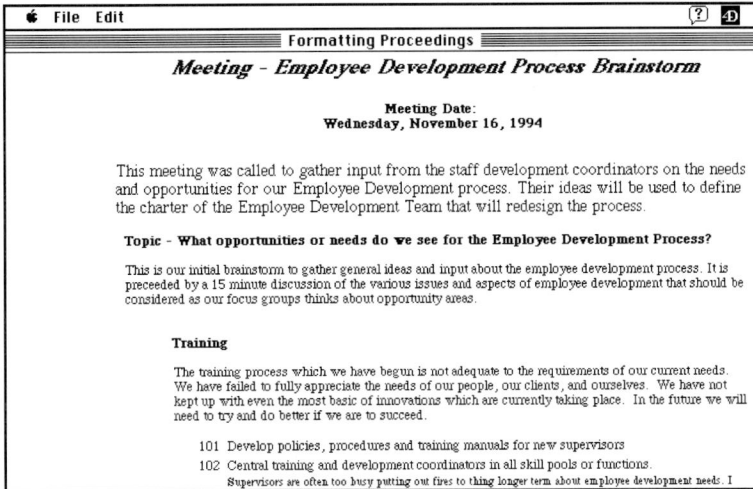

Fig. 7C.7 Sample Meeting Proceedings from an Idea Generation Session

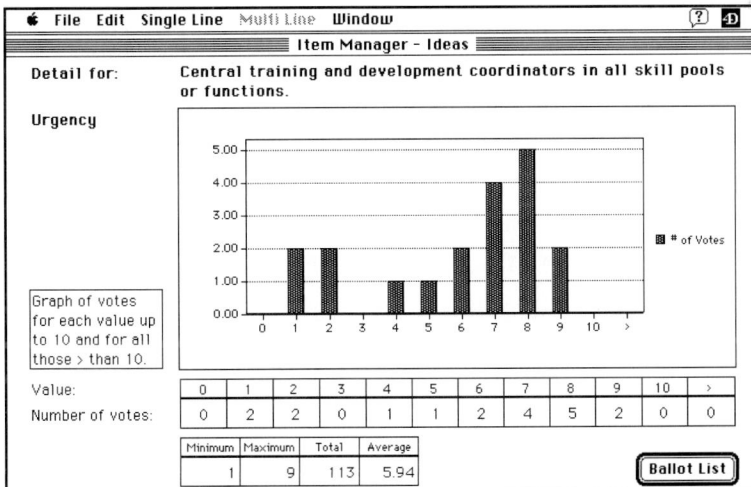

Fig. 7C.8 Sample Meeting Output from a Voting Exercise

7C.3.4 What to Look for in an EMS Tool for Distributed Meetings

Table 7C.3 provides a checklist of things to look for when selecting an EMS tool to support distributed meetings and collaboration.

Table 7C.3 What to Look for in an EMS Tool for Distributed Meetings

Product Features And Other Requirements

- Tools to match your meeting process and the type of work to be done. Examples include brainstorming, surveys, voting and prioritizing, and action plans. Anonymous or identified participation.

- Data management tools that will allow you to manipulate the information collected and export data into other common applications such as word processors, spreadsheets, and document management systems.

- Facilitator training and support availability. Network of facilitators to draw upon.

- Software compatibility with the various operating systems, networks, memory, and speed capabilities of participants' desktop computers. Cross-platform or Web architecture.

- Ability to attach or imbed documents and files for added information sharing.

- Ease of use. A simple set of instruction sent by e-mail is all that is needed to join a meeting and fully participate.

- Ability to run multiple conferences and groups at the same time.

- Appropriate security options.

- Availability of software to all participants. Ability to duplicate client software and freely distribute or access via Web-browser over the Internet or corporate intranet.

- Value for money, in proportion to expected savings and results. Pricing by concurrent users rather than by seat.

7C.4 HOW TO FACILITATE DISTRIBUTED MEETINGS WITH EMS TOOLS

One of the common questions about meetings using electronic meeting systems is whether it is necessary to have a facilitator. The same question may be asked about any type of meeting and the answer is similar. In some form or other, the facilitation role exists for all meetings. Someone needs to call the meeting, define its purpose, distribute information, initiate discussion, collect the data generated, summarize the results, and decide upon next steps. These tasks may be the responsibility of one person called a facilitator or may be handled by several people, members of a self-managed team for example. If these tasks are overlooked, meetings tend to be disjointed, time consuming, and unproductive. The same is true for distributed meetings and EMS tools.

The facilitator's role is to make the most use of participants' time and knowledge to meet the expectations as defined by the meeting owner or the participants themselves. Typically, the facilitator takes a leading role when issues to be addressed are complex, when time is short, or if there are challenging dynamics among participants and a neutral mediator is needed. In the case of distributed meetings, the facilitator's role is particularly important as participants are separated by both time and space, adding to the complexity of coordination and communication. In the case of meetings using EMS tools, someone needs to know the software well enough to be able to set up meetings and topics and manage the data collected. As a team gains experience with an EMS tool and the process of running effective distributed meetings, the facilitation tasks may be shared and there may no longer be a need for a specially trained facilitator.

7C.4.1 Facilitation Model

Figure 7C.2 identified the need for attention to three areas of a successful distributed meeting: the substance or content of the meeting, the people and their interaction, and the technology and its application. Figure 7C.9 incorporates these areas into the classic Plan-Do-Review model.

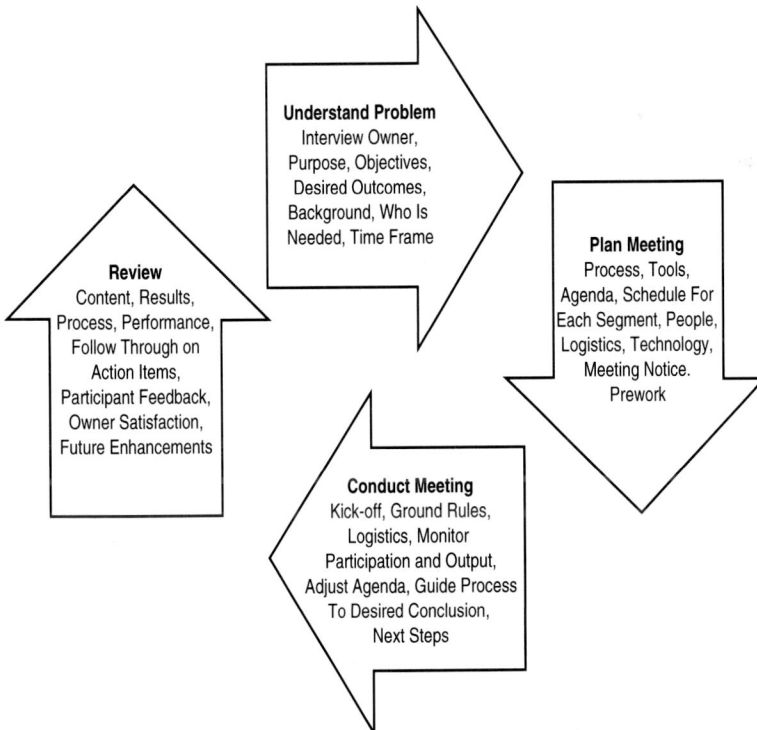

Understand Problem
Interview Owner, Purpose, Objectives, Desired Outcomes, Background, Who Is Needed, Time Frame

Plan Meeting
Process, Tools, Agenda, Schedule For Each Segment, People, Logistics, Technology, Meeting Notice. Prework

Review
Content, Results, Process, Performance, Follow Through on Action Items, Participant Feedback, Owner Satisfaction, Future Enhancements

Conduct Meeting
Kick-off, Ground Rules, Logistics, Monitor Participation and Output, Adjust Agenda, Guide Process To Desired Conclusion, Next Steps

Fig. 7C.9 Facilitation Model for Successful Distributed Meetings

In preparing for and conducting distributed meetings, the critical skill of the facilitator is to translate the meeting objectives into a core set of topics, problem statements, and collaborative exercises that will draw out the desired knowledge and ideas from participants. Unlike a traditional meeting, where the facilitator often relies on his or her impromptu skills to moderate a discussion and draw out ideas, the facilitator of a distributed meeting has a much greater reliance on asking the right questions and providing the right background information. Table 7C.4 lists some of the particular skills of a good facilitator of distributed electronic meetings.

Table 7C.4 Skills and Capabilities of a Good Facilitator

Facilitation Skills and Capabilities for Successful Distributed Meetings
● Ability to establish a meeting framework and discipline that encourages people to participate, keeps them engaged, and results in a high quality of ideas and interaction.
● Ability to create a meeting environment that encourages open dialogue.
● Ability to frame questions. Ability to think and inspire others to think through the written word.
● Ability to communicate remotely using all tools available, both high tech and low tech.
● Confidence and competence with technology and tools. Knowledge of EMS tools and their flexibility to match different meeting requirements. Typing skills.
● Knowledge of the group, their range of abilities and interests in the topics at hand.
● Knowledge of the subject matter and ability to recognize when a discussion is moving off track and away from the meeting objectives.
● Attention to the details of meeting set-up, logistics, project coordination, and team management.
● Confidence to admit when a meeting is not going well, regroup and adjust.

7C.4.2 Meeting Preparation: Planning the Agenda for a Distributed Meeting

There are many types of meetings that can successfully employ EMS tools in a distributed setting (see section 7C.5). Table 7C.5 uses the typical flow of a problem solving event to illustrate the level of planning and preparation a facilitator should undertake to design a good meeting agenda. The better a facilitator's planning, the more flexibility he or she will have in conducting the meeting and adjusting to unforeseen circumstances and results.

Table 7C.5 An Example of Planning and Preparation for a Distributed Meeting

Planning for a Problem Solving Meeting

Problem Solving Steps	Questions for Facilitator Working with the Client
1. Identify and define issues and problem statement	• What does the owner or client want to accomplish? What will a good result look like? What are the products of the meeting? What problem statement or questions will draw out the needed ideas or information?
2. Review background information	• Who are the participants and why are their contributions important? What does the owner know about the circumstances surrounding the problem? How much do participants know or need to know about the problem? What materials can be shared? How can we distribute this information and bring everyone up to speed?
3. Generate ideas and potential solutions	• What kind of ideas will we expect to see? How will we know if the discussion is on track? What level of detail do we need? How much time do we need? How much time do we have?
4. Clarify for understanding	• How can we build in check points and ask follow-up questions?
5. Prioritize and select ideas or solutions to pursue	• What prioritization or selection methods are appropriate? What criteria will we use? How to keep it simple? Should the client or participants select items to pursue further? How many should we select?
6. Identify pros and cons and any killer concerns	• What new questions should we ask to explore the selected issues? What constitutes a killer concern that will remove an item from further consideration?
7. Select an idea, solution, or course of action	• What prioritization or selection methods are appropriate? What criteria will we use? How precise an evaluation method do we need? Should the client or participants evaluate the options? How many should we select?
8. Develop an action plan and take responsibility	• Who should develop the action plan? What input do we need from participants for successful implementation? How to solicit volunteers or appropriately assign next steps? What is the time frame for implementation? How do we distribute/disseminate the results of the meeting?
9. Implement and check effectiveness against original issue or problem	• Did we meet the client's expectations? Did we meet the participants expectations? Were the solutions generated implemented? How effective were the agenda and tools in the problem solving process? What should we do differently next time?

7C.4.3 Meeting Preparation: How to Ask the Right Questions

Asking the right questions is critical to the success of a distributed meeting. Here are is a checklist of suggestions for facilitators.

✔ Know your subject matter, the range of ideas or information you expect, and the level of detail that you need.

✔ Provide examples, good and bad, of the kinds of information or ideas you are looking for.

✔ Test your questions on one or two participants ahead of time.

✔ Keep questions open-ended and at the same time focused and directed to the problem or issue at hand.

✔ Engage the participants in the questions with phrasing such as "How can we...," "What would you do if..."

✔ Ask for examples and explanations, ask participants to be specific and straightforward.

✔ Show participants how to use a headline to attract others to their ideas and then give the full detail.

✔ Use simple, agreed upon words and abbreviations to facilitate data search and sorting, for example: Mktg, Sales, F&A, HR, Manuf, or + for strength, - for weakness.

✔ Start with broad questions to test the range of possibilities. Ask follow-up questions to narrow the scope and focus discussion.

✔ Make sure participants have the needed background information to answer the questions. Let participants know why you are asking the questions. Provide context for the whole meeting and individual agenda items.

7C.4.4 Meeting Preparation: Attention to Logistics & Technology

One benefit of electronic and distributed meetings is that the facilitator no longer has to worry about room size, seating arrangements, flip charts and overhead projectors, room temperature, and the lunch menu. There are, however, several new logistical issues to remember, made more complicated by the distance of participants and the introduction of technology.

✔ Make sure everyone who you want to participate knows the schedule, start and end times for each agenda item, when they have flexibility, and when deadlines are tight.

✔ Make sure that people have enough quality time to spare at the points in the agenda when you need them.

✔ Send out an agenda, background documents to read, or work to prepare. Use e-mail and document sharing tools.

✔ Make sure you know where the owner or client for the meeting is going to be and how you can track them down to discuss the progress and outcomes of the meeting.

✔ Prearrange how participants will check in on changing meeting arrangements or instructions. Don't assume that they will follow instructions, check in and offer frequent reminders. Use your EMS tool as well as all other means available such as the phone, e-mail, and interoffice mail.

✔ Test the software and all the EMS tools you will be using before your first meeting.

✔ Ensure participants are comfortable and competent with the EMS tool and have the correct hardware and networking configurations. Provide a technical support contact.

✔ Set up dial-in or Internet capabilities for people who will be on the road and away from their desks.

7C.4.5 During a Meeting: Attention to Group Process and Emerging Results

As with any meeting, a facilitator needs to manage the mood and productivity swings of the group involved in a distributed electronic meeting. The usual body language signs and verbal cues are not available, so the facilitator must look for other ways to monitor the group process and emerging results. Inevitably, these tend to focus more on the content of the meeting output than the mood of participants.

✔ Check on participation, who has participated, and for how long. Instigate an electronic sign-in sheet or just ask people to let you know.

✔ Work with the owner or client to monitor contributions and determine if things are on track.

✔ Check in with a few participants and ask them how they think the meeting is progressing. Provide a means for participants to ask you questions and broadcast the responses.

✔ Check the output of the discussion topics. Do they have the breadth and depth expected?

✔ Read all the ideas and items that are generated every day. Keep on top of the meeting output and anticipate problems further down the agenda.

✔ Participate in the meeting yourself. Throw in provocative ideas and see what response you get.

✔ Fill in some of the gaps you see and ask participants to add the detail.

✔ Ask follow-up questions to clarify ideas or issues that you and the client do not understand.

✔ Adjust your time schedule if contributions progress quicker or slower than expected.

✔ Manage transitions between process steps. Let people know when to move on to the next activity. Declare an end to each step of the process as you move through the agenda.

✔ Let participants know where you are in the process and how things are going.

✔ Be prepared to stop and change course if the meeting is not achieving your objectives.

✔ Bring closure to the whole meeting. Work with the owner or client to summarize results, confirm decisions, and assign next steps. Ask the owner to provide feedback to participants.

7C.4.6 After a Meeting: Attention to Learning and Continuous Improvement

After each meeting, the facilitator must ensure that the data collected is handled correctly. Reflection on each event also provides an opportunity to learn and improve the effectiveness of the meeting design and tools for next time. Here are some suggestions to consider.

✔ Clean up the data, numbering, and organizing as appropriate.

✔ Print or export the meeting record and distribute to participants.

✔ Manage your data files and archives. Determine who owns the data and where is should reside to be available to those that need it. Are there any confidentiality issues to address?

✔ Check that action items were completed. Did you achieve the meeting objectives? If not why not?

✔ Ask for feedback from clients and participants.

✔ Use your EMS tool to set up a meeting evaluation topic. Keep a general EMS evaluation topic open and encourage participants from consecutive meetings to build up a learning database.

✔ Conduct a self-assessment of the meeting. Take notes for future meetings.

✔ Participate in a distributed electronic meeting yourself. Keep reminding yourself of what it feels like to be a participant working from your desktop or home office.

✔ Participate in news groups and professional associations to keep up-to-date on the latest meeting ideas and tools.

7C.4.7 Measuring Our Effectiveness as Facilitators

Measurement of our effectiveness as facilitators is useful for self-improvement and determining the value that we bring to our clients and the meeting process. We suggest establishing a measurement checklist as part of your meeting preparation and reviewing the results with your clients.

✔ Did the team/meeting achieve the desired outcomes?

✔ Was the client happy with the results?

✔ Which of the stated objectives did we exceed?

✔ Which of the state objectives did we not meet?

✔ What did participants have to say about the meeting format and EMS tools?

✔ Will participants come back for more?

✔ What did we accomplish in this meeting that we have not accomplished in other meetings?

✔ How well did the process flow work?

✔ How did the tools and technology assist or hinder the group productivity and effectiveness?

✔ Did we complete our tasks within the allotted time?

✔ What did the group accomplish because of my contributions as a facilitator?

✔ What could the group have accomplished without my facilitation?

✔ Will I get any repeat business?

✔ Will the client act as a referral for my services and tools?

7C.5 EXAMPLES AND APPLICATIONS

7C.5.1 When to Use EMS Distributed Meeting Tools

✔ To gather ideas before a face-to-face meeting to make better use of valuable time.

✔ When thorough data collection for a disperse group of contributors is critical.

✔ To document group discussions and decisions in a form that can be distributed using document handling and messaging tools.

✔ When there is a need to analyze or prioritize the information collected.

✔ To support ongoing work teams dealing with complex processes.

✔ To get difficult issues on the table.

✔ To manage work of dispersed team members.

✔ To avoid travel costs and scheduling difficulties.

7C.5.2 When Not to Use EMS Distributed Meeting Tools

✗ When the quantity of data that you need to collect doesn't warrant them.

✗ When relationship building is more important that working with the information.

✗ When you don't have a clear idea of your problem statement or purpose.

✗ When people are already in information or technology overload.

✗ When the technology will get in the way.

✗ When talking makes more sense.

✗ When you can't get all the people you need to participate on the same network.

7C.5.3 Work Process Improvement Team Example

"As Is" analysis, benchmarking, "To Be" design, testing, and implementation steps in a re-engineering project all require detailed data gathering and benefit from the input of a wide range of people directly and indirectly involved in the work process. EMS tools, both in a meeting room and distributed over a network, enable teams to gather and analyze work process improvement opportunities and solutions. EMS tools designed for the Web/Internet/intranet have particular flexibility to provide graphical interfaces, linkages to documents, and background information that facilitate data gathering.

Distributed EMS tools provide particular benefit by allowing cross-functional teams drawn from many parts of an organization and many distant locations to collaborate between conventional team meetings. Beyond sharing of messages and documents, team members can continue their idea generation and process analysis activities back at their local offices, including other workers as appropriate. Meetings can be held locally while working off a central database, building from one event to another, avoiding duplication of effort, and sharing ideas and information in real-time. Web-based EMS tools provide the additional opportunity to involve customers, suppliers, and other outside resources with access over the Internet and World Wide Web.

Distributed meetings work best with well-managed teams that have a strong commitment to their common goals, are well-coordinated in their distributed work activities, and have good communication mechanisms in place. Facilitators should first work on building a well-coordinated, well-focused team. They can then take advantage of EMS tools to take the team to an even higher level of productivity.

7C.5.4 Employee Survey Example

EMS tools designed for Internet or intranet have immediate application to employee surveys. Network compatibility allows for wide participation across an organization. Web-based tools provide the advantage of not having to distribute special software with survey participation via the standard Web-browers you are using for Internet or intranet access.

The voting functions of EMS tools allow participants to respond to specific questions and issues and for rapid tabulation of results. Beyond numerical ratings, EMS tools allow for commentary and detailed survey responses adding to the usefulness of the information collected. Responses can be anonymous and can be shared as soon as they are contributed.

7C.5.5 Procurement and Bid Evaluation Example

Procurement of large cost items or projects often involves complex and stringent bidding and evaluation processes. EMS tools have proven particularly useful in allowing the members of an evaluation board to independently review bids while building a common database of comments and evaluations. Evaluation remarks are readily categorized, for example, as major strengths and weaknesses, concerns, and questions. Voting tools provide numerical rating sheets and graphical displays of results.

In this kind of situation, EMS tools allow teams to document their work, facilitating group discussion, and provide a written record of their considerations. Distributed meeting tools enable team members to do detailed work at their own desks while sharing the results of their efforts. Team members are able to build off each others' work without needing to forward files and manage multiple versions of the same document.

7C.5.6 Marketing and Sales Example

Many tools have been developed to provide the remote sales representative with the information they need to sell their products. Tools are available to obtain detailed product information, to electronically check stock or order status, to place the order, and to maintain e-mail links with the regional or main sales office. These tools, however, do not address all of the needs of the remote or traveling sales representative. Meetings are still a vital information and experience sharing vehicle. Unfortunately, distance and time makes such meetings logistically difficult if not impossible.

EMS tools and distributed meetings provide a solution, bringing together representatives from around the world, from office, hotel room, and airplane. Team members can collaborate on a range of customer, market, and product problems and opportunities. Individual sales representatives and the sales manager can pose questions and issues to the group and receive an organized set of responses. Web-based EMS tools allow linkages to documents and information located elsewhere on the Internet or intranet. The benefit that team members receive from group problem solving with EMS tools encourages them to seek out opportunities to collaborate while on the road.

7C.6 FREQUENTLY ASKED QUESTIONS

Q How many people can participate in a distributed electronic meeting?

A The simple answer is that any number can participate within the constraints of the EMS software license, which may limit the number of seats at the meeting or the number of concurrent users (people participating at the same time). The number of people who should participate depends on the meeting objectives, the unique contributions different people can provide, and the extent of participation desired for purposes of buy-in and communication. Typical group size is in the range of four to twenty. For smaller groups, e-mail may be sufficient. For larger groups, survey formats or sub-groups may be appropriate. Forums held over several days or weeks may accommodate several hundred people.

Q How important are typing skills for full participation?

A EMS tools are keyboard tools and require participants to type. However, in the privacy of their offices, even the worst hunt and peck typists can participate and not be embarrassed. Much of the work in a meeting also involves reviewing and commenting upon other people's ideas, which involves more time reading and thinking than it does typing.

Q How long does it take to train to be a facilitator?

A Software vendors typically provide facilitator training for two or five days, depending on the experience level of the facilitator. Two days should be enough for experienced facilitators who are technically adept to get a working knowledge of an EMS tools and how to incorporate them into a facilitated meeting agenda. Beyond two days, we have found that it is helpful to allow facilitators to try out the technology on a friendly audience and practice with some simple meeting agendas. After that, they can return for advanced training in applying the tools to more complex meetings and problems.

Q Do you have to buy a whole system to use these tools? Are they available for rent?

A The latest Internet technology has made Web-server on-line conferencing services available. These services allow you to run trial meetings or rent a meeting space whenever you need it, avoiding set up and maintenance costs.

7C.6 CONCLUSIONS

The potential benefits of distributed meetings and electronic meeting systems are substantial in terms of increased participation, group productivity, and cost savings. Successful introduction requires careful attention to the many aspects of facilitation. Group behavior and readiness is as important as the technology tools that you choose.

Success of computer aided facilitation tools and techniques can be measured in several ways:

By the results achieved:

✔ Time saved, deadlines beaten

✔ Specific results of groups using EMS technology

✔ Collaboration and cooperation achieved among a diverse and distributed group of participants

✔ Acknowledgment by participants of specific outcomes accomplished

By usage:

✔ Number and variety of people and group using your facilities and desktop capabilities

✔ Number of teams incorporating desktop technology into their agendas

✔ Satisfaction index by clients and participants range and applicability of tools provided

✔ Creative ways found to use technology to improve team process and productivity

By availability and accessibility:

✔ Facilitators trained and available to teams and work groups

✔ Technology accessible for planned and ad hoc meetings

✔ Data files accessible and secure

BIBLIOGRAPHY

1. Csikszentmihalyi, M., *Flow, The Psychology Of Optimal Experience*, Harper Perennial, a division of Harper Collins Publishers, 1990.
2. Grenier, R., *Going Virtual: Moving Your Organization into the 21st Century*, Prentice Hall, 1995.
3. Holt, M. E., Kleiber, P. B., and Swenson, J. D., "The Changing Face of Evaluation in Distance Education," a paper presented at the International Evaluation Conference co-sponsored by the Canadian Evaluation Society, the American Evaluation Association, November 1-5, 1995, Vancouver, Canada.
4. Johansen, R., Sibbet, D., Benson, S., Martin, A., Mittman, R. and Saffo, P., *Leading Business Teams,* Addison-Wesley Publishing Company, 1991.
5. Katzenbach, J. R. and Smith, D. K., *The Wisdom of Teams,* Harper Business, a division of Harper Collins Publishers, 1993.
6. Mohrman, S. A., Cohen, S. A., and Mohrman, A. M., Jr., *Designing Team-Based Organizations, New Forms for Knowledge Work,* Jossey-Bass Publishers, 1995.
7. Moore, G. A., *Crossing the Chasm,* Harper Business, a division of Harper Collins Publishers, 1991.
8. Nonuka, I. and Takeuchi, H., *The Knowledge Creating Company,* Oxford University Press, 1995.
9. Rees, F., *How to LEAD Work Teams,* Pfeiffer & Company, 1991.
10. Schein, E. H., *Process Consultation, Lessons for Managers and Consultants,* Addison-Wesley Publishing Company, 1987.
11. Schrage, M., *No More Teams! Mastering the Dynamics of Creative Collaboration,* Currency Doubleday, 1995.

BIOGRAPHY

Julia Szerdy and Mike McCall are the founders of Facilitate.com, Inc., a firm specializing in
collaborative technology and facilitation. They have over 15 years of expertise in the area of
facilitation and have worked with executive level and employee teams to solve problems
ranging from strategy formulation and visioning to organization design and the re-engineering
of work processes. To assist them in their consulting, they designed a software application for
the collaborative work team environment. The application, called Facilitate.com 4.0, is a
multi-platform program that can be used in an electronic meeting room and in a distributed
desktop environment or on the World Wide Web. Since its initial design in 1992, they have
transformed Facilitate.com 4.0 into a commercial offering, which they use with their clients
and market to corporate, government, and educational institutions. A partial list of their
clients includes: the California Public Utilities Commission, EDS, KPMG, NASA, National
Semiconductor, U.S. Navy, Sprint Telecommunications, Texas A&M, The University of
Georgia, Unocal, and the U.S. Federal Government. You may reach them by phone at (800)
423-8890, by e-mail at Julia@Facilitate.com and Mike@Facilitate.com respectively, or at
www.facilitate.com on the World Wide Web.

The Virtual Office Work-Space: GroupSystems Web and Case Studies

Jay F. Nunamaker, Jr.
Robert O. Briggs
Nicholas C. Romano, Jr.
Daniel Mittleman
Center for the Management of Information

University of Arizona

Group Support technology is changing the way we work. The benefits from using computer supported collaboration techniques are so great that these changes must happen. Yet the changes will not be easy. New technologies can cause organizational power shifts, which in turn engender user resistance. Those who embrace change and master group support technology will develop strategic advantages over those who do not. This chapter describes the use of GS_{Web} (GroupSystems for the World Wide Web) technology to support virtual work teams, that is groups of people who collaborate although they are separated in space and time. We then describe a number of case studies drawn from ten years of field experience with GroupSystems. Both successes and failures are discussed because we have learned as much from what does not work as from what works well. The primary focus of the cases is on ways that GroupSystems can improve productivity of the individual, group (team), and the organization.

7D.1 GROUP SYSTEMS DEFINED

The GroupSystems approach uses information technology to enable teams of people to work in concert toward a mutual goal. Its aim is to improve the effectiveness, efficiency, and satisfaction of those involved in group activities. Because everyone using GroupSystems can "talk at once" (if the communication is synchronous), by typing ideas into a network of computer workstations, the system changes the way people interact. As their contributions are made immediately available to other participants, no one has to wait for a turn to speak, possibly forgetting what he or she was going to say.

Participants may contribute their ideas anonymously. Anonymity encourages group members to offer novel-but-embryonic ideas, unpopular ideas, or politically risky ideas they might otherwise be reluctant to reveal to peers or superiors [6,2].

GroupSystems consists of a suite of software collaboration tools. Each tool guides the team through a stage in the decision process. The electronic brainstorming tool encourages a broad discussion of ideas, whereas the idea organizing tool supports a process for rapidly reaching agreement on what are key issues, and electronic polling tools help a group identify areas of consensus and disagreement. Other tools in GroupSystems include a group outlining tool, group writing tools, and multi-criteria decision making tools. GroupSystems collaboration is much more than brainstorming and voting.

7D.2 GROUPSYSTEMS WEB: GS$_{WEB}$ AS A COLLABORATION ENVIRONMENT

Anytime/anyplace interaction for decision making and communication is what everyone wants in today's fast-paced world, but how do we make it possible? Lotus Notes and CollabraShare address several related issues, such as data sharing, but there's much more to interacting collaboratively. To accomplish real work, one needs a team agenda, plus processes and structures to guide the interactions of a group. Why are structure and process so important? Because without them, chaos results. A look at the results of discussion databases and user group discussion sessions reveals no conclusions, no convergence—merely a plethora of disjointed ideas. Certainly, no decisions nor recommendations emerge. In order for decisions to result, both process and structure must be provided to move in an orderly fashion toward a mutual goal.

Every executive seems to want to reduce the time spent by personnel meeting face-to-face in the same location. This means they want distributed anytime, anyplace activities on any platform so they can put action teams together to solve problems from all parts of the world (refer to Fig. 7D.1.). What are the advantages of such a virtual work-place? To start with, it allows work to be accomplished independent of any participant's specific time constraints and schedule. It provides for simultaneous interaction of local and remote teams, as well as acquisition of rapid feedback on routed material and documents that must be reviewed by every member of the group.

Distributed work groups reduce or eliminate the need to establish every type of expertise at each site or location and experience improved information exchange. Instead of attending face-to-face meetings or video conferences, team members can work from their desktops and focus their efforts on areas of interest, skipping those in which they have no interest. They can ask questions as they occur and answer others' questions when they have the desired information. A team is no longer tied to a physical meeting environment and will have the broader participation made possible by special process support features such as anonymity, short-notice participation, and freedom to work on activities on their own time schedules from wherever they are when the need arises.

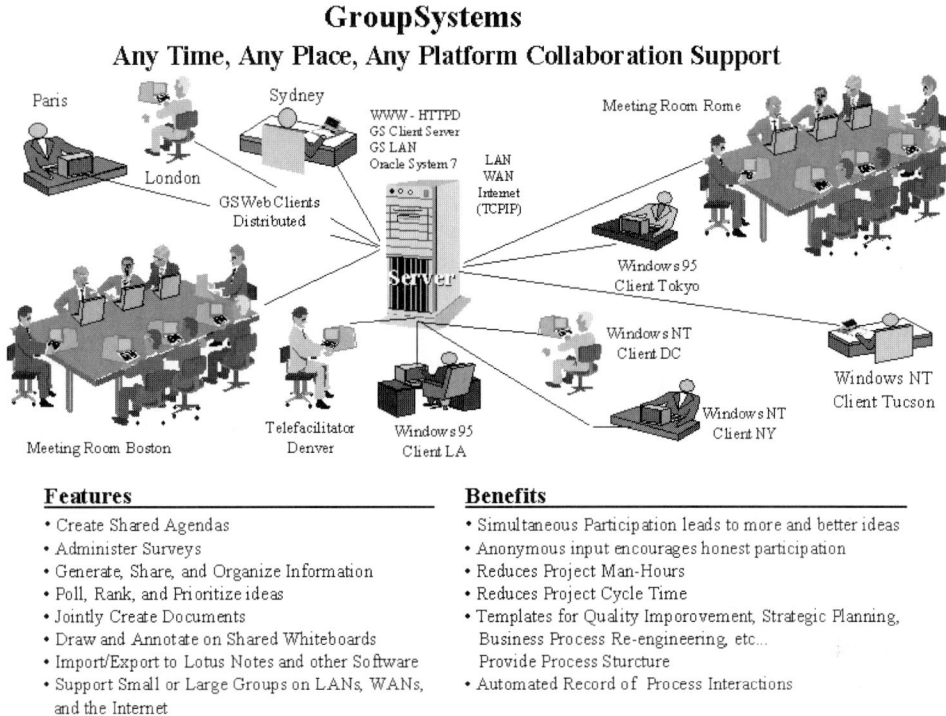

GroupSystems

Any Time, Any Place, Any Platform Collaboration Support

Features

- Create Shared Agendas
- Administer Surveys
- Generate, Share, and Organize Information
- Poll, Rank, and Prioritize ideas
- Jointly Create Documents
- Draw and Annotate on Shared Whiteboards
- Import/Export to Lotus Notes and other Software
- Support Small or Large Groups on LANs, WANs, and the Internet

Benefits

- Simultaneous Participation leads to more and better ideas
- Anonymous input encourages honest participation
- Reduces Project Man-Hours
- Reduces Project Cycle Time
- Templates for Quality Imporovement, Strategic Planning, Business Process Re-engineering, etc... Provide Process Sturcture
- Automated Record of Process Interactions

Fig. 7D.1 GroupSystems Any Time, Any Place, Any Platform Collaboration Support

7D.2.1 What Do We Do in the Virtual Office Work-space?

A wide range of activities can take place in the virtual office work-space. We can get together to set priorities, generate new ideas, discuss ideas, and explore in depth the ones we decide are important. Ideas can be organized and then evaluated. Leading to the development of policies, plans, and documents.

Why don't more organizations and people work in a distributed mode of operation? For one thing, it is uncharted territory. People don't know how to work asynchronously because they are used to resolving issues face to face. People working in a distributed world often do not become adequately engaged in the process. They become observers rather than participants. They often complain, "Am I the only one here?" They experience a low sense of presence and little or no peer pressure or synergy from other members of the group.

The trade-off is associated with the way virtual interactions (VI) differ from face-to-face (FTF) interactions. FTF sessions are characterized by a higher sense of community than VI sessions, in which distractions that occur in the office—need to take a phone call, respond to a fax, or read a brief report—limit the time available to focus on the task at hand. Inevitably, the direction of the agenda in a FTF meeting will change. Visual signals and cues prompt group members to execute new agenda items. These signals cannot occur in a virtual interaction and the group may go marching down, what turns out to be, the wrong path. It is much harder to observe the need for directional changes in a distributed mode because there are no gestures, no eye contact, no body language, no pointing, no rolling eyes, and no handshake or pat on the back. However, these problems can be overcome by using technology to support synchronous dynamics and providing view matching (WYSIWIS), hand-gesturing and pointing, commands for leading and following, pointers for seek-and-match capability, and marker flags to identify locations on a diagram.

One tool will not do it all. Moving beyond data sharing means having access to tools that allow teams to categorize and converge on key issues, evaluate alternatives and make choices, and in the end establish a shared perspective which the group accepts. Since there are very few procedures or protocols for working asynchronously at a distance, those who want to work effectively in a distributed mode must be bold and daring. They must be willing to try a number of different approaches, some of which will fail, and to recognize that one can learn as much from failures as from successes.

7D.2.2 Creating a Virtual Office Work-space

The cases described later in this chapter illustrate the use of technology by teams whose members were working side-by-side, in the same place, at the same time. However, technology for the virtual office work-space—GS$_{Web}$ for geographically and temporarily separated teams—is already here. No longer science fiction, it allows people in different rooms, in different offices, in different cities, and on different continents to work together productively without coming face to face. Pioneers in the virtual workspace report both stunning successes and fantastic failures. So how is it possible to boldly pioneer the virtual frontier without falling into the cyber-quicksand or having an electronic train wreck?

This is the tough question that most "groupware" developers avoid, as evidenced by the fact that current applications of distributed collaboration are more or less limited to news groups, threaded discussions, chat windows, and e-mail. These are useful technologies, but the real needs of distributed teams require much more, and much more is possible. The applications mentioned represent asynchronous information exchange, but they do little to support convergence on key issues, developing and measuring consensus, or joint creation of an end product. A GroupSystems interaction, on the other hand, can focus and structure the efforts of dozens of people through all the phases of problem-solving and enable them to actually accomplish work during the process.

Distributed collaboration requires a complex set of tools, structures, and support to assist the human interactions required to accomplish goals and complete work. Team members must be able to organize and synthesize ideas, generate and evaluate proposed alternatives, plan a course of action, and carry out that plan. Additionally, their environment must support meta-information like date-and-time stamps, authorship, and ownership (refer to Fig. 7D.2.).

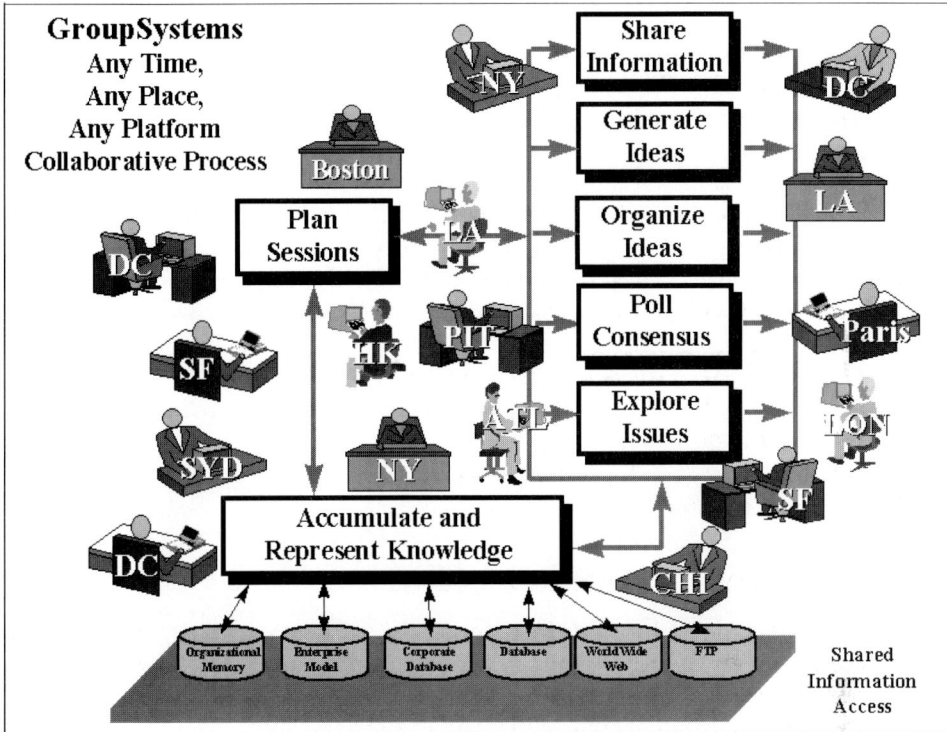

Fig. 7D.2 GroupSystems Any Time, Any Place, Any Platform Collaboration Process

7D.2.3 GS_Web Distributed Collaborative Scenario

The scenario below describes a team using GS_Web technology in concert with desktop video teleconferencing to support a rapid response collaborative effort for a geographically distributed team. The scenario illustrates the value a team can derive from a full-featured virtual workplace.

> Nicholas, the CEO of an aggressively growing software firm, has just learned of a new competitor that poses a substantial threat to his company. This competitor plans to ship its product in a few weeks, so it has become clear that Nicholas's company will have to change its entire strategy very quickly if it is to meet the competition. Nicholas's response must be quick and decisive. He wants an immediate consultation with his board of directors, whose next regularly scheduled meeting is a month-and-a-half away and whose members are scattered around the globe, attending to other business.

Usually the board's development of a new strategic direction requires several meetings over weeks or months. This time, however, Nicholas and the board must gather, organize information, evaluate their alternatives, and plan their actions as soon as possible. They must involve technical and marketing experts to ensure success.

Step One—Preplanning and Goal Setting:

Nicholas establishes a GS$_{Web}$ folder that he names, "Emergency Strategic Session-Code Red." He enters a problem description and defines the team's goal: the "development of a strategic action plan." He selects the people who are to participate, and within seconds the system sends them automatic notification of the calling of an emergency session, using e-mail, beeper, and voice mail as appropriate for contacting each member.

Next, he maps the process the team will use to create a strategic plan. He sets up several collaborative activities on the team agenda (refer to Fig. 7D.3.).

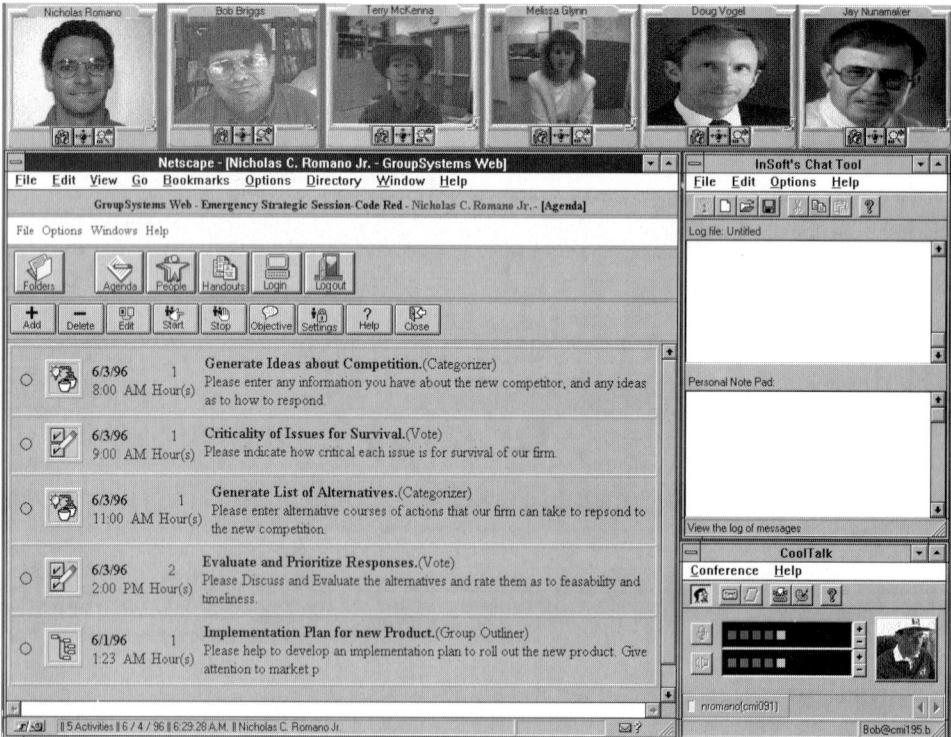

Fig. 7D.3 GS$_{Web}$ Team Agenda Combined with Video-Teleconferencing to Support the Strategic Planning Session for the Board of Directors

Step Two—Distributed Collaboration:

*When the group convenes, members are linked by a desktop video conferencing system and by GS*_{Web}*. Each participant has a set of video windows on his or her computer screen, showing the images of the others. Further, each has the GS*_{Web}* virtual office work-space open. Additionally, they have a chat window facility available for private side-bar conversations.*

After explaining the problem, Nicholas starts an idea generation activity for the group. He asks the members to enter any information they have about the new competitor, and any ideas they have about possible responses. New Topics are highlighted with exclamation points and the number of total comments, along with those that are new, are displayed for each discussion so that team members know what they have already seen and where to focus their attention for new information. As the work progresses, Bob notices that some key themes emerge in the electronic discussion. Bob invites Nicholas to a side-bar chat discussion and suggests that they allow participants to create electronic categories or "buckets" for each key issue. Nicholas gives the team privileges to add categories, and copy ideas, and comments to them. The participants move or copy relevant ideas into appropriate categories to organize their thoughts into meaningful groupings (see Fig. 7D.4.).

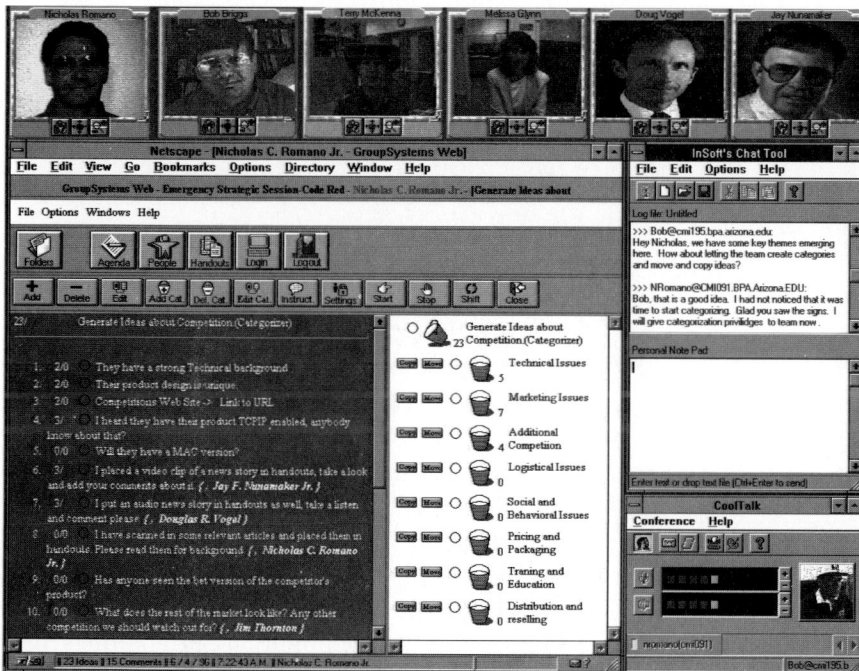

Fig. 7D.4 GS_{Web} Categorization Tool Used for Idea Generation and Organization

The team finishes its first idea generation session with a set of key issues supported by loosely organized comments. Nicholas moves the list of issues into an electronic voting tool and asks each participant to indicate how critical each issue is for the survival of the firm. Team members spend a few minutes rating the issues. Then the team discusses the results. There is broad agreement on some issues, but there is sharp division on others. Nicholas moves the divisive issues into a topic-commenting tool, and the team members go on-line to discuss the pros and cons of each issue and develop detailed arguments for their individual stances.

The team goes through two more vote-and-discuss cycles. Anonymity empowers people to share previously private information. Fundamental assumptions surface and are examined by the group. As the issues are clarified, the group moves toward consensus. A final vote reveals the group's readiness to move forward.

Nicholas has scanned in relevant articles from two trade journals to share with the group. He places them on an electronic handouts list. At the click of a button the members can read the articles. Telecursors let them gesture to one another and highlight key points in the articles as they discuss them. Nicholas sets the system options so that additional members can add relevant reference materials as they become available. A video clip of a news story about the new product comes from Jay, the board chairman. Members view the clip on their local workstations. Links to three home sites let the team view Web-based information about the competition. Finally, Doug adds a link to a streaming audio news story and a press release about the competitor's new product.

Next, Nicholas has the team generate a list of alternatives for the company. The team quickly lists dozens of possible responses. Now, Nicholas invites technical experts to join the session and give expert advice as to the feasibility and timeliness of the alternatives. New cycles of discussion and voting surface the possible implications of each course of action. Based on the information generated, the team finally selects a course of action. Nicholas moves the team into a shared outlining tool where they begin to plan implementation. Marketing groups are invited to provide appropriate feedback on how to position the new product. The entire GroupSystems Collaboration takes only seven hours, yet more is accomplished than at a typical board meeting. Within two days, new policies are sent throughout the company. The marketplace battle is joined. Nicholas's company will respond before the competitor even brings its product to the marketplace.

This GroupSystems Collaboration differs from traditional face-to-face meetings along several dimensions. First, the collaboration occurs in several different physical locations at once. Second, multiple combinations of channels provide support for information transfer and layered communications. Third, participants may contribute to the session either synchronously or asynchronously—sometimes even checking in and out of the session independent of other participant attendance. Fourth, participants may attend multiple collaborations at once on separate computer windows. Fifth, GroupSystems and artificial intelligence software help to structure the collaborative process and sometimes even suggest information relationships independent of human participant contributions. Sixth, the session contains a loosely defined temporal beginning and end. Finally, participants are saved several days that might have been wasted traveling to and from traditional face-to-face meetings.

7D.2.4 Technology for the Virtual Office Work-space

Until the past three years, GroupSystems was used primarily to support face-to-face meetings. GroupSystems was LAN based and bringing in remote participants required technical effort. Now, GroupSystems has moved to the World Wide Web and contains support for distributed teams. Researchers at the University of Arizona have now produced GS_{Web}, the first full-featured Internet-based group support system. Using GS_{Web}, team members working on many different kinds of computers around the world can exchange information and deliberate, working together toward their joint goals.

Participants access GS_{Web} via a standard World Wide Web browser, which provides platform independence. Participants in the same session may be using IBM PCs, Apples, DEC, or SUN workstations. They may use Windows 3.11, 95, or NT; OS/2, System 7, UNIX, or any other operating system that supports a Web browser and all can become a window to the team's GS_{Web} virtual office work-space.

The Technical Details

The GS_{Web} System is based on a special set of integrated HTML frames that act in concert to produce a truly interactive application space that functions as closely as possible to the original GroupSystems environment. The frames are generated dynamically through executable scripts and nested in several layers through a technique called "incursive frame nesting," especially developed for this purpose. A click of a button may launch one or several executable scripts on behalf of the browser client or may cause client side inter-frame communications for error checking and interface updates. This metaphor encapsulates the various hierarchical lists of information within the application space. Additional informational HTML pages and other types of browser viewable objects can also be encapsulated within GS_{Web} or they can be brought up in a new browser window that overwrites the entire GS_{Web} application space.

GS_{Web} has the potential for anytime, anyplace, any-platform sessions among large groups with minimal setup required. There is nothing for the client side to download or install except for a World Wide Web browser. Users simply type in the URL for the server and log into the system with a user name and password. This saves both time and hard-disk space for the user. Another advantage is that maintenance upgrades occur in only one place, at the server. The clients do not have to update anything in order for additional tools or features to be added.

Project Orientation with Folders

The fundamental organizational unit in the GS_{Web} virtual office work-space is known as a folder. Each folder contains all the necessary support for communication and deliberation for a single project. GS_{Web} supports three types of users: administrator, owners, and members. The administrator creates user accounts and passwords and has full control over the system. Owners can create folders and invite others to participate in them. Members cannot create their own folders but can only join those to which they are invited by owners. An owner can also be a member of folders created by others. Thus, the system provides for easy creation and modification of ad hoc teams.

Just-in-time Interface

GS_{Web} uses a set of interface objects to allow for incremental sophistication of the interface. Users are presented with only the options and privileges they need in order to support the task in which they are currently engaged. The owner of a folder can hide all other controls and interface features, which reduces perceptual and cognitive load for users. This just-in-time interface allows a team leader to focus and direct group dynamics, moving the group towards its goal with concerted effort on the specific task at hand.

The GS_{Web} Collaborative Environment

GS_{Web} contains both a suite of electronic meeting tools and a set of components, or building blocks, that allow developers to create new tools quickly. These are briefly described below:

The Collaborative Engine

A set of commonly used routines and utilities for coding, testing, and documenting World Wide Web HTML based electronic meeting systems software tools. These routines include callable forms based parsing routines, list building modules, HTML interface generation routines, inter-frame communication modules, data storage routines, list display option routines, error and warning routines, list layout routines, status bar messaging routines, etc.

Control of the Process and the Interface

The GS_{Web} version of the GroupSystems Control Menu adds new functionality to the various levels of control and extends to users a degree of control that was lacking in the original. This extended control over the granularity of task decomposition and the look and feel of the interface help to overcome many of the problems associated with keeping groups and individuals focused throughout distributed sessions.

Electronic Discussion System

A special environment to allow a developer to create tools that logically partition World Wide Web space into multiple intranets that are subnets of the Internet and become the folders in the GS_{Web} virtual office work-space.

GS$_{Web}$ Administrator

Special tools and routines to create and control user accounts on the Electronic Discussion System. The administrator can add new users, delete users, change passwords, monitor system usage, etc.

People

Tools for populating folders and inviting users to participate in specific activities. These tools interact with virtual business cards, discussed next, to help users sense who else is in the environment and avoid feeling all alone in cyberspace.

Virtual Business Cards

An index of personal information cards for GS$_{Web}$ users. Virtual business cards can contain data in various formats including but not limited to text, audio, video, graphics, hyperlinks, and automatic e-mail links. These cards help folder owners decide who they should invite to a session and also give some sense of having actually "met" or "seen" others with whom they interact in a virtual session.

Folder

A virtual office work-space to contain the collaborative tools and activities and the shared information for a single project. High level tasks are broken down into individual steps in the team process through an activity list known as an agenda. Each folder can have sub-folders that represent sub-tasks within the overall task associated with that folder. Folders are populated with people, who are then invited to participate in the session at varying levels.

Using the components of the collaborative engine described above, University of Arizona researchers have built the following collaborative tools into the GS$_{Web}$ environment:

Handouts

A list of shared reference documents provided by team members for the rest of the group. Once a document has been placed on the handouts list, it is available to all participants in that folder. These shared reference materials may be in several formats, including but not limited to, text, audio, video, graphics, and hyperlinks. Users can upload files of various data formats with the click of a button and a browse feature lets them select the correct file.

Electronic Brainstorming (EBS)

A tool to support rapid generation of ideas by a large group. EBS encourages a group to diverge farther and farther afield from conventional patterns of thinking in search of as many new and unique ideas as possible in a short period of time.

Idea Organizer—Categorizer

A tool that structures and focuses group effort toward rapidly identifying and exploring the key issues raised in electronic brainstorming sessions.

Topic Commenter

A tool that encourages in-depth, detailed exploration of a bounded set of key issues.

Vote

Allows rapid polling by multiple methods to measure consensus and focus subsequent discussion and effort.

7D.2.5 Total Collaboration Through Systems Integration

Earlier, we stated that one tool will not do it all. Teams working together will often need additional channels of communication such as video, audio, sidebar or chat discussions, and even shared drawing space, especially when they are working in a synchronous mode. GS_{Web} is designed to provide the tools, the structure, and the process support to guide teams through collaborative interactions. The World Wide Web browsers are beginning to integrate complimentary groupware features that provide integral communications infrastructure components. Today, Netscape Navigator 3.0 includes a separate application, Insoft's Cool Talk, for audio, chat, and a shared whiteboard. Future versions will have these communications infrastructure components integrated within the browser. Eventually, Netscape Navigator will also include video. Intel's latest Proshare system includes both small room and auditorium work-space environments that will bring video into the integrated virtual office workspace and help to provide a sense of presence in the same room during a collaboration. These infrastructure communications components, when logically integrated with GS_{Web}, will offer a collaborative environment in which teams can accomplish work more efficiently and effectively and allow the involvement of key individuals that could not be involved in a constructive way without this new technology. The technological components for the virtual office work-space, described in the earlier scenario, exist and the challenge for today is to logically integrate them. The keys to success lie in research and development of the core components of the virtual office work-space and the interfaces needed for their integration and coordination. The virtual office work-space will require systems integration of the various components to provide an environment for total collaboration.

7D.3 GROUPSYSTEMS CASE STUDIES

Early GroupSystems work focused on improving the productivity of face-to-face collaboration and addressed the dynamics of traditional group work that were already well understood. The problems of conventional face-to-face interactions were clear, trying to explain asynchronous interactions was impossibly difficult 10 years ago. The first field trials of GroupSystems took place at the Oswego, NY, plant of IBM Corporation in 1986 [8]. In a year-long study, 30 groups used Group-Systems, developed at the University of Arizona, to solve problems in production-line quality. Teams using the technology saved an average of 50 percent in labor costs over those using conventional methods. They also reduced the elapsed time from the beginning to the end of their projects by an average of 91 percent. The results were so dramatic that they were suspected of being anomalous, a fluke of the circumstances surrounding the study, so a second year-long study was conducted at six other IBM sites, each with a different set of business problems. In the second study, which tracked more than 50 groups, average labor costs were reduced by 55 percent and elapsed times for projects of all types were reduced an average of 90 percent [3]. IBM now has more than 120 collaborative installations and the number continues to grow.

In 1991, Boeing Corporation ran an independent study to determine whether there was a good business case for the use of GroupSystems. Over the course of a year, the company carefully tracked the results of 64 groups that were using the technology to define requirements for the shop floor of the soon-to-be-built 777 aircraft. The groups used GroupSystems for problem definition, alternative generation and evaluation, implementation planning, and documentation of group outcomes. The result was an average labor savings of 71 percent and an average reduction of elapsed times for projects of 91 percent. A conservative evaluation of the return on investment for the pilot project was 170 percent the first year [7].

Besides finding quantitative benefits, the IBM and Boeing studies documented improvements in the quality of results and the satisfaction levels of the participants. Since these studies, other organizations have conducted independent evaluations of the benefits of GroupSystems. The US Army reported a total savings of $1 million in eight 1-week sessions to design a new Army-wide personnel tracking system. BellCore realized a 66 percent reduction in labor costs for teams using the technology. The Army National Guard saved over 70 percent in labor costs and 90 percent in project elapsed time over three information systems documentation writing projects.

7D.3.1 Working Together—Not Planning Work for Others

In 1993, the Danish Government decided to hold an electronic conference of more than one hundred of the country's leading citizens—high officials and captains of industry, leading journalists and academics. Their mission: to formulate an overall Danish policy for Information Technology, to prepare for the next century. All the attending luminaries wanted a chance to speak, but they had not come only to be heard. They all wanted to guide the outcome, but they had not come just to recommend directions for a year-long effort. Their goal was to stimulate national discussion, to identify the possibilities, and to actually draft a policy for public consideration. A comprehensive policy, in just three days.

How could such a thing be done? How could one hundred people even be heard in three days, much less jointly produce a document? Under ordinary circumstances, the task they had set could not be accomplished, yet they did it with aplomb. No shouting matches. No long-winded speeches. In fact, more than half the time, no one was speaking at all. They were using GroupSystems.

The conference was charged with excitement as it began, with participants spread across seven rooms, each dedicated to exploring a different theme. Each participant sat before a laptop computer running on a network with special group support software designed to focus and structure the group's efforts. In each room, a task leader gave the group its particular objective. Then, everyone began talking at once, although the only sound to be heard was the clicking of keyboards. All the participants contributed simultaneously by typing ideas into the network. The system immediately made those ideas available to the rest of the participants. In a little more than an hour the participants had presented and discussed every notion they could think of. They had generated more than 4000 lines of comments. Using GroupSystems, it had taken no more time to hear from 100 people than it would have taken to hear from one or two persons participating in a conventional conference.

Because the system passed the ideas around so quickly, participants shook one another loose from familiar patterns of thinking. They ranged farther and farther afield, searching for new and unique ideas. But what does a group do with that much free-form text? It hardly constitutes a finished document. Working in parallel, the participants browsed the discussion material to identify key issues that had emerged. These they posted to a public electronic list. Using an electronic voting tool, team members expressed their opinions about the relative importance of each identified issue. Naturally, there was diversity of opinion on many of the ideas. This, in turn, led to several rounds of focused on-line discussions and voting about several of the key issues, moving the group toward consensus.

Next, the team moved the key issues they had selected, and their accompanying discussion, into a session relying on a group outlining tool, which helped them organize the ideas into a draft document. They finished their work by using a group writing tool.

This case clearly demonstrates how group support technology is fundamentally changing the way we work. A decade ago, it would have been unthinkable that one hundred relative strangers could write a large document in three days. They might have gathered to discuss how to plan a study on how to get the work done. Now, they simply had met to do the work by taking advantage of group support systems (GroupSystems).

7D.4 CULTURAL CHANGES

While many organizations have documented the financial benefits of tools, bottom-line benefits sometimes are not sufficient to motivate permanent adoption of the technology. One heavy manufacturing firm had documented seven-figure bottom-line benefits from the use of GroupSystems. Estimates of the return on investment (ROI) for the project rose to more than 600 percent during the second year. No one disputed the results, and yet at the end of the second year, the project was terminated, and it was nearly three years before another group attempted to use GroupSystems.

Several political problems had developed around the use of the GroupSystems. First, the people involved decided to use the tools in a way that significantly changed the balance of power within the groups. Throughout the history of the company, the senior engineers had absolute authority and autonomy when designing aircraft facilities. The decision was made to include many other stakeholders in the design process. This new approach brought input from many perspectives. The senior engineers were not ready to accept the substantial cultural shift represented by the inclusive design approach. Second, the people who introduced the GroupSystems to the company were not part of the engineering team; they were an internal group of business consultants. Some members of the engineering group regarded the consultants as interfering outsiders even though they were employees of the same firm. Finally, the corporate structure had been changed near the end of the project. The internal consultants were reassigned from their centralized group to a number of locations in the field. Thus, no center of competence remained to support the fledgling GroupSystems project, and so it was canceled.

An important lesson learned during this case is that powerful stakeholders must participate in the planning for early GroupSystems sessions. Busy, powerful people are tempted to delegate GroupSystems planning to others, but choices that appear arbitrary to others may turn out to be critically negative to the stakeholders. GroupSystems is neutral with respect to power shifts. The tools can be used in ways that reinforce the current structure or in ways that create dramatic power shifts. Sometimes a shift is desirable, but changes in power can cause resistance. These issues must be carefully weighed or the benefits of the technology to the organization may be lost.

7D.4.1 GroupSystems Training Must Be Ongoing

A number of organizations have had difficulties maintaining a center of GroupSystems competence for a very different reasons than the aircraft company mentioned above. As people begin to use an GroupSystems to make those around them more productive, the value and visibility of knowledgeable Group-Systems personnel rise rapidly, and they are often quickly promoted, leaving no one with the skills to run the system. One solution to the problem is to make sure that several apprentice facilitators are always in training so that a promotion doesn't strip the company of its GroupSystems expertise. A general in the Marine Corps adopted quite a different strategy: He insisted on being the first person trained with GroupSystems and ran all the early sessions himself. He reasoned that no one would be able to claim GroupSystems was too hard to learn. "After all," he quipped, "if the general can do it, anybody can do it." Others in his command soon acquired the skills, and GroupSystems expertise spread throughout his organization. Minor changes in personnel could therefore neither disrupt nor terminate the use.

7D.4.2 Instilling Group Values Reduces Conflicts

GroupSystems technology can help reduce conflicts between leadership styles. In one situation, a highly autocratic man, who considered himself to be very democratic, used weekly 2 1/2 hour planning meetings to substitute his own agenda for contributions offered by his staff. When his superiors recognized the problem and decided to try using GroupSystems to alter his management style, staff members were enthusiastic about the results, although he was not. Ultimately he decided to abandon the system. When the staff, supported by top management, refused to let him, group morale soared and the team's activities prospered.

7D.4.3 Responding to Stakeholder Concerns

GroupSystems can also be used to identify stakeholders in a project and reveal underlying assumptions. When a national library attempted to develop a computer system, a team of representatives from different departments tried and failed to agree on a shared vision of the project.

After the team leader decided to use an electronic stake-holder and assumption-surfacing tool, it became apparent that both the departments and the computer group had unrealistic expectations. Heated discussions conducted through use of the GroupSystems tools led to common understanding and a shared vision. GroupSystems allowed them to share critical information and correct mistaken assumptions.

7D.4.4 Keeping Criticism Constructive

When they first hear about anonymous input, some people express concern that the discussion will quickly degenerate into "flaming" sessions where participants exchange personal invectives, four-letter words, and slanderous epithets. In tens of thousands of sessions in business and government organizations, however, not a single instance of such disintegration has been documented.

This does not mean, however, that people are not critical in GroupSystems collaborations, they are. Participants often raise issues that would never come out in face-to-face discussions. There is less sting in an anonymous electronic criticism than in a direct rebuke during a face-to-face meeting because the screen buffers negative emotions that may accompany such criticism. Since no one knows the source of a particular idea, people criticize the idea rather than the person who presented it. Even so, egos may get bruised and people may have great difficulty dealing with honest feedback.

For instance, after the feedback on a reorganization plan had been shared in a traditional manner (without use of GroupSystems), the president of one high-tech company was told that there were problems with the plan but that the staff could handle them. In a GroupSystems session, however, he found out what his management team really thought. During the discussion, his staff responded both verbally, as in conventional meetings, and anonymously, by entering comments into their workstations. Everyone started typing at once. A list of ideas scrolled down the large overhead screen behind the podium. Rapid-fire key clicks were an indicator of the energy that the session generated. People suggested options and argued over alternatives, inspiring one another to think in new and sometimes unexpected ways. But it was through GroupSystems that negative comments emerged: "The new plan doesn't stand a chance. It addresses the wrong issues entirely." "Once we've spent all the money to do this, the real problems will still exist, only worse." "We're way off-center with this one." After 40 minutes, the president was baffled. "We've been working on this plan for a year. Why didn't you people tell me this before? What do you think we should do now?"

Anonymity may also encourage group members to view their own ideas more objectively and to see criticism as a signal to suggest other ideas. Sam Eichenfield, president and CEO of FINOVA Corporation said, "I wasn't as uncomfortable when I saw someone being critical of someone else's idea because I thought nobody's being embarrassed here at all."

A Hughes Aircraft manger said, "I noticed that if someone criticized an idea of mine, I didn't get emotional about it." "I guess when you are face to face and everyone hears the boss say, 'You are wrong!,' it's a slap to you, not necessarily to the idea."

Despite the safe haven it provides for most participants, GroupSystems isn't always so comfortable for the leader of a project or enterprise. Sometimes it takes courage for a manager to deal with the issues that surface in an anonymous session. It's hard to learn to deal with unpleasant input, but if problems lie buried for too long, they may become intractable.

In a rare incident, the founder of a very successful medical technology firm called together key personnel from multiple levels in the organization for a GroupSystems session. Thirty minutes into the meeting he turned red in the face and stood up. Pounding a fist on his PC for emphasis, he shouted, "I want to know who put in the comment on the problem with the interface for the new system. We're not leaving this room until I know who made that statement!" He glared around the room waiting for a response. Everyone greeted his outburst with silence.

After a week's reflection he returned sheepishly to the group and said, "I had no idea there was trouble. I guess I'm more out of touch than I ought to be. Let's try again."

7D.4.5 Putting Politics into Perspective

Anonymity reduces political clout. Ideas can be considered on their merits rather than on their source. It is human nature to view problems from one's own perspective but this can harm a project or enterprise. Engineers can be expected to see engineering solutions, sales people to see marketing solutions, and production people to see manufacturing solutions. GroupSystems teams are likely to benefit from the shared vision of problems and solutions fostered by anonymity.

When, shortly after the fall of the Iron Curtain, the newly elected president of Slovenia and his cabinet faced the task of redesigning their economy from scratch, they were able to use an electronic brainstorming tool to separate ideas from old political rivalries, and argue the merits of each suggestion purely on its content. Slovenia now has a thriving and growing economy.

GroupSystems converts negative comments to positive influences. Groups that are allowed to make only positive comments tend to stop looking for solutions after having identified only a few. On the other hand, when people are allowed to criticize ideas anonymously, they are more likely to recognize that they may not have found the best answer right off the bat. They continue to search for solutions until they have exhausted more possibilities. [2].

7D.4.6 Advantages of Electronic Voting

With increasing emphasis on participative management, the need for managers to create and measure consensus is growing. Electronic voting tools offer advantages over conventional voice or paper-ballot methods of voting. Traditional voting usually decides a matter once and for all. Since electronic voting tends to inspire a "vote early, vote often" approach and because it is so fast, teams can use electronic voting to measure consensus and focus subsequent discussion. It may therefore be more accurately described as polling rather than voting. Not only can it shorten discussions but it can also clarify communication, focus discussion, reveal patterns of consensus, and stimulate thinking. The following case studies illustrate some of these benefits.

7D.4.7 Inspiring Confidence

A management crisis loomed for a major telecommunications company after 39 senior managers had wrangled for six months about the rankings of 89 technical researchers and a new vice president had rejected the process they had used.

A new computer-supported voting process, introduced by an outside consultant, required each participant to submit both a ranking of each researcher and a measure of how strongly he or she felt about that ranking. Graphical analyses of their votes found strong confidence in and consensus on some of the rankings and great variation on others.

Subsequent discussion revealed that many managers did not know everyone being ranked and were relying on second-hand information and popularity. After considerable discussion and information sharing, a second vote was taken and a much stronger consensus emerged. After this vote the remaining differences were discussed and the group arrived at an overall ranking everyone could live with. In addition, everyone from the vice president on down accepted the new rankings as legitimate. Confidence-weighted voting and graphic illustration of voting patterns provided a clearer picture than managers had previously been able to see.

7D.4.8 Eliminating Unnecessary Debate

Members of a team sometimes enter into debate when they actually agree. At a health care organization made up of a dozen hospitals in a large city three interest groups—doctors, administrators, and directors—set out to define a mission statement and to allocate how various special services should be distributed.

Some participants suggested that electronic polling might be helpful in allocating resources, and it was decided to perform an experiment. At a meeting of approximately 200 people, each participant was given a hand-held, radio-linked voting box. A facilitator introduced a number of such policy statements as, "When patients need emergency care it shall be given without reservation regardless of ability to pay." Participants were asked to vote on whether they agreed or disagreed with each statement as it was displayed on a large screen.

It had been assumed throughout the health care organization that it was doctors who were responsible for obstructing agreement and that hospital administrators and directors were peacemakers who had to devote a good deal of their energy to persuading the physicians to be less difficult. Analysis of the votes by subgroups revealed that, contrary to everyone's expectations, doctors and directors agreed on every issue but staff administrators were out of step, even though for three years they had been telling the directors that it was the doctors who were causing problems.

7D.4.9 Surfacing Information

Traditional methods of measuring consensus that obscure important group thinking patterns can be costly. A corporate executive who used a computerized voting system to aid the highly charged political task of allocating a budget across multiple corporate sites and projects had asked a number of key associates for their opinions. The results of a first poll were widely scattered. No one seemed to agree on budget priorities, but the president pressed his executives. He wanted to understand why their voting patterns were so dissimilar, assuming all of them had the good of the corporation in mind. Finally, one vice president admitted, "How can we really make an informed recommendation when none of us really knows what goes on at all these places?"

The president then arranged to have electronic comment cards inserted on the ballot, explaining that if a voter knew about a project, he or she should type in what was known but otherwise should read what the others had typed. Within half an hour, a great deal of information about the various projects and sites had been exchanged and the subsequent vote-and-discuss cycle reached substantial consensus on the budget allocation.

As the team left the room, one of the vice presidents pointed out a previous year's investment of $5 million in a project that an eager champion had pushed. Without information to dispute his arguments, the management council had taken a chance. Whereas traditional consensus building had failed to uncover people's doubts, electronic polling had revealed people's true feelings about the project. In the new budget, that $5 million will probably be allocated to projects believed to have a higher probability of success.

Olympic ice dancers' performances are rated on what they have done in a few brief moments, rather than on their potential. Managers also often make decisions that are based on the quality of formal presentations rather than the quality of proposed projects. GroupSystems provides a mechanism for organizing, evaluating, and analyzing information during and after formal presentations. This information is available while voting is taking place so participants can reflect on the facts rather than on impressions received during a presentation.

7D.4.10 Supporting Hard Decisions

Electronic polling can sometimes facilitate painful decisions. A financially hard-pressed corporation used an electronic polling system to help decide how best to downsize. The possibility of eliminating a large but ineffective division had been discussed but rejected for fear of offending the director. No one wanted to hurt the manager's feelings by pushing to have the unproductive division eliminated. The group voted instead to make across-the-board cuts and to sacrifice efficiency in the interests of harmony.

When electronic votes were tallied, however, elimination of the ineffective division was clearly the most sensible and widely supported alternative. It would avoid potentially crippling cuts to critical functions and at the same time correctly attribute responsibility for the cut to all participants in the decision.

Occasionally, when all the electronic votes have been tallied, all the terms defined, and all the hidden assumptions surfaced, some fundamental and irreconcilable disagreements remain. A savings and loan company faced with a life-or-death crisis proceeded on the strength of discussions indicating that most of its leadership was optimistic about reaching a positive consensus. An analysis of electronic votes at one of their meetings revealed that the group was, in fact, made up of several factions with mutually exclusive, deeply held positions. Bitter disagreements had been uncovered, revealing that the viability of the current management team and the company itself were at stake. In spite of this apparent failure to reach consensus, the team was now focused on the most difficult problem and no longer needed to waste time squabbling about other more minor matters.

Electronic voting can also play a critical role in supporting geographically dispersed meetings where it can somewhat compensate for lack of such nonverbal cues as shifting gazes, body positions, and gestures that let speakers sense when it is time for a discussion to move on.

Although electronic voting can be a real time saver, this is not the technology's major advantage. In fact, a group may spend more time deliberating with a GroupSystems voting tool than when using traditional methods. Groups using structured voting schemes and response analyses to clarify communication and focus discussion have been shown consistently to reach higher-quality decisions than groups using traditional voting. Since use of the electronic tool permits participants to change their vote at any time and display group voting patterns in real time, shifts in consensus can be monitored.

CONCLUSION

GS$_{Web}$ should expand remote involvement in collaborative activities. Participants will work from anywhere they can connect to the Web. Geographic limitations are now partially eliminated. Team members can be at their desktops, at home, or anywhere in the world. Will the new-found connections in the virtual office work-space mean people will travel less? Our experience suggests not. Teams using these new technologies report that they still gather frequently. However, they report that they accomplish significantly more during the time they spend together, and they accomplish significantly more during the time they spend apart.

At this point in the development of the virtual office work-space, it is important to understand the technology in order to benefit from it. It is necessary to gain experience to be able to ask the correct questions.

We have a saying when working in a new area and breaking new ground, "Anything worth doing is worth doing badly at first." One has to learn from mistakes and keep trying. There are so many variables to contend with, that it is impossible to lay out a fool-proof plan to start with. The idea is to just get started. Do something useful. There are three approaches to solving the problem of how to get started in the virtual world:

---

1. Throw a hat over the fence.

In other words, set a goal and go after it. Find a champion who will be the leader.

Don't select a toy problem to work on. The problem should be:

◆ Highly visible;

◆ One with a large financial impact;

◆ Difficult to solve with traditional methods; and

◆ Important to stakeholders with a vested interest.

---

2. Fix a broken leg.

Find a problem and use the GroupSystems technology to begin to fix it.

Find someone in pain to be your champion. This approach is low risk and often results in a win/win solution.

---

3. Form a swat team.

Build a team with the necessary skills to solve the problem.

Select a champion and surround him or her with a group that has domain expertise and technology support.

Remember, there is more than technology involved in understanding the virtual workplace. For example, how do you "raise your hand" if you have a question? Don't set unreasonable expectations. A typical video conference is not going to have the production quality of a CNN broadcast. The virtual interactions will not be the same as in FTF sessions. As you move to an environment where you are not in the same place with other team members, group processes must become more explicit. You will need to be more and more explicit in the way you behave at a distance. Your present practices won't work in the virtual office work-place.

What have we learned from distributed virtual office work?

Plan for extreme resistance to change. Even when bottom line benefits can be identified as extremely positive, it is hard for individuals, groups, and organizations to change. Change is painful. New ways of working do not come easily.

There are a number of illusions and realities involved in anytime, anyplace work. One illusion is that groupware will reduce travel. The groupware reality is that more effective travel will be the result. When on the road, one can more easily participate in projects at the home office. One can draft documents and pass them around the organization for approval. One can more or less accomplish all of the tasks that might be done at the home office while traveling on the road. Another groupware reality is better local participation when traveling. Groupware also enables better participation from distant contributors. This involves people you couldn't otherwise afford to involve.

We are not completely dedicated to the concept of interacting with the world through a computer. We do not yet fully understand the social implications of the virtual world we are creating. Work is partially a social activity that is integrated into the practices of communities of people.

We concede that there is no substitute for real interactions and that something is missing in virtual interactions. We need to find the proper balance between face-to-face work and asynchronous distributed work. Although we have the capability to interact asynchronously at a distance, we must learn when and on which topics to meet at the same time and same place. We must also learn when it is productive to work at different times and different places.

The virtual workspace is an unexplored frontier, affording both opportunity and risk. Little is known about what can and cannot be accomplished by geographically separated teams. Little is known about how to manage a project spread across continents. Yet people who embrace change are beginning to map the territory and stake their claims. Can civilization be far behind?

BIBLIOGRAPHY

1. Coleman, D. and Khanna, R., *Groupware: Technology and Applications,* Prentice-Hall, 1995.
2. Connolly, T., J., L.M., and Valacich, J.S. "Effects of Anonymity and Evaluative Tone on Idea Generation in Computer-Mediated Groups," *Management Science,* 36: 6, 1990, pp. 689-703.
3. Grohowski, R. B., McGoff, C., Vogel, D.R., Martz, W.B., and Nunamaker, J.F.,

"Implementation of Electronic Meeting Systems GroupSystems at IBM," *MIS Quarterly,* 14: 4, 1990, pp. 369-383.

4. Nunamaker, J.F., Dennis, A.R., Valacich, J.S., Vogel, D.R., and George, J.F., "Electronic Meetings to Support Group Work," *Communications of the ACM,* 34: 7, 1991, pp. 40-61.

5. Nunamaker, J.F. and Briggs, R. O., "Getting a Grip on Groupware," in *Groupware in the Twenty-first Century,* Lloyd, Peter, ed., Adamantine Press Limited, 1994.

6. Nunamaker, J. F., Briggs, R. O., and Mittleman, D., "Electronic Meeting Systems: Ten Years of Lessons Learned," in *Groupware: Technology and Applications,* Coleman and Khanna, eds., Prentice-Hall, 1995, pp. 149-193.

7. Post, B.Q., "Building the Business Case for Group Support Technology." *Proceedings of the 25th Annual Hawaii International Conference on Systems Science,* IEEE, 1992, Vol. IV, pp. 34-45.

8. Vogel, D.R., Martz, W.B., Nunamaker, J.F., Grohowski, R.B., and McGoff, C. "Electronic Meeting System Experience at IBM," *Journal of MIS,* 6: 3, 1990.

BIOGRAPHIES

Jay F. Nunamaker—Center for the Management of Information, Regents Professor of management information systems (MIS) and computer science—came to the University of Arizona in 1974 where he established the MIS department, served as department head for 15 years, and developed the BS, MS, and PhD programs. As a result of these educational initiatives, thousands of MIS graduates have succeeded in the professional world, bringing distinction to The University of Arizona. More than 50 doctoral students are now on faculties across the country, including Harvard, Carnegie Mellon, Georgia Tech, Texas A&M, Indiana University, and the Universities of Georgia, Michigan, and Washington, among others.

An internationally renowned authority on groupware (computer support for decision making), he is considered the father of electronic meeting systems. He has published more than 200 papers and seven books dealing with these subjects and holds editorial positions on major journals. He has received more than $20 million in research grants over the past ten years. Under his direction, the MIS Department has achieved international recognition as a top program and has been rated fourth in the country for five years by *U.S. News and World Report.*

Jay F. Nunamaker Jr., PhD, McClelland Hall 430GG, University of Arizona, Tucson, AZ 85721-0108, (520) 621-4475, nunamaker@bpa.arizona.edu

Robert O. Briggs—Center for the Management of Information—conducts theoretical and empirical research on applications of technology to group productivity and learning. He earned his BS in Information Systems and a BA in Art History from San Diego State in 1986, graduating *suma cum laude,* and receiving the Outstanding Graduate award. In 1987 he earned his Masters degree in Information and Decision Systems in 1987 from the same institution, and then served three years on the SDSU faculty, where he won the 1989 Outstanding Faculty award. He received a National Doctoral Fellowship in 1990, and received his PhD from the University of Arizona in 1994 and is now a Research Fellow in the Center for the Management of Information. His research on adoption and diffusion of electronic meeting systems received the Best Paper award at HICSS in 1995. His research has received substantial support from NCR, IBM, Intel Corporation, the U.S. Navy, and D.C. Public Schools (DCPS). He conducted a two-year field study in DCPS to demonstrate that a new pedagogy supported by new technologies would re-engage students at risk of dropping out while significantly improving their academic and problem-solving skills. He now serves on the Goals 2000 Technology In Education Advisory Commission for Washington, D.C. Public Schools. For the Navy he developed and demonstrated a technology-supported strategy for real-time crisis management by geographically distributed teams. He is now investigating technology to support real-time crisis response.

Robert O. Briggs, PhD, McClelland Hall 429, University of Arizona, Tucson, AZ 85721-0108, (520) 621-6221, bbriggs@bpa.arizona.edu

Nicholas C. Romano, Jr.—Center for the Management of Information—is a doctoral candidate in the department of Management Information Systems at the University of Arizona and a GroupSystems© Researcher for CMI. His research interests include the integration of multimedia into Group Support Systems (GSS), educational uses of GSS, alternative interface integration for GSS, multicultural and multilingual GSS, and distributed and virtual meetings on the Internet.

He has published papers in the *Journal of Education for Management Information Systems,* the *Journal of Education Technology,* and *IBM AS/400 Systems Management.* He also has several papers in refereed conference proceedings. Nicholas is primarily responsible for the architectural design and development of an Internet-based collaborative groupware tool called GroupSystems for the World Wide Web (GS_{Web}). His dissertation work involves the Design, Development, and Evaluation of GS_{Web}.

Romano holds a BS in General Biology and Genetics (1985), a BS in Management Information Systems (1988), and an MS in Management Information Systems (1992) all from the University of Arizona. He will complete his PhD in Management Information Systems, with a minor in Educational Psychology from the University of Arizona in 1997.

Nicholas C. Romano, Jr., McClelland Hall 428, University of Arizona, Tucson, AZ 85721-0108, (520) 621-8669, nromano@bpa.arizona.edu

Daniel Mittleman—Center for the Management of Information—is a groupware researcher and meeting facilitator for the Center for the Management of Information at The University of Arizona. He has facilitated more than 300 strategic planning, documentation, and process improvement meetings over the past seven years for educational, industry, and government organizations. His research projects include: generation of persistent, distributed, collaborative groupware components on the WWW, development of a groupware support process for architectural planning, design of technology-supported meeting facilities, and development of collaborative writing processes. He has published over a dozen papers in these research areas. He recently coauthored a book chapter "A Electronic Meeting Systems: Ten Years of Lessons Learned" with Jay Nunamaker and Robert Briggs. Dr. Mittleman holds an MBA from Washington University in St. Louis and a PhD from the University of Arizona. He wants to be an architect when he grows up.

Daniel Mittleman, PhD, McClelland Hall 114, University of Arizona, Tucson, AZ 85721-0108, (520) 621-2932, danny@arizona.edu

Using Meetingware and Facilitators: Guidelines and Case Studies

Jana Markowitz
The Collective Mind

People who see meetingware (also known as an EMS—electronic meeting system or GDSS—group decision support system) for the first time and realize its potential impact on the way they work invariably have a laundry list of questions, including these:

- ☞ How many people need to be meeting before an EMS and/or facilitator are needed?
- ☞ How much time will using an EMS save?
- ☞ What *kind* of meetings should I use an EMS for?
- ☞ What are the advantages of using an EMS over unfacilitated meetings?
- ☞ What are the disadvantages of using technology to assist meetings?
- ☞ Can we have meetings from our desks with this (EMS) and not have to meet in a room?
- ☞ Can we use an EMS to support meetings for people in different time zones and countries?

These are valid questions and, like a good consultant, my answer to all of them is "it depends." Since no one (including me) likes that answer, I will try to give generic answers to the questions and clarify them with specific examples from meetings I have run for client organizations.

7E.1 GUIDELINES FOR USING MEETINGWARE

7E.1.1 Size of the Meeting

How many people need to be meeting before a facilitator and/or an EMS are needed?

Usually five or more people need to be meeting before a facilitator or EMS is useful. In groups of five to 20 people turn-taking becomes problematic; a few dominant people will generally take most of the "air time" in a meeting and cliques or factions of two to five people will start to form. A facilitator (even one who is also a participant) can make sure all the voices are heard, smooth over personality clashes, and keep conflicts and debates constructive. By adding an EMS, you allow anonymity, which encourages both candor and participation by those less powerful or less articulate. An EMS also provides automatic documentation of the meeting and instant feedback on votes and decisions.

The business meetings I facilitate have on average eight to 12 participants. I have had as few as five and as many as 25.

7E.1.2 Time Savings

How much time will using an EMS save?

Documented cases have shown a 50 to 90 percent savings of time for meetings over the duration of a project (University of Arizona studies on IBM and Boeing). However, I tell clients the meetings will take about the same amount of time as they had planned for an unfacilitated meeting. The technology-assisted meetings actually take less time than traditional meetings, but I say about the same amount of time they had *planned* because most people schedule half or less of the time they would *really* need to cover the topics in their agendas. Most people are naive or overly optimistic in estimating time for a group to discuss, decide or come to consensus on a topic. I can generally estimate within 10 minutes' accuracy how long a meeting will take.

I am not psychic; two factors play into this accurate estimation: planning and experience. When using an EMS, the facilitator must know exactly what the meeting initiator needs to "leave the room with" to be successful. Once a facilitator knows this, she works backwards to design a process using the EMS tools (brainstorming, idea organization, voting, etc.) to take the group through steps leading to the desired outcome (a decision, group consensus, generation of possible solutions, discussion of pros and cons, etc.) In designing the process, the facilitator can estimate fairly accurately how long each part will take from experience in previous meetings. These "parts" of the process then add up to a fairly accurate time estimate.

Another reason technology-assisted meetings are sometimes not much shorter than their traditional counterparts is that people need to feel they have "discussed" an issue; they need to literally talk about it as well as interacting via computers. My meetings are a balance between leveraging technology to provide meeting efficiency and moderating conversations to meet the psychological need for participants to interact with one another. Leaving out the "talking" part of a meeting all together makes participants feel the meeting was "cold, impersonal, mechanical" and is not beneficial to the participants or the reputation of the EMS.

So when asked about time-savings, I refer instead to the increased quality and detail possible in an EMS-assisted meeting of the same length as the traditional one it superseded.

7E.1.3 Types of Meetings

What kinds of meetings should I use an EMS for?
In meetings of five to 20 people an EMS is especially useful if any of these situations exist:

☞ sensitive issues need to be discussed, which participants might be reluctant to talk about openly

☞ there is an extreme (even violent) difference of opinions among dominant people

☞ consensus is needed before going forward

☞ multiple expertises/perspectives are necessary to make a good decision

☞ there is a very limited time to collect information from a large group of people

☞ a very complex decision, based on many criteria, must be made

☞ the meeting content must quickly be documented and used for desired impact on the organization

Just as important to know are the kinds of meetings you should NOT use an EMS for:

☞ one-way communication; dissemination of information (instead use e-mail, Lotus Notes, intranets, memos, or videos)

☞ gatherings designed to showcase an individual's abilities (these are also known as "grandstanding" and are often necessary precursors to promotion); these meetings won't work with the anonymous environment an EMS provides

☞ sharing the blame (also known as "getting everyone in the boat" with you); when decisions have already been made and the boss wants to garner the group's approval, an anonymous environment is the last thing (s)he needs; all kinds of resistance and "push back" will come out under cover of anonymity

7E.1.4 Advantages Over Traditional Meetings

What are the advantages of using an EMS over "traditional" meetings run by the person who called them?
Vendors of EMS's will list the benefits as these:

☞ fuller participation (with accompanying increase in morale and "buy-in")

☞ time savings (from parallel input)

☞ more candid information (due to anonymity)

☞ more creative solutions (a function of anonymity and synergy)

While all these are true, there are also other, more subtle benefits:

☞ groups seem to go through their "forming" and "storming" developmental stages more quickly

☞ participants get used to high levels of participation and continue the behavior in traditional settings

☞ by requiring detailed pre-meeting planning, EMS meetings are better focused, flow more smoothly, and produce higher quality results

☞ anonymity allows a "face-saving" way for enemies to agree

7E.1.5 Disadvantages of an EMS

What are the disadvantages of using an EMS?
Since I offer facilitated EMS meetings for a living, I would like to think there are no disadvantages, but that's not true. Some of the drawbacks include the following:

☞ a person can leave feeling (s)he was "forced" into a decision the group agreed on, but (s)he didn't

☞ articulate people who can't type often feel they have had less opportunity for input than in a traditional meeting

☞ people who enjoy debate may feel they were denied an opportunity to argue

☞ people who normally dominate meetings feel "unempowered" by the level playing field anonymity provides

☞ very fast typists have been known to key supporting comments for their own suggestions (one person/one vote usually fixes this problem)

☞ a leader may mistakenly feel that letting a group vote on something obligates him/her to accept the decision; unfortunately, the leader is sometimes privy to information that might have changed the group decision

7E.1.6 Desktop Meetings

Can we have meetings from our desks with this (EMS) and not have to meet in a room?
Technically, there is nothing to stop you from doing this and some people already are. Psychologically, there are a myriad of reasons that "distributed" or "same time, different place" meetings can fail.

There is a lot of communication that goes on in a room that is "paralinguistic" and "non-linguistic." Paralinguistic things include intonation and pauses in speech, which communicate beyond the actual words (anger, sarcasm, despair, frustration). Non-linguistic things include eye-contact, posture, and gestures that may communicate a meaning completely different from the words being said. Missing these communication cues can change or destroy the meaning of messages being exchanged. These communication cues are also a reason behind having oral discussions to supplement and clarify the computer-entered comments.

There are circumstances where these missing communication cues may not be terribly important; in a group that has worked together for a long time and that has a very smooth (almost choreographed) flow of ideas, there may be no problem with conversing strictly via computer interaction from different locations. However, these flawless teams are few and far between.

What about combining an EMS with a telephone conference call or videoconferencing facility to bring back in some of those non-linguistic and paralinguistic cues? Great idea and several groups are doing these things as well. The conferencing tools (especially videoconferencing) do address some of the missing cues in communication. However, until we have holographic videoconferencing systems that make us feel the "telepresence" of our remote counterparts, even this technology is a poor second to "being there."

Just as telephones in their 120 years of existence have not obviated the need for face-to-face discussions with associates, no EMS (even with video) can replace a same-time/same-place meeting (but it *can* make the meeting more effective!)

7E.1.8 Across the World Meetings

Can we use an EMS to support meetings for people in different time zones and countries?

Again, our technical capabilities outstrip our knowledge of the human mind. There are EMS systems designed for WANs as well as LANs. Many tools exist (or are on the brink of debuting) that take advantage of the Internet's ubiquitous presence and inexpensive access around the world.

The drawbacks for this type of distributed use include all of the "desktop" meeting concerns with additional stumbling blocks of time zone difference, potential culture clash, and language translation, not to mention the issue of who should facilitate and from where. The complexity of communicating in this environment is staggering.

However, if time, money, and business circumstances make it impossible to be physically in the same place, arrange the situation to avoid as many of the predictable problems as you can. No doubt unpredictable problems will pop up to take their places, but you can only plan, hope, and remain flexible.

Some pre-meeting steps you can take include the following:

☞ Try to be sure participants have met one another at some point prior to this meeting; if this is not possible, distribute photos and short work/personal biographies. The biographies should not only describe education and work experience, but also hobbies, interests, family ties, birthplace, etc. These details are what is exchanged in rapport-building "small talk" at meetings.

While it may seem unimportant or irrelevant, it is often what fosters trust among group members and helps them be productive.

☞ Have readily available technical support and a "fallback plan" for technical failure at each site. If you lose network contact, can a quick phone conference call kept the group going until problems are fixed?

☞ Have a short "ice breaker" or some sort of "warm-up" of the group prior to tackling the issues at hand. This relaxes (most) business people and starts communication flowing.

During the meeting try to:

☞ Allow ample time for input and discussion; no one likes to be rushed into a decision just because connection time is expensive.

☞ Be sure final content is available to all participants, especially if people are entering information at different times (which is likely in different time zones).

☞ Make sure terms used have been defined by the group—people often use the same words when talking about different things or different words to express the same concept; clarity is critical.

After the meeting you should:

☞ Encourage groups to maintain on-going communication via e-mail or telephone, just as they would communicate if co-located by talking in the hallways, eating together, etc.

☞ Distribute all meeting documentation of discussions, decisions, etc. for use in on-going communications as a common reference

7E.2 CASE STUDIES

How can we translate these general guidelines into something that relates to the meetings you will have to attend in the next few weeks? Examples go a long way in explaining ideas. These case studies describe situations commonly found in organizations and the aspects of the situation that made it useful to have an EMS and facilitator.

7E.2.1 FedEx Defines Future IT Employees

Task:

Envisioning the future

Situation:

The FedEx IT organization (about 3000 people) was working with the corporate HR department to define the technical skills and personal characteristics needed in IT employees 3 years in the future.

The situation exhibited these characteristics, which made it conducive to the use of an EMS:

☞ sensitive issues that participants were reluctant to talk about openly

☞ multiple perspectives/expertises were needed to reach a good decision

☞ there was limited time to gather information from a large group

☞ the meeting information needed to be documented and used quickly in order to have the desired impact on the organization

Process:

Brainstorm 3-years-from-now headlines for Computer-World regarding the FedEx IT organization. Define the group's Vision of the FedEx IT organization as it will exist 3 years from now in terms of : 1) Goals of IT, 2) Work Environment, 3) Services Provided, and 4) People. Specify and prioritize the technical skills and personal characteristics of the IT employees in the Vision.

Results:

The headlines the group came up with indicated several things:

☞ the group was optimistic about its success in the next 3 years

☞ the group felt FedEx was "special" when compared to its peers

☞ they anticipated specific problems and pitfalls for their group over the next 3 years

The 25 person group (representing various sections and levels of IT) broke into four teams to define their vision of IT. With this collective vision of the future established, the group proceeded to identify and prioritize (on a 10-point scale) 60 skills and characteristics for the Programmer Job Family and the Business Analyst Job Family.

The group accomplished this work, beginning to end, in approximately 3 hours, using an electronic meeting system. There were discussions, but no heated arguments.

When asked what they thought of using an EMS in this process (it was the group's first use of the technology), their responses included the following:

☞ liked anonymity

☞ non-threatening

☞ good for touchy subjects

☞ effective means of gathering opinions

☞ working in parallel beats working sequentially

☞ people not likely to respond in large groups feel free to contribute

☞ ability to view and comment on others' thoughts provides validity or counter arguments

☞ effective use of technology

7E.2.2 Maybelline Screens New Product Ideas

Task:

Make a series of complex decisions about potential new products

Situation:

Maybelline has to continually create the future by predicting fashions, trends, and needs. They use their "envisioned future" to select product ideas for consumer-testing and launching. After defining 40 or 50 new product ideas, how do you narrow the field to the right 15 or 20 for which to fund further market research and development?

The situation involved these aspects conducive to using an EMS:

☞ consensus is needed before going forward

☞ multiple perspectives/expertises are needed (mfg. sales, etc.) to make a good decision

☞ there is limited time to gather information from a large group

☞ a very complex decision, based on numerous criteria, must be made

Process:

Maybelline developed, through interview and discussion, 14 criteria they felt would accurately predict the success of a new product. They assigned "weights" to these criteria to factor in their relevant importance in the product's success.

They gathered about 30 people from Marketing, Market Research, Business Development, R & D, Sales, and Advertising. These people evaluated the products across all of the criteria and added comments or suggestions about each product. The process was done in three half-day sessions, held twice a year (each person attended only one of the half-day sessions).

Results:

During these meetings, the mood was upbeat and humorous. Some people ridiculed product ideas while others supported them. The process gave them a way to provide both quantitative and qualitative feedback on the products; it also provided a venue for self-criticism. Consistent low ratings across all products in certain areas let management know they needed more advertising to succeed. Low ratings also kept them from entering markets where they had no expertise and little hope of success.

7E.2.3 Sedgwick IT Listens to Field Advisory Group

Task:

Improve IT's support to and relationship with field technical staff.

Situation:

The US Sedgwick IT organization provides help desk support as well as research, system development, network design, and application development for its

60+ field insurance offices. Local Area Network Administrators (Net Administrators) in the US offices do not report to IT. These Net Administrators are the jack-of-all-trades, doing everything from budget to training to installation and trouble-shooting. At a national gathering of Net Administrators, sponsored by IT, the HQ IT organization found there were a lot of negative feelings and comments directed their way. To define and start correcting the problems the Senior VP of IT formed an advisory group, which represented all geographic areas and the variety of different sized offices. The Net Administrators could only be spared from their offices for 2 days.

The situation involved these things conducive to use of an EMS:

☞ extreme differences of opinion among dominant personalities

☞ multiple perspectives/expertises are necessary to make a good decision

☞ limited time to gather information

☞ meeting content must be documented and used quickly for desired impact on the organization

☞ emotional conflicts among participants could derail constructive discussions

Process:

At the initial gathering of the advisory group (seven Net Administrators, three corporate staff attended—including the Senior VP) the stated objectives were:

☞ increase the advantage Sedgwick gains from technology

☞ improve communications between corporate and the field

☞ set the IT direction to best meet the needs of the field

Corporate staff were observers and answer providers, not contributing participants. Participants were asked to list their "Top 3" IT issues. This list was consolidated to 16 items, which were then prioritized by the group. Further consolidation narrowed the list to 10 critical topic areas, the top seven of which the group had time to address in more detail. For each of the critical areas, the Net Admins listed 1) what was good, 2) problems, and 3) anything "missing" in that area (i.e. services, support, products, resources, procedures, etc.)

The group prioritized the problems and missing items. This gave IT a "hot list" of needs and problems to resolve in each area. The "good" items listed in each area served two purposes:

☞ they let IT know what kind of support and resources the field found useful

☞ they softened the "sting" of criticisms in the area

The group proceeded to answer a series of open-ended questions designed to find out what "directions" or trends in IT should change and what should remain. The questions included:

☞ How can we get a better return on technical investments?

☞ What is IT not doing that it should?

☞ How do we get the field more involved in Headquarters ?

The second day was spent identifying actions and responsible parties to address the various issues. The second day, all work was done without an EMS in face-to-face discussions between IT staff and field personnel.

Results:

The IT staff proceeded to take action on many of the issues and problems. Although not all problems had been fixed by the next meeting (3 months later), the atmosphere was warmer and reflected the beginnings of trust on both sides.

IT sent only one staff member to attend the second meeting—the person responsible for the topic being discussed. The group received her warmly and at the end of the day keyed several anonymous compliments commending her for "being open to criticism," "brave enough to spend the whole day with us," and "willing to listen and change."

While there are still problems to solve and relationships to improve, both groups are pleased with their progress.

Their comments on using an EMS for the first time included:

- liked ability to cover a lot of discussion topics quickly

- easy to say what you feel without hurting feelings

- took 15 hours of work and completed in one (8 hour) session

- liked that we were not on the spot to give an answer to every topic

- only way to get corporate and field on the same page

- enjoyed the process of sharing ideas and working together to find solutions

7E.3 INTERNAL FACILITATORS VS. CONSULTANTS

So now we've seen how an EMS can help certain kinds of meetings. Why an outside consultant? How about an internal facilitator? A valid question and much of the time an internal facilitator will work well. However, sometimes the facilitator needs to be an "outsider." Here are some situations where an "outsider" would be preferable:

1) Warring factions need a neutral party to manage discussions and decision-making. Even if the facilitator is from a non-partisan group (frequently HR is a source of facilitators), the groups may suspect him/her of secret allegiance to one side or the other. Often their suspicions are accurate. It is difficult for someone who is part of a company not to have any opinions on internal issues and politics—even if he/she is professional enough not to express them.

2) The groups are so "close to the problem" that they have lost perspective. They need to be prompted to take a different approach. Often a corporate culture will promote one way of solving problems or dealing with issues. When this one method fails to work in a situation, the group often stagnates and can't move forward. Sometimes a fresh perspective or a new way of defining the problem will help the group become productive again. Someone outside of the corporate culture is generally needed as a catalyst.

3) The group needs focused, analytical skills to plan the meeting and draw conclusions from the information gathered. While many groups have these skills in their staff, the resources in "downsized" companies are often over-utilized. Serious problems that can't be put on a back burner may require an outside consultant who can work focused and full-time on taking a problem from definition through resolution.

CONCLUSION

Electronic meeting systems can be a valuable tool in solving many organizations' problems, but don't mistake the tool for a solution. While using an EMS can be invaluable in improving the meeting process, the information in the minds of the participants is the real corporate asset. The skill of the facilitator in planning and managing the meetings is also a critical success factor in EMS use. In the long run, knowing whether to have a meeting at all is the most important matter. After all, the best-planned and most efficiently managed meeting is still a waste of time if it never needed to happen.

BIOGRAPHY

Jana Markowitz is the founder of The Collective Mind, which provides consulting, meeting planning and facilitation, and management seminars to improve business productivity through collaborative work.

Jana has fifteen years of experience in technical consulting, marketing, and developing/ presenting education. She has facilitated and documented numerous meetings (using a groupware electronic meeting system) for clients across many industries including: Acxiom, BellSouth, Dollar General, FedEx, Maybelline, and Sedgwick James. She is a lecturer in the Executive Masters program at Christian Brothers University and teaches the course Groupware for Business Teams. She is a contributing writer for *The Facilitator,* a nationally distributed newsletter for professional facilitators.

Jana worked for the IBM Corporation from 1979 until 1993. She holds a Masters degree in Organizational Psychology from the University of Memphis and a Bachelors in Computer Science and Math from Vanderbilt University. She is a member of the Human Factors and Ergonomics Society and associated with their technical groups for Organizational Design and Management, Computer Systems, and Environmental Design.

Introduction to Chapter 8

What is a collaborative presentation technology? Generally, collaborative presentation products support projecting someone's ideas onto a screen, wall, or whiteboard so that both local and remote meeting participants can interact with the presentation of other people in the meeting. There are a number of these products coming from small innovative companies like Tegrity, Polycom, and LiveWorks.

Dion Blundell of LiveWorks begins this chapter with some meetings strategies that can be enhanced with collaborative presentation products. They examine different types of presentation tools and compare their ability to support collaboration: display tools, electronic whiteboards, remote tools, tools for recorded interactions, convivial tools (support a shared workspace for groups), and finally procedural tools.

LiveWorks is a Xerox spin-off and their technology was developed at Xerox P.A.R.C. (where much of the technology for the computer industry has its origins). Rather than focusing just on their tool, the LiveBoard, they have chosen to educate us about the world of collaborative presentation tools and have reviewed a wide variety of tools in different categories.

Videoconferencing, again, is a tool in this category, and even though this chapter follows the chapter on videoconferencing, LiveWorks brings a very different perspective. They examine videoconferencing rooms and maintain that adding videoconferencing to a presentation technology like LiveBoard is the best of both worlds.

This chapter also looks at Internet downloadable presentations. But these are not real-time interactions, and there is usually no feedback from the audience. Even when there is feedback, it is time delayed. There is a thorough discussion of the pros and cons of audioconferencing, videoconferencing, and document conferencing, as well as a discussion of how these technologies span time and distance for collaborative presentations.

Dion uses case studies to show how collaborative presentation technologies can make real contributions to meeting effectiveness. He revisits the three meetings discussed at the beginning of the chapter to see what differences would occur using collaborative presentation tools and presents case studies from Marriott, the U.S. Army, and Compaq to build a strong case for using these technologies in organizations all over the world.

Finally, the standards that affect collaborative presentations—audio, video, telecommunications, data protocols, and networking standards and protocols— are examined in this comprehensive chapter.

The chapter ends, as it should, with an eye toward the future. LiveWorks expects collaborative presentation functions to move to multipoint over the next year, but more importantly, they anticipate supporting collaboration at an applications level, and expect a standard file format for the distribution of information.

tion. They look at the probable evolution of the T.120 standard, and the challenge of video compression, noting that the WWW is the springboard for many of the new developments in interactive communications. They start to explore the world of virtual meetings and look at the work going on in MUDs (Multi-user Domains), both by the military and the world of on-line games, as technologies that will change the way we have meetings in the future.

Collaborative Presentation Technologies: Meetings, Presentations, and Collaboration

Dion Blundell

LiveWorks, Inc., a division of Xerox, Inc.

Somewhere in the middle of America, a project leader is presenting his team's proposal for a revolutionary new product to a group of senior executives, hoping to leave the meeting with approval for the concept, the work schedule and, most importantly, a budget that will cover a temporary staff increase to provide needed expertise and permit the group to meet its deadlines. He has traveled to this meeting from the coast, with a fistful of overhead transparencies, several sets of handouts, and a laptop loaded with a Gantt chart, a spreadsheet, and a Microsoft PowerPoint slide show.

In the meeting room, he stands at one end of the conference table to operate the overhead projector while making his verbal pitch for the project. He can't use his computer because there is no means of displaying his charts, slides, and spreadsheets directly from it. He's really glad he printed some of them as overheads. During his presentation, he sees only silent faces. At the end, the executives tell him, "We'd like some changes in the timelines and we don't see how you can justify the extra staff. Why don't you go back and rework the proposal and fax us the changes in a couple of weeks?"

* * *

In Connecticut, a sales group is having a strategic planning meeting. Some members of the group have brought information on sales trends in particular territories or market segments. A couple of employees have put their ideas for improvements on paper in the form of handouts. They spend part of their meeting clustered around one end of the table over a large diagram showing a possible reorganization of their group to better meet the needs of their company. In the middle of the discussion, one grabs a marker and starts using the flipchart to record and organize the suggestions that are coming out of the discussion. By the end of the meeting, they have several lists of ideas on flipchart pages, as well as a heavily marked-up diagram. One person volunteers to take charge of putting all the new ideas together to distribute to the rest of the group in order to verify agreement before taking the reorganization proposal forward as a presentation to the VP. If she spends some time in the office over the weekend, it should be possible to get the responses and put the presentation together by Friday of next week.

* * *

In Chicago and Washington, a group of industry leaders is holding a videoconference to agree on a new industry standard for a class of products. They make extensive use of their system's graphics capability to share key parts of the draft document. Some suggestions are written into the pages, but the changes made in Chicago have to be faxed to Washington and vice versa. Several people use the whiteboards at each location to record parts of the standard not covered in the original draft. When the meeting is over, people at both locations have to figure out a way to get all the suggestions and changes from both whiteboards and several different sets of the paper document combined into a single version. They agree to meet again in two days' time.

* * *

Three different meetings, three different kinds of presentation, and three different modes and degrees of collaboration suggest three observations:

☞ A static unidirectional presentation often fails to fulfill the objective of a meeting.

☞ Collaborative interaction involves dynamic manipulation of presented information by more than one person.

☞ A meeting isn't really over when it ends.

Collaborative presentation describes a new way to accomplish business and organizational goals, a shift in the dynamics of traditional meeting components, and an opportunity to apply a wide range of old and new technologies to solving problems, building consensus, and making decisions.

One of the fundamental realizations of management science in the mid-1990s is that collaborative groups have the potential to produce higher-quality results in less time, and at less expense, than either individuals working alone or teams operating in traditional process frameworks. The contribution of technologies that support this kind of collaboration, by facilitating the presentation and manipulation of information and ideas within tight timelines, is to improve productivity, quality of decision-making, and time to project completion. For organizations operating in a highly competitive business environment, these are valuable contributions indeed.

8.1 THE CASE FOR COLLABORATION

Asking almost anyone about meetings is to invite a spate of comments about unproductive time-wasting. People love to hate meetings, and their dissatisfaction is often justified. Many meetings *are* ineffective, and it's not necessarily the fault of the people involved. In view of the marked inefficiency of many meetings, organizations sensitive to the bottom line are paying considerable attention to making meetings more worthwhile.

There is no question that meetings, by bringing groups together, have the potential to be both effective and productive. The University of Minnesota's Marshall Scott Poole [5] summarizes some of the benefits of working in groups, identified by earlier researchers, as follows:

☞ Groups generally have greater knowledge than any individual.

☞ Groups have a diversity of perspectives on the situation, which results in broader thinking.

☞ Group members can check each other's ideas.

☞ [A psychological] social facilitation effect stimulates greater effort by group members.

☞ Participation in group discussions often increases members' commitment to the decision.

☞ Bringing people with different points of view into contact will often surface conflicts that must be resolved for an effective and practical decision to emerge.

These points are generally supported by the comments of meeting regulars, who are keenly aware when meetings work and when they don't. When asked to identify things that make a meeting good, even those with the most negative attitudes will recall meetings where information was presented clearly and succinctly, meetings with lively focused discussion, meetings where they felt their comments and ideas made a difference, meetings where everyone left with a sense of accomplishment.

These views of group work tacitly assume that both presentation (to share knowledge, information, different perspectives) and collaboration (to check and improve ideas, to build consensus) are an integral part of high-quality meeting activity. Effective collaboration needs a variety of well-presented information on which to operate.

Noting that there are many different kinds of meetings, LiveWorks' Frank Halasz, Vice President of Product Development, points out, "There's a function to having everyone get together in one room. Face-to-face interaction can be much more powerful than just getting together from desktops. There's a synergy in a meeting when a group gets together that isn't there when they are separated. Five people in one room and five people in another room is more powerful than 10 people at desktops." High-productivity group work depends not only on both collaborative and presentational activities, but also on the development of synergy within the group, which enlarges individual contributions such that the sum of the parts, in the end, is greater than the whole.

8.1.2 The Business of Meetings

No two meetings are entirely alike, although very different meetings all have at least some elements in common. To begin with, meetings require at least two participants, and most meetings involve more than two people. Meeting participants are engaging in something more than a social encounter—the activity of meeting is a *purposeful* activity based on communication among people. The act of meeting anticipates some kind of product or result. Meeting agendas set out what is expected to be accomplished; what has been accomplished is articulated at the end of the meeting in the form of minutes, decisions, solutions, ideas, and business plans and strategies. Effective meetings *support* the achievement of results.

The more people involved in a meeting, the more likely it is that the meeting will require some form of structure and control. There are many different meeting procedures, each useful for providing a structural framework for particular kinds of meeting. The procedural framework ensures that all those who need to communicate with the other members of the group have appropriate opportunities to do so, while offering at least partial control over digressions and repetitions. In addition, it offers a mechanism for determining group agreement, not only for interim decisions but also for the final product of the group effort.

Communication within a meeting may take several forms. Some individuals may participate as information providers, supplementing verbal information with displays of information using a variety of formats and media. At the same time, some individuals (often the same individuals) work as collaborators, providing informed responses to the presented information as well as new ideas inspired by the dynamic flow of information within the group. For both presenters and collaborators, it is crucially important that their information be successfully communicated to and understood by the rest of the group.

During and at the end of the meeting, there is also a need to capture the results of the meeting in some form. Information presented during the meeting has been manipulated and changed in the course of collaboration. Participants need a record of the outcome or product of the meeting, and may need records of parts of the process of the meeting as well.

That these activities can be difficult to carry out successfully is witnessed by the general discontent with meetings mentioned earlier. Yet the benefits of group work are undeniable, and now, more than ever before, organizations cannot afford to forego the high-quality results that good meetings achieve.

A substantial array of tools has been developed over many decades to assist the meeting process, ranging from procedural structures to presentation technologies. Changes in our modern society have, however, introduced new challenges to the business of holding a successful and productive meeting. The dimensions of a meeting no longer coincide with the walls of a single meeting room. Just as meeting results assume a critical importance for businesses in a competitive environment, high-quality collaborative activity over presented information has to contend with the constraints (or added opportunities) of meeting across space and across time.

8.2 NEW DIMENSIONS FOR COLLABORATIVE PRESENTATIONS

8.2.1 Shrinking Distance

More and more, businesses and other organizations need to use distributed workforces. The decentralization of organizations, coupled with economically advantageous outsourcing for specialized goods and services, has made distance a significant barrier to inexpensive, convenient, and successful interaction among employees and strategic partners.

Meetings, and especially meetings involving collaborative presentation activities, generally bring together people who belong to a particular community of interest. They are purposeful events, and the achievement of purpose requires having all the right people involved. When organizations occupy a single campus, gathering the right people is a simple matter.

The growth of many businesses into branch offices has produced distributed groups. A community of interest may not be clustered at or near a single location, but might involve people who are normally located anywhere in the world. The need to meet over a local office issue does not present any special problems. If all members of a single department are colocated at one site, holding a collaborative brainstorming session is easy. On the other hand, setting up a meeting of all the chief sales reps from 20 or more branches worldwide is a different situation altogether. When customers, suppliers, or other partners come into the mix, none of whom are colocated with the main organization, overcoming distance assumes a new strategic importance for doing business in an effective, efficient, and competitive way.

The two solutions available for the distance problem have been travel and technology. By physically moving all the necessary participants into a single location, travel is capable of providing full support for interactive collaboration. That support comes at an increasingly heavy price, however, in both monetary and human terms. For cost-conscious corporations, travel incurs new expense every time it is used. On the productivity side, travel takes time away from other tasks, creates fatigue and stress, and separates the travelers from easy access to the familiar range of resources they have in their home locations.

Growing concerns about the high cost of travel in tangible and intangible terms have led to strong market forces favoring the development of new technological alternatives to travel. To be most useful in the two-dimensional meeting environment, these technological solutions must simultaneously overcome distance and provide support for the required level of interaction, whether the purpose of the meeting requires nothing more than an effective presentation that ends in understanding, or whether it requires a high level of collaborative activity around presented information that results in a tangible group product.

8.2.2 Shifting Time

The need to work effectively with time is another growing need, complicated further by the increase in globally distributed organizations. In today's business environment, the old adage "time is money" is more true than ever before. As companies flatten and downsize in response to the rapidly changing, highly competitive climate in which business operates today, there is an urgent need to get the most value out of every employee. In the lean, mean organization, the specialized skills and knowledge residing in each individual must be used to support all areas of the operation, whenever they are needed. Most organizations can ill afford to waste their people's time.

The time problem manifests itself in several different ways. One of these relates to the availability of busy people to participate in meetings. Another is the potential for inefficiency in the meeting itself, exacerbated when the right people are not there. The third is that the collaborative presentation activity may have to continue after the actual designated meeting period; as mentioned earlier, the meeting isn't really over when it ends.

Availability of the right people is crucial to the success of many meetings. The more people involved in a meeting, the more likely it is that one or more of them will be unable to attend because of other commitments. In some situations, the person who is not available can assemble his or her unique contribution of information in presentation form, for distribution to other participants before the meeting or for display during the meeting. Technology that supports the use of presentations contributed by people in lieu of their attendance can significantly improve meeting efficiency, as those who are present then have at least partial access to the ideas and concerns of their absent colleagues.

In addition, a report or other record of the meeting can be provided to anyone who was unable to be there. Alone or in smaller groups, those people can then proceed with essential follow-up work identified during the meeting, or provide after-the-fact responses to what happened at the meeting.

Whether the previously prepared contribution of the absent person is shared with the group during the meeting, or whether the essence of the meeting is provided to that person for post-meeting review and action, the participation of the absentee will be asynchronous, *i.e.*, not coincident with the time of the actual meeting. In either event, the use of the right technologies maximizes meeting productivity by facilitating asynchronous as well as synchronous collaboration among the necessary personnel.

8.2.3 The Interactivity Continuum

Interactions among members of a group occur in different degrees and ways, and achieve different results. The full continuum of interactivity extends from the complete absence of communication to one- and two-way communication with varying degrees of understanding, through to total group synergy.

Presentation activity, in the narrowest sense, requires only one-way communication, and simply expresses information with or without understanding on the part of the audience. Further along the continuum, information begins to be exchanged with two-way communication and understanding. Here the processes of education, persuasion, and inspiration come into play, and collaboration begins. In the course of successful collaboration, agreement and commitment begin to lead to productive outcomes. At the highest level of interaction, social facilitation within the group interaction causes each participant to be stimulated to greater effort by the others. The resultant synergy is an essential component of highly productive problem-solving, group creativity, and true collaboration (Fig. 8.1).

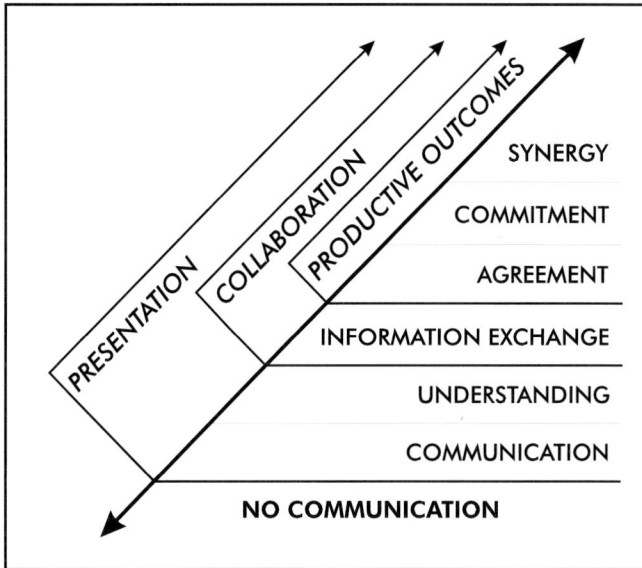

Fig. 8.1 The Interactivity Continuum

With a dynamic group operating at the high end of the continuum, presentation and collaboration merge into a rich interactive meeting process that raises expectations for a high-quality result. To ensure better results or products from meeting interaction, many different kinds of tools have been applied to support the full range of interactions needed to achieve desired outcomes at any point along the continuum. When these tools also support spanning distance and shifting time, they provide real and tangible benefits to organizations that require extensive use of meetings for problem-solving, product development, and decision-making.

8.3 MEETING TOOLS FOR COLLABORATIVE PRESENTATIONS

Meeting tools—aids and supports for presentation, collaboration, and meeting process—are not new. Some of the tools still in use today have an ancient and honorable history. For example, parliamentary procedure as expressed in *Rob-*

erts' Rules of Order has been used to lend structure and control to meetings for almost a millennium. Michael Schrage [6] has commented in *No More Teams!*, *Mastering the Dynamics of Creative Collaboration* that "with the notable exception of colored chalk, there has been no fundamental advance in blackboard technology in over five hundred years. But, like paper, this hasn't prevented the blackboard from being an astonishingly reliable and resilient collaborative tool."

Tools used in meetings serve a variety of purposes. They provide structures to guide the meeting process, interaction where groups are separated by space and time, display capabilities, and shared workspaces for group collaboration. Technological advances and user demand have led to an explosion of new tools to support a high level of meeting productivity while saving time and money. So many new devices are now on the market that users face a sometimes bewildering selection.

Classifying different products on the basis of general capability, such as videoconferencing or electronic whiteboard, is no longer helpful, as many current products incorporate more than one function and more than one technology. The following discussion organizes examples of different kinds of tools in terms of their function vis à vis collaborative presentation, with reference to the interactivity continuum and the distance and time dimensions as presented in Section 8.2. Even at that, some multifunctional products belong in more than one class of equipment.

The first group encompasses such tools as overhead projectors, slide projectors, and other presentation devices that accept computer-generated text and graphics. These are primarily display tools, enabling presenters to accompany their oral presentations with a variety of visual aids. Electronic whiteboards are also part of this group, although their functionality today extends far beyond mere display.

A second, large group of tools enables remote and recorded interactions and communication among meeting participants. Advances in telecommunications technology have led to an ever more sophisticated set of audio, video, and document conferencing tools that permit group interaction across distances. Computer conferencing, both through shared interactive applications and through the Internet and World Wide Web, also provides a form of interaction that can involve groups and operate in both the distance and time dimensions of the modern meeting environment.

For the purposes of collaborative presentations, perhaps the most exciting set of tools now emerging is the third category—what Schrage would class as "convivial tools" for the increasingly collaborative work environment. Schrage is careful to distinguish convivial tools from the vast array of existing work tools—personal computers, telephones, photocopiers, etc.—designed primarily for personal-use applications, arguing that convivial tools will of necessity be qualitatively different. Convivial tools are usable by groups as a form of shared workspace, accessible to different group members, any of whom can import information or manipulate information already displayed or contained in the shared space.

A fourth set of tools is primarily procedural, such as group decision support systems or electronic meeting systems, which provide a computer-based structure for different kinds of meeting processes. Based on a network of personal computers, usually one per participant, electronic meeting systems support both distributed and face-to-face work, often in a specially equipped meeting facility. These systems typically incorporate tools for brainstorming, organizing and exchanging ideas, developing consensus, and making decisions. This class of tools is related but peripheral to the collaborative presentation technologies dealt with in this chapter. An excellent discussion of electronic meeting systems can be found in the first volume of this series, *Groupware: Technology and Applications*, in an article by Jay F. Nunamaker, Jr., Robert O. Briggs, and Daniel D. Mittleman [3].

8.3.1 Presenting Information

The activity of presentation is central to many meetings, where presented information usually becomes the subject of discussion, elaboration, manipulation, and decision-making. Presentations may be formal or informal, previously prepared or offered on an *ad hoc* basis. On the theory that a picture is worth a thousand words, oral presentations are often accompanied by visual aids, consisting of graphics, text, slides, videotapes, even models and demonstrations.

Successful presentations may depend not only on the quality of the information presented but also on the means used to present it. In some circumstances, people will tend to find a handsome color graphic in a slide presentation more impressive than a handwritten scrawl on a whiteboard. Technology has enabled presentation tools far more sophisticated than Schrage's blackboard. Excellent computer graphics and similar applications have made it possible to put a slick and memorable presentation together with minimal time investment. People traveling to meetings may be creating their presentation information on a laptop on the plane. LiveWorks' Frank Halasz wryly comments, "Technology has changed what we expect by way of presentations and in terms of tools like MS PowerPoint slide shows. You used to be able to tell how polished an idea was from whether or not the slides were handwritten, but now you can even update your PowerPoint presentation on the plane."

Presentation tools have also made it possible to present information without being physically present with other participants; many technologies support remote presentations. Indeed, it is even unnecessary to participate in the meeting at all; videotapes and prepared computer presentations do not actually require the presenter's presence, but can be prepared in advance and simply displayed at the meeting. The use of some of these technologies also facilitates interactive manipulation of presented information by the rest of the group. In addition, many users are now making use of the World Wide Web as a vehicle for the provision of presentations on demand. For example, it is common to find hypertext links to prepackaged presentations as part of Web pages.

Display technologies thus not only support rich information transfer but also extend the presentation end of the interactivity continuum along the axes of distance and time.

8.3.1.1 Familiar Presentation Tools in Electronic Form

People meeting face-to-face are accustomed to meeting rooms equipped with a projection screen, a whiteboard, a flipchart, and increasingly a video monitor, where various forms of presentation material can be displayed for everyone to see. Overhead projectors and slide projectors are available for use with the projection screen; presenters write on whiteboards and flipcharts; videotapes are shown using a VCR connected to the video monitor.

Several of these familiar presentation tools have now been translated into electronic versions that not only serve to display information locally but also have the capability of displaying that information simultaneously at more than one location via telecommunications links.

Electronic Whiteboards

Electronic whiteboards have been around since the 1980s, with the original versions providing a no-frills capability of writing on the whiteboard, and transmitting the written image to other locations over standard telephone lines for display in real time on a monitor or projection screen. A typical early electronic whiteboard was NEC's EB-300 Electronic Writing Board System, which included a control unit, a writing board resembling a standard whiteboard with legs, and a pressure-sensitive graphics tablet with attached electronic pen. The main writing board was large enough to suit a normal mid-sized conference room, and presenters could use ordinary whiteboard pens to write on its pressure-sensitive surface. The writing board could not display incoming presentations, but showed only what was written on it directly; everything written on it was, however, transmitted to other locations. At any location, received transmissions were displayed on a monitor or projection screen. The graphics tablet provided an alternative input mode if there were, for example, only one participant at a location. The control unit included a built-in floppy disk drive so that the written material could be stored and subsequently printed using a dedicated thermal printer capable of up to seven copies per minute.

SMART Technologies Inc. of Calgary, Alberta, sees the electronic whiteboard as a very effective way to share computer-generated and handwritten information among the members of a group, whether all participants are at one location or are scattered around multiple sites, as long as all are using the SMART system—ITU T.120 compatibility is not yet available. By connecting a user-provided computer, LCD projection system, and an overhead projector, users of the SMART Board technology can display information both passively and interactively by projecting it onto the front of the SMART Board (Fig. 8.2). Rear-screen projection configurations are also possible, using third-party rear projectors, especially recommended for use under high ambient light conditions.

Fig. 8.2 A SMART Board in use (drawing courtesy SMART Technologies Inc.)

SMART's WriteBoard software allows editing, copying, printing, and similar tasks when used with the SMART Board. It can also be used at a remote location to view material without the editing capability. Presenters can create notes and diagrams during a presentation using ordinary dry-erase markers on the large touch-sensitive board. Anything written on the SMART Board is immediately input into a connected computer—including any IBM-PC compatible running Windows, Apple Macintosh computers, and Sun Microsystems SPARCstations—for storage, from which it can be printed at any time.

What makes the SMART Board more powerful than early electronic whiteboards, however, is the user's ability to combine different components to cover a variety of presentation-related tasks and processes. A SMART Notes application for MS Windows provides a convenient means of preparing presentations by capturing and sorting slides from other computer applications, and gives the presenter an easy-to-use control system as familiar as operating an ordinary slide projector. Multipoint capability over telephone lines is provided by a digital bridge system that supports two to 32 users in one or more multipoint conferences (Fig. 8.3); no additional bridge is necessary for multipoint presentations over LANs or WANs. Presentations may be displayed simultaneously on any combination of SMART Boards (for assembled groups) and connected computer screens (for individual participants). An audio conferencing system must be user-supplied.

Point-to-Point Communications

Site A ☐ ←————————————— ☐ Site B

In point-to-point communications, "A" always receives "B" and *vice versa*.

Multipoint Communications

Site A ☐ **ACTIVE**   PASSIVE ☐ Site B

● **Bridge**

Site C ☐ PASSIVE   PASSIVE ☐ Site D

When the network includes a bridge, the bridge routes information from the active (sending) site to the passive (receiving) sites. The configuration changes automatically as different sites become active.

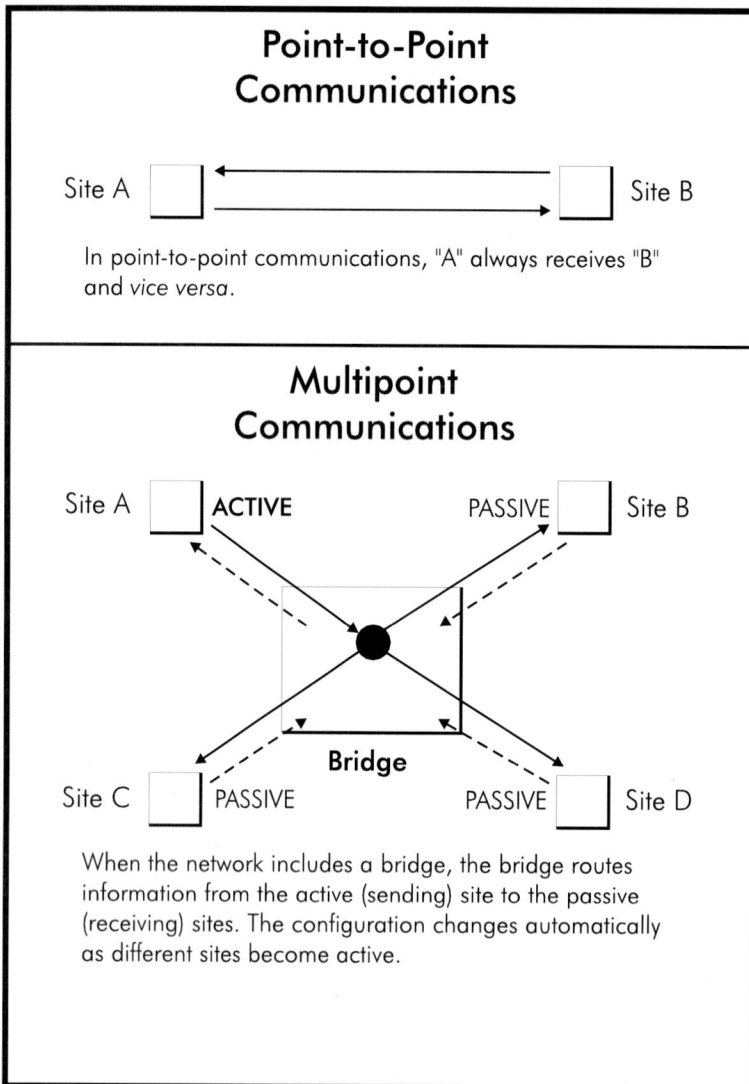

Fig. 8.3 How inter-site communications can be configured using a bridge.

The LiveBoard, from LiveWorks, Inc., a Xerox company, is a similarly powerful display tool also based on the electronic whiteboard metaphor. At present, it is probably the system with the greatest refinement and flexibility, integrating a variety of collaborative presentation capabilities with a display and control system.

The LiveBoard's stand-alone cabinet houses a 67-inch diagonal (about 53" x 40") rear-projection screen, consisting of a color active-matrix LCD display, positioned at a height similar to a normal whiteboard installation. Presentation information can be displayed on the screen from a variety of sources—VCR, CD-

ROM, laser disc, or computer-generated presentations from a LAN or hard disk drive—at local and remote locations. With multiple windows open on the screen, a complex presentation can simultaneously use information from several sources (Fig. 8.4). Cordless infrared pens with built-in controls, that look and feel much like felt-tip markers, can be used to point to, highlight, and even manipulate the displayed information.

Fig. 8.4 The LiveBoard is a stand-alone meeting tool (photograph courtesy LiveWorks, Inc. a division of Xerox, Inc.)

These new electronic whiteboard tools give users a great deal of flexibility and choice in building presentations to suit the occasion, whether full-fledged multimedia productions or simple text and graphics for an internal meeting. As LiveBoard user Ken Conley, manager of telecommunications services at Monsanto headquarters, says, "I can do a dynamite presentation by just pulling my files right off the server." Users also appreciate the ability to capture presentation materials directly, with or without annotations, from tools like the SMART Board and LiveBoard.

Conferencing Projectors

In comparison to the electronic whiteboard as a display tool, the conferencing projector is a new kid on the block, the first being Polycom's ShowStation, introduced in mid-1995. This new meeting tool is modeled on, and bears a strong resemblance to, the ordinary overhead projector, but with some brand-new capabilities (Fig. 8.5).

Fig. 8.5 The ShowStation resembles an overhead projector but has far-reaching capabilities (photograph courtesy Polycom, Inc.)

Polycom's intention in introducing the ShowStation was to add a document-sharing capability to audioconferences using their already successful SoundStation group audio terminal, on the theory that most meetings are primarily intended for exchanging and discussing complex information. Their conferencing projector provides a mechanism for simultaneous multiple-location display of either paper documents or computer-generated presentation materials over ordinary telephone lines.

With the ShowStation, documents are placed on a flat bed where an overhead scanner scans the image and displays it on a neighboring monochrome LCD panel. Like an overhead projector, the ShowStation has a light source that passes through the LCD panel so that an overhead mirror assembly can aim and focus the image on a regular projection screen. Scanned images are simultaneously transmitted to connected locations. Even small objects may be scanned for display.

For setting up the conference, the ShowStation unit has its own keypad, as well as a simple set of controls for managing the image display and changes during the presentation. The presenter can annotate any image by writing with a stylus on the digitizing LCD panel. Presentation materials may also be input directly from a computer. By connecting a standard laser printer, hard copies of the presentation, including annotations, can be made at any time.

One of the most significant aspects of these new display tools is that devices like ShowStation and LiveBoard, being compliant with the ITU's T.120 standards for multimedia conferencing, can communicate with each other if specific common software is used. For example, a LiveBoard can be used at one location with a ShowStation at another if both are running DataBeam's T.120-enabled FarSite conferencing software. Equipment incompatibilities, so long a problem for new meeting technologies, are on their way to becoming history thanks to more manufacturers' acceptance of international standards at an early stage of product development.

8.3.1.2 Information Display in the Videoconferencing Environment

Well-designed videoconferencing rooms usually include an ordinary whiteboard or flipchart, installed within a camera's view, for active use during a meeting. Videoconferencing rooms also typically include a still-graphics capability for showing documents, drawings, or static models to all locations, as well as equipment for slide presentations and videotapes.

Most videoconferencing room layouts locate presentation tools along one end, together with the video monitor(s). Seating is arranged to optimize viewing of the motion video display, together with whiteboard or other display media. The one exception is still graphics, which are captured by a camera above the table or at a graphics stand, and then normally displayed on a separate monitor in the room and at the other locations.

Because some videoconferencing systems do not do a very good job with high-resolution graphics, add-on devices for document conferencing have long been popular alternatives to using the built-in still graphics capability. The new electronic whiteboards and conferencing projectors can be set up side by side with videoconferencing rollabout units, using the same transmission facilities, for easier management of detailed document presentations. Used as an adjunct to videoconferencing, these tools also permit easier connection to computers and printers to display computer-generated information, which can later be provided in hard copy form, a service not possible with videoconferencing systems alone.

Integrating computer-generated images, MS PowerPoint presentations, or similar types of material directly into videoconferencing system transmissions does not always meet with success. Often, a PC or laptop will be equipped with a special video card that converts high-resolution graphics images into the relatively low-resolution images supported by videoconferencing systems. Unfortunately, the significant loss of image quality in the conversion process creates disappointed users.

Whereas the original technology development efforts were directed to adding a document presentation capability to videoconferencing, most recent work has focused on adding a videoconferencing capability to document and computer conferencing applications. Much of this work has spun off from desktop videoconferencing, which provides single users with a feature-rich resource of graphics, applications, multimedia, and, most recently, videoconferencing. Adding videoconferencing to a high-quality graphics system like LiveWorks' LiveBoard maintains the quality and performance of all the information display modes supported, while providing an acceptable motion video in its own user-sizable window.

8.3.1.3 Internet and Intranet Presentations

A number of the software tools developed for use in real-time presentations also offer a medium of distributing presentation material for self-directed, user-selectable access. In other words, presentations on demand. World Wide Web and ftp sites may contain encapsulated presentations, together with freely distributable run-time software, for availability via the Internet to an interested audience. A corporate intranet similarly lends itself to this mode of presenting information, for access by employees at the most convenient time for them.

Microsoft PowerPoint is a particularly efficient and easy-to-use tool for preparing and displaying good-looking slide presentations. Lotus Notes and similar applications can also be used to assemble, for example, training presentations for self-directed use by various employee groups. For self-guided hypertext presentations, the most widely accepted format is Adobe Acrobat. Like MS PowerPoint, Adobe Acrobat includes freely distributable viewers, making it a versatile medium for anything from marketing messages to training.

Generally, this kind of presentation supports no real-time interaction, although its use can be conjoined with other forms of meeting activity, either electronic or face-to-face. Used alone, such presentations are available when needed, in a way that is time- and distance-insensitive but also very impersonal.

Because the presenter may not know the audience, particularly for Web presentations, the anonymity aspect may be said to alter the quality of the interaction from that experienced in a face-to-face or a remote synchronous meeting. Because access is audience-controlled, the presentation does not have to follow a fixed sequence, and parts of it may be not be viewed at all. Each individual, with a uniquely customized view of the world, sees a different presentation, whether the Web page alone, or the complete set of material assembled by the presenter.

8.3.2 Interaction and Communication Across Distance and Time

8.3.2.1 Technology and the Distance Dimension

Whether you enjoy meetings, or whether you hate them, the use of various meeting support technologies has brought about irrevocable changes in the way meetings happen. For most people, the concept of a "real" meeting has long been firmly rooted in the notions, "in-person" and "face-to-face." The growing array of audio, video, and document conferencing tools, however, has expanded the "real" meeting to include participants at other locations.

In today's companies, the people required for a meeting may be down the hall or scattered across the continent (or around the world). They may also be in another building on the campus without fifteen minutes to spare to join other participants in a single meeting room. Current telecommunications and network technologies let groups meet and work together by enabling transmitted audio and motion video, as well as computer conferencing.

Without world-wide acceptance of telecommunications standards for equipment and transmission facilities, meeting across a distance would remain wholly dependent on travel. The first element of meeting across distance to be addressed in a practical way was audio. Extending person-to-person telephone communication into audioconference linking groups allowed group interaction across distances for meetings and discussions.

Audio-only meetings, however, did not provide adequate interactivity, and audioconferences continued to be supplemented by travel to meetings. Being able to present and exchange complex information was a necessary underpinning to productive meetings, and being able to see everyone and everything was also considered important by many users. Both these needs were addressed by the development of new technology to support various forms of document sharing and to provide real-time video so that people could see each other even over distances.

Audioconferencing

Despite the desire to add video, shared documents, and computer applications to remote meetings, audio remains the key component of communications across distances, and the audioconference is still a popular, much-used meeting medium.

The current generation of group audio terminals provides full-duplex audio communication over regular telephone lines with good intelligibility, free of echo and clipping effects. Devices like the Polycom SoundStation, NEC VoicePoint, and others accommodate group-to-group, or group-to-individual, discussions very effectively. Digital audio bridging is a mature technology, allowing interconnection of hundreds of sites with no loss of quality. Bridges can be either leased by the minute from local phone companies and bridging providers, or purchased outright for use with a company's existing phone system.

The high level of interest in the Internet as an alternative communication tool has also led to the development of software that, in conjunction with the right computer hardware, permits audioconferencing over the Internet. Popular PC sound cards like the Creative Labs SoundBlaster, plus an inexpensive microphone and loudspeaker, are all the hardware needed. The addition of Internet Relay Chat (IRC) software to the computer can be done using shareware packages like Winsock IRC, mIRC, Ichat, or Ws-irc, or through commercial software. Real-time discussion requires using an Internet site with a "reflector" or "multicasting" capability, similar to an audio bridge in concept. The quality of Internet audioconferences, however, is still problematic because of bandwidth constraints.

Videoconferencing

The massive amounts of signal data required for good-quality motion video transmission cannot be accommodated over the narrow bandwidth of ordinary telephone lines. Advances in computer technology, however, have made it possible to use sophisticated mathematical processes to derive algorithms to compress and decompress the data. With current video compression methods, however, transmission of high-detail, high-motion images still requires at least a 384 Kbps transmission bit rate to maintain an acceptably smooth rendition of motion.

Processing time for compression and decompression also presented problems, because even very fast computer processors required noticeable amounts of time to handle the video signals; transmission delays incurred when satellites were used compounded the problem. Hapless executives engaging in transatlantic videoconferences gained the impression that their colleagues were a little slow, when they had to wait for answers even to simple questions from the remote location.

The first videoconferencing systems designed for business use were expensive, bulky, and wholly proprietary; that is, equipment would operate only with equipment from the same manufacturer. Over about a 10-year period, the cost of videoconferencing equipment has plummeted, much smaller units are now available, and most of them not only claim compliance with ITU's H.320 family of standards for videoconferencing, but are actually compatible with each other in operation.

Today's videoconferencing systems not only span distance very effectively for groups in specially equipped meeting rooms, but also extend to the desktop to permit real-time video meetings among separated individuals. The desktop environment has presented many challenges to developing affordable systems that still provide adequate performance and functionality.

High-quality H.320-compatible desktop systems are available from companies like PictureTel, the market leader for group videoconferencing equipment. VCON and Zydachron also manufacture good-quality systems that are marketed under a number of different companies' names. In addition, a considerable variety of proprietary desktop systems are on the market, some of which provide good performance while others are quite limited in their capabilities.

The use of desktop video as a remote meeting participation tool has further been hampered by the relatively high cost of providing adequate digital transmission bandwidth to the desktop. Without sufficient guaranteed bandwidth, sound and image quality suffer, and the frame rate for motion is lethargic, to say the least. Many of the systems designed to operate over LANs and WANs have limited functionality because of the inherent characteristics of these transmission environments, designed to handle "bursty" traffic rather than a sustained, continuous data stream. As long as sufficient bandwidth is available, however, videoconferencing systems like Intel's ProShare Video System 200 and Intecom's Incite are capable of providing an acceptable face-to-face meeting experience across distances.

Videoconferencing over the Internet has been available for several years, popularly using MBONE and CU-SeeMe, developed at Xerox PARC and Cornell University, respectively. An improved commercial-use version of CU-SeeMe from White Pine Software has an augmented feature set. Another commercial product for Internet videoconferencing is Connectix's VideoPhone, available for both MS Windows and Macintosh, consisting of software packaged with a simple starter video camera. A number of products, like VDONet Corp.'s Web-based videoconferencing platform, are at various stages of beta test. With these and other Internet videoconferencing tools, users nonetheless may find that the lack of sufficient bandwidth seriously impairs performance, especially for business use. At this stage in its evolution, Internet videoconferencing is not yet ready for prime time.

Whatever form of videoconferencing is used, interest remains high in being able to link more than two sites for a meeting. Standards-based multipoint control units (MCUs) now permit most group videoconferencing systems and compatible desktop systems to be linked in a single conference, even if different sites are using equipment from different manufacturers. Although large organizations typically purchase and install their own MCUs, transmission service providers also offer the necessary video bridging with their own network-embedded MCUs.

Multipoint connectivity is also increasingly possible for videoconferencing over LANs and even the Internet, using software-based multipoint applications running on powerful workstations. Missing from current capabilities, however, is the ability to cross-conference between Internet- and WAN-based videoconferences. It is expected that standards currently under development will mitigate this problem in the future.

Document Conferencing

The need for document conferencing was recognized at about the same time significant efforts were being put into marketing videoconferencing. Improved interactivity between distant locations was wanted because the presentation capabilities of videoconferencing did not create the same meeting process as collaboratively marking up documents.

Among the best stand-alone document conferencing systems of the mid-1980s were DataBeam's CT 1000 and CT 2000 systems. These systems combined a PC, high-resolution monitor, high-resolution projector, graphics tablet, scanner, laser printer, and communications software. Paper documents scanned into the system could be displayed, annotated, and printed at the connected locations. When the industry's attention was diverted from this kind of conference-room device to other means of supporting meeting activities, DataBeam ceased manufacturing these systems. Nevertheless, many users are still finding systems purchased 10 years ago a useful adjunct to remote meetings.

As previously mentioned, most videoconferencing systems include a graphics capability but generally do not support document conferencing beyond the ability to display and discuss documents at two or more sites. The conferencing projector, such as Polycom's ShowStation, includes annotation and capture capabilities that make it an effective document conferencing tool. The new generation of electronic whiteboards, such as SMART Board and LiveBoard, similarly provides solid support for document conferencing.

With computers mushrooming on desktops all over the world, however, far more attention has been paid in recent years to document conferencing by means of shared computer applications. The current leader in capabilities is DataBeam's FarSite, an MS Windows software package providing standards-compliant document and file sharing, and with standards-compliant bridges for multipoint document sharing. Intel's ProShare Personal Conferencing software similarly provides document conferencing capabilities, although Intel has lagged behind DataBeam in including multipoint support.

For Internet users, software specifically supporting document conferencing is rare to nonexistent, given the ease of file transfer and e-mail communication as an alternative.

8.3.2.2 Spanning Time

Users have come to a fairly ready acceptance of audio- and videoconferences as "real" meetings, especially because video permits a remote meeting to remain a face-to-face meeting. It is somewhat more difficult to expand the innate concept of a "real" meeting to include asynchronous meetings. Whether or not we call it a meeting, however, we have no problem expecting asynchronous interaction and even collaboration to continue among meeting participants outside the designated meeting time.

For organizations with offices distributed among different time zones all around the world, the simple ability to use technology to span distance enables synchronous meetings that occur at different times, depending on where any specific group of participants is located. If need so dictates, the meeting itself can travel across both time and distance, letting new sites in later time zones join the meeting as sites in earlier time zones complete their part of the business and drop out. This is the approach taken in Andersen Consulting's "follow-the-sun" network service program, for example, where technicians in France, the United States, and Singapore take turns dealing with network issues, service, and upgrades, using conferencing technologies to communicate.

The incorporation of a capture mechanism, or some means of storing and forwarding messages, gives users the ability to share aspects of a meeting across time. The possibilities exist today for asynchronous communication of both process and product of the meeting, as well as an on-going exchange of responses related to the meeting and its objectives. All or part of a meeting may be captured through recording either, or both, sound and video, so that the process of the meeting may be reviewed asynchronously by people unable to attend at the original time. Alternatively, a message using sound and video may be recorded to initiate an asynchronous meeting that will, at least in part, be conducted through the exchange of such messages.

One of the first supports for asynchronous meetings, apart from straightforward recordings, was MediaMail, a feature introduced by videoconferencing equipment manufacturer VTEL as part of its high-end group videoconferencing system in 1991. A strong proponent of multimedia conferencing, VTEL wanted to address the situation where, for example, North American design staff and production staff in the Far East were not working at the same time because the time zone offset exceeded the length of a normal workday. The MediaMail scenario went something like this:

> You and a group of North American colleagues have just completed a videoconference to finish the design review for a new product. Production is supposed to start soon in your Taiwan plant. At the end of your meeting, the marked-up CAD drawings and revised spreadsheets, plus full-motion video of the discussion with audio and graphics, are downloaded as e-mail on the server at the Taiwan plant, arriving at midnight Taiwan time. When the head of production arrives at work in the morning, the MediaMail message is waiting. The Taiwan staff meet in the videoconferencing room to review the message and prepare their response, to be returned to you in the same way.

The MediaMail system provided a high level of information exchange in a convenient way, at a fairly low cost. In VTEL's words, MediaMail "removed time as a problem" by freeing users from scheduled meetings and by providing the ability to span time zones. The multimedia nature of the messages meant that a more complete expression of an idea could be communicated, especially important for asynchronous interaction in which real-time questions and requests for further explanation simply could not occur.

Although VTEL's MediaMail did not find extensive acceptance, the concept of asynchronous interaction continues to fascinate both users and manufacturers of the new conferencing technologies. With the emerging T.120 and T.130 standards and relatively inexpensive hard disks for storage and lower transmission costs, multimedia mail is now more likely to appeal to a large number of users.

The incorporation of audio and motion video into asynchronous interactions, in addition to text, graphics, and data, is likely to require some new technological features, if users are to be spared the need to adapt their own behavior to make effective use of these tools. The most pressing need is for some method of indexing or searching through a meeting record so that the asynchronous participant can select or find specific significant parts of the record. Without such a capability, users could waste time reviewing discussions that, in the end, turn

out to be irrelevant to the main objective of the meeting. It could also be potentially helpful if it were possible to synchronize the ability to review changes in
accompanying text or data files with the ability to see and hear what other people were doing at the time those changes were made.

In contrast, the asynchronous exchange of single-medium messages is a
long accepted practice, and today's dependence on e-mail messages is little different from an earlier era's dependence on postal services. Technology has speeded
the process, but has not substantially changed the nature of the interaction.
Electronic presentation technologies, many of which already include store-and-
forward or other access capabilities, provide additional enrichment for asynchronous communications.

While the accustomed give-and-take of a real-time meeting is missing, the
exchange and enhancement of information and ideas across time may make up
in thoughtful response what they lose in spontaneity. Participants who would
otherwise have been unavailable are able to make their contributions, in context,
to the work of the group. With time-spanning capabilities, the business of the
meeting can continue in a productive way as long as necessary.

8.3.3 Convivial Tools for Collaboration

In his 1992 book *Liberation Management*, Tom Peters talked about the
emergence of "extended family" project management, noting that, "through the
use of various groupware and other problem-solving tools, the project manage-
ment/brainstorming/idea generation/social integration process is changed forever." [4] He was right. Collaborative presentation, with the support of the right
technological tools, becomes a living exercise in developing concepts, sharing and
weighing ideas, and directing multiple intellectual energies toward specific ends.
The group dynamics operate across time and space, allowing each individual's
presentation to be changed or merged with others. The product of this active collaboration is ultimately captured for application or re-examination in a continua-
tion of similar group interactions.

The different meeting tools discussed earlier in this section all support one
or more aspects of the meeting process, but none is completely capable of repli-
cating the totality of human meeting interaction for transmission across distance
and time. As Peters noted, meetings involve project management, brainstorming, idea generation, and social integration, to which could be added information
sharing and manipulation, debate, negotiation, and a host of other kinds of interaction. As a result, people need not only different types of tools but also many
types of tools, because the meeting itself is intrinsically a multifaceted, multifunctional event.

Some of the most pertinent thinking about the nature and needs of collaborative work is expressed in Michael Schrage's *No More Teams! Mastering the
Dynamics of Creative Collaboration* [6]. Schrage makes a clear distinction
between communication and collaboration, noting that, although dictionaries
define communication as transmitting information, the word itself comes from
the Latin verb *communicare*, which doesn't mean "to communicate" but "to

share." To be effective, exchanging information requires a useful context, so that people can use other aids to construct relevant meanings based both on the available information and on their individual expertise. Consequently, Schrage asserts that "collaboration takes communication back to its roots."

What does this mean for collaborative presentation tools? If Schrage's premise that "all collaborations rely on a shared space" is accepted, his discussion of collaboration design themes allows the derivation of the following list of appropriate characteristics for this shared space:

☞ permits real-time access by all the collaborators;

☞ supports continuous, but not necessarily continual, communication;

☞ supports participation by collaborators from remote sites;

☞ supports selective use of outsiders;

☞ supports or serves as a reference point for multiple forms of representations—mathematical, linguistic, structural, conversational, and visual; and

☞ is freely manipulable by all collaborators

Virtually all the contemporary meeting tools discussed earlier in this section incorporate the first four of these characteristics. Audio, video, and document conferencing tools, including computer conferencing, are designed for real-time interaction. The continuity of communication is user-controlled, although it may be subject to scheduling constraints, due to participants' personal commitments or limited availability of appropriately equipped meeting rooms and transmission facilities. Telecommunications technology supports remote participation and the involvement of selected outsiders to varying degrees, depending on the type of meeting tool, and equipment compatibility issues are now much less likely to present a problem.

Where the more convivial tools begin to stand out among the host of other electronic meeting tools is on the last two points, in essence, multimedia capabilities and full access for interactive manipulation. Until recently, the greatest functional support for collaborative work across distances has been through videoconferencing and through computer conferencing. Each of these conferencing media, however, has limitations for the kind of collaborative work Schrage envisions.

Videoconferencing alone does not provide participants with the capability of jointly manipulating information because its presentation capabilities are more for display than for active collaboration. Even when presentation materials can be annotated and changed during a meeting, videoconferencing lacks its own capture capability. It does, however, provide fairly good support for the kind of social integration Peters talked about as an integral part of the meeting process.

In contrast, computer conferencing now provides good support for all participants to manipulate information and to capture the product at any point in its evolution. Nevertheless, it is a desktop activity, a personal activity, and does not provide the kind of group experience that occurs when a number of participants are together in the same place. It is important to remember that personal technologies like desktop video and computer conferencing do not necessarily scale up for large group use with the same functionality; simply adding a bigger screen for the same application is not a viable solution. While computer conferencing over Internet or intranet connections is an excellent means of collaborating across distance and time, the present lack of support for rich person-to-person contact in the course of that collaboration denies this kind of collaborative presentation activity status as a convivial tool.

The most promising collaborative tools are those that integrate the widest range of capabilities to support a variety of kinds of interaction from all locations. Electronic whiteboards like SMART Board and conferencing projectors like ShowStation provide participants at all connected sites with an equal opportunity to contribute to the collaboration. While an actual group of people can meet around one device, other linked groups and individuals can share in the discussion and the active review and modification of whatever material is displayed. The main medium missing from collaboration using these tools is video, but if these tools are used in conjunction with a videoconferencing system, preferably one that permits connection among both meeting rooms and desktops, Schrage's criteria for shared space are largely met.

Perhaps the most complete realization of Schrage's shared space currently available is LiveWorks' LiveBoard. LiveBoard is essentially a multimedia display device based on the whiteboard metaphor, and is wholly amenable to use in a local-site-only meeting. It can accept and display everything from slides and VCR tapes to multimedia CD-ROM material, integrated with audio and videoconferencing to link remote groups and desktops as needed, in point-to-point or multipoint configurations.

The work of Xerox PARC researchers into improved interfaces between humans and technology underlies many aspects of the LiveBoard design. For example, collaborators can not only write directly on the screen with infrared pens, but can also use the wireless devices to point, write, and control computer applications and other functions from their seats at the table. In other words, equal opportunity to manipulate the developing product of collaboration is fully supported. In addition, the LiveBoard software provides a whiteboard or flip-chart mode, making multiple "pages" available for jotting down notes and ideas, and even rearranging handwritten material on those pages. When computer applications are the medium of collaboration, handwriting recognition supports, for example, changing numbers on a spreadsheet or Gantt chart by hand, then automatically recalculating or adjusting dependent elements within the computer file and displaying those changes on screen.

None of these tools perfectly replicates the whole spectrum of human interaction. Even the development of new standards and capabilities for multimedia communication and collaboration through computers and other devices, for example, in the form of T.120-compatible applications sharing and shared workspace software, will never completely supersede the human need to collaborate person to person and face to face. Nevertheless, the growing availability of devices like these offers a tremendous economic benefit to time-pressed employees in today's far-flung organizations. In the last few years, collaborative presentation technology has made great progress in addressing our meeting needs. Devices like the LiveBoard are not the culmination of the evolution of communications technology, but rather the beginning of the serious evolution of convivial, collaborative technology.

8.4 MAKING COLLABORATIVE PRESENTATION TECHNOLOGIES PART OF THE MEETING

8.4.1 Three Meetings Revisited

Somewhere in the middle of America, a project leader is presenting his team's proposal for a revolutionary new product to a group of senior executives. The executives have gathered in a comfortable conference room with a large electronic whiteboard at one end. The project leader is in a smaller meeting room in his home office building in Philadelphia, with a similarly-equipped large whiteboard. He has his computer hooked up to the whiteboard, so that he can display his Gantt charts, spreadsheets, and organization charts simultaneously at both locations.

The executives can see the project leader in their video window, but they're more interested in the information he's showing them and decide to close the window to see the rest of the information full-screen. The project leader, on the other hand, finds it very helpful to see the reactions of the group in his video window.

One executive takes a laser pen and shortens the time for one of the tasks on the Gantt chart, which immediately changes to show how dependent activities will be affected. The project leader agrees with the change, but points out on the organization chart that extra staff will be needed to meet the new deadline for the prototype. To provide further clarification on the staffing needs, he introduces an MS PowerPoint slide presentation, asking another member of the team, whose office is just down the hall, to come in to talk about the slides. The executives have a lot of questions, but they have the right person in front of them to provide the answers. When agreement is reached among the executives, a senior manager brings up an approval form and signs off on the project. At both locations, those who want hard copies of the relevant information print them out, with revisions. The team members not involved in the presentation will find all the changes on their computers as soon as the meeting is over.

* * *

In Connecticut, a sales group is having a strategic planning meeting. For once, all the members of the group are actually together in one place. Usually, they conduct these meetings using conferencing projectors or electronic whiteboards to display their many charts. For this meeting, a computer diagram for possible reorganization is central to their discussion. When they've exhausted the possibilities for changing the diagram, there are still a lot of unresolved ideas floating around. One of them saves the computer file and then switches the display to whiteboard mode. When they run out of space, they simply draw a line across the screen and push the first set of notes out of the way. It's a lively discussion and there's a lot of dragging words around on the display. It takes surprisingly little time, however, for the group to bring an agreed-on order to what, at first, looked like some really wild ideas. Before the meeting breaks up, copies are printed for everyone. One person is designated to schedule a meeting with their VP the next day to go over the proposal embodied in the whiteboard notes. All participants are satisfied that the notes are good enough to put forward in exactly the form the group created because they will also convey a sense of the process that was used to develop the proposal.

* * *

In Chicago and Washington, a group of industry leaders is having a videoconference to agree on a new industry standard for a class of products. They are using a regular room videoconferencing system, but they also have an electronic whiteboard conferencing system on which they are running a computer conferencing application so that they can make changes in the standard as they reach agreement on each aspect. When new ideas find acceptance, they simply incorporate them into the computer file from either location. Much of the time, everyone's attention is focused on the video monitors, as the debate on some issues is very intense. But once they've talked it through, they make the necessary changes with only minor quibbling over wording. By the time their meeting ends, the completed standards document is ready to print.

* * *

8.4.2 A Sample of User Experience

The people who work on developing collaborative presentation technologies believe that all the advantages illustrated in these hypothetical examples can be realized by actual users of products like DataBeam's FarSite software, Live-Works' LiveBoard, Polycom's ShowStation, the SMART Boards, and a growing array of meeting tools with similar capabilities. The presentation of information and ideas can be simplified while enhancing collaborative activity. The time to achieve a finished product is shortened. Less travel is required, and additional expertise can easily be brought into the meeting to enrich understanding of specific aspects of the problem. Attention is fully directed toward the objectives of the meeting and the quality of interaction is high. Follow-up work requires fewer steps when changes in documents can be made directly, without transcribing them from notes and flipchart pages.

DataBeam's David Panos sees a very broad range of uses for the technology. "At one end of the range are specialized industry applications—petrochemical, geology—where, for example, you might have a remote expert capability consulting around image analysis all over the world," he says. "At the other extreme, you might find the technology used in the product development process for a consumer packaging company. Multiple international company sites all linked to their vendors can run multipoint conferences to walk through packaging issues, including people like tool and die makers to help address all aspects of introducing new lines of product packaging. The product development kind of application tends to have multiple disciplines working together, as well as people from outside the company, people who aren't colocated. Reducing cycle time is really important to that group. You can do things visually on line in a very short time, although many different kinds of meetings may occur."

The Crucial Executive Presentation

For Jeff Comfort, Vice President of Alternative Office Strategies at Marriott Corporation, one trial use of LiveWorks' LiveBoard technology for an important presentation was enough to make him an advocate of collaborative presentation technology. Faced with the challenge of designing a half-day presentation outlining recommendations on new business areas for potential exploration by Marriott International, Comfort knew the presentation had to be powerful and effective to make a lasting impression on his audience of top executives.

In designing the presentation, Comfort and his team used the live videoconferencing capability of LiveBoard to bring in a major supplier to showcase innovative aspects of their product line. They also incorporated a representative application on CD-ROM as well as an MS PowerPoint slide presentation. With its integrated technologies, the LiveBoard provided complete control of all the diverse media, and Comfort credits the medium with the success of his presentation. Indeed, he sees the LiveBoard itself almost as a metaphorical representation of the content that he was trying to convey, saying, "Clearly, the ability to take a tool that embodied what we were trying to get across to the executives had a significant impact on the outcome."

The presentation also had another outcome, in that several Marriott International locations are now equipped with LiveBoards, used for staff meetings, training applications, and, of course, presentations.

Military Meetings

The automation specialists of the U.S. Army's 10th Division (Light Infantry), based at Ft. Drum, New York, turned to collaborative presentation technology to optimize information exchange and improve operational efficiency. Division Automation Officer Major Greg Dreisbach cites an Army cost-benefit study that found computerized presentation technology pays for itself in a matter of weeks by reducing recurring materials expenses such as photocopying and slide production.

In choosing to make more extensive use of the new technologies available, military personnel were seeking flexibility, scalability, cost-efficiency, and mobility. A wide variety of presentation styles and media is needed to support briefings and operational meetings, essentially all computer-based. Sensitive information used in classified briefings is stored on a hard disk that can be removed and stored in a safe when not in use, a more secure approach than reproducing classified material on slides or transparencies, since no duplicates or copy room versions exist. Collaborative presentation tools are also proving an effective support for training soldiers.

Sailing Free of the Paper Sea

A world leader like Compaq Computer Corporation keeps its corporate legal department afloat on a sea of papers—licensing contracts, press statements, trademark documents—with never-ending waves of drafts, many of which require the highest confidentiality. Using integrated collaborative presentation technologies to facilitate the production and review of complex documents leads to quicker consensus on critical legal issues.

The use of the technology is not confined to group collaboration by the legal team within Compaq's Houston headquarters. Attorneys at remote locations can also be brought into a meeting from their desktop PCs, using conferencing software together with an audio connection.

The legal department uses their interactive technology for a variety of purposes. For example, instead of discussing budget projections on paper, forecast budgets and billings are reviewed interactively on the electronic whiteboard at monthly meetings. Multimedia capabilities have also found favor for training, where seamless switching from MS PowerPoint presentations to videotapes and the ability to bring up databases and Windows programs into an interactive group learning environment are seen as enhancing the quality and effectiveness of a variety of training programs.

Compaq's legal team is benefiting from the real-life experience of advantages previously identified in this chapter for collaborative presentation technologies. A number of different departments have worked with the new meeting tools so successfully that the legal team complains, "Now everybody wants to use our conference room!"

8.4.3 Why Collaborative Presentation Technologies Find Acceptance

The preceding are only a few examples of high-value user acceptance of one collaborative presentation product from one manufacturer. Many manufacturers of the new technologies are hearing similar success stories from their users. The ease of finding actual examples of real-world use suggests that people are adopting collaborative presentation technologies at a faster rate than a number of other meeting technologies previously introduced into the marketplace. Why?

One significant reason for swift acceptance is price. A big advantage of simple presentation tools like whiteboards and overhead projectors, and audioconferencing equipment for meeting with people in other locations, has always been cost-effectiveness. With verbal exchange as the key medium of communication, and a place for sharing information where revisions, results, and new ideas can be handwritten as the meeting proceeds, participants can learn, criticize, brainstorm, and solve problems. In other words, most of their meeting needs are addressed by the simple tools. Any new technologies have to add a lot of value, or enhance existing value very significantly, to be worth the price.

Videoconferencing, while an exciting innovation, found slow acceptance until the high costs of equipment and transmission facilities were brought down to affordable levels. And in many meetings, seeing other people's faces is far less important than focusing on documents or other forms of information.

Cost-conscious corporations are looking for more than reduced travel costs. They want flexibility, gains in individual and group productivity, and savings in time and effort as well as money. Collaborative presentation technologies offer all of these advantages in a good variety of products at different price points that permit users to choose what they think will best meet their needs. Interestingly enough, many users cost-justify adopting the new technology on the basis of travel savings, only to find the new tools used even more heavily as support for in-house, on-premises meetings.

The second major force driving acceptance is the incredible flexibility of these technologies to fulfill communication and collaboration needs while requiring minimal adaptation of users' meeting behavior. Because the new tools build on familiar low-tech versions, and integrate other technologies such as computer technology that now has a very large and experienced user base, the best meeting habits are supported.

For LiveBoard, for example, the work of Xerox's Palo Alto Research Center (Xerox PARC) on improving interfaces between humans and technology has unquestionably had a strong positive influence on product acceptance because form and function have been designed with sensitivity to who would use it and how it would be used. Other manufacturers whose products are finding good user acceptance have similarly exercised care in design, paying close attention to users' meeting needs and habits.

Collaborative presentation technologies include a number of more or less mature products with potential for further enhancements as new advances are made. Organizations can be expected to make increasing use of these technologies as the broader development of and compliance with international standards ensures ease of integration of different media and different technological devices.

8.5 THE STANDARDS AND TRANSMISSION MEDIA ENVIRONMENT

Transmission media play a key role in collaborative presentations whenever information or personal presence is being brought in from another location. Once information has been translated into digital form, it may be transmitted immediately or stored for later transmission or access. Even where all participants are together in one place, there is often a need to transfer information from its source to a display device, often an interactive one, and back again. Transmission media therefore can be visualized as the "glue" that connects the various sites and devices to each other.

There is an obvious expectation that all the equipment at any location should be able to communicate with all the equipment at any other location. However, at present, there is no single technology or device that will fully support all the elements that might be desired in a meeting. Users may need a variety of data, applications, graphics, motion video, and audio, each of which has its own requirements for transmission even over short distances. At the same time, there are many different media available for transmitting these kinds of information, not all of which are compatible with each other.

Collaborative presentation technologies encompass a wide range of technologies, most of which evolved more or less independently of each other. In the words of LiveWorks' Frank Halasz, Vice President of Product Development, "Anything involving collaboration makes standards absolutely paramount! We need to communicate with other devices, especially at the desktop. None of that will happen without standards." To avoid frustration on the part of users, the selection of technologies—and the design of new tools—requires an awareness of the standards and compatibility environment not only for the various devices used but also for the transmission networks that link them together.

In technology and telecommunications, there are often a number of ways of achieving a goal or objective which, on their own, are functional and effective. Nevertheless, when different techniques are combined, the result may be completely unworkable. Nowhere does this point strike home more sharply than in telecommunications. At this stage of evolution, collaborative presentation technologies are still coming to terms with the square peg/round hole problem. As standards for interoperability and specified levels of functionality continue to be developed and adopted by manufacturers, it will become easier to achieve uncomplicated interactive communications between different kinds of devices and different kinds of networks.

This section examines the current technologies, their strengths and weaknesses, in light of when and how they can be correctly combined into a working whole.

8.5.1 Standards and Protocols: How Important Are They?

Today, sending a fax across the continent or to the other side of the world is something we take for granted. This is possible because manufacturers and telecommunications providers have all agreed on a single set of standards for facsimile machines, standards that were ratified by the International Telecommunications Union (ITU), an arm of the United Nations.

Not so long ago, sending a fax required having the same make and even model of fax machine at both locations if such a transmission were to be possible. Thanks to universal adoption of a standard method of signal coding and transmission, fax machines can now communicate with each other regardless of who manufactured them.

But today, fax machines do not communicate only with other stand-alone fax machines, nor do they all work the same way, from the user's point of view. A fax can be sent to a machine that is a personal computer, to a machine that reproduces the transmitted image on rolls of thermal paper, or to a machine using sheets of plain paper with ink-jet or laser printing. Some fax machines include electronic document storage, fax-on-demand, group transmission, security, and many other features. In other words, the hardware features, capabilities, and user interface can be significantly different from one fax machine to another, even though they can all intercommunicate properly at a basic level.

The preceding two paragraphs describe two virtual layers of the facsimile machine. The first is the transmission and coding layer, where both connected machines must conform if they are to intercommunicate. This first layer is defined by accepted international standards. The second is the features layer, which is designed on the basis of the needs and desires of individual users, and which does not impact upon the basic capability of communicating with other facsimile machines around the world. This second layer is entirely within the proprietary discretion of manufacturers, dictated by their perception of what the market wants for convenience, flexibility, and ease of use.

The importance of standards is, quite simply, that they are the key to connectivity and interoperability among different devices of the same kind and, increasingly, among devices of different kinds. Without standards, no matter how wonderful the features of any particular device, its users would be unable to use it to communicate with anyone who did not have the same device.

8.5.1.1 When Is a Standard Not a Standard?

The International Telecommunications Union (ITU) standards have already been mentioned with reference to facsimile machines; there are also ITU standards for a very wide range of other telecommunications transmission media and devices. Other bona fide standards organizations relevant to collaborative presentation technologies include the Electrical Industries Association (EIA), the Institute of Electrical and Electronics Engineers (IEEE), and the International Standards Organization (ISO). In addition, a nation may have its own set of specific telecommunications standards, set by its major telephone company and/or government, as well as safety and other standards with which compliance is important. Any communications device typically carries approvals by a number of such organizations, or indicates its compliance with particular standards in its data sheets.

One unique "standards" process is reflected in the on-line community of the Internet. Groups of interested individuals or companies can form a loose association and produce a document known as an RFC xxxx (Request for Comments, plus a number). These are posted on the Internet, where interested parties are free to provide input to the process. Evolving in this less formal way, the Internet has a relatively short standardization turnaround time, complementary to rapid technological change and possibly less influenced by national interests.

Not all things touted as standards are internationally approved and accepted standards. In these days of rapid technological evolution, some manufacturers and software companies occasionally form loose alliances to promote a new technology, often proclaiming that Company X and Company Y have produced a new, improved standard for their product(s). Unfortunately, such proclamations are usually nothing more than declarations of a new proprietary method of doing something. The possibility always exists that a strong promotion of the new "standard" will lead to sufficient market penetration that the proprietary method, through ubiquity of use, achieves some status as a *de facto* standard. Until such methods are approved by the international standards-setting organizations, however, they do not qualify as genuine standards.

Within the computer industry, *de facto* standards have tended to predominate, whereas the telecommunications industry has long depended on internationally agreed-upon standards. The different "standardization cultures" of the two industries have led to some delicate negotiating over the best ways to manage the merger of computing and communications technologies in the new collaborative presentation tools.

Proprietary processes or methods may also be named using the same naming format as is used by one international standards organization or another. The names of ITU standards, for example, take the form of a letter of the alphabet, followed by a period, followed by a three-digit number. Standards for different technologies are grouped together under particular letters: audio standards are G.xxx, motion video standards are H.xxx, multimedia conferencing standards are T.xxx, and so on. At the height of competition for sales of high-speed modems, before the V.34 standard had received final approval, one modem was advertised as a V.FAST modem. The name of the product suggested the name of a standard, but there was no V.FAST standard.

Even more problematic are product descriptions that incorporate the names of actual standards within proprietary references to the product's capabilities. For example, one form of motion video compression has been called "motion JPEG." JPEG happens to be an ISO still-image standard. The motion video products known as "motion JPEG," however, do not conform to the ISO standard, but are wholly proprietary.

8.5.1.2 Standards-Based versus Proprietary Products

Standards-based products and proprietary products each have their advantages and disadvantages. Standards tend to follow the initial introduction of new technologies, which usually emerge first in proprietary form. Set by international committees and subjected to intensive scrutiny to ensure that performance expectations will be reliably met, standards take time, up to several years, to develop. In the interim, proprietary products are usually the approach of choice for the end-user who absolutely must have a certain new feature or capability now.

The one main disadvantage of standards-based products—they are not really state-of-the-art because of the length of the standards-setting process—also leads to a significant advantage. In the process of achieving agreement on an international standard, all the bugs are usually worked out, so that the resultant compliant products tend to be more reliable.

The reliability of standards-based products extends not only to performance but also to connectivity. Part of the product development process usually includes interoperability testing with other manufacturers' standards-based systems. These tests, self-imposed by the industry, often result in manufacturers following a more rigorous debugging process, with the end-user being the beneficiary. In contrast, in the rush to market, proprietary products do not always get properly debugged. With software in particular, users of proprietary solutions sometimes feel they are engaged in an endless beta test, where each upgrade simply exchanges one set of problems for another.

Another serious consideration with proprietary telecommunications and collaborative presentation technologies equipment and transmission methods is whether an organization can accept functioning as an island, potentially isolated from electronic communication and collaboration with strategic partners. Standards-compliant solutions greatly increase a company's potential ability to communicate with external organizations, enhancing the value of the technology investment in both tangible and intangible ways. On the other hand, proprietary systems may offer some performance benefits for in-house applications where external communications are not needed.

The standards-based product is also less likely to succumb to planned obsolescence. The latest and greatest standards-based product can be expected to work properly with a five-year-old standards-based unit, regardless of the manufacturer. Of course, the newer unit may also incorporate newer standards and technology, giving it greater capabilities than the older unit.

Manufacturers of proprietary products are under no obligation to provide backwards compatibility when they introduce new products. The collective wisdom of the marketing department may be the determining factor in whether a new proprietary product will provide any degree of compatibility with older products that have been "manufacturer discontinued." Users may be faced with a choice between undertaking an expensive upgrade of existing equipment at the same time as the new product is acquired, or changing vendors completely.

Protecting a company's investment in proprietary technology against premature obsolescence is possible, of course. Most manufacturers will enter into an agreement to provide customer support, maintenance and parts for five years following the last purchase of a new product. Such contracts may also include a stipulation that the manufacturer will either give one year's notice of cessation of manufacturing the product, or assurances that the product will be available for a minimum of a specified number of years. The cost of such agreements is variable, and companies must evaluate whether the benefits are worth the price.

Cost-conscious corporations, however, appreciate that standards-based telecommunications hardware and software provide a degree of stability and cost control that is not possible with most proprietary solutions. The adoption of international standards means a multiplicity of manufacturers of compatible products, resulting in a wider range of systems from which users may choose, with a corresponding range of prices, features, and service options.

8.5.2 Communications Standards

The proliferation of audio, graphics, multimedia, videoconferencing, and document sharing tools is making the shared virtual workspace a reality. Business, industry, and education have been quick to grasp the benefits, so quick that demand from bandwidth-challenged users has simultaneously driven advances in both transmission and terminal device technology.

The variety of standards for these technologies is bewildering, more so because the capabilities embodied in the various standards are generally not transparent to the user. Not only do different standards do different things, but they also specify different performance standards for the same kinds of end-user functionality.

In combining technologies for integrated tools and applications such as collaborative presentations, providing the most appropriate grade of performance and connectivity, based on the needs and expectations of a particular group of users, presents a significant challenge to manufacturers, service providers, and their customers.

There are two broad groups of standards specifically relevant to collaborative presentation technologies: one for compression of audio, motion video, and graphics images, and one for multimedia conferencing data protocols. Following are brief summaries of the various standards and their roles.

8.5.2.1 Audio, Motion Video, and Graphics Standards

Transmitting audio, motion video, and graphics between terminal devices requires prodigious volumes of signal data, especially for motion video. The transmission facilities used for most business applications do not have the capability of handling such large volumes of data. For this reason, many of the relevant standards focus on ways of compressing the data so that it can be transmitted at the lowest possible bandwidth; the receiving device must then decompress the data for display at the other end.

A codec (COder/DECoder) is a full-duplex (bi-directional) device that accepts the original video and audio signals, processes them to remove redundant information, and transmits them over a digital transmission line together with user data and control information. At the receive end, another codec decompresses the signal for output. Codecs may be stand-alone devices, like many video codecs, but increasingly are being built into the growing variety of collaborative presentation tools.

Many of the standards for audio, motion video, and graphics specify how codecs are expected to operate. They also include protocols for such things as establishing connections, control of multipoint operation, and encryption, among others.

MPEG2

This ISO standard provides the highest quality motion video with stereo audio, with images and motion as smooth as direct broadcast satellite. In addition to its broadcasting applications, MPEG2 has found a place in the business environment, where it is typically used with video servers [2] for such applications as training on demand. MPEG2 needs from 1.5 to 15 Mbps (megabits per second) for transmission, depending on the quality of output desired.

H.320

ITU H.320 encompasses a family of standards for videoconferencing, including standards for motion video, still graphics, audio, multipoint communications, and the transmission of user data and control signals between sites, as well as network interfaces, protocols, and signaling. The motion video quality under these standards ranges from that of a good VHS tape (at bit rates from 384 Kbps to 2.048 Mbps) down to grainy, jerky images (at 56 Kbps). Three different audio coding methods are covered, for adequate to good-quality audio depending on the bandwidth available. For most applications, transmission bandwidth between 256 and 512 Kbps produces good user satisfaction; high-motion images are better at higher bit rates. H.320 is key to incorporating video-conferencing in many collaborative presentation tools.

H.324

H.324 is a new family of ITU standards that addresses videoconferencing over analog facilities at lower bandwidths. H.324 supports a large range of motion video resolutions to accommodate everything from low-resolution, credit-card-sized images to high-quality, exceptionally detailed images for such applications as telemedicine. Good high-resolution images, however, are possible only if there is minimal motion. In multipoint mode, this standard permits any location to choose to view one or several of the bridged sites. H.324 also incorporates backward compatibility with H.320 QCIF (Quarter Common Intermediate Format).

At present, H.324 covers connections between single or dual V.34 modems (28.8 Kbps) using analog phone lines or non-guaranteed-bandwidth LANs with H.323 support. Standards covering cellular radio operation are still under development. H.324 makes provision for transcoding within the network; for example, a call from an analog V.34 connection will be able to connect with a user of ISDN, ATM, or mobile H.324, as well as with H.320. Previous protocols were limited to all-digital circuits with the same type of terminal device at both ends.

MBONE

The Internet standard, RFC-1112, has become known as MBONE, standing for Multicast backBONE. Originally developed by Steve Deering at Xerox PARC, MBONE allows a variety of shared real-time collaborative applications to interact efficiently across the Internet. Software "reflectors" installed at some Internet nodes act as virtual multipoint control units. MBONE supports an ever-growing number of applications including NEtwork VOice Terminal (NEVOT), Network Video (NV), an Audioconferencing Tool (VAT), a VideoConferencing tool (VIC), and a shared WhiteBoard (WB).

CU-SeeMe

CU-SeeMe was developed at Cornell University as an Internet videoconferencing application and can be used in conjunction with MBONE. Still evolving, it is currently available for MS-Windows and Macintosh platforms, allowing the use of consumer-level hardware components. In view of its wide adoption, CU-SeeMe has achieved the status of a *de facto* standard for videoconferencing over the Internet. Like MBONE, CU-SeeMe supports use of reflector sites for multipoint operation. Like H.324, CU-SeeMe can be configured to provide video at a variety of resolutions.

Graphics Standards: JPEG and All the Rest

A myriad of still-image graphics formats, mostly proprietary, are currently in use. The response of software and hardware producers, fortunately, has been to include in their products the capability of displaying and generating multiple graphics formats. For collaborative presentations, then, it is important to make sure that all connected locations and devices have at least one still-image graphics capability in common. When it comes to actual standards for still graphics, however, the standard of choice for new applications is ISO JPEG.

JPEG provides a choice of resolutions and color depth and a variable degree of compression for still-image graphics. It has proven itself a powerful compression tool where a large number of images need to be transmitted, or where the available bandwidth is small. One of JPEG's most powerful compression techniques is lossy compression, with which color depth is reduced and some of the finer details are eliminated. JPEG has been adopted by the ITU in its T.81 standard for use with videoconferencing and other audio-graphic applications.

8.5.2.2 T.120: Data Protocols for Multimedia Conferencing

In the early 1990s, the new availability of inexpensive CD-ROMs created an explosion of interest in making multimedia conferencing available *now*! The resultant rush to market new multimedia products, mostly proprietary and incompatible, laid the foundations for a virtual Tower of Babel of multimedia applications. Farsighted executives and engineers from a number of companies were swift to agree that common standards for multimedia conferencing were essential if these new communication capabilities were to emerge as a useful and ubiquitous business tool.

DataBeam, LiveWorks, and Polycom exercised a significant leadership role, with a handful of other companies, in establishing CATS, the Consortium for Audiographics Teleconferencing Standards. A primary objective of CATS was to gather industry support for the development and use of standards for multimedia conferencing among two or more locations. A series of mergers with other groups sharing similar goals has resulted in today's International Multimedia Teleconferencing Consortium, Inc. (IMTC), which by the end of 1995 had 79 corporate members and 120 observers in 18 countries worldwide. The IMTC has established a formal liaison with the ITU to support the extension and completion not only of the T.120 series of standards for multipoint data conferencing, but also of the H.323 and H.324 standards mentioned above.

The ITU T.120 series of recommended standards collectively defines a multipoint data communication service for use in multimedia conferencing environments. It does not describe the diversity of activities that may form part of multimedia conferencing; video compression, audio coding, graphics, and data transmission are all covered under various other ITU standards. Instead, it defines controls and procedures for applications and their associated protocols, making provisions to ensure interoperability for commonly required functionalities such as file transfer, image exchange, and shared whiteboard.

The development of T.120 has been significantly influenced by the cooperation of vendors, common carriers, and users who participated in IMTC and its
precursor CATS, with the result that T.120 has become a standards suite with
several discrete layers. Varying degrees of T.120-compliance are possible,
depending on how many of the layers a manufacturer wishes to implement. This
series of standards is still evolving and will likely continue to do so for some time
as new capabilities are added.

The foundation layer of the T.120 standards defines an infrastructure for
any multimedia conferencing application. A generic application template (T.121)
provides guidance to developers of user applications on how to use that infrastructure for coherent and consistent compliance. Other parts of this basic layer
cover communications with the network (T.123), multipoint communications and
control (T.122/125), and generic conference control (T.124).

The layer of T.120 above the foundation is an application protocol layer. These
protocols define minimum requirements for interoperability between different
implementations. T.126 covers still image viewing and annotation, shared whiteboard and facsimile, while T.127 covers simultaneous multipoint file transfer. In
parallel with this, outside the standard, there exists also a body of proprietary protocols for the same functions. An actual application may use any combination of
proprietary and standard (as defined in this part of T.120) protocols.

The top layer is actually completely outside the standard, consisting of the
user application itself, which may be developed as software, hardware, or both.
This layer is the chief layer in which product differentiation between different
products and different manufacturers occurs.

Perhaps more than any other set of standards, T.120 is an essential underpinning to the continuing implementation of collaborative presentation technology. Its
early acceptance by such a significant part of the conferencing industry has
enabled the more rapid development of a wide range of collaborative presentation
tools that work together and carry out complementary functions. Perhaps most
important are the standards dealing with the control of multipoint bridging and
service compatibility, T.122 through T.125. With these in place, various manufacturers have been able to produce compliant bridges, an important underpinning to
applications' compatibility. The user's freedom of choice among different products
from different manufacturers is limited only by the desired degree of compatibility.
All T.120-compliant products are not necessarily fully compatible; the greatest
degree of compatibility is achieved among products that comply with T.126 and
T.127 as well as the foundation layer of the T.120 standards.

8.5.3 Networks and Network Standards

Users of collaborative presentation technologies who need to connect multiple devices at one or more locations do this using transmission networks. Only
two main types of network are normally encountered. Local Area Networks
(LANs) are primarily used to interconnect desktop and server equipment within
a single building. The servers act as combination information storage centers

and routers. A second type of network provides links between buildings or around the world. Although the term Wide Area Network (WAN) connotes computer connections to many users, a WAN actually makes use of the same kind of telecommunications infrastructure as telephones, videoconferencing, and a host of other communications applications.

8.5.3.1 LANs

Many corporate LANs evolved piecemeal, often beginning with a single department or group establishing its own network to access a communal printer and perhaps to allow file sharing. The success of these early networks led, in many organizations, to expanding to serve rather large groups of users. Data traffic demands were modest and even large-group usage did not unduly tax the network bandwidth capacity, typically about 10 Mbps. Some standards, such as IEEE 802.1 and 802.3, were developed, covering physical and electrical characteristics of the network together with necessary protocols. Both Ethernet and 10BaseT, for example, are standards-based, the former on 802.1 and the latter on 802.3.

As long as LAN usage was a matter of sending or receiving occasional files, the early LANs performed well. When applications sharing, videoconferencing, and multimedia made their debuts at the desktop, users suddenly needed full-time use of a portion of the available bandwidth. Being designed for bursty traffic and *not* steady-state traffic, these networks failed to meet the new demands. With videoconferencing, for example, audio would be lost, motion images would freeze for a few seconds, or other data might disappear. Today, these early LANs represent what is now referred to as non-guaranteed bandwidth at the desktop.

Network support for the new collaborative presentation technologies requires guaranteed bandwidth availability. There are several possible approaches to providing this support. Perhaps the easiest approach is to leave the old LAN in place to continue its previous function and simply to install a second digital network to provide the necessary guaranteed bandwidth. One solution, currently popular, is to provision desktops with switched transmission technologies like ATM and ISDN, providing the necessary guaranteed bandwidth.

A different approach uses existing LAN wiring for another new guaranteed-bandwidth system known as iso-ethernet, covered under both the IEEE 802.9 and the ITU H.322 standards. This technology permits each user to have access to about 10 Mbps of dedicated bandwidth, allocated in 64 Kbps increments. Upgrading requires colocating an iso-ethernet hub, which also includes some routing capability, together with the existing LAN hub; each connected computer also requires an iso-ethernet adapter. The resultant bandwidth-on-demand capability can fully meet the needs of the audio, video, graphic, and data spectrum of today's applications, allowing collaborative presentations, videoconferencing, and MPEG2 training all to be delivered with ease, without overloading the network.

There is yet another approach that, although it does not provide guaranteed bandwidth, is nonetheless suitable for much of the spectrum of collaborative applications. This solution is simply to upgrade the LAN to a higher-speed network such as 100BaseT, which operates at 100 Mbps, ten times the speed of older

LANs. If a high-speed network like this is kept lightly loaded, with peak traffic at no more than about 25 percent of capacity, the LAN will successfully support the more demanding multimedia applications.

8.5.3.2 WANs

Wide area networks (WANs) are typically shared among a variety of enterprise applications including telephony, data, security systems, and the shared multimedia applications used in collaborative presentations.

WANs are WANs by virtue of their function, rather than by virtue of any particular transmission technology or standard used. Any of several standard interfaces and types of transmission may be used; the actual choice may depend on an organization's communications infrastructure, the degree of availability of specific transmission options at different WAN sites, or the services available from the serving telephone company. Communications links used for WANs include ISDN-PRI (primary rate) and T1 lines (1.5 Mbps), ATM (asynchronous transfer mode at a variety of bit rates), frame relay, and others. Any of these transmission alternatives is specified by a host of standards, governing everything from the physical makeup of the network to the switches and interfaces required for operation.

As with LANs, guaranteed bandwidth or a reasonable approximation thereof is important for the success of collaborative presentation technologies used over WANs. However, ensuring sufficient bandwidth to support the continuous data flow without blocking for many interactive applications, especially videoconferencing, can be problematic. Depending on the capacity of the available telecommunications network and the capabilities needed for a presentation, the necessary bandwidth may or may not be available when it is needed.

8.5.3.3 Switched and Dial-Up Facilities

Where the WAN has insufficient capacity, one alternative is the use of dial-up or other switched facilities at higher bandwidth to support collaborative presentation activities between specific locations. The preferred choice for most collaborative multimedia applications is ISDN-BRI (basic rate) dial-up service at 112 or 128 Kbps, which provides digital data and control signal paths and can access most of the world. Several BRIs can be combined using inverse multiplexers (IMUXs) to derive greater bandwidth if that is required by the application.

8.5.3.4 Internet and Intranet

The world has been transformed into a homogeneous information resource and communications pathway by the Internet, a vast connected repository of diverse information, images, and data available to all. Accessing desired information, however, is often a challenge, requiring a reasonable knowledge of Boolean search methods and use of one of the Internet search tools like Alta Vista, Veronica, or WAIS. The technical key to making the Internet possible is TCP/IP, a protocol for allowing multiple networks and computers to exchange data.

The Internet is simultaneously a network over which collaboration can occur and a source/display for presentation materials. At present, most Internet interactivity is asynchronous (not real-time), although the turnaround time for queries, comments, and messages between people can be remarkably short.

Unidirectional presentations can be as simple as text pages on the World Wide Web, perhaps with still-graphics images. Internet presentations can also consist of slide shows prepared and displayed using such software applications as MS PowerPoint. More complex multimedia presentations, with 3-D and motion graphics, are possible with other software formats. Presentations may be accompanied on the Internet by public domain viewer programs, so that they may be examined by people who do not have the software application that created the presentation.

The Internet has potential usefulness as a distribution medium for presentations, and even though much Internet information is open to the general public, presenters can exert some control over access to their presentations. Private business presentation materials can be stored on a secure server behind a firewall, accessible over the Internet only to those with the correct user-ID, passwords, etc. Nevertheless, perceived lack of security has tended to inhibit widespread use of the Internet for distributing sensitive information. Because of the Internet's explosive growth and stringent US Government restrictions on the export of encryption technology, security was not initially addressed. Now that security is becoming an issue with an increasing group of users, manufacturers are starting to include ever-better security methods in their Internet products.

As a medium for collaborative activities, the Internet currently has few real-time interactive capabilities beyond those of MBONE, MUDs (Multi-User Dungeons, of which more later), and Internet Relay Chat (IRC), none of which are well suited to business use in their current forms, especially because of unreliable, often poor audio and video quality and the potential for lengthy unplanned delays. The Internet excels at storage and distribution of drawings, data, records, statistics, and multimedia presentations.

Intranet is the term now being applied to enterprise-wide versions of the Internet. Each intranet uses an often independent in-house server, usually protected from outside access by means of a firewall. Many organizations are now using an intranet for posting news, discussions, and even for teleconferencing with the help of MBONE and CU-SeeMe. What distinguishes the intranet from the corporate LAN or WAN is its function as a repository for information, including policies, specifications, drawings, prepared presentations, etc. That information can be accessed and downloaded from anywhere within the organization, in a manner analogous to Internet use. With judicious use of passwords and other controls, it is also possible to allow limited access to an intranet by a company's strategic partners.

8.5.3.5 Combining Diverse Networks and Transmission Media

The full use of collaborative presentation technologies integrates such a diverse range of terminal equipment, software, and transmission networks, each seemingly with its own unique set of standards and protocols, that it is difficult to envision how true interactive connectivity can be established to accommodate the full function set available.

Some large organizations might have the needed interconnectivity in the form of gateways built into their LANs, allowing connection to the Internet, the WANs, and dial-up facilities either piecemeal or simultaneously. However, bandwidth-hungry applications like videoconferencing can still bring all but the most modern such networks to a grinding halt.

Bridging devices are important to facilitate the interconnection of diverse networks or protocols. Not only do they provide routing of the signals, but they permit disparate pieces of hardware and networks to intercommunicate. The promise of the T.130 group of standards is that it will eventually be possible to have geographically distributed bridges rather than the current centralized, often dedicated arrangements.

As analog telecommunications are gradually superseded by digital facilities, interconnection incompatibilities will eventually disappear. In this regard, the implementation of T.130's smart-network capabilities will ensure transparent end-to-end connections between different digital transmission media.

8.6 THE FUTURE OF COLLABORATIVE PRESENTATIONS

8.6.1 What Are We Waiting For?

The power of collaborative presentation tools has broadened significantly in the last couple of years, particularly with the introduction of products that integrate an array of technological capabilities into a single device. There remain, however, needs that have not been fully met, and some that have not really been addressed at all.

8.6.1.1 Meeting Management Tools

One pressing need is for improved multipoint and multipoint management capabilities. The problem is not that multipoint usage is impossible with existing devices. Rather, the interactive interchange essential to collaborating and drawing new information into the collaborative environment needs to be easier to use where there is a large group.

Right now, we have three basic tools in addition to videoconferencing—whiteboard, application sharing, and file transfer—all of which will be moving to multipoint over the next year or so. Just as existing meeting procedural systems insert a degree of control that helps to keep meetings on track while facilitating individual contributions, so must collaborative presentation technologies incorporate the means of managing participation, especially when some of the participants are at remote locations.

Some of the early users of experimental precursors to today's systems tended to get into a form of "screen wars" or "window wars," as people vied with each other to present their points or modify materials that others had proffered through the technological media. The more terminal devices simultaneously involved in a collaborative meeting, whether in one location or many, the greater the need for some practical and social means of keeping order.

Solutions to this problem will have to be sensitive to the balance between ensuring the equal freedom to participate and avoiding the inhibition of the flow and process of the collaboration. The quality of personal leadership available within the group is always likely to be the most important factor in effective meeting management, but the right kind of improvements to the technology can greatly enhance the human factors, especially for meetings among several locations.

8.6.1.2 Better Video Capabilities

Another need is for improved video capabilities that provide groups with a better feel of being together. To provide good support for collaborative presentations, video must give people more than a talking head. One of the drawbacks to desktop video implementations at present is that the video window, if it is large enough to be worth watching, covers up too much of the screen for good collaboration over documents and drawings.

Participants in a face-to-face meeting do not look only at the face of the presenter. Their attention shifts dynamically from one focal point to another, from the presenter to the text, and then to the facial expression of someone silently responding to what is happening. As Michael Schrage [6] points out in *No More Teams!, Mastering the Dynamics of Creative Collaboration,* collaboration involves many different elements of human interaction, all of which have their importance for achieving value-added products.

A long-held tenet for videoconferencing has been that the technology should not interfere with the natural behavior of its users. Implementations of videoconferencing integrated with whiteboard and shared applications still have some distance to go before meetings using these technologies really look and feel like meetings as users have come to know them.

8.6.1.3 Asynchronous Continuation of Meetings

Even highly productive meetings—the kind that people leave saying, "Now, *that* was worthwhile!"— do not necessarily stop when the group breaks up. Dialogue and ongoing collaboration begun in the meeting continue through a range of media, including telephone, voicemail, e-mail, and computer conferencing.

Maintaining a high level of dedicated effort and focus for asynchronous collaboration is not easy because time has to be set aside. As Xerox PARC's Tom Moran puts it, "Asynchronous things have a real problem that way. You often find these things where people say, after a meeting, 'All right, we'll handle it on e-mail,' and somebody sends out one message and there's zero response. In modern life, it's hard to set time aside. If you're doing things *only* asynchronously, you find that your attention to responding to something is always competing with something else. My experience is, when you say, 'Let's do it with e-mail,' it just often never happens. One thing a meeting accomplishes is that you slice out a segment of your time, which is your most valuable resource, and commit to devoting that time to this purpose."

In addition, asynchronous interaction is qualitatively different from synchronous interaction, especially face-to-face synchronous interaction. There still exists a need to find ways of shaping asynchronous interaction to become part of the main collaborative activity, despite the fact that it consists of discontinuous pieces of presentation and response.

8.6.1.4 Collaborative Capabilities Embedded in Computer Applications

While collaborative software exists today, the design approach for collaborative software applications has been to require the transfer of graphics, data, and files among users prior to the start of a meeting. Because of incompatibilities, actual applications often have to be distributed as well, so that all participants may work on the file. When required, a massive exchange of programs and data prior to active collaboration can impose unwanted delays and inconvenience.

One ideal enhancement to improve ease of collaboration would be the use of standard file formats, so that all applications could read data from files created by other manufacturers' software. Standard file formats could also aid in overcoming user frustration with insufficient backwards compatibility from the latest version of a software application to earlier versions.

Another need is for a means of ensuring that all team members are continuously aware of and have access to data modifications made by their fellow collaborators. The software development industry, perhaps one of the most team-oriented professions, already uses a standard and vital software development tool, called a version control system. With this tool, developers can always be aware of and have access to the latest versions of their own and other peoples' work. Carrying this concept into end-user collaborative applications would smooth the way to more effective use of collaborative strategies.

8.6.1.5 The Comfort Factor

David Panos of DataBeam identifies one need that will not be completely met by improvements in technology. Quite simply, people don't know how to work together effectively on line yet. Even our current collaborative presentation tools require some adjustment on the part of the collaborators.

The group dynamic can sometimes work against people who are not entirely at home with the tools they are using. Being good on the computer in front of people, while they are discussing the content of what you are presenting, is a distinct challenge to many people's comfort levels. Many would just as soon not be watched. Users of the new technologies can achieve familiarity through frequent use, but the onus is still on producers of the new equipment to design products that are easy and intuitive to use, even for neophytes.

8.6.2 New Technology Development

In the short term, user demand is likely the most powerful force driving new technology development. Some of the collaborative presentation technologies now available were initially implemented to find a use for new discoveries, but more recent developments are much more firmly based on recognized needs in the marketplace. Users of the collaborative conferencing tools that exist today are identifying the additional and improved features and capabilities that they want to see in future products. Corporate managers have recognized that there is a high return on investment in these technologies, particularly in terms of strategic benefits and improved productivity.

User experience has sharply pointed out that there are many kinds of meetings, many kinds of presentations, and many kinds of collaborations. While the most sophisticated supporting technology incorporates significant flexibility, some fine-tuning will permit users to tailor the tools to their specific needs. "All kinds of different interactions may be called meetings," says Frank Halasz, Vice President of Product Development at LiveWorks. "LiveBoard was designed for one kind of meeting, but it's now being used for a lot of different kinds of meetings, from collaborative work at Xerox PARC to business meetings that are stronger on the presentation side."

Manufacturers, including LiveWorks, are in the process of developing families of products at different price points, with different form factors and features. For some companies, this kind of development will likely result in a single core product having a variety of physical and software expressions. Other companies, such as Polycom, have taken a serial approach to developing products for the collaborative presentation market. Beginning with the SoundStation audioconferencing terminal, Polycom first produced a variation more suited to audioconferencing in larger meeting rooms, then added the ShowStation conferencing projector. Will the array of products now expand to enhancing the interactive capabilities of the ShowStation, strengthening its ability to function as a shared virtual workspace? Or will the suite of related products expand to support videoconferencing or other kinds of collaborative activity?

One of the first things users can expect in the next few years is increased compliance with the ITU T.120 and related standards. In March, 1996, Intel Corporation and Microsoft Corporation, with support from more than 100 leading companies, announced an open platform that builds on industry standards to make video, voice, and data communications over the Internet simple and commonplace. The new capabilities will be included in future ProShare™ PC-based conferencing products from Intel as well as in Microsoft's ActiveX™ Technologies in future releases of the Windows operating system and associated developer kits.

In the same vein, the success of DataBeam's FarSite, their T.120 collaborative presentation software product, opens the door for standardized methods of sharing information between many users. Borrowing on its internal expertise, DataBeam also produces "T.120 toolkits" for equipment manufacturers and software developers that are currently the most widely used such product. The toolkits provide all the necessary standards-related protocols and "hooks" for easy integration of the standards to ensure new-product compliance and compatibility. DataBeam is continuing to work on toolkit development, with a T.121 toolkit available in the spring of 1996 and a T.130 toolkit to follow in the future. Other companies, such as Germany's Teleos, are also developing toolkits.

Another aspect under development by many manufacturers is improved provision for multipoint multimedia collaboration. Many current products lack multipoint capabilities altogether; those that do support interaction among multiple sites often do so with limited functionality. The preferred technology currently used to support multilocation meetings is bridging, where a server is equipped with the appropriate software and communications to allow up to 60 sites to interact. The more complete and compliant implementation of the ITU's T.120 and T.130 standards will permit significant improvements in multipoint functionality. With non-standard products, however, multipoint connection will not necessarily be synonymous with fully interactive multimedia collaboration.

In parallel with multipoint improvements is the development of collaborative capabilities embedded directly in conferencing software. SMART Technologies, Inc. have already addressed this problem in Version 3.2. of their SMART 2000 Conferencing System, which no longer requires the application to run on remote sites. Instead, each time a shared file is changed at any site, the site running the application receives a graphic update and automatically distributes it to all connected locations. The current implementation of this feature can unfortunately require a lot of bandwidth, especially if very much of the screen image is being updated or refreshed. The next couple of years should, however, see more efficient implementations of this concept in products from a number of manufacturers.

Too often the importance of audio quality has been overshadowed by the flashier aspects of conferencing technologies such as video, graphics, and other multimedia components. Polycom's SoundStation has demonstrated unequivocally that the marketplace still values high-quality sound with good speech intelligibility. Videoconferencing equipment manufacturers have also made significant strides in improving audio quality for their systems, particularly market leader PictureTel. Other major codec manufacturers are also working on audio improvements, which can be expected to spill over to other conferencing functions besides stand-alone videoconferencing.

Components of collaborative presentation equipment have undergone substantial miniaturization since their initial invention, many of them now expressed as software rather than hardware. Display devices, however, run counter to the miniaturization trend, as groups of users prefer a larger display that they can all easily see and use, especially if the display is expected to contain a lot of information. In the next five years or so, more compact, large-area, flat-panel video screens should be possible as development work on gas-plasma display technology leads to new products at an affordable price. With a thickness of about two inches, the display and its electronics are expected to be suitable for wall mounting, allowing collaborative presentation equipment to be installed in smaller meeting rooms or offices that will be intimate, yet uncrowded, for a natural collegial atmosphere.

Smart-network capabilities are also under development, with the ITU working on defining the network of the future under the new T.130 series of standards. Expected to be complete before the year 2000, T.130 builds on the considerable work done under the T.120 series of standards, opening the door to revolutionary network architecture and concepts, exactly what is needed for collaborative multimedia applications.

Under the new standard, it should be possible to have a virtual network custom-designed for every meeting, with virtual MCUs where they are needed, and transcoding between different types of network and between different video coding technologies. Network management, privacy, and quality of service issues will also be addressed. T.130 networks should automatically make allowance for the potentially different types of terminal equipment installed at various locations, perhaps even accommodating multiple audio and video feeds from a single location for individual participant connection. The people collaborating together will be able to select who or what they want to see, and direct the sending of images where and when desired. In short, T.130 is expected to enable many of the outstanding identified needs for functional and easy collaborative presentations to be addressed.

8.6.3 Future Technologies

The video component of collaborative presentation technologies has long presented difficulties finding a suitable balance point between the image quality and the transmission bandwidth required. All the video compression methods currently standardized make use of discrete cosine transform (DCT) coding, based on the work of mathematician Wen-hsiung Chen, Chief Scientist at Compression Labs, Inc. The quality balance point possible with this technology, however, still requires greater bandwidth than is currently easily accessible at most desktops. Optimizing the benefits of collaboration requires ubiquity of access to the supporting technology, and few organizations can justify the high cost of transmission for the higher quality implementations of videoconferencing except to selected, heavily used conference room locations.

Development efforts are on-going to find more efficient methods of video compression, with the ultimate goal of having excellent picture quality with smooth motion available even over a dial-up voice circuit. At the same time, the speed and processing power of semiconductor devices need to increase to allow the more complex compression techniques to be processed in real time.

Although DCT coding continues to be the compression method of choice, thanks in part to special integrated circuits designed to do the processing efficiently, researchers are examining alternative approaches. Two of the most promising are based on the mathematics of fractals and the wavelet transform. Success with either or both of these is unlikely in the near future, but when and if it comes, the new technology could revolutionize our ability to collaborate in real time, face to face at a distance with full interaction over a complete range of the convivial tools envisioned by Michael Schrage [6].

Speculation about future technological development, however, is seldom confined to the possibilities already being explored in real-world basic research. The glamorous aspects of science fiction futurism are more intriguing, especially now that the world has experienced technological advances barely imaginable half a century ago.

The view of technology in contemporary science fiction is engrossed with issues of bringing people together to meet and collaborate. In the fictional world, this is easily accomplished by means of videoconferencing, virtually instantaneous transmission of people through space, and holographic projections. Videoconferencing is already a success story continuing to evolve through ever improving implementations. Instantaneous transmission of people through space is still beyond our grasp. Some visionaries dream about potential applications of holography and comparable technologies to allow remotely generated three-dimensional demonstrations and presentations that could be manipulated collaboratively during real-time meetings and perhaps even recorded and replayed over time.

If our existing collaborative presentation technologies are limited by the incomplete replication of the full range of human expression and communication over distance, will there be a future where we can completely experience and participate in the process of collaboration without really being there? Michael Schrage [6] has commented on the concept of "faxing" three-dimensional models by means of techniques like selective laser sintering and stereo lithography. A few years ago, scientists at British Telecom's research laboratories in Martlesham Heath, UK, were experimenting with three-dimensional holographic projections of real people that one could actually walk around.

The translation of such technologies into real products, however intriguing to contemplate, is likely to be a long way off. As DataBeam's David Panos puts it, the development and acceptance of new and different technologies is very much an evolutionary process. Even such tools as video phones are still not widely deployed outside of demonstration laboratories. He says, "To get broadly implemented, you need it to look and feel familiar." For that reason, he expects future collaborative presentation tools to be based on existing tools and approaches that are already coming into wider use, for example, the Web browser approach.

Panos' sentiments are clearly shared by LiveWorks' Frank Halasz, who asks, "Why doesn't everyone put on virtual reality glasses?" From his point of view, a meeting has to *feel* like a meeting. He concedes that what people are willing to accept as ordinary and familiar will change over time, pointing out, "We're in kind of the horseless carriage phase, trying to make new technology familiar to people so they can find out how it works in meetings."

There is general consensus among the experts that World Wide Web activity is now a springboard for new developments to make it more interactive, to introduce better ways to work collaboratively using what has now become a familiar and frequently used tool for millions. The first glimmers of the future are already emerging on the Web, where virtual reality may become familiar sooner than many experts expected.

An outgrowth of Silicon Graphics' (SGI) Virtual Inventor software, the Virtual Reality Modeling Language is now available on the Web. VRML (pronounced "vermal") is a leap beyond the Web's two-dimensional, plane-oriented HTML (HyperText Markup Language), implemented in current Web browsers such as Mosaic and Netscape.

VRML adds a third dimension to the Web, transforming the screen into an amazing virtual space, supplemented with audio, where users can travel through complex molecules, between the planets, or even through the multimedia-enabled streets South of Market in San Francisco. Currently, best exploited by users with high-powered workstations and virtual reality helmets right out of the latest science fiction movie, VRML radically expands the possibilities for presenting, for collaborating, for educating, for exploring, and for developing relations in otherwise obtuse data sets. Some of the existing examples on the Web are impressively effective even with just a MS-Windows-capable PC.

Even more experiential collaboration may become possible if virtual reality avatars ever find acceptance outside the teenage computer subculture. The term "avatar" comes from an ancient Hindu myth in which a deity descends to the earth in some manifest shape. Avatars have started to make their presence known on the Web, as user-selectable embodiments of a desired personality that function as a form of communications tool. Wearing the guise of an electronic avatar, users can visit cybercommunities where groups of other people's avatars gather for discussion and interaction. For collaborators who experience difficulties interacting well in face-to-face groups, the avatar concept may one day open the door to becoming fully functioning members of the group.

The term MUD, standing for MultiUser Dungeon but likely to change to MultiUser Domain as it gains respectability, refers to text-based interactive Internet games in which dozens of human players simultaneously wander about, interacting with other human players, computer-generated players, and the usual range of dragons and monsters found in non-electronic fantasy role-playing games. Within the limits of the game's rule-set, players can enhance their powers with weapons, magic spells, and potions, and can amass wealth or power through their encounters with players and monsters. MUDs enjoy great popularity because they combine human interaction with (imaginary) danger and excitement in a controlled, non-threatening way.

At first glance, MUDs seem an unlikely subject for scientific research. At Xerox PARC, however, a team of scientists is exploring the extension of MUD technology for use in non-recreational settings to create a social virtual reality [1]. The strength of MUDs is seen as their capability to provide shared computing with a strong, real-world metaphor; their shortcomings can be corrected by the addition of audio, video, and interactive windows. Social virtual reality has considerable potential for facilitating certain kinds of collaborative activity, including telecommuting activities, by importing characteristics of the essential human interface into the electronic interface. Much of the content of the original MUD concept is likely to be discarded for business applications, however, despite the occasional temptation to import magic spells or weapons into meetings to deal with the dragons sometimes encountered.

It may be a long way off, but a future virtual reality where we will be able to meet and interact with people anywhere in the world, at any time, is not an impossible dream. Whether a fractal rendition of you and your ideas, a moving holographic projection, an avatar, or a knight in shining armor, collaborative presentation technologies will eventually provide participants with a richer sense of presence, a full set of interactive modes, and the capacity for synchronous and asynchronous collaborative activity. Technology is offering a new age of human working relationships.

ACKNOWLEDGMENTS

Thanks to Frank Halasz (LiveWorks, Inc.), Tom Moran (Xerox Palo Alto Research Center), and David Panos (DataBeam, Inc.) for sharing their comments and insights. Thanks also to Polycom, Inc. and SMART Technologies Inc. for providing illustrations of their products.

BIBLIOGRAPHY

1. Curtis, P. and Nichols, D. A., "MUDs grow up: Social virtual reality in the real world," *Proceedings of the 1994 IEEE Computer Conference*, 1994, pp. 193-200.
2. Halhed, B.R., "Video server technology and applications evolve," *Business Communications Review*, 25: 8, Aug 1995, pp. 29-32.
3. Nunamaker, J.F., Jr., Briggs, R.O. and Mittleman, D.D., "Electronic meeting systems: Ten years of lessons learned," in *Groupware: Technologies and Applications*, Coleman, D. and Khanna, R. eds., Upper Saddle River, NJ: Prentice-Hall, 1995, pp. 149-192.
4. Peters, T., *Liberation Management: Necessary Disorganization for the Nanosecond Nineties*, New York: Knopf, 1992.
5. Poole, M.S., "Procedures for managing meetings: Social and technological innovation," in *Innovative Meeting Management*, Swanson, R.A. and Knapp, B.O. eds., Minneapolis: University of Minnesota Training and Development Research Center and 3M Meeting Management Institute, 1991, pp. 53-109.
6. Schrage, M., *No More Teams! Mastering the Dynamics of Creative Collaboration*, New York: Doubleday, 1995. Originally published as *Shared Minds: The New Technologies of Collaboration* by Random House, 1990.

BIOGRAPHY

Dion Blundell brings more than 20 years' experience in all facets of managing and marketing to his position as the director of product marketing for LiveWorks, Inc., a Xerox company. In this position he has held worldwide responsibilities for definition, development, management, and marketing of LiveWorks' systems product line since 1995. Blundell can be contacted at dblundell@lwi.xerox.com

Previously, Blundell was product marketing manager at Polycom, Inc. where he managed the marketing of various product lines, including the SoundStation, the world's leading full-duplex audioconferencing system. Prior to Polycom, he held various marketing and management positions with increasing responsibility for ViTel Communications Corporation, Radius, Inc., Qume Corporation, Northern Telecom, Inc., and Proctor & Gamble International.

Blundell was awarded a BS in chemical engineering from Stanford University in Palo Alto, California and an MBA from Pepperdine University in Los Angeles, California.

LiveWorks, Inc., a Xerox company, develops and markets advanced meeting technologies. The LiveBoard interactive meeting system integrates multimedia presentations, document, and video teleconferencing capabilities with an intuitive shared whiteboard to unleash the power of group collaboration.

Introduction to Chapter 9

Over a year ago, when Groupware: Technology and Applications *was written, it was not appropriate to include a chapter on desktop videoconferencing (DVC) because the field was still in its infancy. However, two events have occurred that make this technology more viable. First, the price of DVC hardware and software has steadily declined over the past year, and second, a common, cross platform interface (the Internet browser) makes this technology more attractive to a broader range of customers. This field is exploding!*

I believe that desktop videoconferencing is going to become so common that it will be part of everyone's desktop toolset before the end of the century. For example, my office is already equipped with ISDN to support two video conferencing systems. One of the systems is an inexpensive Connectix camera with C-U-See-me (free) on a Macintosh. The second is a PictureTel PCS50 PC-based desktop system that is much more elaborate and also, not surprisingly, much more expensive. Vendors such as Intel, Apple, HP, and Compaq are beginning to build these hardware components into desktop systems, adding only a few hundred dollars to the price. Economies of scale will reduce the price, just as it has for CD-ROM drives.

Videoconferencing has become inexpensive enough and robust enough to support mainstream usage and is no longer relegated to expensive videoconferencing rooms. For most of the history of videoconferencing (since the early 80s), people have been using room-based systems. These large and expensive systems are giving way to desktop systems as the technology moves forward and becomes less expensive ($200-$2,000 as opposed to $100,000).

This brings up a second problem—bandwidth. Since most PCs in this country are connected to LANs or to the Internet (via modem), pushing video images and audio clips across a LAN or a modem could bring a network to a standstill if enough bandwidth is not available. With the advent of the Internet, and its apparent graphic nature, many organizations are re-examining their network architectures with bandwidth in mind.

One of the points of this chapter is that people are social and this technology supports social interactions. For example, it may be difficult to discern someone's sincerity over the telephone, but in a negotiation or a sales situation, conveying sincerity and confidence is critical. Videoconferencing is a realistic solution to getting close enough to feel as though you're speaking with a person rather than speaking to a disembodied voice.

Christine includes examples of how to convey authority or sincerity, build relationships, think creatively, and reach consensus using these technologies. She also examines the organizational objectives for videoconferencing and the support structure available in most organizations. She has included a section on how to prepare an IP network (Internet, intranet, or Ethernet TCP/IP LAN) and how to deploy real-time technologies across the enterprise. This section focuses on all dig-

ital videoconferencing rather than analog, and is a fairly technical discussion. Since videoconferencing is so new, it also addresses a number of standards issues, with networking protocols, compression algorithms, and the like. Alternative, all digital videoconferencing networks and other options for analog networks are discussed as well as products that run over the intranet.

Christine is recognized as one of the world's most knowledgeable experts on the desktop videoconferencing industry. Her knowledge covers the technical, business, and organizational issues of using DVC systems. This chapter constitutes an excellent discussion of where DVC is today and where it is going in the future.

Desktop Videoconferencing

Christine Perey
PEREY Communications and Consulting

Desktop videoconferencing is a new collaborative technology with enormous merit and appeal for those revolutionizing their businesses for success in the 21st century. It is a tight integration of real-time video, audio, and data allowing people to supplement the benefits of their face-to-face meetings without many of the associated pitfalls. Videoconferencing, *per se*, is not new. However, combining live video and audio with personal computers and networks is increasingly practical and affordable where escalating workgroup productivity through collaboration is considered a prime objective.

Technology innovators worldwide are demonstrating that in a fast-paced, competitive business climate, both established and new business processes benefit from real-time interactivity at the desktop level. We will examine some of the situations where companies are realizing the most compelling benefits, how the technologies will integrate with today's enterprise information systems, and where this is all going in the future.

9.1 ESTABLISHING A NEED FOR REAL-TIME VISUAL TECHNOLOGY

Corporations are perpetually studying their practices, their people and opportunities and, on the basis of these studies, justifying the integration of various new technologies. The rate of adoption of (and innovation with) any new technology depends on many. For most, the justifications boil down to the need to increase individual, group and corporate productivity, responsiveness to change, and, in general, to reap the maximum benefits from the corporation's most valuable assets, especially its people.

Cost:benefit analyses of introducing real-time technologies and multimedia-enablement are necessary. Most of the complete analyses done to date are tightly guarded and resist examination in a public work such as this book, therefore, a generic case (cost:benefit of real-time multimedia technologies in enterprise) will, when studded with application examples, reveal some points planners should ponder before deciding that the company (its people and the processes they are involved with) can benefit from the deployment of desktop videoconferencing.

We will begin by describing the reasons most commonly cited for introducing desktop videoconferencing and real-time collaboration tools.

9.1.1 Why Desktop Videoconferencing?

There are intangible as well as tangible impacts of adding desktop video-conferencing to the arsenal of collaborative technologies. Depending on the company and particular circumstances (e.g. group responsibilities or priorities, and cost of different options), people will emphasize different advantages.

Fundamentally, humans are interactive, social beings. People with common interests gather to talk, exchange points of view, create new understandings and, on occasion, negotiate agreements. For thousands of years people met face to face to interact. The patterns of "in-person" interaction are essentially programmed into people through genes and culture. With the recent advent of the telephone and its subsequent penetration in enterprise (and, indeed, in society at large), it became very easy and relatively cost effective to talk, share and "meet" in real time using telecommunications. Audio conferencing has extended this model to include more than two participants in a meeting.

Whether by audio conference, two-party telephone call, or an in-person meeting, conference participants' motivations are diverse. They range from "killing time," exchange of information, building relationships to further a particular task, delivery of product or services, or, often, the purpose of a real-time exchange is to persuade someone to adopt a new point of view. Upon introduction, the impact of the telephone was felt in both established business processes (e.g., set up for face-to-face meetings coordinated over the telephone in advance). Most of the significant advantages of the telephone came through the creation of totally new ways of doing business (e.g., conducting meetings without requiring that anyone travel). These translated directly into tangible benefits.

Two-way, real-time video and audio will support interactivity more completely than audio alone. The question is how this will expedite current business processes and how an enterprise will foster the development of entirely new processes to take full advantage (in other words, reap the tangible benefits) of the richer interactions. Historically, the impact of introducing a new tool or technology is particularly high when it results in a discontinuous improvement (i.e., an order of magnitude change) in productivity (e.g., human or productive capacity of a facility).

9.1.2 Intangible Benefits

Energy and emotion of a voice conveys at least as much as the individual words spoken. Nonverbal, auditory communication can be very moving, regardless of the distance from which the voice is emanating. The impact of body language in communications is also very high.[1] Interpersonal dynamics, a combination of verbal and all nonverbal communications, are a part of any community, but they are not equally important for everyone. Nor, for that matter, is any one case of improved interpersonal dynamics necessarily sufficient to justify the costs of obtaining and integrating all real-time technologies across an enterprise.

While the value of seeing the person whose voice we hear varies in individual circumstances, it is evident to most that real-time audio and visual communications more effectively:

☞ convey sincerity and authority,

☞ aid in the assessment of the value of "data" when it is sought for an important decision,

☞ contribute to the bonding of people and the establishment of community,

☞ promote creative thinking through shared spaces, and,

☞ accelerate the process of reaching consensus.

Clearly, there is overlap between these points in any given interaction. Nevertheless, for purposes of this discussion, we will examine each individually. The primary benefit of examining each lies in establishing that there is synergy between two or more benefits.

Translating intangibles into tangible benefits will be important over the course of a company's adoption of technology. A fairly strong body of anecdotal evidence currently suggests that these five benefits of multimedia, and real-time audio, video, and data in particular, are most important when life or money are at stake. The more directly one can improve the quality of life, or the financial health of an organization through one or more of these benefits, the more quickly investments in desktop videoconferencing and real-time interactivity will yield a positive return.

9.1.3 Conveying Sincerity and Authority

A letter or phone call may introduce a concept or establish a presence, but when persuading another or considering a transaction in which relationships count, then conveying sincerity and confidence can make a big difference. Eye contact is a critical component of gauging and communicating sincerity and authority.

---

[1] Stephen Covey, in his book, *The Seven Habits of Highly Effective People* (Simon & Schuster, 1989) estimates that 50% of the communication between people is visual.

Professional services providers and clients regularly meet in person—face to face—to assess mutual interest and respect, both key components of fruitful relationships.

For attorneys, for instance, the case is particularly acute. An attorney must read the sincerity of a witness, the pain of the victim, or the authority of the expert almost instantly through gesture, facial expression, and the dynamics of voice when combined with the person's attire and any other context-setting information that might be available. The New York District Attorney's lawyers in New York City use desktop videoconferencing and data collaboration between police department precincts and the DA's headquarters to determine whether or not to file a complaint and how to prioritize cases based on real-time interviews and remote examination of evidence made possible without moving the suspect, or the evidence.

For the client, or patient, an expert's body language and voice can make a big difference in the outcome of a relationship. Established early, confidence and trust in the service provider may contribute to a productive and positive outcome; all other things being equal, critically ill patients consistently recover more rapidly when under the care of physicians they trust. Faster recovery, or more rapid detection of problems in the first place, translate to financial savings for insurance companies, hospitals, and employers. On the other hand, the unconscious negative signals conveyed between two people in real time may convince one or the other party to seek other alternatives before putting their well-being in jeopardy through the services of a person they don't trust.

In sales, a customer's sincerity when placing an order conveys a great deal. An order placed with agitation or carelessness will, to an educated salesperson, indicate an element of risk. With desktop videoconferencing, particularly between people who have an established relationship, such as a customer/sales person rapport, the unconscious communications can be as important as the conscious.

9.1.4 Collecting Accurate Data for Important Decisions

Indeed, important decisions—about corporate strategy, for example—are often delegated to those who through their carrier have trained themselves to make judgement calls, quickly and with a high degree of accuracy. One of the most time consuming aspects of business cycles today is collecting necessary information, with a high degree of accuracy for the highest likelihood of success.

Executives in a position where they must evaluate data for timeliness, precision, and value like to see the source of their information before making important decisions. The room and group videoconferencing systems in executive board rooms have already proven many times over the value of eye contact in collecting information.

Research companies, and in-house researchers, are in the business of collecting data for others. Currently, most research for casual or rigorous analysis, is being conducted in person, over the Internet and over the telephone. When real-time videoconferencing is widely deployed (in an enterprise or among cooperating companies), research more fully incorporates the nonverbal communications between people.

Marketing research focus groups conducted through members of the Video-Conferencing Alliance Network (VCAN) use live, interactive video and audio coverage of a focus group to save VCAN clients worldwide hundreds of thousands of dollars per study. Independent agencies across the country host focus groups. The video and audio from the hidden research viewing room is transmitted live to the corporate clients' room or desktop videoconferencing systems of key decision makers. Without travelling, the clients can observe the interaction among focus group respondents and even interact with (or provide input to) an independent moderator on site.

Nonverbal nuances (e.g., facial expression, head movements) of focus group respondents supplement the formal qualitative reactions to a proposed product or service. With videoconferencing, the qualitative input of respondents (to an ad concept or a packaging change, for example) come into a single client from many cities and markets without any time lost in moving people to make important decisions. When desktop videoconferencing is in use by more consumers, the focus group's professional moderator will have the benefit of having a face-to-face interaction with individual respondents, regardless of location, and the respondents will be validated (e.g., age, race, sex, and other data critical to the research's accuracy) more consistently and easily.

One particularly strong proof of the value of desktop videoconferencing increasing the accuracy of data on which important decisions are made is in the armed forces. With real-time video, audio, and data conferencing between offices of military leaders, senior decision makers are collecting information about disturbances or potential conflicts without having valuable time elapse during travel. Several local, regional, or national crises have been resolved quickly, or avoided altogether, as a consequence of having individually enabled the decision makers.

The American government also uses videoconferencing in the selection of contractors for special (emergency) services. When decision makers can evaluate their options with service providers quickly through real-time video and audio, risks associated with miscommunications are kept at a minimum.

Even less mission-critical applications of desktop videoconferencing can be justified on the basis of communicating data accurately. In human resource departments using outside or campus-based recruiters, for example, desktop videoconferencing between remote locations is helping fill positions and place qualified candidates. Real-time desktop-to-desktop communications play an increasingly important role when executives are assessing a candidate for a particular position, as exemplified by Cleveland-based Management Recruiters International, which originally tested the principles with small group systems.

9.1.5 Building relationships

In every collaborative experience—be it finding the perfect job for an executive or developing the proposal to make a prospect a new client—real-time interactivity, usually the telephone, is essential. Additional conscious and unconscious communications supported by two-way video serve to build, nurture, and, in some cases, erode relationships.

While relationships should never be neglected, the impact of real-time audio and video in reading the other party and fostering positive relationships is extremely important in cross-cultural situations, or where there are language barriers between team members. As collaboration and cooperation increasingly involve international players, the ability to see the impact of one's words on the other party may mean the difference between offending and complementing the other party.

Companies differ in their approach to fostering relationships. In a world where workgroups are dispersed, and even more frequently virtual, the role of video and audio will become even greater than in today's relatively centralized organizations. People in remote offices and in clusters of activity distributed on a single large campus find that their commitment to a project and overall collaborative potential is easier to direct, sustain, or "tap into" when face-to-face communications occur daily, or even weekly.

Weekly meetings with desktop videoconferencing between distributed offices foster team spirit and strengthen bonds between people. In sales forces of many companies, the weekly videoconferencing meetings include members of marketing and engineering, in an effort to promote cross-divisional relationships. One large computer systems company has demonstrated a 30 percent lower turnover rate and 20 percent higher degree of job satisfaction since deploying desktop videoconferencing on the desks of sales representatives and managers.

9.1.6 Thinking Creatively

The opportunity to share a common "space" on the desktop is one of the little known or explored benefits of people working together in real-time from their own offices. Some analysts believe that true collaboration is only possible when there is a shared space. There needs to be a medium—virtual or physical—in which there are symbols and representations to manipulate. When participants have shared access to a common space at the same time, they have an environment or a context for collaboration because it takes a shared space to create shared understandings.

In all but a few instances, participants in a videoconference between systems of the same manufacturer (i.e., "like points") can share an electronic equivalent of a conference room white board. Interactivity between people looking at the same technical diagrams, an example of "concurrent engineering," typically include a pointer with which the person speaking directs the attention of other meeting participants. Rather than having to recreate an illustration on a whiteboard or print a layout onto paper large enough for many to see, the image appears equally accessible on the screen of all interested parties. Depending on the conference options, one or many meeting participants can manipulate or experiment with a representation on screen while looking for a creative approach to a problem (see Fig. 9.1).

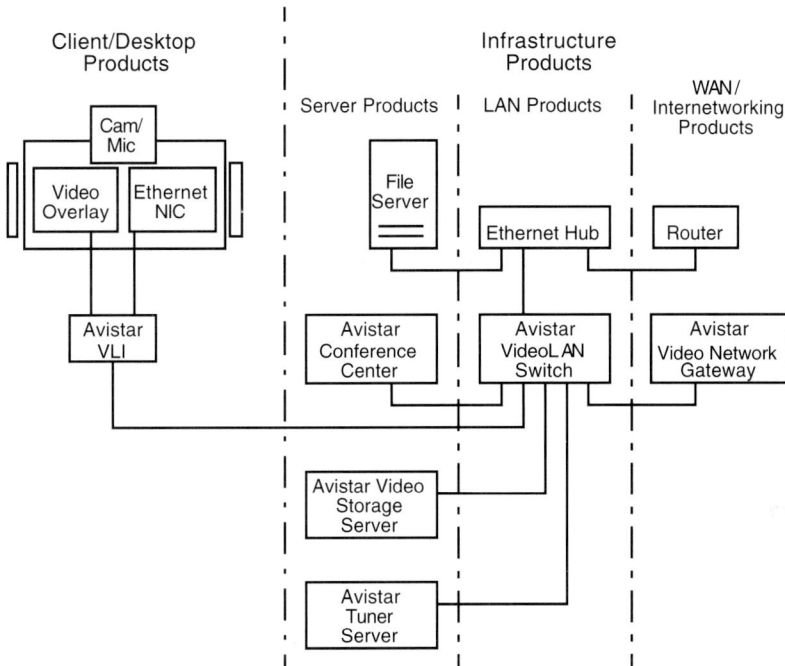

Fig. 9.1 Avistar Video LAN Architecture

Concurrent editing is another valuable application for real-time interactive technologies with a shared space. Application sharing (where two or more people can manipulate an application using their personal computers) with desktop videoconferencing makes it easier for two or more people to see changes they introduce to a document and get the nonverbal reaction of editors, coauthors, or managers nearly instantaneously.

Brainstorming sessions particularly emphasize the creativity of group members. On a shared notebook, or in a shared text editor, participants of a brainstorming session can see the comments captured, and electronically organize them more easily than on paper or during an audioconference. When the session is done, notes are accessible to all participants without delay.

Digital artists preparing visuals for print, television, or electronic media campaigns use real-time collaboration products and services to try out new effects and obtain immediate feedback from one another, or to learn new techniques through experimentation in shared space.

9.1.7 Reaching Consensus

As people encounter new ideas, they do not always agree to change their own strongly held views. In command-and-control management hierarchies, the leader's decision is not open to debate, however, this organizational model doesn't apply in the vast majority of business environments.

Most business processes involve some form of consensus building. Store-and-forward communications prove to be less valuable than face-to-face communications when the interests of two or more parties need to be represented in a settlement or strategy. When people who need to negotiate cannot, for financial or physical reasons, meet in the same room to discuss how their mutual interests will be protected or met, real-time interactivity with desktop videoconferencing offers an alternative.

Visual cues such as rolling eyes and tapping fingers, fidgeting and even leaving a room are hidden from those who can only join via telephone. Without the benefits of seeing others, people are less apt to concede to the solutions of those they think may be adverserial. Conversely, viable solutions may develop when nonverbal communications conveyed between virtual meeting participants encourage a train of thought otherwise abandoned.

9.1.8 Tangible Benefits

Tangible benefits of desktop videoconferencing deployment in enterprise most commonly result from:

☞ Travel reduction (avoidance/substitution)

☞ Higher individual or group productivity translating from reduced cycle time and including increased revenue generation capacity.

The relative importance of each of these tangible benefits will depend on the individual, the workgroup, a company's work processes, and the industry in which the company functions.

Collaborative technologies are also very sensitive to scaling. As more end points and people are enabled, critical mass is achieved and the tangible impact is greater overall, as well as on the individual.

9.1.9 Travel Reduction

Travel reduction, as a result of substituting videoconferencing for an in person meeting, is the most common justification for desktop videoconferencing investments.

The costs avoided are not limited to the air fare, car rental, hotel, and meals. Time that is spent in transit is an important drain on productivity as well, unless the traveller is very conscientious about planning to take work along and the environment is conducive to reading or writing.

For individuals who do not leave an office building or corporate campus in order to fulfill their responsibilities, travel reduction may be expressed in terms of time not spent walking between individual offices on different floors or in different buildings of a campus.

9.1.10 Increased Productivity

Companies measure productivity of individuals and groups in different ways, depending on individual or group's position within the enterprise. Sales people are most often measured by the revenues they generate, though most business analysts understand that the potential for sales is a function of the product/service as well as the markets available.

Increasing productivity is accomplished when the time to complete a task can be reduced, without sacrificing the objectives, thereby leaving more time for other equally important or more productive tasks.

Using real-time video, audio, and data, collaborative tools can speed development of creative solutions to overcome obstacles in mission-critical projects. The people who communicate more clearly and more creatively will reduce cycle times. For example, in situations where natural disasters or fires put structures or lives at risk, real-time collaboration technologies between the emergency personnel in the field and headquarters is proving helpful in devising solutions that will quickly address urgent needs.

In manufacturing, where any downtime on the plant floor costs thousands of dollars per hour, companies select a specialized service provider, or an internal resource, they can rely on for support. New facilities built since the early 1990s, link the industrial equipment in a plant with support staff, vendor, or designer via real-time video. Trained professionals can use a specially mounted camera and a one way video and audio transmission to assess a problem promptly and recommend a new course of action using visual and auditory information and real-time data generated using networked computers.

The same principles are being used in the mining and oil industries. Off shore or remote drilling platforms have the ability to quickly raise a visual communications link to videoconferencing on the desktop computers of the engineers responsible for equipment operations worldwide, without requiring that these engineers travel and delay putting a possible solution into affect (see Fig. 9.2).

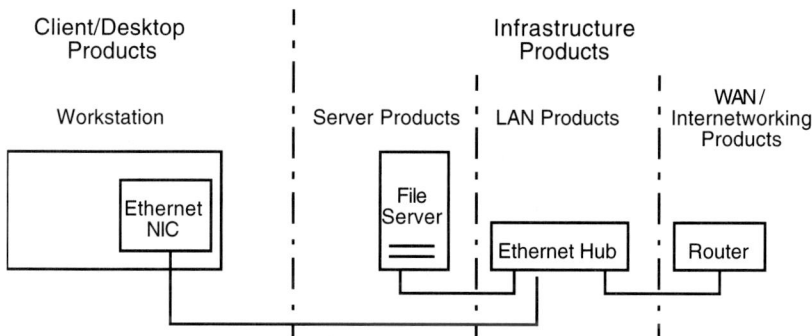

Fig. 9.2 Typical Data Network Architecture

In financial industries, real-time technologies prove to support improved decision making which in turn results closure of more client business. While the impact on increased sales, when enabling sales people with real-time technologies, depends primarily on the cost of the goods or services sold, it is easy to determine the value of enablement by comparing sales volumes before and after technology introduction, training, and stabilization.

9.1.11 All the Above

Based on these intangible and tangible benefits, companies decide if video-conferencing is appropriate on every desktop. Costs:benefit analyses typically emphasize the dollars associated with tangible benefits such as travel avoidance, but a great deal of the true, long term value is realized when companies take advantage of the relatively intangible benefits enumerated above.

It is important to emphasize that the benefits of collaborative technologies will grow over time. The more comfortable people and groups become with working together, and experience first hand their individual or unit productivity without changing locale (and the resources people need to perform their jobs), the more quickly the new business practices will translate to increased revenues or reduced costs for a company or profit/loss unit.

9.2 WHEN TO DEPLOY DESKTOP VIDEOCONFERENCING AND REAL-TIME COLLABORATION

As persuasive and far reaching as the benefits may appear on paper, they are difficult to anticipate, much less measure in absolute terms. Still, assuming that there is a strong potential for benefit, the rate of adoption of desktop videoconferencing is gated by some tangible obstacles such as the sheer complexity of the offerings (which need to be evaluated, purchased, and installed), the cost of acquisition, and the learning curve associated with putting the new technology to use on a daily basis.

If the corporate leaders are prepared to support and accept the changes real-time interactivity introduces, and willing to allocate time and resources new technologies require, then deployment should proceed. How can companies assess their readiness for desktop videoconferencing deployment?

Readiness is expressed at many levels. The following section examines a few of the most obvious signs of readiness.

9.2.1 Survey the Organizational Objectives and Support Infrastructure

Corporations are as unique as people, often adapting to maximize profits, sustain growth, and increase market share within a given economy. Nevertheless, corporations modulate themselves through mission statements and by promoting cultural biases among employees, directors, and management. Within corporations, organizational units (divisions) tend to have their own guiding principles, more specific to the role a unit plays within the larger enterprise.

Corporations, and the organizations they embody, differ radically in their collaborative tendencies. Unlike human beings who have an instinctive urge to socialize and share, 20th century enterprises tend to focus their employees' professional zeal by identifying competitors and polarizing the world view as an "us and them" equation. These patterns probably can not be entirely avoided, and may even have adaptive value for preserving communities in times of crisis.

Most modern companies seek to use a variety of organizational tools (and infrastructure) for managing growth and to motivate people to work towards an overarching corporate mission. Companies encourage innovation by identifying—implicitly or explicitly—creative relationships and collaborative work as targets, but unless there are specific guide-posts for getting there, a competitive and isolating pattern will likely develop within or between workgroups.

A study, either commissioned by management with an outside firm, or using published re-engineering tools, can reveal a great deal about organizational priorities and how much support collaborative technologies will truly garner when the novelty wears off. Below is a short list of indicators useful when assessing an organization's readiness for the changes that desktop videoconferencing requires. They include:

☞ a well-established, well-funded information services staff capable of supporting store-and-forward forms of collaboration; if the company (or IS department) has more than two years invested in people developing tools for collaboration in the sales force, manufacturing floor plant, or corporate management, there are probably already many who recognize the value in and have experimented with (even implemented pockets of) real-time interactivity with videoconferencing.

☞ a commitment to keeping personal computers on the desks and in the hands of employees as up-to-date as possible, regardless of the individual's specific duties; having a text (e-mail) based store-and-forward infrastructure is a prerequisite. In addition, if an organization is already investing in processor upgrades, color adapters, and/or sound boards on a regular basis, then the incremental costs of real-time video to the desktop PC is more in line with a pre-existing corporate policy. When PCs in an enterprise have fallen far behind the "minimum system requirements" for business, the cost of upgrades, combined with the new video hardware and software, will mount.

☞ a well-maintained corporate network, with suitable routers, high-capacity servers and room to expand with a complete corporate information infrastructure; the benefits of desktop videoconferencing are rarely sufficient to justify the cost of deploying an entirely new information system, for the same reasons indicated above.

☞ a human resource department and staff that specifically recognizes its role in selecting people who demonstrate collaborative tendencies, and has objective measures for screening candidates before hiring.

☞ a system for consistently rewarding those who show initiative and, themselves, reduce cycle times, deliver superior products, or perform remarkably (by corporate standards) using real-time collaboration.

Organizational issues are only one facet of the complete picture. A collaborative assessment with an eye towards real-time video-enhanced interactivity needs to include surveys of users, projects, and managers at multiple levels.

9.2.2 Survey Users

While a satisfied workforce is a very clear objective for employee retention and productivity, it may also produce a sense of complacency unconducive to changes such as desktop videoconferencing and collaborative computing technologies will introduce. People who are satisfied with the status quo are among the most difficult to persuade to incorporate new technologies, real-time enabling, or any other for that matter.

A study of groups of people who work together without the technology under consideration can be beneficial to those contemplating technology introduction. In order to assess the (positive or negative) impact of technology introduction on workers and business processes, several groups of prospective users are studied through "shadowing." This technique has an objective third party spending several days per week observing activities in a group. Most user studies need to continue for four to six weeks, some even longer, in order to fully profile the workgroup's processes and priorities in different situations.

A user survey will reveal much that is otherwise hidden from technology evangelists, and those who might introduce or test acceptance of new technologies. For instance, some key indicators of success of desktop videoconferencing will be:

☞ the purposes, frequency, and duration of travel different team members need to do in order to perform their jobs and fulfill their responsibilities. Also important is the amount of stress at the office when compared to the stress born during time out of the office.

☞ the most common measurement of performance by peers in a workgroup. If performance is measured on an axis that is essentially unchanged or reduced by real-time interactivity (e.g., time in a conference room meeting face to face), then either the benchmarks need adjustment or the relative value of other performance indicators (e.g., participation in cross-functional teams) can rise.

☞ users' past experiences with technology introduction has a very significant impact on acceptance of new technologies. If the users in a workgroup are comfortable and motivated to use store and forward collaborative technologies, then the chances of positive outcomes for desktop videoconferencing are higher.

☞ identifying resource limitations early. It is often important to determine if the budgets and resources accessible to the workgroup may be more wisely invested in other productivity or team process enhancing systems (other than real-time enabling technologies). A detailed survey of user's stated and observed needs will reveal the priorities and prejudices of workgroup members and leaders.

All too often, the users who will need to learn and adapt to use new tools are not studied sufficiently prior to technology introductions. Not only is a pre-installation study helpful to isolate potential problems in the user base, but it also may prove useful to establish a control group of people with similar profiles and without early introduction of real-time interactive technologies.

9.3.3 Survey Projects

Over time, as people become more familiar with the tangible and intangible benefits of collaborative work processes, it becomes more evident that certain projects and portions of projects lend themselves more readily to desktop video-conferencing. For instance, projects that require the interaction of people around visually rich media (advertising layouts, or videos for training or sales), and projects with very tight and inflexible deadlines are excellent candidates for the introduction of desktop videoconferencing.

When the objective of a group is to interact with customers and the customers are not equipped with desktop videoconferencing, the impact of these technologies on the individual or workgroup productivity will be negligible, or even negative (as is the case of time and resources are diverted from sustaining customer relationships).

Project surveys generally involve both members of the user community noted above and the project or unit managers discussed below. Through the evaluation of different projects, people will gain consensus around the characteristics of projects with a high degree of collaborative potential and learn to better recognize such projects in the future, without the assistance of researchers or information management systems designers.

9.3.4 Survey Managers

Managing people, projects, and companies requires a great deal of attention to both verbal and nonverbal communications. Successful integration of radically new technology business requires the leadership of respected and dedicated managers.

Champions defy definition except in the most general terms. One of the key characteristics of a champion is the ability to convey potential to many people in such a way that it becomes contagious, creating many champions among the larger community.

Once there is a successful pattern of usage set up with a few people in a company, there will need to be a formal mentoring process. Managers with a high degree of success using collaborative technologies in a variety of situations must be willing, ready, and able to share their expertise with their peers in other workgroups.

Being able to share a vision includes having the time to dedicate to skillfully presenting the new technologies, talking with people, individually or in groups, about concerns, and following through with a strong training program.

9.4 How to Deploy Real-time Technologies in Enterprise

At this stage in the evolution of real-time desktop videoconferencing and collaborative technologies, there is not a clearly defined formula for deployment that assures success in all cases. Every company will formulate their own strategies, based on the results of surveys and the receptivity of the organization to the introduction of desktop videoconferencing.

Deployment plans are typically developed with business line managers, users, and subject-matter experts, including those with business process re-engineering skills and information systems management responsibilities. Plans often include a pilot program in a group or unit of at least 20 to 30 participants with well-established communications objectives and patterns.

To fully appreciate the many diverse aspects of deployment, planners should be familiar with the products and the underlying technologies, and be prepared to make some difficult choices. The following section of this chapter introduces common terms and puts the desktop solutions available today in the context of their room and small group precursors.

9.5 ESSENTIAL REAL-TIME CONFERENCING BACKGROUND AND TERMS

Digital video has migrated from a professional tool accessible to only a few Fortune 100 companies to one that is available on and from any desktop computer.

9.5.1 Room and Group Videoconferencing Systems

Until 1992, anyone interested in using videoconferencing in their businesses had to not only purchase extremely expensive hardware, but they were limited to using their technologies with other end points obtained from the same manufacturer. There was brand loyalty, but no interoperability until, in 1988 and 1989, an International Telecommunications Union (then the CCITT) study group evaluated many algorithms and selected a hybrid coding scheme based on Discrete Cosine Transform, DPCM, and motion compensation techniques. In late 1990, the ITU approved the Video Codec for Audiovisual Services at Px64Kbps (known as H.261).

Before 1992, room-based and group videoconferencing systems were being sold to corporations, primarily on the promise of travel avoidance. "Room systems" refers to an assortment of video and audio capture, transmission, and display components built into a board or conference room in such a way that people sitting around a spacious conference table can all see the monitor and at the same time be captured by the camera and their image transmitted to one or more other room or group systems. Monitors are rarely less than 30 inches wide, camera lenses are controlled digitally, and audio is high fidelity stereo speakers and microphones. In many room systems, microphones are distributed at multiple points around the conference table.

Group systems will be used synonymously with roll-about systems in this discussion. Roll-about videoconferencing systems are generally self-contained units with one or two 25 to 27 inch parallel monitors, capable of being moved among a few rooms in a building. The cabinets with casters house one or more central processing units, an assortment of network hardware, and all the cabling, speakers, and handheld control devices necessary for a successful group meeting.

As these room, group, and small group roll-about systems cost between $40,000 and $120,000 to acquire, their applications are very carefully managed for optimal distribution in mission critical projects. Senior corporate management and others with highly specialized expertise use videoconferencing to supplement face-to-face meetings. Room systems are also popular for business television applications including executive announcements, corporate training, and briefings that would be prohibitively expensive and interfere with normal business processes if all participants needed to attend in person.

After acquisition, the cost of ownership in room videoconferencing mounts quickly. There are special, and occasionally dedicated, telecommunications network connections (e.g. Fractional T-1 or Primary Rate ISDN).

A technician is typically retained in order to set up the calls, maintain equipment over time, and generally do everything necessary to assure high quality conferences at any and all times. In addition, a scheduling application allows users to reserve the room or system with a corporate videoconferencing manager. Including training costs associated with this administrative tool, there are opportunity costs when the person who is called upon to manage the facilities schedule is pulled away from other tasks to schedule, verify, and reschedule meetings using the videoconferencing equipment.

9.5.2 First Generation Desktop and Table Top Videoconferencing

Some might argue that the first generation desktop or table videoconferencing system was introduced in 1964 by AT&T Bell Labs at the World's Fair in Flushing Meadow, New York. Unfortunately, lack of demand, (and, therefore, a market) prevented the otherwise well-thought out system from earning more than a historical footnote in the chronicles of the current desktop videoconferencing industry.

In late 1993 and early 1994, three converging trends met and produced what most will agree was the first generation of desktop and tabletop videoconferencing tools.

☞ Room systems were proving their value and volume sales permitted certain components to be manufactured at less cost. Still, cost of acquisition was not the only barrier. In an effort to make videoconferencing more accessible and lower some of the overhead associated with ownership, vendors began exploring how a personal computer could serve some of the user interface and session management functions.

☞ At the same time, those companies who design and manufacture processors (both central processors and dedicated integrated circuits) saw the possibility of video to the desktop driving continued processor upgrades. Counterparts in operating system design streamlined the file and data management specifically for multimedia.

☞ Growing acceptance of worldwide telecommunications standards (i.e., the
ITU H.320 suite of specifications) offered interoperability among systems,
including rooms of diverse manufacturers, and, potentially, an installed
base that would reach critical mass.

PictureTel Personal Conferencing System was a scaled down version of
room and group systems that the company was already successfully selling into
corporations. The product was designed to run on the IBM OS/2 platform. Within
six months of PictureTel's PCS proof of concept, a number of vendors announced
their intent to create similar systems, hence a true market was conceived. Commercial add-on kits for desktop videoconferencing in Windows desktop computers were quickly introduced by PictureTel, Northern Telecom, AT&T Global
Information Systems (GIS), and Intel. These kits included everything the end-
user needed to add to a standard or high-end PC and begin videoconferencing.

A market was truly born when telecommunications providers in the United
States and elsewhere began offering Integrated Services Digital Network (ISDN) to
medium and small businesses, and residential customers. In order to transmit and
receive the digital video and audio, the systems offered by these and other less well-
known vendors required ISDN. By late 1994, there were approximately 20 companies offering components that in one way or another partially or fully enabled a
desktop computer for real-time video capture, compression, transmission, decompression, and display with synchronized audio. One year later, the field included
solutions for Plain Old Telephone (POTS) networks, and some for IP networks.

Desktop videoconferencing is evolving very quickly. The following describes
typical components of a complete solution.

9.5.3 Today's Desktop Videoconferencing/Collaborative
Computing Systems

A common sense, desktop videoconferencing system for business (assuming
that this means a Windows operating system in an Intel microprocessor environment) begins with a 100MHz Pentium and 16MB of RAM, though some solutions
allow users to retrofit a much lower performance CPU, provided all the critical
compression and decompression is done on dedicated DSPs. Most add-on kits
come with peripherals for video input/output (e.g., a compact but functional analog video camera) and network interface hardware (e.g., Ethernet card for LAN,
modem for POTS, a terminal adapter for ISDN). Finally, speakers are necessary
to amplify the audible frequencies, and the system must also have a microphone.
Often, the microphone/audio source is being incorporated in desktop speakers
specifically designed for personal videoconferencing.

Once assembled, most desktop videoconferencing systems sold to date (e.g.,
Intel ProShare Video System 200, PictureTel PCS50 & 100) follow in the tradition
of the room and group-based solutions from which they evolved and are optimized
for use in point to point communications over a digital wide area network. The
remainder of this chapter focuses on personal computer-based technologies, and
network protocols and topologies that directly support real-time video, audio, and

data communication and collaboration with others on a common corporate campus, as well as with desktop or room-based systems on the Wide Area Network.

Three fundamentally different approaches will be examined, each with advantages and disadvantages.

☞ A digital video approach in which the unique requirements of the video and audio, in otherwise congested conventional data networks, are treated through selective deployment of appropriate protocols and specialized network management in a segment of a corporate LAN or throughout the private LAN, MAN, and WAN.

☞ A digital video approach in which the video and audio traffic runs on an isolated but parallel local area network, thereby keeping the benefits of being digital without compromising data network performance for other users.

☞ An approach in which the video and audio are not digitized before transmission on an isolated but parallel local area network. Though analog in the local loop, the video and audio can be digitized via gateways at the periphery of the enterprise or workgroup for transport over digital WAN services.

These are not architectures in and of themselves. However, it is important to note that some unique video network architectures can include components of each of the approaches and create a total solution. In order to fully understand the first two of these three alternatives, the reader should be somewhat familiar with the basics of digital video and audio capture.

9.6 AN OVERVIEW OF DIGITAL VIDEO AND AUDIO CAPTURE AND COMPRESSION

To capture images for digital desktop videoconferencing requires a camera of some sort. The array of devices for this purpose is quite impressive. Small analog cameras are most popular with add-on kit vendors who want to provide satisfactory quality for very low cost. The camera optics are typically factory set at a fixed focal length and depth of field; the user may have some control over the lens aperture with the software.

In general, a composite video signal (YUV space) delivers images (10 to 30 frames per second) to the video digitizing (analog to digital conversion) circuits on a dedicated board.

Once the video image has been digitized from the analog signal, video compression is necessary for the stream of bits to travel successfully over corporate networks. In an effort to support interoperability, most desktop videoconferencing product manufacturers adhere to international standards. There are no fewer than six vendors currently offering integrated circuits optimized (or programmable DSPs) to perform the discreet cosine transform and ensuing compression following the International Telecommunications Union's H.261 and H.263 specifications on digital video in real-time. These chips are used in a variety of combinations to accelerate compression on PCI, ISA, and NuBus boards. Most real-time H.261/H.263 software-only (motherboard-reliant) video encoding algorithms are far less efficient and, as a result, produce a slower frame rate than hardware supported systems. Conversely, given a high quality stream of frames, hardware-implemented video and audio decoders produce higher frame rates with better quality images in each frame than their "software-only" counterparts.

Audio is also converted from analog to digital signal and compressed using either dedicated DSPs or algorithms running on the motherboard processor (software codecs).

9.6.1 Quality of Service

In contrast to conventional data applications in which data transmission is bursty, digital video and audio applications require continuous data transmission. In IP environments, precise bit rates during the transmission varies with many factors. In Table 9.1, the factors influencing bit rates (and consequently bandwidth) are presented as a function of the media.

Table 9.1 Factors influencing bandwidth utilization during videoconferencing and collaborative computing

video
bit depth (number of colors)
resolution (size of the image being captured, compressed, transmitted, and decompressed; in contrast with window size, which is the size of the image that is displayed for viewing. If the window size is different than resolution, then interpolation is used to generate a new image that fits the window.)
Q factor (sharpness of edges in any given frame)
smoothing (this is a result of—dependent on—motion estimation algorithms and content change from one frame to the next)
frame rate (i.e., frames per second; e.g., NTSC is 30 fps, PAL is 25 fps)

audio
sampling rate (the number of audio samples captured, compressed, and transmitted, expressed KHz, cycles per second; e.g., telephony is 6.3 KHz, FM radio is 36 KHz, music CDs 44.1KHz)
bit rate (the number of bits the system has to accurately represent different tones; 8-bit or 16-bit)
mono and stereo

data
quantity of data (application dependent: refresh rate frequency, sharing real-time graphics, by mouse clicks through the commonly-held files (e.g., send a presentation through FTP in advance of the conference), file transfer)
latency of transmission (how long it takes to send at a given bit rate)

Quality of service is a function of many factors (e.g., window size, processor speed, network bandwidth), which together influence the frame rate, bit depth, image clarity, and resolution, lip synchronization, and latency.

The central processing unit, choice of audio and video codecs, network infrastructure, and network connection directly affect the quantitative factors listed above. Depending on the quantitative parameters, the user's experience (a combination of audio and video) is qualitatively different.

Table 9.2 Components of End User Experience during Videoconferencing

synchronization of audio and video
latency (delay in transmission from end to end)
window size
jitter
richness and clarity of audio
image clarity (bit depth, sharpness, smoothing, and resolution)

The users' experience with bi-directional, live video over any network is a function of the end-to-end quality of service. In order for the interaction to be as close to natural as possible, it is particularly important that both (or all) users in a videoconference experience a uniformly low-latency (minimum delay). Any variation in the frame rate between points is perceived as "jitter" and poor synchronization between lips and audio is also distracting.

9.7 PREPARING AN IP NETWORK FOR DESKTOP VIDEOCONFERENCING

All-digital videoconferencing solutions for TCP/IP networks send streaming data types and real-time packets on the same network where conventional (best-effort) transactional applications transmit their data.

Data networks, including those running Internet Protocols, are vulnerable to network contention and congestion. The relatively low bandwidth available for each user has, to date, made corporate data networks unsuitable for business quality videoconferencing. There are, however, some solutions to evaluate. The Internet Engineering Task Force (IETF) provides guidance and ratifies specifications for managing these networks optimally to prioritize the real-time data types, but there also needs to be agreement between products on the desktop.

The most significant disadvantage for IP-based desktop videoconferencing is the current lack of standards for session set up, management, and video compression. Though these specifications are under development (e.g., ITU's H.323), they are not expected in products until later this year. The direct result of entering IP-based videoconferencing at this stage of the market's development is that the users are confined to communicating with others who are running identical hardware, software, and communications protocols on all end-points. Seamless interoperability is essential for vendor independence, but may be sacrificed for exceptional functionality and quality.

Until interoperability is achieved, either through IETF and ITU ratified standards, through *de facto* standards by one vendor's domination over others, or an industry wide agreement to comply with a common set of protocols, the IP videoconferencing installed base will be thwarted with difficulties.

This said, a number of protocols have been developed to manage the unique requirements of real-time streaming data. Most grew out of experiments with delivering packetized audio and video over a special part of the Internet called the Multicast Backbone (MBone).

9.7.1 RSVP and RTP

The IP-based bandwidth management protocol with the most enthusiastic following to date is known as the ReSerVation Protocol (RSVP). Implemented in end-point and router software on the MBone and currently under review for IETF ratification, RSVP guarantees bandwidth allocation in connectionless networks according to a receiver driven model. It is a fixed bit rate allocation routine, with supplemental provisions to handle "available bit rate" negotiations in the future. Prototype support for RSVP has been demonstrated by a number of different router vendors, is currently the basis for much research by Intel and Microsoft, and will soon be available in many desktop videoconferencing add-on kits and router products.

Unfortunately, current Internet pricing models do not reflect guaranteed bandwidth allocation. As a result, most commercial Internet Service Providers (ISPs) are reluctant to implement or turn-on RSVP in their routers because of the potential for a few users to monopolize router resources. New research at BBN and in the IETF's Internet Services working group promises to address this problem with specific billing protocols built into end-points and routers.

Another development in this field is the IETF Audio/Visual Transport Working Group's Real-Time Transport Protocol (RTP). When end-point applications support RTP, packets will leave the sender's desktop with a time stamp and content identification label. Using this information and through congestion monitoring facilities at either end, the proper sequences of frames can be more reliably recreated at the receiving station.

9.8 ALTERNATIVE ALL-DIGITAL VIDEOCONFERENCING NETWORKS

While IP-based solutions are of keen interest to users today, not all collaborative technologies run exclusively on data networks. Historically, desktop videoconferencing has been most widely deployed over a telecommunications network: ISDN. Basic Rate Interface ISDN provides a 128kbps access to a terminal adapter in the personal computer. Terminal adapters are universally components of commercial desktop videoconferencing systems for ISDN.

9.8.1 Basic Rate Interface to the Desktop

Using existing network interfaces (already provided by add-on videoconferencing systems vendors), a corporation can conduct videoconferences between desktops over a separate network running parallel to that which provides data communications services. An ISDN-based campus video network requires a switch either in the central office of the telecommunications service provider or one that is purchased and running on the premises, much like a voice Private Branch Exchange (PBX). Video-ready networks, such as those supported by Madge Networks' (San Jose, CA) AccessSwitches or Netmatics' (Tampa, FL) Toucan VPBX, provide seamless support to H.320 desktop videoconferencing users. There is also the ability to transfer calls and perform other services (hold, hunt group switching) similar to a voice only PBX.

As long as users are behind a video-PBX, there are no telecommunications charges and no contention with any other data traffic. When the same users want to communicate with other people external to the building or campus, a point-to-point call is easily placed over the telecommunications service provider's basic rate interface ISDN infrastructure.

The principle disadvantage of this solution is the need to install new wiring where eight pairs of shielded twisted pair (that which is required by the Terminal Adapter) are not available in a facility.

There are several other H.320-compliant alternatives.

9.8.1.1 IsoEthernet to the Desktop

The worldwide public telephone network is circuit switched, meaning it establishes connections between calling parties that remain dedicated for the duration of the call. Isochronous Ethernet (IsoEthernet) adapts the isochronous technology for use over Ethernet LANs. It is basically two networks running over the same 10Base-T unshielded twisted pair wiring. A 10 Mbps packet channel carries normal Ethernet data traffic, and an additional 6.144 Mbps of bandwidth is available for isochronous transport when the hardware in the end point is present.

The IsoEthernet hardware (network interface card) provides the additional bandwidth by changing the data encoding system from the 1B/2B Manchester encoding used by standard Ethernet to a 4B/5B encoding scheme. The 4B/5B encoding achieves an 80 percent efficiency from the network clock.

In addition to new hardware at the end points, IsoEthernet must also be supported with new hardware in the hubs. Once converted, an IsoEthernet network is capable of supporting regular 10Base-T mode users, as well those using desktop videoconferencing. Isochronous Ethernet and ATM have a number characteristics in common.

9.8.1.2 ATM to the Desktop

In environments where a migration to ATM (or any other high speed data networks such as Fast Ethernet or Gigabit Ethernet) has begun, desktop videoconferencing can take advantage of the unique Asynchronous Transfer Mode network characteristics.

At the center of an ATM LAN, MAN, or WAN, there is an ATM Switch providing network services. Each workstation (or LAN segment) is like the case with IsoEthernet, connected to the switch using a specialized network interface card in the PC and switch. First Virtual Corporation has been working with the manufacturers of desktop videoconferencing kits in order to use the MVIP connector on a codec board to transfer data over a 25Mbps ATM network interface card.

9.8.1.3 Analog Video Networks for Videoconfrencing and Collaboration in Enterprise

Existing desktop videoconferencing systems on current LANs, even ATM, are incapable of transmitting 30 full screen frames per second indefinitely. Rather, the vendors of all-digital systems for desktop videoconferencing deliver a video stream at the rate of 15-20 frames per second. Many digital video advocates feel that this quality is "good enough." A growing number of companies feel that enterprise users require 30fps, TV-quality (NTSC) solutions.

In order to cost-effectively deliver TV-quality video to the desktop today, companies can use a network distinct from other data types.

A switched, analog network is capable of delivering TV-quality video and accompanying, full-duplex, echo-cancelled audio, with no latency or jitter and no impact on the data LAN. Video and audio are transmitted over dedicated strands of unshielded twisted pair (UTP)—two or four pair—or fiber.

Rather than requiring new network technologies, these solutions leverage existing infrastructure by introducing a separate video overlay network on top of existing data networks. At the center of the network is a data network concentrator (e.g., an Ethernet hub). Each workstation is typically connected to the concentrator using a home run network connection (typically over UTP). For Ethernet networks, the network is terminated in an Ethernet interface board that sits in the workstation.

CONCLUSION

Desktop videoconferencing makes it possible for people who are separated, either by floors in a building, or by thousands of miles, to communicate with verbal as well as nonverbal means. The full potential of combining audio, video, and data conferencing is unclear, however. For some companies, the new business processes enabled with these technologies will provide a competitive advantage well beyond the costs of acquisition, deployment, and usage.

Determining the appropriate time for introducing videoconferencing technologies on the desks of individual users is a critical factor in the overall success of a deployment plan. A number of indicators, technical as well as social, serve to aid planners who are considering desktop videoconferencing. In the end, however, the champions of new technologies are as important as the technologies themselves. With the support of innovative leaders, people will develop entirely new ways of working together without moving from their desks.

APPENDIX A: PRODUCTS FOR DESKTOP VIDEOCONFERENCING OVER LANs AND INTRANETS

Intranet Solutions Vendors

While a buyer's guide is a valuable resource, the information is not suitable for long.

1. WhitePine Software CU-SeeMe
2. VDONet's VDOLive
3. EyeTel Communications
4. Apple QTC
5. Mosaic Information Technology

BRI, IsoEthernet and ATM Solutions

1. Incite
2. Luxcom
3. Ascom Nexion
4. First Virtual Corporation

Analog Solutions with TCP/IP-based Session Controls and NTSC Video

1. Avistar
2. Corel
3. Target Technologies
4. Others

Products and Services for Multipoint Videoconferencing on LANs and Intranets

Bridges

Switches

1. Analog video
2. Digital

De-centralized MCU capability in H.323

Introduction to Chapter 10

A thorough discussion of Lotus Notes begins our vendor section of this book. Notes, the first commercially successful collaborative product, entered the market in 1989 and has changed tremendously over the last several years. Today's product (version 4.0) is fully Web-enabled.

Lotus differentiates Notes from other databases by its ability to deal with unstructured data. I would go further and say that Notes is an "intelligent bucket" in which you can put almost any type of data: phone messages, faxes, documents, presentations, text discussions, e-mail, URLs, pager messages, videos, graphics, etc. Lotus created hooks to almost every type of data in use today, even structured data. Although Notes is not known for transaction processing and work with legacy systems data, they do have ways to import and export data from legacy systems and RDBMS databases.

In fact, the chapter by Oracle, following this one, provides a remarkable contrast in viewpoint on collaboration between a structured database firm to that of an unstructured database company. Lotus's big challenge today is not Microsoft Exchange, but rather tools for collaboration on the WWW, more of which are becoming available everyday!

Lotus Notes is often the product most identified with the term "Groupware" and Lotus has done an admirable job of educating the market about what groupware is and what its benefits are. However, this chapter assumes that replication is a prerequisite for groupware, and that is not a fair assumption. There are many collaborative technologies and functions that do not require replication for collaboration.

Notes is "the Swiss Army Knife of Groupware." It has some of almost every collaborative function, and falls into almost every category in my functional taxonomy. Recently, in Version 4, Lotus has added Organizer for group calendaring and scheduling. Netscape has responded by creating a Web-based group calendaring and scheduling standard, and supporting a group calendaring server. Microsoft, with the best selling scheduler (Schedule +), is also group enabling this product and will make it Web-enabled in the near future.

One of the major advantages of Notes is its rapid applications development environment. Here, iterative development results in a specification for the application at the end of the process, rather than where it is traditionally found, at the beginning. This often drives MIS shops crazy, as it puts the ability to build an application in a few days (for proof of concept) in the hands of the users.

As a matter of fact, the greatest resistance we find in organizations considering Notes is often the MIS group. They see it as a threat, and additional work that does not conform to their agenda. It is these organizational issues that Lotus most has to deal with for the success of their customers, and to their credit, they are addressing this challenge through the Lotus Institute and Lotus Consulting.

This chapter examines in detail InterNotes Publisher, and Lotus's emergence onto the WWW. Lotus has changed their focus from the "enterprise" and "scalability" to "reach." They have positioned their product as a way to decrease Web administration overhead. They also see it as a workflow engine or substrate to support interactive Web-based forms. Their third strength is security. Unfortunately, everyone on either side of the firewall sees security as an issue (see Chapter 2 for details), and I see security as an illusion. The only thing you can do to keep people out is to make it very hard or very expensive to get in.

Lotus focuses on bi-directional replication as an advantage to their server on the WWW. While they do provide good anecdotal support, most Web-based collaborative applications may not need replication at all. Lotus makes a good case for their product as a Web-application development tool. With the integration of their Web Navigator, and the Domino server, Lotus has squarely positioned itself as a player in the collaborative Internet market.

Another interesting discussion is the return on investment that companies experience using Lotus Notes. This chapter includes a cost of ownership study about the cost of Notes vs. intranets. This report shows that Notes is quicker to deploy and easier to maintain than intranet applications with similar functionality. While this information is very interesting, it does conflict with some of the perceptions we found in the Fortune 1000 in our survey work detailed in Chapter 2. In this research, we found that the MIS people perceive that a Notes site is about 5 times more expensive to build and maintain than a Web site.

On the whole, this chapter give you a good feel for where Lotus has been and where they are going. Notes, interestingly, is like religion, everyone has an opinion on it. Still, whatever your position on Notes, it is the prevailing industry leader and this chapter will show you many of the reasons why.

Deploying Second-Generation Intranets with Lotus Notes

Jeff Papows
Lotus Division of IBM

10.1 WHAT IS NOTES?

Just what is this thing called Notes? When I first joined Lotus in 1993, I would have answered that, up close, Notes is shared databases. Step back a few paces and you'll see that Notes is a messaging and groupware infrastructure. Today, my response is that Notes is a platform for developing and deploying high value intranet and Internet business applications. Are the early definitions out of date? Not at all. All three characterizations are valid, and if you posed this question to a handful of customers you would no doubt hear many more equally valid definitions.

10.2 NOTES IS SHARED DATABASES

The fundamental concept underlying Notes is certainly the database: a repository of information, a collection of documents—"notes"—that can be viewed and organized in lots of different ways.

Generally, Notes databases reside on servers where they can be accessed by networked users with just a click of a mouse. The desktop interface seen by the Notes user is shown in Fig. 10.1. On the user's desktop, each database is represented by an icon. Click on an icon and (security privileges permitting) you're in the database, regardless of where that database physically resides. Notice that one of these databases is the user's mail database. (This has some powerful advantages in terms of mobile usage, which I'll discuss a bit later). As these database icons begin to proliferate, they can be organized logically via the user-defined tabs that run across the top of the interface. It's entirely up to the user which database icons reside on the desktop and how they are arranged.

Fig. 10.1 The Notes Workspace

What's so special about making a series of databases available to users? Notes databases are *not* relational. Notes deals with *unstructured* information as opposed to the structured data that most people immediately think of when they hear the term "database." Our customers, for example, store policies and procedures, product brochures, customer records, contracts, sales orders, and so forth in Notes databases, and the information stored within these databases need not be just straight text, numerical data, or some structured combination of the two. Our customers also populate the documents that make up their databases with graphics, audio, software demos, and even full-motion video. This departure from the traditional relational database model gives Notes its initial critical differentiation—its ability to change the way businesses operate. Notes makes important information, the key asset of any large company, readily available for all who need it, when and where it's needed, and in a way that fosters communication, collaboration, and coordination.

The rich variety of information stored in Notes databases can be seen in a variety of different ways. In other words, there can be many different views into a common pool of information. Fig. 10.2 shows a Notes *view* of the numerous documents stored in a Travel Authorizations database. This particular view is organized by the "status" of the Travel Authorizations document. Another user might choose to look at this same information according to the date the Travel Authorizations document was entered into the database or according to the persons requesting authorization. Notes views create a living table of contents that lets users navigate through Notes databases from a variety of user friendly perspectives.

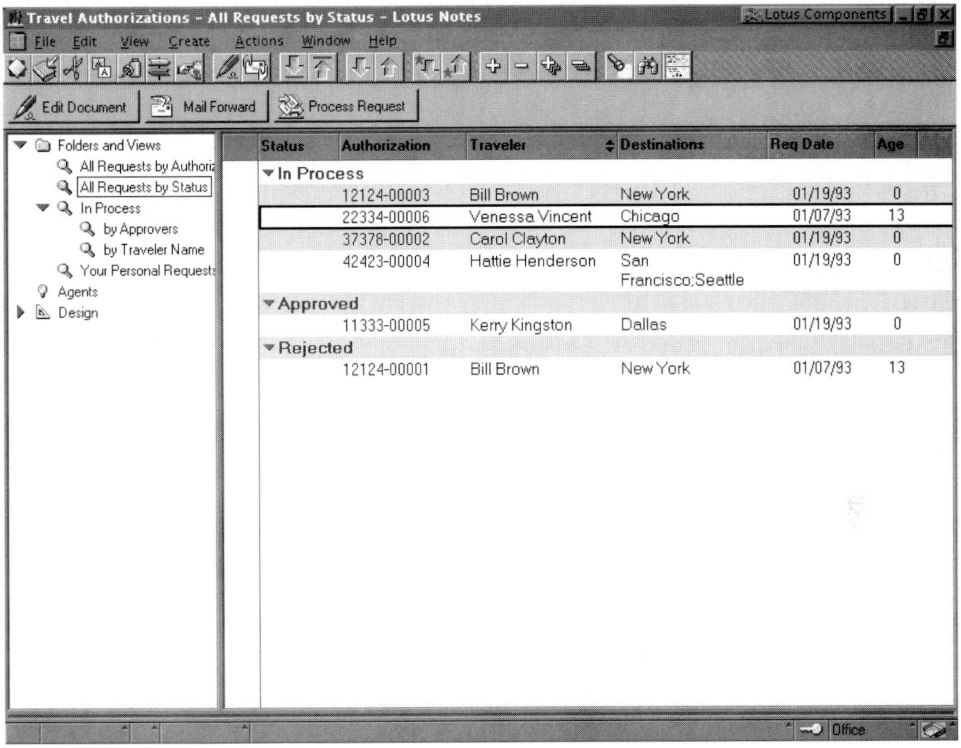

Fig. 10.2 One View of the Travel Authorizations Database

Views can display any number and variety of documents; the amount of detail shown and the sorting conventions used are up to the user. For example, let's say we're looking at a customer records database for the XYZ Widget Corporation. We could ask for a very expansive view—for instance, "all customers with complaints." On the other hand, we could ask for a considerably more contracted view—"all customers in the Chicago metropolitan area who complained within the most recent calendar quarter that they received their widgets order more than one week late." Any view can be either expanded or collapsed: pull-down menus, clicks, and keystrokes are all it takes.

Remember, a user's mailbox is a database too. The "documents" stored here are mail messages. So a view of the messages (documents) in your mailbox can reveal all your messages, or just your unread messages, in date order. You can also view messages by category or by author, or take advantage of the powerful Notes full-text search engine that lets you find any entry, or entries, across the numerous documents in any database.

Once documents have been sorted according to the user's needs, double-clicking on any one of them opens the document itself. For example, say you've just double-clicked on one of the documents listed in Fig. 10.2, perhaps the document that specifies information for Hattie Henderson. Fig. 10.3 shows the document that you'd see on your screen. Each of the items pictured here—Traveler

Name, Employee Number, and so on—is a Notes field. Not only can all such fields be organized in any number of ways, they can also be *encrypted* so that only certain users can see their contents.

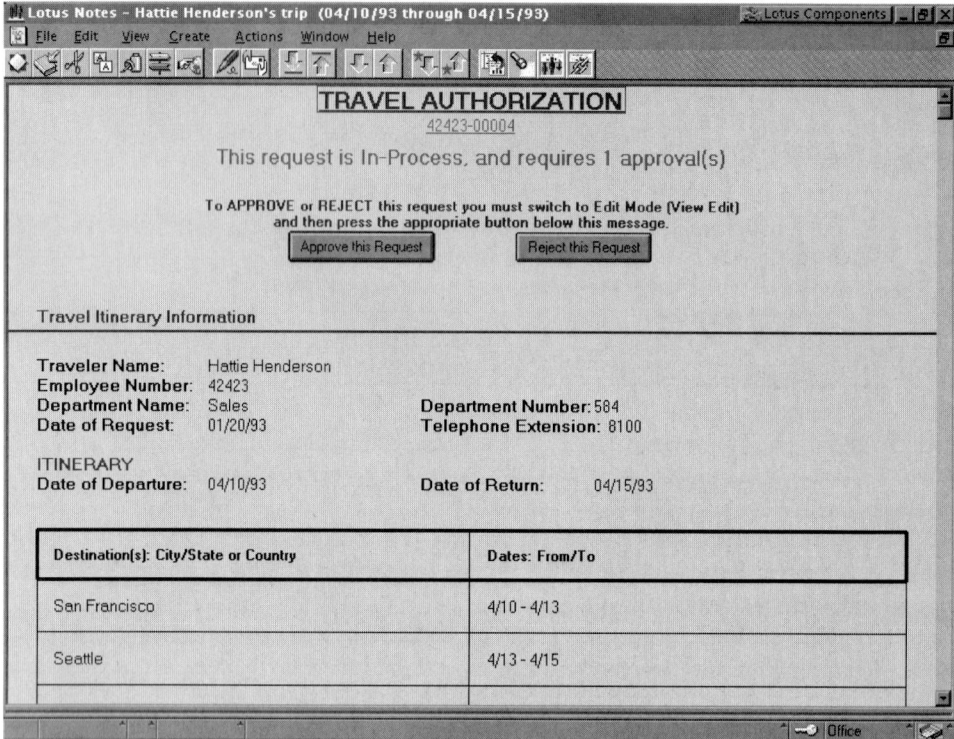

Fig. 10.3 A Simple Notes Document

This is a rather simplistic document. Document structure is actually highly configurable in Notes. You would not, therefore, expect a document in a product catalog database developed for mass merchandising on the World Wide Web (WWW) to look like the one pictured here. I suspect that a Notes database designer, creating a product catalog of this type, would include pictures, or even video demonstrations, of the products being showcased, along with a standardized order form of some sort. Documents (messages) in my mailbox, on the other hand, can run the gamut. Their content and structure is established by the author of each message. Some people send me meeting invitations. The invitation is predictable enough—calendaring and scheduling (C&S) is now an integral part of Notes, so the group scheduling facilities are very well defined. But there are others who include spreadsheets, organization charts, and links to various Web pages in their mail messages. The structure of these messages is limited only by the author's time and imagination.

The database access methods I've described so far, namely *views*, are a text-based user interface (UI) to the documents stored in a Notes database. Users can also access Notes-based information via Navigators like the one shown in Fig. 10.4. True to their name, Navigators are *graphical* guides to the information housed in a Notes database. This particular Navigator incorporates photographs. Click on the photograph labeled "Customers," and the customer database unfolds. Click on the photograph labeled "Contacts," and the contacts database is accessed.

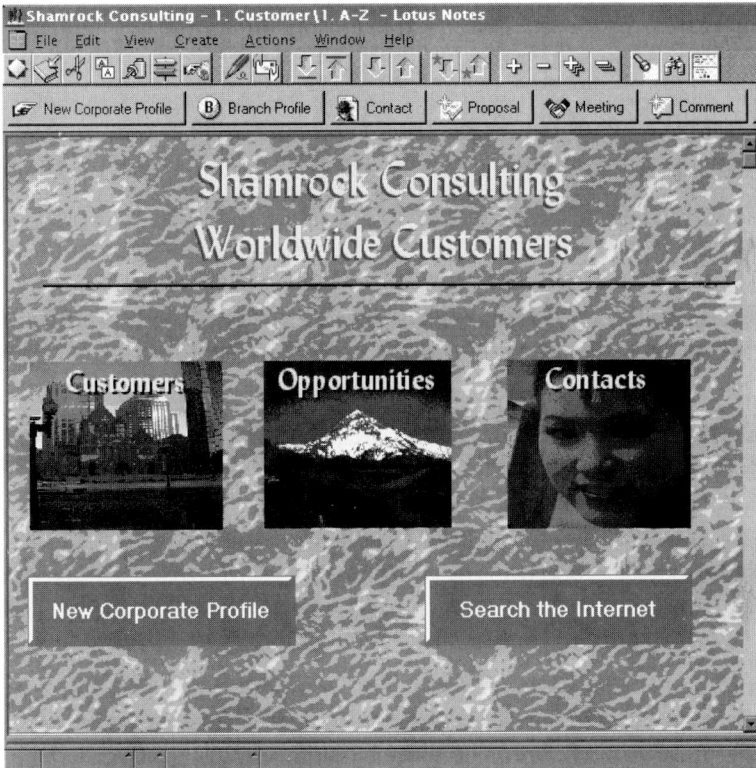

Fig. 10.4 A Sample Navigator

Navigators can take any shape or form. Database designers can copy bit-map images, create their own images, or superimpose one over the other as you see in Fig. 10.5. This is the actual design pane in which a developer can import and manipulate images to create a Navigator for a Notes database. Here, the developer is tracing a map of eastern Massachusetts and highlighting various cities or regions so that a user can, for example, click on the city of Boston to call up information about that city. Click on another portion of this Navigator and information relevant to that geographical location becomes accessible. With just a click on a Notes navigational element, the user is presented with another level of data, a view, or even another application.

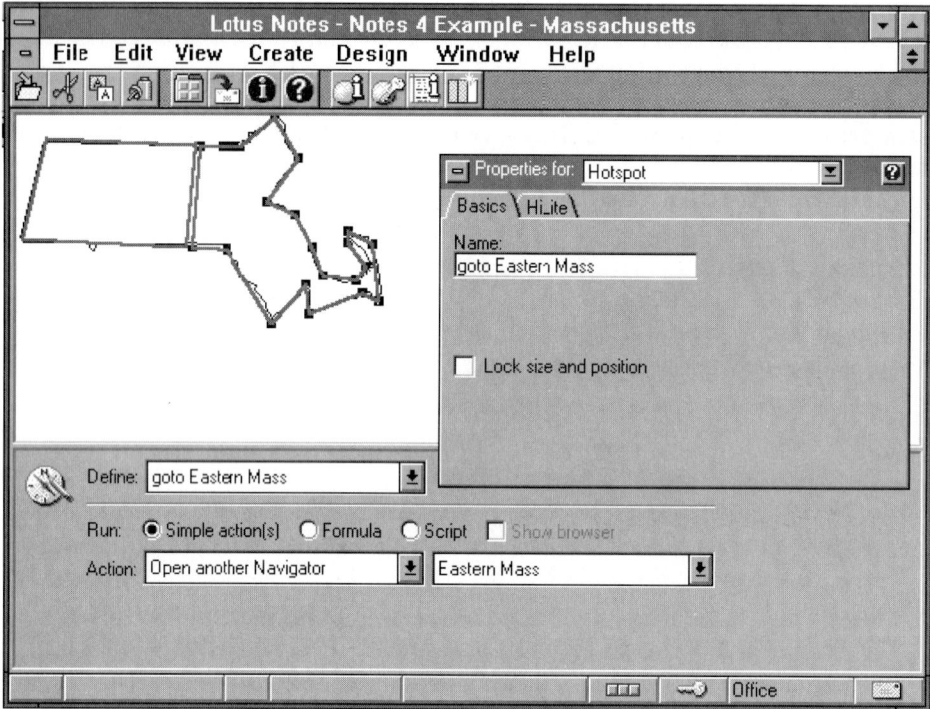

Fig. 10.5 The Development Environment for Creating Navigators

There you have a quick tour of the ways in which information is organized and accessed in a Notes database. But the key thing to bear in mind is that Notes is much more than a means of managing data: It's an application platform upon which we at Lotus and our customers build groupware applications that coordinate and extend the processes by which we run our businesses.

10.3 NOTES IS A MESSAGING AND GROUPWARE INFRASTRUCTURE

The essence of groupware is the provision of electronic messaging support for business processes previously accomplished by means of laborious manual procedures: For instance, hand-carrying an approval form from office to office. Notes applications can be built to replace and improve these workflow processes. Take, for example, an applicant tracking system used by a Human Resources (HR) department. As resumes are received, they are electronically scanned into Notes. HR professionals can then read them, identify department managers who may wish to interview a particular job candidate from a Notes database, and forward the applicable document. The document each interested manager receives contains not only the resume, but two buttons, "interested" and "not interested"; if the former is pushed, an e-mail message automatically goes to HR, apprising the relevant parties of the interest and kicking off the formal interview process.

The Notes messaging and directory services that are so seamlessly integrated into this application are two fundamental prerequisites of a groupware architectural framework. So is the rich suite of application development tools, ranging from simple formulas and agent builders to a powerful scripting language and advanced APIs, which make it possible to *rapidly* create groupware applications.

Another groupware prerequisite is replication—a technology pioneered by Lotus. Through replication, copies or *replicas* of databases can stay synchronized even though the computers on which they reside may not be connected. Imagine one sales tracking database in New York and another in Paris. Users in each location are constantly adding and updating documents within each database. At some predetermined time, one server automatically calls the other, and they (forgive the pun) compare notes; that is, they build up lists of documents or fields within documents that have been altered in any way since the last such reconciliation—called a *replication*—and copy those changes over.

Servers with replicas of the sales database in New York and Paris call each other to determine what information is missing from which replica and quickly fill in the gaps with copies passed to each other.

What if someone in New York changes the same document that someone is Paris wants to modify? Unlike traditional database systems, Notes allows *both* documents to be changed. Mechanisms are in place to guarantee full integrity of data.

Replication is a particular boon to mobile users, who now constitute a considerable percentage of the workforce. Salespeople on the road, for instance, can dial into a Notes server and replicate databases to their laptops. They can replicate a sales tracking database, a product review database, a competitive analysis database, or a budget database—any and all of the databases they need to remain productive while disconnected from their networks.

This is why Notes mail and calendaring and scheduling (C&S) offer superior mobile support. A user's mailbox is, after all, a Notes database. As such, users have full control over how and when they replicate that database. I generally replicate my mail database (or portions of my database—I don't have to replicate it in its entirety) before leaving for a business trip. At that point, my mail database on my laptop and my mail database on my Notes mail server at the office have the same exact information. As I work "offline," that is, disconnected from our corporate network, typically in an airplane, I'm reading my mail, discarding what I don't need, and creating and forwarding messages to colleagues. When I call into work over a modem, or return to the office, these changes all get replicated back to my Notes mail server, and all the messages I crafted while away from the office are delivered to the appropriate addressees. By the way, if I've made appointments with colleagues, meeting invitations go out at that time too. Remember, C&S is now an integral part of Notes mail. I'm not just referring to the fact that users set up appointments, group scheduling, tasks, and so forth from the Notes mail UI shown in Fig. 10.6; I'm referring to a shared back end. A user's Notes mail and C&S information are housed in a common database. That's why when I replicate my mail, my C&S information gets replicated too.

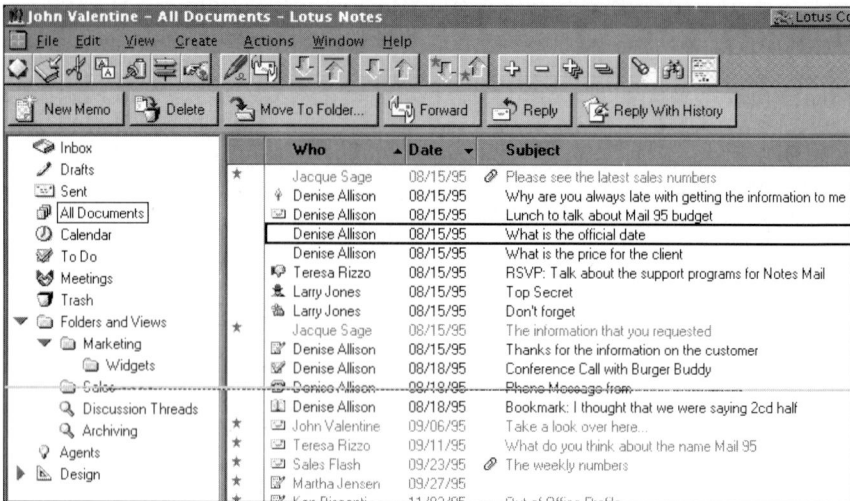

Fig. 10.6 The Notes Mail UI

Ever present behind these messaging, directory, and replication services is Notes security—the best in the industry. Notes features a pervasive and consistent security architecture that's based on public-key cryptography—the technology that Lotus pioneered in cooperation with RSA Data Security—as well as certificate management that's based on international standards. Through Notes' comprehensive security services, a user can encrypt mail or any other document, assign various individuals different forms of access, and build sophisticated workflow applications based on digital signature technology. There is also a thorough implementation of access controls. Access Control Lists (ACLs) are established and maintained by administrators. Every Notes database has an ACL that clearly delineates who is, and is not, authorized to access the information stored in the database, and at what level. Some users, for example, can be given rights to read but not alter documents in the database; some can be given authorization to contribute or edit documents in the database; and some can be denied access altogether.

10.3.1 A Rapid Application Development and Deployment Environment

How quickly and easily can a developer create a workflow or business process application? Let me answer by telling you that Notes is unsurpassed as an environment for rapid application development and deployment (RADD). I base this belief, a belief shared by our customers and business partners, on six specific reasons:

☞   One reason is that the client/server infrastructure is already there and freely accessible. It doesn't have to be reinvented. Developers never need to conduct complex systems integration to build fully functional, mission critical applications. The underlying object store, replication, messaging, security, and directory services can be effortlessly integrated into an application.

☞ A second reason is that Notes offers an incredibly wide range of cross-platform development tools that includes an advanced scripting language called LotusScript, formulas, C APIs, and an agent builder. That's in addition to working with languages such as C, C++, VB, etc.

☞ A third reason is that Notes ships with dozens of templates and ready-to-run applications.

☞ A fourth is Lotus Components. Lotus Components are small, fast, reusable software modules that can be plugged into the Notes environment. For example, there's a Spreadsheet Component, a Charting Component, a Project Management Component, a Draw/Diagram Component, etc. If a member of my team wants me to review a sales forecast, he or she can drop the Lotus Spreadsheet Component into a mail message, enter projected sales figures, and send it to me. Figure 10.7 shows how the embedded component appears when I open that message. I never have to leave Notes to work on the spreadsheet—the data and program are all there at my disposal. These feature-rich components can be laced together by developers and end users alike to quickly and easily create highly customized Notes applications.

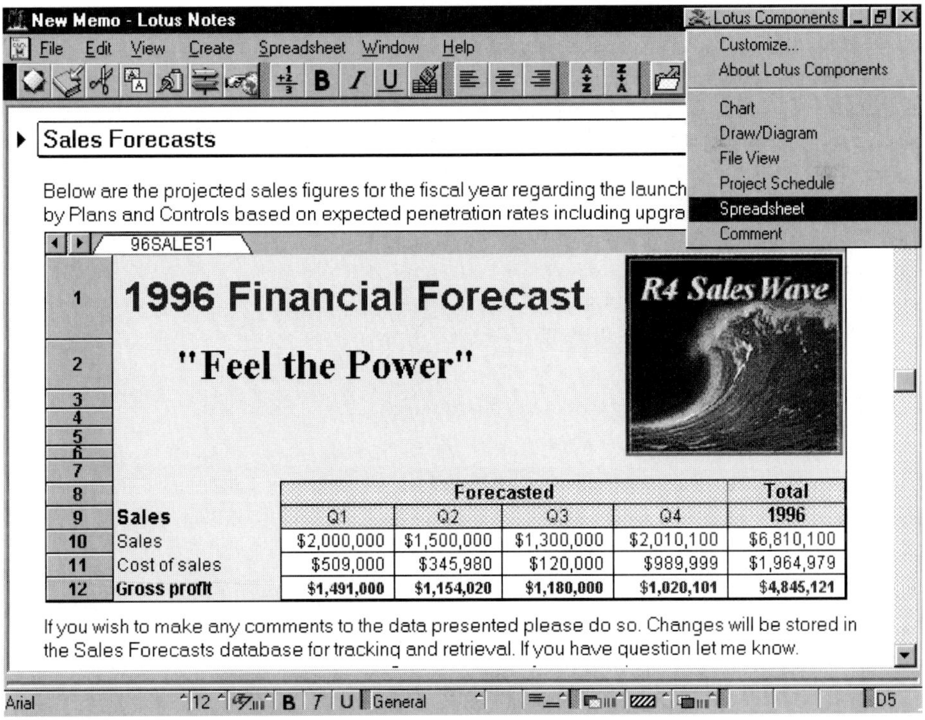

Fig. 10.7 The Lotus Spreadsheet Component

☞ A fifth is that Notes can work with the many, many sources of data that
house corporate information. The larger the corporation, the more sources
you'll find—on mainframes and hosts, on network servers and PCs.
Between native Notes facilities, Lotus add-on products, and a truly impressive array of third-party offerings, Notes can work with virtually all of
these systems. Notes can exchange, synchronize, replicate, and/or share
data with systems from IBM, Sybase, Oracle, and dBase, to name a few. For
example, LS:DO (LotusScript: Data Object) allows Notes access to relational and legacy databases using ODBC. LS:DO allows developers to combine Notes with external databases to link Notes applications with
operational and transaction systems. That is, LS:DO effectively makes
Notes a distributed front-end to traditional systems. Since the LS:DO provides both read and write access to back-end databases, Notes workflow
and replication capabilities are available to developers who want to create
advanced applications that combine relational databases and Notes.

☞ Lastly, once customers deploy an application, Notes' powerful replication
technology *automatically* distributes updates to its design. Secure, reliable,
and automatic application distribution solves one of the most pressing challenges facing IT organizations today—maintaining an application across a
distributed network where the number of clients, servers, platforms, and
operating systems can and will change randomly. By providing deployment
services as a native part of the platform, Notes eliminates the need for additional software management techniques, which are themselves "intrusive"
on the client/server infrastructure.

All of these elements contribute to enhanced user productivity, reduced
time and cost of Notes application development, and more compelling end-user
applications.

10.3.2 An Unsurpassed Applications Infrastructure

There you have it—databases and application development tools coupled
with messaging, directory, replication, and security services—the building blocks
of an enterprise infrastructure. That's precisely what Notes is—a messaging and
groupware infrastructure that offers a powerful framework for "re-engineering"
business as usual, for building applications that truly bring about positive
change in the ways our customers do business.

10.4 NOTES IS A PLATFORM FOR DEVELOPING AND DEPLOYING HIGH VALUE INTRANET AND INTERNET BUSINESS APPLICATIONS

In the 1980s, our industry was focused on "the enterprise." How scalable could
we build an application? How many new users, new resources, new sites could

we add to our corporate enterprise networks and still have them remain high performing, highly secure, and highly manageable? The key word was "scalability." Nowadays, the focus is on "reach." We've replaced the term "enterprise" with "intranet" to convey the expanded functionality we now demand from our networks. It's not enough to be able to grow our networks within the bounds of our own corporations, even multi-national corporations. Today, we want to know how far our network applications can *reach*. Can I establish applications that promote activities between my company and our business partners? Can I keep customer satisfaction high by getting support information to them proactively, rather than after customers experience a problem? Can I promote our latest product offerings on the Web? And can I do all this quickly and easily?

To each of these questions, I answer, "Absolutely." The Notes server—replete with application development and deployment services, messaging, directory, security and administrative services, *and* native support for Internet and Web protocols such as HTTP, HTML, and TCP/IP—addresses each and every one of these concerns. Native support for Internet and Web protocols, and by extension the customer's choice of Web browsers, is a radical departure from the original Notes architecture. It wasn't too long ago that the only thing that could be on the client side of the Notes client/server architecture was the Lotus Notes client. But that's not true today. Today, the "client" can be a Notes client, a Web browser, a cc:Mail client, MS Mail client, any MAPI-based mail client, or POP3 client. The choice is up to the customer.

10.4.1 The Notes Server

I strongly believe that it is the Web server, not the Web client, that will provide the greatest value in a Web-based client/server system. While there seems to be less and less differentiation among popular Web browsers, there is significant differentiation at the Web server level. Web servers that support Web publishing, perhaps the most popular Web application out there today, differ in the amount of administrative overhead they require to manage a large volume of pages. Web applications that go beyond broadcast publishing—from simple forms-based applications to sophisticated workflow applications that support or fully automate a business process, require Web servers that offer a comprehensive RADD environment. And for IT planners, the value of a Web server lies in its ability to reliably integrate with other infrastructure components with a minimum of added complexity. Lotus raised the bar on all three Web server prerequisites when we announced Domino—our code name for HTTP Services for Lotus Notes—back in May 1996. Domino transforms a Notes server into an interactive Web applications server, bridging the open networking environment of Internet standards and protocols with the powerful application development facilities of Notes. There was, and continues to be, a lot of customer excitement about Domino's HTTP support and its ability to render Notes data on-the-fly in HTML format, as well as to serve HTML documents from the file system. This standards support is the reason that any Web client can now access and interact with Notes data and applications.

10.4.1.1 Reducing Web Site Overhead

When I think about the administrative overhead associated with a Web site, four measurements come to mind:

☞ Page management

☞ Supporting interactive activity

☞ Security

☞ Network performance and expense

Let's start with page management. It's one thing to post a handful of Web pages to a Web site. It's another to post and maintain hundreds, or in our case at Lotus, tens of thousands of pages. Every time a new page is posted to a Web server, the author or the webmaster creates a set of links that point to that page. (No link, no access.) Suppose Jane, a sales manager at the XYZ Widget Corporation, posts a page about a new customer on the company's intranet. Users from Sales, Marketing, Accounting, and Support should be able to find that Web page in a number of different ways: by author, by customer, by industry, by product, or by account manager. Jane's sample page has three hypertext links that lead a user from the home page to the customer page itself. It also has three links to other views on the home page. If every page has three links that connect it to the home page and is listed under ten different view criteria, then a site with 10,000 pages will have up to 300,000 links in it, all created in a more or less manual and perhaps inconsistent manner.

The Notes server is a *document* database designed to arrange documents, or pages, into a flexible view structure. It is inherently able to manage Web pages far more effectively than a flat file system. Every Web page stored in a Notes database is *automatically* categorized in a logical hierarchy—the Notes views I described earlier. Every page saved in a Notes database is immediately listed under a set of predefined views (e.g., by author, by date, by customer, by industry) and these views are visible to any Web browser. Notes automatically sets up links to mirror these different views. Manual intervention by authors or the Webmaster is not necessary. This significantly reduces the effort required to make a Web site easy to navigate.

But if posting information is just the tip of the intranet/Internet iceberg, if bi-directional activities are the real potential of this medium, why are the majority of Web sites merely publishing information and not adding truly interactive applications to these efforts? The answer is that this step is complex. After all, you don't ingratiate your company with users by collecting information from them and failing to act on it. Workflow processes must be in place to take information from the user and *do* something with it. If it's a request for product literature, mailing information needs to be sent to a company stock room, complete with instructions about which brochures need to go out. And while you're at it, the marketing folks should get summary reports about the number of information requests being made, demographics about the people making those requests, and how those people heard about the company's products. If it's an actual order for a product, you probably want to send the user's credit card information to a central system to perform a credit check before instructing your shipping department to fulfill the order.

These workflow activities play to the core strength of Notes. They start with a form—the *interactive* Notes interface for collecting data from a user. What is important about Notes forms is that when they are submitted by the user, they are entered into a Notes database and acted upon, unlike basic e-mail messages or files that sit in an in-box or HTML file system on a low-end HTTP server, waiting for someone to open them up and do something with them. Notes forms can trigger a predefined workflow application based upon the value of a particular field within the form. Notes also performs basic validation on forms, to ensure that all submissions are complete. For example, Notes may return the form to the user if the "Last Name" field is not completed.

What about security and the toll it takes on Web site management? You probably want all employees to have access to the company policies and procedures manual on a corporate intranet, but only a select few to be able to access confidential customer information. Most Web servers can only control access to subdirectories. The Notes interactive Web applications server offers Access Control Lists (ACLs), which enable a Webmaster to define not only which specific files can be read, but *how* they can be read. Jane in Sales can be granted security privileges that let her read and post various sales related reports. Mike in Accounting can be restricted to just reading select sales reports. Moreover, Notes ACLs control access to servers, databases, views, pages, and fields within pages.

The fourth factor that comes into play when assessing the overhead associated with a Web site is the network performance and expense. The physical constraints of the Internet and of private internal networks require that individual Web databases be distributed to optimize network performance and minimize costs. The Notes server, a truly interactive Web applications server, is the only Web server that supports true bi-directional replication, which allows a Webmaster to synchronize all pages on all Web servers.

Consider a simple case—a corporate intranet that includes such basic information as an HR policies and procedures manual, an employee benefits directory, a corporate phone book, and some customer profiles. Let's assume that there is a central Web server located at the company headquarters in New York. Most of the material posted to the Web site is also authored in New York, so getting information from multiple desktops to the Web server is relatively straightforward. Of course, the Web database needs to be accessible to all employees worldwide, not only those employees in New York. The company has several options to make this intranet resource available worldwide:

☞ One option is to make the intranet server a node on the public Internet. This is a viable alternative and certainly reduces the cost of distributing the information to close to nothing. But do you feel comfortable putting private, internal information on the Internet?

☞ A second option is to deploy a private wide area network (WAN). A WAN will give the company a high degree of security and performance. On the other hand, private or leased WANs carry with them a necessary expense, and the cost of deploying this intranet server may involve budget items that were not anticipated when it was originally conceived.

☞ A third option is to mirror the intranet server. Many companies opt to mirror their Web server by making an electronic snapshot of all the pages on the server and sending it to all the remote sites. The remote sites, in turn, put the copy of the files on their own local area networks so that everyone has low cost, local access to all the current data. However, this solution becomes painfully complex when there are changes made to the data on all sides of the mirror. That is, if anyone outside New York creates, updates, or deletes a page on the Web server, there is no way to automatically synchronize all the pages throughout the company. The mirroring process, in this case, becomes an expensive and error-prone manual activity conducted by the webmaster.

The solution to this synchronization problem is bi-directional replication, in which all pages on all sides of the synchronization process are updated, so that no changes are lost or overwritten. *The Notes server is the only Web server that supports bi-directional replication.*

10.4.1.2 Building High Value Web Applications

There is no doubt that the greatest value of Web sites lies in their potential to deploy mission critical applications that coordinate specific business processes. Electronic commerce is one of the most commonly cited examples of an Internet application. There are, of course, innumerable other processes that lend themselves to automation on the Web, such as customizing marketing material to respond to specific profiles and inquiries, lead generation and qualification, fulfillment and follow-up, sales meetings, negotiation, contract review and approval, post-sale customer service, account review, and the identification of more sales opportunities. All of these applications represent high value-added activities that can make a Web site an invaluable corporate asset.

Let's use an example to drive this point home. Consider a typical customer service application—a package delivery service company that allows customers to track the status of their packages. As a customer, I can go to the company's Web site, say *http://www.package.com,* and fill in a form with the package billing number and submit the form. The form is returned to the Web server, which in turn makes a call into a back-end database that stores all the package shipping data. The database returns an answer ("The package was delivered at 9:32 a.m., May 10, 1996, signed by Sam Smith.") that is rendered as a Web page. This relatively straightforward application, if deployed well, should prove to be of tremendous value. The shipping company does not have to maintain as many operators to answer customer telephone inquiries, and customers like me get individualized service.

Now consider how this application might be extended to provide even better value. Suppose I visit this site and track my package, only to discover that the package has been lost or that there is no record of it in the system. I would hope that the package delivery company does not want to supply this bad news and not give me some sort of recourse. This otherwise valuable application, in that case, would actually be providing poor customer service, and might discourage me from using the delivery company again in the future. Instead, the Web site should have an application that adds the critical value of turning a dissatisfied (and potentially former!) customer into a satisfied and loyal customer. What would such an application do? I think it should:

1. **Give the customer an opportunity to fill in a form to request that the problem be remedied.** The form would automatically include my customer information: my name, company, package billing number, etc. This is the same information that is provided by the back-end database, which means that the forms tool to create this application is integrated with the back-end database.

2. **Submit the form to an automated "gatekeeper."** As I mentioned earlier, most forms on Web sites are returned as e-mail messages (typically sent to the webmaster as a default) or as files that sit in the HTML file system on a Web server, where they may languish unfound and unanswered for hours or days. That is, there is no automated business process that is triggered by the receipt of a customer service inquiry, regardless of its level of urgency or importance. A more complete Web application would accept the submitted form and process it. In this case, the process would be to check the level of urgency and importance (i.e., Is this a big customer? How bad is the problem? Is this the first time the customer has complained or is this a repeat problem?) and escalate the work item accordingly. In short, this process needs a page store with application logic built into it.

3. **Assign the task to the appropriate respondent.** Once the status of the submittal is determined, the system should assign the task to one or more customer service representatives. This can be done by automatically generating and sending an e-mail message to the right people (not the webmaster!). The e-mail might contain a hyperlink that, when clicked, links the various customer service representatives to the form so that everyone can add comments and suggestions about how to solve the problem in the same place. This process now requires an e-mail system and a directory that contains the names and roles of all the personnel involved (service manager, service supervisor, account representative, missing package warehouse staff, etc.).

4. **Respond to the customer.** Since the system is now "aware" of what is happening to the request, it should let me know of this. It is not enough to tell an anxious customer that the form has been received and that "something is happening." (After all, the shipping company has already mishandled one package. I'm not likely to be overly confident about the shipping company's internal processes at this point.) Rather, the system should give me as much information as possible. It should dynamically create a new

Web page that informs me of the status of the package, who is working on it, how to contact the person working on it directly, and how soon to expect an update about what is happening with the package.

5. **Monitor the process.** Let's face it. Things can always go wrong. Suppose the customer service representative responsible for coordinating the response to this inquiry fails to read his e-mail for some reason. The system should be able to monitor the process to make sure that the service staff is making progress. If the e-mail has remained unopened, or if the service representative did not enter any comments into the appropriate fields in the customer's complaint form, the system should escalate the process, re-sending an e-mail to the service representative, and also alerting others (another customer service representative, the customer service supervisor, the account representative), who now may need to know of a potential customer problem.

What does it require to build this value-added Internet application? This system requires a database with agents that operate without the intervention of a user. It requires a page database, a relational database access tool, a forms editor, a scripting language, a server-based e-mail system, an enterprise directory system, and server-based agents—the very things we provide in the Notes interactive Web applications server:

☞ **Rich forms designer**—This is the core service of the Notes server. Forms are submitted to the Notes server at the API level so that no CGI scripting is required: Forms and logic are maintained together in a single environment.

☞ **A scripting language and high-level development environment**—LotusScript, a BASIC-compatible programming language, is integrated into the Notes database. Developers also have the option of deploying Java applets as part of a Notes application.

☞ **An e-mail system**—Messaging is an integral service of the Notes server. Notes servers support not only Notes Mail clients, but also cc:Mail, MS Mail, any MAPI-based mail client, and POP3 clients, so that virtually any mail client can participate in a Notes application.

☞ **An enterprise directory**—The Notes directory is a flexible Notes database that can include qualitative fields (e.g., "handles urgent customer service inquiries") in addition to simple name and address information, so that Notes workflow applications can include designated roles as well as predefined or hard-coded e-mail addresses. In addition, the Notes directory is compliant with industry-standard protocols, including X.500 and LDAP.

☞ **Server-based agents**—Notes agents range from predefined "simple actions" to fully customized LotusScript programs.

☞ **A database integration facility**—Notes is seamlessly integrated with back end-databases and transaction processing systems, which brings me to the next section!

10.4.1.3 Seamlessly Integrating Web Applications with Diverse Information Resources

One of the great promises of Web protocols and the source of their universal appeal is their ability to simplify and standardize an otherwise fragmented and proprietary corporate information infrastructure without sacrificing functionality. Using a Web browser as a standard desktop client, end-users are free to continue to use whatever operating system platform suits their needs and preferences, whether it is Windows, Macintosh, OS/2, or UNIX.

Likewise, it doesn't matter what word processor or spreadsheet you use. All output can be saved as or translated into HTML, so that proprietary data or file formats no longer hamper the free flow of information throughout an enterprise. By using the standard Web protocols, everyone using a Web browser can get access to every piece of information in the enterprise.

Of course, not all information exists as a Web page on a Web server. Indeed, most corporate information—customer data, employee data, inventory data, financial data—is stored in relational databases and transaction processing systems. For years, the challenge for many IT organizations has been how to make this vast store of information easily accessible to all users, and to marry that structured data to the unstructured information captured in business plans, reports, memos, product specifications, proposals, and other corporate pages. The problem with existing solutions designed to meet this challenge (including executive information systems, decision support systems, and groupware systems such as Lotus Notes) had been that they each required a proprietary client connected to a proprietary server, making widespread deployment costly and difficult to manage or mandate.

The intranet dissolves almost all of these barriers. Web browsers can ubiquitously replace proprietary, special-purpose clients, and HTTP acts as a baseline server protocol. What is needed on top of this basic HTTP server is robust database access tools that will allow every user to access, literally, any piece of corporate information regardless of where it resides—in a database or on a Web page—or in whatever format it is stored.

The Notes interactive Web applications server is tightly integrated with back-end databases. It uses ODBC as a standard interface between Notes and RDBMSs, and it also includes specific integration with Oracle, DB2, and Sybase SQL Server, as well as with SAP and Peoplesoft databases.

Notes is also tightly integrated with CICS-based transaction processing systems through the use of IBM's MQ Series for Notes. MQ Series allows Notes applications to handle semi-structured data and workflow processing that precedes an actual transaction, and then passes control of the transaction from Notes to the CICS application.

Notes also supports integration with image repositories using Lotus Notes:Document Imaging, so that images can be included as part of a Notes application and rendered to Web browsers. And Notes has been integrated with proprietary page management systems, making those pages accessible in a Notes-based intranet.

Lastly, the Notes server is part of an overall systems management architecture through the use of NotesView, an SNMP-compliant management tool that monitors the status of Notes servers throughout an enterprise intranet.

I'm not aware of any other Web server that approaches this level of functionality and integration with this breadth of infrastructure resources.

10.4.2 The Notes Client

Given a choice of popular Web browsers or the Notes client, which includes the Lotus InterNotes Web Navigator shown in Fig. 10.8 (and supports browsers from Netscape and other popular vendors), which one are customers more likely to deploy? The answer is both. There will be a mix of client types. Jane in Sales, for example, might have a Notes client on her desktop. (Being in sales and constantly on the road, Jane requires a mobile client.) In the office next door, Mike in Accounting doesn't need a feature-rich client, only an inexpensive Web browser. Both can browse the WWW. Both can access information on the Notes server.

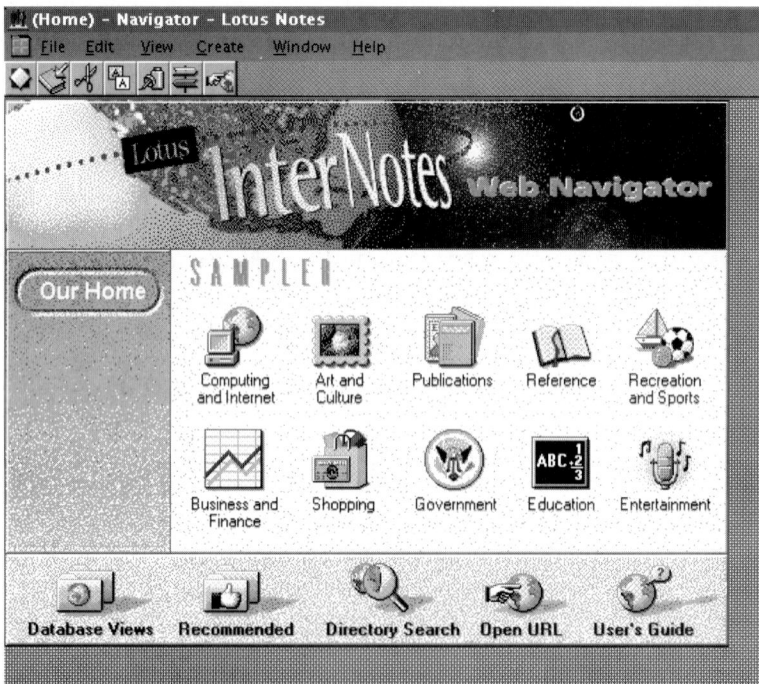

Fig. 10.8 The Lotus InterNotes Web Navigator

Given that both the Web browser and Notes client offer access to the applications that reside on the Notes server, what type of user stands to gain from the Notes client? For starters, anyone with a laptop, like Jane, anyone who wants a single desktop client, application developers and site designers, and Web content providers.

☞ **Anyone with a laptop**—Notes client-to-server replication is unique among clients that run on the Internet and the Web. As a mobile client, Notes allows users to be productive even when not connected to a network.

☞ **Anyone who wants a single desktop client**—Using the single Notes client, users have access to world-class e-mail, conferencing databases, and other groupware applications, business process applications, the World Wide Web, and other Internet applications such as Usenet News, Gopher, and FTP. Browsing becomes a function that supports broader end-user activities. If, for example, I'm writing a competitive analysis, I can retrieve Web pages for future reference, share retrieved Web pages in a folder or database so that colleagues can also view them, capture retrieved Web pages within any other Notes application, such as a Competitor Watch database, mail and route Web pages to anyone as part of an ad hoc or structured workflow, rate, annotate, and categorize Web pages, and create agents that will automatically browse through specified Web pages, saving those that match my specific criteria.

☞ **Web site designers and content providers**—There are a number of axioms that seem to hold true for Web content these days. One is that Web content doesn't necessarily come from just one author. It typically comes from numerous authors. The Lotus Web site, for example, posts content from hundreds of Lotus employees from all over the world. The second axiom is that Web content is authored using many different types of editors—word processors, spreadsheets, presentation graphics tools, databases, specialized HTML editors, and layout tools. Another tried and true axiom is that a review and approval cycle is of paramount importance because Web content is broadcast to such a wide audience. Here again, we're playing to Notes' strengths as a tool that can deliver a controlled and at the same time collaborative authoring environment. Using the Notes client in conjunction with other editors, authors can easily place drafts of content into a Notes document and alert others of its existence. All reviewers and editors can make their changes directly to the content in a single place. When the document is finally approved, Notes can automatically place it on the Web.

☞ **Application developers**—It is the Notes client that gives application developers access to Notes application development tools. Web application developers in particular will find the Notes client to be a very powerful development environment, offering a full editor and debugger, an agent builder, and application templates. All pages in a Notes database can be

designed to conform with one or more specific forms, or templates. If the
Web site designer decides to make a global change (e.g., add or modify a
new logo), this new design change needs to be made just once. The change
will automatically be inherited by all the pages that use that form. This can
save countless hours of repetitious cut and paste activities to each and
every page that needs the update. In addition to forms, Web application
developers using Notes have access to LotusScript, an industrial-strength,
BASIC-compatible, object-oriented programming language. I also want to
mention that the Notes database acts as a container for Java applets.
Developers can create Java applets with their editor of choice, and/or use a
set of Java class libraries, and deploy them in Notes as they would on any
other Web platform.

10.5 COST OF OWNERSHIP: NOTES VS. INTRANETS

With a firm understanding of Notes as a platform for deploying intranets, it's
time to dispel any myths that claim that Notes is a more costly route towards
implementing a corporate intranet when compared to alternative Web tools. The
Business Research Group (BRG) recently completed a report entitled, "Notes/
Intranets: Cost of Ownership Study." The study is based on a survey of IT managers from 100 companies, all of whom deploy intranet applications. Half of the
companies surveyed base their applications on Notes and half use Web software
products from Netscape, Microsoft, Sun, public domain sources, IBM, Oracle,
FTP, O'Reilly, and DEC.

BRG asked these companies about the types of intranet applications they
are running. Most publish documents on their intranets and support e-mail,
nearly half support database access and discussion databases, about a third are
creating workflow applications, and a little less than 20 percent support transaction processing on their intranets.

The study shows that on average, it took IT managers 53 days to deploy
these intranet applications with Lotus Notes, compared to 87 days to deploy
these applications with alternative Web products. The following table shows that
for each and every one of the major intranet uses identified by the participants,
it took less time to deploy, and now takes less time to maintain, applications
based on Notes than those based on other intranet products.

When you consider the Notes server's support for Internet protocols and
open standards, these results shouldn't be that surprising. There are significant efficiencies to be gained by integrating these protocols and standards
with the level of application development and deployment services that are
integral to Notes. I can point to our own Web site as a wonderful example of
these efficiencies. It requires minimal overhead to maintain 10,000 pages that
draw from 83 different databases and hundreds of authors from all around
the world.

Total Hours to Deploy Each Type of Intranet Application

Application	Mean # Hours Lotus Notes	Mean # Hours Other Intranet Products	Fewer hours required to deploy Notes vs. Other Intranet Products
Document Publishing	104	122	15%
Electronic Mail	67	108	38%
Database Access	93	214	57%
Discussion Databases	105	162	35%
Workflow	66	148	55%
Transaction Processing	26	239	89%

Total Hours/Week to Maintain Each Type of Intranet Application

Application	Mean # Hours/ Week Lotus Notes	Mean # Hours/ Week Other Intranet Products	Fewer hours required to deploy Notes vs. Other Intranet Products
Document Publishing	8	16	50%
Electronic Mail	7	12	42%
Database Access	8	27	70%
Discussion Databases	6	14	57%
Workflow	4	17	76%
Transaction Processing	3	18	83%

10.6 ENTERPRISE KNOWLEDGE MANAGEMENT, DISTRIBUTED LEARNING, DEVELOPING THE EXTENDED ENTERPRISE, AND BUILDING EFFECTIVE TEAMS

How did Notes evolve from a messaging and groupware infrastructure to become the industry's best platform for developing and deploying high value intranet and Internet business applications? What drives our technology? Ultimately, it is the business needs of our customers that drive the direction of our technology.

On the cutting edge of identifying customer requirements is Lotus Institute—our research and executive education arm. Its mission is to provide "best thinking and practices" on emerging organizational, technological, and business trends to help customers achieve their business goals.

The Institute concentrates on four critical areas that affect an organization's competitive advantage:

☞ **Knowledge Management:** The Institute investigates and pilots ways to exploit knowledge assets—the ways in which organizations can create value, improve effectiveness, and increase innovation through better management of intellectual capital. Measures, processes, and tools are being developed to help organizations transform information into valuable knowledge assets.

☞ **Distributed Learning:** The Institute is developing new approaches, prototype tools, and methodologies to accelerate individual and group learning. Using Lotus Notes as a uniquely powerful delivery platform, the Institute is collaborating with customers, partners, and universities to develop next generation distributed learning capabilities for business and academic requirements.

☞ **Enabling Effective Teams:** The Institute focuses on issues of team formation, leadership, evolution, and overall effectiveness. It studies optimal ways to support collaborative work within and amongst distributed teams and offers approaches and tools to increase the effectiveness of a wide variety of teams, including cross-functional, executive, ad hoc, and others.

☞ **Developing the Extended Enterprise:** The Institute is investigating how an extended enterprise model can maximize a firm's capabilities, reduce cost of operations, and improve performance through deeper customer and partner relationships. This work is focused on developing useful business models, application frameworks, infrastructure design, and navigation capabilities to support highly interconnected, information-rich, service-oriented relationships.

We recognized early on that technology alone is not sufficient to meet the strategic objectives of any business. Meeting our customers' business objectives requires a detailed understanding of how people work together, how they organize information, and how they employ learning strategies to achieve individual and team goals. This is what led us to originally create the Lotus Institute, which is now at the forefront of this thinking.

10.7 CONCLUSION

I started this chapter by relating my characterizations of Lotus Notes. They've had to change to keep pace with the product. To describe Notes today as merely a database or a groupware and messaging product would do Notes a disservice. It's truly a foundation for deploying *second-generation* intranets—intranets that can be efficiently and effectively created, deployed, and managed with robust tools— intranets that can leverage diverse corporate information systems and that can support interactive, high value Web applications.

Let me end this chapter by asking how you now characterize Notes. I hope that your answer includes the notion that Notes is a platform for developing and deploying *strategic systems*—systems that coordinate the many business activities necessary to achieve broad reaching organizational goals. I hope that you walk away with a sense that Lotus Notes can enable an organization to strategically integrate, analyze, and apply information from within its corporate boundaries and outside of them as well in ways that make it more efficient, more effective, and more competitive.

BIOGRAPHY

Jeff Papows is executive vice president and chief operating officer of Lotus Development Corporation, a wholly owned subsidiary of IBM Corporation. Jeff Papows and Michael D. Zisman share the office of the president at Lotus, both reporting to John M. Thompson, senior vice president and group executive of the IBM Software Group. Prior to his appointment as COO in October 1995, Papows was a senior vice president of Lotus' Communications Products Business Group, sharing with Zisman responsibility for Lotus Notes, cc:Mail, Soft-Switch, and Organizer products.

Papows joined Lotus in 1993 from Cognos, where he was president and chief operating officer for more than three years. Previously, he held senior management positions at Cullinet Software, Software International, and Para Research.

Papows earned a bachelor's degree in biology and secondary education from Norwich University, a master's degree in human resource management from Pepperdine University, and a PhD from CCU.

Introduction to Chapter 11

Novell's rationale for incorporating groupware into its more commonly recognized core competencies, networking, is that groupware increases individual and group productivity. Obviously, this is the same motivation for networking, so the connection makes sense.

Novell's groupware solutions go into a framework called the Collaborative Computing Environment (CCE), which has 5 components, many of which are easy to use "out of the box." Novell seems to have chosen the low road, in terms of price and functionality—they offer some of the least expensive groupware today. GroupWise is reported to have over 6 million seats sold, most likely because of their high value provided.

Novell is also providing innovations that differentiate them from other major groupware vendors. For example, integrating Intelligent Agents, where Novell has more experience than Lotus and the Universal In-Box, which provides users with one place to receive e-mail, faxes, documents, newsgroup feeds, news feeds, URL information, etc.

Novell's CCE, like Microsoft's Exchange, provides many of the components to enable group working without providing the actual applications themselves. Novell sees desktop application as the interface to these group services. This is very similar to Microsoft's strategy, but very different from Lotus'. Microsoft owns the operating system that, they argue, allows them to dominate the desktop from which they can access the groupware. Novell, who currently dominates the NOS on the LAN (which is changing rapidly) feels they can provide group services from this base of strength. Lotus feels their strength is at the applications layer, and Netscape is at the Internet infrastructure layer.

All these vendors are aware of the huge drive towards the Internet and intranets for collaboration, and all of them have different strategies. Microsoft gives Microsoft Internet Explorer away for free and integrates it with their desktop applications. They hope to leapfrog their competitors, and move from Windows 95 as the desktop environment to Explorer as the collaborative desktop environment that their users live in. Lotus has migrated Notes to the Internet and looks at its integrated browser and ability to access data almost anywhere as the logical interface to collaboration. Novell, coming from their core strength of networking and network administration, has provided a framework of services to the user/ administrator which allows them to also integrate with intranet applications and functions. Novell sees Internet and intranets as just another network or LAN to be managed for the individual or group.

Novell made some good decisions early in the process of developing for the Internet. First, they chose to make their product "open," and second, it is cross-platform. Now this is pretty much the same as embracing "mom and apple pie" but saying it and doing it are two different things. Novell supports a large num-

ber of standards, the only ones I did not see in their list are IMAP4, X.500, ActiveX, OLE, and CORBA, and in truth, some of these standards are still being developed, so I am sure Novell is tracking them closely.

Novell's great groupware strength is integrating the "group" functions. The ability to support a threaded conversation whether in e-mail or conferencing, or display messages in a specific order are definite improvements over most e-mail systems. They have also included one of my favorite functions, retraction so if you send a flaming e-mail and have second thoughts later, it can be retracted—but only before it is read! You can also monitor the status of any item, appointment, or task. The GroupWise servers provides rule-based agents, full text search and retrieval, and replication for off-line and mobile working.

Novell has been listening to its customers, and the final part of this chapter examines some case studies of how different organizations used GroupWise to their advantage. Staying close to home, the first organization they targeted was Novell. Everyone at Novell uses GroupWise. Now, I know Lotus uses Notes extensively in-house, but I am not sure everyone at Microsoft uses Exchange, even though they do use MS Mail extensively. In any case, the idea of vendors using their own products is a good one. It not only gives an extensive alpha testing period, but also makes sure the vendor "walks his / her talk."

Novell's Internet strategy is the most interesting piece of this chapter. Novell, is still open and does provide WebAccess Servers for NetWare, NT, and UNIX HTTP server environments. WebAccess has the same tight integration as other GroupWise modules. It allows access to all of the many different functions in GroupWise from your browser. The big advantage of the tight integration is the ability to move data across group functions, making an e-mail into a calendar appointment, or a task into a great time saver.

All in all, this chapter gives a good overview of the GroupWise product and some idea of Novell's direction.

Novell and the Groupware Market

Stewart Nelson
Novell, Inc.

Today's organizations face an environment that grows more complex and competitive with each passing year. Additionally, these same organizations must also do more work with fewer resources than ever before. As competition increases, profit margins shrink. With shrinking profit margins, budgets and work forces shrink as well. In order to remain competitive and be successful, many organizations are looking for software solutions that can increase the efficiency of their employees while better leveraging one of their most precious resources—information.

The boom in PC-based applications during the 1980s is leveling off. Software vendors have done much to increase the efficiency of individuals by providing applications that let them create and process information at the desktop. The increased interest in groupware applications in the 1990s is a natural evolution of expanding individual efficiency into workgroup efficiency through networked applications. People and organizations are looking for better ways to collaborate, and groupware enhances this collaborative work process.

Those who work together to accomplish common objectives approach their work with different perspectives, areas of expertise, and information bases. This diversity among workgroup members is precisely why collaboration is such an effective tool. Groupware enhances collaboration by helping people coordinate, cooperate, and communicate more effectively.

Novell's GroupWare consists of several components, or elements. These elements include e-mail, workflow, document management, task management, imaging, calendaring, scheduling, conferencing, electronic forms, development tools, Internet access capabilities, and remote computing.

The division was formed specifically to help groups more effectively access and share information—whether it is a group of two within a small company, or a group of thousands within several companies. The combination of a strong and focused GroupWare Division, along with today's strongest offering of groupware products, puts Novell in a prime position as a groupware product vendor.

Delivering technology tools that help individuals and groups work more effectively through improved cooperation, communication, and coordination is the mission of Novell's GroupWare Division. Current GroupWare products include GroupWise, GroupWise WebAccess, GroupWise Workflow, SoftSolutions, and InForms. GroupWise is a mature product with a solid customer base. GroupWise boasts six and a half million users with customers such as Nintendo, Nordic-Track, HBO, TRW, and Domino's Pizza.

11.1 COLLABORATIVE COMPUTING ENVIRONMENT (CCE) FRAMEWORK ELEMENTS

As shown in the diagram below (Fig. 11.1), the CCE framework consists of five elements: solutions, client components, service components, network services, and administration and management.

Collaborative Computing Environment

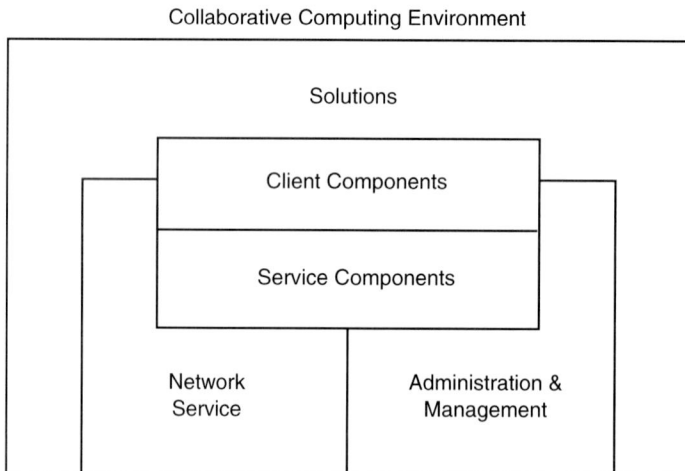

Fig. 11.1 "Collaborative Computing Environment"

Solutions are end-user applications and interfaces that take advantage of all of the service and client components to solve collaborative computing problems and create new collaborative processes. Under the CCE framework, Novell provides several powerful "out-of-the-box" solutions for common collaborative computing needs. These solutions include, among others, an electronic messaging application, a calendaring and group scheduling application, a document sharing and control application, and intelligent agents that can perform many collaborative computing tasks on behalf of users.

CCE framework is much more than the ready-to-use solutions Novell provides. System integrators, third-party vendors, and organizations' in-house developers can use development tools to combine service components and client components in new ways to create solutions to collaborative computing problems unique to an organization or vertical market. CCE will support Novell application development tools, such as InForms and Visual AppBuilder, as well as industry-standard application development languages, such as Visual Basic and C++.

Yet other solutions will emerge in the form of Groupware-enabled applications. These could include all of the applications in desktop application suites, such as Corel's PerfectOffice, Microsoft Office, and Lotus SmartSuite. In this case, the desktop application is the interface to GroupWare component functionalities and services.

11.1.1 Client Components

The client components in the CCE framework provide the base groupware functions that can be used individually or in combination to create collaborative computing solutions. Client components provide the following functions:

- ☞ E-mail, Calendar, Scheduler, Task
- ☞ Workflow, Forms, Database Query
- ☞ Document Management, Imaging Components
- ☞ Address book
- ☞ Conferencing
- ☞ In Box, Out Box, Status Tracking

As with service components, CCE supports the addition of third-party client components.

11.1.2 Service Components

Service components offer a wide variety of base services upon which a wide range of client components and solutions can be built. The following are service components that CCE framework provides:

- ☞ Message Store
- ☞ Message Transport Agent (MTA)
- ☞ Connectivity and Interoperability
- ☞ Workflow
- ☞ Document and Image Store
- ☞ Database Access

The CCE framework also supports and encourages the development of third-party service components. These service components, whether supplied by Novell or third parties, provide a wide foundation for client components.

11.1.3 Network Services

Network Services support the service and client components, which use the network services as needed. Examples of network services that support Group-Ware components include (but are not limited to) the following:

☞ NetWare Directory Services (NDS)

☞ Data Migration

☞ Telephony Services

☞ Security

☞ Print Services

☞ File Services

11.1.4 Administration and Management

Like network services, administration and management services also support the service and client components. The administration and management services eliminate the need for separate administration utilities for the network, servers, and applications by providing a unified and centralized administration model. GroupWare components will integrate administration and management services such as the following:

☞ Directory & Address Book

☞ Configuration (Installation)

☞ Event Notification

☞ Monitor & Statistics

☞ History Analysis and Modeling

☞ Storage Management

☞ Systems Management (FSD/ESL)

In NetWare environments, CCE will use Novell's Administration Services as the native administration platform. A GroupWare-provided administration tool will be used for other network environments.

11.1.5 CCE Design Philosophies

Two basic design philosophies pervade the CCE framework. The first is openness and the second is cross-platform support.

11.1.6 Openness

CCE's open design consists of support for industry-standards, APIs, protocols, and other open interfaces that Novell provides beyond basic services. At the desktop application level, CCE includes support for the following APIs:

• AOCE	• CMC	• ODMA
• IPX	• POP3	• SMTP
• LDAP	• MIME	• IDAP
• DEN	• TCP/IP	• OLE
• SNMP	• DMI	• ODBC
• X.400	• TSAPI	

Any functional extensions that GroupWare provides to our services or components will have a defined interface that will be available to all developers.

11.2 GROUPWISE 5

The audience interested in GroupWise 5 is broadly characterized as anyone interested in e-mail, scheduling, document management, workflow, or groupware. Business managers will be interested in the ability of GroupWise 5 to improve information flow and communications. The focus for the business manager will be the solutions that GroupWise 5 can provide. The universal mailbox and attractive client interface, as well as the cross-platform support, are key selling points. Systems Administrators will want to focus on the reliability, scalability, and manageability of the system. A single directory and common infrastructure are key selling points. The GroupWise VAR is interested in providing a compelling solution to their customers without requiring significant up-front application development. Due to the open interfaces of GroupWise 5, the reseller, integrator, and 3rd-party developer can custom tailor applications to meet customer needs and leverage the GroupWise infrastructure and investment.

Because of the required infrastructure changes as accounts consider the move from simple e-mail to next generation messaging systems, many customers are now actively in the evaluation process. We expect this activity to continue at least for the next eighteen months. Small accounts are usually highly influenced by their reseller. In most medium to large accounts you will find a "technology committee." This cross-functional group is comprised of end users/business managers, system administrators, and information technology executives. The technology committee is given the responsibility to evaluate next generation electronic messaging products. In selling GroupWise 5, it is very important to get access to the members of this committee who are investigating e-mail and groupware products. Because of the trend towards e-mail consolidation, the selling process must include a "top down" sell. One of GroupWise 5's key strengths is the ability to leverage a customer's existing infrastructure (especially NetWare) and support multiple platforms. This contrasts with MS Exchange's complete reliance on NT and Win 95 with the completely separate infrastructure required for Lotus Notes.

11.2.1 Problems and Solutions

"I have too many in-boxes." Most of the users in today's organizations have different In Boxes for e-mail, voice mail, interoffice mail, faxes, calendar items, and workflows. By allowing the user to access all incoming electronic information through the universal mailbox, GroupWise allows users to focus on the work that needs to be done rather than on the rote activities of searching and organizing various in-boxes. Powerful rules allow all incoming information to be pre-categorized or handled automatically.

"Our e-mail is unreliable." Many organizations don't maximize their use of e-mail because of concerns about reliability, security, or even reach. Organizations that use a lot of interoffice mail, voice mail, or fax to communicate may become more efficient by implementing a GroupWise system. GroupWise's status tracking and message retraction capabilities give the user the ability to monitor and control their own outbound mail. Because GroupWise is a fully secure messaging system, even the most sensitive information can be transmitted. With the full complement of solutions for remote users, GroupWise can be used for reliable communication even when users aren't sitting at their desks.

"It's impossible to schedule a meeting." It's nearly impossible to schedule a meeting with busy people without GroupWise as a tool. Personally contacting every person who needs to attend the meeting is difficult; finding an open time slot in a given period of time is nearly impossible. Because GroupWise stores users' personal and group calendar information, other users can easily search for free time when a meeting might be scheduled. This information is available even if a user's workstation is turned off or if the user is out of the office. And, because the scheduling capabilities extend across the breadth of the GroupWise system, the scheduler of the meeting isn't limited to accessing calendars of people within a specific workgroup. The requested participant can then accept, delegate, or decline the requested meeting either from their calendar or directly from the in-box.

"I use e-mail to share documents." Because of the inherent complexity of shared file systems, many people in today's organizations use their e-mail package to share documents. However, while this provides an easy sharing vehicle, it causes other problems including:

☞ No efficiency in storage

☞ Use of outdated documents

☞ Loss of control over documents

☞ Challenges in integrating changes made by multiple users when a document is being edited by a group

GroupWise 5 users will be able to share documents via the easy-to-use e-mail system and storage mechanisms. However, because documents are managed by GroupWise's document management services, all of the previously identified problems are overcome:

☞ Efficiency in storage—A single copy of the document is maintained in the document library. Each recipient receives a document reference that directs them back to the library for document access.

☞ No outdated documents—Because the document is maintained in the library, all updates and modifications are automatically available to anyone who has received the document reference.

☞ Control over the document—The document creator specifies the security for the document. No matter how many times the reference is forwarded, the security of the document remains intact. Only authorized users are allowed to access the document.

☞ Group editing—The GroupWise document library includes check-in, check-out, and version control functions so that multiple users can work on the document without overwriting changes made by others or worrying about manual integration of edited documents.

"I can't find..." All of the full-text indexing power of GroupWise's document management system is used to track all incoming information including e-mail, appointments, documents, faxes, voice mail, and workflow. You no longer have to manually search through all of your folders to find where you filed information on a certain subject. A rapid search allows users to search through their universal mailboxes, all of their folders, and even through document libraries in a single search operation.

"I'd like to share that WWW page with a co-worker." With the integration of GroupWise and the Internet, GroupWise users can send, receive, and store World Wide Web URL references for immediate access from within their GroupWise mailboxes.

"What's the status of the document that I sent out for review?" GroupWise Workflow supports simple document review processes and more complex ad-hoc, administrative, and collaborative workflow processes. Because users can use the familiar GroupWise client, they don't need a lot of additional training to participate in a workflow process. With GroupWise WorkFlow, all participants in a workflow process can easily check the workflow status at any time.

"I need to access my mailbox from an Internet/intranet connection." GroupWise WebAccess allows users to access their mailboxes and all GroupWise services from any Web browser connected to the Internet or to a corporate intranet.

"I need to involve my team in this particular discussion." GroupWise allows the user to share folders of information with other users in the GroupWise system. Sharing of information is not limited by geography or platform. The conferencing features of GroupWise support the many-to-one discussion capabilities very useful in soliciting and analyzing feedback from many parties.

"I can't afford to hire/train new administration personnel for every new product that comes along." Because GroupWise 5 uses the same administration and management tools as NetWare, your NetWare administrator doesn't have to learn how to use new tools. Administrators have a single platform for managing the network and the network applications. Non-NetWare shops must learn to use NWAdmin and ManageWise; but, these management tools are used for all GroupWise components including e-mail, scheduling, document management, and workflow.

"I can't force the other departments to use the same client O/S, application server, or network O/S that I use, but we need to be able to communicate." With GroupWise 5, the same services are available across many different client, server, and network environments. Users are insulated from the heterogeneous network and see a homogeneous solution for communication, collaboration, and coordination.

11.2.2 End User Features and Benefits

The overall breadth of GroupWise 5 functionality covers every facet of collaboration. A summary of those functions follows:

1. **Busy Search:** Any GroupWise user can find an appropriate time for a meeting by doing a busy search. GroupWise checks all user and resource calendars and displays an appropriate time. Confidentiality of appointment information is preserved.

2. **Computer-Telephony Integration:** Users can dial numbers directly from their address book via any TAPI- or TSAPI-compliant telephony connection. Control over telephone functions such as call transferring, call forwarding, and conferencing is also provided. Incoming calls are automatically checked against the GroupWise address book and the user is able to immediately see the identity of the caller.

3. **Conversation Threading:** GroupWise automatically keeps a conversation thread for all messages sent and received. Messages can be displayed in conversation order. This allows the user to easily access messages and replies together for easy navigation of ongoing discussions.

4. **Convert Item:** The user is able to easily convert any GroupWise item to another type. This enables the user to make an appointment or task out of an e-mail message and to block out time on the calendar to work on a document.

5. **Delegate:** Appointments and tasks can be delegated by the recipient. The scheduler of the appointment or task is provided with complete status concerning the item.

6. **Document Control:** Full document management services include check in/check out (for single documents, single folders, multiple folders, selected documents from a single folder, or selected documents from multiple folders), concurrency control, and versioning.

7. **Filter:** With GroupWise's powerful filtering capabilities, users can easily define and execute custom queries such as "show all tasks which have not been completed by the recipient" and "show all tasks which are due this week."

8. **Full Message Control:** GroupWise gives users full control over all of their messages including full status tracking and retraction. Users can monitor

the status of any item, including appointments and tasks, to determine if the item was accepted, declined, delegated, completed, etc.

9. **Full-Text Index:** All information is automatically indexed by GroupWise 5. The index is maintained by the post office agent for each user's GroupWise mailbox and for each defined library. The full-text index includes messages, attachments, and documents.

10. **Graphical Workflow Authoring:** Graphical workflow authoring tools enable users to define serial, parallel, broadcast, conditional, and workflow joins without having to write any code. For the first time, a desktop workflow product gives users the ability to define ad-hoc and administrative workflows that link to mission-critical production workflows.

11. **Integrated Client:** GroupWise 5 features a customizable user environment through which users access, organize, profile/store, share, and communicate information.

12. **Intelligent Search/Retrieval:** GroupWise can search the full text index of any mailbox or defined library to access information. A single server-based search can be conducted for desired information of any type (i.e., messages, attachments, documents, to-do lists, or schedule and calendar events).

13. **Library:** The library allows information to be easily stored and located. The library contains the properties of all stored information (i.e., subject, document type, author, revision date, version number, and security). Information stored in the library can be referenced in any GroupWise personal or shared folder.

14. **MAPI:** GroupWise services can be accessed not only by the GroupWise client but also by any MAPI 1.0 client application. The GroupWise Address Book, Message Store, and Message Transport services are published via MAPI.

15. **Personal Address Book:** GroupWise's MAPI-based personal address books allow users to maintain personal contact information.

16. **Personal Calendaring and Task Management:** GroupWise doesn't just provide tools to support group interaction, it also allows users to manage their personal appointments and task lists.

17. **Phone Access:** All GroupWise 5 information and services can be accessed through any touch tone telephone. Text to speech technology allows e-mail, calendar appointments, tasks, and documents to be read to the user through the telephone. Fax system integration allows the user to request specific e-mail, calendar printouts, or documents to be sent to any fax machine.

18. **Proxy Users:** Proxy Users who need to share information can grant direct access to their universal mailbox through the proxy service. Access can be limited by item type and by allowed actions (read, update, delete). In a client/server system, proxy extends across GroupWise post offices.

19. **Resources:** GroupWise tracks resources such as conference rooms and makes them available for scheduling through the Global Address Book. Server-based rules allow the resource to automatically manage itself by accepting appointments that do not cause a conflict and decline scheduled appointments that cause a conflict with previously scheduled events.

20. **Rules:** GroupWise features both personal and server-based rules to automate message handling and information management.

21. **Send by Reference:** In addition to the ability to attach documents to an e-mail, GroupWise supports a send document reference function. This allows the library to maintain control over and security for attached document references. The recipient accesses the document through the standard GroupWise services.

22. **Shared Folders:** Users can publish/share information from their personal mailbox with other users and assign access controls. Shared folders are based on a server-to-server and server-to-client replication system, which allows them to be shared with any GroupWise user system-wide, including the remote user.

23. **Three-Pane Interface:** With the GroupWise QuickViewer active, users can read messages as they browse through their universal mailbox without having to open each message individually.

24. **Universal Mailbox:** GroupWise 5's universal mailbox allows multiple types of information (i.e., e-mail, voice mail, faxes, calendar events, and tasks) to be received, sent by, or profiled by the user. Mailbox contents can be viewed using message threading, hierarchical personal and shared folders, a "work-in-progress" folder for draft items, sorting, and sophisticated filtering and display.

25. **View Any Attachment:** GroupWise provides full support for viewing attachments via built-in System Compatibility Corporation (SCC) viewers for most document types.

26. **Voice Mail:** When GroupWise PhoneAccess is configured as a voice mail system, voice mail is placed into the GroupWise universal Mailbox where it can be accessed by a LAN client, a Remote Client, a WebAccess user, and/or PhoneAccess user.

27. **WebAccess:** All GroupWise 5 information and services can be accessed through any Web browser. Full information security is maintained by the GroupWise system.

28. **Workflow:** Ad hoc, administrative, and collaborative workflow processes leverage the network infrastructure to transport and track work items created by desktop applications.

11.2.3 GroupWise 5 Architecture

GroupWise 5 Architecture

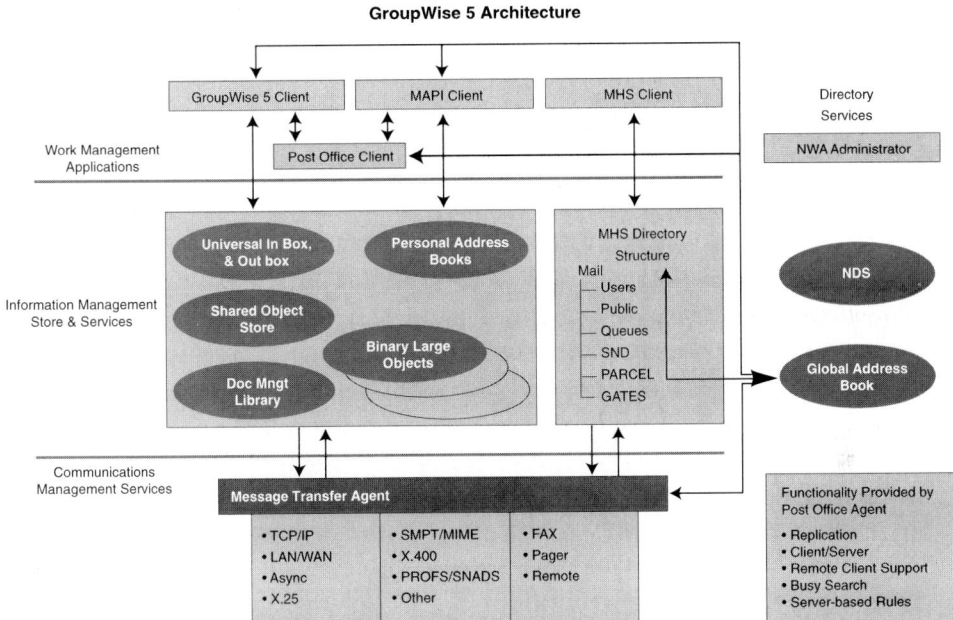

Fig. 11.2 GroupWise 5 Architecture

11.2.3.1 GroupWise 5 Server: Solid Infrastructure

The GroupWise 5 client/server technology is based in large part on the technology found today in GroupWise 4.1; more than two years of fine tuning and production use have resulted in a flexible, scalable, reliable, and manageable product (see Fig. 11.2).

Shared services (i.e., message transport, remote access, replication, indexing and searching): Infrastructure of GroupWise 5 is designed to be open to support additional products and services.

Cross-Platform Server Technology allows GroupWise 5 to bridge dissimilar environments (NetWare Loadable Module (NLM) for NetWare 4 and NetWare 3, UNIX, OS/2, NT), providing a reliable infrastructure even in a heterogeneous environment.

11.2.3.2 Application Specific Sever

☞ Enterprise Message Server

☞ Client/Server Messaging services are offered by GroupWise 5.

☞ Remote User—Master In Box replication/synchronization with highly configurable synchronization filters.

☞ Shared folders are provided through server-to-server replication, allowing users to share any object that is in their own In Box. This technology is also used to share applications and information within GroupWise 5.

☞ Document Management Server—Novell is driving document management to the mass market. By leveraging the GroupWise 5 infrastructure and including powerful document management capabilities, the cost of owner-ship of DMS technology such as document security, check in/check out, and versioning is significantly reduced.

11.2.3.3 Client/Server & File Sharing

Unlike its competitors, GroupWise 5 will offer users both client/server and file sharing models; GroupWise 5 will support both paradigms (both configurations can coexist), making it possible for users to migrate to client/server technology at their own pace.

☞ Client/Server Benefits

☞ No client drive maps required

☞ Used by both network & remote users

☞ Very scalable post office architecture, architected to support today's high-performance servers

☞ File Sharing—Even with the implementation of a file-sharing configuration, GroupWise 4.1 and GroupWise 5 still make extensive use of the server for message handling and other functions as listed.

☞ Uses network file service to allow users to "read" Universal In Box

☞ Database updates can be done either by client or by server process

☞ Allows distribution of processing to client processors when server processing power is not available.

11.2.4 GroupWise 5 Post Office

Many of the distinguishing features of GroupWise 4.1 and GroupWise 5 are made possible by the very flexible object store technology. Following are some examples of functionality delivered by the object store:

☞ Universal In Box

☞ Support of many message types & documents

☞ Attributes and context of In Box items are preserved

☞ Concurrent access to information

☞ Remote user operates off master "Universal In Box"

☞ MAPI 1.0 service provider

11.2.4.1 GroupWise 5 Post Office Agent

The Post Office Agent is the workhorse in the GroupWise 5 system, exposing the power of the post office. Because GroupWise XTD uses a common object store technology, functionality such as that listed below is supported for any application built on GroupWise XTD.

☞ Full-text indexing, search/retrieval

☞ Active disk space management

☞ Server-based rules

☞ Replication

☞ 24x7 operation (on-line maintenance & repair)

11.2.5 GroupWise 5 Administration & Management

The GroupWise 5 management strategy is to integrate GroupWise's management with NetWare management, specifically, NetWare Directory Services (NDS) and ManageWise. All GroupWise 5 components will utilize the same administration and management tools. Third-party applications will also be able to use these same tools. NDS provides GroupWise with:

☞ A single point of administration for applications and the network

☞ A master information repository, eliminating redundant data entry

☞ Security and authentication services

☞ GroupWise 5 NDS Integration:

☞ NWAdmin is the GroupWise 5 management environment

☞ Current GroupWise 4.1 NW administration utilities are extended and integrated into one tool

☞ GroupWise 5 Global Address Book is derived from and synchronized with NDS

☞ Manage users, groups, resources, domains, post offices, and other services

☞ Real-time Management

☞ Management of GroupWise processes utilizing SNMP

☞ ManageWise Snap-in for alarm and process management

11.2.6 GroupWise 5 Open APIs

The GroupWise 5 API Set will enable GroupWise 5 and third-party applications to embrace a vastly improved replicated messaging model. All GroupWise 5 services will be exposed through industry-standard APIs (MAPI, ODMA) where available; where industry APIs don't expose GroupWise 5 services, GroupWise-specific API extensions will be provided. To allow third-party developers to participate and add value to Novell's core products, Novell will deliver an API set in beta format prior to the release of GroupWise 5.

11.3 GROUPWISE SOLUTIONS

11.3.1 Novell Uses What It Sells

The high quality of Novell's GroupWare products is due in large part to the fact that the GroupWare products are used extensively in-house. As a case in point, one of Bob Frankenberg's first objectives after Novell acquired Word-Perfect was to have the new Novell completely connected through GroupWise as quickly as possible. Within weeks, any Novell employee at any site worldwide could send messages and files, as well as schedule meetings, directly with any other Novell employee using GroupWise. And because Novell is committed to multiple-platform product development, the change to a new messaging system did not require additional hardware at the desktop. Novell employees run GroupWise on whatever platform they normally use to do their work.

The idea of extensively using our own products is not a new phenomenon. Prior to the Novell/WordPerfect merger, WordPerfect Corporation used Group-Wise (formerly WordPerfect Office) extensively from its inception. In fact, the WordPerfect Office e-mail product was originally created to solve a business problem at WordPerfect—namely, inefficient communication and information sharing among employees.

The limitations we have found over the years of using our own products are the same limitations that our customers have found. Our own organization provides a very appropriate laboratory to determine how well we resolve these limitations. If a product is not designed optimally or does not work the way people want it to work, we hear about it immediately. The company's insistence that our products be used extensively internally before they are released to the general public has resulted in products that both work and meet customers' needs as well.

11.3.2 Kinko's Case Study

Kinko's Inc., the nation's leading copying and document production chain, recently signed as the five millionth user of Novell's GroupWise and is initiating an ambitious three-phase implementation plan to install the groupware solution at 800 branch offices across the country by the end of 1995. Kinko's has already successfully installed GroupWise at its headquarters in Ventura, California and in several regional offices, where the computing environment comprises an even mix of Intel PCs and Apple Macintosh systems. The GroupWise solution has thrived in this dual computing environment, providing Kinko's coworkers with one central source for e-mail, scheduling, calendaring, and electronic forms management on their operating system of choice.

"Kinko's replaced Microsoft Mail with GroupWise because it needed a more sophisticated and productive integrated messaging system to manage the increasing amount of electronic communication delivered and received by its coworkers," said Dawn Graham, director of information services (IS) at Kinko's. Maintaining a rapidly growing network of branch offices requires nimble, efficient, two-way communication with key audiences, including sales representatives, customers, and suppliers. In the highly competitive copying industry, Kinko's must deliver outstanding customer service and complete large, complex assignments without error on a daily basis. "GroupWise has contributed to our ongoing success in these areas by streamlining our messaging process and ensuring fast, accurate receipt and delivery of messages that are highly critical to our business," said Graham.

Graham says Kinko's coworkers have reported an increase in productivity and efficiency since the GroupWise installations. Users have been particularly pleased with the ability to set rules—a key GroupWise feature that forwards e-mail messages to appropriate back-up personnel. For example, when coworkers are out of the office, they can create a rule so that their messages are forwarded to someone who can respond to them. As a result, the e-mail messages aren't just waiting in the GroupWise InBox unanswered; someone is acting on those messages.

Mobile computing with GroupWise is also popular at Kinko's. The executive team uses it at home and on the road to remotely access their GroupWise messages and route data to company headquarters or regional offices quickly and easily so that information can be accessed in real time. "The Kinko's executives probably use GroupWise more on the road than in the office," Graham says.

Kinko's executive team originally requested a product that would provide calendaring and scheduling support in a dual computing environment, according to Kevin Kekoa, Kinko's manager of communications and computer systems. With Kinko's already using MS Mail, Kekoa and his colleagues first looked at Microsoft's Schedule +, and then evaluated Lotus Notes and cc:Mail. But the only product that allowed Kinko's to support a dual computing environment of Intel PCs and Apple Macintosh systems was GroupWise. "The dual environment is very important," said Kekoa. "We wanted something that provided a fully functional messaging application for both platforms. That was a key issue in our purchasing decision."

To confirm that GroupWise was the perfect fit for Kinko's, Kekoa ran a pilot project in December 1994 using the executive team as the test group. The top executives were so pleased that GroupWise was selected to replace MS Mail by March 1995.

Kinko's three-phase GroupWise implementation plan is 30 percent complete, with more than 500 coworkers now using GroupWise. The final step will be to install GroupWise in all 800 Kinko's branch offices. When implementation is finished, there will be 2,000 GroupWise users in Kinko's branch offices and corporate headquarters nationwide.

After the final GroupWise installation, Kinko's will implement Novell's InForms electronic forms product, which is part of the GroupWare product line. According to Graham, InForms will allow Kinko's to reduce paper usage and dramatically improve productivity in the organization. After the InForms implementation is complete, Graham will explore data warehousing with SoftSolutions, Novell's document management application.

11.3.3 IDC Return on Investment Study

In April, Novell, Inc. announced the results of a return-on-investment (ROI) study of its key customers. This independent, objective study was completed by IDC, a technology market research firm. Among the key findings, the study included analysis of why Novell's NetWare 4.1 is up to 22 percent less expensive to use than Microsoft Windows NT Server. In addition, the research demonstrated significant productivity improvements and cost reductions achieved through business use of Novell's GroupWise and ManageWise products and concluded that cost savings can be compounded when these products and NetWare 4.1 are used together.

In its analysis of groupware solutions, IDC concluded that Novell's Group-Wise generated a typical annual return of 334 percent per user. Furthermore, IDC concluded that organizations have discovered the right choice of groupware can multiply the benefits of investments in desktop hardware, software, and support across an entire organization. A small incremental investment in groupware can pay off in just months—or even weeks—when groupware is used as a platform for linking individual desktop applications to corporate desktop information resources (see Fig. 11.3).

Percent of Mentions

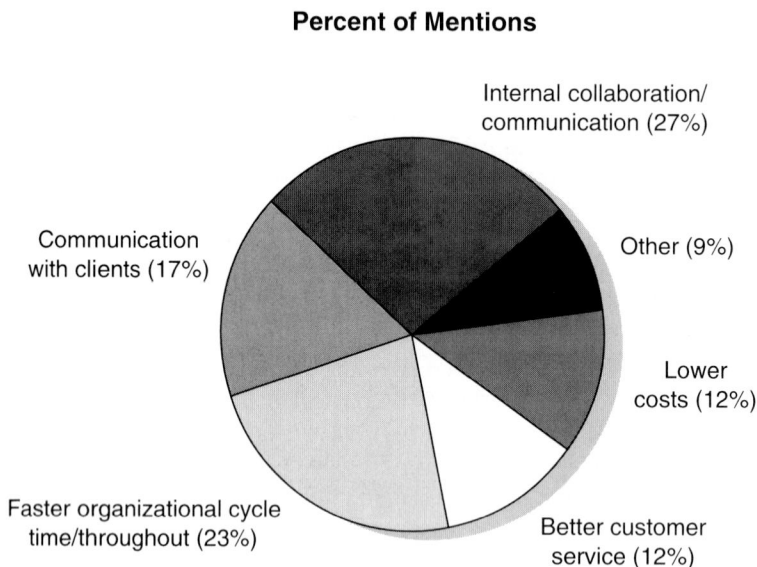

Fig. 11.3 How Users of GroupWise and ManageWise benefit

11.3.4 GroupWise Dramatically Increases Corporate Productivity

IDC's research on the bottom-line impact of groupware applications shows that:

☞ Organizations that implement GroupWise experience a typical annual return of 334 percent per user. For every GroupWise customer interviewed by IDC, return on investment exceeded expectations. NordicTrack, for example, saw a first year return per user of more than three and a half times first year costs.

☞ GroupWise improves individual and workgroup productivity at an incremental cost. At Sheppard, Mullin, Richter and Hampton, a law firm in Los Angeles, GroupWise cut the time needed to set up meetings by 25 hours per week, enabled assistants to support three lawyers instead of two, and saved $16,000 per year in courier costs. Farmland Foods saved nearly $400,000 in communications costs per year. On average, GroupWise paid for itself in only 3.3 months.

☞ GroupWise multiplies the returns from existing hardware and software investments. The IDC research indicates improved productivity, and reduced administration and management costs as a result of the linkages and common components between GroupWise, NetWare, ManageWise, and desktop software.

11.3.5 Farmland Foods Case Study

11.3.5.1 Background

Farmland Foods, a division of Farmland Industries, is the tenth largest meat packing company in America, with annual sales of $2 billion and 6,000 employees. The company's specialty is hog processing, 6 million a year, with its product line including fresh pork, ham, bacon, sausage, and Italian specialty foods, which it sells under the Carando brand name. It also sells some beef products under the National Beef brand.

The business challenge faced by Farmland is one that combines low margins—meat packing companies typically survive on margins of 1–2 percent, commodity products with variable pricing, and rural operations. The company has plants and offices in Kansas, Iowa, Nebraska, Missouri, Illinois, Ohio, and Massachusetts. In addition, it must interface with other Farmland Industries offices in the U.S. and Latin America.

As a result, Farmland is continually looking for operational efficiencies, and the company culture focuses heavily on continual cost cutting and process improvement.

11.3.5.2 Rebuilding the Network

This cost consciousness as a way of life was one of the reasons Farmland Foods chose to migrate from an IBM OS/2-based network to a Novell-based network in early 1992, despite the fact that at the time OS/2 was the accepted standard at the parent company, Farmland Industries. Farmland Food's justification for migrating to Novell related to the lower cost of interface cards, better expected network reliability, and a two-to-one ratio of network administrators that would be required to support OS/2 versus NetWare. In addition, Farmland Foods would be able to put its four AS/400s onto the network as servers instead of having interface cards on each PC and a separate teleprocessing network.

So the company began a million-dollar-a-year migration that is still going on and that now includes 750 PC users, 50 mobile users, 15 file servers, two SAA servers, six AS/400s, a number of 56 Kbps leased lines, and a potpourri of desktop and client/server software, including Novell GroupWise, Novell ManageWise PC Administration software, Microsoft Office, and Novell NetWare.

One of the subsets of this major migration was the upgrade from Novell's WordPerfect Office to GroupWise, with Farmland Foods' Mexico City office being the first to upgrade. The Kansas City headquarters staff followed two months later, and today 100 of the 800 PC users at Farmland Foods utilize GroupWise. Fax, print, and pager gateways were added shortly thereafter.

The advantages of using GroupWise are evident in day-to-day usage. Users can now e-mail a form or message where before they had to write, print, walk, and fax a message. Transaction time for sending a fax has been cut from 15 minutes to 5 minutes. And, while Farmland calculates that one e-mail message costs 25 cents, the phone or fax connection alone costs that much. Line charges are additional. Since voice calls typically include a few minutes of pleasantries before transactions are conducted, these time and line charge savings are non-trivial.

Maybe even more than the cost savings and productivity improvements, just simply being able to keep people in touch has been a key benefit. GroupWise users access the network at Farmland's Kansas City headquarters, at the Mexico City office, at other Farmland Industries offices, and at some of the outlying meat processing plants. The popularity of e-mail is illustrated in Farmland's own polls, which showed about 5 percent of PC users "interested" in e-mail before it was implemented and 80 percent using it after the fact.

In addition, the company has found that, through the integral document management in GroupWise, it has been able to reduce errors in its electronic library of 1,000-odd product recipes, which, by law, must be tightly coupled with product packaging.

11.3.5.3 Looking for Payoff

Farmland is not the kind of company to automate for the sake of automation, so getting a return on what has been a $3.5 million total investment just from 1992 through 1994 is critical and the payoff is there, just look at the GroupWise story. In the total scheme of things, the cost of migrating was minimal, about $40 per user for the license. Since the company was upgrading to Windows anyway, the tax on hardware was nonexistent. Compare this to the savings in fax and phone charges, a conservative $2.50 a day per user, and GroupWise is paid for in a few weeks. Across 100 users, that could be an annual savings of $50,000.

This payoff looks only at lowered communications costs and not at time saved by GroupWise users nor at the qualitative improvements from faster message handling, a more efficient sales process, or better quality information (as with the recipe database). If the time savings and quality improvements yield as much as the costs savings from electronic communications alone, then GroupWise will easily save $100,000 a year for Farmland.

The other costs of migrating, such as training, installation, and support are also minimized with GroupWise, since it is integrated with Farmland's desktop software (WordPerfect and PerfectOffice) with which users are already familiar. In addition, the integration of GroupWise with NetWare makes management and support just another incremental exercise.

11.3.5.4 The Business Benefits

☞ Lower tax and voice telephone charges

☞ Faster document turnaround

☞ More efficient sales process

☞ Improved quality of document database

11.3.5.5 Groupware Cuts Communications Costs

As the tenth largest meat packing company in the U.S., Farmland Foods must continually drive costs out of operations and improve productivity in order to remain competitive in an industry with an average profit margin of 1–2 percent. Since 1992, the company has relied on Novell products to help in this continual process improvement program; and this single application of Novell GroupWise will yield a payoff of over a hundred thousand dollars a year.

11.3.5.6 Lessons Learned

What's clear from the GroupWise application is that hard savings alone can justify the adoption of collaborative and communicating software. It's also clear to the folks at Farmland that doing so with products that all work together, from the desktop to the workgroup and on up to the enterprise, makes life simpler in a tangible way. Driving down the cost of doing business through electronic communications is just another part of driving down the costs of producing a pound of bacon.

11.4 NOVELL AND INTRANETS

11.4.1 Strategy

Intranets are central to Novell's strategy to enable a Smart Global Network that connects today's private and public networks into a single, integrated information resource for both business and consumer use. A major component of this strategy is GroupWise, the first and only enterprise-wide, collaborative computing application to integrate electronic mail, personal calendaring, group scheduling, task management, Internet messages, faxes, rules-based management and voice mail into one place called the Universal In Box. This universal mailbox allows users to access and act on information in one place, eliminating the need to piece together information and types of data from a variety of sources.

GroupWise WebAccess, Novell's first full-featured intranet product, enables collaboration and communication via the Web. GroupWise Web Access is implemented as a home page on the Internet so users can access the GroupWise client with the look and feel of the Internet browser they are using. Users can now read and send e-mail, check their calendar, listen to voice mail, view tasks, attachments and faxes—all from the Internet.

11.4.2 GroupWise Web Access

GroupWise WebAccess provides users with advanced messaging and collaborative services through any Web browser. With its browser access, GroupWise WebAccess makes GroupWise as pervasive as the Internet, letting users access information anytime, anyplace.

GroupWise WebAccess combines the power of the Internet/intranet with superior GroupWise collaborative computing tools, including a Universal In Box and calendaring, group scheduling, task management and voice mail integration. WebAccess makes it easier to communicate and collaborate, to manage schedules and complete tasks, and to work more efficiently and effectively, unhampered by time and distance limitations.

GroupWise WebAccess offers much more than just Internet e-mail, including the following:

☞ Voice Mail Capabilities—Listen to voice mail messages received in the GroupWise Universal In Box.

☞ Fax Integration—Send a message to any fax machine worldwide.

☞ Calendaring—Keep track of personal appointments, tasks, and notes.

☞ Group Scheduling—Schedule meetings and track whether invitations to meetings are accepted or declined.

☞ Task Management—Assign tasks to other GroupWise users and track the status of those tasks.

☞ Attachment Viewing—View text files and other MIME attachments.

☞ Message Morphing—While composing a message, change it into another message type (mail message, appointment, task, note, or phone message) without losing information already entered.

☞ Screen Customization—Modify HTML source files to include graphics, company information, or links to other URLs on the Internet or intranet. Also, extend calendar views and restrict or modify data delivery.

All this gives users and administrators a complete set of tools for communicating, collaborating, and working more efficiently within their Internet/intranet environment.

11.4.3 Provides More than E-Mail

With GroupWise WebAccess, users can access most forms of communications that they receive on a daily basis through the GroupWise Universal In Box. The rich store of information available on the Internet or intranet can be effortlessly linked to GroupWise E-mail, scheduling, and task management messages, and advanced encryption techniques offer high security for GroupWise WebAccess. All of this is available within a seamlessly-integrated point-and-click environment.

11.4.4 GroupWise WebAccess Extends Access Points to GroupWise

GroupWise WebAccess (see Fig. 11.4) lets users access information, communicate and collaborate, and manage scheduling and tasks at any time, from virtually anyplace on the Web. Intranet users and remote/mobile users can work more efficiently than ever before, and online service providers can provide these same capabilities to their subscribers. WebAccess also promotes the use of under-powered workstations and heterogeneous desktops. If it can run a Web browser, it can run GroupWise WebAccess.

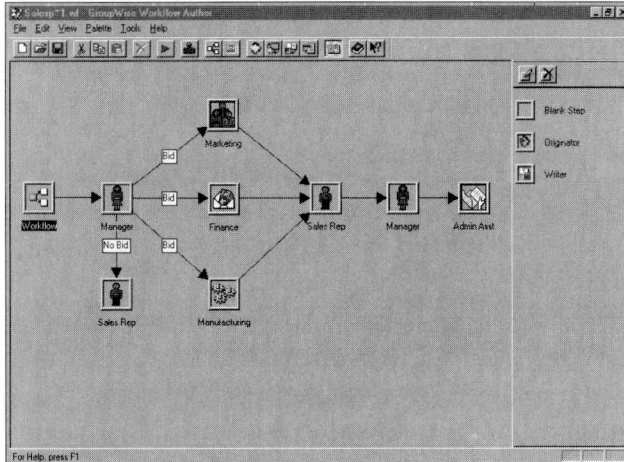

Fig. 11.4 GroupWise Web Access

11.5 FOUNDATION PRODUCTS FOR GROUPWISE 5

11.5.1 GroupWise 4.1

GroupWise messaging software provides electronic mail, scheduling, calen-daring, and task management for the workgroup and entire enterprise from a single application. GroupWise provides collaborative solutions today by helping people to:

☞ Communicate and share information via e-mail (with attachments);

☞ Track personal and group appointments;

☞ Quickly and easily schedule group meetings by checking free and busy times of attendees and resources;

☞ Assign personal and group tasks and track them through completion;

☞ Route documents and messages for approval or review from one person to the next in a distribution list;

☞ Configure rules to act on messages automatically on the user's behalf;

☞ Connect to PROFS, cc:Mail, SMTP, and X.400-based systems; and

☞ Be accessible from anywhere by using remote (mobile) technology, whether by fax, telephone, or wireless technology.

GroupWise provides one of the most powerful and comprehensive e-mail, group scheduling, and task management solutions available on the market today, as well as a solid messaging foundation for enabling other GroupWare applications.

11.5.2 GroupWise WebAccess

GroupWise WebAccess provides users with advanced messaging and collaborative services through any Web browser. With its browser access, GroupWise WebAccess makes GroupWise as pervasive as the Internet, letting users access information anytime, anyplace. GroupWise WebAccess combines the power of the Internet/intranet with superior GroupWise collaborative computing tools, including a Universal In Box and calendaring, group scheduling, task management, and voice mail. WebAccess makes it easier to communicate and collaborate, to manage schedules and complete tasks, and to work more efficiently and effectively, unhampered by time and distance limitations.

11.5.3 Remote Services

GroupWise 5 has been designed specifically with the remote or mobile user's requirements in mind. It allows the user to operate in fully disconnected, occasionally connected, and fully connected environments. The premiere client for the mobile user is the GroupWise Remote client. GroupWise Remote (available for Windows, DOS, and Macintosh client platforms) continues to use the in-box and the same program executable that the LAN client uses. Now with GroupWise 5, the occasionally connected user can more easily change between the remote and LAN connection modes. The GroupWise client automatically detects on startup whether or not the network post office or post office agent is available. If so, it will function as a network client. If not, it will function as a remote client. Remote mailbox synchronization is done automatically upon startup if there are pending requests to transfer to the master mailbox. Prior to leaving the office, the user is able to activate the "hit-the-road" feature to update the Phone Access remote mailbox with the most current information from the master mailbox.

While the Remote client is the principal tool used by the mobile user, many of GroupWise 5's other services enhance the mobile user's capabilities. For example:

☞ The sales representative can call in to GroupWise PhoneAccess via the telephone on the way to an account visit to replay the directions to the meeting location.

☞ With WebAccess, a sales representative can access a GroupWise account and schedule a follow up meeting with a systems engineer using a customer's Internet connection.

☞ The Pager gateway can be configured to notify the sales representative anytime a message is received from his target accounts.

☞ The FAX gateway can be used to deliver the latest product information to the customer.

11.5.4 GroupWise Workflow

The concept of workflow is not new. As long as business has needed to manage information, there have been business processes and workflow. In a paper-based or manual system, workflow is the flow of information or work through an office, department, or workgroup. It is the established procedure for managing information critical to the core function of a workgroup or department. Electronic or automated workflow is new to the industry and can be summarily defined as intelligent routing of work and information. Figure 11.5 shows the GroupWise workflow interface.

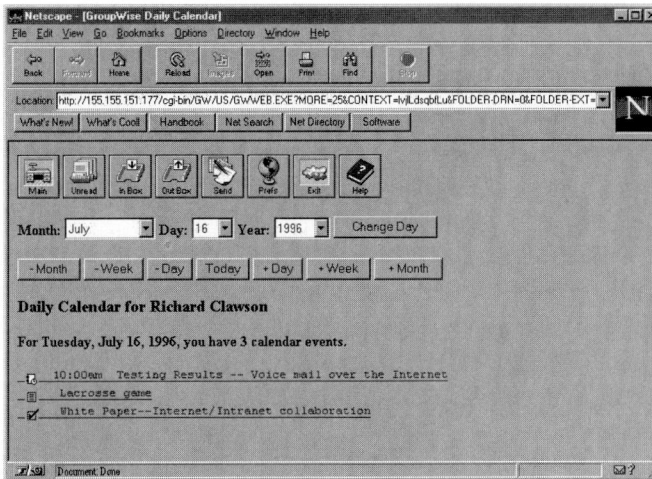

Fig. 11.5 GroupWise Workflow Interface

A work process usually consists of people, procedures, and information. Workflow refers to the physical movement of work through an organization. Processes that currently rely on the routing of paper can now electronically automate and coordinate the actions and tasks used in daily business operations. A workflow management system supports and tracks the flow of work by automatically integrating and routing documents, primarily forms and files from workstation to workstation throughout the organization.

Automating workflow requires understanding how existing and anticipated processes, policies, and practices can be best modeled and implemented in an electronic environment.

Review and approval is a common workflow that involves a number of individuals, and in most cases an electronic forms function. For example, a manager can create a workflow to route a project proposal along with an electronic sign-off form. The proposal and sign-off form is sent to a number of department individuals for review and comment before the proposal is officially presented to the board of directors. The workflow route might include review of the proposal by the engineering department for accuracy, review by an account supervisor for proposal content, review by an editor for proper style and grammar and then finally to the board of directors for their review and final decision.

By enabling rules-based or dynamically defined sequencing of tasks that mirror human and task interaction, workflow applications determine how information is handled and modified according to business conditions. Workflow redefines the flow of documents and tasks to improve quality and productivity at all levels within the organization.

Work can usually be divided into two parts: task time (the time it takes to do a task) and transfer time (the time it takes to move the work and associated information to the next person). Transfer time typically takes ten times longer than task time. Workflow automates and coordinates the movement of tasks and information to the next processing step and consequently reduces transfer time. In addition, workflow helps present the work and associated data to the user in a more logical way, thereby reducing task time. With workflow, customers can improve business productivity by designing, automating, and managing the more effective and timely use of information.

11.5.5 Workflow Market Segments

The key to Novell's workflow for groupware strategy is to provide products that meet the needs of various market segments. Users can leverage the strength of e-mail, forms, document management, and workflow products in one environment to create workflow applications that can span structured and unstructured business processes. Workflow processes, or market segments, can be broken down into four categories: Production, Ad Hoc, Administrative, and Collaborative (see Fig. 11.6).

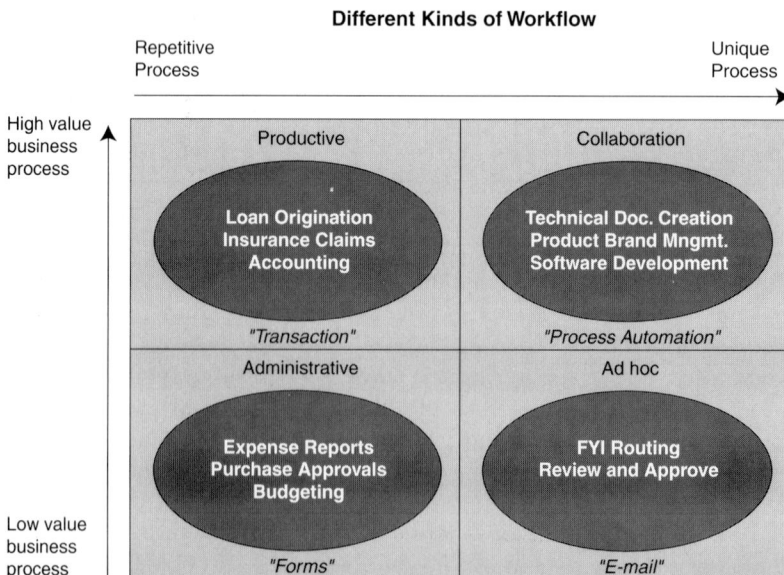

Different Kinds of Workflow

Fig. 11.6 Different Kinds of Workflow

11.5.5.1 Production Workflow

Production workflow involves transaction-oriented, high-value, repetitive processes that are locally audited and typically involve some form of transaction processing, such as insurance claims or accounts payable. Critical to the core business, production workflows directly influence and support the mission of a company or workgroup.

11.5.5.2 Ad Hoc Workflow

Ad hoc involves more unique, less complex and "low risk" processes. In a groupware environment, the focus for ad hoc workflow is the desktop. The workflow is e-mail-based and is used to track, route, or distribute information or to incorporate information as part of a document review and approval process.

11.5.5.3 Administrative Workflow

Administrative workflow supports the day-to-day business operations and services of a company, department, or workgroup and deals with low-value processes. This workflow represents routine office activity such as travel authorization, expense reporting, or purchase order approval and is essentially electronic-mail forms. Administrative workflows typically involves knowledge workers that coordinate and integrate human activity.

11.5.5.4 Collaborative Workflow

Collaborative workflow software supports unique, joint work efforts that involve a group of people whose efforts are mission critical, high value, and generally nontransaction-oriented. Collaborative workflows are core business functions of a department or workgroup. The work effort is generally non-repetitive and varies in length. New product development, sales force automation, or technical document publishing are examples of collaborative workflows.

The Novell workflow solution focuses on the automation of procedures to achieve, or contribute to, an overall process goal. Documents, forms, information, and tasks are passed between people via workstations according to a defined set of rules. Novell's workflow management system manages the sequence of work activities and invokes the appropriate human and/or technology resources associated with each activity.

11.5.6 SoftSolutions

SoftSolutions is a sophisticated document management system that enables you to track information and documents on all networks throughout your enterprise. Advanced capabilities, like automated document archiving and deletion, version control, activity tracking, and fax integration make SoftSolutions an outstanding network automation tool.

Other specific document management solutions that SoftSolutions provides include:

☞ Fast, easy location of information in any document using a powerful full-text search engine

☞ Extensive document security to control access of shared documents

☞ Dynamic document maintenance

☞ Enterprise-wide management

☞ Tight integration with many popular applications

With the power of SoftSolutions working in your organization, you may never lose a document.

11.5.7 InForms

InForms works as the front end of your database and lets you design, create and use electronic forms to automate the gathering and storing of information in any of more than 20 different database formats.

InForms provides the following forms solutions:

☞ Easy and professional design of both electronic and printed forms

☞ Automatic calculations eliminate errors created using manual means

☞ Query capabilities allow fast analysis on any linked data.

☞ Advanced database field and form linking, including cross-database joins

☞ Intelligent Workflow

☞ Ability to use most major E-mail systems as Workflow transport vehicles

☞ Digital signatures with high-level security using RSA Digital Signature

InForms can almost put an end to paperwork. Invoices, employment applications, employee records, requisition forms, purchase orders, or expense reports can be filled in quickly and accurately. In addition, the information can be immediately routed and sent to databases that will automatically create the data records to help gather, analyze, and share information quickly, efficiently, and immediately.

InForms is another powerful GroupWare tool to help automate and reengineer the way businesses process and use information.

11.5.8 GroupWise 5 Key Differentiators

Unlike other advanced messaging systems, GroupWise can leverage the existing network system environment, reducing the cost of ownership and making GroupWise a cost-effective electronic messaging system to buy, administer, and maintain. Furthermore, Novell offers a tightly integrated set of products that facilitate collaborative computing and enable users to act on information to work more effectively and efficiently. Because GroupWise 5 offers a component-based, open messaging environment, users and third-parties can develop collaborative computing solutions that best meet their needs.

11.5.9 Next Generation: GroupWise 5

GroupWise 5 is Novell's next generation messaging and collaborative services solution. Novell defines collaborative computing (or groupware) as software products and technologies that help people work together, share information, or collaborate on documents, information, schedules, and more. Collaborative computing products should provide solutions to enhance individual and team productivity and facilitate or enhance collaboration. The following list of functions, services, and tools was derived from models put forth by International Data Corp. (IDC), the Gartner Group, and Avante, among others. A comprehensive groupware offering should include the following products and features: (see Fig. 11.7)

- E-mail
- Task management
- Forms creation, processing, and routing
- Document management
- Development tools
- Remote support

- Calendaring and scheduling
- Workflow management
- Database access
- Imaging
- Conferencing
- Internet access

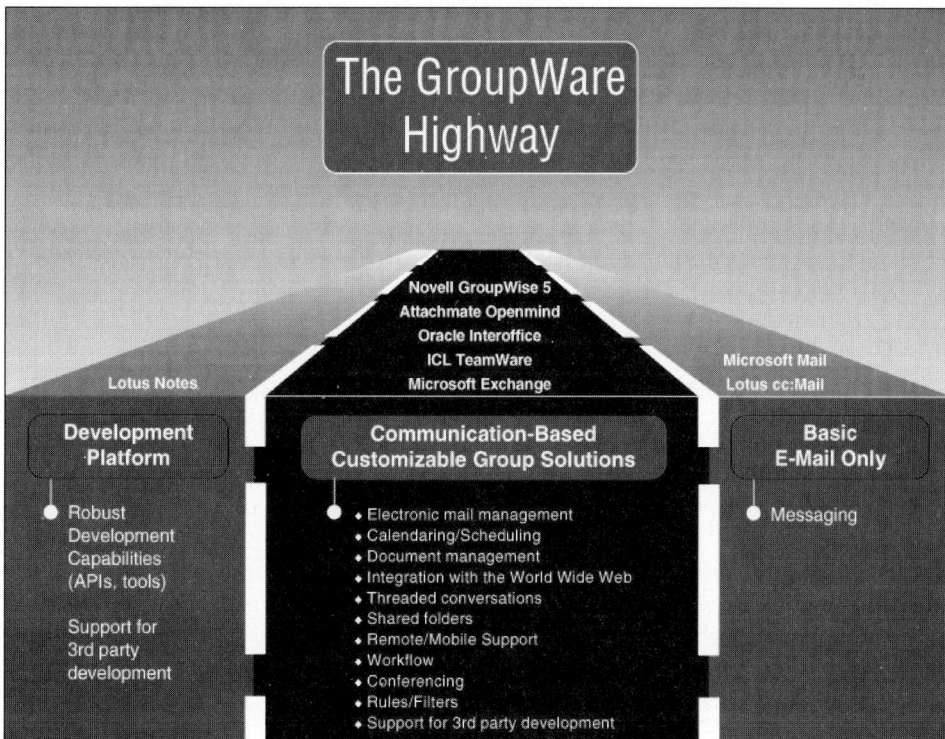

Fig. 11.7 The GroupWare Highway

GroupWise 5 represents the continued fulfillment of the CCE strategy. GroupWise 5 advances the state-of-the-art in collaborative computing technology. GroupWise 5 is also an open platform upon which Novell's partners, 3rd-party developers, Independent Software Vendors, Value-Added Resellers, Consultants, and Systems Integrators can build applications and solutions. With GroupWise 5 users can communicate, collaborate, and coordinate with others on their internal company networks, intranets, external public networks, and the Internet.

GroupWise 5 will be available on most popular computing platforms including Win 95, Win NT 4.0., Win 3.1, Mac, and UNIX. Novell will continue to deliver a homogeneous solution for collaboration across heterogeneous platforms. Regardless of the client or server platforms chosen by the customer, GroupWise 5 allows users to work together, share information, and collaborate seamlessly.

GroupWise 5 provides an integrated messaging and collaboration environment with support for open APIs so that custom solutions can be provided to enhance the off-the-shelf e-mail and collaborative services. Support for document management, group calendaring/scheduling, and workflow is provided in the basic architecture. No additional infrastructure is required to extend the GroupWise 5 system (see Fig 11.8).

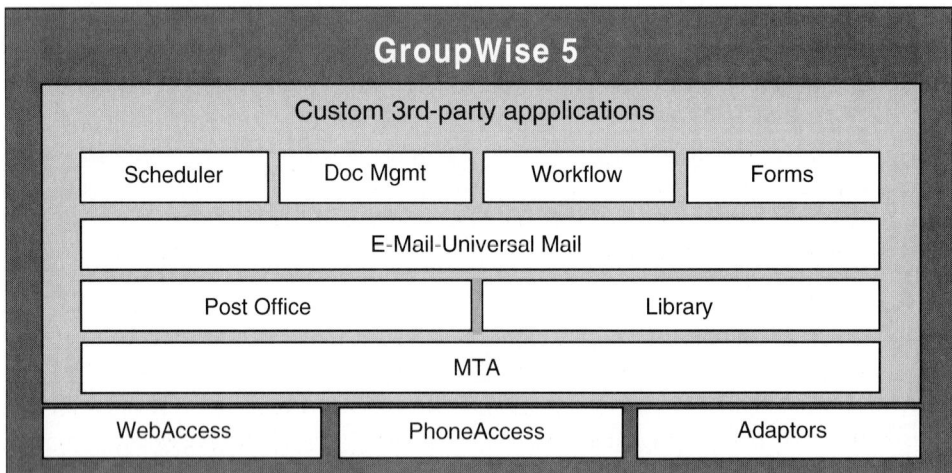

Fig. 11.8 GroupWise 5

The development of GroupWise 5 products has focused around providing enhanced customer solutions. Many customer enhancement requests have been incorporated into the product, and as new technology has been added, Novell has been careful to ensure that it enhances the overall customer solution. The key benefits that are at the core of Novell's GroupWise 5 strategy are:

☞ Provide compelling end-user value

☞ Reduce total cost of ownership

☞ Increase scalability

☞ Provide messaging and collaboration infrastructure with open APIs

☞ Allow the "remote" user full access to all information and services

11.6 GROUPWISE DEVELOPMENT ENVIRONMENT

All GroupWise 5 services will be exposed through industry standard APIs (where available), including MAPI (Microsoft Application Programming Interface), ODMA (Open Document Management API), DEN (Document Enabled Network), and ODBC (Open Database Connectivity). Novell will also support the Microsoft MAPI Workflow API. Where industry APIs limit GroupWise 5 services, GroupWise-specific API extensions will be provided in common development environments such as Delphi and Visual Basic.

11.7 COMPETITIVE ENVIRONMENT

11.7.1 Novell Compared to Microsoft

GroupWise 5's major competitors are Microsoft Exchange and Lotus Notes. While this is not a complete competitive analysis, this information highlights some of the key differentiators between these products and GroupWise.

Microsoft is releasing its next-generation, client/server messaging product over two years behind its original schedule. This first generation product features strong e-mail capabilities and moderately strong collaboration services. It has no document management capabilities and its remote capabilities are much weaker than GroupWise's.

☞ Exchange does not, contrary to MS's claims, provide an integrated scheduling system. Schedule+ is a separate application and uses a separate store and a "custom message" integration with the Exchange InBox. Scheduled items, once accepted, can only be accessed from Schedule+ (they can't be seen in the Exchange InBox). And, unaccepted appointments can be seen only in the Exchange InBox.

☞ The document management capabilities of Exchange are limited entirely to the referencing of OLE objects in the Exchange InBox. There is no support for document sharing, check-in, checkout, version control, or document security.

☞ The separate store that Exchange uses for scheduling and for personal folders limits it as a remote solution. With GroupWise, the remote client synchronizes against the master mailbox. With Exchange, users must copy their Schedule+ calendar file and personal folders file to all remote client workstations and then manually synchronize them. In addition, Exchange doesn't support access to the Exchange InBox via the WWW or via telephone.

☞ Microsoft Exchange is a Windows-only solution.

MS Mail customers must make a significant architectural change to migrate to Exchange. Exchange requires that NT application servers be installed to support the Exchange Server. This increases the administrative overhead by requiring that administrators manage not only Exchange, but also the NT servers domain directory—including the inherent problems with trusted domain relationships. Exchange also requires a client/server configuration.

11.7.2 Novell Compared to Lotus

Lotus Notes Release 4 is an outstanding product for application development and customization. Its weaknesses are that it requires a completely separate infrastructure than the network, and it has no built-in support for calendar/scheduler functions. While Notes can be used for limited document management, it requires custom development to do anything more sophisticated than a discussion database, and, it is known to have problems with document control in replicated databases.

Prior to the Notes 4 release, the e-mail capabilities of Notes were very limited. With Version 4, Lotus implemented the cc:Mail user interface for e-mail and significantly strengthened their e-mail capabilities. However, the cost of using Notes as an e-mail system is prohibitive because of the overhead. Another characteristic of Notes is that it requires the user to work within its confines for all Notes related activities.

11.8 SHAPING THE FUTURE FOR CUSTOMERS

CCE embodies Novell's vision of collaborative computing and is the core foundation for GroupWise 5. With features like document management, imaging, calendaring, task management, e-mail, and a full-scale intranet product, GroupWise has helped today's organizations to streamline communication, increase efficiency, share information, and make demanding business decisions.

Novell continues to move forward with its vision of CCE and GroupWise 5. Continual advances made by Novell's GroupWare Division will prove to greater enhance an organization's productivity, customer service, global reach, and competitiveness.

GroupWise not only empowers people so they can handle the volumes of information they receive, it makes it possible for them to make the best use of that information, thus providing users and their organizations with the competitive edge that is critical to succeed in today's business environment.

BIOGRAPHY

As vice president and general manager for Novell's GroupWare Division, Stewart Nelson leads the marketing and development of Novell's line of collaborative computing products, including the rapidly growing GroupWise product line.

Prior to accepting the general manager position in June of 1995, Nelson held the position of Vice President of Research and Development for the GroupWare Division. In this position, Nelson was responsible for leading the transition of GroupWise from a simple e-mail solution to an advanced messaging product capable of enabling users to collaborate across local area networks as well as wide area networks.

Nelson joined WordPerfect Corporation in 1987 as a programmer where he worked to develop WordPerfect for the IBM 370, WordPerfect 5.1, and LetterPerfect. Prior to joining WordPerfect, Nelson worked as a database programmer for IBM.

Nelson earned bachelor and master's degrees in computer science from Brigham Young University.

Introduction to Chapter 12

TeamWARE is one of the best selling groupware products suites in the world. However, it is still relatively unknown in the U.S. This chapter is a chance for the U.S. TeamWARE team to let us know about what TeamWARE can do and how it will be developed in the future.

TeamWARE is a "framework" product, much like Lotus Notes, OpenMind, HP Open Mail, and Novell GroupWise. It uses a messaging backbone to integrate islands of collaboration. What distinguishes TeamWARE from better known products is that each function module is available separately. This enables users to purchase the modules most appropriate to their business needs. The result is a tightly integrated group of function modules, tailored to each organization's unique requirements. Needless to say, this is very attractive to users.

The case studies in this chapter point out the need to integrate groupware with business processes. TeamWARE uses a library metaphor (as opposed to Notes' database metaphor) to explain their discussion databases. TeamWARE libraries have various levels of messaging, from individual through forum levels. Individual messaging is the lowest level; chains of messages together with their replies and attachments constitute a discussion, and a forum is a group of discussions focused on a central theme or topic. This type of hierarchy allows you to summarize at each level.

Each forum is assigned to a manager or facilitator whose responsibility it is to avoid building new roach motels for information, those discussion databases into which people pump information (that's the good part), but from which nothing is taken—no decisions, no action items, essentially, no benefit of the database other than basic communication and archiving (that's the bad part). The forum manager or facilitator is like an administrator who keeps things moving—a real step in the right direction. The goal is to turn the information into knowledge that is used by other people in the organization.

Although this chapter covers each of the TeamWARE modules, there is particular attention paid to the Workflow component, TeamWARE Flow. In Ronni Marshak's chapter (Chapter 6), she presents a workflow taxonomy that is also used by TeamWARE: production, ad hoc, and collaborative products. TeamWARE Flow is a collaborative workflow product that focuses on continuous improvement. In other words, TeamWARE Flow supports standard workflows but can easily be changed to support ad hoc flows. It is transaction-based, i.e., there is a database behind it.

TeamWARE is currently LAN-based, but has recently been positioned to capture the current interest in intranets by including support for X.500 messaging and LDAP directory standards. Also, TeamWARE plans to add videoconferencing, voice integration, and 3D effects. Just as Microsoft and Netscape are moving into this arena, so is Fujitsu.

*TeamWARE is a great product for a site that currently has no groupware. There are not a lot of those in the U.S. because our infrastructure is older. Almost everyone has e-mail, and many companies have already implemented other collaborative functions. However, not **all** U.S. companies are using groupware, and the TeamWARE messaging backbone will make it easy for them to add modules as needed. The modules integrate well, offer low administration overhead, and integrate with the WWW.*

The U.S. TeamWARE team is very capable and we expect them to gain significant market share over the next few years, especially multinational firms based outside the U.S., which are already using TeamWARE.

TeamWARE: Managing the Transition to Intranet-based Groupware and Messaging

Mika Enberg
Director of Marketing, TeamWARE

TeamWARE has now been in the North American market for over two years, but many people are still unclear about where we came from and what we do. The reality is that TeamWARE is an established vendor with products that have proven to be extremely successful in Europe and Asia, and we are still completing the process of introducing ourselves to the American market.

12.1 WHY TEAMWARE?

TeamWARE's products are all about facilitating, managing, and improving the flow of information inside and outside an organization. The portfolio includes e-mail, a complete suite of groupware applications that can function independently or as an integrated whole, messaging servers for transporting information in a variety of formats throughout an organization, and an advanced workflow product that allows for the continuous refinement of business processes by the individuals responsible for doing the work instead of a programmer.

TeamWARE has taken a modular approach to implementing groupware, messaging, and work flow, so each piece can be used by itself or with other modules to form a more complete solution; all of the products were designed from the beginning to integrate into a whole that would be more than just the sum of its pieces.

The components of the TeamWARE Office groupware suite are:

☞ TeamWARE Mail and TeamWARE Mail Professional—an electronic mail application that includes task routing facilities to help automate office routines and bi-directional fax capability.

☞ TeamWARE Library—a collaborative information management system that lets users share, store, update, and retrieve any type of document.

☞ TeamWARE Forum—an enterprisewide information exchange system that allows users to share valuable, up-to-the-minute news quickly and easily.

☞ TeamWARE Calendar—an electronic calendar providing time management functions for personal, group, and resource scheduling.

☞ TeamWARE Imaging—a horizontal component of TeamWARE Office that image-enables the other applications.

☞ TeamWARE Alarm—a component that can be configured to notify a user when any event relevant to that user occurs in the system. For example, TeamWARE Alarm can be set to activate when new mail is delivered, a Forum message is received, a calendar appointment is set, or when a preset personal reminder is scheduled to alert a user about an impending event requiring action.

The products are all based on a client/server architecture, with the front ends of the different modules residing on individuals' desktops and the underlying databases and messaging infrastructure implemented on server systems. An important benefit of TeamWARE's approach is that it is structured with "thin" clients on the front end; in other words, the software has been designed so that the storage and processing-intensive aspects of the different modules draw on server resources rather than those of the desktop clients. This is the same model that Internet browsers are based on, and the design optimizes network bandwidth utilization to provide for an efficient flow of information (see Fig. 12.1).

While the breadth, scope, and level of integration of TeamWARE's product offerings are unique in the industry, TeamWARE had another, almost accidental advantage in its European origins. The present day TeamWARE organization has evolved from its beginnings over seven years ago as a part of Nokia Data in Scandinavia. The early focus on the European market, with its emphasis on open systems standards to enable multinational interoperability, meant that TeamWARE started life with a standards-based approach to messaging that would later become increasingly popular on both sides of the Atlantic.

Today, TeamWARE is parlaying that headstart into satisfying user demand for incorporating Internet-based technology into corporate intranet solutions with products like the TeamWARE Internet Messaging Server. The implementation of X.509 directory services, planned support for the Lightweight Directory Access Protocol (LDAP) that will enable LDAP directory access via browsers and other interfaces, support for SMTP/MIME, IMAP and POP mail exchange standards, and active participation in the Workflow Management Coalition's efforts to define standard APIs for workflow products are all examples of how Team-WARE has taken a leading position in implementing and helping to define international standards.

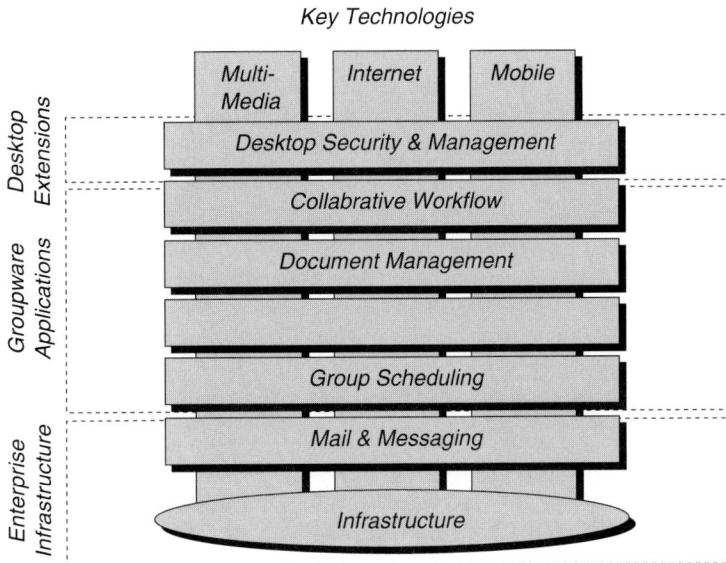

Fig. 12.1 Collaborative Computing Environment

As TeamWARE moves forward, it will continue to build on its standards-based strengths to use Web-based technology to deliver groupware and messaging functionality. For example, Sun Microsystems' Java technology will be used to develop applet-based groupware modules that will provide all of the benefits of the different modules in today's TeamWARE Office suite, but with the added capabilities of support for rich audio and video content, hyperlinks, and more easily implemented remote access for designated users outside of a business organization.

TeamWARE is a part of the Fujitsu corporate family constituting the second largest computer company in the world. The international TeamWARE development and marketing organization was recently streamlined into three groups representing North America, Europe, and Asia-Pacific. The TeamWARE Division of Fujitsu in the United States is based in San Jose, California, and has the main responsibility for Internet-related product development, the TeamWARE Flow collaborative workflow product, and TeamWARE Imaging.

While TeamWARE's operation in the United States continues to expand, the global organization currently has 900 employees at work in Europe, America, and Japan, making it the largest groupware-focused organization in the world. Although TeamWARE's market recognition is just beginning in the United States, the organization is the largest groupware vendor in Europe and now has over 1.3 million user licenses in place worldwide.

12.2 MESSAGING—A BRIEF HISTORY AND EXPLANATION

Messaging products lie at the heart of an organization's infrastructure for sharing information electronically and fall into three broad historical categories. The first group of products are generally referred to as office automation systems and enjoyed their highest point of proliferation with the peak of proprietary minicomputers in the mid-1980s; the two most widely recognized packages are probably IBM's mainframe-based PROFS and Digital Equipment Corporation's All-In-1. The systems are host-based and typically combine e-mail with document routing capabilities, an electronic library, and popular office applications such as word processing. While we write of these systems in the historical sense and their volumes are no longer growing, office automation systems have a very long life cycle and will probably remain in use for the next decade.

A second generation of product arrived with the rise of PC LANs. Products such as Microsoft Mail and Lotus' cc:Mail utilized file sharing technology to enable users to transfer messages and files across a LAN from one user to another. UNIX-based packages such as Uniplex extended this capability by building on the Simple Mail Transfer Protocol (SMTP) as the e-mail carrier to allow the exchange of messages over TCP/IP networks.

Messaging servers are the most recent development in the growth of information-sharing infrastructures. They reach beyond the basic e-mail exchange; a directory element is usually included, as well as more versatile connectors for linking all kinds of mail systems into the active part of the messaging backbone and for synchronizing their directories. Messaging servers are increasingly being deployed by large commercial users who require a reliable and robust information-sharing backbone. As they become more widespread, what were originally PC LAN e-mail products are being transformed into PC e-mail clients.

Currently, a fourth stage of messaging products based on Internet standards is emerging in the commercial environment, and TeamWARE has taken a leading position in that segment with the recently introduced TeamWARE Internet Messaging Server. The TeamWARE Internet Messaging Server is the first Internet messaging server that supports enterprise requirements.

The TeamWARE Internet Messaging Server and TeamWARE EMBLA Internet mail client provides native support for Internet Mail Access Protocol (IMAP), a leading remote client access standard, Post Office Protocol (POP), a standard protocol for downloading Internet electronic mail from a server, Simple Message Transport Protocol (SMTP), a TCP/IP protocol governing electronic mail transmission and receipt, Multipurpose Internet Mail Extension (MIME), SMTP extensions that enable audio and video electronic mail attachments, Pretty Good Privacy (PGP) encryption for security, and Whois++ and X.500 user directories.

Mark Levitt, an industry analyst with the market research and consulting firm International Data Corporation, observed in a recently published report: "TeamWARE's Internet Messaging Server is significant in that it is one of the first relatively low cost complete Internet/intranet messaging solutions sold and supported by an established e-mail vendor."

TeamWARE's future product direction will be to merge the TeamWARE Internet Messaging Server with its more mature commercial product, the Team-WARE Messaging Server.

12.2.1 Messaging Server Backbones

A messaging server backbone allows connected subsystems to communicate with one another. The backbone maintains directory services that integrate all connected user directories to maintain a consistent address base for users of all connected subsystems. The directory also eases system administration and provides basic security functions such as user authentication and access control.

Directories have gained importance in messaging systems of all types because they are not just used for maintaining user addresses, but also critical data concerning the connected e-mail subsystems, such as alternative native address and file format information. The typical requirement for the messaging backbone of today is to be able to synchronize the backbone directory with well-defined standard or de facto standard directories. The most important of these are X.500 and Novell's NetWare Directory Services (NDS).

PC-based LAN e-mail and groupware systems typically maintain proprietary directories and user address or distribution lists. Synchronized interchange with these systems must also be possible, since they represent the messaging infrastructure's front-end systems. The interchange can either be provided over dedicated system-specific connectors or across standard messaging gateways, such as X.400 or SMTP/MIME.

The messaging infrastructure should be constructed so that front-end systems connect transparently and relay messages between the systems through the backbone unchanged, appearing at the receiving end exactly as sent, although they may be transferred between two dissimilar systems.

Mainframes and minicomputer hosts must also integrate with the backbone, although it is usually sufficient if message interchange and batch-mode directory interchange are facilitated. However, it is usually very difficult to integrate legacy office automation systems because of their large variety; at one time, every systems vendor had their own package, and they share few common denominators. In most cases, specific connectors must be created or provided by the original vendor.

12.3 TEAMWARE MESSAGING

Today's mainstream commercial TeamWARE Messaging Server Backbone is centered around a distributed company directory that can automatically be synchronized to maintain the integrity of data stored at multiple server sites consisting of one or more servers. The server sites can be connected over a wide-area network (WAN) or LAN, and provide messaging services to client PCs that are connected by a LAN (see Fig. 12.2).

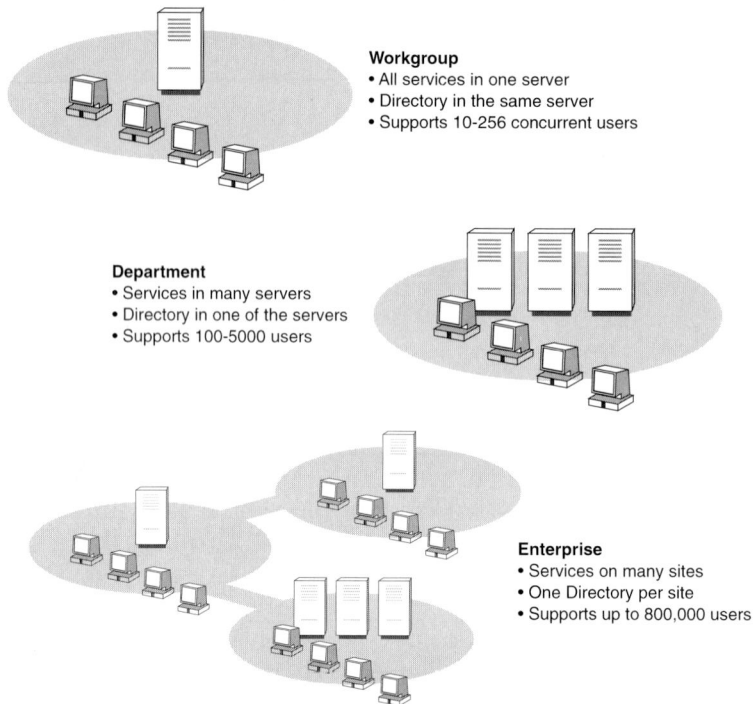

Workgroup
• All services in one server
• Directory in the same server
• Supports 10-256 concurrent users

Department
• Services in many servers
• Directory in one of the servers
• Supports 100-5000 users

Enterprise
• Services on many sites
• One Directory per site
• Supports up to 800,000 users

Fig. 12.2 TeamWARE Messaging's Scaleable Implementation

The TeamWARE Directory contains the user address information necessary for message routing and can also contain user profile information including title, position, office address, telephone and fax numbers, and other user-defined entries. The directory is hierarchically structured to provide a single point of management and administration for the entire enterprise. The central Team-WARE Directory provides a master point for collecting, controlling, and disseminating user information drawn from other server sites. The interval of directory replication between sites is defined by the system administrator. However, users are typically managed--added, removed, or modified--at the local server site level. Modified directory information is automatically cascaded through the organization to the central TeamWARE Directory and back to the server sites by means of the directory replication mechanism.

TeamWARE Messaging Server is based on the store-and-forward principle, which means that a message is passed on from the originator to the recipient in steps. Each step is secured by storing the message in the previous stop until a positive delivery acknowledgment is received from the next stop. If there are transmission errors or a server malfunctions along the way, a copy of the message will always be stored somewhere along the route, and the node maintaining that copy will either try to forward the message via alternate routes, or if that is impossible, it will return a negative acknowledgment to the originator. As a result, there will always be reliable information available on the status of the message, regardless of the transport mechanism used between intermediate nodes.

12.3.1 Standards Support and Interoperability

The TeamWARE Messaging Server supports the major transport communication protocols typically implemented in front-end LAN environments today. TCP/IP, NetBIOS, NetBEUI, IPX/SPX, and X.400 protocols are supported, enabling the TeamWARE messaging environment to encompass virtually every network configuration a customer may have in place. NetWare, LAN Manager, Windows NT, and LAN Server network operating systems can all interface with the TeamWARE Messaging Server, as can networks of UNIX-based workstations through the TCP/IP and NFS protocols. Macintosh clients are supported by the Mail and Forum modules.

The TeamWARE Messaging Server is available on a variety of platforms, including the Windows NT for Intel, OS/2, NetWare NLM, UnixWare, Solaris, HP-UX, Tandem's UNIX SVR4-based operating environment, and ICL NX operating systems.

12.3.2 Connectors

While the TeamWARE Messaging Server is a routing message switch, connectors provide added capabilities to the TeamWARE messaging system that address message interchange and directory synchronization. Support for SMTP/MIME connectors make it possible for the TeamWARE Messaging Server to exchange mail and mixed-media files containing audio, video, or graphic images with any system connected to a TCP/IP network.

TeamWARE Connectors for X.400 and X.500 are available. The X.400 Connector provides a full switching Message Transfer Agent facility when required for multiple X.400 links or as a gateway from TeamWARE to X.400 when a system without high level enterprise capabilities is being implemented. The X.500 Connector serves the same functions as the X.400 Connector, but also adds the ability to create a separate X.500 directory to complement the TeamWARE directory.

However, connectors are also available to address other messaging needs that go beyond the server's support for industry standards. The TeamWARE Connector for MS Mail provides native messaging exchange and directory synchronization between TeamWARE and MS Mail; another Connector for Lotus Notes provides the same services for Lotus Notes users with the message exchange based on X.400.

A Connector is also available for adding bi-directional fax capability to the server, allowing users to send and receive faxes through their PCs.

TeamWARE has also created a Connector Software Developer's Kit that contains the tools, libraries, and facilities required to build connectors between the TeamWARE Messaging Server backbone and other systems, providing message interchange and directory synchronization between the two systems.

12.4 GROUPWARE

Why build a messaging infrastructure in the first place? Although simple e-mail has revolutionized the way people work and exchange information, the answer goes beyond this basic form of electronic communication. A relatively new product category, groupware, is expanding the foundation of e-mail to provide tools that further facilitate collaboration and coordination between individuals and groups.

TeamWARE Office is a complete suite of groupware modules that can be implemented independently or as an integrated whole. TeamWARE's solution is scaleable, making it useful for LAN-based workgroups or entire enterprises consisting of a maximum of 800,000 users; beyond that, multiple enterprise-level organizations can also be linked together using TeamWARE. Like the Team-WARE Messaging Server, TeamWARE Office is easy to administer centrally, regardless of the platforms it may be running on. All servers can be administered from a central point using the administrator's tools provided with TeamWARE Office, enabling remote system administration.

Currently, TeamWARE's largest Office installation is the United Kingdom's Metropolitan Police Service (MPS), which is now in the middle of a three-year project to implement TeamWARE Office on a TeamWARE Messaging infrastructure that will support 21,000 users.

John Leary, Deputy Director of Network Projects for the MPS, summarized the need for TeamWARE Office as fundamental to accomplishing the mission of the organization: "The driving force behind our information systems and communications strategies is the need for distributed, timely, and appropriate information. This organization captures a tremendous amount of information, but uses only a small portion of it. Officers who come into contact with the public acquire a great deal of information. If this is not archived, valuable data that could be of benefit to a colleague is lost."

John Townsend, Commander of Operational Technology for the MPS, cited the ease-of-use and intuitive feel of TeamWARE Office as a critical factor in the success of the project. "We offer training and courses constantly, but because officers' time is valuable, the less time we need for training users on IT the better. TeamWARE Office does not frighten users. It is reasonably easy to train people to use it and they get rapidly used to it."

Jörgen Ostersehlte, head of the German Bremer Landesbank's PC systems and electronic services operation, concurs on the importance of ease-of-use in gaining widespread utilization of groupware applications within an organization once the software has been installed. "When TeamWARE Office was introduced, we encountered no acceptance barriers. A good deal of the credit for this is due to the user-friendliness and simplicity of TeamWARE Office, and to the ease with which it can be mastered."

In a study of TeamWARE users at the Kimitsu Works at Nippon Steel in Japan and users at the County Council of Blekinge in Sweden, industry analyst Geoffrey Bock of the Patricia Seybold Group reached similar conclusions regarding those two very diverse groups of users. Bock observed: "Once TeamWARE is deployed, end-users quickly embrace it in their everyday work. As users repeatedly describe, individual TeamWARE applications become natural extensions of their desktop tools, providing increased capabilities for communicating and sharing information within particular workgroups or across entire organizations. These capabilities serve to supplement and enhance existing modes of communication."

TeamWARE Office constitutes a full set of ready-to-use groupware applications, which include facilities for electronic mail, document management and retrieval, personal and resource scheduling, information sharing and conferencing, and task routing. The applications are designed to be user friendly, providing tools for managing personal productivity and the activities of a group working as a team.

While most people use and understand electronic mail today, the other elements of the TeamWARE Office suite may be less familiar to the typical user.

12.4.1 TeamWARE Library

TeamWARE Library is an electronic information system that enables people to organize and share valuable documents in the TeamWARE Office system. The TeamWARE Library server can contain several separate libraries, with each one being dedicated to a specific theme or topic; for example, different projects can have their own libraries. Within a library, a hierarchical organization of folders can be constructed that contains documents arranged by function or topic. The system allows for direct communication with most popular applications, including Microsoft Word, Excel, Lotus 1-2-3, and WordPerfect. Other applications can be integrated with TeamWARE Office through the use of TeamWARE Link, an application programming interface.

The MPS' John Townsend describes one way his organization has customized TeamWARE Library: "A good example of process automation with TeamWARE Office is found in one division which has developed an electronic case prosecution system. After arresting a person, officers fill in a list of information on the screen and type up the statement. The case papers for court are then made automatically through the system, and TeamWARE Library is used for filing them. This is one of the procedures that have shown considerable savings in time."

Documents organized in a library may contain one or more files in addition to a document profile. Provided by the owner of a document, the profile indicates the name of the document, the folder it is stored in, its author, file types, version number, and creation date. The profile may also contain a description of the contents and keywords in the document. TeamWARE Library displays the latest version of a document by default, with preceding versions arranged by date. When updating an existing document, a user can lock it from others to preserve consistency during the update.

The TeamWARE Library user has a few different search methods at their disposal to locate a document or documents. For a quick view of what a certain library or folder contains, a user can browse through document lists in the main window of the user interface. TeamWARE Library also supports document search functions based on a keyword, a fraction of text, author, owner, approximate creation date, or document version. To standardize and simplify the search process, a whole library can be given a set of workgroup-specific keywords that will automatically prompt the user.

TeamWARE Library is password protected, which makes the libraries and their contents accessible only to a selected group. Each individual TeamWARE Office user can be given the right to read, update, or only insert documents on a folder-by-folder basis. Alternatively, they can be granted no rights at all. The users can also be organized into user groups, and the user rights concerning libraries and folders can be defined for an entire user group.

12.4.2 TeamWARE Forum

TeamWARE Forum is the electronic bulletin board and conferencing medium of the TeamWARE Office system. Like the other TeamWARE Office modules, TeamWARE Forum can be implemented at the LAN level or across an enterprise-wide WAN using an X.400 connection.

The TeamWARE Forum hierarchy consists of forums, discussions, and messages. Discussions are chains of messages and their corresponding replies and attachments. Each TeamWARE Forum system contains multiple individual forums that are structured based on the variety of topics at hand and the need for information security. Like TeamWARE Library, authorized users can search forums by subject, keyword, message type, author, or creation date.

Each forum has a manager who has the right to modify the forum profile, grant user rights, or delete the forum entirely. Users can be granted three different levels of forum-specific rights: the right to read and write messages in a forum, the right to read messages in a forum, and the right to view the forum in name only so that a user could contact the forum manager for access to that forum's contents.

The TeamWARE Forum system can be utilized for a variety of purposes. For example, many inquiry and discussion forums usually have restricted access and are limited to the exchange of information regarding a project that may involve many people who are physically widely dispersed. Another example would be a department forum, where all employees of a department or organization have both read and write rights and messages are set to expire after a specific period of time.

12.4.3 TeamWARE Imaging

TeamWARE Imaging is a complete imaging application including support for scanning, indexing, storing, viewing, annotating, and retrieving images. With TeamWARE Imaging, users can replace any manual paper-based system and/or process with a complete electronic document management system that is tightly integrated with the other modules of TeamWARE Office, enabling a user to move images between groupware modules without actually opening and closing each individual application or module. Support for industry-standard drivers and formats means that TeamWARE Imaging can interoperate with any other device, system, or software that also supports those standards.

12.4.4 TeamWARE Meeting

TeamWARE Meeting is a desktop conferencing application that allows users to conference, share files, and share applications to facilitate group efforts when team members are geographically dispersed. The working meeting can have a chairperson who controls the session, or a free-style mode can be used where every participant is equally empowered to take action. Through a modem, TCP/IP, or IPX network connection, multiple users can discuss and interactively make changes to the same file on their desktop, with each user's changes clearly linked to that user.

The module also has flip chart functionality, enabling users to write notes in the same way they might use a white board in a meeting room. TeamWARE Meeting also supports desktop video conferencing, although it is not necessary to implement that portion of the module to take advantage of the other functions.

12.4.5 TeamWARE Calendar

TeamWARE Calendar is an enterprise-wide group scheduling and resource management application that can be used to reserve the time of people and resources concurrently. In TeamWARE Calendar, the calendars of several users, groups, and resources can be seen in one window regardless of their location on a server. A user would then define a convenient time for a meeting by reserving a room, equipment, and booking the time of the other participants. Each requested participant would then be able to accept or reject the proposed meeting.

12.4.6 User Customization

Users have other tools in addition to the TeamWARE Alarm feature to use in customizing their working environments. Definable, free-format to-do lists can be configured to remind users of important tasks. TeamWARE Office also offers a configurable tool bar for all groupware applications. A Preferences feature also allows the user to personalize groupware applications. For example, criteria for listing TeamWARE Library documents and TeamWARE Forum messages can be set by the user as can the time intervals used in TeamWARE Calendar.

12.4.7 System Administration

The TeamWARE Office system administrator program includes tools for customizing user directories, log files, and alarm functions. The administrator can monitor the functioning of the system by collecting statistical information about mailboxes, library documents, and folders. TeamWARE Mail also has features that allow the administrator to consolidate information about mail usage; he or she can collect a mail billing log, or monitor and configure mail sending times.

Administrators maintain the workgroups' servers, the users' mailboxes, and the TeamWARE Office applications. They keep a record of the members of a workgroup, as well as assign and maintain the usernames. In TeamWARE Library and Forum, the administrator can define and maintain the list of keywords that can be used for document searches. In an enterprise-wide Team-WARE Office implementation, replication enables application availability for dispersed members of a team. According to the size of the TeamWARE Office system, the administrative functions can be divided among several individuals.

12.4.8 Security Features

TeamWARE DeskTop is a security and administration tool for managing PC Windows desktops in networks. DeskTop enables secure single login to the PC, network, and TeamWARE Office. Administrators can control whether users can load and run programs from outside sources on their system, and can prevent users from copying applications programs loaded on their PCs.

Several users with different software desktops can share one computer, and a user's desktop will remain the same should they move to another PC. Users can be allowed to set their preferences or modify their personal desktops, or the system administrator can design the layouts. TeamWARE Desktop enables administrators to manage users' personal desktops remotely on a global scale.

File replication with TeamWARE DeskTop management eases the task of software installation. An administrator installs the software on their system and then replicates the program files to users' systems while defining the program icons and the initialization settings.

TeamWARE Crypto is an easy-to-use security extension for the Windows environment that encrypts files on hard disks, floppy disks, and on the network. Crypto automatically decrypts and encrypts data as the application program reads and writes files, so users can work normally with sensitive information without worrying about security.

12.4.9 TeamWARE Flow

TeamWARE Flow is a workflow management tool, a separate product category that owes its existence to thinking that originated with groupware. Workflow products fall into three main segments: production workflow, document routing, and groupware workflow. Production workflow products are mainly used for fixed, predefined processes. Document routing products are somewhat more flexible, but generally lack the planning capabilities, rich functionality, and programming environment required by large organizations.

Alternatively, TeamWARE Flow is a groupware workflow product, enabling teams and individuals to plan and manage complex processes that do not necessarily conform to a fixed and predefined set of steps. TeamWARE Flow is designed for the type of work processes that can be continuously improved as a team learns how to improve its processes, making a true learning organization possible.

Consider processes that involve complex interactions such as purchase orders, loan applications, order fulfillment, or software bug tracking. Instead of a single programmer designing the entire process, it is composed of pieces supplied by different users. Rather than force every group in the organization to work in exactly the same way, different individuals or groups have different plans to achieve the same goal, thereby allowing each group to find the plan that works best for them. Process plans are modified even while being enacted, allowing people to start with incomplete plans and finish them as they go. The group needs to respond to exceptions as they arise, rather than being forced to make conditions for all possible exceptions up front.

To support such complex work activities, we need to be very concerned about the exact way that things are done. More often than not, the way in which a goal is accomplished depends on the specific goal. For example, closing a large sale with an important customer will depend very much on that particular customer, on the products, and on the sales people. It is not possible to write a single, fixed sales process that will support this activity.

TeamWARE Flow supports an organization's business processes by enabling collaborative planning among group members. With TeamWARE Flow, every process or major sub-process has an owner who determines which users have the right to alter the process, mimicking the way the external world works with process and authority. Every worker involved with the process can see the entire flow diagrammed on their system's screen and can also track where a given item or project is in the process. The structure of the flow can be modified at any time by any user with the appropriate rights. Because TeamWARE Flow is transaction-based, it maintains a record of the date, time, and individual taking action at each stage of the process or altering the work flow model. The database recording the transactions is a relational database.

As noted by customers in the discussion of TeamWARE Office, user resistance can be the major factor determining the success or failure of a given software application. Because TeamWARE Flow is based upon the user's involvement in creating the process, it avoids the pitfall of user resistance that has ensnared products designed to impose externally contrived procedures upon an individual or organization. With a system that empowers the user to refine and modify processes as necessary, the user becomes the driving force behind the process rather than a programmer's afterthought.

There are two main tools within TeamWARE Flow, the Viewer and the Graphical Planner. The Viewer element allows a user to see worklists, forms, historical data, and messages associated with a given task. The Graphical Planner is a tool that provides a visual representation of the actual work process and makes it easy to diagram plans, allowing a user to grasp work processes easily and identify ways to improve the workflow (see Fig. 12.3).

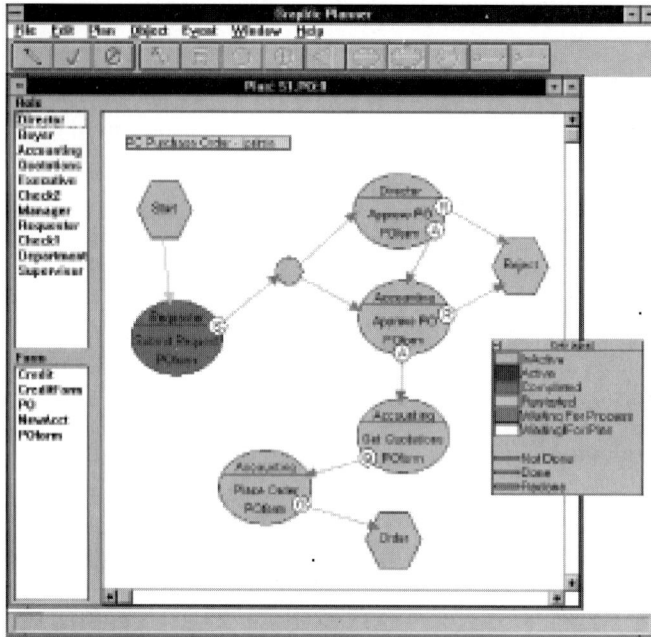

Fig. 12.3 TeamWARE Flow's Graphical Planner

12.4.9.1 The TeamWARE Flow Model

The TeamWARE Flow model takes a task oriented approach. Plans are composed of a network of stages; each stage represents one or more tasks, or questions, as a specific step in the process. Stages in a plan can be invoked serially, in parallel, or in any combination. Each stage has roles assigned to it.

Roles are simply variables that hold lists of names of people or groups assigned to an activity. A given individual may play one or multiple roles simultaneously in any process.

Activities are defined as requests from one person (the process owner) to another person or persons (assignees). The description of the task is free form text; it is not constrained to a set of predefined tasks. A lengthy description of the job may also be included. An activity is either considered to be active or inactive. When active, the people assigned to complete the tasks are aware of the assignment and have accepted the responsibility. Strictly speaking, activities are not tasks but rather the interpersonal communications needed to coordinate tasks. Sometimes it is necessary to implement a split-stage activity, or a request that is duplicated for every assigned individual so that each person may take action independently.

After an assignee has accepted an activity, he or she is then free to specify a sub-plan to be used to accomplish that activity. The sub-plan—a network of sub-activities—may be created on the fly to handle that specific need. The last activity in a sub-plan activates an exit node, which deactivates the entire plan and sends a message to the parent activity with the result of the subplan.

An activity includes one or more choices that the assignee may take to respond to the requested action. Selection of a choice causes the completion and, usually, deactivation of one activity and the activation of the next.

Since activities can be accomplished in parallel, any number may be active at a given time within a particular process. When a user views a process, that process is searched for all open activities and they are presented as a set of pending tasks. If the user is playing a role that is responsible for one or more activities, the actions for those activities will be presented to that user. A user may not take any action on activities for which they are not responsible.

One of TeamWARE Flow's main design goals is to facilitate communications between the users of the system. Choosing the "Done" choice from a menu on an active task will tell others that the task is done, but little else is communicated. Therefore, with every action, users may include a message summarizing whatever they feel the others participating in the process will need to complete their tasks.

A record of all actions and their associated messages can be browsed at any time by any participant in a process. This is the history list and can provide a way for a new participant of the process to catch up on what has happened up to the present. Equally important, it provides a means of looking back at a project to see what really happened, so users can learn from experience. By making processes visible, people can evaluate and improve the way they work.

Since processes can evolve with TeamWARE Flow, there is no need to ensure that any process is completely correct before starting a project. Most of the costs involved with implementing traditional workflow solutions are associated with defining and verifying the correct process. TeamWARE Flow lowers that cost barrier while providing workers with the degree of freedom necessary to do a job correctly.

Because each group has their own segments of the larger process, they do not need to get signoff from the entire organization just to make a small experimental change. The result is that individuals are empowered to automate their own processes and continually improve them.

12.5 TeamWARE and the Internet

In the past three years, the Internet has become a mainstream technology, serving as a sort of global messaging infrastructure for disseminating information from e-mail to newsgroup discussion forums. As tools are added to the Internet environment to make it more secure, manageable, and reliable, the technology is expected to be adopted increasingly by commercial users who will implement it in the form of intranets, or private Internet-based networks dedicated to the use of a single organization.

The TeamWARE Internet Messaging Server is intended to address issues that have prevented many commercial users from adopting Internet e-mail as a standard, providing the enterprise-class features that such users have come to expect and demand. In addition to a basic SMTP mail engine, the TeamWARE Internet Messaging Server provides message delivery receipt or failure notifications and retries, and has connectors for passing messages and synchronizing directories with proprietary e-mail systems such as MS Mail, cc:Mail, MHS, and VAX Mail. The TeamWARE Internet Messaging Server supports all major open industry standards, including IMAP, POP, MIME, and LDAP.

The server is scalable and can support thousands of users through sophisticated clustering technology. Windows-based administration tools enable either centralized or decentralized system administration and tuning from any server or Windows desktop. Mailboxes can be managed, allowing the system administrator to move users from one server to another and to impose mailbox or message size limitations. It also provides for intranet user directories containing user phone, fax, physical location, and e-mail address.

TeamWARE has also licensed Java technology from Sun and is actively exploring how that technology will advance the state of groupware applications. TeamWARE has plans in the near term to provide access to its groupware applications with a Web browser to better facilitate the communication process with individuals and organizations on the outside of a corporate structure.

For example, consider an advertising agency that uses TeamWARE internally for improving effective teamwork and communications. The agency also works with a number of small subcontractors, with each of them implementing one part of a complex project. The subcontractors do not have groupware, nor do they have the budget, skills, or time to install a project-specific software product on their LAN.

By implementing TeamWARE through the Web, the advertising agency can easily establish project-based communications that will allow employees and subcontractors to be linked together in a way that enables all basic groupware functions without installing the software at the subcontractor's site.

In this scenario, the agency has a project manager who creates discussion Forums, a group Calendar, document folders in the Library, and workflow routing schemes. The manager then grants access rights to the system as needed by in-house employees, and subcontractors use a standard browser to access TeamWARE through the Internet using a URL the project manager has established.

All TeamWARE services will be implemented inside the browser as an HTML document, allowing the Web-based users to read and reply to TeamWARE Mail items, make TeamWARE Calendar requests, read and participate in TeamWARE Forum discussions, and update or view TeamWARE Library documents from any server on the network. All the functionality previously available only to LAN-based users will now also be possible from within the Web browser.

When the user connects to the URL representing the TeamWARE Web server, a log-on dialogue will be displayed. If the user is authorized and has an active password, all the services that the user has rights to access will be displayed along with the latest developments relating to that individual, starting with the most critical item. This Event application will serve the same function as TeamWARE Alarm does in a LAN environment today, keeping a user posted about important events directly related to them.

Users will also be able to store links back to external HTML documents inside TeamWARE documents. Access between TeamWARE and Web documents will become transparent, except where access rights to sections in TeamWARE have deliberately been restricted due to privacy or security concerns. For example, mail and workflow access will always require a valid user ID and password for authorized use, while public documents might be set to allow access to anyone with a standard Web browser.

Above and beyond the functionality found in today's groupware modules, TeamWARE will also incorporate Java-based technology from Sun Microsystems in future releases. The intention is to turn today's groupware modules into Java applets that will support multimedia enhancements along with enhanced capabilities for interactive computing. In the future, the portability of Java also promises to deliver the ultimate in multi-platform support; any authorized user running a Java-enabled browser on any desktop platform will be able to connect directly with the TeamWARE database and run the groupware applet. Java-based groupware applets will also have the ability to absorb software updates dynamically as opposed to the conventional method of loading new software revisions on systems.

Going forward, development of TeamWARE products will also focus heavily on the integration of multimedia content and support for mobile users. Video streaming, voice integration, and 3D virtual reality are all part of TeamWARE's development efforts, as is enhanced support for mobile users, whether they are laptop users that are occasionally connected to the network, completely wireless, or using handheld devices.

CONCLUSION

As secure transaction standards are more widely deployed within the Internet community and capabilities such as authentication and certifications gain wider acceptance, selling open and cost-effective transactional Web-based services will become a new business model in business-to-business and business-to-consumer markets.

TeamWARE has historically supported intra-group and intra-organizational information access, while the Internet has supported self-selected interest group-oriented information access. TeamWARE emphasizes the dynamic information interchanges that are routine parts of ongoing business activities. The Web, by comparison, focuses on ubiquitous information access and multimedia document dissemination.

As TeamWARE moves ahead with new product development, the focus is on combining the strengths of the two environments. By taking the degree of access, standards support, and multimedia capabilities inherent in Web technology and combining those features with the need for control, structure, security, and manageability required by commercial users, TeamWARE intends to remain at the forefront of vendors supplying messaging and groupware solutions.

The end result of the synergy between TeamWARE and the Web will be the development of a comprehensive business computing environment for both Internet and intranet users. Today, TeamWARE has an Internet Messaging System based on native Internet e-mail protocols and standards, and it plans to offer a browser-based groupware system enabling users to access all TeamWARE collaborative services through the Internet environment. TeamWARE's ultimate goal is to provide a secure, scaleable, and manageable intranet solution combining the best of the proven LAN-based and continuously evolving Internet-based solutions.

BIOGRAPHY

Mika Enberg is currently director of marketing for the TeamWARE Group in North America. He has previously served in a variety of development and marketing positions in Finland and the United Kingdom since joining the organization in 1989. Prior to his experience with TeamWARE, Enberg was responsible for developing internal business systems for Digital Equipment Corporation in Finland and gained significant experience with Digital's All-In-1 and VAX Notes products. Mika Enberg is a graduate of the Finnish Business Institute with a major in Information Science.

Introduction to Chapter 13

Although Hewlett-Packard has offered its OpenMail messaging backbone for many years, HP is perceived as a hardware vendor. This chapter may change your mind.

HP has put a great deal of time and effort into developing a groupware backbone for collaboration. Their recent alliance with Netscape, and subsequent reselling of Netscape's product, is evidence that HP is serious about collaboration in both LAN and Internet/intranet environments. Interestingly, HP also has a strong relationship with Microsoft, and so is aligned with both camps in the browser wars.

HP's philosophy and approach to collaboration is through enterprise tools. Their tools link people, processes, and information in communication and collaboration. HP's collaboration tools take a semi-custom approach to collaboration providing ways to capture the expertise that went into initial customization and development across a company if needed.

HP's model for collaboration is called ICS for Internet Collaboration Services. These products are open, and the architecture to support them is flexible and supports a variety of standards (X.400, MIME, IMAP4, POP3, CMC, and NNTP). ICS is enterprise-focused, runs on a messaging backbone, provides multiple levels of security, and supports mobile workers. HP sees on-line discussions, forms, and workflow as essential to making businesses more productive. Not only do they support the implementation of processes, but the monitoring of processes. ICS also supports a variety of clients including Mac, PC, and UNIX, and is focused around open Web-based browser standards. It also allows both a "push and pull" information model.

Our studies show that security is seen as critical issue today for all IP network applications, and that no one is very happy with the current levels of security available. HP offers security at both the application and corporate infrastructure levels and supports such security standard protocols as SHTTP and SLL. However, even these protocols only make it more difficult and expensive for an unauthorized person to get to your data. Security is an illusion many of us like. Truly, nothing is secure, however, you can make it so expensive and hard to get to that the economic incentive for accessing this data is minimized. This is much of the role of today's security systems. As someone looking at collaboration in your organization, you must decide where you sit on the continuum of collaboration vs. security. The more open the system is to support collaboration the less secure it is. The more secure the system is, the harder it is for true electronic collaboration.

Into its messaging architecture, HP has integrated other Web-based applications for forms, document management, workflow, and database support. In actuality, HP's architecture supports both the Netscape Navigator, and the Microsoft

Explorer, as well as other popular groupware products like Eudora for e-mail, FileNet for Workflow, and links to Lotus Notes (through an API). OpenMail supports threaded mail conversations.

HP also has OpenTime, a calendaring and scheduling program, and uses the UniPlex OnGo document management engine for group document management and version control. Additionally, filters and search engines like Alta Vista, Magellen, and Lycos can be incorporated as objects into the HP object store, making HP's standards oriented architecture compatible with a wide range of groupware products and functions.

HP has built their infrastructure on this industrial grade messaging backbone, however the architecture is modular enough to be able to plug in a variety of Internet/intranet functions and products as they evolve. HP's future involves calendaring on PDAs, support for voice mail and a universal in-box, EDI, support for new server platforms like NT, better security through encryption and other technologies, LDAP directory support, and support for the semi-custom "software factory" concept.

This well written chapter shows why HP is a force in computing today and will become a force in the future in the area of enterprise collaboration. It also shows that the Internet infrastructures are being taken very seriously by HP and that they have evolved their LAN messaging backbone into a tool to support collaboration on the Internet and intranets.

Increasing Business Performance with Internet Collaboration Services: HP's Communication & Collaboration Strategy

Raul Mujica
Hewlett-Packard

Companies pursue new business approaches as they try to keep a step ahead of rivals, foreign and domestic. Technical innovations have provided tools to assist in implementing new business strategies. Many companies have chosen to pursue the innovative family of tools, generally called "groupware," or more accurately described as "communication & collaboration," to provide a structured way to address these issues.

Communication & Collaboration (C&C) tools electronically create links between workers, data, and processes. Whether a company seeks to automate a process on a PC or a mainframe, different C&C solutions are available to meet unique business needs. Vendors offer a choice of C&C strategies, each appropriate for a different scale of business. The right selection involves choosing the right tool for the business problem (see Fig. 13.1).

Most vendors coming from the PC and LAN applications market have designed their C&C tools to work with small workgroups. These tool vendors believe that a company can begin from the workgroup and generalize to the enterprise. Many companies have discovered that this approach leads to cost and performance problems. Hewlett-Packard has developed a unique approach to C&C development and implementation, focusing on enterprise-level implementations and scaling downward to workgroup applications.

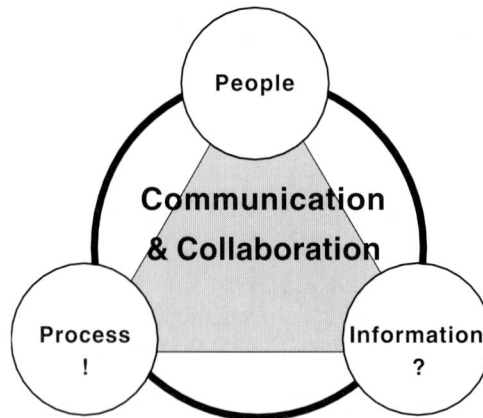

Fig. 13.1 C&C Architecture links people, process, and information

13.1 How Business Benefits from Communication and Collaboration (C&C)

The modern business operates in an information-rich environment. Today's organizations must react to information quickly. Consider the following business examples:

☞ A fast food company evaluates ways to improve its customer response process. Each customer can use a call-back number listed for product complaints, purchase problems, or other issues. The current system works fairly well, but the company could improve the process by using a computing system to track each call, tally statistics, and show trends. In addition, the call log would be used as a knowledge base for future customer issues. The expected returns include advanced knowledge about process issues and better knowledge about customer issues.

☞ A casualty insurance company wishes to exploit a competitive advantage in speeding up claims processing. The well-trained staff can complete an average claim within two weeks. Recently, a competitor announced plans to reduce the processing time by thirty percent (three days). This company sees an opportunity to reduce claims processing time by 50 percent, utilizing a new process and new computing tools. This will reduce paperwork delays and provide opportunities for the company to service a greater number of customers.

☞ An automobile parts maker wants to reduce its warehouse inventory. The company serves a variety of aftermarket chains whose business is rivetingly competitive. Delivery is the key. Winning delivery means having parts available on demand. The retailers also want to minimize inventory, so they will work with several aftermarket parts companies to ensure prompt delivery. This parts maker wants to tie itself more closely with its sales force of manufacturers, representatives and direct salespeople. By understanding and building a better sales model, along with regular updates, the company hopes to predict demand far better than the capabilities of the existing system.

C&C architectures provide an environment for implementing each of the systems described above. Each example involves links among people, process, and information. In older generations of information technology, companies developed applications specific to these problems. The new generation of C&C tools offers a more standardized and leverageable architecture for building these integrated applications. C&C solutions provide a facilitation engine for communication and collaboration, connecting people via message dissemination and conferencing, linking to process with workflow and time management tools, and integrating information through a variety of sources. Table 13.1 shows examples of the tools used to link people, process, and information.

Table 13.1 Elements of Communication & Collaboration

People Connections	• Electronic Mail • Fax • Conferencing • Shared Folders • WWW
Process	• Workflow • Calendar/Time Management • Development Environment
Information	• Database Links • Document Management • Forms • Filters/Search Engines • Security

On top of the integration tools, good C&C incorporates sample applications, showing how to link people, process, and information in an intelligent manner.

The business benefits of a C&C solution are threefold:

1. Flexibility with reduced cost
2. Rapid prototyping
3. Computer-aided process management for a variety of business activities.

13.1.1 Flexibility with Reduced Cost

The typical implementation for a customer response system depends on the system being obtained. A prepackaged, "shrink-wrapped" solution has the lowest implementation time, but it is also the least flexible for meeting business needs.

A C&C solution incorporates the standardized architecture of a prepackaged software product, but targeted towards flexible group projects. In contrast, a custom solution can be much more flexible, but typical implementation time far exceeds that of either the prepackaged or C&C solutions.

As prepackaged software, C&C tools are available at a cost comparable to other "shrink-wrapped" products. With C&C solutions, most of the cost involves resource allocation, implementation, and management. Since C&C provides a structured approach to implementation, C&C tools are much less expensive than full custom products. As an added benefit, the expertise used to develop a single C&C application can be shared throughout the company. A company can reuse the structured C&C approach for many applications.

In the fast food franchise above, the company can choose to computerize its customer calls with either a prepackaged software product from a fictitious company called Help Solutions, a C&C product, or a custom package to be developed by a consulting firm. The Help Solutions implements a specific process, runs on a set of databases and platforms, and is optimized for a specific environment or set of environments. The C&C product provides flexible people connections, information connections, and process setup, and a team can design a custom call management process, or find an existing groupware design from the vendor or a third party. The custom solution requires all the parts to be designed and integrated, without guarantees that the parts can be reused anywhere else in the company (see Fig. 13.2).

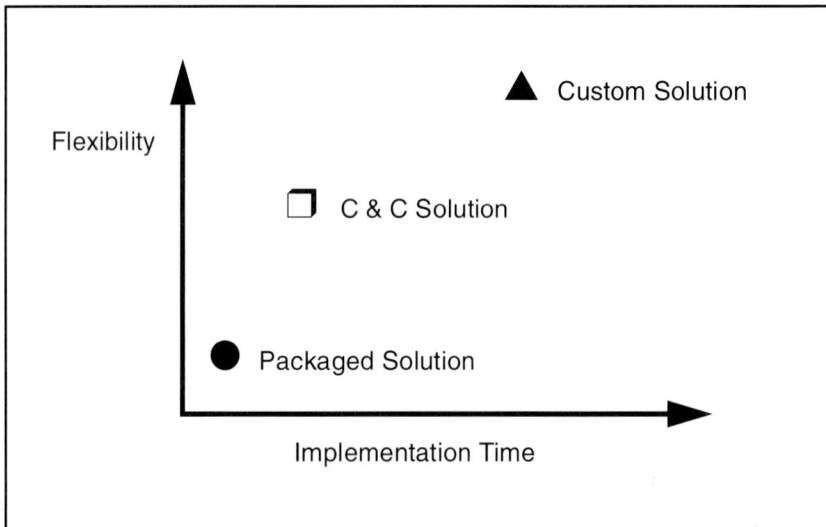

Fig. 13.2 C&C Solutions are flexible with short implementation times

13.1.2 Rapid Prototyping and Implementation

C&C solutions offer a structured approach to connecting computing resources in process design. Using C&C allows companies to focus on process design only because resource access is built into the C&C product. A design team can use the structured C&C approach to prototype a specific process, validate the prototype, and quickly develop an implementation. C&C tools speed up application prototyping regardless of scale, from workgroup to enterprise.

In the insurance example, the company can evaluate a number of different prototype processes as it models the claims management system. The C&C implementation allows the company to demonstrate the information flows in a given prototype. By identifying key bottlenecks in a design, the company can redesign the process to reduce or eliminate the bottleneck and reduce overall process time.

13.1.3 Computer-aided Process Management for a Variety of Business Activities

C&C allows a number of processes to profit from computerization. These include discussions and "group histories" online, allowing group members to review business notes, charts, graphs, and other relevant information. With form-based entries, users can tailor the information entered into a business process, and with workflow management, relevant information is transmitted to the correct user.

C&C gives its users not only a process for problem solving, but also a way to view and modify the process electronically. Once a process is in place, design teams can monitor the process to determine where it can be improved. Also, as inputs to a given process change, the effect of those changes can be identified and appropriate process changes implemented. The following diagram shows a general approach to processes. The typical process inputs are people, information, and a process to be solved. The process implementation creates a process that generates a result from these inputs. C&C allows electronic process monitoring to identify areas for process improvement (see Fig. 13.3).

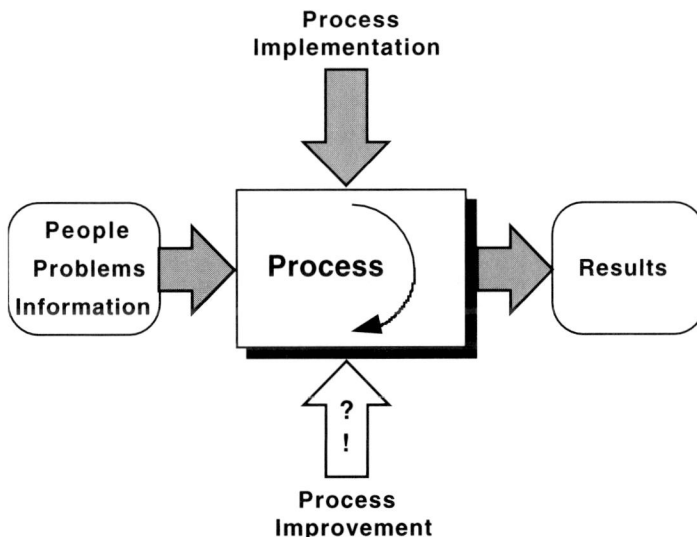

Fig. 13.3 Dynamics of process development

13.2 WHAT C&C MEANS TO HP

Hewlett-Packard has designed a C&C solution based on an enterprise-ready, scalable software model called the HP Internet Collaboration Services (ICS). ICS encompasses the communication and collaboration tools that today's professionals need to work with their teammates. At the heart of the model is a core of open technologies, allowing companies to deploy a flexible C&C architecture, based on industry standard input, output, and communications tools, with key components that meet specific business needs.

HP C&C is designed to address the following principles:

Enterprise Down	Enterprise-ready, scalable and afford-able for the workgroup
Communication-Driven	Message delivery for the backbone technology
Diversity	Open standards designed in product core to integrate the most diverse set of applications, Internet-ready
Security	Validate users and protect information
Mobile	Anywhere access to information

HP has designed ICS around the basic concept of "enterprise down." With an enterprise-down approach, resources and infrastructure are designed at the enterprise level, then scoped for a specific task at the workgroup level. This contrasts with other C&C products that target the workgroup, then attempt to scale up to the enterprise. Enterprise down is the most cost effective and people inclusive, eliminating the costs and difficulties of "scaling up" a workgroup-based application for enterprise functions.

An additional principal of ICS is use of message delivery as the core of the enterprise C&C tools. HP made a conscious architecture decision. A C&C solution can center either on its database or its message delivery server. Due to its proven, distributed, standards-based architecture, messaging scales easily to address enterprise or workgroup requirements. Database-centered tools are more difficult to scale, having trouble in a distributed server architecture; to be enterprise-ready, a database-centered C&C must use an enterprise-scale database (see Fig. 13.4).

HP offers a truly open C&C system. Unlike other tools that use proprietary interfaces, ICS internalizes standard message formats such as MIME and X.400 and interface protocols such as MAPI, POP3/IMAP4, P7, CMC, and NNTP to link users and third-party applications. The ability to support diversity is critical for successful C&C implementations. Individuals and business units will always have unique needs that will drive their desktop application selections. For companies to cost effectively support C&C, they must deploy services that run in the background and can be shared by many desktop applications. What are these services? Messaging, directory, security, and management come to mind. Why? Because all C&C applications utilize these basic services while sheltering the end-users with their own presentation. (Similar to how Windows-based applications utilize the printer drivers that are supplied by the Windows OS.) In addition to being the most cost-effective approach, the support for diversity is critical to maximize collaboration between teammates. Who is on the team? Well, that is constantly changing as the business does. Teammates may be from different departments, companies, industries, and countries. It is nearly impossible for a company to standardize company-wide on a particular desktop C&C application because individuals and business units have valid business reasons for choosing their own. It is definitely impossible for every potential business partner to be using the same desktop C&C application. Yet you need to collaborate with them in a cost-effective manner. How do you do this? Implement core infrastructure services such as messaging, security, and management company-wide that are standards-based and can natively support the widest set of desktop C&C applications.

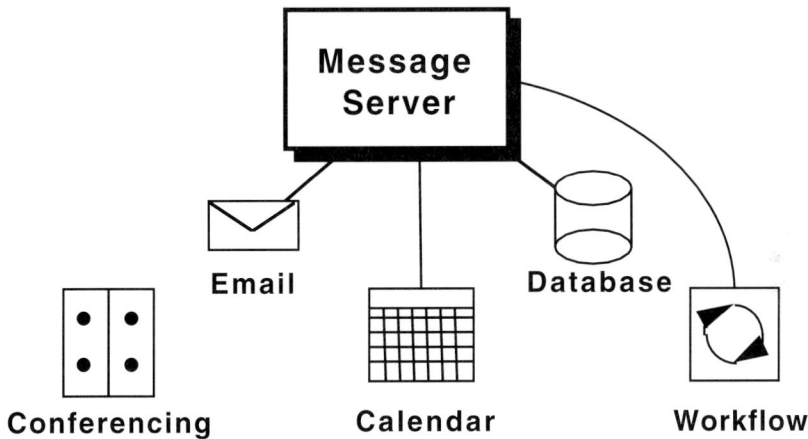

Fig. 13.4 Message Server is central in ICS

Users access ICS through a variety of clients traversing the thin-to-fat spectrum on a range of platforms including Windows, Mac, and UNIX. Due to their pervasiveness and platform independence, Web browsers, or as they are now being called, "Internet Clients," are an exciting development. While competitors are providing a browser view or "window" to their services, ICS takes this a large step further. In ICS, Internet Clients are fully empowered for interactivity on the same par as MAPI or MAC based clients. ICS competitors are unable to match this level of functionality because their business models are predicated on controlling the desktop. Internet clients break this stranglehold (see Fig. 13.5).

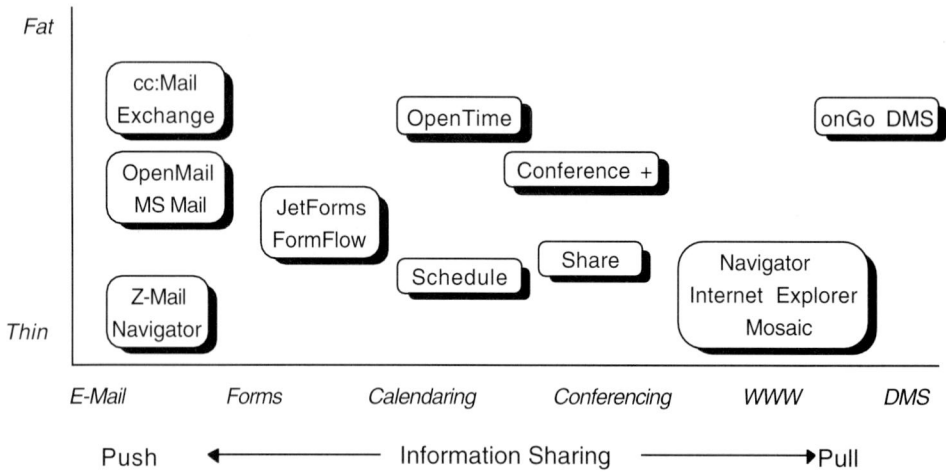

Fig. 13.5 Some popular desktop applications integrated with ICS

Internet services are core to ICS. This internalization is significant for two reasons. First, Internet standards such as POP3/IMAP4, SMTP/MIME, NNTP, FTP, DNS, and TCP/IP are the most pervasive worldwide. Adherence to these standards results in maximum participation of professionals in collaborative undertakings. Second, C&C architecture requires a mix of "push and pull" information delivery and access. Certain interactions are best suited by "pushing" information, while others are best suited for being "pulled." The WWW fills the "information pull" side of the C&C architecture. The WWW is an ICS design choice for two reasons: "minimize data redundancy, maximize access." Minimizing data redundancy ensures data consistency and is the lowest cost to manage. WWW browsers offer the most universal access to any information that is presented through a WWW server.

Security is a major requirement in any enterprise-level architecture. Security covers many areas, some of which are more appropriate for given applications. Basically, you want to ensure that data is kept private (encryption), data isn't altered during transmissions (data integrity), the sender and receiver of information are who they say they are (digital signatures, non-repudiation, private/public keys), and users have access to those resources for which they have been granted permission (access control).

By offering security at the application and the corporate infrastructure level, the ICS approach differs from that of other C&C vendors. Most utilize application-specific security only, requiring that all business transactions take place within their C&C product. This is a fine approach for a small company attempting to build a well-bounded application, but larger companies will have difficulty integrating existing procedures or partners into this security system. By integrating ICS with a corporate security infrastructure such as Nortel's Entrust, security services such as authentication, non-repudiation, data integrity, data privacy, and access control are shared among many applications. This reduces the operational costs and simplifies management, benefitting the company and IT. The end-user benefits because a security infrastructure allows for the maximum number of participants in a process, fostering collaboration. With the development of public certification authorities, security infrastructures will be extended between companies without the need for predefined agreements. Additionally, secure Internet communications are implemented through SHTTP and SLL protocols and HP's Web Security Technology Virtual Vault, for process control above standard firewalls.

ICS completely caters to the mobile requirements of today's workforce along three fronts. First, all ICS services are designed with a local synchronized copy of the server stores, such as e-mail, calendars, and directories. Second, ICS services are made available beyond the PC. Increasingly, mobile professionals are using PC alternatives such as palmtop computers and telephones for their mobile computing. Third, ICS covers the complete set of connection options both tethered and untethered.

13.2.1 Messaging, an Essential Foundation for C&C

As discussed in previous sections, C&C products integrate people, information, and processes. The key internal piece that binds all the C&C tools is message delivery. Message delivery automates user connections with other users, information, and process activities. Whether the process requires routing a document to a manager for approval, accessing a discussion conference for designers to evaluate alternative product specifications, or tying into a government-required regulatory database, the message delivery mechanism provides the vehicle for information transfer.

C&C applications can have a heavy data storage requirement, and some C&C vendors have chosen to focus on the database component as the center of their software. Database-centric systems depend on users accessing identical databases. To ensure system consistency, the database-centric tools rely on database replication, another form of information transfer. As many users of these applications have discovered, databases and database replication provide challenging management problems at the enterprise level. The key to database replication is minimizing and optimizing the replication process, but a database-centered C&C application provides management difficulties in determining which sections of the database should be replicated (see Fig. 13.6).

Managing Database Replication

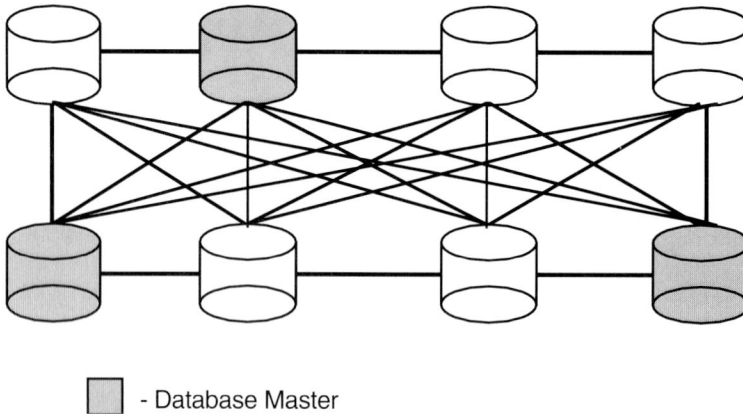

☐ - Database Master

Fig. 13.6 Database Replication complexity with multiple master information

For database data management, the ICS approach eliminates excessive database copies throughout the enterprise. To HP, databases are information repositories, not process managers. The proper level and scale of information, from customer contact information to full financial transaction information, is managed as a separate enterprise resource. Data redundancy should be minimized with data access maximized. Due to its ubiquitous access, the WWW is ideal as both storage for unstructured information and presentation of both structured and unstructured information. The latter is accomplished through the CGI interface into the ICS message, calendar, shared folder, and conference stores and RDBMS (see Fig. 13.7).

Databases and HP ICS

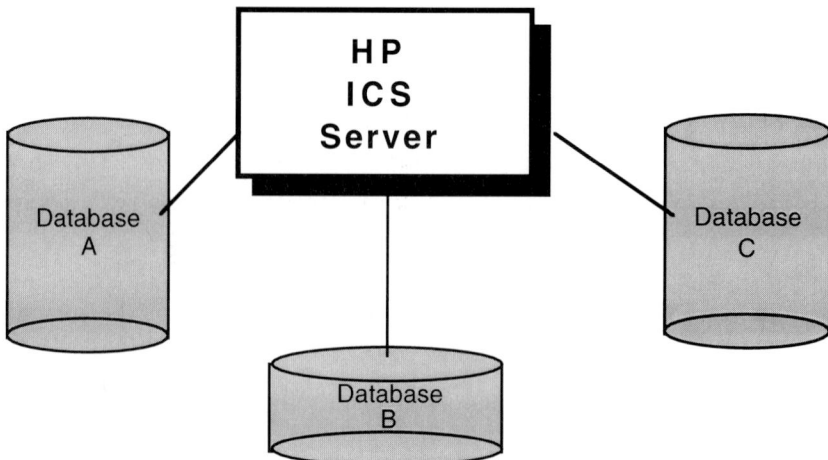

Fig. 13.7 HP ICS utilizes different enterprise databases

13.2.2 Enterprise-Level Messaging

To ensure enterprise-capable C&C applications, the infrastructure must provide reliable, robust, and timely message delivery. A robust messaging system means:

☞ Reliable: Zero lost messages

☞ Fast: 5 minute delivery time guaranteed anywhere in the world

☞ Scalable: 1.6 million messages a day on 50 servers

☞ Low Cost: 25 administrators for over 80,000 users

A robust messaging system provides the communication foundation for high-speed information transfer for C&C and business applications.

The HP messaging architecture acts as a foundation for enterprise-level C&C. HP OpenMail provides C&C-ready message delivery. In addition to e-mail, OpenMail incorporates group-level conferencing, shared folders, and bulletin boards. OpenMail integrates with other Internet-ready applications to ensure secure, timely delivery of database information, workflow activities, forms, and documents (see Fig. 13.8).

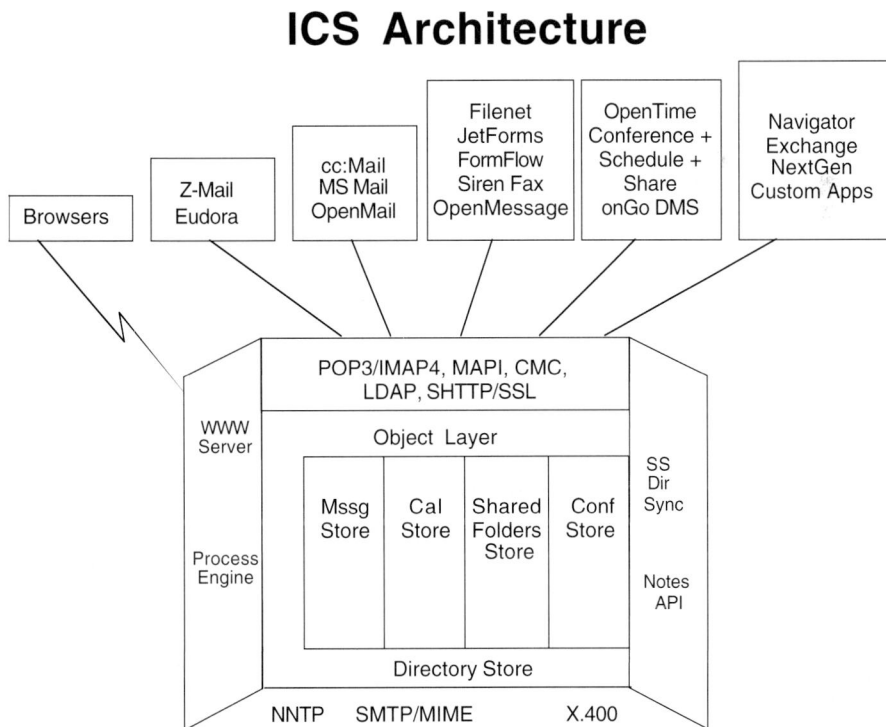

ICS Architecture

Fig. 13.8 ICS Architecture

The cost of enterprise messaging is primarily dependent on the administration and management of the systems. Various cost of ownership studies by analysts have concluded that 2/3 of the cost of messaging systems is in the administration and management. The cost of managing is primarily dependent on two factors, scalability and management tools. The scalability concept is simple. The more users you can load on the server, the less servers you will have to manage. Fewer servers translates to easier, lower-cost management. OpenMail is unsurpassed in its scalability for corporate messaging, achieving 5 to 10 thousand users per server and supporting company environments of over 100,000 users. As with security, OpenMail provides management tools at two levels: application-specific and corporate infrastructure. Application-specific tools are object-based, graphical tools and come in two flavors. One flavor is for department administrators where functionality can be regulated. A typical usage would be to allow the department secretary to edit names and the transfer of a user's mailbox to another department. The second design set is for IT administrators who require single console administration of multiple servers and sophisticated administration such as designing naming and routing schemes. At the corporate infrastructure level, OpenMail is integrated into OpenView, which provides object-based, graphical, single-console administration and management of hundreds of applications, network devices, and hardware. The advantage of utilizing a management corporate infrastructure such as Open-View is that management overhead is reduced and simplified and operational costs are lowered.

13.2.3 How to Implement C&C—Who Should Do What

The key to a low-cost and effective C&C architecture is the leverage of common services across the whole organization. Services that are good candidates for cross organizational use are those that many applications utilize and are "invisible" to end-users. Appropriate candidates are messaging, security, directories, and management services. These services are sometimes called infrastructure or back-end services. In a client/server computing architecture they reside on the server and are largely invisible to end-users.

As mentioned earlier, different professionals and business units will require different C&C applications at the desktop level. However, you cannot let the desktop applications determine your infrastructure, rather your infrastructure should be open and flexible to seamlessly accommodate a wide diversity of desktop applications. A large organization cannot escape diversity and should therefore embrace and prepare for it. Among other services, desktop applications will require messaging, security, directory, and management services. If you implement each of these on an application-specific basis, your costs and management will grow out of control. Plus, you will have incompatibilities at the infrastructure (back-end services) level, which will at best severely hamper the free flow of information and surely spiral costs upwards for any attempt to deploy enterprise-wide processes.

Thus, IT should select and implement a C&C infrastructure that will be low-cost and manageable for their benefit as well as flexible in delivering its services to a wide diversity of desktop applications benefitting end-users. Business units and end-users can then select the desktop applications most appropriate for their needs with the confidence that they will integrate and leverage the company-wide infrastructure services provided by IT.

13.3 HP INTERNET COLLABORATION SERVICES (ICS)

The HP Internet Collaboration Services (ICS) provides a full suite of Internet-based C&C tools. The C&C functionality was based on basic research exploring what today's Global 1000 professionals require to effectively work with fellow professionals. Table 13.2 shows the components of ICS:

Table 13.2

People Connections	• Electronic Mail • Conferencing • WWW • Shared Folders
Process	• Workflow • Calendar/Time Management
Information	• Document Management • Forms • Filters/Search Engines
Management	• Synchronization • Security • Clients of choice • Groupware of choice • Administration Tools • Network Tools

Here is a brief description of each component in ICS. (Refer to the Open-Mail Solutions Catalog for a complete listing of the many Partners who provide products integrated with OpenMail.)

People Connections

Electronic Mail	OpenMail provides secure, fast message delivery, clients of choice, and remote access all within a manageable environment at the lowest cost.
Conferencing	OpenMail also provides threaded conversations on multiple topics. These conferences are synchronized between OpenMail servers and other C&C applications such as Netscape's Collabra, Exchange, Internet Usenet, and Notes.

WWW	Provides a secure Internet access point into the ICS C&C services through standard WWW browsers and tools. Beyond a simple view or "window" into the ICS services, standard WWW browsers are fully empowered as interactive clients.
Shared Folders	Provides a document sharing and editing environment that is based on the ICS object store and replicated between OpenMail servers. Shared folders also have the capability of "publishing" documents to the WWW with simple "drag and drop" actions.

Process

Workflow	ICS provides workflow tools for process management. This allows users to automate their information delivery and transfer steps in a C&C application. Workflow is provided at two levels: Workgroup and Enterprise.
	Workgroup workflow is for processes where the originator can bound the process participants, such as review of a new personnel policy or budget setting. The architecture is client-based where objects containing all the process logic and status are routed to the process participants. ICS will provide the process modeling, definition (roles, routes, responsibilities), and execution tools required for end-users to graphically implement workgroup workflow.
	Enterprise workflow is for processes that breed exceptions, such as expense reimbursements approval, where the participants cannot be bounded by the originator. HP's Process Management Engine (Montana) has been designed to efficiently handle hundreds of processes with hundreds of sub-routines. This scalability at the process level (as opposed to just simply the number of users that can be supported) is unique in the industry. Montana centralizes all the process logic and orchestrates the execution of the process. Montana is integrated with market leading modelling tools such as Meta Workflow Analyzer and ICL Process Wise. For maximum leverage of legacy applications and process flexibility Montana integrates with RDBMS (where process data is stored), business applications, and transports including X.400, SMTP/MIME, and CORBA.

| Calendar/Time Management | HP OpenTime provides wide-area calendar management featuring real-time, free-time map lookups across servers and resource scheduling for C&C applications. |

Information

Document Management	Through HP's Gold Certified Partner, Uniplex, OnGo DMS delivers a high-quality document management system for entering, version control, natural language searching, on-the-fly summaries, and archiving compound documents.
Forms	Supports a variety of forms, including forms developed for use with MAPI message delivery systems
Filters/Search Engines	Incorporates filter and search engines into the ICS Object Store and Internet resources.
Security	Application-level security includes end-to-end encryption, read/write protections, access controls, and password authentication. With OpenMail Gold Certified Partner, Nortel, Entrust provides an enterprise-level security infrastructure including encryption, digital signatures, and private/public key management. And with HP's Web Security Technology, access control is achieved on the Internet without firewalls and secure transmissions are implemented through SHTTP and SLL.

Management

Synchronization	Graphical synchronization, configuration, management, and scheduling of the ICS Object Store.
Clients of choice	Support of the widest variety of clients on popular platforms, including Windows NT, Windows 95, Windows 3.1, Macintosh, and UNIX. (Refer to OpenMail Solutions Catalog)
Groupware of choice	Supports a variety of Web browsers including Netscape's Navigator and Microsoft's Internet Explorer and partners' specialized clients incorporating the latest in Web technology, including database access and forms generation. Also, integrates other C&C tool packages, such as Exchange, Notes, Share, and Conference +.
Administration Tools	Tools for managing and monitoring C&C applications and message delivery leveraging a management and administration infrastructure provided by HP OpenView.

Network Tools   Tools for managing and monitoring hardware and
                                 network operation and performance leveraging
                                 HP OpenView and the Network Node Manager,
                                 PerfView, and MeasureWare products.

13.3.1 Collaboration with Business Systems

ICS can be integrated with existing business applications to form a new
generation of business systems. In fact, the messaging infrastructure, user interfaces, management, and security of ICS provide much of the foundation for business systems deployment. ICS combined with Inter-Application Messaging, App-
Link and a Process Management engine (Montana) to form the Internet Business Architecture. IBA is an architecture for developing and deploying business
systems that are characterized by their leverage of legacy applications and flexibility in adapting to new business models.

Inter-Application Messaging will emerge as a preferred data communications technology for many business applications. What makes Inter-Application
Messaging attractive:

☞ Worldwide, well understood, and proven standards for messaging interfaces
  and structures make messaging a great integration platform between business applications

☞ Queueing architecture frees the process from having all resources 100 percent available

☞ Message stores can handle large and unpredictable data streams efficiently

☞ Messaging works over a distributed computing environment

App-Link will leverage much of the OpenMail technology and add Business
Object Wrappers for integrating applications for batch file transfers. Further
out, "near-real-time" performance transports options will be integrated.

To orchestrate the business system, a Process Manager is necessary. This
concept and HP's productization (Montana) are unique. Montana manages processes from a central server that coordinates the execution of transactions
through the business process. The workitem objects that are routed through the
nodes of a process do not contain all the process logic. The process logic is maintained in a centralized process engine, Montana. This fundamental architecture
choice is one of the reasons that Montana can scale to manage hundreds of processes. While current workflow products can scale to many users in a process,
they cannot scale to many processes. This is largely because current workflow
products encapsulate the process logic with the data in the workitem object. As
the number of processes and subroutines increases, the workitem objects become
larger and more inefficient. Plus the ability to manage process or subroutine
changes becomes unmanageable as all the workitem objects must be correlated
and updated (see Fig. 13.9).

Process Management

Captures the flow of
business value

Business Model

Process
Model

Application Model

Data Model

Groupware

Structures data into
knowledge pools

Workflow

Coordinates data
with people & time

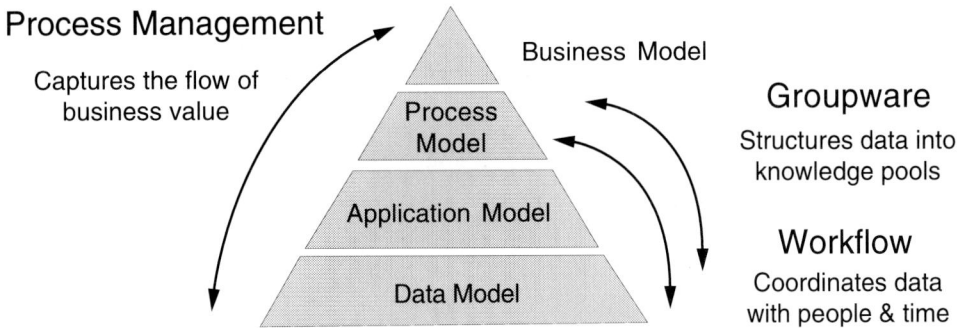

Fig. 13.9 Process management versus workflow and groupware

Montana treats existing legacy applications as subroutines that are "objectized" so they can be utilized in many business processes. Since the business process logic is maintained in Montana, the business process itself can be refined or dramatically re-engineered with reconfigurations of existing process objects (applications) or the introduction of new process objects (see Fig. 13.10).

IBA offers IT with a flexible architecture for providing the technology necessary to support evolving businesses. In particular, IBA:

☞ Facilitates incremental improvements to business processes

☞ Leverages the ICS infrastructure

☞ Mirrors emerging business models

Value

Process Management
Architecture

Current IT
Architecture

B_3, A_3

B_2, A_2

B_1, A_1

B - Business Model
A - Application Model

Time

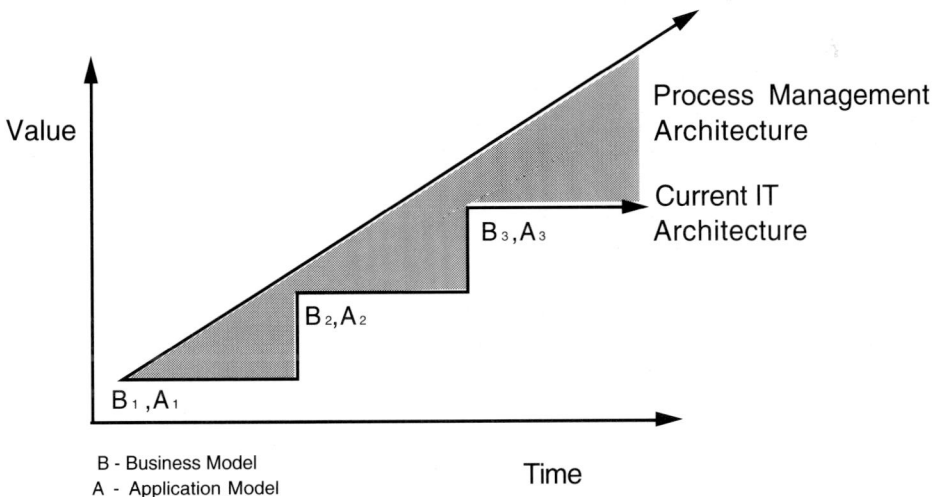

Fig. 13.10 Process management architecture aligns the technology with the business model

Business Example:

The Internet Business Architecture can manage complex enterprise-level processes. For example, a complete application may incorporate the process engine managing business processes that include manufacturing resource planning (MRP), general ledger (G/L), and order processing (O/P) applications. The integrated engine utilizes existing, off-the-shelf systems that may already be in use inside the company (see Fig. 13.11).

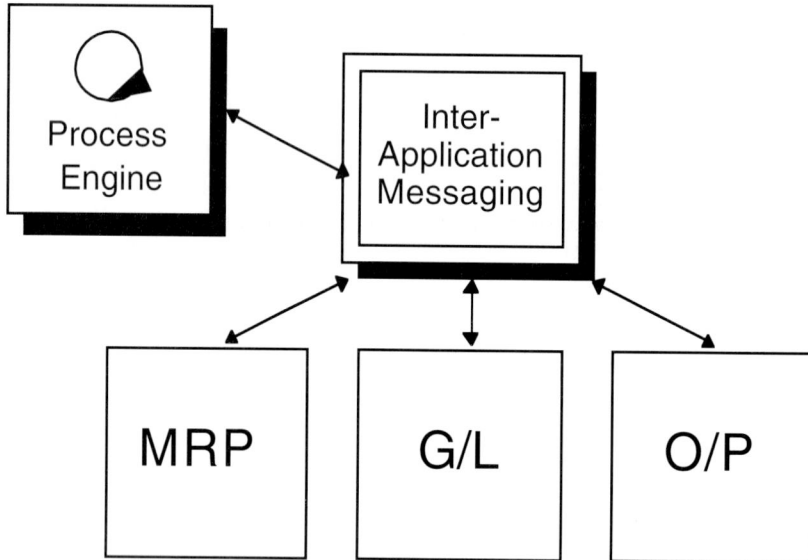

Fig. 13.11 Example: Business Processes

In this example, the process engine drives a manufacturing process that integrates order processing for manufacturing materials, an MRP management system, and links to the company's general ledger system. As the MRP system calculates materials requirements, it communicates to the interapplication message system, which signals the start of a purchase process. In turn, the order processing is automatically initiated and a placeholder is generated in the general ledger system.

Until the order is completed, the order processing system can be set to identify unfulfilled orders for automatic checks; such as time-outs or esclation routines. As materials are received, the MRP system is manually updated, and the process engine transmits a fulfillment message to the order processing system and sends the invoice amount to the general ledger. Once the general ledger shows the check is sent, the final order can be closed.

In this example, the order processing, general ledger, and MRP systems are all capable of sending and receiving business messages to each other through the inter-application message system and coordinated by the process engine.

To program such an integrated application, a business systems professional uses process modelling tools which are fed into the process engine. Process results and emerging business conditions will drive alterations and improvements in the process that, once modelled, are incorporated in the process engine. The process engine then redirects existing resources and incorporates new resources in the process to service the new business requirements. The end result is a cost-effective and fast approach to synching the technology with the business model.

Summary

Business professionals have recognized the value of empowering teams, creating closer links with customers, and integrating processes previously managed as separate disciplines. A pervasive C&C architecture is key to enabling such business initiatives. Today's IT organizations must provide their business sponsors with the technology infrastructure for C&C. This infrastructure needs to be deployed on a company-wide basis for maximum leverage and minimum cost. The C&C infrastructure needs to be open to serve the most diverse set of desktop applications that business units will require and flexible to allow business to take advantage of future developments. Through intelligent deployment and usage of a company-wide C&C infrastructure, aggressive businesses will drive competitive advantages over the laggards.

13.4 FUTURE DIRECTIONS

HP's charter is to provide unique, valuable technology to improve our customer's communications:

☞ internally, and with customers and partners

☞ between individuals and to link business applications

☞ with absolute reliability, security, and privacy

☞ in a tightly managed environment at the lowest possible cost

13.4.1 People Collaboration

Communication combines spoken and written messages. Those messages come to people today through three channels: phone, fax, and e-mail. HP's Internet Collaboration Services (ICS) is an innovative approach to workgroup services based on Internet standards. The technologies within ICS simplify conducting business: conversing, planning, sharing information, and holding meetings. Future directions include the following:

Global Calendaring: Driving open calendaring APIs through standards bodies and agreements with other groupware vendors. Our products can then share information with other calendaring servers. By 1998, robust desktop PCs and network-integrated PDAs will manage calendaring directly. Then, e-mail messages will generate calendar lookups directly to the wireless PDA or office desktop. Users can respond immediately or defer until later, with all communication through e-mail.

Voice Mail and the Universal In-box: The "universal in-box" is an essential first step to integrating voice and electronic messaging. However, real efficiency comes to business by reducing the effort for individuals to link up across organizations. HP's approach is to integrate voice messaging with other services at the application level. For example, callers can log meeting requests through voice mail, which will forward those requests to the calendaring system and deliver notification through a wireless pager (see Fig. 13.12).

Integrated Voice-Mail and Scheduling

on Messaging Backbone

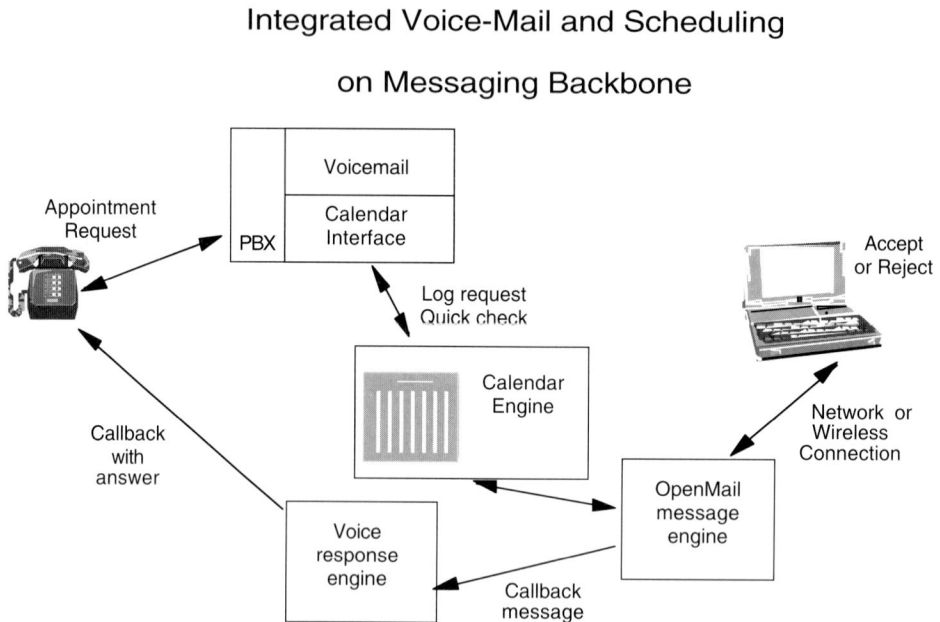

Fig. 13.12 Integrated voice-mail, calendaring, and messaging

Extending Tools Integration: OpenMail's shared folders, conferencing, and object stores will be integrated with shared white boards and videoconferencing. This will provide complete support services to cross-functional development teams, all based on Internet standards.

New Collaboration Tools from the Internet: The Internet will continue to breed new collaborative, multimedia standards and technologies. If past trends continue, these innovative suppliers will focus on the needs of workgroups and base products will lack enterprise scalability. As these technologies become mainstream, wide-area collaboration will become a requirement. OpenMail will support them and their users with reliable transport, high-speed directories and security. Business teams will be able to choose the most appropriate tools from an emerging, ever-changing menu rather than being limited to a single vendor's product release schedule.

13.4.2 Application Collaboration

The pervasive adoption of personal messaging technologies provides a solid base of standards and protocols for inter-application messaging. With today's reliable, high performance transports, customers can standardize on messaging as the preferred technology for integrating business processes. Standards-based, easily modified, message-based systems are important alternatives to complex solutions such as transaction monitors and custom EDI. Corporate mail systems will support transaction messages as well as today's personal e-mail traffic. HP will continue investing to support performance, security, and deployment of business application and transaction messaging. HP has invested in several areas to ensure widespread adoption of messaging for business process integration.

Performance: The OpenMail product provides the message throughput capacity to support application messaging in batch mode. Throughput will be enhanced to support transaction processing as well as end-user interactivity. With "open systems" mainframes, customers will adopt message routing technology to support inter-application communications. This will function within a server or server cluster as well as between networked servers. Today, OpenMail can take advantage of the high performance, availability, and cluster technologies provided by HP's HP-UX operating system and SMP platforms. OpenMail on NT and other UNIX platforms provides our customers a choice of vendors, pricing, and service levels (see Fig. 13.13).

Messaging Platform Architecture

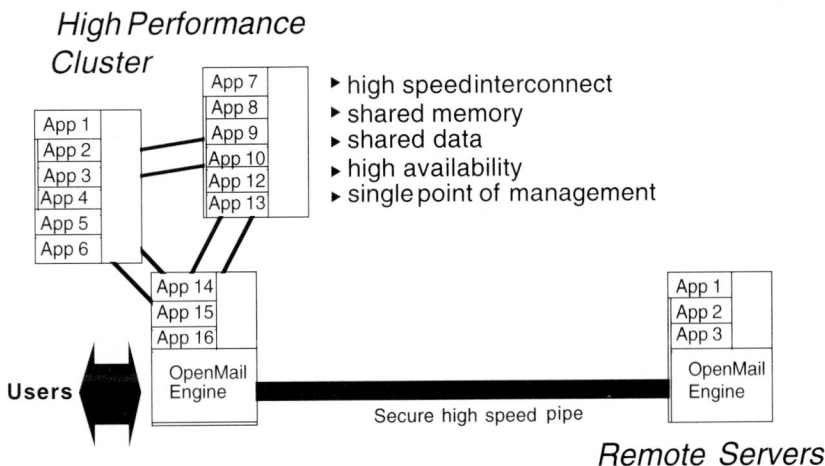

Fig. 13.13 Hardware clustering architecture

Security: HP provides a complete set of security services that support global, secure messaging across the Internet. Security technologies areas within HP that support electronic commerce include smart cards, flag (encryption) cards, and integration with authorization servers and certificate authorities. HP's security services will be delivered as a set of building blocks that customers can deploy to meet business requirements. Components can be combined to provide increasing levels of security, as described below.

OpenMail encryption already provides secure "message tunnels." Our customers depend on this technology for secure communication across open networks. Today, this solution requires firewalls to isolate the OpenMail server from the open network (see Fig. 13.14).

Manufacturing Supply Chain
Datastream Security Across the Internet

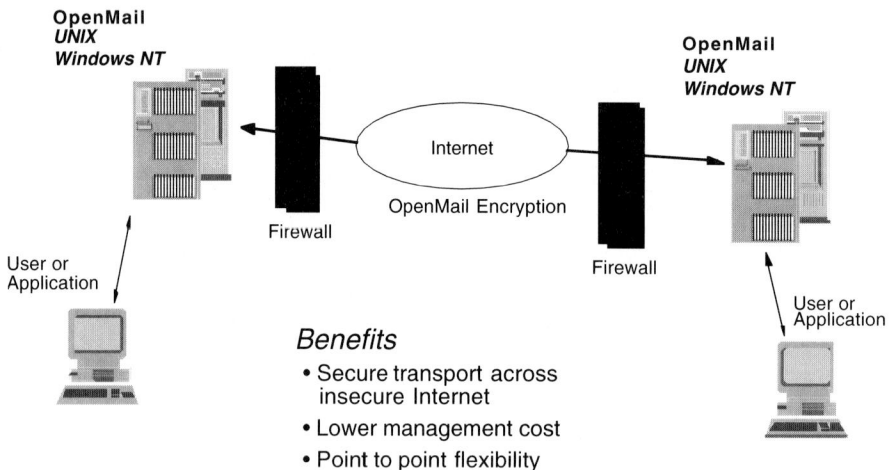

Fig. 13.14 OpenMail encrypted messaging through the Internet

Our Internet Service Provider customers want to provide secure dial-up access to e-mail from any location. HP's solution will combine three technologies:

☞ Third party solutions enable strong authentication and cache protection for Web browsers. This eliminates hacker access to the mailbox from unauthorized network nodes.

☞ HP's "Virtual Vault" will provide OpenMail with a protected environment to host mailboxes directly on the Internet. This is the same technology used by HP's financial services customers to provide secure banking on the Internet.

☞ Integration with SSL 3.0 encrypts communications between the browser and OpenMail's HTML interface (see Fig. 13.15).

Internet Service Provider
Secure Dial-up Access

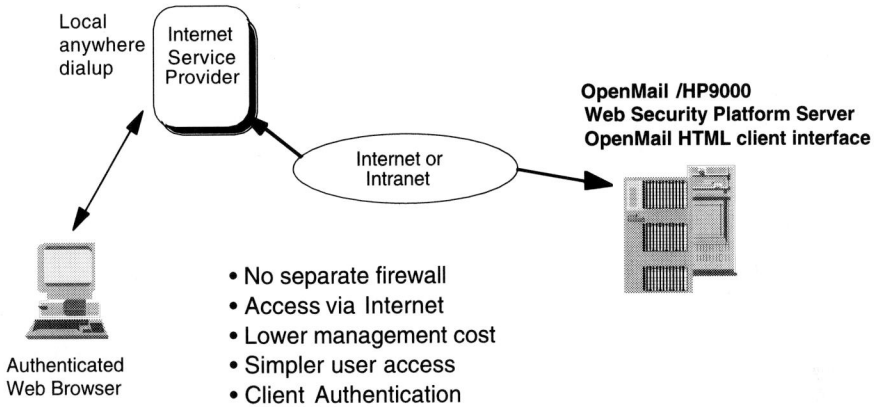

Fig. 13.15 Secure dial-up access

Public key technology provides a very efficient mechanism for securing a wide range of message-based communications. EMO has recently integrated NorTel's "Entrust" technology to integrate public key technology and support enterprise certificate authorities. In addition, EMO will integrate smart card authentication/authorization. This will provide the secure "end-to-end" services that support electronic commerce on the Internet (see Fig. 13.16).

Global Trading Firm
Secure Document Transmittal

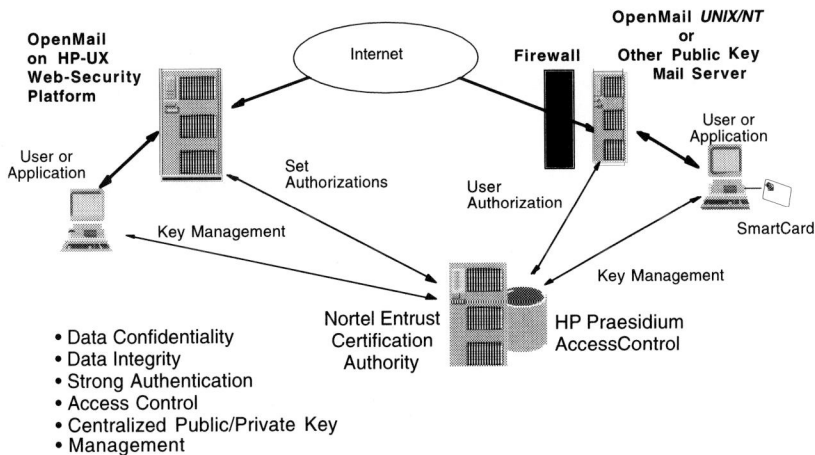

Fig. 13.16 Secure end-to-end document delivery

HP is committed to the success of our G1000 customers in deploying global, secured messaging. To support an open messaging infrastructure, HP will provide the following:

☞ Interoperability with other applications that support public key standards

☞ Seamless links to public key "certificate authority" providers and third party X.500 directories

Process Management "The Software Factory": As businesses update processes to improve efficiency, they will use HP's technologies to reduce "wait time" within those processes. For example: WWW search engines have made it simple to gather comparison data from a wide number of sources quickly and automatically. To further automate business processes, the next problem is to execute similar transactions across dissimilar business application sets. This means applying the same business rules to a variety of linked application architectures and changing business rules and architectures quickly in response to new opportunities and challenges. In addition, developers can incrementally improve application processes instead of replacing large components. This demands a "software factory" approach that can produce a large number of semi-custom applications that all support a core business process (see Fig. 13.17).

The HP Software Factory
HP Montana Process Manager

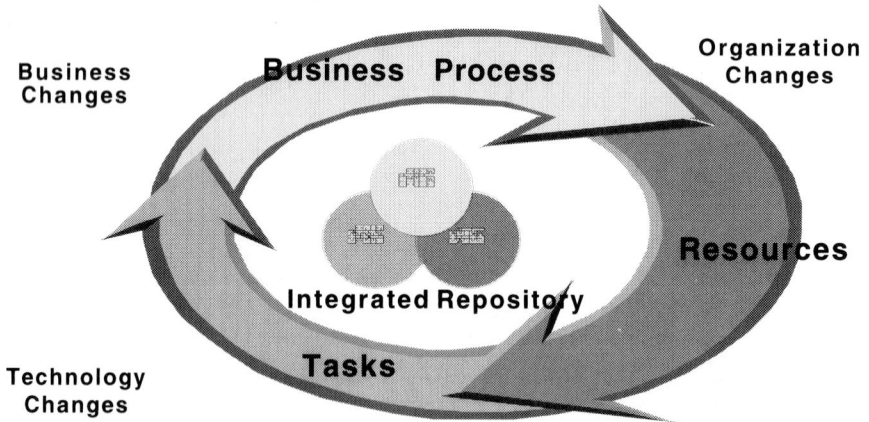

Fig. 13.17 The software factory

The total solution encompasses more than messaging and groupware. Our customers require a process management component to define core processes and deploy applications to support them. Previous reuse strategies, such as metadata repositories and object stores, focused on the implementations rather than the processes. This never provided payback because the focus on code implementation neglected process improvement capture. HP will deliver the process management design and monitoring technology to support the process reuse model. In parallel, HP, with its partners, will develop a series of industry-specific solutions to help customers adopt this new technology quickly. Candidates include manufacturing (supply chain integration), insurance (claims processing), and telecom (service provisioning).

The process monitor will be transport independent. Customers can choose from synchronous and asynchronous mechanisms to link applications in a business process. Separation of process flow models from technology will enable businesses to re-implement or modify applications while maintaining tight control of the overall business process. In the past, many large retailers have solved this problem by creating a fixed solution and dictating processes to their vendors. HP will deliver process definition and deployment solutions that provide much greater flexibility. This will make automated supply chain efficiencies available to enterprises with "mix and match" vendor relationships.

Directories: Global businesses must leverage resources cost-effectively. Directories are a key component of identifying and utilizing resources. No technology area is more vital to the collaboration of business teams or the integration of business applications. X.500 provides the fundamental specification for corporate and global directories. HP is investing heavily to ensure that our products and solutions leverage the X.500 standard for personal messaging and application messaging applications.

HP will extend the usage of the Lightweight Directory Access Protocol (LDAP) to ensure synchronization with, as well as access to, other applications and enterprise directories. This will enable our customers to leverage their investment in legacy directories, such as NDS, when deploying new applications. OpenMail, as the backbone messaging technology, can provide replication services to local directories supporting business units and/or applications.

Government and telecom suppliers have announced intentions to provide X.500 services in concert with certificate authority services. HP will work closely with these service providers to deliver complete solutions. This will support our customers in deploying secure global solutions rapidly. This means that our customers will be able to leverage those services with minimal short-term investments and realize significant long-term payback.

Management: The explosion in messaging volume over the next five years requires a messaging architecture that balances security, availability, and performance. As large organizations expand their internal networks, they will face the following challenges:

☞ Security—Growth of intranets puts a strain on network management budgets. HP's secure messaging platform allows transfer of message traffic to the Internet. This outsourcing of bandwidth will greatly reduce internal network management costs.

☞ Server Consolidation—EMO's client/server approach to messaging pioneered high performance through user consolidation to a few, large platforms. With fewer servers, there is inherently less network traffic, limited replication requirements, and lower administration costs. Messaging becomes a bounded solution with fixed costs that can be easily outsourced. HP will work closely with service providers to help them develop strategies for e-mail, workgroup services, and application messaging outsourcing strategies.

☞ Low-cost Management—HP has developed a wide range of management tools that integrate directly to HP's OpenView IT/Operations management platform. HP will continue to invest in management technologies and assist customers to create lights-out data center environments. Our vision is to deliver a monitored, self-sustaining messaging environment that guarantees message delivery regardless of individual system failures. Over time, business will be able to outsource increasing amounts of server administration while continuing to deliver privacy and security to corporate users (see Fig. 13.18).

Messaging and Network Investments

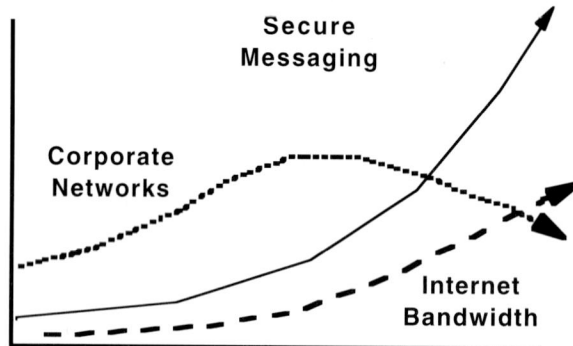

Fig. 13.18 As secure messaging and Internet bandwidth develop, corporate network investments decrease

13.4.3 Conclusion

The objectives of business are to improve process efficiency, individual performance, and customer satisfaction. The demand for flexibility will move integrated business applications towards a strong process model and supporting messaging technologies. By improving personal and business collaboration, we will provide our customers with new opportunities for growth and profit. By providing messaging services at the lowest cost, we enable our customers to free their corporate resources to build customer value.

HP's secure messaging platforms and flexible process integration tools will provide business with the means to bind closely with suppliers and customers.

By providing scalable solutions and Internet-secure communications, HP enables IT to reduce investment in corporate network infrastructures. The combination yields a comprehensive solution for business collaboration over the Internet (see Fig. 13.19).

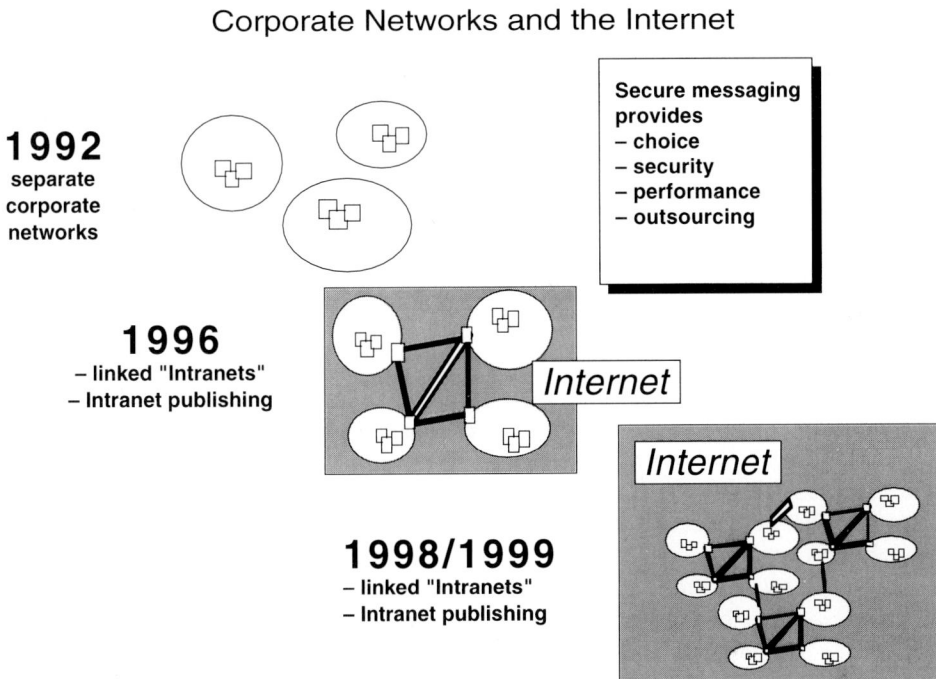

Fig. 13.19 Internet evolution as a secure business resource

BIOGRAPHY

Raul Mujica is Marketing Manager for Hewlett-Packard's Administration Flow business. He has been in the information technology industry for eight years driving collaborative computing projects such as data warehousing, messaging, workflow, and Internet marketing. As a Product Marketing & Planning Manager, Raul has defined and developed businesses for Hewlett-Packard's Intelligent Warehouse, OpenMail, AdminFlow, and Internet Marketing Framework. As a Technical Consulting Manager, Raul and his teams have enabled many large customer implementations. A broad range of opportunities, close customer interaction, and the collaboration of talented colleagues at Hewlett-Packard and the industry have placed Raul in a good position to continue to develop profitable businesses that advance the competitiveness of Hewlett-Packard's customers.

Introduction to Chapter 14

Oracle is the last chapter in this section because they are the newest entry into the groupware market. Oracle InterOffice can be seen as the fruit of many years of development. Oracle's perspective reflects their history as a database vendor, their core strength, technology, and business. Oracle has the advantage of entering the market late and being able to develop directly for the Internet.

Oracle maintains that there are two distinct types of computing. The first is the desktop-based single purpose application. The second type is universal access to information. This environment is Web-centric, and Oracle has architected InterOffice for it unlike the other groupware vendors who have had to retrofit their LAN-based software to take advantage of the Internet and intranets.

InterOffice is closely integrated with the Oracle 7 database server. This brings me to discuss the architectures for most commercial groupware products. Although many of them started out with a messaging architecture, most have been converted to a hybrid (messaging-database) architecture or moved to a database architecture. Although products like Notes do not have an underlying relational database, they are more focused on unstructured information (which comprises about 90 percent of all the information in the world today) managed by a database. Oracle contends that collaborative information, like the information for sales force automation, is unstructured, but account information, product purchase information, buying patterns, etc,. is structured.

Oracle sees Groupware as a second generation application (e-mail being the first) that allows the communication of information but not a pattern or process for that communication. This seems problematic in light of workflow, BPR, and re-engineering efforts over the last several years, which used groupware tools to not only communicate, coordinate, and collaborate, but also to optimize collaborative processes. Oracle claims that the second generation groupware allows users to automate collaborative processes and communications.

Oracle's third generation solution uses a discussion database and a reporting and escalation strategy based on database triggers set to defined field limits. Again, this is focused on audit trails, reporting, and accountability. While accountability is important, groupware can also be interactive. Oracle's focus on the database look-up model ignores a large class of groupware.

The next section in this chapter focuses on database management and groupware—a worthy topic. Oracle claims that 80 percent of a workers time is spent documenting or communicating business processes against goals. If only this were true, we would be much more productive. The figures I have heard from the MIT study on productivity, detailed in Scott Morton's book The Corporation of the 1990s, *shows that our business environment is very complex and we no longer do most tasks alone, requiring others to work with us. Morton focuses on communication and collaboration as ways to be more productive. Metrics are nice, but you have to establish the relationship first and make sure it works before concentrating on the metrics.*

Oracle claims a symbiosis between groupware and database technology. I agree that these two technologies can enhance each other. Oracle chose a database architecture as the way to integrate the group function, allowing users to communicate and share information by connecting to shared databases. InterOffice seems to offer collaborative functions similar to other groupware vendors.

The Divergence of Two Worlds: Oracle's InterOffice

John Bartlett
Oracle Corporation

As a collaborative application designed to address business problems in heterogeneous environments, Oracle InterOffice is worth understanding well, and this chapter will help you do that. But its suite of functionalities also reflects every major trend in the larger world of business computing. It is in this role—as a microcosm of the present world of information management and an indication of how its future will evolve—that Oracle InterOffice is most interesting.

What is visible in information management right now is the divergence of two economic worlds based on entirely different philosophies regarding the role of information in business. The first world is the world of single-purpose applications and functional islands of information. The islands have expanded over time, to be sure, from single machines, to small LANs, to entire companies. But they are still islands. The software in this world is not Internet-aware, and traces its genealogy back through LANs, to master/slave architectures, and to the dim past of paper-based information management. What is surprising about a lot of groupware, which is putatively concerned with sharing information, is that it can be found firmly in this tradition of proprietary data and application types.

The second world is the world of economics based increasingly on electronic information. It rests on the assertion that to be truly useful, information must be accessible using any appliance in any computing environment anywhere on earth. This world is characterized by multipurpose groupware applications that are architected from the beginning to exploit the expanding capabilities of the

Internet. Oracle InterOffice is an example of a collaborative application designed for this kind of environment.

The Internet is one major area of difference between Oracle InterOffice and many other groupware applications. Oracle focused on the Internet as an enabling technology for information-sharing early in the evolution of InterOffice. Hence, the application has Internet functionality that is designed from the beginning rather than added on later. But this is not the only area of difference.

Oracle InterOffice's scalability mirrors that of the Oracle7 relational data-base management system, with which it is closely integrated. Unlike some groupware applications, which were conceived as workgroup productivity tools, InterOffice can scale to the level of the entire enterprise.

Its functional openness is another difference. Some groupware has an impressive list of functionalities it can deliver to users in what are essentially dedicated environments. Oracle's focus on the need for universal access to information made the "dedicated environment" strategy impossible. Instead, InterOffice supports multiple computing appliances and environments, and has an interface that supports all standard Web-browsers.

The largest difference between InterOffice and other groupware, however, is undoubtedly the application's close integration with the Oracle7 database server. Because of this integration, it has the ability to incorporate structured data from a fully-evolved relational database management system into InterOffice's six basic functionalities: messaging, directory services, calendar and resource sched-uling, discussions, document management, and workflow facilities.

A good example of the benefits conferred by groupware that has this kind of access to structured database information is sales force automation. E-mail, scheduling, and other kinds of unstructured information are clearly important for this task. But information typically resident in databases—information on the purchase history of a given account, whether their buying patterns are sea-sonal, what their last order was, and so on—can help sales managers improve the productivity of their sales forces because it can give salespeople the precise data they need to focus their efforts on areas that will yield the greatest returns in any given season, product cycle, or geographic region.

This kind of application could also be integrated with information in inven-tory and MRP databases so that salespeople can not just sell a given product, but can also determine whether it is in inventory or, if not, when a likely delivery date would be.

14.1 THE EVOLUTION OF GROUPWARE

In a sense, groupware is just the latest step in the evolutionary trend of comput-ing environments away from small numbers of huge centralized CPUs accessed via terminals, and toward those in which large numbers of small dispersed CPUs predominate. In other words, groupware is an outgrowth of dispersion.

In both environments, the need to collaborate exists. Using electronic infor-mation to do so in the old master/slave world, however, was essentially impossible. True electronic collaboration was enabled first by the advent of local area networking, and then by applications that allowed the sharing of unstructured information in the form of documents and other files.

E-mail is the archetype of a kind of "first generation" groupware application. It allows the communication of information, but nothing else. What's missing from an e-mail-based groupware solution is any idea of establishing a pattern or process for that communication, and therefore being able to automate it as much as possible.

That is essentially what groupware in the "second generation" does, if only in a dedicated environment; allows users to build a process around various kinds of communications to enable the automation of collaborative business processes.

A good example showing the difference between first- and second-generation groupware might be an auto company that has produced a car with which owners are having some troubles. A first-generation response to this situation could have the customer service manager send an e-mail to everybody on the design and manufacturing team for that model car, asking them to tell the manager everything they know about what this problem might be. Possibly, this would be effective in the long run, but it has some horrendous inefficiencies built into it, including the need for lots of time to send the e-mail, gather the responses, evaluate them, re-send to those who didn't respond the first time, re-gather and re-evaluate the second round of responses, and finally write some kind of report and funnel it back to the design or manufacturing operations, depending on what kind of problem it turns out to be.

A second-generation response might automate some of this process, include some relatively inflexible reporting mechanisms going from one predetermined point to another, be auditable, and occur all within a dedicated environment.

Still missing is the integration of structured database information and the use of the Internet. What would be really useful in this situation is a "third-generation" groupware solution with the ability to integrate the application functionality on top of an existing database that would be easily accessible over the Internet. Using this kind of system, the customer service manager would be able to set up a process for automatically reporting customer complaints into a simple discussion database and making that database available over the Internet to any company site, no matter how geographically remote. The company could have user-defined limits for an acceptable number of complaints of any given type, and a well-designed process for ensuring that once the number was exceeded, a report would be automatically generated and sent to all of the relevant decision-makers. It would be easy to ensure that nothing would slip through the cracks, and that complaints would generate a usable audit-trail.

14.2 GROUPWARE AND DATABASE MANAGEMENT

The market forces driving the development of this kind of collaborative solution are based on the fact that in today's business environment, nearly 80 percent of the average worker's time is spent documenting or communicating business processes and progress against goals. Clearly, the automation of these activities—which requires groupware—would yield such potentially enormous gains in employee productivity that the groupware opportunity as such requires little explanation.

But why has Oracle, a company known for its relational database management systems, tools, applications suites, and related technologies entered this market? The reason is that seen without labels, groupware and database management technology are very closely related. Each is concerned with managing information. Each relies on access to shared data. Each depends on networking technology to realize the fullest range of its potential benefits. And most important, each is the other's missing piece.

Groupware alone cannot give users all of the information they require. And databases alone cannot automate business processes. But working together, groupware and database technology provide a complete solution: They automate communications and business processes, thereby offloading a tremendous amount of drudgery from employees within the corporation; they help facilitate consistent interactions with business partners outside the corporation; and they integrate structured, mission-critical data from central database engines into the world of groupware, where it can be used to streamline the response of the company to changes within the organization, changing market conditions, or a changing competitive environment.

Because of this close symbiosis between groupware and database technology, Oracle regards collaborative applications as an extension of its core competencies in information management and universal information access. This approach is consistent with Oracle's database focus because in InterOffice, users communicate and share information by connection to shared databases—either single databases residing on central servers in a single location, or replicated databases residing on multiple networked servers in different locations.

14.3 INSIDE INTEROFFICE

InterOffice is a third-generation collaborative application developed by Oracle to include six collaborative functions: messaging, directory services, calendar and resource scheduling, discussions, document management, and workflow facilities, all accessible through a single user interface. The design of the product expresses the desire of Oracle's developers to include two fundamental capacities. First, the ability to build core collaborative applications, both inside the corporation and on external networks such as the Internet, wireless networks, and corporate intranets. (These applications can be built using tools from Oracle like Developer/2000 or Oracle Power Browser Objects, or any tool supporting MAPI, OCX/ActiveX, OLE, ODMA, C/C++, or the World Wide Web.) Second, the ability to extend existing applications with new collaborative capabilities.

The first generation of Oracle InterOffice was an e-mail product called Oracle Mail that was developed in 1989. This was successful as an e-mail product for Oracle environments, but as the workgroup environment began to evolve, it became clear that users were demanding more than just e-mail. They wanted an application that would let them communicate on an ad hoc basis when that was appropriate, but that would also let them begin to codify business processes whenever possible.

In order to meet that need, Oracle released a collaborative application called Oracle Office that included scheduling and coordination functionality. This product was also well received in the Oracle community, but it remained somewhat limited. With the sudden emergence in the mid 1990s of the Internet and World Wide Web as a business tool, the development team responsible for Oracle InterOffice looked into the future and made a guess about the role this network of networks would play in the information management strategies of commercial enterprises.

What they saw was that the World Wide Web had effected a fundamental change in the dynamics of the application software market. Instead of being tied to computing environments defined by operating systems and chip architectures, users of the Web had a standardized environment in which they could access any and all information that could be translated into a Web-browsable format. Web browsers, themselves cheap and stable software platforms, would be important new information gateways in the coming information environment.

What Oracle did was extend the existing elements of Oracle Office and engineer new ones, all with the capabilities of the Web in mind. The end result is a collaborative application that uses the Internet: 1) as a way to extend its functionality across a private intranet; and 2) as an enabler for incorporating partners and customers into established corporate business processes.

They also incorporated it into the Oracle Universal Server, which is designed to allow the management of every type of digital data, including relational data, text, images, sound, and video. The role of Oracle InterOffice in the Universal Server is to serve as the fundamental link between the world of documents and the world of relational data. With Oracle InterOffice integrated on top of the Oracle7 database, the database can be used to manage not just data, but also messages, the library, workflow rules, and schedules.

14.3.1 The InterOffice Messaging Server

The Oracle InterOffice Messaging Server has four elements or components that give it its functionality: Messaging, Directory Services, Calendar/Scheduling, Messaging Interoperability.

14.3.1.1 Messaging

Architecturally, the Oracle InterOffice Messaging Server is a database agent, which makes the parallel processing and database management capabilities of Oracle7 available to it. This gives users a range of functionality that would otherwise have to be written into the application.

Once a message is composed, it becomes part of the database. As a result, messages can take advantage of full recovery capabilities, and can be managed in much the same way as relational data. The message server stores aliases, distribution lists, attachments, folders, and other information about the messages in database tables, and users can employ standard database indexing techniques to retrieve specific messages or folders.

The Messaging Server is client/server by design, and allows the client portion to run on PCs, Macintoshes, UNIX systems, Motif systems, character mode terminals, and extremely thin clients like the Network Computer or the Philips Screenphone. Because every client connects to the messaging element of the InterOffice server, the designers have optimized the management of a very large number of simultaneous connections. Those connections are made among Oracle7 databases using SQL*Net, the Oracle networking protocol, or to the outside world using mail gateways.

Another outgrowth of the Messaging Server's integration with Oracle7 is that all InterOffice messaging traffic is covered by the database's security features, including encryption and the same single-system log-on authentication used by other InterOffice collaboration services.

The message client connects directly to the database server. Other messaging functions, however, are implemented as a set of server processes that are given access to the messaging database. For example, the postmaster server process updates inbox folders when new mail is received and the gateway server process forwards mail to other mail systems when necessary, including Internet mail using SMTP/MIME, MHS, X400, and IBM PROFS. This architecture allows InterOffice to scale easily, and to handle wide variations in the amount of mail being processed. When large volumes of messages coincide, additional postmaster processes or gateways can be initiated. Oracle7's inherent linear scalability enables this approach, ensuring that adding more postmasters and gateways will in fact provide enough additional processing capacity—up to thousands of users on a single processor.

The essential messaging server processes included in Oracle InterOffice's Messaging component are described below.

The Guardian Process serves two functions. First, it is the controlling process for all other server processes. In order to start or stop any process, the Messaging Server administration tool (OOMGR) sends a request to the Guardian Process. Second, it is the "process manager" that continually checks the database to make sure that enough processes are running to handle the existing load.

The Postman Process is responsible for managing all of the details necessary to get message and information traffic—including traffic destined for gateways to other messaging systems—through the Messaging Server.

The Directory Synchronization Process is responsible for a crucial bit of electronic housekeeping necessary when other directories need to be updated outside of Oracle InterOffice: synchronizing the InterOffice's Messaging Server directory with the directory of the outside messaging system. Also involved in this process is a foreign messaging system translator, which works with the directory synchronization process to translate directories between the messaging systems.

The Replicator Process is also involved in the tasks of directory synchronization. It propagates directory and configuration information throughout the

InterOffice Server community, communicating with other replicator processes to synchronize system and directory information.

The Scheduler Process is a backup process for handling some scheduling requests. In some cases, an InterOffice client may want to try to schedule a meeting with a user on a remote node, but the client will be unable to connect directly to that node using SQL*Net. The Scheduler Process is designed for this situation, stepping in to handle the scheduling itself in a way that is transparent to the user.

The Alarm Process handles the routing of warning messages to any Inter-Office user logged into an operating system account.

The Statistics Process collects basic information about system utilization. It will gather data on such indicators as message delivery times and use of data-base space and store it in the database, where other processes use it to enforce space quotas, determine network efficiency, and diagnose problems.

The Monitor Process is one of these processes, the first-line manager of sys-tem utilization in InterOffice. It analyzes the flow of messages, the use of database space, and the status of all relevant processes to ensure that users get the level of service they require. It also looks for any configuration mistakes or missing objects and references. Not just reactive, the Monitor Process has the intelligence to keep tabs on potential problems, suggest preventive steps, and send reports to either one user or a designated distribution list.

The Garbage Collector Process frees up disk space by removing such elec-tronic detritus as deleted mail messages, scheduler events, and the internal records of the Replicator Process.

The InterOffice Messaging Server also contains a set of messaging objects that help define the capabilities of the system. These objects include: private and public folders, which help users organize and manage access to messaging infor-mation; private and public aliases, which allow addressing shortcuts; private and public distribution lists, for streamlining communications among members of various groups; private and public templates that let users request informa-tion from each other in a structured way; and attachment types that let users attach files to mail messages in various ways.

14.3.1.2 Directory Service

InterOffice supports a number of directory services, including Directory Classes, Filter Operations, Viewing Operations, Editing Operations, and Copy-ing Operations.

Directory Classes include: public and private aliases, public and private distribution lists, domain, people, equipment, gateway, location, organization, role, and room.

The Filter Operations supported by InterOffice include "starts with," "con-tains," and "exactly matches." Using these two services, users can implement the third: Viewing Operations. For example, a user can choose to view all people whose last name starts with the letter "J." The list of searchable attributes sup-ported by InterOffice is listed in Figs. 14.1 and 14.2.

Directory classes	Searchable directory class attributes
Alias-private	Name Email Adress Description
Alias-public	Name Email Adress Description
Distribution Lists-private	Name Description
Distribution Lists-public	Name Description
Domain	Name Description

Fig. 14.1

Directory classes	Searchable directory class attributes
People	Name Last name First name User name Phone Organization Role Manager
Equipment	Name Description Location
Gateway	Name Description
Location	Name Description
Organization	Name Description Cost center
Role	Name Description
Room	Name Description Location

Fig. 14.2

The Editing Operations allow users to create, edit, and delete private aliases and distribution lists.

The Copying Operations allow users to locally store directory data by configuring a personal MAPI address book and then copying the server data to that book.

Also included among Directory Services is the Directory Synchronization Server, which is the element responsible for automatically synchronizing information between a Messaging Server directory and an external data source. Directory Synchronization allows users to import and export the following Directory Classes: public aliases, equipment, locations, organizations, people, public distribution lists, roles, and rooms.

Another function of directory synchronization is to combine information from different sources in a single location. Using directory synchronization, a person could therefore collect in a single document or report user mail addresses from a foreign mail system, employee records from a personnel database, and office location information from a facilities database.

14.3.1.3 Calendar/Scheduling

Anyone who has ever had to set up a meeting with more than three people knows that calendar/scheduling capabilities are a groupware function that yields substantial benefits. Oracle InterOffice provides a full set of scheduling features, including daily, weekly, and monthly views of a given schedule, with to-do lists and notes for each, and the ability to print whatever view is necessary. It also allows users to employ the monthly calendar as a quick overview, and to click on any day of the month to retrieve the more-detailed daily view for any given day.

The range of event operations supported by InterOffice is complete. To create a new event, they can open a new event window that allows the creation of all event-types within InterOffice. To open an event, the user opens a window similar to the new event window, and can edit various parts of the event, depending on which type it is. Users can delete events, or move them to other dates and times. They can also use InterOffice to write a given event text into the file system. The event bodies support the RTF format and attachments.

Other functions, referred to as "preferences," let users customize InterOffice to fit their particular work-styles. The user interface, date and time, calendar, scheduler, alarms, and security can all be modified to suit individual requirements. Calendar access can be very finely graduated, from no view, to view free, to view all with other privileges, including: create events, modify/delete events, accept invitations, modify/decline invitations, send invitations, reschedule/cancel meetings, and owner access.

A set of capabilities designed to make using the calendar/scheduler easier has also been developed. The View Free Time capability lets people trying to set up a mutually agreeable time for a meeting concentrate only on periods not yet scheduled. The Attendee Status lets users check to see who has been invited to a meeting, and among those who has responded. InterOffice lets users open calendars on one node and across many. It lets users save predefined searches. And it supports off-line access to scheduling information.

14.3.1.4 Messaging Interoperability

In the ideal messaging environment, people would be able to communicate with each other regardless of the technological barriers imposed by differences in mail systems. The concept of interoperability seems inherent in the very idea of sending messages back and forth, particularly in today's world of balkanized communications systems.

Oracle InterOffice has addressed the problem of interoperability by providing gateways to virtually any major mail system, and to fax systems. The mail systems include: SMTP/MIME, X.400, MHS, and PROFS/OfficeVision VM. The intent in supporting these various messaging environments is to allow InterOffice users to be able to communicate transparently with parts of their own enterprise that may use one of these different systems, and with users or resources outside the confines of the enterprise.

14.3.2 SMTP/MIME

What the SMTP/MIME gateway enables is transparent linkage of Inter-Office users to the "sendmail" utility included with all major variants of UNIX. Why Oracle made this one of the first gateways provided with InterOffice is because communications support for SMTP/MIME means that Oracle Inter-Office users can exchange messages and files with other Internet users across what amounts to the most extensive e-mail network in the world.

The SMTP/MIME gateway is able to handle messages with an unlimited number of binary attachments, which means that sending documents, spreadsheets, graphical images, audio files, video clips, or other objects can be accomplished with no additional steps. To be able to handle such attachments, all the recipient has to have is a MIME-aware mail-reader.

In many environments, gateways impose their own technological limitations on what can be successfully sent to a given addressee. Oracle InterOffice has minimized that problem by allowing the administrator to create addressing rules for public aliases. These rules allow the automatic routing of a given kind of message through the appropriate gateway.

This gateway provides another kind of functionality in that it allows the connection of isolated pockets of SMTP/MIME users over non-TCP/IP networks, as well as over the SMTP-compatible TCP/IP networks for which it was designed. Again, it is the addressing capabilities of InterOffice that make this kind of routing seamless and transparent.

Once a gateway to a different messaging environment is in place, the tendency has been for organizations to begin to rely on it in much the same way they have come to rely on local area networks or other communications facilities. Gateways must therefore provide high availability, which means they must be easy to manage. Oracle has made it possible to manage the SMTP/MIME gateway centrally or remotely from a single administrator's interface.

14.3.3 X.400

The importance of the X.400 messaging system is obvious. It is the International Standards Organization's standard for exchanging messages among store-and-foreward mail systems.

Building this gateway for InterOffice, therefore, gives InterOffice users a fair amount of leverage: direct access to X.400 systems and indirect access to the many private e-mail systems that also have X.400 gateways. This includes: support for messaging products from vendors such as Hewlett-Packard, IBM, and Digital Equipment Corporation; gateways from vendors such as Soft*Switch, and Boston Software Works; and services from providers such as AT&T, MCI International, and various other national PTTs.

The X.400 standard was defined to include both P1 (envelope) and P2 (contents) data. Making this distinction allows X.400 clients to send not just simple messages, but also word processing, spreadsheet, or graphics documents as binary attachments. InterOffice supports both the P1 and P2 features of X.400.

Two other features of Oracle InterOffice's X.400 gateway are intended to increase the efficiency of communicating with X.400 clients. The first is the ability to use the Private Alias feature to set up simple address names for X.400 clients frequently contacted, allowing InterOffice users to address large numbers of X.400 users with simple addresses. Or InterOffice users can add X.400 clients to the system with native InterOffice addresses, and who therefore act as "foreign" users (from another system) who are visible from the InterOffice directory.

The Oracle InterOffice X.400 gateway conforms to all of the following standards (based on ISOCOR ISOPLEX):

- Australian GOSIP version 2.0
- CCITT (1988/1992) X.200, X.208, X.209, X.217, X.218, X.219, X.227, X.228, X.229, X.400, X.402, X.407, X.413, X.419, X.420
- ENV 41 201 (CEN/CENELEC A/3211)
- ENV 41 202 (CEPT A/311)
- FIPS 146-1 (U.S. GOSIP versions 1 and 2)
- ISO 7498, 8072, 8073, 8073/AD2, 8348/AD1, 8348/AD2, 8473, 8802-2, 8880, 9542
- NIST SP 500-183
- Nordic GOSIP
- POSIX
- TOP 3.0
- U.K GOSIP version 4.0

14.3.4 MHS

NetWare MHS is Novell's messaging engine for smaller, less-complex networks in workgroups, departments, or small to mid-size companies. It is a store-and-forward system for enabling multiple front-end applications to communicate over LANs and wide-area networks.

The primary purpose of the MHS gateway is to allow the exchange of messages between an InterOffice server and MHS-compatible mail servers. Messaging in the MHS environment itself is based on a set of APIs called the NetWare Standard Message Format (SMF), which are supported both by NetWare MHS and NetWare Global Messaging.

The gateway between MHS and InterOffice runs in the MHS environment and accesses the InterOffice Server over SQL*Net.

In a situation where two InterOffice nodes are connected using an MHS backbone, the gateway designers have made transparent communication possible by implementing a "tunneling" mechanism in the gateway. Any InterOffice message features that cannot be mapped to MHS messages are encapsulated by the tunneling mechanism as a body part of the MHS message at the originating InterOffice node. When the message reaches its destination, the mechanism interprets encapsulated elements and inserts them back into the InterOffice message. If multiple MHS networks have to be accessed from one InterOffice Server, multiple MHS gateways can be defined on that server.

The biggest advantage of Novell's adherence to the SMF message format is that the nature of the application originating a message is invisible to the gateway and will not affect its operation.

14.3.5 PROFS/OfficeVision VM

With the huge installed base of IBM PROFS and OfficeVision VM users, a gateway to these environments is a logical requirement for any company seeking connectivity to legacy mail systems. Oracle InterOffice's PROFS/OfficeVision/VM Gateway uses the NJE protocol over IBM SNA to connect InterOffice and OfficeVision/VM users. With this gateway, IBM users see InterOffice users as if they were on a remote OfficeVision/VM node. Using InterOffice's foreign directory entries, administrators can merge OfficeVision/VM user addresses into InterOffice's directory services. These foreign addresses appear to Oracle users as InterOffice IDs, and can be automatically replicated to other InterOffice domains.

Once connectivity is established, the next task is the exchange of messages and documents. The gateway allows the synchronization of directory information, which enables communication with other e-mail services or even other information resources such as personnel databases. Oracle's PROFS/OfficeVision/VM Gateway is architected to make message exchange as transparent as possible. The gateway gives messages destined for IBM environments OfficeVision/VM-style headers and footers, while messages destined for Oracle environments appear in native InterOffice format. The gateway also preserves such message attributes as return receipts and included messages.

For documents, the gateway allows IBM users to send to InterOffice users DCF and RFT documents, PC ASCII or binary files, and fixed- or variable-length CMS record files. CMS sendfile users can send CMS notes, VM/CMS EBCDIC text files, and native CMS files. When InterOffice users send to OfficeVision/VM users messages with binary or text-file attachments, they are received as documents. Conversions between EBCDIC and ASCII are performed automatically wherever necessary.

The gateway also provides functionality for other kinds of groupware tasks. Meeting invitations exchanged across these two environments always appear in a familiar format. Notifications from OfficeVision/VM appear in InterOffice users' inboxes as InterOffice Meeting Invitations, which they can accept or decline in the usual manner. If accepted, the meeting appears automatically in the user's calendar and the recipient is given the option of replying by e-mail to the person sending the invitation. Invitations going the other way appear to OfficeVision/VM users as native meeting notifications.

The gateway software itself runs on dedicated PC-compatible systems with no special host software. One gateway can manage multiple InterOffice servers or OfficeVision/VM nodes.

14.3.6 Microsoft Mail

Communications with Microsoft Mail is a straightforward process using the InterOffice SMTP Gateway.

14.3.7 cc:Mail

Messaging connectivity to cc:Mail can be accomplished by sending messages first to MHS using the MHS Gateway, and then to cc:Mail via the cc:Mail/MHS gateway available from cc:Mail. An operational MHS installation is necessary to be able to access cc:Mail users.

Lotus Notes

The Lotus cc:Mail Gateway is now in the process of being ported to OS/2 by cc:Mail in order to integrate it with Lotus Notes. Once that gateway is available as part of the Lotus Notes server, then the gateway program can be used to exchange SMF message files with the MHS gateway on one side and Lotus Notes on the other.

14.3.8 Fax

In addition to messaging environments, InterOffice provides a gateway for communication via fax.

The fax gateway works with the Oracle Siren fax server to transmit all outbound faxes in the TIF class F format. The outbound gateway generates an ASCII file for the message body and submits it—together with all TEXT, PS, and TIFF attachments—directly to the fax server.

Using these facilities, faxes are sent by InterOffice as e-mail messages, and received as incoming e-mail messages in the InterOffice inbox. InterOffice and the Siren server support as many modems as the number of serial ports available on the server machine for simultaneous inbound and outbound fax calls. Users normally map the outbound modem pool to individual phone lines. The inbound pool can be mapped either from individual lines or from DID trunks. To avoid contention, users usually configure disjoint outbound and inbound modem pools. Of course, any modem can be configured to send or receive faxes.

For security and cost-control, the InterOffice fax gateway implements two levels of access control: fax-gateway access privilege and long-distance dialing privilege.

14.4 THE INTEROFFICE DOCUMENT MANAGEMENT SERVER

Document management has become one of the most significant challenges facing businesses today because of the confluence of two trends and the existence of a technological shortcoming. The two trends are the growing importance of documents stored in electronic form and the increasing ease with which ever-more-complex types of such documents can be created.

Electronic documents have become more important to businesses worldwide simply because of the proliferation of software for word processing, spreadsheet, desktop publishing, and other applications. Businesses have embraced these personal productivity tools and employees have responded by using them to create information critical to the success of the enterprise. These unstructured documents are now a fundamental element of most organizations' information infrastructure. They contain an important record of a company's past. They serve as the medium through which much of its most significant present business is conducted. And they are the forum in which future plans are conceived, modified, approved, and implemented. In fact, these unstructured documents constitute what is in effect a highly detailed blueprint for any given organization's value proposition and way of doing business.

The second trend, the growing ease with which complex documents are created, is evident in the proliferation of personal productivity tools and the steady inclusion in them of richer and richer data types. Electronic documents used to just contain text and data. Now they can contain text, data, graphics, audio clips, video clips, computer animation—any kind of information that can be expressed in digital form.

The net result of these two trends is that at the same time unstructured information is becoming more important to the typical organization, the efficiency and capability of those creating these documents is steadily rising.

Which brings us to the technological shortcoming. Given the importance of unstructured documents, it is surprising that they have so far been so difficult to manage. The ideal solution would make is possible to manage unstructured documentary information with the same degree of reliability, security, integrity, and availability commonly afforded the structured data in relational databases. Oracle has addressed this issue with the creation of the InterOffice Document Management Server, a server that brings six different kinds of functionality to bear on the challenges of managing unstructured documents: organizing, sharing, loading, general operations, storing, and searching. The following section examines each of these in detail.

14.4.1 Organizing Documents

InterOffice accomplishes the organization of documents through a number of mechanisms, the most basic of which is the division of a document into a content element, which is unstructured, and structured attributes that are used as "card-catalog" information to help categorize and retrieve the document. Examples of attributes include a document's owner, title, and the date it was created. These attributes are always stored in the database.

14.4.2 Document Classes

InterOffice uses document classes to help organize documents according to their unstructured content. A typical set of document classes might include Specification, Schedule, and Budget. Because InterOffice segregates this unstructured content from structured attributes, different attributes can be assigned to each document class. The result is a great deal of flexibility in organizing and managing documents.

Consider the three document classes listed above. If a company has a project to reengineer a product component, it will use Specification, Schedule, and Budget to help organize the documents associated with this project. Specifications are tied to a given project and a given component. Schedules are also tied to a project. They are not, however, tied to the component; they are tied to a version of the component instead. Budgets are tied to cost centers that may very well contain more than one project, and have a list of approvers associated directly to them. What each class shares are the attributes title, creator, and creation date. A model of this situation in the Document Management Server would therefore look like this:

☞ Specification (title, creator, creation date, project, component)

☞ Schedule (title, creator, creation date, project, version)

☞ Budget (title, creator, creation date, cost center, approvers)

14.4.3 Inheritance

This kind of flexibility is clearly desirable for organizing the many different kinds of documents associated with major business undertakings. Assigning such attributes every time, however, could become burdensome. InterOffice includes a functionality called inheritance that obviates the need to do this. As its name implies, inheritance allows users to create a class that has inherited all the attributes of another class "plus" specific others. Using inheritance, the above attributes could be modeled like this:

☞ Specification (title, creator, creation date, project, component)

☞ Schedule (version)

☞ Budget (cost center, approvers)

A class is the "subclass" of the class above it and inherits all of the attributes of that class.

14.4.4 Folders

Folders are another organizing functionality offered by InterOffice. By now, this metaphor is a familiar one for allowing users to organize large numbers of documents according to whatever criteria suit them best. InterOffice's folders, however, offer standard folder capabilities plus one other necessitated by the need to use and modify documents in a shared environment.

In most systems, when a document is put into a folder, it exists only in that folder. In a shared environment, however, a document may belong in several different folders, or may be used by different users in different ways. InterOffice accommodates these differences by using a "foldering by reference" scheme. In foldering by reference, the document is never actually put into a folder; the folder merely refers to it. This distinction is transparent to the user, but it allows the document to reside and be managed in one environment, yet be accessible to users in many other environments. All folders that refer to a given document refer to the same version of it, which ensures that if a document is changed by any user, the changed document will be available to all users in all folders that refer to it.

14.4.5 Virtual Folders

A variation on this foldering scheme is InterOffice's ability to create "virtual folders." A virtual folder is a search definition that is saved as a persistent object. Using virtual folders, users can search across all of the information contained in other folders without being limited by that hierarchy. They can also place new documents in a searchable structure without having to physically go through the process of putting them into all of the existing folders to which they might be relevant. Virtual folders also convey benefits when an attribute of a document is changed. For example, if a draft document is approved, the change in its attribute from "draft" to "approved" can cause it to automatically appear in the folder containing all approved company policies.

14.4.6 Versioning

In order to control and manage changes made to documents, InterOffice uses a "check-in/check-out" protocol. If a user wants to change a document, he or she checks it out for revision. The user then has a "lock" on that document, which allows other users to read it but not make any changes. After making the changes, the user checks the document back in, which saves the changes and makes a new version of the document. The next time a user wants to read that document, they get the new version by default. This does not mean, however, that the previous version is destroyed. InterOffice does not write over the old version when it creates a new version of a document. All of the revisions are saved and are available to be read or edited whenever they are requested.

14.4.7 Searching with ConText

Of course, the main reason for organizing documents in the first place is so information can be easily searched for and retrieved. Oracle InterOffice is unusual in this area because it is integrated with a software facility—called the ConText Option for Oracle7 Release 7.3—which is designed to let users manage, search, and retrieve unstructured text information using tools evolved to manage the structured data in relational databases.

The business, scientific, and technical information that exists in text-form represents a huge potential competitive advantage to business. This advantage has been unachievable in the past, however, because the tools for managing text either have not existed, or have existed in the form of small proprietary applications incapable of dealing with the scale of the text-management challenge in large organizations.

Oracle started to look at the problem of text management several years ago, and developed a strategy of creating a solution that would allow users to incorporate unstructured text information directly into an Oracle database. That solution is accessible through Oracle InterOffice, which gives InterOffice an unusually comprehensive text management capability.

The intent of Oracle's strategy is to allow companies to reap twin benefits. End-users can manage text using the industrial-strength tools of a fully evolved database environment. And IS can easily put text into that database, therefore avoiding the training, development, and administrative costs associated with supporting a wholly separate development environment for text management.

The benefits of this kind of text management fall into four categories:

☞ First, it is fully integrated into the Oracle7 Release 7.3 relational database, so users can manage unstructured text with the same scalability, security, integrity, fault-tolerance, and administrative ease that they have always had for structured nontext data. The Context Option is not an application; it incorporates text at the data-repository level. As a result, text incorporated in the database can be used by existing and new Oracle7 applications, and text-management can occur in robust, parallel, distributed, multiprocessor architectures.

☞ Second, it allows the management of text in a standards-based environment. The ConText Option supports retrieval using standard SQL, and treats text data as a peer to relational data. Developers can therefore use standard tools to define queries combining structured data with intelligent text searches. In other words, all of the familiar features of the database environment remain the same, but the scope of what kind of searches a user can do in it has been expanded significantly.

☞ Third, the ConText Option provides a suite of text retrieval facilities that allow users to intelligently manage amounts of text in the terabyte range. It includes all of the standard text retrieval capabilities, including multi-lingual stemming, proximity searches, relevance ranking, Boolean logic, term weighting, thesaurus support, soundex/fuzzy matches, and stop lists. In addition to these capabilities, however, the ConText Option includes facilities based on sophisticated linguistic analytic software that has been under development for 15 years. Using this software, the ConText Option can execute a range of complex tasks. It can reduce large documents to summaries conveying the main points of the original without human intervention. It can provide even smaller summaries that give users the gist of large documents. It can automatically classify documents in user-defined trees of subject-areas based on the preponderance of text in a given document on a given subject, and can then route the document to the appropriate group of people. And it supports user-defined dictionaries of jargon or terminology specific to particular areas.

☞ The fourth benefit is an extensible framework designed to protect customers' investments. The ConText Option allows the integration of new languages, formats, and specialized search engines within the same unified relational database. It now supports full-text retrieval in English, French, German, Spanish, Dutch, Italian, and Japanese. As new multilingual capabilities are developed they also can be incorporated.

Applications using the ConText Option include: news and multimedia archiving at a major television network, delivery of World Wide Web information for a Canadian government ministry, back-article archiving for a large U.S. information services provider, help desk and customer support for several large Oracle customers, and the archiving of research text, commercial and government intelligence, library information, and legal information.

14.4.8 Loading Documents

For documents to be manageable by the Document Management Server, they must first be loaded into Oracle InterOffice. This can be accomplished in two ways. For existing documents, the Import Document command will load it as the contents of a newly created document. For creating or editing a new document, using the New Document command launches an appropriate application. If that application has been extended with Document Management Server functionality, then the user can load the document directly from it. If not, the user can save the document to an operating system file and then use the Load Document command.

Users can also employ the Open Document Management Architecture (ODMA) standards to load documents. If they choose this option, saving files from their desktop application will automatically and transparently store the contents in the Document Management Server.

14.4.8.1 Document Storage

The information used to store and retrieve documents is always kept in the Document Management Server. The documents themselves, however, can be stored either in this environment or in another file system. When stored in the database, the document's contents are stored in a series of rows in a "content table" inside the Oracle7 server. When stored in a file system, a document's contents are stored in a file within an operating system directory. Storing a document in the Document Management Server enables its protection against unauthorized modification and viewing using the Oracle7 database architecture.

14.4.9 Document Size and Format

Any kind of electronically stored data that can be manipulated by a computer can be a document in InterOffice—a word processing document, an image, a sound, or a video. And it can be any size, from a short note to a long video clip.

InterOffice also places few restrictions on which applications can be used to create documents. Formats can be application-specific (e.g., Word for Windows) or non-application-specific (e.g., TIFF, PostScript). Operations in the Document Management Server can be either format-specific or independent of format. Adding a document to a folder can be done regardless of the document's format. But indexing text in a document for the purposes of content-based retrieval is format-dependent.

The system administrator is responsible for setting up the proper associations between the format of a document and the applications to be launched for viewing or editing that format, which is all that is required for the Document Management Server to "support" a given format.

14.4.10 Document Sharing

The default assumption for access control in the Document Management Server is that all objects are public and can be seen by every user unless the objects are made explicitly private. If the administrator does not want an object to be public, he or she can use the server's access control mechanism to specify the privileges of the document's owner, people in the same organization or role as the owner, and other specific users, organizations, or roles.

The Document Management Server also defines the concept of a "workspace" to which every document belongs. All documents created in a workspace share the same access control characteristics as the workspace itself. This is a convenience intended to reduce security problems. If a user creates a new document while reading documents in a "highly confidential" workspace, then the Document Management Server will assign that new document to the same "highly confidential" workspace.

The interaction of access control privileges and the workspace concept means that whether a user can perform an operation on a given object depends on two things: whether the controls on the object itself allow that user to perform the operation; and whether the characteristics of that object's workspace allow that user to perform the operation.

14.4.11 Document Management Operations

The previous information has been provided to interpret the range of functionalities provided by Oracle InterOffice's Document Management Server. Following is a simple listing of the various operations defined for this software element.

Folder Operations

☞ Create new folder

☞ Open folder

☞ Delete folder. This operation will act as a "soft delete," allowing the folder to be retrieved in the event of an accidental deletion.

☞ Copy folder. The copy operation copies both the folder and its contents, including any subfolders.

☞ Create a shortcut to a folder. This creates a reference to an existing folder.

☞ Move folder

☞ View/edit folder attributes

☞ Rename folder

☞ Sort based on attribute values

Document Operations

☞ Create new document. The attributes of the document must be specified as part of the creation process.

☞ Open document

☞ Delete document. Another "soft delete."

☞ Copy document. This results in a new independent document object within the Document Management Server based on the contents and attributes of an existing document.

☞ Create a shortcut to a document. Similar to copy document, except a new independent document object is not created. A reference to an existing document is created, though, so that changes in either the document object or the reference will be reflected in both places.

☞ Move document

☞ View/edit document attributes

☞ Rename document

☞ Sort based on attributes. This sort can include which documents a user has checked out.

☞ Import a document from file system. Using this operation, a user can retrieve a document without putting a "lock" on it.

☞ Check in a document

☞ Lock a document (without checking it out)

☞ Check out a document

☞ Unlock a document

☞ Edit a document in place. This is similar to the check out function except that when the document is checked back in, it replaces the previous version of the document so that it cannot be retrieved.

☞ Print a document

☞ Mark a document read/unread

☞ Forward/send a document. This allows a user to send a message to another user with the document as an attachment.

☞ Reply to a document

☞ Index a document. This function is required so that the "content indexing engine" becomes aware of the document.

☞ Remove document index

14.5 THE INTEROFFICE WORKFLOW SERVER

In one sense, workflow is the essential capability of collaborative application software because it enables the automation of business processes that is the largest potential benefit conferred by groupware. It unifies messaging, document management, calendar/scheduling, and directory services components into a coherent workspace where standard workflow tasks can be performed with little or no human intervention. And if a given workflow solution is flexible enough, it also affords a workspace where the requirements of unusual or unique workflows can be easily accommodated.

Oracle has developed a Workflow Server that is integrated with the other functionalities of InterOffice in order to provide such a workspace. It has three essential characteristics. People can use the Workflow Server to design ad hoc process workflow; it is not locked into certain patterns. People can use it to monitor workflows in progress and to modify a given process while it is running. And, people can use it to integrate documents and data from the InterOffice environment and from other Oracle enterprise databases. The Workflow client software is integrated seamlessly into the InterOffice client software, so that all of the functionality of InterOffice is available to someone constructing workflows.

Building Workflows

Workflows are built in InterOffice using a process that is less like programming than it is like GUI Rapid Application Development. A single window, which holds the workflow process painter, is used for the purpose of workflow design. The window is divided into two "panes": one that displays the workflow under construction, and one that displays a tree-view of available Item Types, Messages, or Lookup Types that can be used in the workflow.

A tabbed toolbox visible in the workflow window contains four tabs, one for each class of activity (process, notification, PL/SQL function, and Java function). In addition to the "from-scratch" tool that is used to build each new process, function, or notification activity, the tabs also contain completed processes, functions, or notifications that can be plugged into designed workflows where necessary to speed the development time. An example is an "AND" function for conditional branching: "If user X can approve this stage of the project AND approve budget, then forward to Department Y."

Any activity that a user builds can also be made to appear as an icon in the toolbox. This allows users to build what are essentially activity "objects," reusable components that can be dragged from the toolbox and dropped into a workflow under construction.

14.5.1 Integration with Messaging

The fundamental capability for workflow is messaging. InterOffice's Workflow Server is integrated with its messaging component to allow the delivery of workflow items to any user accessible via InterOffice.

In Oracle's approach to messaging, the importance of how the work item presented to the user looks is paramount. Oracle believes it is important that the user should be able to intuitively know what to do with the work item—which may have arrived as either a notification or an e-mail message. The same is true for any of the supporting items attached to that work item.

InterOffice therefore uses E-Forms for viewing work items, which clearly display the message, source, expected response, any comments, and a space for routing the message to other users.

When someone constructs a message object using Oracle Workflow, they can associate a standard MAPI-Forms-compatible message-class with that object (which can also be used with the Web client). InterOffice allows users to assign message-classes in two ways: by creating their own message-classes and associated form-views; or by using a predefined library of message-classes for common message-types.

14.5.2 Integration with the Document Management Server

The InterOffice Workflow Server does not have its own generalized document store, which makes tight integration with the Document Management Server an absolute requirement. This solution allows the Workflow Server to be smaller and more focused, and removes the possibility of document management conflicts that could arise from having two document repositories operating in the same collaborative application. Oracle has chosen to bind the two together in two ways.

When defining a workflow, the workflow designer is able to see and select any document in the Document Management Server as the item to be routed by the workflow. The reason is that the workflow engine treats documents as first-class workflow item types, which are peers to all other workflow item types in the system. The workflow designer is able to see and have access to all of the attributes of a given document, and can therefore base routing decisions on those attributes.

When defining a workflow notification message, users can specify particular documents as attachments to the message or as the message itself. Recipients of these messages can view or modify the attached documents as they wish before responding to the notification.

14.5.3 Integration with Other Services

Oracle has used essentially the same approach to solving the problem of how to provide directory and calendar/scheduling services to workflow designers. Both of these functions already exist within InterOffice, so the task was not to create them again, but to provide access to the existing functionality.

For directory services, access is provided using a button labeled "Directory," in the notification activity property sheet of the Workflow Server. The button makes the InterOffice directory available to the workflow designer for routing message objects. It also can be used by third-party developers to link the Workflow Server to their own directories. And at run-time, the button can be used by people on the workflow route to perform ad hoc routing, adding other workers to the list of recipients wherever necessary.

For calendar/scheduling services, workflow designers are able to specify whether to communicate the notification due date to the schedule of the recipient. If yes, the workflow engine automatically invokes the calendar/scheduling API and adds the entry to the recipient's calendar, and informs the schedule to notify the user periodically as the due date approaches. When the task is completed, the notification engine lets the schedule know, and the item is closed.

Integration with Navigator

InterOffice has a software facility called the Navigator that allows users to browse various parts of the application. One of those parts contains workflow "stores," connections to an Oracle database that has the Workflow Server installed on it. Once the Navigator has connected to the store, it displays two folders in the part of the window devoted to file trees: a process definitions folder and a process instances folder. By giving users access to both of these folders, InterOffice makes it possible for them to see either how a given workflow was designed, or how a workflow process is working at the moment, or how workflow processes have worked in the past.

One inherent difficulty in building complex workflows is the amount of time it takes to do so. One way to reduce that cycle time is to make it possible to reuse processes built for one workflow in other workflows. InterOffice uses a feature called a "template" to enable this kind of leverage. Templates can be as complex as a patient-tracking process for a large hospital group, where the documents might have to go to literally any department in the hospital. Or they can be as simple as sending a document from one requester to one approver.

We've already seen how users can monitor the status of a workflow in progress. In addition, InterOffice's monitoring viewer lets users with the correct privileges not just see the workflow, but dynamically change it to fit changing requirements. Using this tool, workers are able to add new activity nodes and new transition edges, and specify whether such modifications affect only the present instance or all instances of this process class.

InterOffice includes facilities for workflow administrators as well. It includes a set of commonly used reports on workflow processes, both active and completed, and a facility that allows users to generate their own custom reports. Administrators can assign specific privileges to specific users, ranging from those who can only view to those who can modify a workflow. InterOffice also allows organizations to set up different classes of administrators, e.g., those who can restart a workflow process and those who are allowed to kill an entire workflow.

The design of its workflow engine is likely to have a large impact on the overall performance of a collaborative application for two reasons. Workflows interact with potentially every element of the application, so all of its interactions must be efficient. And workflows use information contained in other elements (e.g., directories, documents), so the application designer has to choose whether to use existing facilities for managing that information or to build new ones just for the workflow engine. Oracle InterOffice has chosen the first strategy and concentrated on integrating the Workflow Server with the servers responsible for managing the information it requires as seamlessly as possible.

14.5.4 System Management and Administration

All collaborative applications have tools to help administrators set up and maintain them. These are nontrivial tasks, and the tools to do them tend in general to be sophisticated pieces of software. Oracle InterOffice provides three tools to help administrators do their jobs: the Oracle InterOffice Manager Utility (OOMGR), monitoring reports, and server logs.

The Oracle InterOffice Manager Utility is actually a set of tools accessible through the same GUI used by other Oracle applications. Using this utility, system administrators can do all of the basic configuration and troubleshooting tasks necessary to keep InterOffice up and running, providing communications and information-access services across the enterprise. These tasks include:

☞ Configuring the machines that handle the flow of messages and information for InterOffice;

☞ Populating the system with people, organizations, locations, and equipment so that users can send messages, schedule meetings, and reserve resources;

☞ Developing the correct configuration of server processes so the InterOffice can handle all of an organization's messaging and information traffic;

☞ Responding to the system operation reports that alert administrators to potential system problems; and

☞ Monitoring reports.

OOMGR contains a set of tests and reports that administrators can use to monitor the health and efficiency of the InterOffice system. These tests and reports are presented in a list, from which the administrator chooses the ones necessary and how often they should be run. Results are sent automatically to the user or group of users designated by the administrator. If the tests uncover situations that could lead to problems in the future, OOMGR has the ability to suggest actions that could help the administrator either avoid those problems or solve them once they have occurred.

Server Logs

In addition to specified reports, InterOffice makes the actual logs of server activity available to administrators. These logs provide another way to get a regular view of system activity, information that can help round out the overall picture of how various server functions and processes are working.

14.5.5 The Oracle Universal Server

Oracle has based InterOffice on the Oracle7 Server, which means that a copy of the Oracle7 Server is included in every copy of Oracle InterOffice. This inclusion allows other InterOffice elements to be built on top of—and to take advantage of—the Oracle7 Server's various functionalities. It also means that Oracle's SQL*Net networking product is the foundation for all of InterOffice's communications tasks.

An example of how InterOffice employs Oracle7's capabilities is when the Messaging Server uses the shared pool of pre-processed SQL statements provided by Oracle7. This shared pool is a buffer that allows repeated requests to be executed many times faster than if each statement had to be reprocessed. In messaging, where many users share a common application, the shared pool effectively "hides" the multifunction nature of InterOffice's messaging application, and lets it perform with the efficiency of a single-function program.

Another example is the Messaging Server's use of Oracle7's Multithreaded Server (MTS) feature, which allows a single "dispatcher" process to manage up to 50 TCP/IP connections. When messaging loads on the server increase, the dispatcher has the ability to forward some of the work to an idle shared server process. The purpose of this kind of load-balancing is to ensure that each time a messaging client accesses the database, an unloaded server is assigned to service the request. With its multithreaded capability, each of the Messaging Server's dispatchers and shared servers can be on a separate processor, so the load can be scaled across every available processor of a multiprocessor system. In order to match the amount of processing power to the demands placed on it, MTS can also start additional servers as the load increases, and shut them down when it decreases.

InterOffice's use of SQL*Net for its many communications tasks offers users of collaborative applications some basic advantages.

First, it gives InterOffice users transparent connectivity across a range of different protocols and platforms. SQL*Net supports a large number of transport protocols, including TCP/IP, Novell SPX/IPX, IBM LU6.2, DECnet, OSI, and others. Its MultiProtocol Interchange option allows the transparent bridging of protocols, thus facilitating communications in typically heterogeneous networking environments. The purpose of such connectivity is to allow the Oracle7 Server to interoperate across different systems, operating environments, and networks so that InterOffice users can essentially access data no matter where it resides.

Second, SQL*Net works with Oracle7 to provide a shared-server architecture. This architecture offers some efficiencies in handling large numbers of clients. SQL*Net also allows multiple connection routes from clients to a given data source, which gives it the capacity to balance networking loading when necessary and provide fail-over capabilities.

Finally, SQL*Net helps deliver network fault tolerance. During setup, it can detect component failures on a given pathway and switch to an alternate route, and it detects abnormal client terminations without automatically locking the server, which can increase the average availability of server resources.

14.6 OPEN PROGRAMMING INTERFACES

Almost by definition, collaborative applications must be standardized and use standardized means of accessing information in other environments. Just as it is difficult for people speaking different languages to collaborate, so it is hard for computer systems with no shared means of communication to work together. Oracle InterOffice relies on a number of strategies to allow for electronic cooperation. It supports standards in messaging, directory services, and collaboration. It supports standard Web browsers such as Oracle Power Browser and Netscape Navigator. It supports portable interfaces for Windows 3.1, Macintosh, Motif, and character-mode terminals.

None of these, however, allow for the integration of InterOffice with existing enterprise systems. To do that, InterOffice must support a series of open programming interfaces, including core standards like HTML/HTTP, MAPI, OLE, OCX/ActiveX and C++, and ODMA. It also supports interfaces like CMC1.0, POP3, IMAP4, XAPIA-CSA, SMTP/MIME, and LDAP.

The HTML/HTTP programmatic interface in InterOffice's Web Connector offers users a standardized way to integrate InterOffice services into Internet-based applications. As such, it allows users to access global information resources in an application environment that is familiar to them.

The Web Connector contains components that provide mail, scheduling, directory, and document management services to users over the Internet (Fig. 14.3). This architecture helps the Web Connector preserve some important benefits of Internet applications.

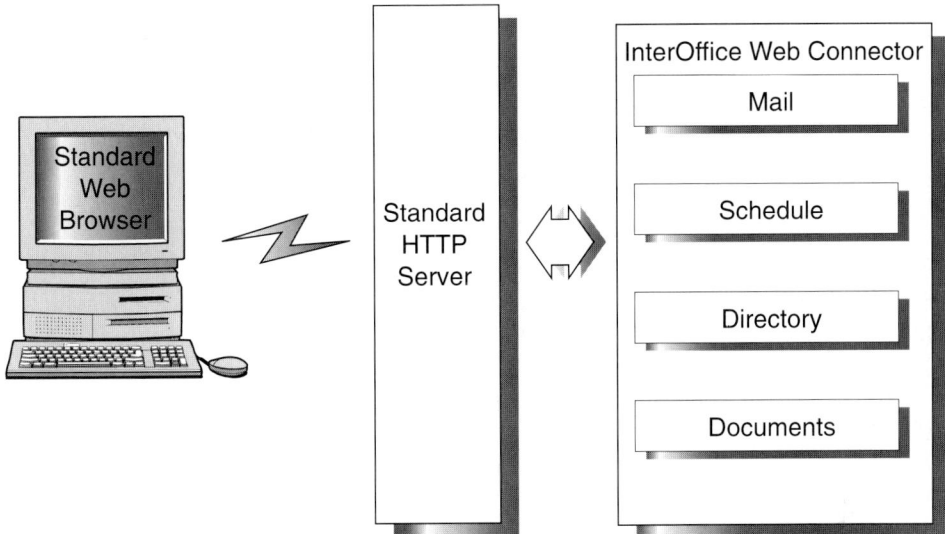

Fig. 14.3

It provides a generic client that is able to execute any Web application. It preserves the ability of Web browsers to access any Web application anywhere on the Internet, and it ensures application portability because Web browsers run on many different client platforms.

The Web means access to global information resources and a new way to communicate inside and outside an organization, both of which make the HTML/HTTP interface important. Microsoft's Messaging Application Programming Interface (MAPI) is important because it has become an industry standard that is used by many applications. With MAPI, an application does not need to understand the messaging protocols necessary to reach a given environment; it just has to know how to make use of the standardized API.

MAPI has grown in popularity for a number of reasons. It has an object-oriented interface. It offers a clean division between front-end and back-end functions, and it has an infrastructure designed to support both servers and clients. This makes it a good fit with InterOffice and other such client/server collaborative applications.

MAPI is used to create, manipulate, transfer, and store messages. It supports three kinds of so-called "service providers": message store providers, which offer facilities for storing, organizing, and recalling messages; address book providers, which offer addressing and distribution facilities; and messaging transport providers, which actually move the messages among clients.

Messaging applications communicate with these service providers through MAPI's client and service provider interfaces. This division allows the selection of services by MAPI from different providers to be entirely transparent to the client application, which sees only one combined address-book container for the actual routing of messages.

14.6.1 OLE Automation

InterOffice supports Microsoft's Object-Linking Environment (OLE) because it is an industry standard for object-oriented application programming interfaces. One of the advantages conferred by Oracle's support of OLE is the ability of programmers employing Oracle development tools (such as Oracle Developer/2000) to seamlessly access parts of the InterOffice server through OLE automation.

OLE Automation is, together with all of the other APIs supported, a good illustration of Oracle's strategy with InterOffice. Oracle decided to support high-level object oriented APIs and visual APIs so that people can integrate the collaborative functionality of InterOffice with existing applications, and create new collaborative applications that also integrate well with InterOffice.

In the Microsoft Windows environment in particular, OLE automation and OCX/ActiveX provide excellent ways to do that. The APIs provide access to libraries and the user interface component, ensuring that InterOffice applications will interoperate well with other applications that are also written to the OLE API.

Oracle InterOffice's support of these open standards and interfaces is the foundation of two of its important characteristics. First is its ability to be a good "plug and play" citizen even in diverse and complicated computing environments. ODMA, SMTP/MIME, POP3, and other such standards allow InterOffice to seamlessly interoperate with a wide range of other desktops and application environments. Second is its ability to help users extend the functionality of existing systems, or program collaborative functionality into new systems—MAPI, HTML/HTTP, OLE, OCX/ActiveX, and other are examples of this kind of interface.

The combination of the two in InterOffice is simply an assurance that this collaborative application really can collaborate in many different environments and can extend existing software into applications with whatever groupware capabilities are necessary.

14.7 INTEROFFICE AND INTRANETS

The rapid evolution of groupware applications like Oracle InterOffice has been a response to a set of business pressures that have put a premium on collaboration, no matter what technological or geographic obstacles might exist in a given situation. Another response to those pressures has been the rise of corporate intranets, Web sites designed largely as either operational clearinghouses for routine internal business processes or as inexpensive and easy-to-deploy alternatives to classic wide-area networking systems.

Given the tremendous investment companies have made in heavy-duty transaction-processing and decision-support systems based on client/server architectures, the swift move to Web technology seems puzzling. But Web technology offers strong advantages that companies discovered they could use to help them build useful intranets. Many of those advantages have to do with lowering the overall cost of operations, decision-support, and collaboration.

The Web has open, non-proprietary standards developed by standards bodies and not controlled by any single vendor or coalition of vendors.

The Web also enables a lower cost of application deployment and management because of a simple arithmetic truth. When client/server applications are installed or upgraded in large companies, it has to happen on hundreds or even thousands of desktop systems. Intranet applications, which are based on simpler technologies, are also generally installed on only a few tens of servers. The administration and management advantages are obvious.

Web-based information systems tend to partake of the Web's underlying philosophy of self-reliance and independence. Applications, therefore, tend to be extremely easy to use, tending toward the creation of a "self-service" information systems model, as opposed to the "experts-only" model of having to rely on IS departments to find, compile, or interpret the information a person needs.

An outgrowth of this "self-service" ethos is a radical reduction in training and support costs. Once users learn how to use a Web browser, they have most of the capability they need to access any of the information resources on the Web.

All of the above advantages point to what could be the biggest benefit of all: universal access to information and applications. Given the computers and servers already connected to various LANs and WANs, most corporations have the majority of the building blocks necessary for an intranet already in place. Information and applications already on the Web are accessible using standard Web browsers. So the two pieces still missing are: a link between Web applications and powerful database management systems; and the kind of groupware that is designed from the beginning not to just coexist with the Web, but to bring its specific advantages of standardization, simplicity, self-service, and universal access to corporate intranets.

Initially, the two responses—collaborative applications and the Web—paralleled each other. But as each has evolved, these parallel approaches to helping people work together across many different barriers have begun to converge. Oracle InterOffice sits at their point of intersection, a collaborative application designed from the beginning to take advantage of the Web's standardized environment and ease of use. It is a fundamental piece of Oracle's intranet strategy, which is itself a crucial element of Oracle's overall product strategy for information management.

Reduced to its essential element, Oracle's intranet strategy is to bring commercially meaningful transactions to the Web. The company has other intranet goals as well: to make the Web more extensible, to make the Web more manageable, and to enrich the data types accessible on the Web by enabling real-time multimedia that includes streamed video, dynamically classified text, spatial data visualization, maps on the fly, and so on. But these goals are all secondary to the essential task of forging a link between Web-based applications and the vast stores of data that exist in industrial-strength database management systems. Once that link is created, the Web will provide more than just a novel way to access and present static data; it will support on-line business transactions, provide advanced tools for managing data, and be the crucial enabling technology for worldwide collaborative applications.

Oracle believes corporate intranets provide new benefits in operations, decision-making, and collaboration, which, when they are all realized, will provide a solid business-systems foundation for electronic commerce using the Web. Oracle has products that play a role in each of these areas, but as we will see, InterOffice can play a role in all of them.

Operations

Streamlining everyday business operations is a goal toward which corporations have been working for years. The essential strategy in this area has been to automate paper-based, labor-intensive tasks. This strategy is now being facilitated by the appearance of the Web, a standardized and effective way to connect dispersed business functions, and groupware designed to actually implement whatever tasks are necessary for the degree of automation desired.

Oracle's strategy in operations rests on the Oracle Universal Server, the WebServer 2.0, the Designer/2000 WebServer Generator, Oracle Web applications, and InterOffice.

The Universal Server is a database management engine based on Oracle7 that has the ability to integrate other elements (called "Options") designed to manage specific data-types: video, text, spatial data, OLAP, and the Web.

The WebServer 2.0 is Oracle's intranet applications platform. It is based on an element called the Web Request Broker, which uses a cartridge architecture for building applications, which can then be plugged into the WebServer to extend its functionality. All server cartridges are run as individual processes, providing true asynchronous independent processing and guaranteeing that third-party cartridges will not affect the rest of the system.

The next release of the Designer/2000 WebServer Generator lets developers do two things central to Oracle's Web strategy. First, they can build Web applications that contain complex transaction processing. Such applications will be deployable using the transactional capabilities of the Web Request Broker. Second, and they can create transaction processing applications with dynamic HTML documents who will be able to query—as well as insert, update, and delete data from—the database.

Oracle Web Applications are new applications built expressly for the Web's inherent suitability for untrained, unsupported users. Oracle believes Web applications must exploit the easy-to-use features of browsers so that users require little or no training to use these applications.

Decision Support

All of the software elements that play a role in operations—the Universal Server, WebServer 2.0, Designer/2000 Web Generator, and Web applications—play a role in decision support as well. The challenge in decision support, as it is in so many other aspects of business, is getting access to exactly the right information for the task at hand. How to enable access to exactly the right information—but not swamp people with so much data that it's impossible to find anything—is the balancing act corporations have to accomplish every business day. Tools necessary to make information easily accessible follow:

14.8 DATABASE SERVERS THAT MANAGE MANY DIFFERENT DATA TYPES

1. Online analytical processing software, which allows users to create applications that either include these different data types (e.g., graphics, video, maps and charts, analytical data staged for multidimensional analysis), or that present data in ways that are easier to interpret or comprehend;
2. And collaborative applications built to use the power of the Web.

14.9 COLLABORATION

In the pre-intranet world, transaction processing and decision support were paramount among the various types of business computing. With the advent of intranets, however, the classical collaborative processing functions of messaging, scheduling, document management, and workflow have come into their own, and are now considered to be every bit as mission-critical as these other functions.

The need for powerful collaboration software is where the capabilities of Oracle InterOffice resemble most closely the opportunities of the intranet environment. Intranets today are essentially mechanisms for facilitating the internal use of shared information. InterOffice's document management capabilities, combined with the Internet, allows the creation of a system for sharing documents that is based on Internet standards and functionality, and is available through a standardized, easy-to-use Web browser. As companies add the ability to do transaction processing to their Web sites, then the intranet opportunity will expand significantly. A good example would be a large mail-order clothing store putting its catalog up on the Web. But instead of having it just be a static display of descriptive text and graphics, it could be dynamic, including facilities for querying the inventory and pricing tables in a back-end database and, in the not too distant future, facilities for actually making the purchase electronically.

14.10 ELECTRONIC COMMERCE

When a company has all of the infrastructure necessary for using intranets to streamline operations, support the decision-making process, and collaborate across disparate computing environments, then it is standing on the threshold of true electronic commerce. The only other necessary functions are an end-to-end solution for electronic payment, and strong security capabilities to safeguard financial and transactional records in an open network environment.

Many companies are working on the former challenge, including VISA and MasterCard with their Secure Electronic Transaction (SET) protocol. Creating such an end-to-end solution is not a trivial challenge, due largely to the fact that there are two elements to it: creating a viable payment-link between banks and merchants and creating a viable payment-link between merchants and customers. The bank-merchant link is relatively easy due to the relatively small numbers of merchants and banks who must commit to a software-based solution. The merchant-customer link is another story because to function, millions of customers would have to commit to the system. It is difficult to predict, but some industry-watchers believe we are within a couple of years of seeing the beginnings of such a system.

Oracle has a number of solutions for the latter challenge. In fact, one of the advantages of having intranet solutions integrated with fully evolved enterprise relational database management systems is that any financial records generated over the intranet are protected by the database's security features.

In the case of Oracle's Universal Server, confidentiality and integrity are based on the control over access provided by system privileges (e.g., the ability to create a table) and object privileges (e.g., the ability to update, delete, insert, or select from a specific object in the database). Privileges may be encapsulated into roles or transactions for ease of administration. Another means of managing access is provided by granular access controls, which help enforce "least privilege," a principle that ensures users receive the minimal privilege set they require to do their jobs. Data integrity is maintained through data consistency mechanisms. For example, one such mechanism provides that all parts of a transaction are committed or none are. Oracle's database servers can provide authentication through database-specific passwords, or through reliance on host or network authentication mechanisms such as Oracle Security Service or Kerberos.

If customers require still more database security for intranet applications, Oracle will offer the Oracle WebServer on a number of higher-assurance (B1 and B2) operating systems, including Sun's Trusted Solaris and Data General's DG/UX with DSO.

And finally, to secure data actually in transit from the user to the Oracle WebServer, and from the WebServer to Oracle7, Oracle is developing a security server that will issue digital certificates, enabling encrypted communications between Web browsers and servers over a corporate intranet or the Internet. From the user to the WebServer, security is based on open standards such as the Secure Sockets Layer (SSL), X.509, and LDAP, and will provide Certificate Authority capabilities. From the WebServer to the Oracle7 server, security is provided by the Oracle Advanced Networking Option, which uses industry standard encryption techniques (e.g., DES, and RSA Data Security's RC4 (128-bit) with MD5) to provide data confidentiality and integrity.

When these last two capabilities are finally in place, and companies have end-to-end payment solutions that work, together with security features that can protect valuable data on an intranet, then the creation of what Oracle calls "business-critical intranets" will be possible, and the age of electronic commerce will begin in earnest.

Oracle InterOffice should play a significant role in the arena of intranet-based electronic commerce. Because its combination of functionalities—messaging, document management, and workflow—enables users to combine Internet-based applications with sophisticated stores of data. InterOffice therefore serves as a kind of electronic "glue" to unify all of the processes that have to happen to make electronic commerce real.

14.11 ORACLE INTEROFFICE IN USE

InterOffice occupies a position in Oracle's overall product strategy as a pure expression of Oracle's fundamental mission: to make information of any kind accessible to people in any computing environment, any place in the world. The servers that Oracle builds manage the information. The tools allow its manipulation. The networking software makes it possible to move information wherever it's needed. But Oracle InterOffice is the "glue" whose specific functionalities—messaging, document management, workflow—bring that managed information into the collaborative world.

At the most basic level, then, Oracle views InterOffice as an enabling technology for making information accessible. But in today's environment, where users have to find what they want among terabytes or petabytes of data, the term "accessible" needs some qualification. In this world, any successful collaborative application cannot be the software equivalent of a blunt instrument. It cannot only make it possible for people to somehow "get to" vast stores of undifferentiated data. It has to allow users facing real-world challenges on tight deadlines to manage, find, manipulate, and transmit exactly the information they need.

Oracle's overall product strategy has been directed at this challenge since the company was started in 1977. The strategy's goals are to provide users with an information management environment in which they can manage, access, and write applications that use any type of data. Sitting at the core of that strategy is the Oracle Universal Server, which is the Oracle7 RDBMS with a set of extensions that allow the management of many different kinds of data: video, text, spatial data, OLAP, and the Web.

The Oracle Video Option, when used with a utility called the Oracle Video Server Web Plug-in, provides full-motion, full-screen streaming (not downloaded) video to intranet applications over corporate networks.

The Oracle ConText Option for text management has already been described in detail (see p. 473).

The Oracle Spatial Data Option allows spatial data to be stored, accessed, and manipulated in the Universal Server in the same manner as structured data. And all of this information can be converted into charts, graphs, and maps, and be made accessible to any Web browser across an intranet.

The Oracle OLAP Option lets users perform on-line analytical processing on data stored in data warehouses, RDBMSs, and legacy systems.

This architecture makes it possible to integrate special-purpose functionality into the Universal Server without the need for specialty servers like bitmap indexing servers, star schema servers, specialty Web servers, and so on.

Even sophisticated data management, however, is not enough for today's complex environments. Users need integrated tools that let them write universal applications that can incorporate many different data types. Using standard, open interfaces, Oracle's software lets users create applications for client/server access, of course, but also for Web access and messaging access. This is one of the unique advantages of having a collaborative application integrated on top of a sophisticated database engine. It not only allows messaging, document management, workflow, and the other classic functionalities. It also allows users to apply development tools and other utilities to integrate groupware functionalities into non-collaborative applications integrated with the database.

The standards on which the Universal Server are based include SQL, HTTP/HTML, ODBC, JAVA, and OLAPI, in addition to the standards supported by Oracle InterOffice (see p. 460). Open standards are implicit in the concept of systems for universal data management cooperating with collaborative applications. Oracle has shaped its product strategy to adhere to the standards that will make this cooperation possible. Oracle's overall approach to data access and management focuses power and functionality in the server, while leaving the client side with only minimal tasks to perform. This "thick server, thin client" strategy is evident throughout the Oracle product line, including Oracle InterOffice.

14.11.1 Case Study: The Oracle Corporate Repository (CR)

One example of how the "thick server" approach can be made to work in a sophisticated data-management application is the Oracle Corporate Repository. A kind of digital library, the Corporate Repository is an application that allows multiple methods of information organization, from strict hierarchies to more flexible ontological models. It also allows several different kinds of transactions, including view, download, e-mail, fax back, FTP transmission, and network print.

The application has two major purposes. The first is to help enterprises of all kinds deal with the demands of distributed information management. The heart of the system is the Oracle Universal Server, which serves as a centralized repository for both structured and unstructured information. Using this technology, the CR is not limited to character-based files. It can (and does) store and retrieve collateral, presentations, graphical images, self-launching multimedia demonstrations, code, and spreadsheets. If an information item can be stored electronically, it can be stored and retrieved from the Corporate Repository.

The second major purpose is to give organizations that rely on e-mail another model for information distribution. E-mail is a "push"-oriented strategy that sends information from multiple points to multiple points—a pattern that puts significant stresses on network capacity. Before the advent of the CR Oracle was, in the words of one observer, "an intensely religious e-mail culture"—a culture that ends up putting a significant strain on networking resources. Oracle wanted to move away from that to an "information on demand" strategy, where users who need information go out to a central repository and find it, and then use the functionality of the "thick server" repository to do what they need done.

An example of how these two scenarios work can be found in a sales representative with a mobile client and a 9600 baud modem who wants to send a batch of collateral material to a prospect. In the e-mail model, the representative would call up the central repository over phone lines, find what she wanted, download the files to her mobile client, and then use e-mail to send those files to the prospect—with every function having 9600 baud as the performance ceiling. In the Corporate Repository model, the representative would still use phone lines to contact the repository. But once she had found what she wanted, she could use the distribution logic in the database to send the files directly to the prospect, completely avoiding the download to her mobile client and using the high-bandwidth part of the network to accomplish the transfer.

The Corporate Repository that Oracle designed is distinguished by its accessibility to multiple clients, its organization and user model, its use of business rules, and its use of Oracle InterOffice as a foundation for its management and messaging functionality.

Users can access the Corporate Repository through multiple clients, including Web browsers, the Oracle Forms/GUI, Forms/character mode, and Oracle mobile agents.

The CR is organized into sources, which are analogous to Dewey Decimal System numbers in a library that group together books on a common subject. An example of a source in the Oracle CR would be "Sales and Marketing," in which all sales and marketing information items are stored. The next level down is the foldering construct of Oracle InterOffice, in which folders can contain other folders and individual files.

The overarching purpose of this kind of organization is to give people ownership and control of the information that is closest to them. To accomplish this goal, the CR has a user model in the shape of a pyramid. At the base of the pyramid is the Requestor Community, defined as anybody who requests information from the CR or, in other words, almost everybody. The job of the requestor community is to have access to the multiple client-types supported by the CR, to go online to get information, and to provide feedback. Just above the base of the pyramid is the Provider Community, whose job is to upload and maintain online information, and provide quality assurance for that information. At the apex of the pyramid is the Sponsor Community, whose job is to define the content of, access to, and structure of the Corporate Repository.

The business rules embedded in the structures of the Corporate Repository are designed to provide the structure, communications standards, and data integrity/consistency necessary in distributed enterprise environments. Examples of how this works include: the primary index of a folder requiring users to define expiration dates, rules about who can see the information inside that folder, rules defining who has maintenance privileges, rules ensuring indexing is completed before a folder is accepted, rules ensuring that the targeted users actually have the correct application-types to access and use a given kind of information, and rules on output ensuring, for example, that people will not indiscriminately copy and fax information covered by various copyright restrictions. All of these rules are inherent in the structure of the Corporate Repository, which eases the administration of this very large (9+ gigabytes and rising) database.

Oracle chose to build the Corporate Repository on top of Oracle InterOffice because InterOffice has a fully-evolved toolset for document management and messaging, two capabilities central to the usefulness of the Corporate Repository. The foldering construct already exists, as do facilities for doing document searches and contextual searches, an extensible architecture that can be used for rules-based manipulation of data, and facilities for storing large binary chunks of data.

The alternative to using an engine like Oracle InterOffice would be to store documents in a file system, which would place some severe limitations on the functionality available to users. Here are a few examples. The data store would be quite limited compared to the underlying capacity of Oracle7 used by InterOffice. The number of file attributes is also quite limited, perhaps only file size, owner, and primary path information. The number of attributes listable in a database, however, is essentially unlimited and could include such information as the document's owner, provider, sponsor, creation and expiration dates, format, language, and whether it is associated with multiple versions that include the original, textual version, PostScript version, compressed version, etc.

And of course, a file system will never provide a DBMSs facilities for multi-purposing of information, which allows you to provide a document once in the database, and make it available from there to multiple information mechanisms throughout the company and beyond. In the Corporate Repository, a document that Oracle first makes available to its sales force can then be made accessible to the public via a tunneling service to the World Wide Web. All of these information items, which are managed by functionalities built on Oracle InterOffice, can be distributed in a surprising number of ways—but only have to be administered in their centralized Corporate Repository once.

The Corporate Repository is a good demonstration of how Oracle InterOffice can play a role in the "thick server" part of the architecture, and allow a shift in an organization's information-distribution model. But what about the "thin client" side of things?

14.11.2 Case Study: The Oracle Network Computer

The Oracle Network Computer™ (NC™) provides a good example of how a thin client might work in a world of easily accessible thick servers. Oracle's NC is firmly in the mainstream of present thinking about network computing appliances. It is an extremely cheap computing engine that discards much of what defines the functionality of today's PCs, including leading-edge microprocessor technology, local disk space, large amounts of RAM, very large and sophisticated operating systems, and indivisible applications that can only offer users all of their capabilities, even if they are never employed.

Instead of including these costly and hard-to-manage features, the NC is a very thin client indeed. Its entire design is based on a fast, cheap processor; a lightweight OS kernel; limited application "componentware" or "applets" downloaded over high-bandwidth networks on an as-needed basis; and a modified version of Oracle InterOffice serving as its messaging interface to the outside world. This is not the multipurpose corporate PC to which users have grown accustomed; it is a limited, special-purpose machine that people can use to browse the Web and do lightweight word-processing, spreadsheet, and other basic office tasks.

The question is, why are people so excited about the Network Computer? The answers fall into two basic categories. The first is that, thanks to the development of some key enabling technologies, such a device is now possible. The second is that the NC holds the promise of drastically reducing not just the initial cost of personal computing, but also the surprisingly high ongoing cost of ownership entailed by large, fully capable PCs.

There are a number of technical developments that made the NC possible, but first among them without doubt is the World Wide Web. Before the Web existed, networks were relatively limited in bandwidth and extremely limited in the kinds of information they could practicably transmit. The Internet, the descendant of a collaboration between university research laboratories and the Defense Department called DARPAnet, had evolved to the point where widespread connectivity was possible. But the only thing available on it, in essence, was text. With the development of the Web, this text-based, character-mode world metamorphosed rapidly into an environment where graphics ruled, and interactions with remote information were vastly simplified through familiar (or at least understandable) graphical user interfaces.

Because of its graphical nature, the Web is also starting to drive improvements in network bandwidth and data-rate, both of which are important for another essential characteristic of the NC—the fact that it does not load 100 percent of a large application but use just 10 percent of it. The Network Computer is relying instead on a computing model in which the user downloads "componentware," essentially a piece of an application with precisely the functionality the user needs at that time, and is able to use that smaller "applet" to do whatever task is at hand.

The componentware model depends on platform-independent programming languages, of which Java is the most familiar. A high-level interpreted language that insulates applications from proprietary characteristics of OSs and hardware platforms, Java enables the creation of vast storehouses of small applications focused on specific computing challenges, all of which can run on a Network Computer with a Java engine, but none of which have to be stored there. The applets reside instead on a server, and are downloaded over the network when they are needed.

The net effects of this model on the industry are hard to predict, although some have said the ability to have platform-independent applications available over the Web will go a long way toward destroying the business model used by Microsoft—ever larger applications designed for particular operating environments—for the past 19 years. The effects on Network Computers are easier to see. It absolutely relieves them of the requirement to have lots of RAM and disk space to accommodate these large applications, and it poses some questions about the kind of system software that will be necessary to both run the computer and attract developers to write the applets necessary to make it viable in the marketplace.

That system software has been conceived as a lightweight kernel that provides the essential subset of the much larger set of services provided by conventional PC OSs. The reason is that the hardware environment in which it will be running does not have all of the resources necessary to make large operating systems viable, hence, the industry's consensus that the NC kernel must weigh in at 1 megabyte of memory or less. Oracle's NCOS is a microkernel that runs in considerably less that 1 MB.

Attracting developers to write for such an operating system is another challenge because most developers now rely on the kind of APIs that exist for UNIX, Windows, and the Macintosh's System. Oracle's NCOS has none of the big APIs of mainstream operating environments. Oracle has addressed the problem of providing such high-level functions through the use of class libraries of Java objects and other separate subsystems.

Finally, at the heart of the cost/functionality balance is the microprocessor. Larger PCs set the tone for the processor debate, and they of course are living proof of the inclinations of the hardware design community for leading edge (or even bleeding edge) CPUs. State of the art processors double in speed so fast, and the trade press trumpets these advances so loudly, that people forget that the same dynamic of increasing performance that defines the leading edge is at work on the trailing edge of the performance curve as well. The benefit to the Network Computer is that surprisingly good performance is available for really astonishing prices on that trailing edge. Oracle has specified Advanced RISC Machine's ARM 7500 as the CPU of the NC, a 32-bit RISC chip equivalent in performance to a 66 MHz Intel 486 that will cost a great deal less than $100.

14.11.3 Case Study: The Philips Screenphone

If the NC is a very thin client, then the Philips Screenphone is an ultra-thin client. Produced by Philips Home Services, a division of the Dutch electronics giant, the Screenphone was conceived as a way to bring the e-mail function back from the relatively rarefied world of computing to the world of consumer electronics and home telephony. In the future, the Screenphone is also intended to show how the model of using a cheap and very thin client works not just for e-mail, but for a whole range of online services.

In order to do this, Philips had to create an information appliance whose functionality was accessible with essentially no training whatsoever, and with no controls more complex than a push-button.

On the outside, the Screenphone looks like a standard telephone with some unusual extensions, including a 5" backlit liquid-crystal display (that can handle 16 lines of text, each 40 characters long) and a pull-out keyboard.

Internally, the differences are more pronounced. It includes an Intel 8086-compatible processor, a 2400-baud modem, and a special support processor dedicated to running a modified version of Oracle InterOffice, which serves as its messaging engine. InterOffice is integrated with a client/server-based software application called the Philips Home Services Delivery System (PHSDS), running on a network of three types of Sun UNIX machines: Terminal Controllers, which provide session connections and session-state information; Support Processors, which provide services to the sessions; and Interchanges, which provide messaging between Terminal Controllers and Support Processors. In Philip's scheme,

InterOffice sits on its own Support Processor, using SQL*Net to handle the messaging traffic between itself and the Interchange.

Paul Chapple, the media relations manager for Philips Home Services, describes how the company got into the Screenphone project through research that indicated there was a market for such a device. "People want reliable e-mail, and they don't want to have to buy a computer for it," he says. "It was originally intended to be a communications function. It just got taken over by the computer community." With the Screenphone, Philips hopes to start reversing that trend.

Chapple said Philips decided to go with Oracle "because Philips has a history of going to the experts in a given field when they need expertise, and Oracle is clearly committed to providing industry-leading messaging software."

Just creating the phone wasn't enough, however. Philips also wanted a large-scale test to see how amenable average telephone users were to adopting e-mail. The barriers to entry in the e-mail world are surprisingly high in the standard model. First, users must have or have access to a computer. Then they must contract with an e-mail service provider for the service. Finally, they have to take the time to learn how to exploit the e-mail software.

Philips wanted to use a different model and came up with an idea for removing the usual obstacles. They chose a population of 6,500 users in Garden City, New York, decided to give them Screenphones for free, and then monitored what happens to e-mail usage.

The project started in January of 1996 with a series of meetings at the Chamber of Commerce, Teacher's Association, hospitals, and every other community forum they could think of, telling people about the project and asking them to participate. They started shipping phones April 2, and by the beginning of June, the first of the online services—e-mail based on Oracle InterOffice—was ready. All users had to do was dial an 800 number to download the software, and they had e-mail, and it is a different approach to e-mail than those based on computers. To use e-mail on a computer, you have to first start the computer, and then boot up the messaging software—a considerable delay. On the Screenphone, e-mail is always up and ready to go. People can just work off-line to create their messages, dial the destination number, and send them off.

Chapple says the response has been good, with over 2,000 households (approximately one-third of the population with phones) choosing to download the InterOffice software. Of those, "nearly all" are active users, he says.

Philips believes that, ultimately, there will be three screens in the typical household: some kind of computing engine for productivity; a television for entertainment; and a Screenphone for communications. Oracle InterOffice plays a role in two of these screens today, and will perhaps offer functionality in all three in the very near future.

14.12 FUTURES

Structures like the Oracle Corporate Repository, and devices like the NC and the Screenphone, would not exist without a collaborative application like Oracle

InterOffice. The fact that they do exist suggests just how far the two economic worlds discussed at the beginning to this chapter—the world of single-purpose applications and functional islands of information, and the world of universally accessible electronic information—have diverged.

This second world, the world of potentially universal information access, is shaped by one trend that has already transformed the present information-management environment, and that will undoubtedly characterize its future as well.

This trend is the reduction in the number of interfaces people have to employ to manage and use the largest possible range of information.

The reduction starts with the underlying server engines. The world of specialized database servers for video, for bit-map indexing, for star-schema, or for specialty Web applications and data is suffering from its inherent complexity, interoperation and performance penalties, and management problems. The new world superseding it is one in which people access a single fully evolved database management engine that has the capability to manage any kind of information that can be encoded in electronic form: structured data, text, graphics, video, audio, spatial data, online analytical processing data, and others. The benefits of reducing the number of server engines necessary to fully manage all types of information are obvious, and include the possibility of closer application integration, simplified maintenance and administration, and quicker application development cycle-times.

The reduction in the number of interfaces continues with the expanding abilities of groupware to be integrated tightly with sophisticated database management systems. Integrated collaborative applications such as Oracle InterOffice allow the management of documents, the automation of business processes, and the creation of workflows that are all based not on static data downloaded for periodic updates, but on dynamic online data that ensures all such processes are using absolutely the most up-to-date information possible. Because they are tightly integrated with the underlying server, these applications, designed to support and automate typical ongoing business activities, can be used as a single familiar interface for database access. If the application is flexible enough to handle all of the tasks it is asked to perform, it will yield the benefits of reduced training costs and improved information access to everyone who becomes familiar with its capabilities.

A third example of how the number of interfaces is declining is the industry-wide focus on openness. During the period when the number of data types and specialty storage mechanisms were proliferating, the number of applications a person needed to know to manipulate and manage it all was also quite large. All developers agree this is an insupportable trend, and have labored for years to provide the standards necessary to make interoperation economically viable. InterOffice attacks the problem by supporting the data, messaging, networking, and application programming interfaces necessary to allow it to be used to access information wherever it might be. As a result, InterOffice can serve as a single interface for remote information access across all standard computing environments. The quest for openness and standardization has been a consistent industry trend for the last decade and a half. And no matter what other technological surprises may lie in wait, it will undoubtedly shape all of the industry's conceivable futures as well.

Finally, Oracle InterOffice demonstrates the trend in information management toward using the Internet as a stable, inexpensive, and standardized way to provide access to global stores of information and application functionality. Web browsers, which are cheap and stable software platforms, are already clearly important gateways to information. InterOffice's support of not just the letter of their specifications, but also the spirit of self-service and ease-of-use that characterizes the Web, is a reflection of how important the Internet will be in the coming environment of evolving collaborative applications.

In the future, Oracle believes this major trend toward fewer interfaces to the world of information available will no doubt continue. We are therefore committed to continuing to make it easier to develop new applications and extend existing applications to include sophisticated collaborative functionality. We will continue our efforts to support the widest possible range of data types, and to incorporate them smoothly into future collaborative functionalities. And of course, we will also continue our close integration of InterOffice into Web-based collaboration and development environments, which we believe supports the larger trend of the rapid transformation of all collaboration—and indeed most application-types—into software that is aware of, and relies on the functionality of, the Internet and World Wide Web.

A world of flexible and multifunctional servers. A world of Internet-based collaboration. A world where—no matter the platform, operating environment, networking system, or data type—there is universal, inexpensive, and simple access to information for everyone. That is the future Oracle sees in which all information management systems, and all collaborative applications, are going to have to work.

Introduction to Chapter 15

It would not be surprising if a chapter about groupware design would be technical, full of macros, code chunks, and object libraries. Although Geoffrey and David are systems designers and implementors, they understand that groupware is a socio-technical system and therefore managers and business users need information on the economic realities of groupware situations.

This chapter is full of case studies and examples about how collaborative technologies are used, and provides a management primer for many state-of-the-art practices for groupware development. They also look at how to determine which technology is appropriate in a given situation as well as how to leverage the technology for maximum return. For example, we accept that there are times when it is worthwhile to use videoconferencing, and other times when videoconferencing is excessive. The same is true with other groupware technologies; they should be used in the circumstances where their functionality adds value to the interaction. Videoconferencing adds value when meeting participants can see the same document, in real time, on a shared whiteboard, or where actually seeing someone's facial expression conveys information necessary for decision making. But using videoconferencing technology for routine calls, such as setting up a meeting or leaving a message, is not a good use of the technology. Still, we do like to use technology just for technology sake, but doing so often makes things worse rather than better (see Groupware Reengineering: The Human Side of Change, Chapter 17).

One of the major themes of this chapter is the relationship(s) between technology, business, and people processes. With this in mind, the authors talk about mindsets, *not only how they influence design, but how the designer's mindset filters what he/she sees of the world. Culture, the way a group of people thinks, is the result of a mindset. The authors believe there are four design mindsets: designing from understanding, designing according to form, designing using rules, and designing within a context. These mindsets, they argue, shape the groupware design process.*

Bock and Marca also examine design methods, i.e., examine the information transactions and then define the groups by the types or frequency of the transactions they handle. They also recommend a long assessment phase before designing a groupware system, as "understanding and trying to satisfy social and technical requirement generate a host of issues during a design effort."

This chapter contains case studies of successful groupware deployment. The heuristics derived from working with their clients parallel the 20 rules for groupware success in the introductory chapter of this book. Their ideas include: addressing deployment issues early in the process, getting everyone involved and participate in the design process, and making sure the system is customizable for the process, participants, management and administration, user interface, etc.

Examining social protocols is not something you would expect in a technical chapter. However, these protocols are as critical as the collaborative technologies that support interaction. Social protocols enable human-to-human interaction just as messaging protocols enable messages to be transferred from one system to another. They cast this process in the light of learning, and note that learning takes place when people work together (see Chapter 20 on Groupware, Knowledge Creation and Competitive Advantage) and then look at how groupware supports teams.

This chapter is filled with examples of the most common problems and issues encountered when implementing a collaborative system on any of the current infrastructures available. This chapter is excerpted from Designing Groupware, *by Geoffrey Bock and David Marca (McGraw-Hill 1995), which I recommend reading for more information on this subject.*

Designing Groupware: A Management Primer[1]

Geoffrey E. Bock

Geoffrey E. Bock
Patricia Seybold Group

David A. Marca
OpenProcess, Inc.

15.1 INTRODUCTION

Journey through the technical field now being called "Computer-Supported Cooperative Work," or CSCW. This emerging discipline is concerned with bringing computing technology face-to-face with groups of people as they work together. Supporting human collaboration is the vision for CSCW, and from this challenge comes software that enhances cooperation, augments interpersonal communication, and supports distributed teams. Naming these new capabilities is more difficult than describing what they do and how they function. For lack for a better choice of words, we call this software "groupware."

Unlike traditional computing technology, which has a strictly technical focus, groupware has strong social and organizational dimensions. This new way of thinking about people, work, and technology is making substantial strides at utilizing the capabilities of existing technology, as well as forging new innovations. By focusing on the underlying business situations and organizational frameworks, we distinguish groupware from the computing technologies that we have experienced in thc past.

---

[1] Adapted and extracted from G. E. Bock and D. A. Marca, *Designing Groupware: A Guidebook for Designers, Implementors, and Users,* New York: McGraw Hill, Inc., 1995, and reprinted by permission.

This chapter provides a management primer and summarizes many of the state-of-the-art practices for groupware development, recognizing first and foremost that groupware is both social and technical in nature. People need to coordinate ongoing work activities, and seek environments that support teamwork and collaboration. Groupware designers must therefore focus on the problem of group work itself, and must design software that harmonizes business tasks.

15.2 IDENTIFYING GROUPWARE SITUATIONS

15.2.1 Recognizing Groupware

What is "groupware" anyway? For systems designers and implementors, we must begin by focusing on the problems our organizations are facing. Managers confront multiple challenges to remain competitive in the marketplace. Certainly, they struggle to control costs while maintaining quality. Equally important, markets are now global and competition intense. Effective businesses must be able to respond flexibly and quickly to changes in market conditions, to the advent of new competitors for existing products, and to the development of new products and services. Effective managers must focus on time to market, meeting market demands, the quality of goods and services sold, and customer service. They need to create sustainable competitive advantages for their goods and services, insure customer satisfaction, and enhance quality and responsiveness to changes in market conditions, while continuing to improve productivity and seeking to reduce costs.

Increasingly, these changes mean that managers must find new ways to organize their operations. Rather than formal organizations with fixed hierarchies, teams of people are more effective. They are geographically dispersed and convene on an ad hoc basis to resolve particular problems. They are to communicate and share information in new and different ways.

Coordination, cooperation, and competition drive managers' efforts to restructure the work environment, to improve organizational effectiveness and job satisfaction. Critical assets include just-in-time information—getting the right information to the right people just when they need it—maintaining networks of personal relationships, and being able to adapt quickly and flexibly to the business situation at hand. Increasingly, managers are turning to advanced information technologies to help them bridge time and space, to integrate diverse parts of their organizations, to forge (appropriate) linkages with both customers and suppliers, and to compete profitably in the global market.

Enter "groupware"—software designed to support groups of people working together, often at a distance. It is fueled by profound changes in enabling technologies—ubiquitous, affordable desktop computing devices, expanding communications bandwidth, networked information access, and global connectivity. It is ignited by the ability to connect to anybody, anywhere, at any time, remembering of course that we first must know their address or how to reach them. Groupware combines enabling technologies with notions of organizational design and interpersonal effectiveness. Groupware is sometime described as "a bad name for some good stuff."

Herein lies the rub. Users face a confusing collection of alternatives to find the best approach for sending and receiving information.

☞ When to phone or send a fax?

☞ When will a mail message be good enough or when to organize a meeting?

☞ How can the sender of a message be sure that the receivers not only received it, but understand its content and take appropriate actions?

☞ How can the receiver sort through all the available information to manage activities, and achieve particular goals?

Groupware must provide some rules of thumb to structure alternatives for sending, organizing, and receiving information.

Groupware includes many different kinds of information technologies—electronic mail, online discussion groups, distribution lists, document management systems, and world wide (or corporate wide) access to shared information stores as recently embodied by the Internet and the World Wide Web. Rather than dwelling on the features and functions of particular groupware products, we will emphasize a different perspective. Groupware is about the power of information systems technologies, together with its *effective* application to ongoing work in organizations.

Assuming a distributed computing environment is in place, what then? Certainly, broadening the bandwidth of communication is an initial step—sending and receiving mail, organizing threads of ongoing conversations through conferences, perhaps publishing timely information in a newsletter. But beyond sharing information, people work together by interacting with one another: making requests, stating commitments, keeping promises, delivering results, and arguing about outcomes. The enabling information technologies for groupware should enhance these ongoing group and organizational activities. Effective groupware focuses on productive business outcomes, utilizing appropriate technologies. Groupware depends upon a wide and ever expanding set of systems technologies, including a communications infrastructure, messaging capabilities, shared filing systems, and access to shared data (in all likelihood stored in shared databases). These capabilities are designed to work together seamlessly, so that groups might quickly and easily construct varieties of interactive environments, supporting the business tasks at hand.

Groupware requires innovative approaches for designing systems, anticipating breakthroughs between conflicting requirements for change on one hand, and stability on the other. Emerging technologies provide some aspects of the solution. Distributed computing environments enable decentralized management and control—systems cooperating with one another according to defined sets of rules. Groupware applications depend on a core of common systems services.

15.2.2 The Business Context for Groupware

Groupware provides conscious links to a work setting, to both the management tasks and group processes of a business team. It focuses on the general flow of information (and authority) in a workgroup and a business context.

Viewed as a snapshot into an existing organization, groupware enables us to focus on the dynamic flow of information within a workgroup, particularly as it is linked to business processes and operational activities. We seek to deploy information systems that foster appropriate connections to business environments. As we do this, we must consider innovative ways to redefine both specific work tasks and general management procedures. With rapid access to the right information at the right time, we can envision innovative management processes and new ways to structure work activities.

15.2.2.1 Bridging Time and Space

First, we can view groupware as a map for understanding technologies to bridge time and space. People might work together to share information in terms of four different kinds of activities:

☞ When they can coordinate their schedules, the group might organize a meeting in a single place so that everybody can get together to share information. Arranging a meeting may be difficult—with a distributed workgroup, some people will have to travel to the meeting.

☞ If they decide not to schedule a meeting, group members might develop their ideas through a series of memos, and then send them to one another. Everybody can respond when they are able.

☞ If they cannot all travel to the same place, they might meet "over the telephone" so that people are talking to one another at the same time while located in different places.

☞ If they are working on a specific project in one place but at different times, such as a shift-work situation, they might log their activities in a shared notebook to which everybody might access during their shift.

Each alternative represents a different kind of time commitment as well as a particular style of communication—oral or written; face-to-face with "body language" or at-a-distance when reading (or hearing) words transmitted on the network; or all together in "real time" or synchronously, whenever personally convenient. Each alternative enables certain kinds of group conversations and information sharing.

Groupware promises to support anytime/anyplace communications, commensurate with the work-related needs of a workgroup. Innovations in communications technologies represent a major driving force, enabling people to consider new ways to communicate across time and space—global connectivity, ubiquitous e-mail, intuitive access to shared information repositories, video to the desktop, and other innovations of advanced information technologies. Most important, these innovations must serve to enhance ongoing workgroup activities and enable progressive managers to structure innovative business practices.

15.2.2.2 Integrating Information into Group Processes

When people work in groups, they seek to accomplish a variety of tasks. Some of these tasks lead to results, the "outputs" of an organization, while others are associated with the processes needed to do the work. We must develop an understanding about how groups function. Groupware provides a framework for integrating organizational information with group processes.

Groups within business organizations exist to help the larger enterprise achieve its specific tasks. For instance, a group of salespeople are part of a sales organization, selling a company's products and services in the marketplace. A group of software designers are part of an engineering organization, creating and maintaining a company's products and services in the marketplace. In order to achieve these tasks, the groups must engage in a variety of group maintenance activities.

Groupware connects information access with group processes in a number of ways. On the simplest level, groupware can assist with many routine maintenance activities, freeing individual members to spend more time to focus on significant tasks. Scheduling meetings, tracking action items, circulating status reports, and flashing updates about critical events are often time-consuming group maintenance activities, requiring extensive communication and coordination. Groupware will help people organize frameworks for sharing information by providing a single membership list for all activities and a simple way for an administrator to update it.

On a more comprehensive level, groupware has the potential to extend beyond maintenance activities and to support core business tasks. An information system can capture knowledge about individual users' roles and responsibilities, such as the organizational relationships among members of a workgroup, their job titles, their expertise, and their prior experiences. This system can encode specific activities by defining the information required to complete particular tasks and the business rules for processing various activities. When taken together, these steps provide a dynamic sense of business process, or workflow.

15.2.2.3 Tying Information Needs to Group Conversations

When people work in groups, they need to discuss the various issues at hand, share points-of-view, develop insights, make decisions, and communicate the results. Group work consists of an ongoing series of interpersonal conversations: discussions, debates, fact-finding analyses, small-talk, humorous encounters, and what not. Exchanging, managing, and directing the flow of information is a crucial aspect of group life. Groupware provides environments for people to manage their personal needs for interpersonal conversations.

People are often overwhelmed by the volume and velocity of information available to them at their desktops, in their meeting rooms, and within their cognitive purview (limited only by the 24 hour day). People have the opportunity to participate in many conversations, but individuals must know which ones are central to their interests and which ones are only of tangential value. Groups can initiate discussions with many people, but tracking conversational threads and distilling important information often becomes a hit or miss affair. With easy access to a wide range of information and with the ability to send and receive documents almost at will, interpersonal communication needs are more critical than ever before.

Getting in touch, staying in touch, and knowing when to move on, becomes the central issue for interpersonal communication. Groupware provides people with opportunities to first structure and then restructure their ongoing series of conversations in two very important ways. Groupware requires us to recognize the pull-push paradigm for information exchange.

Sharing information is a two-way street. On some occasions, people need to find information and bring new knowledge into the group. They must query various sources, sort through conflicting reports, consult authoritative repositories of information, research alternatives, and generally search for critical elements within larger pools of general information. Typically, they seek to access all kinds of relevant facts and figures, to find things as needed, with a modicum of effort. In this mode, people are trying to pull information from the various pools (or information repositories).

On other occasions, people need to communicate with one another to achieve a group goal or advance a group objective. These are directed conversations, requesting action, describing alternatives, taking a point of view, offering an opinion, soliciting feedback, or trying to advance the group's agenda. Typically, they seek to communicate decisions, delegate actions, track commitments, and broadcast conclusions. Group information represents a stream of conversations. Group members **push** information along the stream.

Information streams are integral parts of information pools. Similarly, information pools are integral to information streams. Groupware leverages two interrelated kinds of technologies—those that help focus and direct the actions within a workgroup and those that enable people to retrieve the right information, just when they need it.

Modeling holds great promise for representing group processes and for building effective workgroup computing environments. Group working depends on a continuing series of interpersonal conversations. Modeling these conversations and interactions provides a business context for groupware. Effective workgroup computing environments requires us to understand the impacts of group conversations.

15.3 A DESIGN PROCESS FOR GROUPWARE

15.3.1 Design Mindsets

We have already stated that one of our goals is to impart knowledge about how both ways of thinking and uses of language can have a very strong influence on the design of groupware. This section is devoted to different ways of thinking.

Some people refer to "the way one thinks" with terms such as "fundamental perspective," some use the term "essential viewpoint," and some use the word "mindset." We have chosen to use the latter because it conveys the sense that people have a complex set of elements of feeling, perceiving, thinking, and reasoning that, when combined, define and guide one's way of thinking. We will now explore this, the most basic, concept of groupware design. We hope that you will take the opportunity while reading to examine your own way of thinking about computers, and to consider how your own mindset influences the way you design groupware.

Those who practice traditional software design have a particular way of thinking about computers. At the core of their mindset is a notion that the computer is a mechanism for manipulating and exchanging data. At the core of effective groupware design is a different way of thinking, which sees the computer as a medium for allowing people to collaborate. By seeing computers as a medium, groupware researchers and practitioners have begun to expand their scope of concerns during design. They are now concerned as much with the human relationships and endeavors computers can support, as with the information computers can carry and manipulate. One could say that these new concerns come from a different mindset. Within this new mindset, non-traditional approaches have been invented for designing groupware. Before we investigate today's major design approaches, let us take a look at the realm from which these approaches were created—the Design Mindset.

15.3.1.1 Mindset Influences Design

Design is a fundamental human activity. One could say that people are, in fact, constantly designing the world around them—their families, their buildings, their governments, their computing technology—just to name few. One could also say that it is one's mindset that is at the heart of this design activity. This essential element can be thought of as a filter through which a person interprets and interacts with their world. Culture is a good example, for it is an outcome of a particular way of thinking that has been adopted by a group of people. Culture is the result of the way a group of people thinks about life, other people, and the world at large. One could, in fact, say that mindset is at the root of everything in our lives. For example, right now, people pay a lot of money for diamonds, and this price has been relatively stable for many years. However, the value people have currently placed on diamonds could be thought of as designed. One could say that this price was made up from the mindset people created about scarcity—something rare (e.g., diamond) is worth more than something common (e.g., slate). In other words, design is an activity that comes from one's mindset. To say it another way, a design is the result of an innovation conceived, created and expressed within a particular mindset. Design and mindset are intimately connected. In sum, mindset is at the heart of design. Mindset influences both the design process and the resulting design artifacts.

This powerful, overarching concept called "mindset" gives us a vehicle for exploring the various ways people design computing technology. In fact, researchers have found that people typically choose one of four fundamental

mindsets: understanding, form, rules, or context. It is from these mindsets that
the cultures of the world have evolved. To say it another way, people have used
these mindset to create an interpretation about the world in which they live.
Researchers have also discovered that one, and only one, of these mindsets is
chosen and kept because people require a consistent interpretive framework in
order to give meaning to their life. As a result, each mindset profoundly influences the way people design life, work, and technology. Let us briefly look at each
of these mindsets, see how they differ, and discover how each influences the
design of computer systems (refer to Table 15-1).

15.3.1.2 The Four Design Mindsets

The prior discussion gave a sense of the concept called "mindset," and noted
that there were four basic kinds. One could summarize the discussion by first
saying that a design mindset is a deeply held set of assumptions, beliefs, and
viewpoints concerning the nature of people, work, and technology. Second, while
not everyone has the same mindset, the mindset of a particular person is a way
of thinking that is held onto very firmly. When it comes to designing groupware,
the same concept applies—people approach the design with a set of very strong
biases, which have enormous impact on both the design process and the final
result. Let us now take a look at each of the four basic mindsets to see how they
influence the design of, for example, a computer system for supporting meetings.

Design From Understanding—In this mindset, the designer uses a
holistic, systems approach, with an intention to develop a broad understanding.
Using this mindset, designers would study meetings from such places as a con-
cealed glass observation room. These designers see collaborative work as the
consequence of complex and integrated human activities. Complexity, interaction, and evolution are some of the issues dealt with during the design process.
Their detached observations would generate enormous amounts of data in all of
these areas, which would be carefully collected and analyzed before beginning
the design. In other words: understand first, design second. A typical design
often depicts such things as collections of data that change over time (e.g., a
shared distributed database), and software as modules requiring interface definitions and coordination (e.g., distributed applications used by multiple people). To give a purely technical example, general systems theory comes from
this mindset.

Design According to Form—Here, the designer employs the tool of simi-
larity to classify various parts of a system. Meetings are still observed, but the
focus is on its form—agendas, action items, where people sit, and so on. These
designers see collaborative work as being very stereotypical in nature, and something that can be unambiguously ordered and labeled. The format of agenda
items, how ideas are linked together during discussions, and what information
should be kept confidential are some of the issues dealt with during the design
process. A typical design often depicts meetings in terms of a fixed set of repeat-
able patterns such as highly structured agendas, hyper-information that links
together the results of all prior meetings, and so on. As a purely technical example, object-oriented programming comes directly from this mindset.

Table 15.1 How Mindsets Influence Groupware Design

Design the Mindset	What Is Collaboration?	How Is Groupware Designed?	What Does Design Represent?
From Understanding	Complex and integrated human interactions.	Detached study. Note complexity of inter-actions.	Purpose, goals, behavior, connec-tions, equilibrium.
According to Form	Stereotyped work. Tasks that can be labeled or ordered.	Detached study. Focus on form.	Types of objects, object relationships, and object states.
Using Rules	Autonomous tasks coordinated by a set of rules.	Detached study. Analyze according to a model/theory.	Input, output, control, workflows, functions, rules, procedures.
Within a context	Work that occurs within existing human relationships.	Study only within a given context. Note uniqueness.	Viewpoint, context, experience, action, conversations.

Design Using Rules—In this mindset, the designer uses predefined rules to study a system. For example, the behavior of people in a meeting is described using a cause-and-effect explanation (i.e., so-and-so dominated the meeting because they sat in the chair that gave them the most power and control). These designers see collaborative work mechanistically, often describing it as tasks that react with one another. Analysis into component parts, quantifying system properties, and identifying underlying mechanisms are some common design issues. For example, a typical design might attempt to coordinate individuals via a set of rules that assumes the tasks are done in a completely autonomous fashion. In such designs, information is represented in terms of hierarchies and contains rules about how information must be manipulated. This design mindset is often used to create software that supports the status quo, authority structures, and controlling environments.

Design within a Context—This mindset is quite different than the others. Here, the designer studies a system from within a specific context. For example, a designer would evaluate a particular software program as it is being used to support an actual meeting. In this mindset, systems are never analyzed independent from the context in which they occur. This is because designers have the orientation that the context gives meaning to each and every thing or event. For example, no two meetings are ever considered to be the same. Using this mindset, designers see collaborative work as activities that occur within established human relationships. Discovering social situations and creating how technology can support those situations are common design issues. For example, a typical design defines an artifact created from a meeting in terms of: who created it, why it was created, and how it will be used in the future.

In short, context is the essential ingredient for groupware. Designing groupware in the context of its use is the key to producing an effective solution.

15.3.2 Design Methods

We have just dealt with questioning our traditional way of thinking during the design activity. We looked at how the concept of "mindset" governs the design process, we investigated an alternative mindset, and covered some associated approaches that have proven useful for designing groupware systems. Embarking on a groupware design effort, however, requires not only a mindset and an approach for shaping our way of thinking. We need more than just a fundamental perspective! A groupware design effort also requires a corresponding method for actually creating the design. The method is practiced within the context of the fundamental perspective. Therefore, the perspective provides a way of thinking about people, work, and systems, while the method defines the set of design practices appropriate to that way of thinking. Before we investigate some specific groupware design methods, we need to set the stage by taking a look at the nature of design methods.

15.3.2.1 What Is a Design Method?

A groupware design method is two dimensional—it has both representations and practices. Regarding representations, a design method is used to create a model—some kind of picture—of the intended system. Therefore, since groupware is socio-technical in nature, a groupware design method must be made up of a set of logical structures capable of representing both the social and technical aspects of the system. A "good" method must therefore provide a seamless connection among the structures so the design always ties together social and technical aspects of the system. Regarding practices, using a design method results in a set of activities—design events—which, in turn, produces the resulting logical structures. Since groupware design is a human endeavor, and since human endeavors are strongly influenced by the adopted mindset, a groupware design method comprises a set of practices consistent with the chosen fundamental perspective. Let us take a closer look at each of these dimensions.

The representational dimension of a design method can be thought of as a kind of language. The design language uses symbols, such as words or graphics, to represent the underlying assumptions and essential concepts about a group of people, how they work together, and the technology they need to support their work. It is important to note here that the use of this language is an expression of the people and their work as it is interpreted within the particular approach. For example, the Human Augmentation approach strongly suggests expressing group work as a set of human skills and how those skills build upon each other. One of the resulting representations would therefore be interrelated skill sets. In addition, a design language often uses different sets of symbols to denote different levels of abstraction. For example, "logical" designs depict the operational intent (e.g., create agenda) while "physical" designs spell out the actual implementation of that intent (e.g., use the Calendar tool). It is crucial to note here that if the design language does not contain the symbols to express concepts or assumptions, the designer is, at best, unable to articulate these notions and, at worst, unable to even recognize particular system aspects. In other words, without language, there is no "people," "work," or "system."

The practical dimension of a design method comprises the activities people engage in to create a design. These activities, or practices, are carried out by designers within the design mindset they have chosen. For example, you may choose to design a system: 1) by relying solely on your knowledge of similar systems, 2) by observing that system in operation, or 3) by asking the users to help you design the system. Since groupware is socio-technical in nature, today's groupware design practices almost always involve users. However, the nature and extent of this involvement is vastly different because they arise directly from the chosen mindset and approach. For example, one could start designing a software system for supporting the day-to-day office work of a large corporation in a variety of ways. You could:

1. Look at the information transactions and then define groups by the transactions they handle.
2. Study all the documents and identify the information common to those artifacts.
3. Describe the office tasks and then define how the software will affect those tasks.
4. Sit down with the user and learn how they do their work.

Read the list carefully and you will notice the particular mindset behind each design practice: 1) Design From Understanding defines the organization by how groups handle information, 2) Design According To Form creates information objects based on documents, 3) Design Using Rules defines cause-and-effect relationships between office tasks and software, and 4) Design Within A Context starts with a first-hand experience of the way people work. While all of these practices have a role during design, it is important to clearly distinguish what, fundamentally, is driving the design activities. Let us now take a look at how mindset influences a design method.

15.3.2.2 How Mindsets Influence Design Methods

One could say that the way people are thinking about the workplace is shifting from "individual work" to one of "team work." The nature of work in today's office is far more collaborative in nature than that of office work a decade or two ago. For example, draft passing, a traditional work practice that comes from seeing people as individuals exchange information, is giving way to real-time co-authoring of information artifacts. During co-authoring, a group of people simultaneously create portions of a document or spreadsheet and then make those contributions publicly available. The group evaluates the portions, selects some for inclusion, and combines selections into a final artifact. Co-authoring is highly interactive, often takes unplanned directions, requires almost continual conversation, and creates a rapidly evolving work product. All these aspects of co-authoring make it hard to do without a social structure for coordinating the work and technical infrastructure for supporting the tasks. Even with these structures in place, each co-authoring event occurs very differently from the one that preceded it.

These aspects of co-authoring give evidence for the notion that each and every collaborative work event is unique. Unique work events place special demands on designing computer support for collaboration, and these demands necessitate the adoption of a non-traditional mindset. For example, design practices within the Design Using Rules mindset are devoid of understanding of the unique context of each work event: its history, the work society, and specific circumstances that surround the event. In contrast, The Design With A Context mindset advocates design practices that create an awareness of the constantly changing social aspects of the work. Asking questions that begin to reveal the unspoken aspects of the work, participating in the design of the larger organization, and letting the users define the software interface are examples of practices that come from the Design Within A Context mindset.

The Design Within A Context mindset also strongly suggests the use of design languages whose elements are capable of expressing non-technical and non-informational aspects of the system. Such elements provide ways to articulate very important aspects of a group work situation—intention, commitment, action, dependency, coordination, and learning—to name just a few. It is this kind of language that allows a designer to recognize and express the human, and action-oriented, aspects of the work. By using such design languages, people have a opportunity to design a system that actually enables the intended action to actually happen. In contrast, when technology is built without concern for the social factors, it often disables intended action.

15.3.2.3 Three Important Design Questions

The complexities around simultaneously gathering, understanding, and trying to satisfy social and technical requirements generate a host of issues during a design effort. Some issues reside in either in the purely technical or the purely social spheres of concern. However, a large number of issues exist inside the overlap of these two domains. These issues are concerned with how the technology does or does not match the way people work. For example, one organization told people to use a coordination tool that required the use of special, non-customizable, language for electronically making requests and promises. On the first day of its use, people became frustrated with this tool because it did not allow them to express the way they negotiated their work. This tool was such a misfit with the way these people worked that it was rejected. One person, in fact, threw the box of software right out of his office! Other issues are concerned with how social norms restrict or demand the use of certain technology. For example, in the above case study, the great disparity between user communities regarding secretarial support prevents tools like automatic meeting scheduling systems from being adopted. In other words, both kinds of issues raise questions about the fit between technology and the workplace. To assist groupware designers in getting some handle on these issues, we suggest using three questions during every groupware design effort they undertake:

Augmentation: What mechanisms will be most effective in increasing the ability of people to coordinate their actions?

Language-Action: What will people say and do so that it makes a positive intervention in their work lives?

Metaphor: What core concept can be created for bridging the cultural and language gaps between designers and users?

15.4 ENABLING CAPABILITIES FOR GROUPWARE

15.4.1 Building the Groupware Infrastructure

Groupware utilizes advanced information technologies—communication networks, databases, client/server protocols, distributed computing systems, and the like. When well implemented, users are scarcely aware of the infrastructure. Rather, their focus is on their immediate tasks at hand. The underlying technologies are important only in so far as they help people to better work together. The groupware infrastructure helps people to define the boundaries of the group—how people share information within the group and how they communicate with others outside their immediate team.

The enabling infrastructure requires three sets of interrelated services. First are the services supporting the basic communications among systems—the network connectivity and bandwidth. Then, once connected, people need to be able to define their identities—who is a member of which group, who has what kinds of roles and responsibilities. The infrastructure needs to identify and control group membership through security and access control services. Finally, the environment needs to maintain a catalog (or a basic directory) about who is a member of what group and who has what level of privileges and responsibilities. Directory services are the third part of the enabling infrastructure for groupware.

Networks enable people to communicate and share information in many different ways, depending upon their business tasks at hand. Key elements are flexibility of the network and the speed with which the information can be transmitted from place to place. Network bandwidth has a profound effect on the groupware infrastructure. Technically, bandwidth describes the speed of the connection between client and server, or between server and server—the amount of data moving through a network connection. Practically, bandwidth is a measure of throughput, similar to the phenomena of water flowing through a large water pipe. The higher the speed, the more data transmitted across a network connection between any two systems. With high speed networks and high network bandwidth, we can foster a greater degree of group interactions. As bandwidth increases, people can send and receive larger documents in the same amount of time, or the same sized documents more quickly.

Groupware leverages the capabilities of client/server computing environments by tailoring the flow of information to meet the specific needs of individual work groups. Networks provide the basic connections, like the highways linking two neighboring towns. But we need more than connectivity. We need policies and procedures for managing the flow of information, just like we need the "rules of the road" in order to ensure a safe journey along a highway. These policies and procedures define the boundaries of a group—certain people have privileges to access share information databases, but only a few people can change them. Or certain people have authority to send specific kinds of messages, but all can read them.

Security policies and access control procedures pose a thorny set of issues for groupware. They define the relationships among users. They determine which users can access what information when working in the groupware environment. Users seek an environment where they only have to enter a single password and then have authenticated access to many different servers. Individual servers, in turn, have mechanisms in place to verify users' identities. System managers seek an environment where they can centrally manage many servers, and where they implement a security scheme for an entire client/server environment. There is an obvious trade-off to establish a "good enough" security for users' tasks at hand—one that will also preserve the flexibility required for workgroup computing. The underlying technologies and security mechanisms must be balanced against the values and norms of the workgroup.

To support group communications, an authoritative source within the networked environment needs to assign addresses and ensure that they are unique. Somebody needs to maintain a set of directory services, listing users' names, addresses, and any other computational resources that are shared. Enter the third part of the enabling infrastructure for groupware: directory services.

Directory services for groupware begin as an authoritative list of workgroup users, maintained in a central location. They provide both the central definition of the group and the local definition of group activities. They extend to include the names, addresses, and core attributes of many computational objects—such as printer queues, file systems, and databases. Most important, they are quickly and readily accessed. Thus a single, centralized database is often inappropriate. Directory services need to be readily available so that users can quickly find the information when needed.

15.4.2 Using Groupware Applications

Groupware applications are based on metaphors for office work. Computer supported information technologies offer some intriguing possibilities for restructuring and improving basic business activities. Groupware applications comprise a broad range of information technologies that enable people to work together around a common set of activities and to accomplish specific business goals. These applications enable people to find the information they need, just when they need it, and to communicate with one another as required. Ideally, they should become essential tools for group activities, as unobtrusive and as functional as the telephone.

15.4.2.1 Electronic Mail

Electronic mail supports interpersonal communication on a broad scale. The underlying metaphor is the postal system where people are able to communicate with one another, regardless of time or distance. Certainly, the most mature and pervasive set of capabilities, e-mail applications enable people to send and receive messages on their computer systems. People experience very tangible effects of using e-mail. They can attend to specific tasks more quickly, as little time is lost in the transmission of information. Sometimes messages are "wrapped" in electronic envelopes to distinguish addressing schemes and delivery mechanisms from the actual content. This is important when people want to mail messages that contain more than plain text (or simple characters), such as financial spreadsheets, formatted documents, graphs, or pictures. In some instances, the e-mail applications recognize the content and open the envelope automatically, invoking the appropriate application in the process.

15.4.2.2 Information Sharing Tools

Information sharing applications enable people to organize, access, find, and exchange information in a work group. When people work together, they need to share many different kinds of information, beyond sending and receiving mail. Shared file cabinets are a recurring metaphor for groupware applications. They are just like the familiar physical objects found in offices around the world. Users can open these computerized cabinets and access collections of electronic "file folders." Information is organized hierarchically; users have to discover the organizing schema in order to understand how to find things.

A computer conferencing application provides another approach to information sharing. This kind of application seeks to emulate ad hoc information exchanges of group discussions. The basic idea is a simple, two step process. Like entering a conference room and stating a position, people first post documents on particular topics in a shared area. Other people then read the information and post their replies. The application structures the exchange into a "topic" "reply" hierarchy, much like a conversation in a meeting. To find things, people can sort documents into various views, related to the terms used to describe everyday activities.

An electronic library application is another approach to information sharing. It models both the organization and the ready access to published information found by walking into a traditional library, a place where books and documents are catalogued and stored. Many people can simultaneously access a single electronic document. An electronic library facilitates information sharing on a broad scale.

15.4.2.3 Using Time Management to Organize Group Work

Time management applications capture an elemental aspect of groupware. Scheduling meetings, planning activities, coordinating events, and tracking commitments are essential to supporting group interactions. These kinds of tasks represent an overhead to group life—things that must be done for the group to actually do its work. Time management applications seek to expedite group coordination. Online systems are an option, provided that they are easy to use and are well integrated with the overall work environment. Users must see immediate benefits: everybody in a workgroup must agree to maintain an on-line version of their personal calendar. In addition, beyond simple scheduling, time management applications might coordinate workgroup activities, reminding people when tasks are due and synchronizing a project schedule with personal calendars and task lists. Potentially, these kinds of time management applications can reduce the overhead of group life. But people must realize that they derive a direct benefit to themselves and to their workgroups by keeping their schedules online, and these benefits must outweigh the costs.

15.4.2.4 Real-time Meetings

When meeting in different places, everybody needs to hear and see one another, and view the information that is the subject of the meeting. Desktop conferencing provides both audio and video links between people in different physical locations—perhaps in an adjacent office, perhaps thousands of miles apart. The video link can display all kinds of electronic information in real time: people sitting in one place can actually view a slide presentation or a product demonstration, originating from another location. This kind of groupware is as simple as ensuring that everybody in the meeting sees the same information at the same time. At the end of the meeting, one or more persons can quickly prepare the meeting minutes and action items, including perhaps the agenda for a follow up meeting, and send them to all the meeting participants. The results of the meeting thus become a set of on-line documents distributed via e-mail, catalogued in a computer conference, or stored in a shared file cabinet.

15.4.2.5 Structuring the Flow of Business Information

Work processes in organizations depend upon the flow of business information—from person to person, from place to place, and from task to task. Groupware applications serve to facilitate the flow of information, focusing first on business documents and then on the nature of the work itself.

Shared document management applications go beyond simple information sharing. They focus on the document life cycle, the interrelated set of workgroup activities for producing a shared document. They help people organize and structure the document production process. Shared document management applications provide uniform methods of access and retrieval throughout the document life cycle. Based on a centralized repository, these applications support standardized document naming, indexing, and security policies. As people work together to produce a document, they need to coordinate activities at various stages in the process.

Recognizing the importance of organized processes leads to another kind of groupware application—workflow. When people work together in a group, their work activities flow from one person to another. With many different systems interconnected on a network, the applications can serve to structure the flow of business information. Workflow describes the connections between one person's tasks and another's. Workflow encodes the business rules that identify how people are supposed to work together around a common task. It also captures the roles of individual people—based either on their individual identities or their responsibilities within an organization.

Groupware needs to be tightly connected with the business activities of the workgroup—both the objectives and the recognized operating procedures. These workgroup technologies need to be appropriate for the tasks at hand; they also need to fit the values and norms of the business teams.

15.4.3 Advancing Groupware Environments

When we communicate and share information, we must focus squarely on the business benefits: who needs to talk to whom and for what purposes. We must be able to identify the added business value of enhanced communications and information sharing technologies. Building the infrastructure and creating an electronic work environment is only the beginning.

How can we separate the wheat from the chaff of electronic information? Enter notions of *filters and agents,* software assistants that "live on the network" and can help us manage our information space, adapted to our own particular needs. Our problems are complicated by the realization that chaff to some people may be wheat to others. We need to be concerned about both the management of information and the organization of work.

Filters and agents are the glue for living in a networked world. Once we are wired to one another via some combination of LANs and WANs, we can literally share information with anybody on the network. (And thanks to the magic of the Internet, this could be more than 30 million people all over the world.) Raw information sharing, however, becomes a very unruly affair, where everybody might wind up shouting, or broadcasting, or sorting through huge heaps of information, just to find the golden nugget.

Filters and agents capture essential information about the operational policies and procedures of business teams—in effect, the meta-knowledge about how an organization functions. Filters and agents utilize the definitions about organizational policies and processes to support workgroup collaboration, enabling people to structure the flow of information from one person to another—and from one business team to another. They enable both people and computer processes to proactively take actions—and direct the flow of information—when specific criteria are met. They "push" information through interconnected networks of people and information systems, facilitating the flow of information to support business processes. In effect, filters and agents serve to "distribute" the knowledge about specific business procedures and activities to many different workgroups within an organization, and to enhance the coordination of business teams.

Filters describe the selection criteria needed to identify specific "items" of electronic information. They enable us to find various bits of electronic information. Some filters examine simply the structured information fields, or header fields, that are integral to any electronic information environment. Other filters process both header information and the actual content of the information, to detect when specific words or phrases occur. Eventually, sophisticated filters (still in research and pilot testing phases of development) will go beyond matching specific words and phrases in an article, and detect information based on an understanding of the underlying context, including knowledge of related concepts.

Agents are software processes capable of taking independent (or autonomous) actions, provided specified criteria are met. They are typically comprised of a collection of simple rules, a choice of appropriate subsequent actions, and an understanding about triggering events. Sophisticated agents can check for two or more related conditions. The actions taken by any specific agent depends on the capabilities of the underlying environment. For instance, e-mail agents will be able to forward, refile, or do other commands that you would typically expect from an e-mail system; they will be triggered by the arrival of new mail, by message counts in a particular folder, or by other common e-mail related events. A database agent, by comparison, will query a database, construct reports, automatically send faxes, or perform other activities relevant to the database, again triggered by related events.

We can proceed to build communities of context sensitive agents that not only interpret the information they are processing and understand what to do with it, but also develop an awareness of other agents operating within the general environment. As agents learn about one another, they become increasingly more capable to perform useful activities with electronic information. Filters and agents require a business context. They tailor the flow of information through various steps in a business process.

Communities of agents do not follow a formal master plan; activities are hardly managed in a rigorously defined, closely controlled environment. Quite the contrary, these communities emphasize the diversity of activities in an distributed electronic environment, stressing the importance of decentralized control. No one person or central management entity creates and updates all of the filters and agents. Rather, each person or group has responsibility to manage the filtering criteria and agent actions at his/her individual node in the networked community. There is just enough structure in the system to make things work, to establish basic social conventions about permitted behaviors.

15.5 SUCCESSFUL DEPLOYMENT OF GROUPWARE

15.5.1 System Evolution

So far, we have introduced and discussed analysis, design, and implementation aspects of developing groupware. We suggested ways of recognizing groupware, presented non-traditional design methods, and touched upon some of the more important parts of the technical infrastructure. Now, we come to that portion of a system development effort where deployment is traditionally done. This is the point where developers turn their attention to the matter of getting the system into actual operation. Typically, issues such as parallel operation and system cut-over, reorganizing workgroups or departments, implementing new work procedures and document flows, and data conversions and information backup take precedence. For groupware, however, resolving such issues at the time of traditional system deployment is a formula for failure. As we will see in subsequent sections, addressing deployment early in a groupware effort allows for the proper handling of issues at design time. Let's see why.

15.5.1.1 Addressing Deployment Issues Early and Continually

We have already introduced and discussed how our traditional notions of single-user systems do not translate to groupware situations. We have also pointed out that we cannot anticipate all aspects of collaborative work and that we cannot always predict how a system will actually function in every group situation. Adopting a different development strategy, one that continually considers deployment, is a key to successful groupware. Such a strategy can be created by using the Design Within a Context mindset—by considering and doing deployment during all stages of development. Doing so enables groupware developers to take into account system operation and usage as the system is being designed, thereby allowing for the opportunity to adjust the current design in a straightforward manner. In this way, the design process is an evolutionary one, resulting in an ever-changing solution that addresses every deployment issue as it manifests itself during the actual use of the system. In short, a groupware design must continually evolve so as to address deployment issues as they manifest themselves.

This strategy suggests an evolutionary process of system development, guided by every new requirement that surfaces as a result of the system being used in actual group work situations. Many successful groupware efforts have reported this kind of process to be highly effective in guiding design activities. Their experiences point to two key practices. First, the design process is done in a way so as to be a highly participatory one—users and designers work together to evolve the design of the system. Second, a series of increasingly complex prototypes is designed and tested in the context of real system usage. When used continuously and in conjunction with each other, these practices create a total method for system evolution. Let us now look at the role of participatory design and rapid prototyping during the system development process, and see how these practices can lead to successful groupware systems.

15.5.1.2 The Nature of Participatory Design

Participatory design is first and foremost. It embodies all the design concepts and methods previously covered. When we think of technology design, what usually comes to mind are module interconnections, calling hierarchies, user interface styles, etc. Participatory design, however, is concerned with a broader range of issues, such as: the character, pace, and organization of people's work, the extent of people's privacy or isolation, and the freedom people do or do not have in taking an active role in shaping their work lives. Traditionally, decisions in these arenas have been left to managers or technologists. In contrast, participatory design suggests widening the circle of decision makers to include people who are directly affected by the technology and whose expertise is essential to making the technology work.

With traditional practices: 1) technology is designed in one physical locale while it is used in another, and 2) one set of people design the technology while another must use what is built. In contrast, participatory design brings together designers and users in the place where the technology will ultimately be used. It is an action-oriented practice, enabling all parties to make their own mark on the final system. It is a way of thinking about design that continually creates a collective voice throughout the entire design process. We can think about participatory design as bringing the user into the design process. On further examination, however, participatory design could be thought of as bringing the designer into the use process. We advocate this latter way of thinking as it fosters a point of view where the user and the usage locale dominate the design process. Couple this viewpoint with the socio-technical nature of groupware, and you obtain a set of practices for the ongoing design and adaptation of: the systems, the work policies and procedures, and the overall work environment.

Participatory Design is therefore an integrated set of practices that emphasize the interrelationship between technological advancement and social change. It addresses issues about using computers different than those that immediately come to mind when people think about designing work group systems—issues such as: privacy, priorities, language differences, bias, ownership, autonomy, formality, power, consensus, metaphors, skill, and space. Participatory design also comprises methods quite different than those used by traditional technology designers—story telling, keeping diaries, thinking out loud, learning by doing, video recording, drawing rich pictures, and theatrics. In short, the nature of Participatory Design acknowledges the value of investigating the totality of life at work as a prerequisite to the design of technology.

15.5.2 Customization and Usability

We have showed how and why groupware systems evolve, and tied this evolutionary phenomenon to the matter of the system being altered during its use. We introduced the notion that groupware applications were, in fact, their own development environment because they had to be constantly changed as they were used. We used computer supported meetings as an area of collaborative work to begin explaining this way of thinking and how it produces extremely effective results. This way of thinking is actually founded on a basic tenet:

Group process (e.g. meeting agenda)	+
Simple tools (e.g. clock, editor, spreadsheet)	+
Group visibility (e.g. projection of computer screens)	+
Participatory design (e.g. immediate reflection and alteration)	=
Very high payoffs.	

This tenet goes counter-intuitive to traditional groupware design (which is very technology oriented and technology driven). It is an approach that focuses on the work first and foremost, and places the activity of design squarely inside of the work. It is an approach that lets end-users modify their own system as they use it. In other words, the users become the designers. But this approach requires something very special from technology—it must be *highly* customizable.

We all have a sense of what "customizable" means. For example, spreadsheet software lets just about anyone create tables of interrelated data, adjust the formulas, and vary the formatting of the resulting computations. But this is not what we mean by the phrase "highly customizable." The level of customization required to have groupware be successfully altered during its use is well beyond what is available today. The Clock tool in Windows 3.1 is a good example. The Clock is the basic time-keeping tool. As such, it should be customizable so it can keep track of time during any kind of group work event. For example: it should have an alarm, which can be audible or silent. It should be capable of setting the time clock in the computer system. It should be able to label and simultaneously display one or more other time zones in the world. It should have adjustable fonts so it can be seen under any kind of projection situation. It should be able to display either analog or digital time. It should have a stopwatch mode and display the countdown in analog or digital forms or via a graphic metaphor. The Clock tool in Windows has none of these functions.

Some technologists think these kind of capabilities fall into the "nice to have" category. However, over three years of research by one of the authors suggests that at least one business meeting per month (on average, the work of six people for one hour per month) was significantly impeded because one or more of the clock functions were not at people's fingertips during the meeting. These functions are not "nice to have." They are crucial for supporting human needs during collaborative work. For example, stopwatch mode is needed to allow those who need to speak a way of stating their concerns within an agreed to amount of time. This use of the clock is good for minimizing the "off the point" discussions that sidetrack a meeting so much so that nothing gets accomplished. The degree to which groupware can be immediately adapted will ultimately define how usable it really is. Let us investigate the kind of customization usable groupware is required to have by considering how it used and altered during meetings.

15.5.2.1 Customizations for Group Usage

In group work events such as meetings, people are not trying to use computers. Instead, they are trying to get their jobs done in a collaborative way. Computer technology has demonstrated potential in magnifying a group's ability to work together, but this potential is far from being realized. One of the impediments is that software is still being designed for personal (i.e., desktop or laptop) use, not for group use. In other words, technologists have not yet fundamentally changed their way of thinking about how to develop computer systems for use by groups of people. For the purposes of this chapter, we will look at the usability of groupware as it pertains to meetings because real-time meetings provide some of the most stringent usability requirements for software as it is used by groups. In this section, we will cover usability issues that have the widest scope. These issues arose by studying hundreds of computer supported meetings. The study concluded that the user interface presented by current personal computer software is far too detailed and complicated for use in a group setting.

- ☞ Dynamically adjustable list boxes of non-standard size so extra, and detailed, hand actions are minimized. (Customizations during operation.)

- ☞ Readjust execution priority for changing usage situations. (Customization prior to operation.)

- ☞ Allow people to switch to their favorite tool during the manipulation of a particular file. (Customization during hand-offs.)

In sum, a groupware system must: provide familiar tools, have simple functionality, operate without delay, and minimize typing and hand movements.

15.5.2.2 Customizations for Managing Group Work

Many of us are familiar with windowing software and the standard software applications they contain: Clock, Calendar, Mail, Notepad, and so on. As we said before, these applications have been designed for individuals—for personal use—they were not designed for workgroups. Extensive research by one of the authors in the software capability required to support real-time meetings has uncovered a large number of needed customizations to standard windowing software. You can think of these customizations as capability for managing specific group work situations. It is important to note that these capabilities should not become the standard. Instead, they should be always and immediately available, in the event a software application is chosen to support a particular workgroup event. The remainder of this section presents some standard windowing software tools and the amount of customization they need to better support an electronic meeting.

☞ Central panel of alarms, always keep clocks visible, setting the clock resets all active applications and all computers on the network.

☞ Calendars map time into multiple continuums, thus allowing groups to reflect on past events, manage current events, or plan future events.

☞ Mandatory simultaneous delivery of sensitive mail, lock out general distribution lists when people send sensitive or confidential mail.

☞ Users can turn off pending delete and automatically provide text wrapping and intelligent cut-and-paste capability.

In other words, groupware must operate correctly even though people are prone to use computers in group situations in just the same way as they do when working alone.

15.5.2.3. User Interface Customizations

For computer supported meetings, the fact that groupware is projected on walls dramatically changes the nature of the software and the user interface in general. Some argue that this fact has no bearing on user interface design. However, three years of studying electronic meetings by one of the authors has provided large amounts of data that call for customizing various aspects of the user interface. The research showed that the readability of the projected screen is extremely different from the readability of a personal computer screen. Let us now take a look at some portions of a user interface in the context of their being projected onto walls for the purpose of group viewing in meetings.

☞ Adjustable sizes of buttons and indicators in all toolbars and dialog boxes

☞ Adjustable fonts for all application, tear-down, and pop-up menus

☞ Customizable size, thickness, and color for all cursors

☞ Let users turn on or off the informational display inside their icons, and any associated audio signals as well

☞ Let users always choose the format of the icon display to best suit the work at hand.

15.5.2.4 Other Important Customizations

Group work events places special demands on the people who must operate the technology. Speed, accuracy, and error-free operation are some of the high usability standards that must be met to technically support workgroup events such as real-time meetings. The design of current windowed environments and applications is heavily influenced by the personal use of computers. So, it is natural to expect that the user interface of the windowed environment and its applications will not necessarily provide capabilities for supporting people in operating computers with ease and grace during meeting situations. This chapter closes with a set of other important customizations that provide capability not commonly found in current windowed environments or applications. Experience in, and observations during, hundreds of computer supported meetings have shown a clear need to provide such capability to those operating computers during the very dynamic setting of face-to-face or distributed real-time meetings.

☞ Application control panel, customizable tear-down and pop-up menus

☞ Let users easily customize or fixate the shape, identification, and layout of all windows at any time

☞ Automatic marking and storing of event sequences with just one keystroke or mouse click

☞ Application functions must always be at the user's fingertips while application displays must be easy to visually locate.

15.5.3 Solution Emergence

Emergence is the process of groupware deployment—a process within which an appropriate solution comes forth. An appropriate solution does not emerge with just good intentions and hard work. We have already introduced Participatory Design and Rapid Prototyping, and discussed why these methods are essential for evolving a groupware system. Using participatory design, groupware designers involve the user throughout the development effort. Using rapid prototyping, groupware developers are able to iteratively change a system so that an appropriate solution can emerge. These methods are not sufficient, however. We have also discussed why technology must have the capability of being radically customized. Only highly customizable technology will enable changes to be made fast enough so that people can evaluate how well the altered system does or does not fit within the present social situation. Thus, it is the combination of participatory design, rapid prototyping, and highly customizable software that enables groupware development to be successful.

Groupware solutions emerge when iterative development methods and highly customizable technology are used. With iterative development methods and customizable technology, we can now discuss some important aspects of how groupware solutions emerge. Now, we will take a look at the deployment process. Central to this process is the notion of iterative refinement. One could say that this notion is a "fine tuning" process, where changes are made in a way so that people "hone in on" an appropriate solution. This way of thinking is in marked contrast to the notion that groupware systems are designed *a priori*, that is, they are totally designed before they are deployed. Effective systems are the result of people's changing work experiences and their interpretations about which solution is now appropriate for supporting their work.

We now present how successful groupware solutions emerge when groupware designers and users fine tuned their social protocols, their learning, their technology, and the way they coordinate with each other. We first explain how people iteratively refined their social protocols so that the final result was a far more participatory way of working. Second, we discuss how people used software to capture and share their learning. Third, we present how people tune the performance of their technology in order to obtain a workable solution. Lastly, we describe how teams can design a way of coordinating their work that allow them to be successful when other teams who previously faced that same situation failed. Each point shows how the emergence process is an intentional one—where people are determined to create an appropriate solution, even though they do not know exactly what that solution will ultimately look like.

15.5.3.1 Fine Tuning Social Protocols

Every group of people has a set of social protocols that enables the members of the group to work together. These protocols are an established set of norms and procedures people follow to do their work. More often than not, the bulk of these protocols are unspoken, are initially designed and iteratively refined without conscious thought, and for the most part, go completely unexamined. In other words, the social protocols are so ingrained in the day-to-day work, people are blind to their influence. Usually, the only time social protocols are noticed or examined is when a problem arises between or among members of a group. This, by the way, is not an incorrect way to work—it is, however, the ordinary way people work. This ordinary way of working is a risky one. Lacking an ability to identify and distinguish social protocols, people often create a working environment where conflict can jeopardize working relationships, project objectives, and even the prestige of an entire corporation. Thus change the work metaphor first. Social protocols are refined in the context of a change in the fundamental work metaphor.

15.5.3.2 The Emergence of Learning

We all know that learning takes place when people work. However, what is not well-known is that this learning usually applies to only the task level. In other words, people rarely have deep knowledge about the work they are doing. They rarely know anything about how their task was designed and what larger purpose it serves. The emergence of deep learning, like the emergence of social protocols, happens when people are, or become, aware of something fundamental about their work. Regarding deep learning, it emerges when the fundamental aspects of work (i.e., the unspoken assumptions about the work itself) are made known. Usually, these unspoken assumptions sit in the background and form a tacit collection of interpretations (i.e., a culture) about how work should be done.

Learning is dramatically accelerated when people become aware of, then accept, and then communicate the basic assumptions behind their work. This is the first step. The second and equally crucial step is when people learn about their work from each other through a series of sometimes complicated dialogs. During these discussions, people share their understandings about the work they are doing. Deep learning happens when people have specific dialogs about the whys behind their work. They become more aware of the forces that drive the work, which allows them to either incorporate fundamental assumptions into their work, or alter those assumptions in some way. Groupware can facilitate these kinds of dialogs, as well as give people more opportunity to have them. Hence, groupware systems represent learning—an implemented set of work rules and business information.

15.5.3.3 Technology Refinement

As the social protocols and the organizational learning portions of a groupware solution emerge, the technology component is correspondingly refined. As we discussed in the last section, part of this refinement process involves using customization features to adjust the "look and feel" of the user interface (e.g., very large buttons in the toolbar) or the way particular functions operate (e.g., intelligent cut-and-paste). But numerous other refinements are also done—most notably changes to underlying functionality and refinements commonly known as optimizations. In this section, we will give a real-life example for each of these refinements, both in the area of the computer networks. First, we will show how a worldwide, real-time electronic meeting demanded a non-transparent network. Second, we will discuss how the nature of meetings require optimizations to that network.

Network Non-Transparency

There is so much emphasis today on transparent computer networks and the value that transparency gives users. Transparency is vital to *personal* computing. But collaborative work alters the very nature of what is needed from a network. In fact, the usability of some groupware solutions may actually suffer if the transparency cannot be *removed*. In other words, a transparent network makes it impossible to develop some kinds of groupware solutions. For example, take the case of a worldwide, real-time electronic meeting that was designed for the 200 person law department of a Fortune 100 company. The technical goal was to link each law office around the world with telephone and computers. The goal of the meeting was to resolve a particular international legal issue that had multiple legal interpretations—one for each country! This prompted the following design question: "How could computers help lawyers manage an international, real-time conversation for fully understanding a legal issue and taking appropriate action?

Computer conferencing (e.g., Notes) was an inadequate technical solution—it could not keep pace with the verbal conversation, electronic input could not be coordinated with the verbal conversation, nor could people instantly tell which country was currently contributing their point of view. A script writer was hired to work with the lawyers to draft a meeting process and agenda. The groupware developers participated in that scriptwriting to understand the social protocols and business assumptions. The social protocol of the meeting was designed around some one country hosting the meting. The host country would describe the legal issue and then take input from the participating countries as each felt ready to speak. To signify when they were ready, a country would "raised its hand." The fair thing to do was to call on each country in the order their hand was raised. Since the company had an extremely fast wide area network, electronic mail was chosen to implement this social protocol: 1) Requests to speak are sent by mail. 2) Electronic mail queues each request. 3) The leader of the meeting handles each request in order of receipt. 4) The next law office in the queue takes the floor.

As a general technology, electronic mail is designed with network transparency in mind. Most of the time, people want to know the person sending the message, not where they are located. This general design was entirely inadequate for this electronic law meeting—the location was even more important than the person! Why? Because the location established the context within which the person was speaking. Lawyers came from cities in India, Australia, Japan, Canada, South America, the United Kingdom, France, Germany, Spain, Switzerland, Sweden, Denmark, Holland, Israel, and the United States. Meeting participants would literally not be able to understand their colleagues unless they first understood where they were located!

Thus, e-mail had to be modified to communicate the location first and the person second. Now, the component of a standard e-mail header that identifies who sent the message has the format "computer::account." The groupware designers chose to eliminate network transparency, by creating a mail header that would indicate first the city and then the person (e.g., "Zurich::Johansen"). Since their version of electronic mail does not allow its users to create network aliases, the solution required renaming all the computers and accounts that would be sending mail messages during the meeting. Clearly, this required special effort on the part of technicians to prepare the network, but the need for location was so high that it far outweighed this additional development cost.

Network Optimization

The design team for this electronic law meeting knew that the complexity of the legal issue, the number of people involved, and the world-wide scope of the event warranted testing both the social and technical components. They chose to conduct two tests before the actual event. The first focused on the technology (e.g., telephone and computer connections). The second tested the social components (e.g., the script for the meeting, the "hand raising") and the technical components (e.g., sending mail requests) together in a dress rehearsal setting. Each test identified the need to optimize the computer network. During the first test, designers discovered the central computer had insufficient memory and processor speed to handle electronic mail while running meeting recording software. They decided to dedicate a separate computer to the task of receiving, queuing, and displaying mail. Also, some remote computers were slow to connect, or could not connect, to the central computer because of partial network failures in their home country. This required reconfiguring the network by creating dedicated connection paths to the central computer. During the dress rehearsal, the real-time, simultaneous transmission of the meeting record to 34 sites was too much of a load for the software. This required breaking the network up into three areas, Pacific Rim, America, and Europe, and having yet another computer dedicated to just transmitting the record to specific computers in each of these three areas.

This case study is rich in groupware design problems. Problem one was how to utilize a network originally designed for asynchronous transmission of electronic mail messages to create a solution that demanded synchronous communications. (This technical situation reinforces our claim that fundamental assumptions about group work are embedded in technology!) To explain, the assumption that it is acceptable for people to wait for transmissions was directly embedded in the wide area network of the Fortune 100 company. In most cases, if a portion of the network fails, it's perfectly OK for electronic mail to arrive a day late. This much latency was totally unacceptable for the electronic law meeting. Lawyers needed to have their mail messages arrive within seconds of sending it. Problem two was how to simultaneously transmit a live meeting record around the globe, and the unpredictable delay time in seeing that meeting record. When computers are used as the focus of the meeting, and a transmission delay is greater than several seconds, people get disoriented. They cannot follow the verbal conversation when the computer record lags too far behind. It would be better if they did not see the screen at all. It was for these and other groupware design problems that the wide area network of the Fortune 100 company had to be reconfigured and optimized to reduce transmission delays.

In other words, network latency is a shifting requirement. Network latency is always a matter of interpretation. "Slow" for one workgroup is not the same for another.

15.6 HOW GROUPWARE SYSTEMS EVOLVE AND CHANGE

15.6.1 Business Process Teams

In contemporary business situations, we seek to organize work around integrated business processes. These are the specific activities that *add value* to an organization, without necessarily supporting the formal structure. People are empowered by their organizations to achieve identifiable results. They are involved in multiple aspects of a process, and their jobs are redesigned to fulfill specific roles within a process. Individual workers are more than just single links in the production chain to create a product or deliver a service. Their work activities extend across the functional boundaries of their business enterprise. Working in process teams, people do more than perform a set of defined tasks in a repetitive fashion. If anything, assignments are hardly repetitive and people need to adapt to changing situations. A flexible organizational structure with ready access to essential information is key. Groupware is an important part of the picture. It facilitates the redesign of business processes.

We can identify three different approaches for using groupware to support business teams, each emphasizing different ways that team members can work together.

One approach facilitates online discussions. Conferencing software provides methods to structure and organize electronic conversations, making them much more useful than simple e-mail or basic computer bulletin-boards. A second approach organizes shared electronic documents. A document sharing environment provides team members with an organizing framework about what needs to be done and in what order. It enables a process team to track tasks and measure accomplishments by monitoring the ongoing flow of documents. A third approach focuses on procedures for supporting process teams. In many instances, team members need to understand the overall picture about the linkages among activities to support the business process. They need to focus on the underlying sequence of tasks, the flow of individuals' actions required to accomplish a particular business process. They need to clarify responsibilities, identifying who is accountable for producing particular results.

15.6.1.1 Supporting Process Teams

Groupware supports process teams in three ways. It can enhance group discussions so that teams can meet online, in effect continuing the give-and-take of real-time meetings. It can enable teams to share group documents so that all have ready access to timely project information, in effect providing a bookshelf devoted to a particular business task. It can help coordinate the flow of actions and activities, identifying process steps and monitoring results, so that each person can manage his or her own commitments to the team.

Groupware provides a focus on business communications, enabling people to share information as needed. The steps for supporting process teams combine business insights with enabling technologies. These steps build upon an attention to business process reengineering and organizational design by clarifying management goals and defining business objectives. To implement groupware and identify an appropriate strategy, teams need to build three catalogs that describe their processes and functions: catalogues of business activities, information requests, and communication techniques.

A process team has a business purpose related to the core activities of the organization. Team members need to describe their work in their own terms—what they do, how they do it, and when they consider a task complete. Certainly, individuals' accomplishments and business objectives change over time, and work assignments may change as well. What is important is having a place to begin, an initial catalog of activities that participants can revise and update.

Next, team members need to identify the essential information required to achieve their core business tasks. They need to describe their requirements for different kinds of information, together with the methods they use to find essential information and to communicate it to others. A catalog of business activities can lead to a catalog of information requests. Within a process team, these information requests are often difficult to describe with any degree of precision and are likely to change as situations change. Teamwork is dynamic and little remains constant. Typically, team members get the information they need from telephone conversations and voice mail, from business meetings and informal discussions, from timely delivered private reports and public documents, or from utilizing their time effectively and interacting with one another. They hardly want to replace these mechanisms and yet they need to adapt to changing work requirements, to have the flexibility and accountability of working together in new ways.

Finally, this catalog of information requests leads to a catalog of communication techniques. Team members need to structure their methods of communication to meet their core business needs. They also need to manage their communication processes. At a very simple level, this means understanding when e-mail or a memo might be sufficient and when it is necessary to schedule a face-to-face conference (particularly one that would require travel and an extensive time commitment). This means understanding the business requirements and the business processes being supported by the process team, and to support effective group communication processes accordingly. A team-based approach needs to include flexible communications methods and be easily adaptable in light of changing circumstances.

Introduction to Chapter 16

Case studies of how groupware and collaborative strategies are being used in companies provide us with the benefit of others' experiences. The Big Six consulting firms were some of the earliest adopters of groupware and intranet technologies, so their implementations are as mature as any others in the market. These companies have capitalized on the routing and sharing of intellectual capital across their organization and applied that knowledge to client problems. Additionally, these firms are very competitive, if one adopts Notes, the others do also. It's not a case of follow the leader, it's a question of adopting solutions that work. In the case of groupware and collaboration, once one firm discovers how to implement successful programs, the others must respond to neutralize that competitive advantage.

This chapter contains interesting information and insights and is well worth reading. In the consulting world, clients are king. Getting the right solution to the client in a timely manner is critical to their business. Also, the authors do an excellent job of explaining the need for knowledge management. In fact, several of the Big Six firms have established knowledge management practices, discussed further in Chapter 20. It is clear that the groupware infrastructure has been used to store, create, and leverage knowledge for the client's benefit in these organizations.

It seems most of these consulting firms have similar infrastructures. If that is the case, what makes one groupware and knowledge management implementation better than another? Could corporate policies about such things as training, incentives to include knowledge, sharing knowledge (tacit and explicit), and corporate loyalty determine the effectiveness of these collaborative infrastructures?

Although most of these firms have thousands of Lotus Notes seats, that doesn't necessarily mean that Notes is being used to its best advantage. For example, is the most critical information actually making it into the best practices' databases? Is the culture supporting the technology, or are a few experts hoarding knowledge? What is the ROI for discussion databases? Are they monitored or facilitated, or do they become the "roach motel for information," i.e., information goes in, but nothing ever comes out! Is there a sufficient knowledge architecture in the organization to support a document repository and directory of who's who. Further, can explicit knowledge be matched to the people who have implemented it? What about tracking the tacit knowledge that went into making client decisions? These and other questions are answered in this chapter.

This chapter focuses on the practical, and looks at how Notes deployments changed both organizational and cultural systems. The authors very clearly present how the Big Six learned to deploy Notes successfully within their organizations, including a wide variety of technical tips for Notes deployment. The suc-

cess of the deployment was determined using the formula in the introductory chapter of this book.

Notes is used to support consultants and keep them connected to the knowledge of the firm at all times, especially when they are at a client's site. Notes and the Web are also being used to link directly to the client, essentially bringing them into the corporate infrastructure. However, at this point, the Web requires a "connected model," which is not sufficient for consultant's needs. Therefore, a hybrid infrastructure is being created to support knowledge management. It is important to ensure that the new infrastructure does not conflict with Notes but supplements Notes in the spreading of knowledge.

Although the Big Six have adopted collaboration technologies in a big way, they still have a long way to go. This chapter reports on their progress so far.

Groupware at Big Six Consulting Firms: How Successful Was It?

Andrew S. Clark
Arthur Andersen
Charles E. Downing
Operations and Strategic Management Department, Boston College
David Coleman
Collaborative Strategies

This case study chapter focuses on the internal use of groupware products at Big Six consulting firms. Through interviews with several prominent groupware players from Big Six Management Consulting firms, the authors were able to explore why groupware was implemented, what challenges the firms encountered, the lessons learned from their deployment efforts, the changes and benefits obtained, as well as where groupware is heading at the Big Six.

Big Six Management Consulting firms, by their very nature and size, acquire and store a wealth of intellectual assets at all levels of the firm. These firms have recognized that the dissemination and availability of these intellectual assets to the entire organization are what provide them with the competitive advantage needed to survive and prosper in today's market. Groupware was identified as a prominent vehicle to propagate this information/knowledge.

While deploying groupware products, these firms faced a number of challenges regarding roll out, training, technical infrastructure, and culture that provide lessons for any organization interested in participating in this arena.

Through the initial deployment and beyond, these firms embarked on these projects with the simple notion that to survive in the competitive marketplace of management consulting firms, they had to be able to leverage the knowledge of all their employees.

Although [2] had a chapter with much the same name, its focus was different. That chapter was written by executives involved in groupware at the Big

Six. This chapter leverages that one and takes it a step further. We had a much less biased view, and interviewed a wider range of firms. Because we see these companies as knowledge driven and innovators in the use of these collaborative technologies, we see the information gathered in this chapter as a bellwether of how other firms will use groupware in the future.

16.1 RESEARCHING THE BIG SIX: GOALS, PARTICIPANTS, AND PROCEDURES

How are Big Six firms using groupware today? Is it helping them to achieve their objectives? What difficulties did they encounter in implementation? What lessons have they learned, and what subsequent plans do they have for groupware? To answer these and other questions, prominent groupware players from several Big Six Management Consulting firms were interviewed (see Table 16.3 in Section 16.11 for a list of interviewees). Individuals closer to the operational level were spoken to as well. All of the discussions offer insight into the unique world of management consulting and the past, present, and potential future uses of groupware. Interviews averaged over one hour, and were often followed by shorter discussions for clarification.

The remainder of this chapter is organized into eight sections starting with a summary of the forces driving the Big Six firms. Section 16.3 describes the need for knowledge that arose because of the forces being placed on consulting firms. In section 16.4, the role of groupware at consultancies is described within the life cycle framework of consulting engagements. Section 16.5 identifies the challenges consulting firms faced when rolling out the groupware applications discussed in 16.4. Lessons learned from the process are discussed in section 16.6. The changes and benefits the consulting firms experienced through their efforts to build and deploy groupware are described in section 16.7. Section 16.8 presents a summary of the findings that provides insights into the success of groupware at consulting firms. Finally, section 16.9 focuses on some of the areas where groupware is heading at the Big Six.

Throughout this chapter, special attention has been given to highlighting the perspectives of the interviewees at the various firms. These perspectives, titled "Discussion Snapshots," are direct quotes and are identified by the following box:

Discussion Snapshot—Interviewee Name, Firm "Title"
"Quote"

16.2 FORCES DRIVING THE BIG SIX

16.2.1 Competitive Forces Driving Big Six Consulting

Understanding the competitive context in which Big Six consulting firms operate is critical when exploring groupware uses and plans for usage within these firms. Porter's model [1980] provides a well-known framework from which to begin (see Fig. 16.1).

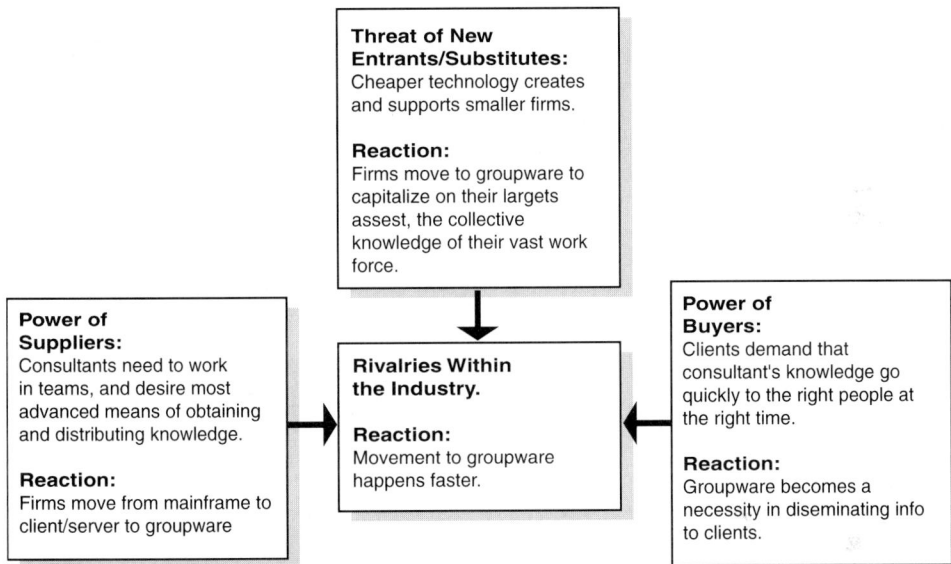

Threat of New Entrants/Substitutes: Cheaper technology creates and supports smaller firms.

Reaction: Firms move to groupware to capitalize on their largets assest, the collective knowledge of their vast work force.

Power of Suppliers: Consultants need to work in teams, and desire most advanced means of obtaining and distributing knowledge.

Reaction: Firms move from mainframe to client/server to groupware

Rivalries Within the Industry.

Reaction: Movement to groupware happens faster.

Power of Buyers: Clients demand that consultant's knowledge go quickly to the right people at the right time.

Reaction: Groupware becomes a necessity in diseminating info to clients.

Fig. 16.1 Groupware's Role in the Competitive Context of Big Six Consulting Firms.

The product of management consulting firms is ideas and advice, both which originate from a variety of sources and locations. As Mike Blum of C&L puts it, "we do it in a form that we need experts and disciplines combined. So, immediately you're looking at putting together a team."

The "suppliers" in this environment are the consultants and the consulting teams themselves, including consultants from other areas of the firm. With knowledge dissemination as their primary function, these individuals and teams have proven to be strong proponents of technical change; if technology facilitates the quick and easy collection and distribution of knowledge, the consultants are obviously in favor of it. These suppliers have, not surprisingly, been a driver behind the switch from a mainframe environment to a client/server environment, and now from a client/server environment to a groupware environment.

The "buyers," on the other hand, are of course the firm's clients themselves. These clients represent the strongest force in the Big Six consulting world. In an increasingly downsized corporate world, the buyers expect, and in fact demand, that the consultant's knowledge be given to the right people at the right time. The increased expectations for speed and distribution of the consultants' services necessitated groupware solutions.

"New Entrants" and "Substitutes" in the Big Six consulting world are smaller consulting firms and independent start-ups. The client/server era saw these entities faring quite well in competition with the "big boys." With the price and power curves of computing moving rapidly in opposite directions for many years, these companies were able to leapfrog larger, more inefficient organizations in service/price ratios. Just about anyone could purchase a PC and fax machine and post an "Open for Business" sign in the front yard. However, larger firms have several extraordinary advantages over their smaller counterparts: their huge base of competent professionals and their name recognition as proven providers of information technology. Big Six firms are beginning to leverage the knowledge of their professionals as was discussed in the introductory chapter section on preservation of intellectual capital. Groupware is being used as the facilitator of this knowledge transfer. If the knowledge, experience, and expertise of 30,000 or more professionals is pooled and made easily available to those professionals exclusively, how can smaller organizations hope to compete?

And finally, the competition amongst rival Big Six firms is helping to make all of this happen faster. In all the firms interviewed, none had a problem (or in some cases even a recollection of) building a business case for groupware deployment. The need was obvious, and the push or pull from these competitive forces was overwhelming.

16.2.2 Market Move from Mainframe to Client/Server Computing

As the buyers in our competitive context model have moved from a mainframe environment to a client/server environment, a change has had to occur at consulting firms to align their project teams to the needs of client/server computing and management. This shift in team structure has meant that fewer consultants have to carry more knowledge than their predecessors. Where once a project team consisted of 40 or more consultants, client/server projects may now only involve 10 or fewer consultants. For example, a client server project might consist of a systems architect, a network architect, a distributed database designer, a GUI designer, and GUI developers, as well as project management personnel. The architects and designers have a much broader knowledge base requirement and fewer people under them than a traditional mainframe development environment required.

In addition to project team size, consultancies are now having to provide expertise in a wealth of new technologies and project management that did not exist in the world of the mainframe including topics such as networking, distributed RDBMS, and GUI technologies, as well as networked project organization.

This shift in project team compositions and breadth of new technologies has meant consulting firms have had to find the best ways to disseminate information that ensures the buyers are provided with the value added information they are looking for. Groupware has provided them with that ability.

16.2.3 Market Focus on Providing Value-Based Consulting

Another market force playing a role in shaping Big Six groupware use is the emphasis being placed on providing value-based consulting. Clients are asking consultancies to deliver *value* to them, not just a product.

As Charlie Paulk, CIO at Andersen Consulting, pointed out, Andersen's mission statement: "to help our clients change to be more successful," and vision: "to be one global firm committed to quality by having the best people with knowledge capital working for the best clients to deliver value," clearly associate the ability to provide value to the client by maintaining a staff of people with sufficient "working capital." This once again points to the need to disseminate information to consultants.

Providing value to clients also means being able to support threaded activities where work is moving from place to place with an incremental value being added at each point. This requires consultancies be able to collaborate in a semi-structured format. John Parkinson at E&Y described it this way, "...increasingly our work for clients requires us to be able to pilot something at one place and move the results on to other places, modifying and adding incremental content each time we do it."

16.3 THE NEED FOR KNOWLEDGE

With the various forces at work, as described in the previous section, Big Six consultancies have recognized the need to create a communications infrastructure that will enable them to deliver knowledge to their clients. For a more thorough discussion of building a knowledge based company, refer to Chapter 20, "Groupware, Knowledge Creation, and Competitive Advantage"

16.3.1 Factors Driving Groupware Projects at the Big Six

The factors driving the groupware surge at consulting firms are identified below. The major factor cited first by all interviewees was the need to leverage professional expertise given the wealth of knowledge spread over the globe.

Forces driving the use of groupware at consultancies:

☞ Leveraging professional expertise

☞ Increased productivity

☞ Fewer meetings

☞ Automating processes

☞ Integration of geographically disparate consultants

Consulting engagements by their very nature require consultants be on the road. Integrating geographically disparate consultants became a central factor in deploying groupware.

Discussion Snapshot—John Parkinson, E&Y, "The Bigger Need for Groupware"

"What we need is a family of technologies that support asynchronous collaboration. Because we have people who need to work on related topics who are dispersed in geography obviously, but because of the extremes of the geographic disbursement, they're also disbursed in time. And, if you look beyond the United States, you look at the global business, then the simple view of groupware, which is that it allows synchronous collaboration, because we can't drag people out of bed at two in the morning to participate in a conference."

16.3.2 Bringing the power of the practice to People Who Need It

The Big Six firms are national organizations with offices in major cities around the world. To get their products and services out, they need to be able to work in a "virtual mode." Whether that is putting together presentations or proposals, the power of the practice needs to be accessible to the people who need it.

Discussion Snapshot—Rowan Snyder, C&L, "The Essence of Groupware"

"Client needs are often so complex, the answers so difficult, and the time so short that you need to focus the best resources you can as soon as you can. This is what groupware does. And it works."

To address the complex needs of clients with the best possible resources, groupware solutions were examined. Lotus Notes and SoftArc's FirstClass were chosen by the firms interviewed for this chapter. Once these products were selected, their growth into the firms' practices grew at an extremely rapid rate.

At Andersen Consulting, for example, groupware deployment went from a 40 member global management group of Lotus Notes users to a pilot group of 6,000 users to their current count of 25,000 seats in less than 3 years. At Coopers & Lybrand, a nine month pilot effort of Lotus Notes preceded the rollout to the current 35,000 seats. At Ernst & Young, total seat count went from 600 seats of Lotus Notes to 9 or 10 thousand in about 15 months. KPMG has ramped up to 17,000 seats of SoftArc's FirstClass since 1992.

The following table (Table 16.1) should help give an idea of how many and how rapidly consultancies have "ramped up" their Lotus Notes and SoftArc First-Class deployment. Total seats represents the projected seat count when all deployment efforts have been completed. Deployment represents the current status.

Table 16.1 Lotus Notes and SoftArc FirstClass deployment

		Deployment			
Firm	Total seats*	Partner	Manager	Consultant	Staff
Andersen Consulting	25,000	100%	100%	40%	By next FY end

*Consulting practice only

		Deployment		
Firm	Total seats*	Us consultants	US overall	Worldwide
Coopers & Lybrand	67,000	4,000	16,000	35,000

*Target for all practices

		Deployment
Firm	Total seats*	US consultants, tax practice, and support staff
Ernst & Young	22,000	10,000

*Target for all practices

		Deployment		
Firm	Total seats*	US all practices	US consultants	Overseas consultants
KPMG	20,000	17,000	4,000	2,000

*Target for all practices

16.3.3 Convergence of Groupware Tools, Knowledge Needs, and Technology

The rollout of Notes and SoftArc FirstClass at Big Six firms did not happen overnight. The convergence of three major factors helped lead to the introduction of groupware in late 1989 and early 1990 (see Fig. 16.2).

1. **Technological advances**—For the most part, Big Six firms had already been bulking up their network infrastructures in the early 1990s. While far from ready to support the current or future needs of Notes, the groundwork had been laid.
2. **Knowledge needs**—As outlined in the previous section, the knowledge needs of consultants were exploding with the changing face of computing. Most firms were reexamining their practice's strategy for sharing knowledge in the early 1990s.
3. **Groupware Tools**—The release of the alpha version of Notes in 1989 coincided with the previous events.

Big Six Groupware Development

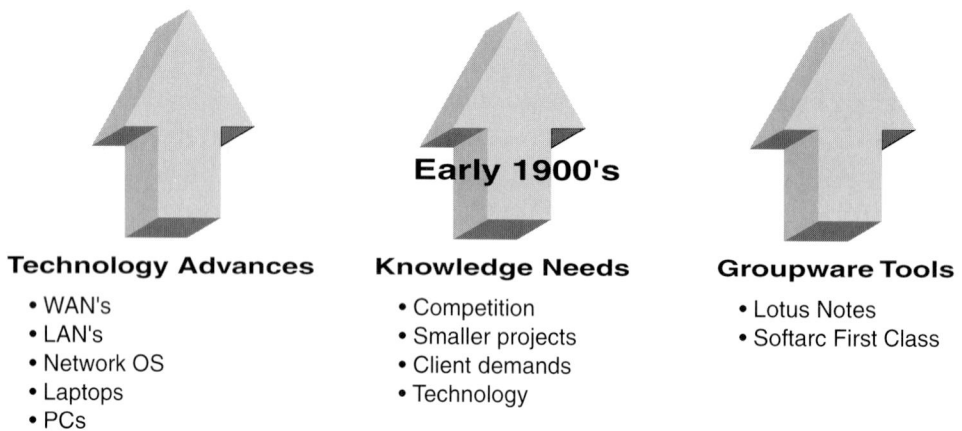

Early 1900's

Technology Advances
- WAN's
- LAN's
- Network OS
- Laptops
- PCs

Knowledge Needs
- Competition
- Smaller projects
- Client demands
- Technology

Groupware Tools
- Lotus Notes
- Softarc First Class

Fig. 16.2 Big Six Groupware Deployment

To help meet their knowledge needs, Big Six firms were assessing their strategies to better leverage the knowledge capital of their work force. Anderson Consulting, for example, had concluded research on knowledge transference through technology about the same time it was reexamining its strategy for delivering consulting services. As a result of these independent efforts, they decided to move forward with research specific to their practice involving groupware. Notes was evaluated during this nine month study in late 1991 and matched up well against the criteria Andersen had identified. Charlie Paulk described the result of the converging events this way: "We felt that Notes gave us an opportunity to use technology to achieve our vision, which ultimately created a competitive advantage for our firm."

16.4 THE ROLE OF GROUPWARE AT CONSULTANCIES

Groupware plays many roles at Big Six firms throughout all phases of consulting engagements. This section starts with general information about the use of Notes at Big Six firms that were interviewed. Next, we examine KPMG's selection of SoftArc FirstClass to meet their groupware needs. This section then moves on to identify the components of their Notes and FirstClass applications within a framework of the consulting engagement life cycle as depicted in Fig. 16.3.

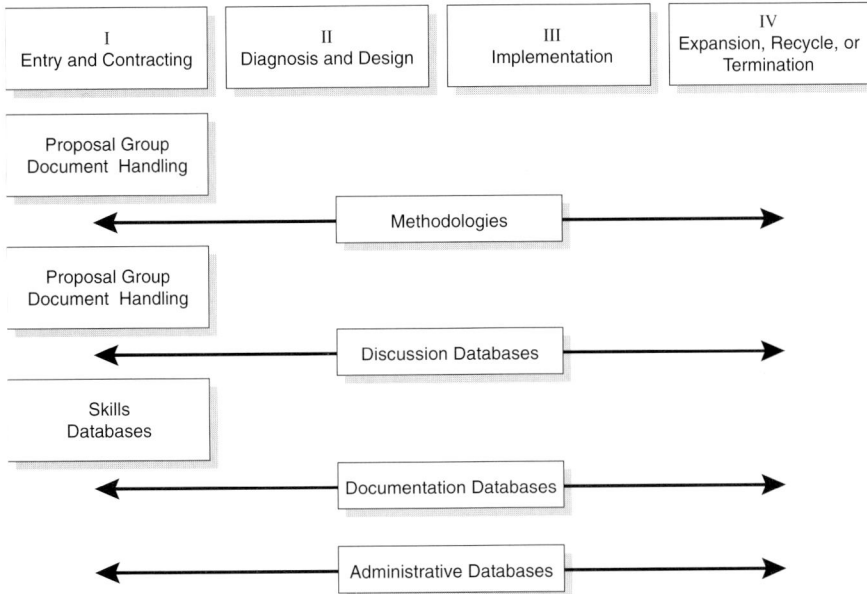

Fig. 16.3 Consulting Engagement Life Cycle and Groupware

16.4.1 General Notes Deployment Information

Big Six firms represent some of the largest users of Notes. As pointed out in section 16.3.2, Notes seat counts are in the tens of thousands. Database counts range in count depending upon what is counted as a database. Ernst & Young for example, reports about 600 "production databases." They also report about 250 development or local/private databases that reside on sandbox servers. No counts are maintained of individual (on the client only) databases. Andersen Consulting reported maintaining over 1,000 databases. Coopers & Lybrand has over 2,000.

Server counts range in the hundreds with Andersen Consulting reporting a total of 360 servers to support their operations.

Most Big Six firms run the Notes Server on OS/2. The OS/2 platform originally had the best administration tools and third party management and administration utilities. Both Coopers & Lybrand and Ernst & Young reported a migration to Windows NT.

Most Notes development was done in house with support from Lotus Consulting reported as the only 3rd party vendor to participate.

Initial databases were generally deployed at the partner level first, to gain "buy in." Each Big Six firm reports progress towards outfitting the entire consulting practice in the near future or has already achieved full rollout. Andersen Consulting had their consultants rolled out with Notes in the Spring of 1996. The roll-out progression from partner to staff was somewhat influenced by the need to provide laptops to each successive level within the firm.

16.4.2 FirstClass Deployment at KPMG

While most firms selected Lotus Notes to address their groupware needs, KPMG chose FirstClass from SoftArc to address their knowledge management needs. FirstClass is an easy-to-use communication system that allows you to send and receive electronic mail, share files, use electronic conferencing to exchange ideas, and participate in on-line chats. FirstClass works in a client/server model with a client component to connect to the server using either a modem or a network. To use FirstClass, you need a settings document for the system that you want to connect to and the FirstClass Client application.

Our interview with Allan Frank, partner of Enabling Technologies at KPMG, provided a different perspective on the role of groupware at Big Six firms and why FirstClass fit into their short and long term plans.

Some of the reasons KPMG selected FirstClass:

☞ Met their knowledge management needs now and provided a migration path for their future needs

☞ Wanted more open, client/server approach that did not require use of proprietary database used in Notes

☞ Consistent with their goal of maintaining a single source or "glass house" approach to sharing data rather than propagating data through replication techniques

☞ Wanted data to be separate from the tool used to view it

☞ Low per seat costs of FirstClass

As Allan Frank put it, "Lotus Notes is the antithesis of the appropriate architecture for our needs." KPMG wanted a groupware tool that could point to the information sources in their original format (CD-ROM, database systems, files on a server) without having to tie the data to the tool used to view that data. By keeping the data separate from the tool, they felt they would be better able to move to new platforms (intranet, Internet, and beyond) because the data would be in its original format and not in a proprietary database such as Notes.

KPMG looked at FirstClass as a migratory, client/server implementation to their groupware needs since FirstClass clients could dial into the KPMG WAN and access data in whatever format it was created. The idea is to store the data in one place and have the client find it wherever it resides. This is aided by FirstClass's ability to distinguish between a native document that requires an application to be launched and Web pages that require a browser. In either of these cases, the user does not need to be aware of how to get at the information using FirstClass.

To KPMG, Notes represented an end-state because of the proprietary nature of the underlying database used to support Notes and the replication strategy. FirstClass allowed them to keep their knowledge content in its native format and in a single location for expanded usage. KPMG plans to be fully Web based in 1997 with all clients using IP for server connectivity. FirstClass usage will not cease once KPMG is totally Web based; it will remain a part of their tools as long as it is still being actively used by the firm.

16.4.3 Discussion Databases

Discussion databases have been set up to parallel industry groups (products, services, etc.) within each firm. These databases provide the opportunity for information to be posted and read in a manner that facilitates collaboration.

> **Discussion Snapshot—John Parkinson, E&Y, "Networks of People"**
>
> "We want to set up networks of people who have shared interests, and who therefore share, or contribute to, a shared experience. Like a knowledge base, a whole series of overlapping, interconnected knowledge bases, where you can't really predict in advance what's going to go in them, or what they'll be used for, so what you want to do is provide the people who are interested with the tools to support their collaboration."

At Coopers & Lybrand, catalogs of databases are made available to users to help them locate discussion databases or topical databases (skills, proposals, and qualifications areas). At Andersen Consulting, there are knowledge integrators within each of the industry groups who synthesize raw data pertaining to a technology, process, strategy, etc. into meaningful information for their industry group. As Charlie Paulk put it, "they present the information, on object technology for example, in context of what is important to that community."

16.4.4 Documentation Repositories

To provide repositories for knowledge documentation, Notes databases for a variety of information were set up. These databases, along with newly developed software agents, which begin to pinpoint the information consultants are looking for, provide a means for consultants to find the right information.

Inherent to these repositories is the "passive nature" of the documentation.

> **Discussion Snapshot—Mike Blum, C&L, "Passive Versus Active Sharing"**
>
> "Now [with Notes], you basically have a passive mode of sharing versus an active mode of sharing. In the old days, you had no way of doing it other than active, meaning you had to broadcast it, you had to send a memo out, you had to send something out. Here, in essence, you can build repository and it becomes a passive mode, which is a lot more amenable to people who have so many things to do. In other words, when I feel like it, I'll go in and get the information, but it's not piling up on my desk and I'm not forced to look at it."

Samples of the types and variety of documentation repositories maintained are listed below:

1. Client proposals
2. Leads and Prospects
3. Administrative repositories for
   • Voice and mail directories
   • Time reporting
   • Expense reporting
4. White papers
5. Presentations
6. Project deliverables
7. Internal training curriculum and booking
8. Lead tracking
9. Contact management
10. Messaging
11. Regional news
12. Methodologies
13. External information sources

External information sources are an interesting implementation of documentation repositories. As well as documentation produced from within a firm, consultancies are obviously interested in tapping into external information sources.

> **Discussion Snapshot—John Parkinson, E&Y, "Hook Up to External Resources"**
>
> "We want to hook people up to external information sources, in three ways. One way is on-demand search and browse, so if I'm interested in who's writing books about groupware, I could go out and look specifically for that topic. The second way is what we call notification and alert mode. So, I express an interest in something, but I don't want to spend all my time sitting and waiting for that interest to be satisfied, I just want to know when something that's interesting to me shows up. And then the third mode is what we call serendipitous discovery, where I want to be able to find things I didn't know I was interested in, but which are important to me."

Consultancies have also incorporated access to their methodologies into their Notes and SoftArc FirstClass environments. As with any other documentation, access to the most recent versions of their methodologies means they can take advantage of the latest revisions to engagements. In the past, the distribution of methodologies was slow and resulted in different versions of the methodology being applied.

16.4.5 Messaging

All of the consultancies that use Notes adopted Notes messaging as their standard. Ernst & Young and Coopers & Lybrand both started with existing e-mail packages in house that were replaced by Notes. Andersen Consulting replaced their Wang office systems with Notes. The Notes messaging capabilities have been expanded to include receiving and sending of Internet e-mail. The ability to add attachments to messages was a well-received and now well-used capability.

16.5 CHALLENGES FACED IN GROUPWARE DEPLOYMENT

Many unique challenges were faced by consultancies in their deployment of groupware. This section highlights some of the categories that were identified by the interviewees.

16.5.1 Roll Out

The roll-out of the first groupware applications was different for each firm.

Table 16.2 Notable Differences—Initial groupware deployment

Firm	Method of initial groupware deployment
Andersen Consulting	Small strategic pilot initiative with 40 partners
Coopers & Lybrand	Audit practice pioneered groupware use at the firm
Ernst & Young	Client driven experiences which spawned internal use
KPMG	All practices participated in deployment

In the Andersen Consulting case, a group of 40 partners who represented the global management practice were introduced to the early versions of their Knowledge Exchange, a loosely grouped organization of Lotus Notes databases and applications, to help facilitate meetings. At Coopers & Lybrand, Audit moved to groupware as a means to facilitate the entire audit process. Management Consulting saw the benefits, and followed suit. At Ernst & Young, Management Consulting was first to use Notes. Clients had problems that Notes provided a perfect solution for, and consultants on these project spread the positive word.

Once it became apparent that these tools could provide the mechanism consultancies were looking for to disseminate knowledge, large scale efforts were made to deploy the tools to all of the practice.

With a global work force, the roll out of Notes was a major challenge to Big Six firms. These firms learned the hard way, in many cases, that the logistics of getting Notes client and communications links were more challenging than had been anticipated. At E&Y for example, initial problem rates with the hardware and software for running the Notes client and communications link were estimated to be 10 percent. In the end, a problem rate of nearly 40 percent was observed.

Determining what parts of the default Notes installation to roll out in the initial phases was also identified as a challenge. Initial Notes rollouts that offered highly usable applications that resided on Notes was the approach ultimately arrived at by firms. How they got to that decision was interesting. The discussion snapshots below from E&Y elaborate on these points.

Discussion Snapshot—John Parkinson, E&Y, "Rolling Notes Out"

"Lotus shipped a whole bunch of example databases with the tools, and if you sat down with the instructions, or with basic training, you could certainly start building versions of your own, and we didn't want that to happen...we went out and talked to a lot of people when we were planning the implementation and tried to figure out what had worked and what hadn't for people, and basically we got two messages.

One message was that it's better to do a few useful things very well, then a whole lot of not very useful things. So we decided that we would not deploy Notes, but we would deploy a number of applications implemented on Notes that people would find useful.

The second message we heard was that you had to do it fast, get a lot of people in, so that you create critical mass, build momentum, but more than that, build connectivity between users. If you only have 100 people using it, then they're the only 100 people that can talk to each other."

Discussion Snapshot—Gene Cort, E&Y, "Put the Applications First"

"The problem with rolling Notes out, or any major rollout, but I think Notes in particular, is that what you think you're going to deploy and how you deploy it aren't necessarily the same thing. In retrospect, the initial feeling and focus was to roll Notes out. That was amended to decide to roll out applications that, by the way, used Notes...a very subtle but different approach. If you decide to roll out Notes, but haven't thought about the cultural changes or what people are going to do with it, you're kind of all dressed up and no place to go."

16.5.2 Training

Trainers for the consultants required a wide range of skills to be successful. In addition to traditional training skills, the trainers needed to be able to teach collaboration skills to a variety of users. Some trainees felt comfortable with the idea but others needed to see how it would work before they would feel comfortable. Ernst & Young found that paid trainers were great at training consultants on Notes, but not so great at training consultants on E&Y-specific applications.

16.5.3 Technical Infrastructure

While many firms were in the process of upgrading WAN and LAN infrastructures, few were prepared for the infrastructure requirements needed for deploying Notes. Currently, Andersen Consulting has nearly 360 servers deployed to meet their global needs. Three tiers of servers were set up to support replication needs: area servers, regional servers, and office servers. Figure 16.4 depicts the replication structure at Andersen Consulting. The majority of the 360 servers are stationed at the local office level with a significantly smaller quantity at the regional level and a handful at the area level. This diagram is not complete, but represents the breakdown of the Americas' area into a sampling of the regional and a sampling of the office.

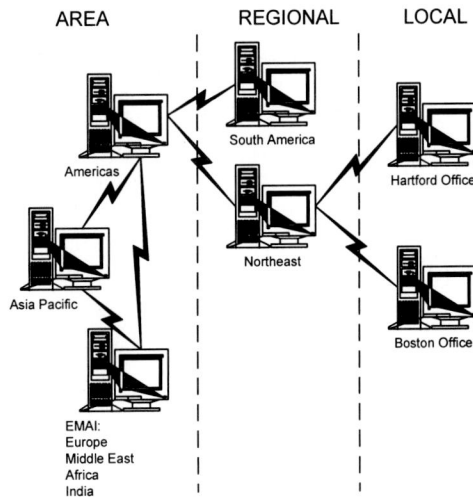

Fig. 16.4 Replication Structure at Andersen Consulting

Another component of the technical infrastructure that caused telecommunication challenges to firms was the ability to connect to and replicate data in countries where their communication capabilities were not reliable. Andersen Consulting, for example, is using satellite communications to replicate with their offices in South America.

16.5.4 Management Paradox: Empowering Users Requires Tight Central Management

Groupware is a powerful tool, which "empowers" consultants at Big Six firms to do their jobs. However, empowerment should not translate into a surrendering of control. Indeed, as Rowan Snyder describes below, empowerment through groupware necessitates *additional* management control.

Discussion Snapshot—Rowan Snyder, C&L, "The Hidden Irony"

"One of the problems with a large enterprise groupware deployment is that it is a complicated technology. Therefore, it puts strong upward pressure on the skills necessary to support it. This translates to direct expense for the training and ongoing costs for more skilled people to support it. The best way to offset these costs is to manage the deployment centrally with fewer people. This can often more than offset new costs, it can reduce total expense. However, this takes expensive tools and engineering of solutions for central management. The irony then is that to be successful in the "ultimate" in end-user computing requires the ultimate in central management. This hidden shift of activities isn't clear when you go in."

16.5.5 Willingness to Contribute Knowledge

One of the "themes" that had been expressed about consultants was their unwillingness to share information with each other because they needed that special piece of knowledge to help them get promoted. During our interviews we found this not to be true for a number of reasons, including:

☞ Reward and recognition systems put into place

☞ Tools that cut down on time to resolve problems will be embraced

☞ Management support

☞ "Can't do it alone" thought process

Discussion Snapshot—John Parkinson, E&Y, "Incentives to Share"

"It was a recognized issue, back when we started, and we've done a number of things over the last four years to attack that, one of which is providing a technology that makes it easier to share things, but equally important is the fact that we have a reward and recognition system now that you can't max out in unless your contribution to the shared environment passes a threshold. So you have to submit things."

16.6 LESSONS LEARNED FROM GROUPWARE DEPLOYMENT

As a result of the challenges faced with their deployment of groupware, Big Six firms learned many lessons about what works and what doesn't. This section highlights lessons that were shared by one or more of the Big Six firms we interviewed.

A special Notes-specific technical section from Rowan Snyder at Coopers & Lybrand is also included in this section. These eleven items should prove extremely useful to a technical manager responsible for the deployment of Notes. Special thanks to Rowan and Coopers & Lybrand for allowing us to incorporate these technical tips in the chapter.

16.6.1 Identify Project and Groupware Champion

Every listing of project success factors stresses the importance of a champion who will sponsor and support a project, and all of the interviewees identified the need for a project and groupware champion. The groupware champion must be actively involved with groupware and understand the benefits it can provide. He or she must also understand what changes groupware will bring and what changes in culture groupware may bring about. For a more thorough discussion about groupware champions, please refer to Chapter 1.

In the case of the Big Six firms, the CIO, Enabling Technologies Partner, or equivalent in each firm was charged with the rollout of groupware. These groupware champions included Charlie Paulk at Andersen Consulting, Rowan Snyder at Coopers & Lybrand, John Parkinson at Ernst & Young, and Allan Frank at KPMG.

16.6.2 Culture Plays a Large Part in Groupware Success

The success or failure of groupware has a lot to do with the culture that exists at a company. For the most part, Big Six consulting firms have a history of sharing information (internally). This foundation helped pave the way for groupware but did not guarantee the complete success.

> **Discussion Snapshot—John Parkinson, E&Y, "Cultural Impact of Groupware"**
>
> "Don't underestimate the cultural impact [of groupware]. If you don't have a sharing culture, you are in trouble. At E&Y, the concept of sharing comes from very high. The firm pushes sharing."

16.6.3 Raise Internal Awareness Before and After Deployment

A corporate culture that supports sharing is vital to groupware. To ensure that employees embrace groupware, sufficient efforts must be made to raise the awareness of employees about the changes that groupware deployment might bring about. Users who are aware of what to expect will be able to transition to the tool and achieve productivity gains faster.

After groupware has been deployed, continual efforts have to be made to ensure that employees understand what is available to them and how it can contribute to the success of the individual and the company. Andersen Consulting, for example, employs Knowledge Exchange Champions to help facilitate the use of Notes. These individuals operate in a region and help facilitate the use of the Knowledge Exchange through newsletters, one-on-one training, Notes database monitoring, and facilitation sessions. At Ernst & Young, moderators are assigned to special discussion databases. Moderators are middle level practice support staff from their Center for Business Knowledge, who have broad responsibilities for supporting "networks" of people with common interests.

16.6.4 Do Not Deploy Groupware for Groupware's Sake

Big Six firms identified a business need that was addressed by using groupware tools. They concentrated on producing a small number of high impact applications and progressed from there.

Projects that start with the selection of a groupware product and then look for a problem to solve are destined to fail. Decide on a groupware tool based on a specific business problem. Groupware tools should be chosen because their functionality provides a solution that is not achievable through other "standard" tools.

16.6.5 Don't Forget the Non-Technical Infrastructure

Infrastructure needs to be built correctly from the start, to ensure the successful deployment of groupware. Infrastructure is not just the technical aspects, it also includes:

1. support
2. help desk
3. administration

These need to be put in place one at a time. They may increase apparent costs, but will allow a company to react to problems and support demands of users.

16.6.6 Consider Adopting a Two-Pass Deployment Approach

In a large scale roll out of Notes, rapid deployment is worth pursuing. This deployment approach would have two phases to it:

1. Clean up the client PCs in terms of software and hardware requirements
2. Deploy Notes and train the users

This approach ensures the true deployment of Notes in step 2 has a greater chance to succeed. By identifying and resolving client PC hardware/software problems before training resources and dollars are committed, Notes deployment goes smoother and training can happen as planned.

16.6.7 Place Special Emphasis on Training Remote Users

With any new technology, good training helps to ensure users will adopt and use the software. In the case of groupware, this is especially true. Users unfamiliar with groupware concepts need to be introduced to the way groupware works before the semantics of a tool can be introduced.

Several firms emphasized spending more time coming up with quality training. John Parkinson at Ernst & Young pointed out the need for extensive training for remote users. Training for remote users is critical so that they continue to believe in the system if/when it breaks.

Discussion Snapshot—John Parkinson, E&Y, "Importance of Remote User Training"

"Remote users need to be given enough training so they believe in the system and continue to use it even when it breaks down. That is a big thing because in consulting we have a 90 percent mobile population, so they were all going to be using dial in, at some stage, and that's a much harder piece to figure how to do....You need to benchmark how knowledgeable the population you're going to deploy to is, and build training that brings them up the confidence curve quickly. The stuff is easy to use, and as an application it's not unreliable, but it's the application plus infrastructure that people need to be trained in."

16.6.8 Synthesis of Information into Knowledge

All of the Big Six firms noted the value their clients placed on receiving quality information representing the best the firm had to offer. To ensure that firms are delivering the right information at the right time, a synthesis of information into knowledge needs to occur within the groupware environment. A mechanism has to be put in place that gives structure to the information to ensure it can be used.

Charlie Paulk at Andersen Consulting pointed out how they apply the concepts of their Change Management practice group to make this happen. These concepts helped Andersen identify the need to present information in the context of what is important to the community using the information. If this synthesis process was not to occur, the information may not be presented in a manner that is retrievable or useful to the user community.

16.6.9 Identify the Point of Diminishing Returns for Groupware in Your Organization

It is important to understand the point of diminishing returns for groupware in your organization. What is the appropriate usage level? When do physical meetings need to take place? If groupware is seen as the collaboration answer in all circumstances, people will become dependent on it, and ideas will get stale.

Discussion Snapshot—Mike Blum, C&L "Avoid Over-dependency on Groupware"

"You ultimately will have very stale things and very flat things that are highly dependent on what was done before and sitting in some database."

16.6.10 Coopers & Lybrand Technical Tips for Notes Deployment

The following eleven technical tips come from Rowan Snyder, Chief Technology Officer of Coopers & Lybrand. They were developed from extensive experience. Special thanks again to C&L for allowing these to be reprinted here.

1. **Design for the maximum end-state from the beginning**—The Notes topology should be thought through carefully. Notes does not scale easily and changing the topology is a demanding exercise.
2. **Implement a Lotus Notes organization**—This would include an administration/support group and a planning/design group. These could be combined according to the size of the organization. Application development is usually done at the business unit level.
3. **Implement a standardized Notes platform and configuration**—This enables one to create a template server from which all other servers can be built. It further simplifies maintenance, upgrades, customizations, and problem diagnosis.
4. **Implement a standard client workstation for Notes**—This simplifies maintenance, upgrades, problem diagnosis, and enhancements to the work station.
5. **Implement IP or other WAN routeable protocols on all servers and work stations before rolling out Notes**—This ensures efficient routing via the WAN instead of the servers.
6. **Implement a separate domain for development databases and a Q/A process using standard database templates for deploying databases in production**—This ensures stability of the infrastructure by ensuring that new requirements are stable before being implemented in production.

This also enables developers to test applications in a pseudo production environment.

7. **Implement a change control process**—This ensures the registration, documentation, approval, and tracking of changes that affect the technology infrastructure are processed properly.

8. **Implement separate mail and database servers**—This simplifies manageability and increases the number of sessions on a server.

9. **Implement mail routing point-to-point**—This will increase the efficiency of mail delivery.

10. **Do not customize the Name and Address book**—This will ensure that your Name and Address book is compatible with all new releases of Lotus Notes. This also simplifies manageability of the Name and Address book and facilitates future upgrades.

11. **Implement a centralized and automated administration system**— This enables one to automate the process of deploying databases, ACLs, IDs, name changes, verification of backups, dead mail notification—simplifies manageability of the environment. This also ensures a more secure environment.

16.7 CHANGES AND BENEFITS FROM GROUPWARE DEPLOYMENT

16.7.1 Cultural Changes

While many companies cite the changes that occur in culture as a result of groupware deployment at their companies, consultancies do not share the same degree of cultural change. All of the interviewees stressed that groupware was an extension of the way they already worked. Consultants by their very definition are in the business of intellectual capital.

The cultural change that has occurred is the willingness to share information. Consultants at all levels of the firm have come to recognize that no one person can do it alone.

To a degree, the discussion databases have helped foster the willingness to share information by moving consultancies further towards a non-hierarchical structure. Because access to the discussion databases are not restricted, it provides an opportunity for consultants at all levels to post and respond to questions. This gives seniors and staff an opportunity to interact with partners and vice versa. This has not always been the case. See Fig. 16.5 showing the local regional communications channel prior to the introduction of groupware and the discussion databases. It shows the various levels communicating with their peers on other engagements.

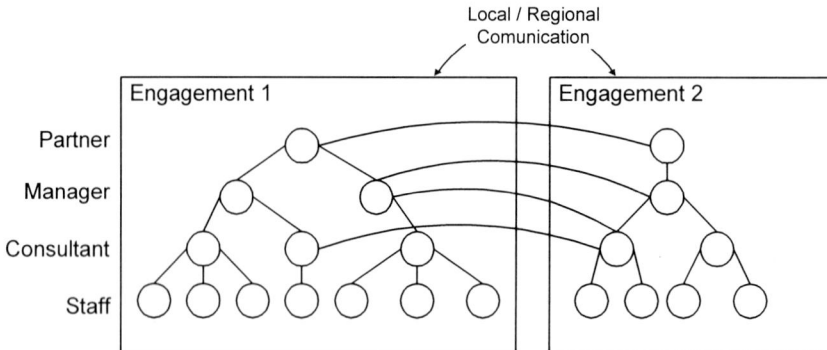

Fig. 16.5 Previous Communication Channel at Big Six Firms

With the introduction of the discussion databases, the communications channels have opened to allow for potential global communications between all levels as depicted in Fig. 16.6.

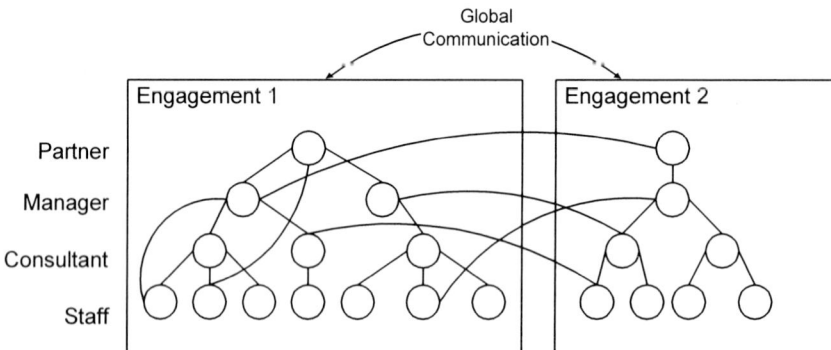

Fig. 16.6 Discussion Databases Have Allowed for Open Communications

16.7.2 Workflow Changes

The most dramatic workflow changes at consultancies is the preparation, development, and approval of proposals and presentations. What might have taken weeks to coordinate in the world of voice mail and faxes can be reduced to days by making use of documentation databases, software search agents, and messaging capabilities. Replication capabilities eliminate the need to version drafts of proposals and presentations. As a result, meetings and conferences to discuss and review documents can now be replaced by mobile reviews and updates.

Increased importance has been placed on administration tasks involved with project work. Engagement papers, for example, now need to be completed accurately and promptly to ensure that project information is available to the rest of the world. As Chuck Dean at Andersen Consulting put it, "Before, if you didn't complete your engagement papers, your files were incomplete. Now, if you don't complete your engagement papers, the whole firm's project papers are incomplete."

16.7.3 Benefits

Many benefits were discussed during our interview sessions. Some were directly related to client approval, while others related to cost benefits. Below are the most common benefits mentioned:

16.7.3.1 Supports Strategic Direction

The benefits of providing a medium for the distribution of knowledge capital of the firm was stressed by all interviewees. It is the benefit that all firms felt they had to achieve in order to stay competitive in the market.

16.7.3.2 Responsiveness to Client/High Value to Client

Several interviewees related stories of how groupware has increased the responsiveness to clients. For example, many firms now have startup templates for projects pre-packaged. These pre-packaged templates might include GUI standards or generic data and process models. By searching for and incorporating existing templates from engagements with similar backgrounds, consultancies were able to get projects up and running quicker for their clients.

Another example of client responsiveness cited by interviewees is the ability to get "up to speed" on new technologies or management processes in a short time frame. If a manager is asked, for example, to give a brief presentation on a subject area not familiar to him/her, he/she can do research in an efficient manner to report on the best information the firm has available. This enables consultants to quickly respond to the needs of clients.

16.7.3.3 Reduced Administrative and Overhead Costs

Firms are moving toward "hoteling," i.e., virtual office setups at their branch offices. Consultants get an assigned area (may change each time) in a physical facility that is smaller than current facilities, which they share with others. Overhead expenses are reduced, and to stay on par with previous work methods, they need something to make up for the lost process support. Notes can make up that gap.

16.7.3.4 Increased Mobility and Portability

Groupware has enabled consultants to work in a virtual mode on the road, in a hotel, or at a remote client site and still be productive. Prior to Notes, the ability to get work accomplished while mobile was dependent on having a large briefcase with project documentation. Now, replication and off-line review of material make keeping informed and adding value much easier to accomplish.

16.8 HOW SUCCESSFUL WAS IT?

Groupware projects at the Big Six have been, and continue to be, success stories. All of the interviewees identified links between the implementation of groupware and their ability to sell work.

Put in the framework of the success formula identified by David Coleman in Chapter 1.

Groupware success = Technology + Culture + Economics + Politics

This is not surprising. The two major challenges of groupware, technical and organizational, are well addressed by consultancies: They deal with and implement technology for their clients, so they have the resources to address technological issues. Further, organizationally they have a corporate culture in place that already was based on collaboration.

Economically, the strategy, mission, and vision statements adopted by consultancies in the early 1990s made the need to exploit their knowledge capital a primary objective. In fact, financial measurement, e.g., ROI, was not part of the picture. There was simply a belief that a collaborative work environment serves the business goals and directly impacts the bottom line.

Discussion Snapshot—Gene Cort, E&Y, "Collaborative environment serves the business goals"

"The decision was made pretty much on knowledge sharing, and believing in a gut decision that opening up information, sharing it, and being able to make available the intellectual capital of the firm was the right thing to do. And, I don't think anybody had put an ROI on it. We're in the business of intellectual capital, and this was minimal entry to be in that business."

Politically, the firms interviewed all spawned these projects from the top with commitment from partners and the assignment of the resources needed to make it a success. Incentives were put in place to make sharing of information a rewarding experience for the individual and the firm.

16.8.1 Big Six Consultancies Take the Groupware Challenge

Applying the groupware challenge from Chapter 1 to Big Six firms at a point in time around the early 1990s shows that the chance for success was stacked in their favor from the beginning. A score of 80 or better indicates a situation where groupware is likely to be successful (see Table 16.2).

Table 16.3 Early 1990s Snapshot of Big Six Success with Groupware

Technology	Culture	Economics	Politics	
Score = 7	Score = 8	Score = 9	Score = 9	
Weight = 1	Weight = 2	Weight =3	Weight = 4	
Subtotal = 7	Subtotal = 16	Subtotal = 27	Subtotal = 36	Total = 86

16.9 WHERE IS GROUPWARE HEADING AT THE BIG SIX?

16.9.1 Migration to Notes Version 4.0

With the release of version 4.0 of Notes, Big Six firms are faced with the daunting task of upgrading thousands of Notes users and hundreds of servers spanning the globe. Most firms have been testing Notes 4.0 for 6 months or more in preparation for the upgrade.

From discussions with interviewees, two approaches to migration are being followed:

1. Big Bang approach of migrating all servers and clients to version 4.0
2. Staged approach where servers are migrated first and clients second

The big bang approach is being adopted by Ernst & Young. They have already switched approximately 10 percent of their servers and 20 percent of their users as a conversion test without any problems. The majority of their people will be upgraded as they move to Windows 95.

The staged approach is being adopted by Andersen Consulting. They plan to migrate their server pool to Notes 4.0 as part of their 6 month release schedule. The migration of the servers to 4.0 will help Andersen to improve performance, allow for bigger databases, and provide better replication capabilities. Andersen also plans to deploy Windows 95 as part of their release schedule. In the spring of 1997, Andersen will migrate all users to version 4.0 over a 3 to 5 month period.

16.9.2 Notes vs. the "Web": A Big Six Perspective

Interviewees at the Big Six shared the opinion expressed in the introductory chapter that the World Wide Web will not make groupware obsolete.

They see a hybridized future in which the strengths of each are exploited. For example, mobile consultants can work with Notes information off line so data may be populated in a Notes environment where it can be best used in an off line mode. Rowan Snyder, at C&L, described the strengths of each environment this way, "...the Web is better for static information dissemination, and Notes is better currently for more dynamic, more mobile, more secure types of applications. It is also a richer development environment. This will change as the Web technology improves."

Ultimately, interviewees felt that a convergence in groupware and Web environments would occur that would provide a "transparent" interface. Users will not know what they are using to access information (a Notes client, a First-Class connection, or a Web browser), they will simply access the information they need to get in a format that is easy to understand and visually stimulating. An indicator that this convergence needs to occur is the mechanism firms are using to populate Notes and Web-based servers. In many cases, firms have the same

feeds of information going to Web servers and Notes servers. A tool that can combine the off-line strengths of Notes with the advantages of the Internet will ultimately be adopted in the long term.

Discussion Snapshot—John Parkinson, E&Y, "Web vs. Notes"

"You look at what you can do with the WWW, or to be more specific,
with Web servers and a client browser, and that has some advantages. First of all, it's pretty good at information linking, the structural hyper links that you can put into documents, the ability to
link dissimilar things together once you've discovered that you
need to, and the ability to run agents over it were very attractive
from an Information Management/Knowledge Base Management
point of view. The fact that the browser has a very low footprint on
the client and doesn't require you to store things locally unless you
really want to was also an advantage. But that technology is
essentially sessional…if you're not connected, then you can't do
anything with it.

Whereas with Notes, there's quite a lot of things you can do when
you're not connected. So, although Notes was a relatively expensive answer, it looked like it was also quite useful, when a large
percentage of our population is basically mobile."

Finally, many interviewees discussed software agents as being the next big
step in determining how the Notes vs. the "Web" debate will be resolved. The
company that can produce a workgroup application that combines software
agents in a multimedia environment was identified as the next big winner in this
battle. Some of the tasks that software agents would need to accomplish include:

☞ Actively search or browse on the user's behalf

☞ Actively link to other workgroups and collect information

☞ Passively identify topics of interest to users and report as needed

☞ Passively identify groups of topics that appear unrelated, but when combined are of great interest to users

16.9.3 Linking to the Client

Several factors are helping promote the idea of electronically linking the
consultant and client in a workgroup environment. A few long term engagements
were cited by interviewees that involved the linking of the client to consulting
resources maintained in Notes databases, and conversely linking the consultants
to client resources. While most of these links were terminated at the end of an
engagement, some firms felt it would be beneficial to have more permanent links
set up to help foster longer term bonds with the client.

Discussion Snapshot—John Parkinson, E&Y, "Client Access"

"We have a big, long-term reengineering project running with a client, and the group there has a network environment that they operate in, and the group is both E&Y's people and the client's people. That network is visible as a common segment to both the client's wide area technology and ours. So, somebody working on that team can use E&Y's Notes infrastructure to some controlled degree. They can use their own Notes infrastructure to some controlled degree. But if you're on the client's internal network, you can't see ours, and vice versa."

Factors promoting electronic linking (see Fig. 16.7):

1. Electronically networked consultants can augment smaller core project teams to provide expertise to the project at a reduced cost.
2. Electronically networked clients can bring more perspectives on the needs of the company and can increase the success of a project.
3. Costs related to client reporting and work-in-process can be reduced.
4. More permanent connection to clients helps foster long term bonds.

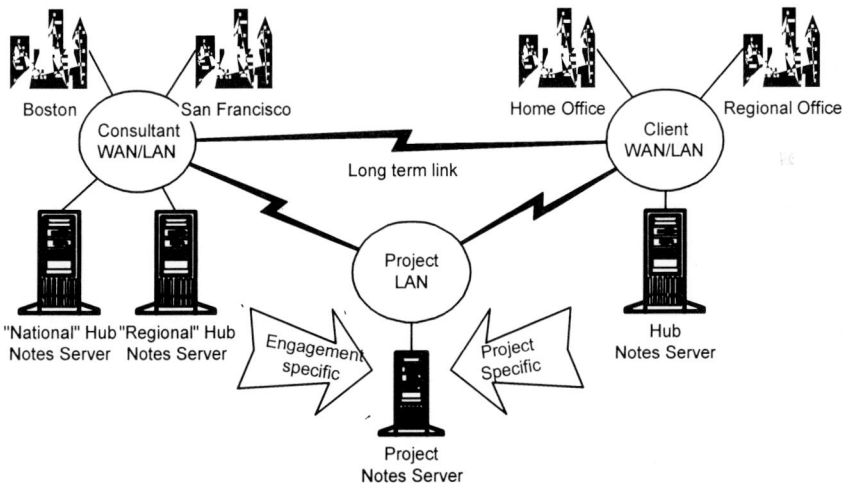

Fig. 16.7 Electronic Linking to the Client

Reporting status and work-in-process is a major component of the consulting process. Checkpoints, management reviews, status reports, and other forms of project related reports can represent a fairly significant expense. By providing clients with engagement specific information originating at the client site, or from regional offices who are contributing to the project, can greatly reduce the costs of administration personnel and provide more timely information.

16.10 CONCLUSION

Big Six firms began with a sharing culture, which made the use of groupware more logical and the implementation smoother. However, firms interviewed still experienced a variety of roll out problems, and learned much along the way.

The discussion of these problems and lessons in this chapter, as well as an enumeration of the benefits firms were able to attain, will hopefully be helpful to any organizations contemplating either the implementation or advanced usage of groupware.

16.11 APPENDIX

The following Table (Table 16.3) lists the participating individuals and their firm.

Table 16.4 Groupware Interviewees.

Firm	Individual	Title	Date of Initial Interview
Andersen Consulting	Charlie Paulk	Chief Information Officer	1/24/96
	Chuck Dean	Associate Partner, Regional Knowledge Exchange Champion	1/23/96
	Ben Torrey	Manager, Regional Knowledge Exchange Champion	1/5/96
Coopers & Lybrand	Mike Blum	Consulting Partner; Strategic Business Unit Leader	1/30/96
	Gary Clair	Director of Collaborative Computing	1/30/96
	Hamid Sabet		1/19/96
	Rowan Snyder	Partner; Chief Technology Officer	1/25/96
Ernst & Young	Gene Cort	Chief Information Officer	1/16/96
	Jon Parkinson	Consulting Partner; Director, Emerging Technologies Research	1/15/96
	Randy Russell		1/18/96
KPMG	Allan Frank	Partner, Enabling Technologies	4/26/96

BIBLIOGRAPHY

1. Block, P., *Flawless Consulting,* Pfeiffer & Company, 1981.
2. Coleman, D., *Groupware: Technologies and Applications,* Prentice-Hall PTR, 1995.
3. Gewirtz, D., *Lotus Notes 3 Revealed,* Prima Computer Books, 1994
4. Johansen, R., Sibbet, D., Benson, S., Martin, A., Mittman, R., Saffo, P., *Leading Business Teams; How Teams Can Use Technology and Group Process Tools to Enhance Performance,* Addison Wesley Publishing Company, 1991.
5. Olson, M. H. *Technological Support for Work Group Collaboration,* Lawrence Earlbaum and Associates, 1989.

INFORMATION SERVICES

1. Black, G. "Taking Notes, Big Sixer Aims for Head of the Class." [CD-ROM]. *Software Magazine,* Mar. 1995.

2. Fryer, B. "When Users Take Notes." [CD-ROM]. *Computerworld* Magazine, Aug. 8, 1994.

BIOGRAPHIES

Andrew S. Clark is a manager in the Business Consulting practice at Arthur Andersen in Boston where he is a member of both the technology and financial services groups. Mr. Clark provides information systems planning consulting services to middle market companies throughout New England. His areas of expertise include client/server architectures, collaborative computing, and data warehousing.

Prior to joining Arthur Andersen, Mr. Clark spent 4 years at a major financial services company and 4-1/2 years with Andersen Consulting. While at Andersen Consulting, he worked on one of the first major implementations of an object oriented system. Mr. Clark also provides independent systems integration consulting services to local companies through his business, Andrew S. Clark & Associates.

Mr. Clark holds a B.S. in Computer Science from Rennselaer Polytechnic Institute and is pursuing a Masters in Business Administration from Boston College where he has completed graduate work on the use of groupware at Big Six firms. He was awarded a grant from the Boston Chapter of the Society for Information Management for his work on the use of groupware tools at consulting firms.

Arthur Andersen
Voice: (617) 330-4178
Fax: (617) 439-9731
E-mail: Andrew.S.Clark@ArthurAndersen.com

Andrew S. Clark & Associates
Voice: (617) 545-7345
Fax: (617) 545-7346
E-mail: ASClark@tiac.net

Charles E. Downing is Assistant Professor of Management Information Systems (MIS) in the Wallace E. Carroll School of Management at Boston College. His research focuses on measuring the effectiveness of information systems, the implementation and evaluation of Decision Support Systems which employ advanced analytical techniques, and group communication and collaboration using information technology. Professor Downing worked in the financial services industry as an information systems specialist for several years, and has served as a consultant to a variety of corporations.

David Coleman is the founder and Managing Director of Collaborative Strategies. He has been involved with groupware and collaborative technologies since 1990 and is the author/editor of *Groupware Technologies and Applications* (Prentice-Hall, 1995). He also was the founder and conference chairman for the GroupWare '92-'95 conferences that were held in San Jose, Boston, and London on an annual basis. Mr. Coleman was the editor and publisher of *GroupTalk*, the newsletter of workgroup computing. He is the founding editor of *Virtual Workgroups* magazine, and currently a columnist. He also writes a monthly column on groupware for *Computer Reseller News,* and for *MainSpring* (an on-line resource for intranet and Web developers). Mr. Coleman has written for many trade and business publications such as *Network World, Datamation, Fortune,* and is a frequent public speaker worldwide. He has consulted to groupware vendors on product marketing, positioning, market research and competitive analysis, and for groupware users in assessing their organization groupware readiness as well as tool selection and the human factors involved in a successful groupware project. Mr. Coleman can be contacted directly at 415-282-9197, or at davidc@collaborate.com. More information on Collaborative Strategies can be found at www.collaborate.com.

Introduction to Chapter 17

This chapter is one of the most controversial in this book. The authors contend that groupware only makes organizations worse! The argument is that the people in organizations have established habits of interaction, many of which are counter-productive. However, we learn to work around these behaviors to get our jobs done. The problem with collaborative technologies is that they facilitate these bad habits. In other words, they make bad communication better. Additionally, the cost and effort required to implement a collaborative infrastructure, whether it be groupware, e-mail, or the intranet, are futile without first dealing with the issues that are characteristic in human-to-human communications.

Further, the authors contend that even in companies where groupware has been implemented successfully, groupware's benefits are only marginally realized. In order to fully harness groupware's potential, organizations much first focus on the people who will use it. Easier said than done. Addressing technical issues is always simpler than human issues, in part because the "soft" issues are much harder to identify in the first place than are the "hard" issues. Still, the problem remains: How do you focus on the people and make your intranet more effective? The authors contend that managers must understand the interpersonal dynamics of teamwork in order to effectively implement their technology solutions.

There are four ideas generally recognized as necessary for success with human issues in collaboration. They are called the 4 Cs: communication, collaboration, coordination, and corporate knowledge. In order to teach managers how to focus on the people, the authors discuss two of the four, communication and collaboration, as examples of how to deal with some of the human issues in collaboration. They note, as have I in the introductory chapter, that people are not generally skilled in collaboration. I would go further and say that our society gives us mixed messages about collaboration. When we are young and in school, collaboration is called cheating. Can you imagine being rewarded for working on someone else's test answers? Then, when we enter the corporate world we are asked to be a team player, *but even then, we are rewarded for our individual effort while being told that the only way to be successful is to collaborate with others. It's easy to be confused!*

In our experience, working with organizations that are having problems with groupware implementations, we often have to teach collaborative behaviors. This frequently requires that people un-learn the "rugged individual" behaviors they have used for many years. This is often a very uncomfortable process, akin to cliff jumping with an untested bungee cord.

The authors contend that people's fear is the stumbling block for collaboration, not any technology glitch or lack of functionality. But, focus is important as well. By focus, we mean the ability to see options other than what is immediately in front of you.

This chapter will show how people's fear not only rules their mindset, but how it determines behaviors. A collaborative mindset is necessary to get the most out of groupware and any type of electronic collaboration. Creating a collaborative organization is more than laying down a technical infrastructure, it is a commitment to a collaborative mindset and the behaviors fostered by that mindset.

I have often contended that groupware is like a magnifying glass. Unlike a database, where you work against the data from your desktop, the nature of collaborative software requires interaction with at least one other, and often many other people. Groupware is by nature more public, and has the tendency to magnify individual character attributes or deficiencies. These behaviors often reflect the organization, its policies, goals, and beliefs. Sometimes it reflects the style of the person who heads the organization; and reflecting his/her behaviors, thoughts, and goals, it imposes them on the rest of the corporate culture.

In any case, the authors tell us how to make the best of this magnifying function and how to use it productively in our organizations, using NLP techniques. I must say that I have experienced classes and workshops from these authors and have seen the effectiveness of their techniques. Also, I believe that any focus on enhancing human skills relative to collaboration behaviors can only increase the effectiveness of interpersonal communications systems.

This chapter's message is that focusing on interpersonal communication skills is essential to getting the benefit of collaboration technologies and that is an idea I can get behind 100 percent.

CHAPTER 17

Groupware & Reengineering: The Human Side of Change

Gerald O'Dwyer
Harvard Brown & Co.

Art Giser
NLP Associates

Ed Lovett
Associate, Harvard Brown & Co.

17.1 INTRODUCTION

The costs of implementing groupware—in time, money, effort and employee "change capital" (their patience and willingness to change)—can be very high. It is critical that the return on this investment, financially and in terms of intangible benefits such as teamwork and creativity, be high enough to make it worthwhile. Upon examining how successful companies have been in doing this, a mixed portrait emerges. In some companies, employees fight groupware's introduction and refuse to use it. Other companies initially embrace groupware but then use tapers off or stops. Stuart Woodring of Forrester Research, quoted in Glenn Rifkin's article "A Skeptic's Guide to Groupware," describes this "predictable cycle": "They go from skepticism to excitement to enthusiasm to disillusionment and back to reality." ([13] p. 78)

In most cases, groupware is more successful; most companies that use it reap some of the many benefits it promises. But all of these companies, even those that enjoy some success, are failing to harness the full potential of this powerful technology. How is this the case, given companies' good intentions, their investments of energy and resources, and the high quality of these products? What is missing from the current ways of thinking about collaboration in general, and groupware in particular, that would cause a quantum leap in ful-

565

filling the promise of this technology? How can organizations cope with the new problems groupware creates as they use it to solve current ones? The answers to these questions are critical if we are going to get the maximum value out of groupware. This chapter answers these questions by exploring the human side of groupware—its importance relative to technology and its role in fully realizing groupware's promise of helping create, as Thomas W. Malone writes, "[W]ork organizations that truly engage the intelligence and creativity of thousands or even millions of people." ([4] p. xix).

17.1.1 People: The Missing Link

David Coleman, while delivering the keynote address at the 1995 Tools and Methods for Re-engineering Conference in Arlington, VA, said:

> When I ask groups of people what is stopping them from being successful with groupware, I get two responses. The first is on the technical side, and very few people seem to have major technical issues, or they are easily solved. When I ask, "Who has major people issues?," almost everyone raises their hand...

Companies are failing to unleash the full potential of groupware because they are not giving the "people side" of the process the attention and commitment that it demands. The core premise of groupware is that enhanced collaboration is a key, if not *the* key, to sustained competitive advantage in the emerging business environment. Yet technologists and managers are often completely uninformed as to the inner workings and dynamics of teamwork and collaboration. As Glenn Rifkin writes in his article, "A Skeptic's Guide to Groupware":

> Most corporations are ill prepared or ill suited for the dramatic cultural shifts...that groupware spawns, and many end up getting only partial or little benefit from the implementation. ([13] p. 77)

Perhaps the reason the term "groupware" has stuck as an umbrella term for these products is that it combines the two ideas at the heart of its conception and implementation: "group" + "ware" = people + technology [Note: David Coleman discusses this concept in detail in Chapter 1 of this book. -*Ed*.]. But current implementation efforts tend to focus, in design and practice, much more on the machines—application design, compatibility with legacy systems, etc.—than the people. They pay more attention to the tangible over the intangible, the tool over the user, the new toys over the old communication patterns that are integral to collaboration. Lesley-Ann Schneier discusses this imbalance in her description of groupware implementation at The World Bank:

> IS management now recognizes that while the hardware and software issues can be solved relatively easily, it is the people issues that are the hardest and most intractable to resolve. Nonetheless, the support and training functions remain underfunded...and managers in general do not believe that they need to spend more time and money on these crucial people areas in order to gain the full effectiveness and potential of the technology that they have deployed. ([15] p. 383)

The technology, already quite powerful, will only get better and better as the groupware market matures. As this happens, the side of the process that technology alone cannot fix—the human side—becomes an even more critical factor for success. An appropriate strategy not only creates a balance between the technological and the human, but actually spends *more* time and energy on the people issues, as they are both more important and more difficult. As Kenneth W. Lyon writes in "Why Groupware is Tough to Love":

> Groupware deals with the core behaviors of groups that arise out of the organization's culture. The skills needed to exploit groupware are 90 percent organizational and cultural change management and only 10 percent technology management. ([9] p. 80)

The importance of human issues in successful implementation of groupware—which, after all, is supposed to empower people in working together better—makes sense and requires neither an imaginative leap nor a "paradigm shift." Many contributors to *Groupware: Technology and Applications,* especially in the chapters on implementation, mention the importance of the human element to groupware. Because this human element was not their central area of focus or expertise, these comments are essentially an informed caveat—"Hey, watch out: Don't underestimate the people side of all this...."—between discussions of the technology and strategy issues. This chapter picks up where they leave off. In it we will:

☞ Examine the human issues involved in groupware;

☞ Discuss why and how the failure to deal with these issues has kept companies from unleashing groupware's potential; and

☞ Propose new mindsets, attitudes, and skills that handle these issues effectively so that you avoid the pitfalls and maximize the benefits.

17.1.2 Why Don't Companies Address These Human Issues Already?

Some executives tend to place little value or prestige on people issues, thinking them superfluous, "touchy-feely" or "soft." These people do not attempt to educate themselves in these issues. Executives who do see the importance of people issues do not address them because they do not know how. They feel helpless in the face of them because these issues seem hard to understand and even harder to influence. Perhaps some hope that technology will ride in on a white horse with a quick solution.

A second reason for this failure to address human issues is the belief that there is not enough time ("We'll get around to it as soon as things quiet down a bit....") and waiting for someone else to do something (e.g., for senior management to issue an edict). Sometimes companies invest in improving people skills but in too limited a fashion, in effect only paying them lip service, which fails to produce any lasting benefits. Whatever the reasons, this failure to address human issues has an extremely high cost in time and money.

> ## *People don't address human issues because...*
>
> ☞ *"I don't believe in that touchy-feely stuff."*
>
> ☞ *"This great new technology will take care of them."*
>
> ☞ *"I want to, but I don't know how."*
>
> ☞ *"There's not enough time."*

People issues take on an added importance in the context of any organizational change program. This is especially true for groupware, which is both a tool for change and a kind of change program in itself. The most common pitfall in this case, in addition to the general ones discussed above, is the view of technology as somehow being outside the context of corporate culture. In fact, breaking down barriers to the flow of information, the main effect of groupware, carries significant implications for corporate culture.

Technology and culture are intimately connected, and IS people must, like everyone else, develop people skills. They need to understand that their primary function is to work with people, not machines, to help them get the most out of these tools. A recent column in *ComputerWorld,* a publication known more for "hard" technology than for "soft" people issues, drives this point home. Titled "What the Heck? Two Findings That Left Some *ComputerWorld* Editors Wondering," the piece comments on a statistic from the annual Computer Sciences Corp. (CSC) survey of IS management issues:

> **CSC asked:** What are the three greatest contributors to the success of your IS organization?
>
> **Respondents:** Only 4.6 percent list communication skills.
>
> **We say:** Only 4.6 percent, no wonder so many users think IS doesn't understand their needs.

In groupware, human issues can make the difference between success and failure or wasted potential, due to the errors, delays, resistance, low morale, frustration, and miscommunication that occur when they are ignored.

17.2 BACKGROUND

The hard-won lessons this chapter teaches are the product of our extensive consulting work with various companies in the areas of organizational learning and change management. Our methodology is based on Organizational Development research conducted in the past few decades, particularly that of Dr. Chris Argyris of Harvard Business School, and on Neuro-linguistic Programming. We help companies develop new concepts, procedures, and skills that unleash the intelligence of their employees and make them more productive. Our approach to technology is based on the premise that technology implementation issues are merely a subset of the basic human issues involved in collaboration, communication, and change.

The human barriers to success with groupware mentioned throughout this book and *Groupware: Technology and Applications* vary, but beneath the surface they fall into the exact same patterns that we see in all parts of all companies (we will discuss these patterns in the following pages). Fortunately, this same dynamic technology being a subset of the larger organizational and human issues—applies to the solutions as well as to the problems. Successful collaboration strategies, and the skills that support them, work for any kind of organizational change, and their benefits are good collaboration in general, not just over a computer network.

17.3 THE TWO CS OF GROUPWARE: COLLABORATION AND COMMUNICATION

The benefits of groupware—all of which serve the ultimate goals of greater productivity and profitability—are numerous, far-reaching, and range from simple automation to enabling profound cultural changes in the organization. For example, closer to the surface you have benefits such as:

☞ Automation of otherwise time-consuming routine processes;

☞ Reduced reliance on paper: information is easier to organize and it is less likely to get lost;

☞ Better coordination with employees, clients, vendors, and strategic partners; extending the organization to these groups;

☞ The ability to access information without having to go through a hierarchy;

☞ Streamlining of operations; and

☞ Improved meetings.

Deeper, more cultural benefits include:

☞ Helping to create a learning, creative organization;

☞ Global coordination;

☞ Supporting major change programs such as BPR, TQM, and other programs that aim to flatten hierarchies and create the kind of flexible, quick company that succeeds in the current business climate; and

☞ Leveraging expertise and enhancing knowledge-transfer.

The common threads that run through most of these benefits, especially the deeper ones, are collaboration and communication (see Fig. 17.1). The overall promise of groupware is that it will enhance the sharing of information (communication) and improve people's ability to work well together (collaboration), which increases productivity and profitability.

Better Communication

$\uparrow$ $\downarrow$ $\longrightarrow$ Increased
                                        Productivity

Better Collaboration

Fig. 17.1 The Two Cs of Groupware

Better Collaboration

Collaboration and communication, as mysterious and intangible as they may initially seem, have been studied and the critical success and failure factors—which appear to transcend cultural differences—have been identified. This chapter applies this body of knowledge, which is well-developed but not widely known and even less widely applied, to groupware. In order to understand the human side of groupware, and thereby increase your chances of getting the most out of this technology, it is necessary to understand collaboration and communication issues in general.

17.4 THE FIRST "C": COLLABORATION

The simple fact of the matter is that people are not naturally skilled at collaborating. We Americans have the added disadvantage of having been born into an individualistic culture. In earlier times, people had to collaborate more in everyday life, as in a barn-raising. Even then the goals were simple and the organizations were mainly hierarchical. Nowadays, we admire the "rugged individualists," entrepreneurs, mavericks, and superstars as if they do it all alone, oblivious to the fact that most of their success depends on good collaboration. As offensive linemen in football have said, "let's see how great that star quarterback is if we don't block the defense."

Although we are naturally unskilled at collaboration, we can learn how and why this is; i.e., what it is in our thinking and behavior that accidentally blocks collaboration. Most importantly, we can learn the new mindsets and behaviors that support it. "Behaviors" are visible, tangible actions and "mindsets" are the thoughts, beliefs, and assumptions behind them. Behaviors are like the tip of an iceberg—clearly visible, discernible, etc.—while mindsets are like the submerged part of the iceberg (see Fig. 17.2).

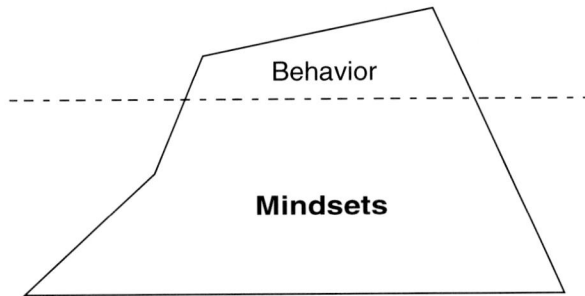

Fig. 17.2 Fear-Based Behaviors and Mindsets

We will call the behaviors and mindsets that block collaboration fear-based and those that spur collaboration collaborative. The reason for the term "fear-based" is that the fundamental psychological motivation for these mindsets and behaviors is some kind of fear, usually of threat and/or embarrassment.

17.4.1 Fear-Based Mindsets and Behaviors

The Effects of Fear-based Mindsets and Behaviors

Fear-based mindsets and behaviors impede collaboration and learning and therefore keep people from solving persistent problems in their organization. They also keep companies from getting maximum value from groupware. It is important to emphasize that people are largely unaware of these mindsets and behaviors and their effects—and they are unaware that they are unaware. Most people want to do their best and would not consciously intend to sabotage the success of their own organization. But this is exactly what happens in some cases, and what could happen to any company. Newspapers and magazines contain many examples of how certain fear-based mindsets and behaviors—in most cases, escalating "defensive routines" and cover-ups—severely harm or destroy even the mightiest institutions, such as Barings Bank, Drexel Burnham, and the Orange County Pension Fund. These are not isolated anomalies. All organizations, big and small, young and old, contain the seeds of their own downfall. We call these seeds organizational defensive routines.

Here is a list of fear-based mindsets and behaviors, along with some examples of how these behaviors show up in groupware:

17.4.1.1 Fear-based Mindsets

☞ **Avoid situations you are afraid might embarrass or threaten you.**

☞ **Focus on the task.** This mindset grows out of the fear of not completing a task successfully. The most important thing becomes "getting the job done" at all costs. This mindset can be seen in statements such as: "All we need to do is hunker down and re-focus;" "if we just follow the process...;" and "if they would just do what is in the plan...." This emphasis on the task comes at the expense of an emphasis on relationship and collaboration in completing the task. When people think their goal is being threatened and they are behind time, they don't think that they have time for communication issues, or they think that they will look bad or be punished for asking questions.

☞ **Defer to those perceived to be "above" you.** This mindset comes from the fear of embarrassment, or of losing your job. Carl Di Pietro, in his chapter on EMS in *Groupware: Technology and Applications*, uses Hans Christian Andersen's fable *The Emperor's New Clothes* to illustrate this deference to authority:

> Why didn't the Emperor's closest advisors, his staff, or his subjects expose the hoax [that his "new clothes," instead of being invisible, didn't exist, so that he was actually naked]? According to Andersen, to challenge the emperor's perception was to be seen as "stupid" or "not suited for their jobs." ([5] p. 438)

☞ **Being perceived as vulnerable or fallible is bad; "showing strength" is good.** This comes from a fear of looking bad or weak. This mindset steers us away from discussing some things thoroughly with others because we fear that asking questions will make others think we don't know our job or what we are talking about. This can take place in any groupware context (e-mail, EMS, etc.).

☞ **You're on your own, it's a competition and you have to win, dominate and avoid being dominated.** This comes from a fear of losing the perceived "competition."

☞ **Behave rationally; downplay feelings or emotions as much as possible.** This comes from a fear of exposing emotions in yourself and others, and the embarrassment that such a display might bring. People also cling to rationality and "logic" in advocating their position, assuming that others will be more likely to agree ("you can't argue with logic"). But ideas that are rational and logical to one person may not be to another; they are not unshakable external truths but rather can be just as subjective as emotions.

☞ **"Surface" Learning.** Surface learning is learning that is focused only on solving the immediate problem, or "putting out the fire." It does not look behind this problem to find the root causes or to detect a pattern. Like bypass surgery, it only treats a symptom (clogged artery) while ignoring its *fundamental* causes (bad diet, not enough exercise).

17.4.1.2 Fear-based Behaviors

☞ **Defensive Routines** or actions that bypass potentially threatening or embarrassing situations or otherwise help you save face. For example, not showing that you don't know something; blaming others (individuals, departments, etc.); distancing yourself from people with whom you have difficult issues and making these issues "undiscussable." What makes these issues "undiscussable" is the fear of threat or embarrassment discussing them might cause. Defensive routines keep persistent problems in place because "that which you resist, persists;" i.e., if you do not talk about the root causes of these problems, they will not get solved. They also cause misunderstandings and distortions that kill productivity. Finally, they are self-sealing processes: We cover up that we are covering up and dancing around issues.

Groupware examples can be found in all the different products. Simply not responding to someone's e-mail is an example of a defensive routine. Or, if someone contributes to a discussion database and requests feedback, and the others either don't respond or respond vaguely (waiting for someone else to put his/her neck on the line), it is likely that they thought their honest feedback would produce some "negative" reaction from the original contributor. Not responding or responding vaguely attempts to avoid this reaction.

☞ **Rush to emphasize agreement and conformity, be a "team player."** This mindset is akin to Professor Irving Janis' notion of "groupthink," which he defines as a "concurrence-seeking tendency" found in cohesive groups ([8] p. 129). This tendency places the harmony of the group over the need to inquire and challenge assumptions.

In an EMS meeting, if people's comments during the meeting combine to create a momentum in a certain direction, a participant wanting to disagree or understand better may not act on this desire because of the pull of consensus.

☞ **Tell people, especially those perceived to be "above" you, what you think they want to hear.** For example, if someone has data or input that seems to go against what he/she thinks is his/her boss' "pet project," he/she probably will not participate fully in a discussion database about that project.

☞ **One-directional communication: telling, dumping, monologue, advocating your opinion, debate instead of dialogue.** People who rely on this persuasive, dominant behavior may refuse to participate in or sabotage an EMS meeting if, as Carl Di Pietro writes, they feel "their power or influence is compromised" ([5] p. 455).

☞ **Withhold information and act as if you aren't.** People often do this because they think their knowledge is their "power" ("I'm paid to know"). This common behavior is a huge barrier to success with groupware, whose central premise is the sharing of information. For example, when Price Waterhouse installed Lotus Notes in 1989–90, this behavior was a major force in the corporate culture initially resisting the project in that employees didn't want to share their knowledge because they believed it was their "worth."

☞ **Water cooler talk, gossip.** This kind of behavior can grow out of people's fears about security and privacy in conjunction with e-mail ("Who owns my e-mail?") and group calendaring ("Big Brother is watching!"). People will gossip around the water cooler instead of fully using groupware if they have security fears.

☞ **Advocacy combined with coercion, covert antagonism.** An example of this kind of behavior is when someone states and restates a position without inviting feedback, thinking that if others would just listen and think "logically" about what he/she is saying they would see that he/she is right.

☞ **When overwhelmed, stop communicating/inquiring, blame someone or something other than yourself, complain.** E-mail overload, common when people receive up to a hundred messages a day, can cause this overwhelmed state, as can the proliferation of meetings brought about by the ease of group calendaring. "Flaming" e-mail is often a vehicle for blame. With the technology they are using (e-mail, EMS, Discussion Database, Conferencing, etc.), people tend to withhold feedback if they think that the other person "can't handle it," or may "blow up" because the feedback is about his/her "pet project."

☞ **Make assumptions and attributions and don't share them and/or test them publicly.** This behavior is exacerbated when people feel constrained by time and when the boss is around. People talk about another person or group (perhaps over e-mail) but do not check out the attributions they are making, which leads to bad decisions and other problems.

17.4.2 Three Ironies of Fear-based Mindsets and Behaviors

The first irony is that many of these fear-based mindsets and behaviors are distortions of "good" interpersonal rules we were all taught as children. "If you don't have something nice to say, don't say it at all" seems innocuous enough but, reincarnated in organizations today, it keeps people from communicating anything that isn't considered "nice" or "positive"—holding another accountable to his/her word, inquiring into another's reasoning, etc. The old lesson, "respect authority," causes excessive deference to perceived superiors in the form of telling them only what you think they want to hear, which prevents a true feedback loop and blocks learning.

This last example concerning employees telling their boss only what they think he/she wants to hear leads to the second irony. The key word here is "think": the last thing most managers want to hear is what their reports think they want to hear. This is because managers need the highest quality information possible from their team to lead well and make the best decisions. The authors once facilitated a meeting of the Senior Partner of the Auditing department of a Big Six accounting firm and a group of partners and their direct reports. The Senior Partner had proposed a new opportunity and direction for their business. He had had numerous conversations with individuals about it, and they had already spent an entire day as a group working on it. It became clear to us, using the communication principles that we operate with and that we discuss in this chapter, that they were not all talking about the same project. They all used the same name for it, but clearly they didn't have the same definition. None of them was aware of this (at least none of them gave any indication of being aware of it).

When we surfaced the misunderstanding they were shocked, especially the Senior Partner, who was counting on full and honest engagement in the project. There were at least four significantly different versions of what the project was. In this case, there were other causes besides deference to authority for this misunderstanding, such as not challenging assumptions, not inquiring, not seeking to understand, and not knowing how to assess whether or not they were communicating. But it is a good example of employees telling the boss what they think he/she wants to hear—and of how, ironically, this is the last thing the boss wants.

The third irony is that intelligence, education, and rank do not make someone any less likely to think and act anti-collaboratively. Robert Putnam calls this a "central paradox of organizational learning: good members, acting rationally within the organizational world they know, create, and maintain defensive routines that prevent the organization from learning" [12] and, we would add, collaborating. Fear-based mindsets and behaviors are so deep-set that they show up equally in management consultants with MBAs as they do in factory workers.

To get the most value out of their people and out of groupware, companies must acknowledge that fear-based mindsets and behaviors exist in their culture and actively seek to replace them with collaborative ones.

17.4.3 Collaborative Mindsets and Behaviors

The Effects of Collaborative Mindsets and Behaviors

Again, we human beings are naturally not good collaborators. But when people and organizations commit themselves to collaborative mindsets and behaviors, they work together more and better. This enhanced collaboration is not just a "plus" but a necessity given the challenges of the emerging business climate. Enhanced collaboration promotes "deep" learning—looking underneath business problems (symptoms) to find the root causes (disease)—which is the only way to solve persistent problems in organizations. Fear-based mindsets and behaviors only allow surface learning. Collaborative mindsets and behaviors also stave off the damage done by fear-based mindsets and behaviors such as organizational defensive routines. Finally, because they empower true collaboration, collaborative mindsets and behaviors help you get the maximum value out of groupware.

Another way to talk about the effects of collaborative mindsets and behaviors is in terms of the collaborative organization. The foundation of a truly collaborative organization is a deliberate, systematic commitment to cultivating collaborative mindsets and behaviors. The relevance to groupware is in the fact that a collaborative organization is in a sense both the goal and the requirement of groupware. Figure 17.3 depicts a symbiotic, circular relationship or "virtuous cycle": companies install groupware to improve collaboration, and improved collaboration is necessary to maximize the benefits of groupware.

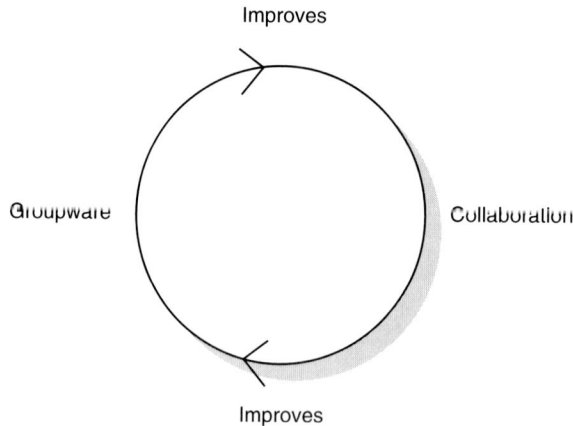

Fig. 17.3 The "Virtuous Cycle"

Here are some characteristics of a collaborative organization:

☞ **Emphasis on innovation and the discovery of new ideas**—Paul Romer's influential New Growth Theory [also mentioned in Gordon Stone's chapter on groupware and knowledge management. —*Ed.*], along with other commentators such as Don Tapscott (in *Paradigm Shift,* 1994 and *The Digital Economy,* 1996), propose that growth in the emerging economy is based more on ideas than objects; i.e., to capital and labor must be added a new factor, discovery, to complete the growth equation. Groupware can be an engine that drives discovery, but only when used with the collaborative mindsets and behaviors described below.

☞ **Trust**—In a collaborative organization, trust is a company-wide condition. It neutralizes the fears that produce fear-based mindsets and behaviors, and propels collaborative ones. When there is trust, people are much more likely to inquire, check assumptions, etc. and hold others accountable to doing the same.

☞ **Individual commitment, accountability, ownership**—The importance of individual commitment to success with groupware or any other type of change cannot be overstated. The shift from fear-based to collaborative mindsets must happen on an individual level. It cannot be mandated from above because people will only do what it takes to change when they discover for themselves what is in it for them. When enough individuals generate the momentum for change, a critical mass is reached and organizational transformation can occur.

The idea of the "collaborative organization" describes a constant process, not a finished state. The development of the Boeing 777 is an example of a project that combined technology and teamwork to achieve success. As Rochelle Garner writes in her article, "Flight Crew":

> Don't tell Larry Olsen that teamwork is an empty platitude. Olsen, director of information systems at the Boeing Co.'s 777 project, and his staff worked with, listened to, and pitched in alongside thousands of employees who created the world's newest airliner. ([7] p. 66)

Convinced of the importance of people issues in collaboration, senior managers at Boeing met weekly with an Organizational Behavior specialist for almost one year. The goal was "to teach managers the art of teambuilding" ([7] p. 66). They interviewed thousands of candidates for the IS positions involved in the 777 project. Those hired were selected for their technical abilities and for their ability to work together. The managers looked at their past job performance and got feedback from their peers on how well they functioned as team members. The results of this approach were extremely positive:

> IS became a better, stronger organization. Everyone in Olsen's group agrees that people can speak honestly to each other at any level of the hierarchy. Barriers taken down, after all, are hard to rebuild. ([7] p. 67)

17.4.4 Collaborative Mindsets

Now that we have talked about their effects, here is a list of collaborative mindsets (followed by behaviors):

☞ **Publicly testing assumptions is necessary for learning and good decision-making.** Explain the reasoning behind your conclusions and ask others to examine this reasoning. Encourage others to do the same with their reasoning. Though few people use it this way, groupware provides an environment for testing assumptions.

☞ **People have a capacity for self-reflection and integrity.** This mindset encourages you to discuss with others what normally could go undiscussed because you are afraid it will upset them. Anything that is not discussed will continue to cause problems and harm productivity.

☞ **Inviting inquiry into your own ideas is a demonstration of strength.**
Collaboration depends on honest and open discussions. Inviting inquiry creates an environment that allows others to examine your assumptions and
thinking.

☞ **A willingness to try new things and make mistakes leads to learning.** Experimentation is a key to learning. There can be no experimentation
if there is no room to make mistakes.

☞ **Rapport, compassion and empathy lead to trust.** Knowing others'
thinking and appreciating the intent behind their behavior spurs trust and
open inquiry.

☞ **Inquiry is necessary for retrieving high quality information.** Inquiry
is to organizations what radar is to navigators of ships or airplanes: a tool
with which to avoid dangerous and unnecessary obstacles to your desired
course. It allows you to elicit the crucial information from others that they
would ordinarily keep private so that you know their reasoning, their level
of commitment, etc.

☞ **Synergy, spirit of curiosity, and discovery need to be embraced.**
Growth in the emerging economy is based more on ideas than objects. A
mindset of curiosity and discovery aids collaboration and helps groupware
live up to its promise.

☞ **Individual commitment to/ownership of company's success; self-
responsibility.** In a sense, this is the mindset behind all these other
mindsets. Again, this cannot be mandated from above. Despite artificial
groupings such as "departments" and "teams," all organizations are just a
collection of individuals. Real change only comes from momentum generated by these individuals. People must take active responsibility for their
role in creating successful collaboration for it to happen.

☞ **"Deep Learning."** Surface learning is dealing with symptoms and "putting
out fires." Deep learning looks at the underlying "why" and "how" of the
problem at hand in an attempt to find and address its root causes. It asks:
"What caused the fire? How do we prevent it in the future?" It is a systematic approach to problem-solving that relies on surfacing the otherwise hidden assumptions and reasoning of which the current problem is a
manifestation.

17.4.5 Collaborative Behaviors

☞ **Uncover and test the assumptions, sacred cows, and underlying reasoning on an individual and organizational (policies, processes)
level.** This is central to deep learning. This behavior causes people and
organizations to be constantly self-reflective and to learn from the high

quality information that this process surfaces. The results are good collaboration, better use of groupware and higher productivity.

☞ **Inquire to get high quality information.** High quality information, so integral to collaboration and good decision-making, usually resides under the surface. The only way to get your hands on it is to ask lots of questions, in all situations/groupware contexts and with all of your colleagues.

☞ **Encourage yourself and others to discuss the "undiscussable."** This behavior is simple but initially not easy, because it arouses fundamental human fears of threat and/or embarrassment. But it gets easier, especially in light of how beneficial it is to good collaboration and problem-solving. "What you resist, persists;" i.e., you can't solve a problem if you don't talk about it.

☞ **Advocacy combined with inquiry, dialogue instead of debate.** When making a joint decision, advocate your position but constantly inquire into how others are interpreting what you say, as well as their thoughts on your position, and invite objections ("Do you see any gaps in my reasoning?").

☞ **Creating rapport.** Rapport is essentially a state of mutual trust. All of these collaborative mindsets and behaviors help create rapport with others. Rapport fuels collaboration in general, and is central to good collaboration over the computer.

☞ **Model these behaviors, be the example for others.** This is a key premise: People are more likely to think and act more collaboratively if they see it in their colleagues than if someone tries to mandate it from above.

17.5 THE SECOND "C": COMMUNICATION

As with collaboration, human verbal communication has been studied at its most basic levels of psychology, neurology, and language. There are unavoidable patterns in how we give and receive information of which we are largely unaware. These patterns by themselves are not "bad"; they are simply the subtle processes by which we exchange information. Becoming aware of these patterns and skilled in how to deal with them, however, is critical to using groupware tools as effectively as possible.

Here is a brief introduction to these fundamental communication patterns, with special attention to their particular manifestations in and relevance to groupware:

☞ **Language is inherently incomplete, ambiguous, and abstract.** Language is a set of symbols that stand for or "mean" something else. To communicate, we try to cram our thoughts, ideas, and emotions into these symbols so that they represent as closely as possible our original intent. Best used, language can come close to conveying this intent. But it *is* never the original intent, and is merely an approximation of it. We use non-verbal cues (body language, tone of voice, etc.) to try to fill in the blanks, but this doesn't recover all the lost meaning. Knowing these limits of language—and how to deal with them—are essential to best use of groupware. Groupware products range from having no non-verbal cues (e-mail, EMS, non-real time conferencing/discussion database, workflow) to having, at best, some (audio and video conferencing), making it even more crucial to become skilled in inquiry to get the most out of these products.

☞ **As human beings, we are compelled to try to figure out what things mean, and we assign meaning to what others say and do.** We think and behave as if this interpretation were objectively "true" and reflected exactly what the other person meant, forgetting that we just made it up. We use non-verbal and visual cues—gestures, facial expressions, tones of voice—to try to improve our interpretation. The problem is that this interpretation often has little relation to the other person's intent. Checking this interpretation against what the other person actually meant is crucial to all good communication, but we tend not to do this. Most forms of groupware, being purely text-based, do not transmit non-verbal cues, exacerbating this problem. When all you can base your interpretations on are the text of what people say, without visual or non-verbal cues, the likelihood of misunder- standing is higher. "Emoticons"—such as ":-)" for lighthearted or happy and ";-)" for winking or tongue in cheek—were developed because of this absence of non-verbal cues in electronic communication. But these elec- tronic gestures hardly take the place of the real thing; much is still left to interpretation.

☞ **People do two things when they give and receive information: delete and distort.** As is the case for all of these tendencies, this habit is, for the most part, unavoidable and unconscious: we are unaware of it and of our own unawareness. A giver of information unknowingly omits part of the original thought in speaking or writing (deletion), because he/she could never verbalize *all* of the thoughts and emotions behind what he/she wants to say. The receiver unknowingly fills in these blanks (distortion). Deletion and distortion are graveyards of high quality information.

For example, the writer of an e-mail usually limits the number of words he/she uses, deleting even more information than he/she would in a con- versation. The recipient, without the aid of non-verbal cues, then tries to fill in the missing information, thus distorting it. If the recipient passes on this information to someone else, it is likely that he/she will leave out some of the original message before passing it on, causing further dele- tion. (Even if he/she simply forwards the original e-mail, it is still dis- torted because the second recipient reads it out of context.) If this second recipient is not skilled at inquiring into the context of or reasoning behind the message, he/she will fill in the blanks with his/her own meaning, further distorting it, and act upon it. These kinds of situations can cause upset, disappointment, and confusion. On an organizational level, these errors can become self-multiplying and escalate into significant losses in productivity because people are making decisions without checking the accuracy of and reasoning behind the information on which the decision is based.

☞ **Low quality vs. high quality information.** Groupware revolves around information-sharing, but this information varies from low to high quality. Low quality information comes from debate and opinion, i.e., without the search for underlying reasoning and thoughts. High quality information comes from dialogue and tells you how the other person arrived at his/her conclusions, promoting deep learning. This distinction is essentially identical to that between low and high "context" communication, mentioned frequently in this chapter.

Low Quality Information	High Quality Information
Comes from debate and opinion.	Comes from dialogue.
Devoid of underlying reasoning.	Rich in underlying reasoning.
Allows only surface learning.	Promotes deep learning.
A.k.a. "low context."	A.k.a. "high context."

People generally believe that they give and get a lot of high quality information. Our experience working with teams in organizations is that, while they *think* they are exchanging high quality information, most of the information exchanged is low quality. Groupware often can exacerbate this tendency toward low quality information because of the perceived need to limit the length of electronic messages and because of the "get the job done quickly" mindset.

Because groupware can exacerbate the effects of these four communication issues, employees must (1) be aware of these issues; and (2) learn and practice the skills of inquiry and testing assumptions (defined more thoroughly below).

17.6 A Closer Look at Groupware Products

The central themes of groupware are collaboration and communication. The above explanation of general collaboration and communication issues paves the way for a better understanding of the human side of groupware. Now we can focus the discussion a bit and look more closely at where and how these general collaboration and communication issues and groupware intersect.

17.6.1 Groupware's Effect on Communication and Collaboration

People are still the critical resource in an organization, and groupware and other technologies only augment what people do. ([4] p. 19)

Groupware advocates claim that this technology changes the way people communicate and share information. This is true, but this change is only superficial. Beneath the surface operate the same, age-old patterns of thought and behavior, which in most cases are fear-based. If people weren't questioning their and others' assumptions and sharing high quality information before using groupware, chances are they aren't doing these things now. Furthermore, it is not even true that the worst case scenario is simply not improving people's mindsets and behaviors: groupware can exacerbate the status quo. Groupware's powerful applications can magnify exponentially fear-based behaviors and their effects. For instance, people's tendency to assume without publicly testing their assumptions is generally worse in electronic communication. The speed at which information moves is a mixed blessing in that it spurs on the task-oriented, "get the job done" mindset, with all its barriers to learning. In addition, speed, coupled with another of groupware's main features—the ability to extend the range of information across the globe—often only spreads misinformation faster and farther.

17.6.2 The Skills of Collaboration and Communication: "The Hard Skills of the Soft Side"

Collaborative mindsets and behaviors remain merely attractive concepts without the practical skills that support them in "the real world." Here is a definition of the main collaboration and communication skills needed to use groupware most effectively. The comments on the individual groupware products below will refer to these skills. These skills enable you to avoid common problems of using groupware and to unleash the power of this technology. They are crucial to maximum success with groupware because they are the bridge between theory and action. You will notice when we list the skills needed in the different groupware categories that, for the most part, these lists are very similar. That is because these are the core competencies that are critical to collaboration, no matter what form it takes. Finally, these skills are separated for the sake of discussion but in "real time" they are intertwined and overlapping. One needs to use them all interchangeably to improve communication and collaboration.

☞ **Inquiry**—Inquiry is the skill of asking questions to recover the high quality information that would otherwise stay beneath the surface due to the basic communication tendencies discussed above. By inquiring you can unearth mixed messages, contradictions, etc. that create problems when they stay unsurfaced. Our research shows that people see the importance of inquiry but they do not do it. It also shows that the reasons why people do not inquire or invite inquiry from others come from the speaker's or listener's private assumptions. For example, a recipient of an e-mail message may not inquire as to the sender's reasoning if he/she assumes that the question may threaten or embarrass the sender, and thereby prove to be "career-limiting" for the recipient.

☞ **Identifying and examining assumptions**—As few people realize, we all make assumptions about everything (including others' assumptions), we typically do not share them, and we do not inquire into others' unshared assumptions. Even if we are aware of others' unshared assumptions, we are afraid to identify and examine them, so instead we guess. This is a major communication problem. Though we've been taught to "assume nothing," that is not a realistic goal. Instead, the goal should be to check and identify our and others' assumptions with each other, constantly and publicly, using the skills of inquiry. What keeps us from doing this already are fear-based mindsets and behaviors such as not wanting to seem presumptuous, fear of embarrassment, etc.

☞ **Calibration**—Calibration is the skill of attuning yourself to the cues people give that add a great deal of meaning to their words. These cues can be verbal (one's vocabulary) and non-verbal (voice tone and tempo, body language). Calibration requires: (1) experience with the other person and (2) inquiry (a good example of the interconnectedness of these skills).

Due to the fear of threat and embarrassment, people rarely say everything that they're thinking and feeling. Calibration allows you to observe and address these hidden messages. For example, if someone asks a colleague to do something for a project and he/she says, looking down after a short pause, "Yeah, uh, O.K.," the first person, if he/she is skilled in calibration, will detect unspoken reservations and inquire into them to work it out. Someone unskilled in calibration will probably move on, only to be surprised and disappointed when the other person doesn't do what he/she "agreed" to do.

Since in e-mail you can only calibrate to people's words, an example would be if this same scenario occurred over e-mail and the colleague responded, "yeah, I'll try." Someone skilled in calibration would want to know what the word "try" means for the colleague: Does it mean "yes" (this is rare!) or does it mean something less than a 100 percent commitment? By inquiring into this choice of words, the first person will surface the colleague's thoughts and assumptions and address them.

You can calibrate over a video conference, but our experience is that people can act differently in this medium, so it requires a better mastery of these skills.

17.6.3 Groupware Products: Benefits, Problems, and Skills Needed

While all the issues discussed so far—fear-based mindsets and behavior, basic communication tendencies, etc.—come into play in all groupware products, here is a more specific application of what we have been talking about to some of these products, with special attention to the following:

☞ how the collaboration and communication issues we have been talking about manifest themselves in each;

☞ in the context of collaboration and communication issues, what are the typical benefits and potential problems of each product;

☞ the skills each product requires to maximize these benefits and minimize these problems.

17.6.4 Electronic Mail

E-mail is a convenient and useful tool for linear, back and forth, one-to-one or one-to-many communication of messages and documents. It is also an enabling technology for other forms of groupware itself. Research shows that people tend to be more honest and more willing to "discuss the undiscussable" in e-mail. A deep learning approach would find out why this is. One possibility is that the lack of face-to-face contact lessens the fear of embarrassment and threat, as when getting the answering machine makes a difficult call easier.

E-mail messages are usually high in content and low in context, i.e., the thoughts, assumptions, and reasoning behind what is explicitly stated ("content"). As suggested above, others' non-verbal cues—body language, tone and tempo of voice, etc.—are an excellent source of high-context information. This source is cut off in electronic communication because people can neither see nor hear each other. People's neglect or misuse of the subject line, and their tendency to compose e-mails out of short statements, are other reasons for the shortage of contextual information in e-mail. There is even more room than normal for the recipient to make up what the sender means without checking it out.

Due to this lack of context, e-mail is easily misunderstood and distorted, creating escalating errors that lead to hurt feelings and low morale. People also complain about being deluged with information ("I get copied on everything!"), which leads them to withdraw and distance themselves. A survey of Fortune 500 companies by Chicago-based EdWel & Co. found the average e-mail user gets fifteen messages a day, and spends nearly fifty minutes just reading them. We have heard of cases in which companies declare a moratorium on e-mail, a sure sign that something is missing from the implementation strategy that would help ensure that this technology lives up to its potential. As one of the authors is fond of saying, "E-mail can be just a faster way to miscommunicate."

To minimize these problems and get the most out of e-mail, the sender of an e-mail needs to be deliberate and specific in inviting inquiry and checking out what meaning is being made out of his/her words. He/she must also step into the mindset and perception of the recipient as much as possible. These skills improve the communication greatly and teach the sender how to use e-mail effectively. On the other end, the receiver must (1) inquire and (2) step into the sender's mindset to fill in the context of the received message.

E-mail is best-suited for short, quick requests and responses during the middle to later stages of a project. This applies to the overall project of implementing groupware and to projects simply using groupware. At the beginning of a project, people need as much high-context information as possible so that they understand their role and goals and visions are shared by all. Face-to-face interaction ensures the best chances of this happening (though it does not guarantee it!). Then, in later stages, e-mail is effective for rapidly furthering the action towards the goal.

One of the authors interviewed members of an international (U.K. and U.S.) team in one of the largest pharmaceutical companies. Many of them mentioned that, until there was some face-to-face contact that allowed them to get to know their co-workers in projects, it had been very frustrating, time-consuming, and inefficient to work together via e-mail and voice mail. They felt like messages went into a "black hole" and they were rarely sure what, if anything, was being done about a request. After they felt they knew each other from face-to-face meetings, they found that e-mail and voice mail enhanced efficiency. The writing of this chapter provides an example of this model in action. At the beginning we met face to face and on the telephone to decide together what we wanted to say in the chapter. Once we had drawn this big picture, we used e-mail to send the work-in-progress back and forth, exchanging feedback.

Summary	
Benefits	Speed of communication
	Ease of use compared to paper-based communication
	Ability to transmit files
	Access to people across hierarchies, distances, and time zones
	Many people can participate in a discussion
	Ability to broadcast messages one-to-many
	"cc:" function useful in keeping people informed
	Greater willingness to discuss subjects that people are reluctant to discuss face-to-face
	Can increase asynchronous collaboration across departmental and functional boundaries
Problems	Can be just a faster and more efficient way to miscommunicate
	There can be serious misunderstandings due to an increase in the tendency to make assumptions/jump to conclusions and not check them out.

Summary

Messages are "low context," making them much easier to misunderstand and distort than telephone, video conferencing, or face-to-face
communication.

Misunderstandings can lead to "flaming," distancing, conspiracies, and
gossip.

Less "human connection." Unless e-mail is supplemented with "high context" communications, it becomes easier for some people to say "no" to
requests and to treat the other person as if he/she were not a human
being with feelings, needs, etc.

High volume of messages, and a high percentage of non-useful messages,
can waste time and discourage users. Additionally, senders assume that
the receiver will have read their message soon after they send it. Due to a
high volume of messages, it may never get read.

Senders assume their message has been received and may never find out
that there is a technical problem. File attachment can incur technical
problems as well. This can cause serious practical and relationship problems (resentment, feeling ignored, etc.).

Long discussions, or short ones involving more than two people, can get
confusing and create misunderstandings.

Some types of communication are not well-suited for e-mail: e.g., expressing anger, complex group discussions (for which discussion databases are
best suited), urgent communications. These situations require more high
context communication (face-to-face), though some people use e-mail
because it is easier or less uncomfortable.

People can use e-mail to hide and avoid difficult conversations and
decisions.

**Skills
Needed**   Inquiry

Identifying and examining assumptions

Stepping into the mindset and perception of the reader

Stepping into the mindset and perception of the writer

Knowing what types of communication are appropriate for e-mail

17.6.5 Electronic Meeting Systems (EMS)

One of the most popular features of EMS applications is anonymous feedback and voting, which creates a risk- or fear-free environment. Again, a deep
learning response would be: "What does it say about your corporate culture that
employees will only give honest feedback—the information most vital to building
growth and competitive advantage—anonymously, especially when this anonymity comes from such an expensive product?" Also: "What is going on in a culture
where people wait for new technology to come along that hopefully will improve
communication and collaboration instead of tackling these issues themselves?"

One of the authors recently attended a meeting using EMS where people did seem to be more willing to discuss the "undiscussable." However, the EMS setting did exacerbate other anti-collaborative tendencies. Again, speed was both a blessing and a curse. Participants began generating and selecting ideas as rapidly as possible, with this rapidity being the main criterion, not the quality of the ideas or the effectiveness of the meeting. Because of this momentum, clarifying these ideas did not occur to most participants. Those to whom it maybe did occur did not speak up because there was no room for it. This decreased the amount of inquiring into and checking out people's underlying assumptions, resulting in increased miscommunication.

It is crucial to understand that most of the participants in this electronic meeting, including the facilitator, were probably not aware of these communication problems, and their response to the technology could be positive. This is because the communication patterns and issues causing these problems—e.g., the unspecificity of language, our tendency to make up what others mean instead of ask, etc.—are so natural and inherent to all of us. We are like fish who don't know they are in water. Therefore, even though the role of the facilitator exists to minimize miscommunication and maximize the benefits of EMS, unless he/she is trained in the particular issues discussed here and the skills needed to handle them, the problems will still arise.

Summary

Benefits	Faster and more productive meetings
	Anonymous feedback and voting promotes honesty in challenging ideas, especially those of senior participants, and "discussing the undiscussable."
	More variety and higher quantity of ideas
	Increases creativity
	Increases participation
	Decreases "groupthink"
Problems	Increases the tendency to make speed the goal, spurring the "get the job done" mindset.
	People often think they know who said what and assume it is true. They then act accordingly towards that person without checking it out.
	People can comment on their own proposals as if they were someone else ("I think X is a great plan!").
	Can increase the tendency to assume and guess at what other people meant, rather than checking it out. While people are more likely to challenge ideas, they are less likely to challenge their assumptions about what the other person really meant. This problem can be exacerbated by the rapidity of discussion in EMS.
	Accountability in regard to decisions: Who will do what? By when? Who will follow up on these commitments?

Summary

Electronic discussions, like any kind of discussion, can degenerate into debate.

Skills Needed

Inquiry

Identifying and examining assumptions

Stepping into the mindset and perception of the reader

Stepping into the mindset and perception of the writer

Knowledge of what types of communication are appropriate for an electronic meeting

Supervision by a highly skilled facilitator is extremely valuable. Even competent facilitators overall are generally not skilled in fundamental communication and collaboration issues, such as challenging assumptions.

17.6.6 Video/Audio Conferencing

Video and audio conferencing software is useful because it transmits voice qualities and non-verbal cues, making the communication higher in context than purely language-based media like e-mail. In addition to raising the level of communication, this also increases the sense of connection between participants. This sense of connection is highest in video conferencing, followed by audio conferencing, e-mail, and discussion database. Although video and audio conferencing are higher context, they are not the same as a face-to-face meeting, and require an adjustment in communication style for a participant to be persuasive. Someone could be skilled at meetings but not be less effective in a video or audio conferencing situation. Finally, some participants, including the team from the pharmaceutical company, mentioned to us that it is more difficult to "read" people and that many people seem to put on a false front, making it difficult to know if people are truly agreeing or are just being agreeable. If there was agreement, they weren't sure what had been agreed to, and later actions often clashed with what they thought had been agreed to.

Summary

Benefits

Higher context communication (voice qualities and non-verbal cues)

People feel a greater sense of connection.

Problems

Video is often delayed in relation to what you hear, so you see others' reactions to what has already been said, not to what you are actually hearing.

Requires adjustment of communication style to be used effectively. Most people do not make this adjustment so they come off quite differently from how they would face to face.

Summary

The difficulty of "reading" people, and their tendency to act differently, make it difficult to know whether they agree or are committed, calibrate to them, etc.

Video conferencing, especially internationally, can be expensive and strain budgets. Even in large corporations, facilities can be limited and difficult to book, sometimes taking months for people who are not senior enough.

While many facilities have special cameras for showing documents, the normal size text is often hard to read.

Skills Needed

Ability to "work" this medium

Calibration

Inquiry

Identifying and examining assumptions

Stepping into the mindset and perception of the listener

Stepping into the mindset and perception of the speaker

Knowledge of what types of communication are appropriate for video/audio conferencing.

17.6.7 Discussion Database or Non-Real Time Conferencing Software

One potential benefit of this software is increasing the organization's ability to share intelligence. Yet this intelligence is only as good as the information in the database. Unless there is trust, people will tend to withhold, tell each other what they want to hear, and practice other face-saving behaviors with the justification of wanting to win, reducing hurt, being strong, etc. These behaviors inhibit the flow of high quality information and therefore make the software less effective.

Summary

Benefits

Threaded conversations make it possible to have complex discussions with multiple participants.

Increases the efficiency and speed of business processes by routing messages to the right people in the right order, and notifying the sender if someone is not available.

Can be used to help transform information into knowledge, and distribute this knowledge.

Can capture knowledge, insights, techniques, solutions to common problems, and make them available to others, including future employees.

Summary

Can increase the sense of relationship between employees if it is used with higher context communication.

Can increase collaboration across departmental and functional boundaries, without having to go through a hierarchy.

Helps create environment of synergy that creates knowledge and gets disparate groups to share information and experience.

Problems   Can be just a faster, more efficient way to miscommunicate.

There can be serious misunderstandings due to an increase in the tendency to make assumptions, jump to conclusions, and not check out assumptions.

Electronic communication is "low context," making it much easier to misunderstand than telephone, video conferencing, or face-to-face communication.

Misunderstandings can lead to "flaming," distancing, conspiracies, and gossip.

Less "human connection," unless it is supplemented with "high context" communication.

Long discussions, or short ones involving more than two participants, can get confusing and create misunderstandings.

High volume of messages and a high percentage of non-useful messages can waste a lot of time, discourage users, and cause "information overload." Additionally, senders assume that the other participants will have rapidly read their message. Do to a high volume of messages, it may never get read.

Senders assume their message has been read and may never find out that there was a technical problem. This can cause serious practical and relationship problems (resentment, feeling ignored).

Accountability in regard to decisions: Who will do what? By when? Who will follow up on these commitments?

Electronic discussions, like any kind of discussion, can degenerate into debate.

Skills Needed   Knowledge of how to set up complex discussions so that they work well; e.g., how to divide the topic into digestible pieces.

Inquiry

Identifying and examining assumptions

Stepping into the mindset and perception of the reader

Stepping into the mindset and perception of the writer

Knowledge of what types of communication are appropriate for this kind of software

17.6.8 Workflow

Since it automates business processes, in some ways workflow seems to have less of a human side than, say, e-mail or EMS. Though this may be true, workflow still has its share of people issues. After all, at the heart of workflow is still the transferring of information in an organization.

In sports terms, workflow is like a team in a relay race, whereas other groupware products are more like a football team that huddles together before the next play. Both models involve collaboration, but in workflow, "where only one team member at a time is actually running, the hand-off of the baton spells the difference between success and failure" ([10] p. 71). It is in this crucial moment of the hand-off of the baton that most of the people issues reside. The better the task—and the information associated with it—are handed off to the next person, the more likely it is that the overall sequence of individual achievements will reach the goal. Finally, because the foundation of re-engineering is that you capture assumptions and inquire into them, people skills are especially important in designing the workflow.

As with other groupware products, speed can be a mixed blessing. While saving time is good, this gain in efficiency can be offset by more subtle collaboration and communication problems. Although the old ways of processing a form, with people physically handing it off to each other, is slower than workflow, the human connection at the point of hand-off can help deal with unexpected problems and unusual situations better than a computer can.

Summary	
Benefits	Increased efficiency and productivity
	Can be a good way to capture valuable information and the assumptions underlying how a company operates. Can enable company-wide self-reflection about why it does things a certain way.
	Better decision-making resulting from the right information being routed to the right person at the right time
	Can use it to establish control, authority, and accountability. For example, it helps you know when people did what and helps you track commitments.
Problems	Potential reduction in flexibility and creativity
	Passing information between different groupware products is problematic, despite efforts to create an industry standard.
	There could be a tendency not to re-examine the process after automating it because of the view that, once the process has been cemented, it would be too expensive or difficult to change.
	Making processes faster can be a mixed blessing by spurring the task-oriented, "get the job done" mindset.
	As e-mail can be a component of workflow, all of the problems of e-mail can apply to workflow as well.

Summary

As non-real time conferencing can be a component of workflow, all of the problems of non-real time conferencing can apply to workflow as well.

Problems in communication and collaboration, especially lack of inquiry, can lead to automating poor processes.

Workflow applications can be sabotaged by unprepared and resistant users.

Successful implementation relies on everyone knowing how the application works and what is expected of them.

Skills Needed   Inquiry

Identifying and examining assumptions

17.6.9 Groupware Frameworks

Groupware Frameworks tie together the individual groupware functions so that it doesn't have many human issues by itself. In another sense, however, it has them all, because all groupware products are involved in groupware frameworks.

As in the case of workflow, design is the key stage for human issues. The groupware framework needs to be designed so that it works well with how the employees work. Finding out how employees work—i.e., the underlying assumptions and thinking beneath what they do—requires that the designers, including the technologists, be skilled in inquiry and identifying and examining assumptions.

Summary

Benefits   Helps coordinate the enterprise

Integrates "islands of collaboration" into a productive whole, bridges gaps between platforms, operating systems, etc.

Since groupware frameworks encompass all the other products, most all of the benefits associated with these products can apply to groupware frameworks.

Problems   Security can be a problem.

Authority and control issues can be a problem.

Since groupware frameworks encompass all the other products, most all of the problems associated with these products can apply to groupware frameworks.

Skills Needed   Inquiry

Identifying and examining assumptions, especially in designing the framework

---

17.7 CONCLUSION

If you get only one message out of this chapter, let it be this: To maximize the potential of groupware, everyone involved—those who champion, design, and use groupware—must:

1. Become aware of the communication and collaboration issues in groupware
2. Learn and practice the skills needed to address them

In the past, organizations have been blind to or have ignored this human side of groupware, or have lacked the required expertise in collaborative skills. They have paid for it, either through failure or lost opportunity. It is our hope that more and more organizations will acquire the expertise they need to anticipate and avoid the minefields human issues can create, such as delays, lost momentum, resignation, and wasted time and money.

Instead of waiting until the technology is in place before tackling cultural issues, companies need to implement new technology and new mindsets/skills simultaneously. Moreover, it is best to approach this simultaneous dual re-engineering not as two parallel but separate processes but as two parallel and integrated processes (see Fig. 17.4).

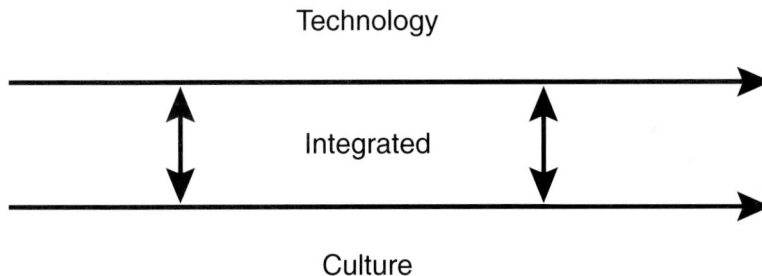

Technology

Integrated

Culture

Fig. 17.4 Simultaneous Changes to Technology and Culture Improve Chances for Success

What happens when this isn't done is what happened at Young & Rubicam, the large advertising agency. Writes Glenn Rifkin:

> Y&R's three-year plan has now dissolved into a less aggressive six-year roll-out. And Rudd has learned a valuable lesson about neglecting the all-important people side of the equation. The Field of Dreams approach, a popular method of implementing groupware, didn't work. Said Rudd: "If you build it, they won't necessarily come." ([13] p. 76)

Because technology was introduced without a companion effort in cultural issues, employees "didn't understand the underlying fundamentals of groupware." ([13] p. 76) Rudd summarized the problem: "The strategic thinking, as clever as it might have been, was inappropriate to the reality." ([13] p. 76)

You need to plan for cultural impact—you either pay up front, in the form of training in communication and collaboration skills, or you pay dearly. As Glenn Rifkin writes:

> Companies that drop collaborative technology into cultures unaccustomed to sharing are in for serious disappointment if they fail to address organizational demands up front. Consultants like Alan Witty, president of Productivity Partners in Petaluma, Calif., [now at KPMG.—*Ed*.] are constantly amazed at how little attention is being paid to the human side of the groupware equation, despite the powerful changes the new technologies bring to an organization. "Ultimately, the success of groupware projects depends on people, not technology…. It's incredible how few companies seem to understand this." ([13] p. 80)

In an age in which we are all increasingly interconnected, and in which we *need* to be interconnected, groupware has immense potential to help us face future challenges, both in business and in society. As Thomas Malone writes, "The companies that figure out how to use these new technologies wisely will be helping to create a better world for themselves and for the rest of us." [4]. Our success in harnessing this potential depends on our ability to confront and master the fundamental human forces in how we communicate and interact that are involved in groupware. Groupware carries a lot of promise, but it is a promise that only we who use it can keep.

BIBLIOGRAPHY

1. Argyris, C., *Knowledge for Action: A Guide to Overcoming Barriers to Organizational Change*. San Francisco: Jossey-Bass, 1993.
2. Argyris, C., *Overcoming Organizational Defenses*. Boston: Allyn and Bacon, 1990.
3. Cameron-Bandler, L., Gordon, D. and Lebeau, M., *The Emprint Method: A Guide to Reproducing Competence*. Moab, Utah: Real People Press, 1985.
4. Coleman, D. and Khanna, R., ed. *Groupware: Technology and Applications*. Upper Saddle River, NJ: Prentice-Hall PTR, 1995.
5. Di Pietro, C., "Meetingware and Organizational Effectiveness" in *Groupware: Technology and Applications* (see above), pp. 434–473.
6. "Downside of e-mail," in *Crain's Chicago Business*, April 1, 1996, p. 20.
7. Garner, R., "Flight Crew." *ComputerWorld*, Feb. 5, 1996, pp. 66-67.
8. Janis, I. and Mann, L., *Decision-Making: A Psychological Analysis of Conflict, Choice and Commitment*. New York: The Free Press, 1977.
9. Lyon, K. W., "Why Groupware is Tough to Love." *Forbes ASAP*, June 5, 1995, p. 80.
10. Marshak, R., "Workflow: Applying Automation to Group Processes" in *Groupware: Technology and Applications* (see above), pp. 71-96.
11. O'Connor, J. and Seymour, J., *Introducing Neuro-linguistic Programming*. London: Aquarian/Thorsons, 1990.
12. Putnam, R., "Unlocking Organizational Routines that Prevent Learning." *The Systems Thinker*, vol. 4, no. 6.
13. Rifkin, G., "A Skeptic's Guide to Groupware," *Forbes ASAP*, June 5, 1995, pp. 76-91.
14. Robinson, P., "Interview with Paul Romer." *Forbes ASAP*, June 5, 1995, p. 66ff.

15. Schneier, L., "The Implementation of Enterprise-Ware at the World Bank: A Case Study in *Groupware: Technology and Applications* (see above), pp. 378-407.

16. "What the heck? Two findings that left some *ComputerWorld* editors wondering...," in *ComputerWorld*, April 15, 1996, p. 90.

BIOGRAPHIES

Gerald O'Dwyer is Founder and Principal of Harvard-Brown & Co., a San Francisco management consulting firm specializing in organizational learning and change management. He is a trained communication professional certified in advanced communication studies. His clients range from small firms to large corporations such as Arthur Andersen, LensCrafters, and Ashland Chemical.

Art Giser, Senior Consultant at Harvard-Brown & Co., specializes in training professionals in communication, decision-making, skills transfer, leadership, team-building, and organizational change. He is a trainer and developer in Neuro-linguistic Programming (NLP), the Founder and Director of NLP Associates in San Francisco, and co-developer of Imperative Self Analysis. His past clients include Glaxo Wellcome, Intel, and Sun Microsystems.

Ed Lovett is an Associate at Harvard-Brown & Co.

In addition to in-house work with clients, Harvard-Brown & Co. offers two public courses, Leadership: Driving Change in your Team, Department, and Organization and Motivation, Negotiation and Influence, through the University of California at Berkeley Extension. Mr. O'Dwyer and Mr. Giser recently collaborated with David Coleman to deliver a course on Groupware: Combining Teamwork and Technology for Competitive Advantage, also at Berkeley.

The authors welcome your response and comments to issues raised in this chapter. They can be reached at:

Harvard-Brown & Co.
3255 Broderick Street, Suite 2,
San Francisco, CA 94123
(415) 928-1875/1833 fax
E-mail:
Geodwyer@aol.com
AGiser@aol.com
ELovett420@aol.com

Introduction to Chapter 18

The construction industry is very mature, especially when compared to groupware. With minor changes, buildings, roads, and dams have been built the same way for generations. There are several reasons why the construction industry has not aggressively sought out technology solutions, but much of that is changing. The pressures of global operations and business goals are challenging traditional construction industry business practices. There are three primary reasons why construction companies are employing electronic tools. First, increased competition has made delivering projects on time and on budget even more important. Second, the scope of construction projects has become much more complex and third, the rise in construction claims-related litigation means that documenting every step of the project in a timely and efficient manner can mean the difference between success or failure in the market.

PRC was motivated to introduce technology (groupware and other collaborative technologies) to change the traditional construction processes. Although the chapter focuses on PRC's experiences, Frank Lancione also brings in vignettes about collaboration in many other industries—from a chain of coffee houses to the oil industry. The focus of the chapter is Genesis, a project PRC initiated for internal project management, but which has been commercialized for clients.

Genesis looks at the collaboration between the three parties contractually responsible for any construction project; the builder, the architect, and the owner. Although, in an earlier chapter we talked about fear-driven behaviors blocking collaboration, in this case, fear-driven behaviors (fear of liability) are driving the move toward collaboration.

In the case delineated in this chapter, the contractor is still paper based, the owner, PRC, is electronically based, and the architects are somewhere in between. PRC found that the lack of automation in construction operations was increasing costs through rework, delays, and duplication of effort. Frank uses the example of moving a door to explain the new workflow process. Using a Lotus Notes template for the construction workflow processes, he shows how the use of these collaborative tools can change a process cycle time from one week to one day.

PRC understands that the "technology as aspirin" approach to process engineering, or re-engineering, is not sufficient to reach the goal. People and processes must be considered in tandem to gain success. Although Genesis looks suspiciously like re-engineering supported by collaborative technologies, Frank debunks both TQM and Hammer's philosophies and inserts a more practical philosophy of his own.

Frank takes us into the future of 2001. This is not a future where HAL takes over the world as in 2001: A Space Odyssey. *Instead, he presents a more realistic future, where the construction firms that survive are the ones linking with their customers to reduce costs and cycle times. These firms overcame technophobia and resistance and were able to move ahead. Frank concludes with his observations and provides some good tips to managers who are thinking of implementing any type of collaborative technology for a complex project.*

Applying Groupware to the Architectural Design and Construction Industry: PRC's Genesis Strategy

Frank A. Lancione
PRC Inc.

A West coast coffeehouse chain that has sown franchises across the U.S. like a modern Johnny Appleseed, now seeks to build a network of stores in Japan. How do they manage the construction of the new stores half a world away?

A large piece of a major oil company's next year's profitability depends on launching 200 new gas stations in the Middle East before its rivals can secure their position in that market. How do they ensure that the architectural and engineering work on their new sites gets done in time for their stations to come on-line before those of their competitors?

Back in the U.S., the Pentagon is betting what's left of its budget for new technology on a handful of large, complex weapons system construction projects. The success of these projects—and the future security of our country—rests with the ability of literally hundreds of suppliers, engineering firms, government personnel, and prime contractors to work in unison despite the fact that they are physically dispersed across the country.

* * * * *

Project management provides an almost perfect setting for testing the ability of groupware to redefine team based work. Imagine that you are the project manager for a complex global project like the ones described above. How do you keep everyone moving in the same direction? How do you keep on top of issues and problems? How do you spot opportunities? How do you learn from and prevent mistakes?

At PRC we are using groupware to change the way we work with the architectural firms, construction management firms, and general contractors that carry out major construction projects for us. We've named this effort Genesis because we intend to totally reinvent the way we manage ourselves and our suppliers.

Our Genesis story is very much a work in progress. We are evolving our methods and making sure each phase works before we move to the next step. The sections that follow describe the vision we have of how Genesis will work when it is fully implemented. Section I explains how we got started. Section II shows how the technology enabled workflows we envision under Genesis compare with business as usual in the building design and construction management industries.

When groupware fails, it's usually because the implementors succeeded in getting the servers to talk to each other but failed to get the people talking to each other. Section III describes a holistic framework for relating leadership strategy and change management concerns to process innovation and technology deployment. This is the conceptual architecture we are using to guide our Genesis implementation.

Finally, even though we are still in the early stages of fully realizing our Genesis vision, our in-house staff and the vendors working with us on the Genesis project team have already begun to talk about how groupware could reshape their industry. Section IV presents excerpts from an electronic brainstorming session in which Genesis project team members speculate on the impact of groupware on the design and construction business in the year 2001.

18.1 THE GENESIS OF GENESIS

Genesis started as an idea to improve the management of PRC's internal facilities construction and real estate operations. PRC is a major systems integrator operating as a wholly owned subsidiary of the Litton Corporation. We are involved in everything from weapons systems to weather systems to the U.S. postal system. The wide diversity in PRC services and the types of people and facilities required to carry them out creates an ever changing set of office and laboratory space needs.

Mark Herbert is PRC's Vice President of Facilities and Real Estate. To Mark and his staff, PRC is best understood as a nearly endless succession of requirements to lease, refurbish, and maintain facilities. Mark and his group do this while also continuously relocating large blocks of employees and their possessions with minimal disruption of work for our clients. One of the many units that Mark relocated over the past year was the group of which I am a part, PRC Management Consulting.

In preparing for our move, we had many discussions with the facilities team about our group's technology infrastructure needs. Mark learned about our methods for using technology to help clients redefine business processes. We learned about how construction projects get managed. Between us, we quickly concluded that applying our methods to Mark's mission was a match made in heaven. The Genesis program grew out of our collaboration.

18.1.1 Facing the Future with Yesterday's Tools

As sophisticated as the design and construction management process is, it is surprisingly lacking in the use of groupware for collaborative decision making. In the usual construction office, computer networks are for getting to the printer, or maybe e-mail. Heavy duty construction office computing usually consists of individual performers operating word processors, spread sheets, computer aided design, and project planning packages to produce personal work products. There is rarely an automated link between a firm's accounting system and the software programs its project managers use to track costs, or manage schedules. Reentering the same data into different programs for different purposes is a way of life— as are data reentry errors. Paul Himes, President of Himes Associates Construction Management Company, put it this way:

> Over the past 10 years, we have won and managed an average of 30 construction projects a year. In nearly three hundred projects, I have yet to see anyone who is using technology in any but the most rudimentary ways. The first one who can routinely operate the way we have defined in Genesis will be the 900 lb gorilla in the market.

The design and construction industry's cavalier treatment of information transfer is in stark contrast to its actual need for discipline in collaboration. Construction project success requires maintaining an accurate and timely flow of data among the owner; the project A&E (architect and engineering) firm; the construction management firm representing the owner; the general contractor responsible for the project; and the sub-contractors executing the work.

In a construction project, time really is money. Because schedule slippages on major construction projects can generate cost overruns, each potential delay is treated like a law suit in the making. If cost increases actually do arise, it kicks off a kind of mini-Watergate investigation. All sides join in a witch hunt to determine what each respective participant in the project knew about the problem and when they became aware of it. The answer is the basis for determining culpability and liability for damages. Everyone is a potential target for litigation.

Because of the liability issues, the flow of communications on a major construction project can resemble war time message traffic in terms of frequency and intensity. CYA (cover your assets) memoranda are disseminated through endless faxing, courier runs, and overnight mail. The participants find themselves literally buried beneath stacks of paper documentation on requirements, notifications, change orders, and progress reports. It doesn't have to be this way. Contemporary collaboration technologies, judiciously employed, provide opportunities to avoid this paper nightmare altogether.

If construction management is stuck on the paper based side of the methodological continuum, PRC Management Consulting overall, and my Workgroup Technologies team in particular, is firmly ensconced at the other end of the pendulum swing. The top management of our company has specifically chartered us to apply the most advanced methods and tools to 1) the process redesign solutions we develop and implement for clients, 2) PRC's own methods for delivering solutions to clients.

We employ a broad range of products for our internal and external workgroup technologies consulting activities:

☞ Lotus Notes for shared data repositories;

☞ Workflow and document routing software such as Quality at Work, Action Technologies workflow, GroupWise by Novell, and Lotus Notes;

☞ Face to face and same time/different place electronic meeting software and group decision tools like GroupSystems by Ventana;

☞ Desktop video and document sharing a lá Intel ProShare;

☞ Shared whiteboards like Xerox's Liveboard that can communicate images to and share applications with remote PCs;

☞ Web browsers and e-mail;

☞ Integrated personal productivity suites that combine individual word processing, spreadsheet, graphics, and database packages with collaborative features;

☞ Installation of gateways to decision data resident in corporate information systems in other parts of the organization; and

☞ Installation of gateways to bulletin boards, on-line news services, and research data bases.

18.1.2 How Groupware Changes the Way Teams Work

One of the great rewards of management consulting is the diversity of projects you get to work on. In my unit alone, we're helping a hospital implement a 250 seat installation of Lotus Notes in a remote desert location. We're helping one of the leading national software companies use electronic meeting software to accelerate its strategic planning on application development priorities over the next three years. We're helping a billion dollar energy company develop computer simulations of the costs and capabilities of moving to a new business model that will employ technology in a radical redesign of its business processes. The list goes on and on. The unifying theme of all these engagements is the application of groupware to decision making, data sharing, and communications and work flow.

Whether you are managing a construction project or serving on a task force assembled to tackle a specific problem, the dynamics of how groupware changes work group interactions are very similar. A good example is a project PRC carried out for a team of regional office personnel in a client's organization. This group had been charged to accelerate development of a new policy manual for nationwide application. The effort had high priority because of the need to control costs quickly by changing policy in a high visibility program area. This is a very typical business situation and illustrates the kind of technology leverage groupware brings to process redesign.

The project kickoff meetings were held over several days in Washington, DC. Everyone was flown in to participate. At the kickoff meetings, we used Ventana's GroupSystems electronic meeting software to facilitate the group process. Ventana's product put every participant in front of a PC through which they could comment, vote, and contribute to shared work products. The results were displayed on public screens. Our facilitators gathered group input with the technology and then guided the group's analysis and decision making. Work products were documented electronically throughout the process. Using these tools we were able to help the participants rapidly 1) develop the outline for the policy manual and 2) come to agreement on the issues to be covered in each section.

Each client participant brought their laptop to the kickoff. While the electronic meeting sessions were underway, our staff loaded Lotus Notes on each laptop. This included setting up special "chauffeur driven" menus to make it easy for participants to get into Notes. With marginal effort, participants would be able to access our Notes server in McLean, VA, from their home duty stations over dial-up telephone connections. As the group came to closure on the outline for their policy handbook, we created project databases in Lotus Notes that contained complete records of the decisions made and served as a repository for the work products of the team. We trained the participants on how to use the custom applications we developed and then sent them back to their home duty stations. Over the next two weeks, we provided extensive telephone help desk support for participants.

Back at their home offices, as each member of the team worked on their assigned chapters of the new policy manual, they periodically dialed into our Notes server and deposited their results. Because Notes keeps remote worker's files synchronized with the master records on the server, all participants were able to see how the work on the parts of the policy handbook that were being completed by members in other locations was progressing. Using discussion databases they were able to pose questions to each other and maintain an audit trail of issues and issue decisions. At the end of two weeks they reconvened in Washington, DC.

At the second face-to-face meeting, we again used GroupSystems to facilitate decision making and get closure. The final word smithing of the policy handbook was completed in facilitated discussions that used GroupSystems voting and commenting tools to drive decisions to closure. The group was able to finalize its product over several days of work.

The process, as well as the product, was considered highly successful. Previous handbook development projects conducted in the client organization had required temporary reassignment of regional personnel to headquarters full-time for periods of up to four months. The four week cycle time of our sponsor's project was considered a breakthrough. It allowed the group to reduce travel costs, and required participants to spend less time away from their families. It also made it possible to get needed guidance to the field more quickly—thus helping top management control costs in a high visibility program area.

For permanent workgroups and project teams that work together over longer periods of time, we implement gateways so that team members are able to view all of their e-mail directly from their Notes desktop even if it comes from the Internet or from other users in their corporation who are not on Notes. We also install Web pages to allow outside customers and stakeholders to answer surveys and receive information updates on a project's progress.

From our prior experience working with teams like the one described above, we knew with certainty that groupware could dramatically improve results in traditional organizational settings. In asking us to undertake the Genesis project, Mark Herbert was challenging us to apply the groupware redesign methods we use for teams to the flow of work, communications, and group decision making for the key players in the architectural design and construction process.

18.2 THAT WHICH IS AND THAT WHICH WILL BE: THE GENESIS STRATEGY

You're in any big city in the U.S., on the street, looking up at the skyscrapers. You think: "Surely, the people who conceive and build such magnificent structures must run their projects with precision and coordination that the rest of us mere mortals can only aspire to reach one day!" Unfortunately, god-like organization is not exactly how typical architectural design and construction projects operate.

The sections that follow trace out two workflow scenarios: 1) the steps in the process for an action such as changing the location of a door following the "As Is" processes carried out in most design and construction projects today, and 2) the "To Be" processes for carrying out the same procedure that we are implementing under Genesis. What's remarkable is that despite the extreme sophistication you see evident in the end product on a complex construction job, the reality is that the workflows for coordinating and managing the project are in most cases only minimally automated. This lack of automation creates numerous opportunities for rework, delays, and duplication of effort.

18.2.1 Moving a Door: The "As Is" Strategy

Executing large scale architecture and construction projects requires close coordination among a team of players: 1) the owner is, obviously, the end client, 2) the architect and engineering (A&E) firm does the design and engineering drawings, 3) there is often a separate construction management firm that represents the owner's interests and provides oversight of the project, 4) finally, there is a general contractor who coordinates the activities of the sub-contractors and supplier firms and provides the field project manager who runs the construction job site. Figure 18.1 shows the players and gives examples of the types of information that passes among them.

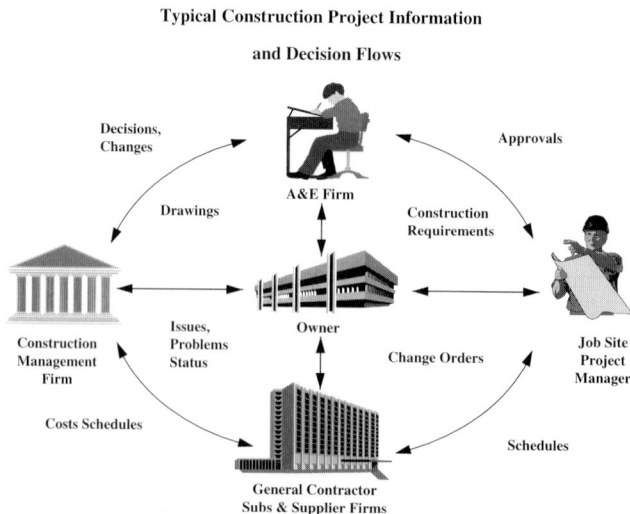

Typical Construction Project Information and Decision Flows

Fig. 18.1

Construction projects typically deploy millions of dollars of heavy equipment. Architectural firms are virtual seas of young men and women perched in front of Computer Aided Design (CAD) terminals—the twentieth century version of architectural drawing boards. However, when you come right down to how decision making is carried out in construction projects, it's done the old fashioned way—and in this case that's not a virtue.

As shown in Fig. 18.2, project binders, overflowing file cabinets, and inordinate faxing and overnight mail characterize the way things are communicated today. Want to generate a change order, redirect something that has already been agreed to and planned for? Look out Nellie! Every principal in the decision chain will receive a paper copy as well as generate several additional copies for the files and for internal distribution. Meetings to debate how to make the change and who pays for any resulting overruns will generate still more memoranda for the file.

Today's "Tools of the Trade"

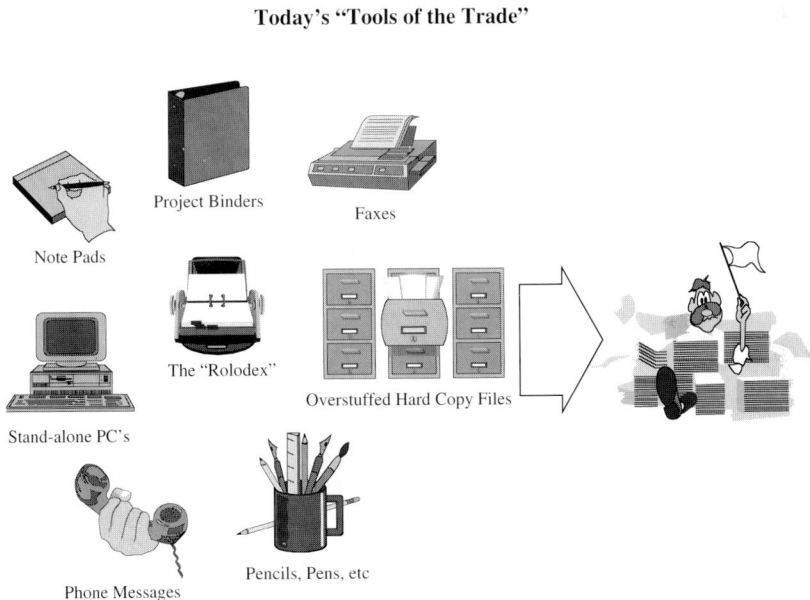

Note Pads

Project Binders

Faxes

The "Rolodex"

Stand-alone PC's

Overstuffed Hard Copy Files

Phone Messages

Pencils, Pens, etc

Fig. 18.2

18.2.2 Moving a Door: The "As Is" Strategy

PRC's Genesis team used the process of requesting and implementing the relocation of a door in a renovation project as its sample process for modeling "As Is" work methods. On a building job worth millions of dollars, something as small as moving the location of a door a few feet might be handled informally if the change came before the space was built out. On the other hand, the movement of the door could become a major issue if it required expensive changes in the routing of plumbing or air ducts. It might also generate controversy if the change requested conflicted with fire or building codes and thus required adjustments to be made in other parts of the design to compensate. And what if the door just happened to be in a custom paneled executive conference room that had just had been completed and expensively carpeted? You can almost hear the sound of the cash register ringing when a change like that is proposed.

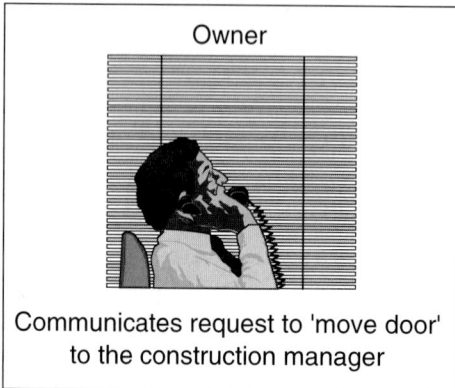

Owner

Communicates request to 'move door' to the construction manager

Fig. 18.3

Fig. 18.3 shows the first step. On a Monday morning, the owner identifies the need to make a change from the originally agreed upon layout. Most likely, this has occurred because of a change in the plans of the tenants slated to be moved into the space that is being renovated. The owner telephones the construction manager to let him know of the requirement to relocate the door.

Moving A Door: The "As Is" Strategy (cont.)

Construction Manager

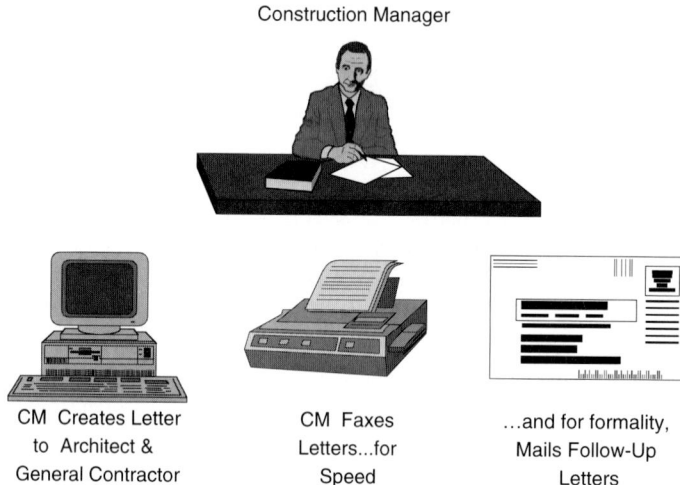

| CM Creates Letter to Architect & General Contractor | CM Faxes Letters...for Speed | ...and for formality, Mails Follow-Up Letters |

Fig. 18.4

Figure 18.4 shows the construction manager responding to the owner's request. Using today's tools: a standalone PC, a fax machine, and regular mail, the construction manager a) reduces the request to writing, b) sends notification copies to the A&E firm and General Contractor for action by fax, and c) sends each of them an original signature hard copy to document the requirement for the record.

Moving A Door: The "As Is" Strategy (cont.)

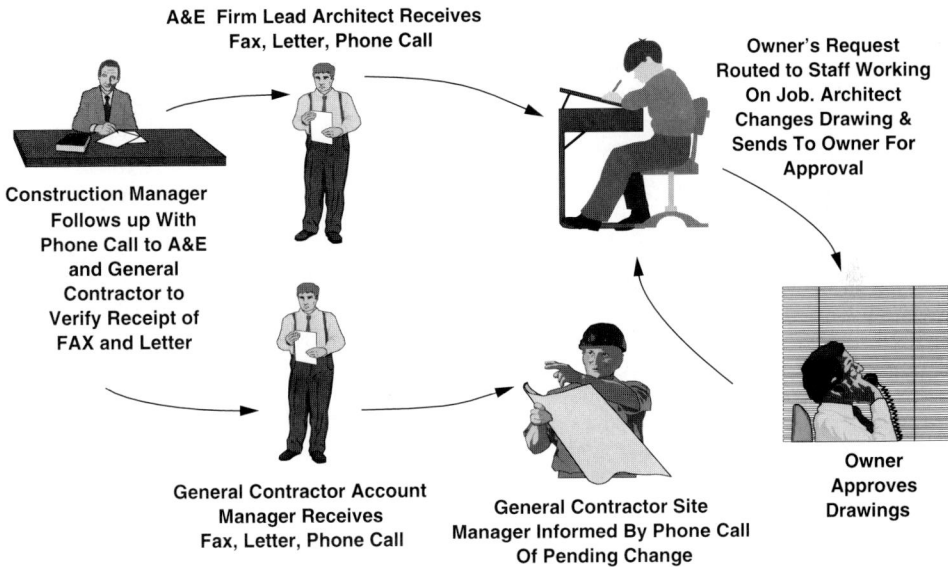

A&E Firm Lead Architect Receives Fax, Letter, Phone Call

Owner's Request Routed to Staff Working On Job. Architect Changes Drawing & Sends To Owner For Approval

Construction Manager Follows up With Phone Call to A&E and General Contractor to Verify Receipt of FAX and Letter

General Contractor Account Manager Receives Fax, Letter, Phone Call

General Contractor Site Manager Informed By Phone Call Of Pending Change

Owner Approves Drawings

Fig. 18.5

As Fig. 18.5 illustrates, the construction manager can't simply send a message about the proposed change. It's his job to make sure the change happens. So, in the real world, not long after the fax is sent, the construction manager follows up with a phone call to the A&E firm and the General Contractor. This extra step verifies that, "Yes, indeed," they did receive the fax requesting the change and are aware that changes need to be made in the project plan.

Inside the A&E firm, the fax and eventually the mailed paper copy of the request are routed to the staff architect who is assigned to work on this job. It is at this point that the first actual work on the change of the door begins as the staff architect revises the drawing to accommodate the owner's request. All time and effort expended up until this act has been devoted primarily to communication of requirements, back-checking, and documenting actions with a paper trail to create proof that the messages were sent and received.

Once the owner approves the new drawing and the word is passed back to the A&E lead architect. The team is able to swing into action once again. The A&E architect instructs the general contractor site manager to have the subcontractors move the door. The construction crews complete the necessary work. The construction management firm verifies that the work was correctly performed. The construction management firm then notifies the owner that the work has taken place and meets the requirements set for the project. The project that began with the owner's request on a Monday is completed on the Monday of the following week.

Moving A Door The Genesis Way

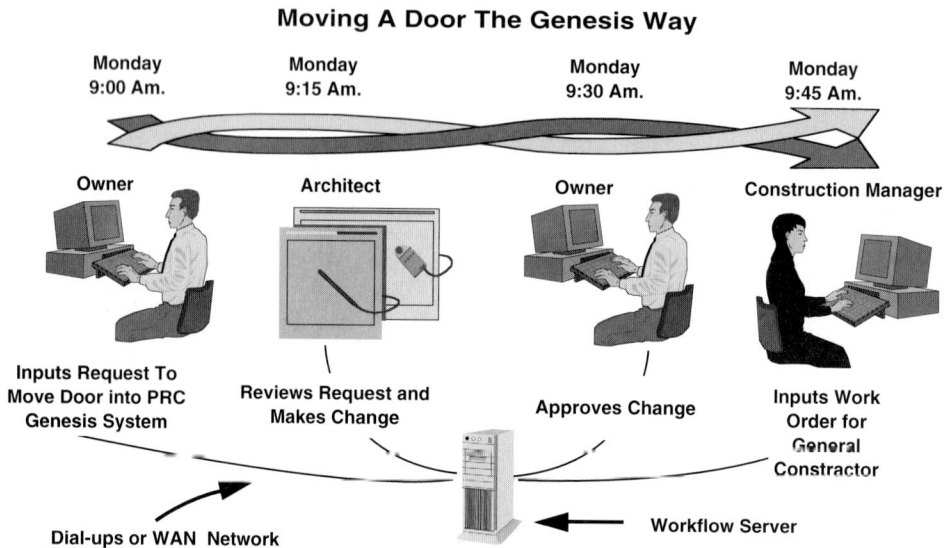

Fig. 18.6

18.2.3 The "To Be" Strategy: Moving a Door the Genesis Way

As Fig. 18.6 shows, cycle times can be drastically different when key decision makers are linked using workflow tools operating over dial-up or wide-area telecommunications networks. In our internal implementation, PRC is creating workflow templates using Lotus Notes to cover virtually all of the standard construction project workflow procedures approved by the American Institute of Architects. The principals on project management teams can use Genesis to initiate and track the status of important action requests. Project documents are automatically date and time stamped and archived for audit trail purposes. Because they are operating in a networked environment, all members of the project management team can see and work on actions in parallel. These technology implementations are far from exotic, but they totally transform the process.

Instead of calling the construction manager on the phone, the owner (or one of his staff) simply enters a change order request into a pre-designed Genesis electronic change order form. Pull-down menus and built-in edit routines minimize the amount of input required and help prevent entry errors.

The moment that the requester hits enter, an electronic message is generated to alert the construction manager and the A&E firm that an owner request is pending. At the same time, the Action Item list that the management team uses to track key events on the project is updated to show when the request was made, who has to respond, and the current status of the request. Finally, a date and time stamped electronic copy of the request is stored in the project database for archive purposes. All members of the project management team can access the forms for generating requests, the Action Item tracking and status list, and the document archive, from their Genesis home page screens.

At the A&E firm, the lead architect handling the owner's account and the staff architect doing the actual design for this project both receive notification of the owner's change request. Genesis workflow applications can be set up with questions on the original input form that trigger varying levels of review/change authority as the request moves through the process. In our example, the cost and schedule impacts of moving a door fall below the thresholds the A&E lead architect has determined require his pre-approval before staff can work on the design. The request shows up on the staff architect's desk as a high priority work item ready for action.

The architect calls up the appropriate Computer Aided Design files, makes the change, attaches the revised drawing to the request, and forwards the document to the owner for approval. He includes a verification that there are no unexpected impacts such as the need to reroute plumbing, which would cause the cost to exceed the range agreed to by all parties as having minimal overall budget or schedule risk. The A&E firm's design archives and the Genesis project management archive both are updated to reflect the changes in the location of the door. Anyone on the project management team who happens to be checking the Action Item list sees that the A&E firm has completed the design and the request is now pending owner approval.

While the design change was underway at the A&E firm, the construction manager also was receiving electronic notification of the request to relocate the door. As soon as he learned of the proposed move, the construction manager immediately checked the master plan to make sure no finish work was scheduled in the area where the door is being moved. This early notice enables the construction manager to prevent the onsite crews from proceeding with work that might have to be redone because of the change in the location of the door. As soon as the owner approves the A&E design, the construction manager will be notified electronically. The construction manager then initiates a work order authorizing the general contractor's onsite project manager to proceed with the work.

Moving A Door The Genesis Way (cont.)

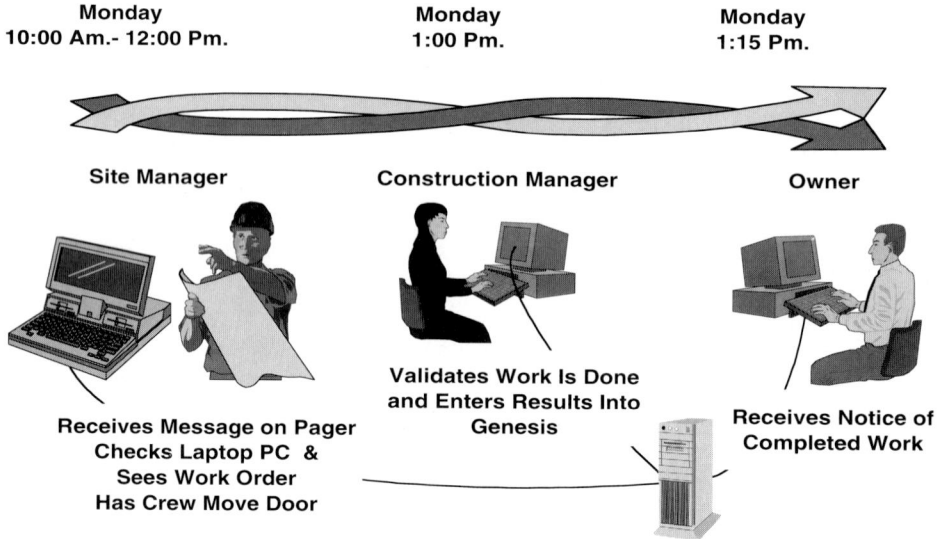

Monday 10:00 Am.- 12:00 Pm.	Monday 1:00 Pm.	Monday 1:15 Pm.

Site Manager

Construction Manager

Owner

Receives Message on Pager
Checks Laptop PC &
Sees Work Order
Has Crew Move Door

Validates Work Is Done
and Enters Results Into
Genesis

Receives Notice of
Completed Work

Fig. 18.7

As shown in Fig. 18.7, when the owner approves the change order, Genesis generates a pager message to the site manager informing him that a new work order is waiting for him. He walks to the office trailer on the site and uses his laptop to pull up the information on the new work order. Since it is simple and the crews are just finishing other tasks, he decides to schedule it right away. Within an hour, the construction manager is checking the work to ensure its quality and completeness and using Genesis to "sign off" on behalf of the owner. The construction manager's sign-off triggers a message to the owner and updates all Action Item lists and repositories informing all players that the task has been successfully completed.

18.2.4 Initiating Action During the Progress Meeting with Genesis

Figure 18.8 shows the Project Management team conducting a progress meeting to review status and address issues. A decision to move the door could easily have originated in this type of a meeting. As Fig. 18.8 describes, Genesis can be used directly during the meeting to access the floor plans for consideration by the group. At the meeting, Genesis's electronic polling and commenting capabilities are used to get closure quickly on issues and document decisions. Once the group agrees, a message is generated to the site manager who schedules and executes the move of the door. The construction manager validates completion and the owner gets notification that the work is finished.

Moving A Door The Genesis Way
The Progress Meeting Scenario

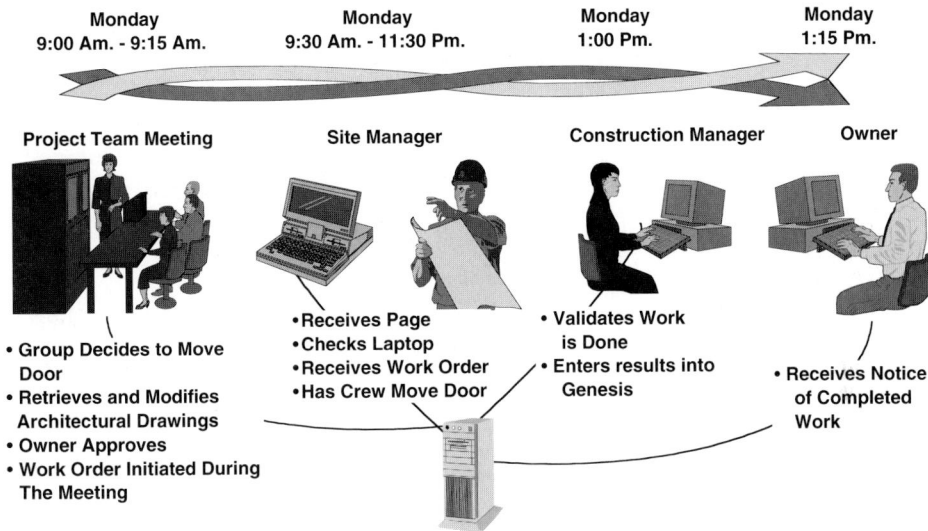

Fig. 18.8

18.3 THE THEORY BEHIND THE PRACTICE

It is easy to see how workflow and other groupware tools can quickly make a difference in highly paper based systems like those currently operating in most architectural design and construction projects. However, there are legions of organizations that have bought and implemented technology by itself only to see no measurable change in results. This is the technology as "aspirin" approach: "Buy two servers, and call me in the morning." To understand PRC's approach to Genesis, it is helpful to understand PRC's approach to enterprise engineering overall.

If Total Quality Management was the reigning "magic bullet" of management consulting in the 1980s, business process reengineering became its spiritual successor in 1990s. Dr. Deming and his quality acolytes argued that change is achieved through grueling, incremental, bottom-up continuous improvement. The payoff, Dr. Deming used to say, will come over the long term. This was tough medicine to swallow for American managers for whom any quarter's financial results could signal the end of their jobs if the profits were judged unacceptable by Wall Street or their bankers. Enter Dr. Hammer and his camp followers.

Hammer argued that dramatic improvement could be produced quickly with bold, "obliterate don't automate" management reengineering campaigns. Ever driven by the next quarter's bottom line, American managers bailed out in droves from the long term life style change prescriptions of Dr. Deming. Dr. Hammer's new crash diet credo of reengineering became the new "buzzword de jour." This shift provided an opportunity for everyone in the field of management consulting to reconsider their approach to bringing about change in organizations—particularly their approach to using technology to generate change.

In theory, upgrading technology should almost automatically net you gains in productivity. After all, vendors only get money to develop new products when they are able to convince investors that the clear benefits of their new mousetrap will generate sufficient buyers to turn a profit within a reasonable period of time. Seemingly, every new product launch is accompanied by case study data and testimonials. How many times have you seen brochures making claims that the "Improved Furbutz Workflow Connector Product" (or some equally fancifully named new technology) produced miraculous results in company XYZ during the test trials? If XYZ got such great results from the "Furbutz," how is it that your organization might spend a bundle and get "nada" in return? As Shakespeare writes in *Julius Caesar*: "Men at some time are masters of their fates; The fault, dear Brutus, is not in our stars but in ourselves."

In our experience, there is enough knowledge readily available on how to successfully handle the technology side of implementing established groupware products like Lotus Notes. When a mature technology doesn't do what it promises, it's rarely the networks or computer platforms that are the source of the failure. When technology is not meeting our expectations, we need to look as Shakespeare said, not "in our stars, but in ourselves." Usually, getting the soft stuff right—providing enough training, making sure there are relevant applications, removing the disincentives and creating incentives to use the new tools are the fatal flaws in project execution. Getting these things right, it seems, is much harder than stringing wire, or getting the bits, bytes, and data packets to talk to each other.

PRC's strategy for enterprise engineering is summarized in Fig. 18.9. Perhaps the most notable feature of our approach is that process innovation by itself is seen as only one element of a much broader framework for achieving changed results on a large scale within an organization.

The chart shown in Fig. 18.9 is actually a sort of methodology "home page." Each horizontal and vertical band, and each intersecting cell shown on the chart, is backed up by more detailed supporting charts. These describe the deliverables produced at each step and the interrelationships among all of the activities. The horizontal bands represent functional areas of focus that PRC believes must be enjoined for success in getting broad scale organizational change. These are:

☞ Leadership and Strategy

☞ Change Management

☞ Process Innovation

☞ Technology Program Management

☞ Technology Delivery

The vertical bands on the chart represent phases in the life cycle of reengineering efforts. These phases are:

☞ Strategic Planning, which is driven by the organization's Strategic Vision and shapes the organization's Enterprise ReEngineering Plan;

☞ BPR Projects, which are driven by the Enterprise ReEngineering Plan and lead to a Process ReEngineering Plan;

☞ Information Technology and Change Management Delivery, which are driven by the Process ReEngineering Plan and lead to Pilot Site Implementation; and

☞ Roll-Out, which is driven by Pilot Site Implementation and leads to Full Scale Implementation.

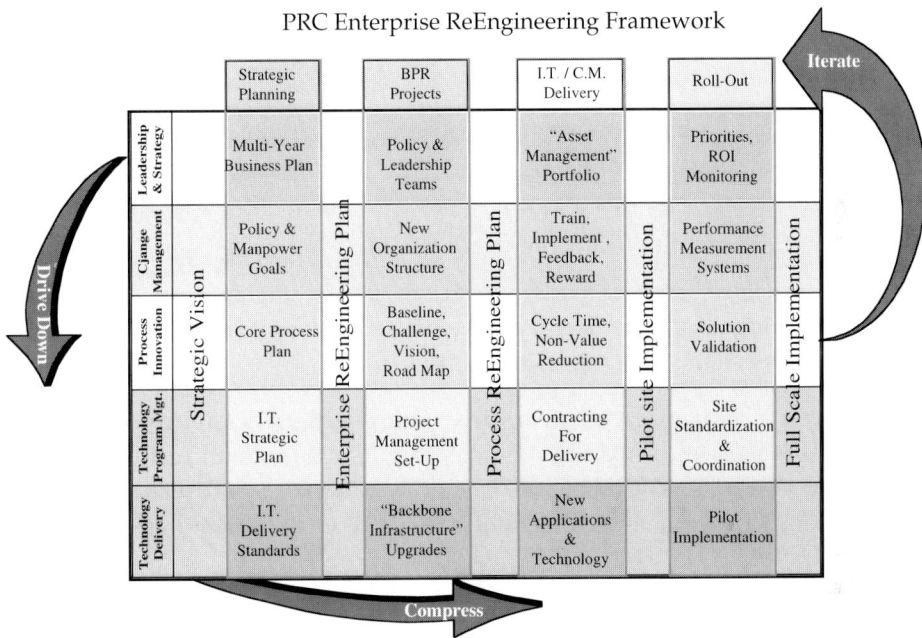

PRC Enterprise ReEngineering Framework

	Strategic Planning	BPR Projects	I.T / C.M. Delivery	Roll-Out
Leadership & Strategy	Multi-Year Business Plan	Policy & Leadership Teams	"Asset Management" Portfolio	Priorities, ROI Monitoring
Change Management	Policy & Manpower Goals	New Organization Structure	Train, Implement, Feedback, Reward	Performance Measurement Systems
Process Innovation	Core Process Plan	Baseline, Challenge, Vision, Road Map	Cycle Time, Non-Value Reduction	Solution Validation
Technology Program Mgt.	I.T. Strategic Plan	Project Management Set-Up	Contracting For Delivery	Site Standardization & Coordination
Technology Delivery	I.T. Delivery Standards	"Backbone Infrastructure" Upgrades	New Applications & Technology	Pilot Implementation

(Left column: Strategic Vision; between column 1 and 2: Enterprise ReEngineering Plan; between column 2 and 3: Process ReEngineering Plan; between column 3 and 4: Pilot site Implementation; right: Full Scale Implementation. Arrows: Drive Down, Iterate, Compress.)

Fig. 18.9

I am extremely skeptical of people who promise that if you slavishly follow their "10-step" process, or simply install 2000 of their new and improved "Net-Blaster XL" software suites, you will painlessly transport yourself to enterprise-wide change. Everyone starts with some level of articulated leadership business strategy. Everyone starts with some level of staff capability and beliefs about what behaviors are incented and which are not. Everyone who is carrying out business has at least some formal or informal process in place now for doing so and some level of technology they operate with, even if it's only fax, phone, and word processing. It's unlikely that anybody's change checklist will exactly match your situation. Further, it is unlikely that you will achieve lasting change if you only address one of these elements and ignore the rest.

To get lasting and significant change in an organization, you need to focus on the relationships among all of these elements. Thus, for PRC, Genesis is not simply a technology installation, it is a rethinking at a profound level about how to interact with our suppliers, manage ourselves, and approach the market.

18.4 IMPLEMENTATION ISSUES

As Adam and Eve found out in the Genesis story as told in the Bible, there are snakes even in paradise. In the modern day technological Eden, the snakes are the people who promise you infinite gain with no pain. As we continuously work towards full implementation of our "To Be" Genesis vision, we get daily confirmation that success requires taking care of the basics. The lessons we have learned applying groupware in other arenas are equally true in the world of architectural design and construction:

☞ **Installing the hardware and software is just the first step.** Changed results come from changed behaviors. Changed behaviors come from ensuring that:

  ☞ Your pilot applications get used because they provide clear benefits for users and demonstrable payoffs for the customers using the outputs;

  ☞ You train users to their level of comfort not yours—they typically need a lot more training than you think would be necessary; and

  ☞ You continuously work the incentives issues—again, you must deal with things from the user's and customer's view in terms of what they think is incented vs. what your intent is.

☞ **Make sure you maintain an enterprise-wide perspective.** Only very small projects can be executed in isolation. If you are working on something important, chances are you will need to understand and be able to articulate how what you are doing will affect the critical influence streams at work in your organization. As described above, in PRC Management Consulting's enterprise reengineering methodology we look at projects in terms of the following:

  ☞ **Leadership & Strategy:** *How does this project relate to the business goals the leadership has set for the organization?* If the answer is loosely, or not at all, expect to have trouble getting funding, priority, and cooperation as you try to implement. You might be better to rethink your choice of process.

  ☞ **Change Management:** *How does this project fit into existing change management initiatives that may be underway?* Do the proposed implementation's training, incentive, and customer outreach initiatives complement or conflict with programs already underway? If they conflict, is it possible to demonstrate that the proposed initiative is actually better aligned to leadership goals than existing "status quo" initiatives?

☞ **Process Innovation:** *Will there be clearly demonstrable process innovations after the new technologies and methods are fully implemented?* One of my favorite presentations to executive audiences is a talk I give entitled: "What To Ask In The Program Review." Virtually all of the executives in the groups I address have some type of technology based reengineering effort underway even if they describe it by another name. Surprisingly, many of these high powered leaders say that they are not receiving the types of data on proposed projects that they need to be comfortable that the results will justify the funding that is being requested. Whenever you are asked to approve technology-based process redesign proposals, you should demand to know if the proposed changes will allow your organization to:

☞ *Compress Time*—Will you see dramatic reductions in the time it takes to execute the process if the proposed changes are implemented?

☞ *Neutralize Space*—Will your people be able to work on the reengineered process through electronic networks without regard to where they are geographically located?

☞ *Hire The Customer*—Will the reengineering proposal integrate customers into its methodology the same way that automatic teller machines and on-line banking have integrated customers into the cash deposit/withdrawal processes of modern banks? On-line banking and ATMs give customers 24 hour access to their money at a fraction of the cost of teller service. If the redesign you are being asked to approve isn't employing similar strategies for the customers it serves, it is not fully exploiting one of the highest benefit reengineering opportunities available to you.

☞ *Know It All*—Who will own the knowledge on how to execute this process properly in your organization if this redesign is implemented? Will this knowledge reside primarily with the employees who designed the process? Will the knowledge be a personal asset of the people who operate the process? Will this knowledge walk out the door when they leave? Or, will the knowledge be captured as an asset of your organization? Will the redesign codify the critical rules, tools, and references needed to perform the job and make these available in the form of context sensitive help screens? Will the redesign provide "goof proof" step-by-step scripts and just-in-time training for executing the required tasks? Will the process feed the creation of a corporate base of knowledge that becomes an organizational asset in its own right?

☞ *Electrify Decisionmaking*—Does the proposed redesign take advantage of workflow technologies and techniques? Does the redesign utilize electronic meetingware tools and structured facilitation routines for recurring group decision activities such as requirements analysis, status reviews, and prioritization activities?

☞ **Technology Program Management & Technology Delivery:** *How does the proposed redesign fit into the present and planned technology architecture of your organization?* In some organizations, the internal information systems shop is regarded as an obstacle rather than an asset. Line managers in these organizations will frequently instruct reengineering teams to "do their own thing" without involving personnel from IS in the planning. In our experience, this is usually not an optimal strategy. The best IS departments provide central management of data, networks, and infrastructure in much the same way an electric utility provides power. The power company doesn't tell you what appliances to install, but it does set standards for the type of equipment you can operate using the service it provides. You could install lamps throughout your home that run on other than the standard residential 110/220 electrical service. However, you would trade away the convenience of simply buying power through the standard electric lines already attached to your home.

In the same way, if you are truly committed to leveraging technology in your process redesign, it is critically important to know what assumptions you can make about the general capability of your organization's technology architecture. Can you assume that there is connectivity to staff in geographically remote sites? What computers do the workers you plan to link electronically have now? How are they using them? What technology upgrades are planned? When are planned upgrades expected to come on-line? Proceeding without this kind of information could easily lead to creating an "island of technology" that can leave work units: a) cut off from corporate maintenance services, b) not in compliance with corporate data standards and therefore unable to fully utilize corporate data maintained in other systems, c) unable to avail themselves of the benefits of future hardware and software upgrades paid for with corporate dollars.

18.5 GENESIS VISIONARIES/GENESIS VISIONS

From the earliest stages of the Genesis project, we have received enthusiastic participation and valuable input from the design and construction suppliers that support PRC: HOK Architects, Himes Associates (construction management), and Clarke Construction (general contractor). We have electronic access to these firms through the Genesis workflow applications we have developed in Lotus Notes (Fig. 18.10). Representatives from these firms also work with PRC staff to identify ways of fine tuning the design of Genesis workflow screens like the one shown in Fig. 18.11. Most encouraging to us has been the fact that in addition to participating in PRC's implementation of Genesis, our suppliers are asking us to partner with them to introduce Genesis concepts and technologies into their service delivery for other clients.

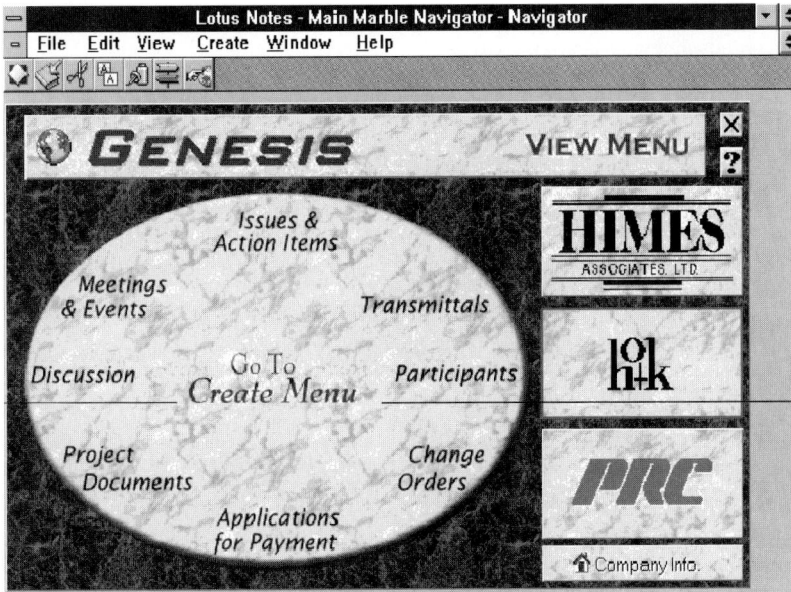

Fig. 18.10 The Genesis "Homepage" *Navigation Menu*

In keeping with Genesis methods, we frequently use electronic meeting software to facilitate group interaction and problem solving during Genesis team meetings. In a Genesis electronic meeting, participants are able to brainstorm by inputting their comments into laptop computers that are linked into a local area network. Input can be identified with the authors or collected anonymously. All ideas entered are fully documented and easily displayed on a front screen display so that the group can quickly review and analyze the results.

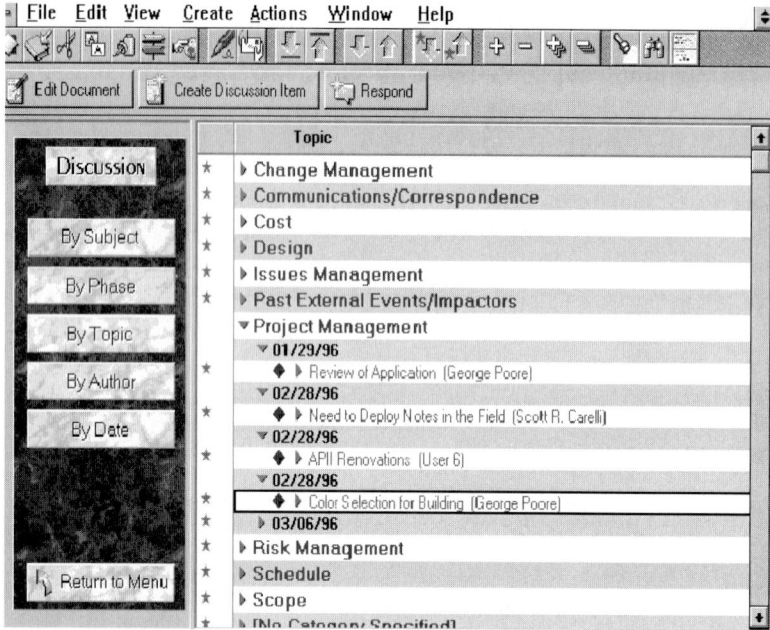

Fig. 18.11 Genesis Discussion Database

The first time Mark Herbert, PRC's Vice President for Real Estate and Facilities, used Genesis tools to conduct a requirements programming meeting he was amazed at the results:

> The savings are unbelievable. In less than two hours, the five of us generated over 300 items, organized by type of requirement, that we needed to address in Phase II of our renovations plan. This would easily have taken a full day using flip charts and traditional methods. We not only completed the task faster, the product we got is much more thorough and better in quality than we would ever get using flipcharts or post-it notes.

Several overlapping groups participate in Genesis. Day-to-day operations are carried out by members of Mark Herbert's staff and the people directly assigned to working on PRC design and construction projects from our supplier organizations. In addition, senior managers from PRC and our supplier organizations meet periodically as an advisory forum to assess whether the methodology of Genesis itself is on track and evolving appropriately. At a Genesis advisory meeting, we asked the management group to speculate on the impact of Genesis-like technology strategies on competition for and delivery of design and construction services in the future.

The specific questions we asked are shown below in Fig. 18.12. A sample of the participant comments collected on electronic meetingware during the brainstorming session appear below.

> ## Genesis Vision Exercise
>
> Imagine that it is the year 2001, and that all of the Genesis project goals for applying groupware to the architectural design and construction process have been met.
>
> ☞ Who in the architectural design and construction industry is using Genesis style groupware technologies? How are they using them?
>
> ☞ What was difficult to do in 1997 that groupware technology has made easy to do by 2001?
>
> ☞ What has groupware changed in the way people compete for architectural design and construction work in 2001?
>
> ☞ What happened to architectural design and construction firms who chose not to adopt groupware?
>
> ☞ What obstacles had to be overcome in order to implement groupware within the architectural design and construction industry?
>
> ☞ What specific benefits has groupware brought to the management of global projects and accounts by 2001?

Fig. 18.12

It's 2001. Who in the architectural design and construction industry is using Genesis style groupware technologies? How are they using them?

☞ The companies that remain in business will be using groupware.

☞ 60 percent of our clients, but only 10 percent of our competitors. Because of cost and technophobia, there is a great deal of reluctance to adopt technology in the industry.

☞ Multinational corporations with multinational locations. Groupware will be critical to handling global accounts.

☞ Mid-size to large corporations will be using groupware in in-house real estate and facilities groups. They will make implementation of groupware a selection criteria for architecture, engineering, and construction firms.

☞ Most of the major companies in the world will be using groupware.

What was difficult to do in 1997 that groupware technology has made easy to do by 2001?

☞ By 2001 cross-platform incompatibility should no longer be a major handicap in transferring information electronically. Ease of intermachine communications will be at the "Pick up the phone and make a call" level.

☞ Use and application of technology on the user level is many times a generational thing. In 1996 the architecture, engineering, and construction industry was not technologically adept/comfortable with groupware technologies. By 2001, more technology savvy people will have moved up into leadership roles.

☞ Lack of anything close to an industry standard in 1996 means that each company's response and resulting benefits in 2001 will be unique.

What has groupware changed in the way people compete for architectural design and construction work in 2001?

☞ Groupware is now an entry barrier or hurdle: "Gotta have it to play the game."

☞ If the client has the commitment before we show up, then we will need to have the product to compete. This may be the case in 2001. In the interim, I look for groupware to be an added value both internally and externally. If it can help us to be better, faster, cheaper, then we win.

What happened to architectural design and construction firms who chose not to adopt groupware?

☞ Whole market segments became closed to those who did not keep up.

☞ Those who did not pursue are no longer fee competitive because of inability to be efficient.

☞ You won't find them in the yellow pages, and no matter how good James Earl Jones sounds, their # won't be on 411 either . . .

☞ They are still working in the Dark Ages!

☞ Groupware will be necessary by the year 2001 in order to compete on a national or global market for the architecture industry. This technology is going to be similar to computer aided design (CAD). If you don't have it you will not be able to compete.

☞ By 2001 will there be a choice? Compare how extensively e-mail is used today [1996] vs. how little it was used just 3 years ago.

What obstacles had to be overcome to implement groupware within the architectural design and construction industry?

☞ Lack of vision

☞ Good opportunities require: the hardware and software, a dexterity with the use of technology, and all team members being literate.

☞ Statistics to sell it

☞ There will be many software systems in the market performing similar functions, each claiming to be better than the other. Different clients will have selected the software they prefer. A firm like ours is going to have to be able to support multiple software systems.

What specific benefits has groupware brought to the management of global projects and accounts by 2001?

☞ Shortened processes, and greater efficiency

☞ Increased speed and delivery of projects. A reduction in the number of meetings held, and a reduction in meeting time by over 30 percent.

☞ Groupware will greatly augment delivery of standardized services when global clients request us to support them in remote locations.

☞ Seamless communication amongst team members

☞ "Real time" project control

☞ Labor reduced by 20 percent due to shortened time line. Less non-contributing man hours. More standardization.

☞ Flattening of project management structure. Greater interactivity among team members at all levels.

☞ More direct access to resources/people in geographically dispersed locations.

☞ Empowers design studio concept—standards development, preferential service

☞ More verifiable audit trails. Greater ability to verify decision making processes and justify conclusions.

☞ Enhanced communication between client and project team through groupware will ensure continued working relationships on global agreements.

☞ Reliable communications will reduce the impact of the global horizon. Tracking issues and actions on the other side of the globe should become as easy or difficult as tracking the same activities on the other side of town.

☞ There will be smaller core project teams with easier short-term access to "experts" who fill clearly defined niches.

☞ Uniform reporting on all projects.

*   *   *   *   *

18.6 CONCLUSION

As I stated at the opening of this chapter, Genesis is a work in progress for PRC. We have done the basic As Is/To Be analysis work and we are carrying out evolutionary design, deployment, and refinement of our workflow applications. Along the way we have run into some interesting issues.

People who make their living in the design industry—like the principals on our advisory group—are highly visually oriented. We started developing Genesis in Lotus Notes, release 3.2. We introduced graphics wherever we could, but, the applications were still highly text-oriented in their fit and feel. When the project advisors saw the new Notes Version 4 with its graphical navigators, it was a classic case of "upgrade fever." We quickly migrated the early applications to Notes 4, and along the way expanded the features and functionality.

A second issue we have grappled with is infrastructure. Anyone trying to implement a new technology knows that whenever your project requires changes in the networks and information systems owned by other parts of your organization, you have many policy and priority challenges to overcome. In Genesis, we faced this situation in multiples. Not only did we have to negotiate with the information systems people within PRC, we also had to help the Genesis team members from our supplier organizations work with their respective bureaucracies. Fortunately, we have had senior level personnel from each supplier company participating in an advisory role on the Genesis project. Even with this top level backing, though, it took multiple briefings and much cajoling to get the needed infrastructure in place for all players.

Working in a collaborative vs. arm's length way with our suppliers has provided substantive benefits, but it's raised challenges as well. PRC periodically recompetes its design and construction contracts. In the last round, one of the key participant firms in the early work on Genesis was not selected. This led to a soul searching dialogue for all parties on whether or not this firm would continue promoting the use of Genesis in its work for clients outside of PRC. Perhaps the best indication of the loyalty Genesis has generated is that this firm decided to stay involved with PRC, even though it is no longer working as a direct supplier to us.

Do Genesis methods really have the potential to achieve the widespread industry acceptance envisioned by PRC and its Genesis team mates? It's easy to see how Genesis could be adopted by architects, engineers, and Facilities Vice Presidents when you are in an executive conference room talking to other people in business suits over a mahogany conference table. But walk into a dusty trailer at a construction site and the prospects suddenly shift.

At the construction site, you are most likely to see a group of people running around with walkie-talkies and clipboards that will tell you with great pride that they are more comfortable with checklists than they are with laptops. Even when computer literacy is not an issue, investment capital is. In both the design firm and the construction firm, the level of communications infrastructure that Genesis demands requires a level of technology sophistication that is for most part not in place today. Getting funding for the necessary upgrades and training means competing against other, more seemingly immediate, priorities in the annual scramble for a share of your company's capital dollars.

What makes widespread acceptance of Genesis probable, in fact most likely inevitable, is that Genesis is more than a faster way to execute today's construction management processes. It is, in fact, a transformation of a communications process into a model based collaboration process. Literally, Genesis moves a design and construction management group from passing discrete bits of data in a serial fashion where no one really has a complete picture, to using shared data base repositories and electronic decision tools to create an on-line workspace.

When our implementation is complete, you will be able to dial into the Genesis workspace and see all of the work packages proposed, pending, and required to execute your project. A mouse click away will be data on each action item's history, present status, and what each of the other principals in the management team is saying and doing about them currently. A record of the items covered at the last face-to-face meeting of the management group and all the decisions made will be there for your perusal. So will the agenda for the next face-to-face meeting, including a tailored list of the items you personally need to be ready to report on. A time stamped, threaded database will record the dialogue of the key players on the critical issues. You will be invited to contribute on-line in a distributed meeting or asynchronously through chats, e-mails, or formal transmittal workflows. You can't see or participate in all of these interactions in the same way when you are serially faxing, filing, and phone calling your way through the project management process.

As Michael Schrage has observed, shared workspaces exert a powerful effect on group results:

> Communication is a necessary but not sufficient condition for collaboration. The key element, the key ingredient, the key medium for successful and effective collaboration is the creation and maintenance of a shared space. You cannot create shared understandings without shared space. That is the real challenge.[1]

In Schrage's view, shared workspaces enable innovation by attracting the right people into the dialogue and allowing them to interact in the right ways. Whether it is a flip chart or a home page, successful groups utilize the power of shared workspaces to iterate and prototype ideas. After the fact, we ordain their results to be "innovative."

---

[1] "Leading Lights: Technology Designer: Michael Schrage," *Knowledge Inc*, Vol. 1, No. 2, Mountain View CA: Quantum Era Enterprises, June 1996, p.8.

The near term barriers to broad adoption of Genesis type methods are likely to be "resistance to change," and "resistance to investment." Both these barriers are surmountable. For example, as we close in on the year 2000, every PC literate eighth grader knows that the benefit of writing on a computer is the ability to interact with your own ideas in real time. This allows iteration, fine tuning, and produces higher quality written products. Today, it seems hard to imagine a professional operating in a white collar business setting without a personal computer. Go back to the early 1980s when PCs were first coming into widespread general office use, however, and the situation was almost reversed. There were few personal computers available, and to the budget boys, few legitimate reasons why the organization should spend its precious resources buying you one.

Early in the life cycle of any new technology, corporate finance types have the upper hand over early adopters seeking funding. If you are truly an early adopter, there aren't many good examples of how the new tool you're recommending has already proved successful elsewhere. Really unfortunate is the truth that the benefits may not make sense in terms of the old ways of doing the task. The trick—and you will need to resort to tricks—is to satisfy the bean counters by demonstrating the costs vs. benefits of new methods in terms of payback concepts that were derived from the methods that are being superseded.

White collar early adopters in the 1980s resorted to justifying the purchase of computers for general office use in terms of the number of secretarial positions that would be eliminated if professionals had PCs to "do their own typing." Typing was understood. Replacing secretaries was understood. The impact of word processing on the creative process was neither understood, nor considered a reason to part with money.

"Resistance to change" is an equivalent challenge. In the early stage of every new technology, there is a period when the effort required to master it is high compared to the benefits you get. Once new technologies are widely deployed and infrastructures are already paid for, however, chain reaction dynamics kick-in. The performance gains the new technology makes possible create a survival advantage for the firms that use them that late adopters cannot offset by trying to compete with yesterday's methods.

The "mud on the boots" image of the construction management process belies the reality of complex collaboration workflows, requirements for shared access to records, and the need for data synchronization to bring large projects in on time, on budget, and to everyone's satisfaction. The long view is that Genesis-type techniques will inexorably prevail over the near term funding and change issues. This will occur not because the current incumbents of the jobs in these industries want it to happen, but because they will have little choice.

Like the bean counters who so valiantly tried to defeat the introduction of computers into the work place during the early 1980s, the naysayers to collaborative computing in the design and construction industry are fated to lose in the end. The cycle time compression and unity of action achievable by management teams collaborating in shared workspaces like Genesis will generate innovations unattainable by the old methods. The hold-outs will not be able to attract the people with the intellectual capital necessary for the most challenging work. If you doubt this, try recruiting an MBA from a leading school to your firm by telling him or her that your company doesn't believe in using computers and that he or she will be expected to operate without one.

Those few companies where resistance to change or bean counting succeed in preventing investment in collaborative technology will find themselves with a Pyrrhic victory—exile to narrow niches of the market or potentially extinction. In the end, the adoption of groupware by the design and construction industry will prove not only to be a new business strategy, it will serve as a catalyst for a major evolution of the methods we use to build and shape our physical world.

BIOGRAPHY

Frank A. Lancione is the Director of Workgroup Technologies for PRC Management Consulting. He brings a mix of high level commercial and public sector engagement experience and over 10 years of "Big 6" consulting background to his strategic planning and enterprise reengineering work for clients. Frank has written and spoken widely on the use of electronic meetingware and other groupware tools to dramatically compress cycle times for group decision making. You can reach him at lancione_frank@prc.com

Introduction to Chapter 19

The goal of this chapter is to examine how hardware and software development environments use collaborative technologies. The chapter reports on research performed by The Institute for Distributed Work and Collaborative Strategies. We began with the premise that development environments in general, and computer hardware and software development environments in particular, benefit from collaboration. Further, because we were looking at technologically oriented organizations, staffed with computer engineers, we anticipated they would welcome the electronic tools that support collaboration.

The first major surprise of this project was that in many organizations, the only collaborative product in use was e-mail. Many people reported that they thought SCCS (source code control system) was a collaborative product, however, it is not. Many also said that groupware was not for programmers, and that if they wanted or needed a collaborative solution, they would build one themselves.

Even so, we did locate several organizations that were using groupware in their development process. Generally, they were also selling groupware or collaborative products, and therefore, trying to "walk their talk,"

The organizations using collaborative technologies reported a 25–40 percent improvement (estimated) in productivity. Given such dramatic results, why aren't all, or certainly most, product development organizations using collaborative software to decrease cycle times?

Some of the answers will be found in this chapter, but not all. Much of the research that was done for this chapter has led us to ask other questions, and therefore, into new lines of research. For example, what comprises the "agile" or "collaborative" office? What are the physical traits of a workspace that will support collaboration? If an organization has a "fishnet" structure, where people are assigned to multiple projects (common in computer R&D groups), how does their space reflect this and if it does, will it enhance their productivity?

Experiments are taking place relative to this work as we speak. Sun, HP, and other high tech firms, have a suspicion that dealing with collaboration as a gestalt treatment *will make the greatest improvement in productivity.*

This chapter brings up a larger problem, managing and preserving the intellectual capital created during the product development process (see Chapter 20). It is the role of an R&D organization to create knowledge. Productively applying this knowledge to the product development process makes an R&D organization successful. Yet today, organizations squander their intellectual capital. They have no infrastructure to capture or disseminate the knowledge developed by past experience. Neither do they chart their knowledge flows in hopes of tying this development process to other business processes.

The ability to tie collaborative technologies to specific business processes was one of the greatest insights we have gathered from our research and working with our clients. If the technology is implemented and not tied to a process that benefits those that use it, and the technology is not used every day, it gets lost, and is a poor investment. If it is tied to a process and will clearly benefit those in the process, and is used frequently, we find that collaborative technology is often wildly successful. The same is true about change in general. People are resistant to change, but if they can see the benefits, they are generally willing to work for those benefits. It may not be any easier, but the participants are more willing.

Since this research was done, emphasis on collaboration on the Internet and intranets has grown. This is particularly true with R&D groups, which are (1) collaborative by nature and (2) often interested in new technologies. Many of these groups have been using the Internet for years, collaborating with researchers at academic institutions. Now, all of a sudden, there are a wide variety of tools for collaboration available on a medium they are intimately familiar with. We see increased pressure for expanding Internet and intranet usage.

One key impact of using the Web for R&D is that it dramatically increased cycle times for product releases. This change in product philosophy is best exemplified by Netscape, who seems to release a new version of their Navigator about every month. They put it up on their Web site, thousands try it, hundreds send in bug reports, they fix them and then release another version of the beta. This type of interactive development is actually getting the customer to be part of the product development process. Making the customer a partner is a smart move by Netscape and others, it's more collaborative, and insures that when the production product is available, you have buyers for it.

Groupware in Hardware and Software Development Environments

Charles Grantham
Institute for the Study of Distributed Work

Judy Carr
The Fielding Institute

David Coleman
Collaborative Strategies

If groupware boosts productivity and communication effectiveness in routine business applications, why isn't it used more in computer system development environments? We set out to answer that question by finding a few test cases of this application of groupware and asking what was really going on. Not surprisingly, we found only a few cases of actual use—and these were experimental, pilot phases of use. We believe that using a management framework like the Carnegie-Mellon Software Maturity model can guide developers to appropriate uses of groupware.

We found that many variations are being tried from typical Lotus Notes and GroupWise for e-mail and project tracking to file sharing with Team Links and CollabraShare. We also found use of Live Links and Synchronize for bug tracking and scheduling. In our small sample of development team groupware users, they report a 25–30 percent increase in productivity because of groupware. We conclude that this increase comes from increased speed of communication and decreased cost of coordinating activities.

However, groupware applications have not yet found their home in development teams. UNIX is a standard development environment and existing groupware products don't integrate smoothly into UNIX platforms. This objection (along with security issues) can be solved, we believe, with the use of more Web-based groupware applications where hybrid platforms are used to promote communication across time and space boundaries.

We think that the future portends a battle between three groupware platforms for use in the development environment: Novell's GroupWise, Microsoft's Exchange, and Lotus' Team Room extension of Notes. The winner will be the platform that adds functionality to promote effective group interaction. The groupware product that provides a flexible method for structuring team interaction, and its evaluation, will be the groupware platform that becomes the *de facto* standard for developers.

There have been numerous articles about how groupware enabled success in sales and marketing organizations, customer service, and even back office operations. However, we have seen very few reports of groupware being used by software and hardware development teams.

To us, this is an obvious place to use groupware as these groups are often already organized into teams, the teams are often very flexible and distributed, and they are always under pressure to get product out quickly while still maintaining high quality. Groupware would seem an ideal candidate for such teams, but when we investigated this we found it was not so!

But before we get to the specifics of what we found, let's look at why software development groups should want to improve their internal coordination. Obviously, we thought that teams of developers would want to decrease cycle time, reduce costs of coordination, and stay in closer contact with customers driving the design process. Well, when we consulted the experts in software design and engineering we found some surprising insights into how the real world of development works. For example, when we talked to M. Lynn Markus about why software developers don't seem to use groupware products we got the following opinions:

> Even experts sometimes run afoul of the technical and project management challenges in system development . . . . Failures like these are surely regrettable, but much more disturbing are failures that occur when people do not use systems that work well technically.

> Everybody talks about failed software systems development projects. Some people even go so far as to point out that "since its inception, the software industry has been in crisis . . . software is unreliable, delivered late, unresponsive to change, inefficient, and expensive."

19.1 THE INDUSTRY VIEW ON SOFTWARE DEVELOPMENT

James Martin, the industry pundit, cites a history of technically led development projects as a key factor leading to the development of software systems that are unresponsive to the needs of the user. Although technically successful, software systems that are designed from a technical perspective rather than from a user perspective are often unused or under-used and cost organizations millions of dollars each year. In all our searching, no one would cite a specific figure of failed projects, although many say a range of 40-60 percent of all projects is a reasonable estimate.

There is much speculation as to the root cause or causes for the dilemmas facing software development organizations. It seems to those who have studied the problem that the issues lie not with the technology but with the organizational and human resource components of the development process.

19.2 A FAILURE TO COMMUNICATE!

So why do systems designs fail? Current wisdom holds that they falter in the design of the business process because designers often fail to diagnose and understand the root business need that requires the development of a technical system in the first place—a lack of close coordination with users throughout the design process. Not surprisingly, when systems fail to address the business problem for which they were commissioned, users tend not to use the new technology.

When system developers are not held accountable for the ability to implement a system but rather for the technical proficiency of a system, the projects are doomed to failure. In short, from a technical perspective, a systems development project can be deemed a success if it technically works, even if does not provide a functional solution for users. It seems this would point to a need for closer coordination within the development team and with users.

Working on the premise that communication is critical to the design of a software system, researchers have focused on the role of effective communication in the software systems development of software to the number of communication links incorporated into the development process. Customer-developer links are the techniques or channels that allow customers and software developers to exchange information.

Others maintain that communication at the requirements development phase is key to the overall project design. So we went to the experts at Carnegie-Mellon and asked them what role communication and communication actions should play in software development—a natural role for groupware products.

19.3 THE MATURITY MODEL

The Software Engineering Institute at Carnegie Mellon University leads the engineering community in the conceptualization of software development models, which are sensitive to these human factors. The Institute has developed a model consisting of five (5) levels of process maturity and is based on the premise that improving a software organization requires continual improvement of its people and the conditions that empower their performance.

While many organizations have discovered that their continued improvement requires significant changes in the way they manage people, most improvement programs for software organization have emphasized process or technology, not people. The "People Capability Maturity Model" provides a combined focus on people, process, and technology to produce high quality products and services. Table 19.1 below outlines the components of the model and you can see that communication/coordination rank very high as techniques to improve software development.

Table 19.1 Five maturity levels of the People Capability Maturity Model.

Levels of Maturity	Purpose	Key Processes
Initial	Starting place for process	None
Repeatable	Instill basic discipline into workforce activities.	• ***Work Environment*** • ***Communication*** • Staffing • Performance Management • Training • Compensation
Defined	Identify primary competencies and align workforce activities with them.	• Knowledge and Skills Analysis • Workforce Planning • ***Competency Development*** • Career Development • Competency-Based Practices • ***Participatory Culture***
Managed	Quantitatively manage organizational growth in workforce capabilities and establish competency-based teams.	• Mentoring • ***Team Building*** • ***Team-Based Practices*** • Organizational Competency Management • Organizational Performance Alignment
Optimizing	Continuously improve method for developing personal and organizational competence.	• Personal Competency Development • ***Coaching*** • ***Continuous Workforce Innovation***

Source: Summary of concepts from Paul M., Weber, C., Curtis, B. and Chrissis, M., 1995, p. A-28

So we have all the background that points to why software development teams should coordinate their activities more closely; why they should be interested in using tools to help them do this.

19.4 INTO THE WILDERNESS

We interviewed several key development efforts to collect real-life experiences in the use of various groupware products. In this primary research, we made may calls and found very few development organizations using groupware. From the eight organizations we did talk to, we were able to generalize and draw some conclusions. We will look at how groupware technology is really being used today and what we see for the future.

We will also look at a major limitation we have found with current group-ware product offerings—namely lack of smooth integration with UNIX plat-forms, which is often the development platform of choice with these groups. We expand the discussion by focusing on two major groupware products: Notes and TeamLinks. Finally, we will offer three brief case studies of Novell, Hewlett-Packard, and DEC, and draw some controversial conclusions from these interviews as well as making some recommendations for the future.

19.4.1 What Are People Really Doing?

We found more software companies using groupware than hardware compa-nies—not surprising. Often the software companies were producers of groupware and used their own software to help in the production of their product. Group-ware was not often used in the actual coding process but rather was used as adjunct software to help in other tasks that require close coordination, such as:

☞ Discussing problems in the coding process or a particularly difficult or development problem

☞ Developing and storing technical notes and documentation

☞ Routing forms and documents for approval or sign off, groupware was also used more frequently in shops that had a TQM or ISO 9000 oriented devel-opment processes

☞ Scheduling meetings with other developers, marketing staff, and managers

☞ To support group decisions regarding product strategy, direction, and func-tionality

☞ Groupware was also used to help convey feedback from the customer indi-rectly to the development groups

Basically, groupware is used in product development in the same way it helps in other complex knowledge work. It speeds communication, helps people cross time and space boundaries, and provides a written record of decisions, questions, and background information needed by others on the team or in the future.

What we didn't find is even more striking. Hardware and software develop-ment are very creative tasks usually carried out by small groups of people. The types of tools that developers use are very different from the underlying struc-ture of common groupware tools. This, we believe, is creating a barrier to more widespread integration of groupware into the development environment

19.4.2 Problems in UNIX Environments

All of the organizations using groupware usually (with the exception of DEC) had introduced groupware to the development staff over the last two years. So this a relatively recent diffusion of a new technology. We received many reports that Notes did not work very well in the UNIX environment (the environment currently in favor in this market segment), but that many development teams were eagerly looking for the V4 UNIX iteration of Notes to solve many of the problems they currently have.

UNIX programmers tend to have a bias against groupware, they see it as cute, and fluffy, and not a real programming tool, and therefore how can it be of any use to them. However, when one of their own people shows it has some functional value to programmers, then they are willing to drop this prejudice and are willing to come on board, use the software, and become enthusiastic proponents of the software and integrate it into their development process. Groupware was not always used in a true collaborative manner, but was used as a storage place to share information of a dynamic nature.

Group Calendaring and Scheduling, a relatively mature groupware technology, has been used in some development organizations. Again, it has run into some cultural difficulties with the UNIX developers.

With any implementation of Group Calendaring and Scheduling, the groupware is only as effective as the data it shares. The managers of business groups or development teams do keep their electronic calendars up-to-date, but the developers don't. This makes it difficult to use this software effectively. Why don't developers keep up their electronic calendars? Often they have problems with the GUI interfaces.

Programmers want as much control as possible, they want the "stick shift" of interfaces where they can feel the engine (operating system) directly. They don't want the "automatic shift" that an interface like Windows or Notes provides. They want a command line interface. However, when they find out that groupware products have functionality they can't get elsewhere, they will begin to use it. This was a strategy we found was used successfully at Sybase. We conclude that groupware products need to be better integrated with the commonly used tools in these workgroups to be successful. In talking to some of the groupware vendors who participated in this research, we found that they were aware of the problem and were working on a variety of solutions.

19.4.3 Product Focus

Overall, we found encouraging evidence of the business effectiveness of groupware tools for hardware and software developers. We found, in our limited set of eight interviews, that teams that did use groupware found that they had about a 25-30 percent increase in productivity, i.e., they were able to get the product out that much faster, or they were able to get the product out in the same time but with better quality. Groupware significantly impacts the time it takes to develop new products. Getting a software product out on time is almost unheard of these days, and these development groups usually used the increased productivity they found from using groupware to add more functions to their product or to provide a higher quality product, rather than getting the product out early. These decisions had nothing to do with groupware, but rather with the design philosophy of the development teams.

19.4.4 Flirting with Lotus Notes

Notes was used briefly by Intel's management team about 3-4 years ago. However, since Notes did not meet the needs of the management team running the pilot, it was dropped. Specifically, Intel's management is highly mobile and Notes was seen as a vehicle for both communication and collaboration. Since Notes did not support the diverse e-mail systems at Intel or provide easy log-in for management, it was deemed ineffective. However, Notes has been used successfully at Intel in sales and marketing groups for several years, helping the sales force publish current and sensitive information such as price lists, release dates, and technical notes for sales people and field sales engineers. Given the development of Notes in recent years, Intel decided to try Notes again with their management team and is currently implementing Notes for their whole staff (including executives) world wide. Intel's arch competitor, AMD, is also implementing Notes throughout their organization for many of the same coordination reasons.

In many development organizations, Notes was often used with key customers to get feedback directly into the development environment, as well as decreasing the time needed to respond to their community of users. Rather than replying to each individual e-mail message, the comments are put into a Notes database and can be answered by a wide pool of developers, marketing people, etc.

Often, Notes was used to isolate projects, with each project getting its own Notes database. In this way, everyone in the organization could see where the project was, track its progress, and add information that was available to all who access or have security clearance for it. This kept the project focused, while the information was not isolated but a complete record was available.

Many of those interviewed are looking forward to Notes 4.0 to fix some of the scalability and platform issues they were currently having with Notes. We didn't find anything to indicate these issues were any different than in other applications.

19.4.5 Coordination for the Ultimate Engineering Organization—DEC

For DEC, groupware and e-mail have always been a grass roots push, not mandated by management. The network at DEC is pervasive and e-mail is a way of life for both administration and development teams. Groupware has a long history at DEC and is well integrated into the business process.

We talked with Tim Sager who has been with DEC for 20 years. He feels DEC's culture is very groupware positive. He has used a wide variety of groupware tools for development. Teamlinks is the tool used most frequently now. His group helps produce TeamLinks, which provides developers with a variety of functions that they can use to collaborate, including shared draws and file cabinets, shared folders, and e-mail. In DEC, we have an example of a groupware product being used to create more groupware products—a true test of groupware's usefulness.

Since the development environment for TeamLinks is distributed (40 developers in New Hampshire developing the client side to TeamLinks, 40 people in Reading, England, developing the server side of TeamLinks, and 13 people in Galway, Ireland, developing VTX (another related groupware product that allows the publishing of static documents)).

TeamLinks is used the most as an e-mail backbone, for document routing, shared files, and group conferencing (like a BBS). It is used heavily as an internal BBS because, like Notes, it allows keyword searches and offers threaded conversations. It is often used as a repository, and DEC has threaded conferences on every product in Tim's organization. This BBS mechanism is also used for interactions with the field sales forces, and other internal people. It allows you to identify an internal expert on any DEC product or topic by searching through the directory of conference titles, then searching topics, and finally narrowing down the search to messages in that topic posted by experts.

In cases where you can not wait for the person to look at the document, TeamLinks provides document routing facilities, where the document is forced through a process in a workflow-like manner by TeamRoute. Using TeamRoute, the user can define the path for the document, who is a reviewer and who is the improver, etc., and set time limits on the document, cause escalation of the document, etc. TeamRouter already comes with a variety of routable forms such as: travel requests, document reviews, meeting announcements, purchase requests, etc. It also supports document tracking through reports to see where the document is in the process.

TeamLinks supports Mac, PC/Windows/UNIX, and VMS environments and is already working on an NT version. It also has shared files that now work with Notes. TeamLinks is both a collaborator and a competitor to Notes. The Lotus Notes TeamLinks connection package (prototyped but not released yet) allows TeamLinks and Notes to exchange data at different levels. This should run on OSF UNIX and other servers.

19.5 STUDIES IN EARLY SUCCESS

Products are fine; but where are people finding value for groupware in the hardware/software development world? We found several instances and report three here that really show what can happen.

19.5.1 Novell—Using Groupware to Make GroupWise

We interviewed Paul Smart, Director of Novell's R&D effort for GroupWise. Novell has a large and distributed development organization and currently uses GroupWise internally as well as CollabraShare for the development of Group-Wise XTD.

The GroupWise division has the challenge of using Novell GroupWise to schedule meetings between developers, documenters, and testers as well as marketing meetings for the review and approval process (that require human signatures). They currently use CollabraShare to share ideas about feature or products functions. Many of the discussions focus on obstacles they need to overcome, as well as what bells and whistles are needed on the project.

CollabraShare conferences, when resolved, are used to develop a design document. They extract the latest pieces of information from CollabraShare into a design document for the features in discussion. This information is put into a WordPerfect for Windows document and it is stored in SoftSolutions for document management, to index the document, as well as to manage access and modifications. Novell also uses a system of read-write privileges as part of their security.

The GroupWise development team then uses the GroupWise mail component to inform people about changes to a document that has been previously approved, and sends them the document reference number or identifier so they can see what changes have occurred to the document. In this way, they currently have not worked out a true workflow process for the development environment and don't move documents around. They have recently started a partnership with FileNet and are looking at FileNet for workflow solutions at a later date.

Novell is very aware of their customer feedback and in the software develop process they track input from customer base through customer support and large account conferences. This feedback is stored in an internal database. When it becomes time to coordinate the next release of the product, the marketing group goes through the database and looks at the frequency a feature is requested or if a bug is noted to be fixed. They also look at the size of the account making the request and then give a weight to each feature and prioritize them. A features list is incorporated into a draft of a marketing requirements document that is passed to the engineers. The engineers then craft an architecture and start the conversations again in CollabraShare. The whole process takes 12-18 months with this development group of 300 people. We were left wondering how this compares with development processes at Microsoft or IBM, which have even larger groups of developers. Are they using groupware to speed up their development processes?

When asked what kind of productivity increases Novell had seen from using groupware, they reported anecdotally that the product development life cycle has gone from four years to get all the client software out on all the different platform's for GroupWise 3.x to 18 months. Very significant results!

19.5.2 H-P: Using Groupware to Schedule Developers

Although HP is a large Notes user, they are not really using Notes at this site; management is, but the developers are not. Developers are using a groupware product called Synchronize, which is a group scheduling system from CrossWind Technologies that runs on UNIX. It is used in the development group to keep track of individuals and calendars. It is currently used on UNIX workstations and PC's Windows 3.1 and is used to schedule developers, managers, and administrative assistants in meetings and for meeting resources.

They have been using Synchronize for four years, their division is split geographically with one group in Cupertino of 285 users, a 300 user group in Ft. Collins CO., and a group of about 300 in Chelmsford, MA. Collaboration is currently done by teleconferencing. They use Synchronize to schedule the conference call as scheduling is difficult because of time zones, so the group calendaring system helps in scheduling the meeting and when to call into the conference line. They do not currently do videoconferencing but are looking at this technology for future use.

Right now, they have no conferencing software but use Internet news, i.e., newsgroups, and post stuff on their own internal network. The developers use a grass roots approach—use Web software—to publish on the internal network for internal people. Their infrastructure is Ethernet TCP/IP with T1 links between geographic sites and NFS to mount software between machines at different sites.

However, they realize that collaboration software has moved ahead quickly in the last few years and are starting to look for better solutions. One of those solutions is Clear Case (Atria Software), a configuration management system—to keep track of all parts to make up a product—including documentation. They are using Notes for some of the division management personnel. They are not using any workflow products currently.

Why are they successful with Synchronize? Before that, they used paper calendars—DayRunner, etc.—engineers were easy to schedule, it was the managers, etc. who were difficult to schedule. As the project moved on, there were more meetings and more people needed in the meetings. It got so bad that at development meetings with 30 or more people in them, it took 20 minutes to schedule the next meeting. They rolled out Synchronize to each project group. They used Synchronize to set up the next meeting and it took no time away from the meeting. They then put conference rooms into Synchronize, which saved people from going to the AA desk and determining when the room was free.

Once a month, HP has a 1/2 hour training on Synchronize. If the people have unusual requirements, they may need another 1/2 hour training to learn special features. Support for Synchronize is from the IS support group. They currently have a person designated to do this support and maintenance.

How much time has Synchronize saved? No quantitative measure, they just know it works and saves time. Management will not go back to doing it the old way, that is the best metric they have.

19.5.3 Odesta: Using Workflow to Build Workflow Tools

Odesta has been in the Macintosh environment for many years. When we interviewed them, they were 40 people with a development organization of 11 people. Since then, they have become part of Open Text Corporation, who went public in 1995 and used some of the money generated in the IPO to buy Odesta.

Unlike some of the larger companies we talked to, Odesta's development team is all in one geographic location. The development organization uses a mixture of Macintoshs and PCs. The current groupware products they use is their own LiveLinks product as well as CE Software's QuickMail, Intenet mail, AOL, WWW, and CompuServe.

LiveLinks is used as a bug tracking system, where bugs are assigned to a specific developer with a given priority. Developers can update the bug status in LiveLinks as well as add comments. When a bug is closed, it is routed by the LiveLinks workflow to the testing group. The testers verify that the bug is fixed and certify it. The bug description and comments are then routed to the product manager or product marketing manager, and he determines what documentation is needed to publicize this bug fix. Usually, the bug fixes are incorporated into end-user documentation or release notes.

LiveLinks is used for technical documentation, which can be stored in the LiveLinks database repository and can be accessed by anyone in the company. However, it is read/write protected—for security—so only those with the appropriate level of access can read this documentation, and only a few have the ability to change the documentation.

LiveLinks also provides automatic version control. Anyone can check a document out and then check it back in it. LiveLinks increments the version number. Prior to LiveLinks, they used ODMS (Odesta Document Management System) and Projector—a Mac-based code management system.

Today, LiveLinks provides a framework for Odesta's code management. Code modules are stored in the database and can be retrieved with read/write protection.

LiveLinks also provides discussion areas for developers, which have helped a lot in solving problems or brainstorming topics. These discussion areas do not eliminate face-to-face meetings, but what they have found is that they can have pre-discussion of the agenda and in the meetings really focus on the problems at hand and make the meetings more efficient.

Odesta is also using LiveLinks as group project management software. The project area on LiveLinks is organized by project, it acts like a BBS and is organized by topic, but not threaded (they are currently looking at Notes for this) but in a hierarchical file structure.

Although almost no one could give us accurate metrics on what their productivity gains were from using groupware in the development environment, when pressed, Odesta said that using groupware in bug tracking had made them 30-50 percent more productive. Groupware in the code development process has made them 25-30 percent more productive. This productivity comes from the fact that the developers are not making modifications to the same module simultaneously and there is less redoing of work. Table 19.2 illustrates the summary of findings.

Table 19.2 Summary of Findings

Company	Product	Use	Effect
Intel	Notes	E-mail	Project Tracking
DEC	Team Links	File Sharing, E-mail, Document Routing	
Novell	GroupWise CollabraShare	Scheduling, E-mail, File Sharing, Brainstorming	Decrease in development time from 4 years to 18 months
H-P	Synchronize	Scheduling	Saves time
Odesta	LiveLinks QuickMail	Bug tracking, Version control	30-50 percent increase in team productivity

19.6 OVER THE HORIZON

What is coming next for groupware in hardware or software development environments? First of all, we believe this is an important sector to watch. It may not be a market for millions of users, but it is critical to groupware's diffusion into the mass market. Look at it this way, if automobile manufacturers begin to use certain tools to build cars, then those cars will need to be maintained, modified, and have changes in functionality made using those VERY TOOLS!

Since development organizations seem to be very dynamic, with developers often having multiple projects, or being moved from one project to another based on a wide variety of reasons, strict workflow packages that enforce a rigid static process will probably not be successful in these environments, rather workflow products that incorporate some document management features, and offer the ability to change the flow or role assignments or tasks on the fly (ad hoc workflow), will be more useful.

Development groups were often separated in time and place. Here, groupware was not only used to schedule teleconferencing and videoconferencing, but was also used to support discussion and coordination between these geographically disparate groups.

Next up, we believe groupware scheduling products and those which offer more fidelity in direct communication will enjoy acceptance. We also noted that developers do not always enjoy the luxury of proprietary telecommunications networks within their geographically disperse groups. Therefore, groupware products need to be available on public networks and security of information flow will become a major concern. IBM/Lotus (Global Link), WorldCom, and others

Baby Bells will be offering these as commercial services, but such services often run into the NIH factor in development organizations.

What about CASE tools, which are often used by developers? Will the CASE vendors extend their tools into the groupware, or will certain groupware companies begin using their own tools to build development environments? We think the latter because the very experience of using groupware tools to do your own job is the most powerful.

The bottom line is that groupware has not really been widely accepted in hardware and software development environments. However, as it becomes clear that this software provides an additional productivity tools to developers, it will start to get incorporated into their bag of tools. We believe that by the turn of the century, groupware will be a standard tool for development environments. With the increased use of low cost programmers from Eastern Europe and India, better coordination across larger landscapes will be critical to a project's success, and groupware has the functionality to provide this type of coordination on a global basis.

Another issue to look at is Web-based or intranet-based collaboration for development environments. Will companies start to store code on their Web servers serving their intranets? If so, will something like SCCS (Source Code Control System) be available for the Web? It probably already is available at the time of the writing of this chapter and we just don't know about it.

In Chapter 7A, David talked about the large number of electronic meeting systems that are now available on the Web. This coupled with Web-based workflow tools, and the distributed nature of many hardware and software development teams, leads us to believe that if the security issues can be worked out, Web-based collaborative software development is not far in the future. This type of platform would remove many of the UNIX objections and would allow a variety of platforms to be used in the process.

Although we believe that all developers will use the same platform (i.e, PC, Mac, or UNIX), the people they have to interact with may not be on the same platform. For example, if all the developers in a company are on UNIX-based platforms, but the marketing department is on Macintosh and executive management is on PCs, using the Web provides a transparent solution to this collaborative problem. Additionally, developers as well as marketing people seem to be in love with the Web.

Many of the high tech firms we work with as clients have a hybrid strategy right now for collaboration. That is, a Web-based front-end, usually Netscape Navigator, and a collaborative back-end, usually Notes. Until the new Web-based tools become more robust, and development groups realize the productivity enhancements they can get from these collaborative tools, we do not see a broad acceptance of collaborative tools for software and hardware development until close to the end of this century.

In doing the background research for this article, we also became sensitive to the forthcoming battle of groupware platforms: Lotus Notes, Microsoft Exchange, and Novell GroupWise. This competitive battle will be very intense and is a harbinger of a larger shakeout in the PC software industry. We believe that the winner will be the platform that best facilitates group interaction over the network. It's more than e-mail and scheduling as we have shown, but what is the "killer app" for groupware? We think it is team facilitation. Notes has just announced Team Room and we are sure others will follow.

The critical element here is not just enhancing the flow of communication among team members, but giving it some structure. But not the structure we saw in early products like the Coordinator I; instead, a structure that is formed by team members to fit their goals, desires, and wants. More emphasis needs to be placed on the "soft" side of groupwork.

BIBLIOGRAPHY

1. Bailey, J., Swigger K. and Vanachek, M., "Computer Supported Collaborative Work and Its Application to Software Engineering," Olfman, L. ed., *Proceedings of ACM SIGCPR Meetings*, 1995, pp. 249–250.
2. Cole, P. and Johnson, E.C., "Lotus Deploys Team Rooms," presentation to the ACM SIG Computer Personnel Research Annual Meeting, Denver, CO, April 1996.
3. Grantham, C.E. and Nichols, L.D., *The Digital Workplace: Designing Groupware Platforms*, New York: Van Nostsrand-Reinhold, 1993.
4. Humphey, W., "Characterizing the Software Process: A Maturity Framework," *IEEE Software*, 5(2), 1988, pp. 73–79.
5. Kraut, R. and Streeter L., "Coordination in Software Development," *Communications of the ACM* 38(3), 1995, pp. 69–81.
6. Markus, M.L., "Intellectual Teamwork: Social and Technological Foundations of Cooperative Work," *Administrative Science Quarterly*, 39(1), 1994, pp. 179–183.
7. Martin, M., "The Human Connection in Systems Design," *Journal of Systems Management"*, 37(10), 1986, pp. 6–29.
8. Paulk, M., Weber, C., Curtis, B., and Chrissis, M., eds., "The Capability Maturity Model: Guidelines for Improving the Software Process," Carnegie Mellon University Software Engineering Institute, Reading, MA, Addison-Wesley, 1995.

BIOGRAPHIES

Charles Grantham, Ph.D. is President of the Institute for the Study of Distributed Work in Oakland, CA. The Institute conducts a program of applied scientific research focused on telework, distance education, and intellectual capital formation. Currently he is engaged in a joint venture with a consortium in Sweden for distribution of organizational analysis products in Scandinavia. His most recent book is *The Digital Workplace: Designing Groupware Platforms*, (Van Nostrand-Reinhold, 1993). He can be contacted by e-mail at ISDW@AOL.COM and his web site address is http://www.isdw.com

Judy Carr is the Director of Automation for the Interstate Commission on Employment Security Agencies in Washington, DC. She is also a doctoral student at The Fielding Institute in Santa Barbara, CA, where she is completing a dissertation on the relationship of human factors approaches and successful software development projects. She may be contacted through the Institute for the Study of Distributed Work.

David Coleman is the founder and Managing Director of Collaborative Strategies. He has been
involved with groupware and collaborative technologies since 1990 and is the author/editor of
Groupware Technologies and Applications (Prentice-Hall, 1995). He also was the founder and
conference chairman for the GroupWare '92–95 conferences that were held in San Jose,
Boston, and London on an annual basis. Mr. Coleman was the editor and publisher of
GroupTalk, the newsletter of workgroup computing. He is the founding editor of *Virtual
Workgroups* magazine, and currently a columnist. He also writes a monthly column on
groupware for *Computer Reseller News*, and for *MainSpring* (an on-line resource for intranet
and Web developers). Mr. Coleman has written for many trade and business publications such
as *Network World, Datamation, Fortune,* and is a frequent public speaker worldwide. He has
consulted to groupware vendors on product marketing, positioning, market research and
competitive analysis, and for groupware users in assessing their organization groupware
readiness as well as tool selection and the human factors involved in a successful groupware
project. Mr. Coleman can be contacted directly at 415-282-9197, or at davidc@collaborate.com
More information on Collaborative Strategies can be found at www.collaborate.com

Introduction to Chapter 20

Although this chapter is the final chapter in this book, it is not the end of the story—rather the beginning. Groupware, the Internet, intranets, and collaborative technologies are only a few years old. Most of our LAN networks are only 10 years old.

We see the introduction of new technologies for collaboration increasing rather than stabilizing. So, how can we determine ROI numbers for these technologies? Is determining ROI even a worthwhile effort? What impact will groupware have on your organization? How will the introduction of an intranet that allows collaboration with your peers throughout your company change the way you work? If we assume that change is the only constant, than how do you adapt to an environment where the rate of change is continually increasing? If, in the course of collaborative interactions, knowledge is created, how is it stored, indexed, and used in the right place at the right time? As collaborative infrastructures mature, how do we create an organization and culture that can optimize the benefits of technology. And last, but certainly not least, how do we store both the tacit and explicit knowledge that is the intellectual capital for the organization?

Groupware and collaborative infrastructures are enabling technologies for knowledge management. In other words, collaboration generates a lot of information, or knowledge, which needs to be captured and disseminated in an appropriate way. Otherwise, it is not retrievable when needed and essentially goes to waste. This is why we often find ourselves reinventing the wheel. Knowledge management allows organizations to leverage the learning of past experience in order to be more effective in the future.

If knowledge is the key, then business processes are the lock. The most benefit is gained, note the authors, when knowledge is tied to a business process. Preserving intellectual capital today will make the future difference between companies that are competitive and those that are not. Looking at the value of knowledge, knowledge is tied directly to money. In an information driven society, knowledge is critical not only for prosperity, but simply for survival.

When reading this chapter, keep in mind the following definitions. Data is the bits and bytes, information is derived when someone gives meaning to those bits and bytes, knowledge exists when the bits and bytes are applied, and wisdom results when experience is used in the application of knowledge. There are many systems on the market to deal with data and information, but only few that deal with knowledge. I don't know of any that deal with wisdom.

Hongo and Stone focus on creating and managing knowledge. Many of the examples in this chapter come from their work with clients. The chapter is rich with examples of how knowledge management was applied at high tech firms, manufacturing companies, and financial organizations. Because both authors have a background in organizational design and consulting, they look at knowl-

edge management as part of the trend toward organizational learning where the ability of individuals to learn and collaborate has been leveraged. Much of the chapter focuses on organizational learning and how to use groupware as the loom on which the fabric of organizational learning can be woven.

One of the strengths of this chapter is the articulation of how knowledge creation equates to creation of wealth, and ultimately results in a significant competitive advantage. The "real work" examples are not only useful metaphors but provide a way for us to see how these changes affect our lives.

Finally, Hongo and Stone look toward the future, at how collaborative technologies on the Internet and intranets will support these knowledge architecture. They tie knowledge management to work processes and examine some of the barriers to success. This comprehensive, and well annotated chapter, is an apt beginning for the next focus for collaboration technologies . . . knowledge management!

Groupware, Knowledge Creation, and Competitive Advantage

Ellen Hongo
Gordon Stone
GroupWorX L.L.C.

Since the launch of Lotus Notes in 1989, groupware has become the hot buzz word in the business community. The promise of global collaboration, true team working, and open communication across the enterprise has created a whole new industry that expects to reach $5.5 Billion by 1998.

For corporations in the throes of downsizing and organizational restructuring or redesign, groupware offers the ability to help increase productivity and to achieve more with less. It is also a tool for the grass roots—something that can be implemented without huge IS infrastructure or support. For the last six years, groupware applications have been springing up in companies to help solve discreet problems such as issues tracking or document management.

However, the seeds of tomorrow's problems lie in today's solutions. In the case of groupware, organizations begin to see the benefits of these applications and attempt to use the groupware tool to achieve broader, more strategic goals. The barriers they encounter are rooted in their initial successes—because the initial projects were discreet in nature and only focused on single processes or issues, scaling up the applications to encompass multiple processes or groups can be extremely difficult. The existing applications are not based in a common view of the work process. Common vocabulary is necessary to allow easy access to the insights and knowledge contained in the system, but it has never been established. Expectations about how to work together collaboratively have never been set. The architecture of the knowledge itself (how each piece relates to the others in a logical, visualizable whole) is unclear.

For example, at a high tech Silicon Valley manufacturer, we found they had been creating new computers for almost 20 years—by starting from scratch each time. They were operating without any formal processes or tools to help capture learning from each product development cycle. Individuals in the firm were learning, but in this high turnover industry their learning didn't benefit the company for very long.

Worse than their failure to capture the learning of past experience, they were reinventing the wheel during each product development cycle. Project Management in this company was a nightmare—no one could easily say where a given project stood. Some projects had managers assigned full-time to just find current status information on their own and related efforts. So many different organizations contributed their knowledge and expertise to the project and product that when a new project started it took weeks to untangle who knew what and where to find it. Our role was to untangle these knowledge flows in the development process and enable the client to see that they needed electronic collaborative tools to build an architecture for this critical knowledge. Only through the use of current generation collaboration technology could they create an environment where 4,000 engineers and managers could easily collaborate on development problems, and capture what was learned in these collaborations so that the company can benefit.

20.1 KNOWLEDGE IS THE KEY

The idea of linking together the knowledge held by discreet parts of the enterprise for greater collaboration and learning is now becoming a strategic focus of many organizations. Companies are realizing that business process engineering is not enough.

Harvard Business Professor Dorothy Leonard-Barton has written a new book entitled *Wellsprings of Knowledge*,[1] which focuses on the role of knowledge in enterprises. She stresses the need for organizations to manage their knowledge assets if they are to remain competitive in this global environment. Leonard-Barton writes:

> Companies, like individuals, compete on their ability to create and utilize knowledge; therefore, managing knowledge is as important as managing finances. In other words, firms are knowledge, as well as financial institutions. They are repositories and wellsprings of knowledge. Expertise collects in employee's heads and is embodied in machines, software, and routine organizational processes. Some of this knowledge and know-how is essential simply to survive or to achieve parity with the competition. However, it is core or strategic capabilities that distinguish a firm competitively. Management of these strategic knowledge assets determines the company's ability to survive, to adapt, to compete.
>
> Products are physical manifestations of knowledge, and their worth largely, if not entirely, depends on the value of the knowledge they embody. The management of knowledge, therefore, is a skill, like financial acumen, and managers who understand and develop it will dominate competitively.

---

[1] Leonard-Barton, D., *Wellsprings of Knowledge,* Harvard School Business Press, 1995.

The emerging technologies called *"groupware"* or *"collaborative technologies"* combined with the power of current and future generations of personal computers and networks, inherently provide the ideal technical enablers for organizations attempting to manage their intellectual assets. Organizations, once they have installed these tools, are ready to tackle enterprise issues, and groupware is reaching a level of maturity that will allow it to successfully support and facilitate these objectives.

20.2 KNOWLEDGE = MONEY

So what makes businesses successful? What does it take to grow a business? For years, the economists answered: Capital and Labor. These were the measurable parts of the equation, the ones that can be quantified, observed, weighed, measured. They seemed to be an irreducible minimum—you couldn't have a business without them. Capital turned into buildings, equipment, raw materials. Labor took these tangible things and animated them—brought them to life by producing products or services and selling them. Management, entrepreneurship, and the skills of the craftsman all translated into the commodity called Labor—so many hours at so much per hour.

But if it were true that given capital and labor any business could be successful, why aren't all businesses successful? Why can't every manufacturer produce high quality products? And why does anyone work for wages, other than to save enough capital to open a (sure to be successful) business?

It seems clear that business success cannot be explained by capital and labor alone. Even in labor intensive industries, the role of ideas and information is now important. As Don Tapscott discusses in his book *Digital Economy*, even traditional work such as agriculture and factory production are quickly becoming knowledge intensive.

> In the new economy, more and more of the economy's added value will be created by brain rather than brawn. Many agricultural and industrial jobs are becoming knowledge work. Already, almost 60 percent of all American workers and eight of ten new jobs are in information-intensive sectors of the economy. The factory of today is as different from the industrial factory of the old economy as the old factory from the craft production that preceded it. Farms are operated with agricultural equipment brimming with chips. Cargo is shipped in containers loaded by computer-controlled cranes or in jumbo jets loaded with software.

Therefore, economists have evolved their thinking to include a third major factor of production—another basic input to production—knowledge and ideas. Under the heading of "New Growth Theory," Paul Romer, an economist at U.C. Berkeley, argues persuasively that ideas, knowledge, and intellectual capital are not only essential ingredients in the mix, but are in fact the key factor in determining which businesses prosper, grow, and thrive and which do not survive in the marketplace.

In support of these ideas, Peter Drucker, during an interview for *Industry Week*,[1] said:

> International economic theory is obsolete. The traditional factors of production—land, labor, and capital—are becoming restraints rather than driving forces. Knowledge is becoming the one critical factor of production. It has two incarnations: Knowledge applied to existing processes, services, and products is productivity; knowledge applied to the new is innovation.

> Knowledge has become the central, key resource that knows no geography. It underlies the most significant and unprecedented social phenomenon of this century. No class in history has ever risen as fast as the blue-collar worker and no class has ever fallen as fast. All within less than a century.

Seems only reasonable that knowledge would play a role in sorting out the winners from the losers. But if knowledge is that important, if it is the single most important factor in delivering growth to a business (or a national economy), then shouldn't businesses and nations be managing it as a resource? Shouldn't we be studying and learning a great deal about the nature of this intangible but critical resource?

Companies who are worrying about this business of managing knowledge are prospering. Some of the better known examples include:

☞ Oticon, a Danish hearing aid manufacturer, grew from $27 million in revenues in 1991 to $436 million in revenues today by scrapping a traditional management hierarchy for a very flat, very knowledge based set of roles, supported with groupware technology to tie it all together. (See Chapter 1 for a more comprehensive view of this case study.)

☞ Arthur Andersen's Global Best Practices (GBP) knowledge base is a central repository of knowledge about world-class business practices. This knowledge base captures qualitative and quantitative information about how companies achieve best-in-the-world standards of performance in activities that are common to most companies, regardless of their industry, for use by more than 40,000 Arthur Andersen professionals to provide clients with an ever-growing body of knowledge as a reference point for performance improvement.

☞ Dow Chemical Company has calculated that the cost of maintaining its portfolio of 30,000-plus patents was $180 million over a 10-year lifetime. This realization led to the charter of an "intellectual-asset management" organization, which has since developed a methodology for classifying, assessing, and investing Dow's patent portfolio in line with its business strategy. As reported in Industry Week Magazine, this knowledge management system has already saved Dow $40 million in tax maintenance costs and promises to enhance the licensing value stream from $25 million in '94

---

[1] "Peter Drucker: Managing in a post-capitalistic market-place" by Tom Brown, Industry Week, January 3, 1994, Penton Publishing

to a projected $125 million in the year 2000. The real bottom line will be directed technological resources toward value creation . . . through business alignment with the technology organizations—potentially worth "billions and billions."

20.3 KNOWLEDGE IS POWER!

As you can see from the examples we have cited from our client base, we believe passionately that knowledge is the key to competitive advantage in an information oriented economy. Our goal in writing this chapter is to explore the role of knowledge in today's new and more collaborative organizations. Our goal is to expose you to new ideas and ways of looking at your business. If, as Peter Drucker believes, we are entering a knowledge economy and one of the key economic drivers of business is knowledge, how do we maximize our ability to capitalize on our knowledge assets for competitive advantage?

20.4 GROUPWARE AND KNOWLEDGE MANAGEMENT

How can groupware and Web-based collaborative tools help organizations to capitalize on their knowledge assets? As we will discuss later in this chapter, knowledge creation happens at many levels in any organization. Individuals, teams, groups, and departments all create and consume knowledge. Larger enterprises need to find ways to collaborate and share knowledge beyond the traditional boundaries of geography and time. They also need to find ways to capture existing knowledge so that they are able to create a corporate memory for others in the organization to access, utilize, enhance, and evolve the knowledge and thinking of the company.

How many times have you started a project from scratch, just knowing that somewhere in your organization, someone else had done a project that was very similar to yours? They have solved many of the problems you now have to contend with and if they were successful, could probably provide you with a template that would enable you to finish your project in a fraction of the time. But where do you find this information/knowledge/experience? Often asking your colleagues isn't enough, and posting and e-mail will sometime get no answers or many false trails.

Wouldn't it be easier to look into an indexed corporate repository, rather than try and "reinvent the wheel." Such a repository would not only have documents and "explicit" information, but it would also contain the "people map" to help you to find the experts on this subject in the organization.

Groupware provides a set of technology enablers to facilitate the knowledge sharing process. Although technology is only one enabler to a knowledge management process, it is a critical one. Today's global organizations cannot maximize their knowledge assets without tools to facilitate the capture and sharing of information and ideas across all boundaries of space and time.

20.5 WHAT DO WE KNOW ABOUT KNOWLEDGE?

Well, we know that the human race has gotten better and better at generating the stuff. By some estimates, the sum of all the knowledge in the world doubles every seven years. Each time a new doubling begins, the rate of growth must double, because it is starting from a higher base. And in some areas, knowledge is growing even faster! In electronics, for example, the technology generations fly by so fast that the knowledge in today's product offerings will be obsolete 6 to 18 months from now.

We know that knowledge is different from capital and labor in important ways. First of all, it has the ability to multiply. A dollar bill, once spent, is no longer in your pocket, but in someone else's pocket, an hour of labor, once worked, is no more. Knowledge, once you share it with someone else, belongs to each of you. You can sell it, or give it away, and you still have it.

One implication of this ability to multiply is that global free trade may be far more important than we realized because it spreads ideas and knowledge that help the world as a whole prosper. Which boats do best on this rising tide of knowledge-driven prosperity will be determined by how well they are able to manage knowledge.

Another unique characteristic of knowledge is the fact that it costs little to reproduce, but a great deal to create. This is perhaps most evident in the world of the Internet, where you can send a message to thousands of people—almost for free. To take a journalistic example—the wages, travel time, and support staff for an investigative reporter add up to thousands of dollars per story. The cost of the paper and ink to print the story are trivial in comparison. Those who take the risk of investing in creating new knowledge are the ones who will reap the rewards.

Knowledge is difficult to measure, weigh, or count. Like the wind, we see its effects, but cannot see the thing itself. We have elaborate systems to measure, allocate, and control capital. We have personnel appraisal systems to track labor. We can only count and measure knowledge in very indirect ways, like numbers of patents issued, and that hardly captures all the learning and knowledge creation in the business.

If knowledge is being created at increasingly rapid rates, it follows that some knowledge is becoming obsolete and diminishing in value. This "time value" is another key characteristic of knowledge. Knowledge and insight hold their value only for a short time—they must be replenished.

Knowledge comes in several "flavors"—for example, tacit and explicit. Tacit knowledge is the set of skills, understanding, experience, and insight that each of us carry around with us. We may not be able to consciously say all that we know, but we can respond to a very wide variety of circumstances based on life-long learning about our craft, our industry, people, and organizations. Often, tacit knowledge is embedded in products (we know how it works, but no one can tell you why it was done that way) or in a company's business processes.

Explicit knowledge can be written down, or can be described—it is often found as black ink on white paper, bound in books—this book is a good example of a collaboration between people with explicit knowledge of groupware. Of course, today, we find explicit knowledge on our computer hard disks, and all over the Internet as well. What interests us here is that explicit knowledge can be owned by organizations, individuals, or groups.

20.6 MALTHUS GOT IT WRONG . . .

Thomas Malthus, in 1798, said that, "left unchecked, the growth in human population, which increases exponentially, would outstrip the world's ability to increase its food supply, which was increasing linearly. At this point, the growth in population would be checked by starvation."

At least so far, the burgeoning population of humans has not outstripped the human race's ability to create new knowledge—and use it to increase food supplies at a rate faster than the growth of the population. In fact, more of the world's people eat better now than when the world population was far smaller and our ability to manage plant and animal yields was far more primitive. In addition, human knowledge has created the ability to reduce the growth in population through birth control. That is the power of knowledge, creation to create competitive advantage. Malthus fell into the trap identified by Paul Romer, who says: "We systematically under-appreciate the potential for new things to happen."

So, since knowledge is the most basic factor in production, the fabric against which capital and labor do their jobs, they who have the best knowledge win...

And, since they who have the best knowledge win—they who do the best job creating, acquiring, and managing knowledge will have the key to competitive advantage...

And, this is not a one-time game, it is played out all over the organization, all the time, with knowledge that is constantly changing in form and content. The speed of this game requires computer assistance—there is just too much stuff changing and growing too fast to trust it to the #2 pencil and a legal pad—or worse yet—to human memory. The level of complexity in our society is increasing at alarming levels. This too is a by-product of our ability to rapidly create knowledge.

Groupware, with its special characteristics for managing the knowledge creation processes (communication, collaboration, coordination, and corporate memory—initially described by David Coleman in his introductory chapter) is the key enabling technology for achieving competitive advantage in this knowledge-based world.

20.7 KNOWLEDGE CREATION FOR COMPETITIVE ADVANTAGE

To win at business requires that you know more about some crucial aspect of your business than your competitor. To consistently know more means that you cannot just rely on what you can learn from others—you must constantly generate new knowledge. New insights into the market, new developments in your technology, new understanding of your customers, in groups or as individuals.

There are two types of learning in organizations—receiving wisdom and generating new insights. For most of us, learning brings to mind pictures of sitting in a college classroom listening to a lecturer drone on. This is receiving wisdom. In day-to-day business operations, quickly accessing the knowledge of others can be critical to avoid "reinventing wheels" and to stay in front of competitors. This "received" organizational learning is important in that it keeps the firm from operational disadvantage, but it does little, by itself, to create strategic advantage.

20.7.1 Creating New Knowledge in Day-to-day Work

The most strategically critical learning is innovation—the generation of new knowledge. New ideas, both breakthrough and incremental, help create competitive advantage. Work that generates new knowledge often starts with a question, as in: "What we've got to figure out here is..."

Every product development project is designed to create new knowledge embedded in a new product. Sales people generate new knowledge as they prospect for new customers and try out new sales pitches. Business strategists find new ways to look at products and markets. The ability to capture and act rapidly on this kind of learning can be supported with thoughtfully designed groupware applications. Knowledge creation is ultimately where the game of business will be won or lost.

For example, in the automobile business, the ability to design the next generation of cars quickly and well is more important to the survival of the company, and more worthy of investment and management attention, than is the current generation of vehicles coming off the assembly line.

In another example, the geographic expansion of a fast-growing retail chain was threatened because its new managers and executives weren't getting the benefit of the learning that their parent company predecessors had gained in growing the first generation of the business—they were "reinventing the wheel" rather than breaking new ground. The rapid expansion of the firm had kept them from capturing and using their knowledge of where to put new stores, how to penetrate new markets, and how to select and train new staff members. This led to significant profit under performance while the executives in the new geographies discovered the operating methods that the first generation of leaders already knew.

20.7.2 How Is Knowledge Created?

If knowledge is critical to business success, and if the creation of new knowledge is the single most important thing in differentiating one firm from another, then it is important to understand how new knowledge is created.

The creation of new knowledge is the point at which individual and organizational learning come together—the act of working and that of learning are the same. The way that learning is connected to working is in the learning spiral of conceive, act, reflect (see Fig. 20.1 below).

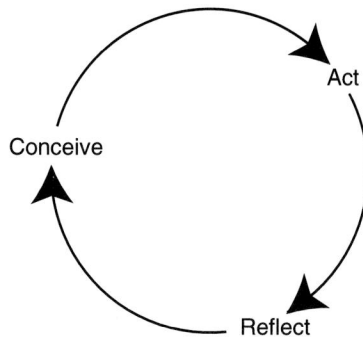

Fig. 20.1 Reflection Is Key to the Learning Spiral

In learning spirals, the single element that Western organizations do poorly is the element of reflection. We know how to conceive great plans for action and we know how to go out and do, but we often fail at looking at what we have done compared to what we wanted to accomplish, and drawing the lessons about what to be sure to repeat next time, what to avoid at all costs, and what, if only we had invented it in time, would have made a huge difference to the outcome.

In contrast, in Japanese firms today, very little information is captured "explicitly." People rely on interpersonal communications and the sharing of tacit knowledge. The Japanese document very little of their processes and practices and rely on knowledge transfer through interpersonal sharing.

During a project with a Japanese client, we wanted to gain a better understanding of how Japanese firms deal with capturing the intellectual capital of their firm so that the organization doesn't lose the knowledge if the individual leaves the firm. We asked our client team what they would do if someone in their firm left and they needed that person's knowledge. Their first response was that they would contact the individual and have a conversation—in fact, they had a program to hire retired individuals on a part-time basis to share knowledge and experience. The idea that they would lose this knowledge didn't strike them until we finally had to kill off (for the sake of the argument only!) their ex-employee and then ask them what they would do.

The dichotomy of knowledge management styles between the East and the West becomes most apparent when the two need to work together. An example is the joint partnership between Caterpillar and Mitsubishi Heavy Industries, which created a global line of hydraulic shovels. As soon as the two companies started to work together, they found that their respective R&D processes clashed with each others'. Japanese engineers shared tacit, experiential knowledge on a day-to-day basis as they worked together and therefore they did not document their work. On the other hand, the American engineers kept looking for the manuals so that they could learn how the Japanese engineers worked.

Mitsubishi learned that they needed to devote more time to documenting and making their knowledge explicit if they are to work effectively with global partners. Relying solely on the interactive sharing of experiential information does not work in a multi-cultural environment.

Finding ways to make reflection an active step in Western business processes, rather than something to do only when there is quiet time (almost never), is an important task in knowledge management process design. One retailing chain, for example, designed into their planning process a detailed replanning of each season after its results are known. From this replanning, lessons are drawn and applied to the next season to be planned. This step happens in every store for every season. The store managers learn, the buyers learn, and the executives learn. New line strategies and new display practices are invented and shared throughout the chain. All of this because the business process includes an explicit step of reflection, and then captures the individual learning for the corporation.

It is true that most new knowledge is incremental. It is more in the nature of invention, of putting together known pieces in new ways, than of true discovery—finding ideas, approaches, and technologies that are truly revolutionary. The breakthrough idea must be nurtured, but the cumulative impact of many incremental gains is, in most organizations, at least as valuable.

Groupware can help to facilitate the reflection process but only when the process of contributing to the system is well planned and facilitated. One common mistake is to assume that just creating data fields for people to fill in will facilitate the contribution of insightful and well-reflected knowledge. What most systems designers don't realize is that they need to help facilitate the qualitative input of information—not just the quantitative.

As people reflect on events, they tend to input discreet, succinct comments into a groupware system—like Lotus Notes Discussion Databases or Collabra-Share Forums, for example. These comments will usually highlight the key points of the action or event but don't explore why, where, how, etc.... By framing the questions in ways that have the user explore their responses with more reflection, the value of their responses will provide additional insight and learning to both the user and to the other members of the team. Below are some examples of qualitative questions:

☞ We are now at the midpoint of the project—If, at the end, we are bemoaning the fact that we got badly off track and did not achieve our goals, why did this happen?

☞ A competitor has just announced a product that will compete with our new offering, but at half the price we had anticipated charging. What should we do?

☞ What have we done in the last month that has contributed to our staying on schedule? What have we done that has slowed us down?

☞ What are three things that "we've always done that way" that we should challenge in our design process?

Another groupware tool that helps to facilitate reflective learning is Electronic Meeting Systems (EMS—see the chapters in this book in the Technology Section and also in this section about how people are using EMS to generate and capture knowledge). Through group brainstorming and group reflection, new ideas are created and perceived barriers are defined and removed. Electronic Meeting Systems help to break down communication and personality barriers and create a safer and more democratic environment for knowledge sharing and idea generation.

The initial limitation of this tool, though, was the fact that all of the learning and ideas stayed in the system or were printed out for people to take away. There was no way to use the technology to facilitate action from the session. You also couldn't put the outcome from the meeting online so that others could learn or continue to add to the discussion. Its purpose was only "same time, same place."

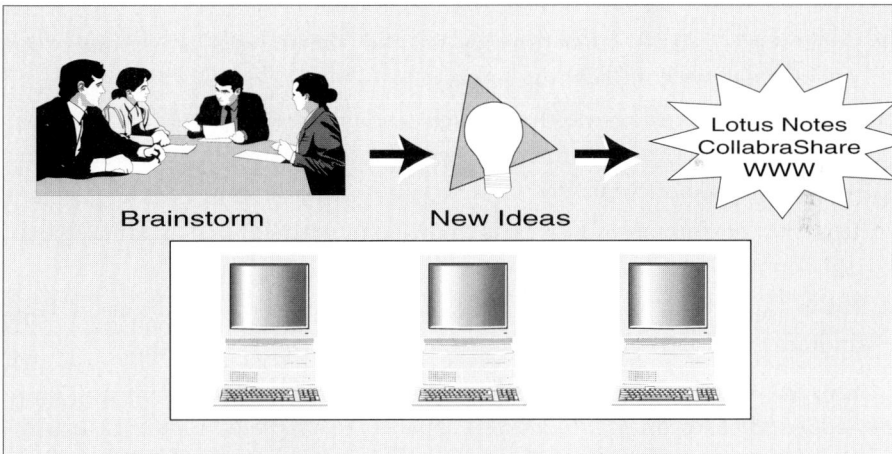

Fig. 20.2 Electronic Meeting Systems—Anytime, Anywhere

Today, most Electronic Meeting Systems have (or are planning to have) the capability to export the knowledge created during the group session into another groupware tool or Web server so that the learning is captured for future use (see Fig. 20.2 above). These tools are evolving in functionality so that teams will have the ability to conduct not only "same time, same place" but "anytime, anyplace" meetings and idea creation activities.

20.7.3 How Do Organizations Create Knowledge?

"An organization cannot create knowledge on its own without individuals. It is, therefore, very important for the organization to support and stimulate the knowledge—creating activities of individuals or to provide the appropriate contexts for them."[1]

What can organization do to leverage individual knowledge and to provide an environment for knowledge creation? This section proposes a set of tactics to facilitate individual, team, and, ultimately, organizational, knowledge creation. It involves changing how organizations think about learning.

Organizations create knowledge by setting in place processes and infrastructures that make it possible to share and amplify new knowledge created by individuals. The test of whether an organization (or individual) has learned is whether there is new competence; can the person or team do something it couldn't do before? Until insight is translated into action, it is just information. Once we can act or perform differently, there is evidence that we have created new knowledge. Based on our work in knowledge management, we observe that:

- ☞ Knowledge creation leads to continuous innovation, which leads to competitive advantage

- ☞ Knowledge creation takes place at three levels: the individual, the team, and the organization

- ☞ Groupware creates opportunities for the sharing and spiraling of knowledge, which we call learning loops

- ☞ Learning involves knowledge, which leads to action. In order to act on new insights, an individual must internalize it, context it, and add their own values and beliefs to it.

- ☞ It is the interaction of our tacit knowledge with explicit business problems that creates new knowledge.

- ☞ Groupware supports communication, collaboration, coordination, and the building and sharing of corporate memory.

Our focus on knowledge and learning is based on the belief that well-managed knowledge increases an organization's capacity to produce results. Learning does not exist without action. Learning involves doing things we couldn't do before. The evidence of learning is a new skill, demonstrated in action.

The elements that need to be orchestrated, as we think about organizational learning, start at the core—the individual—and then move outward to the team and the organization against a backdrop of organizational climate created by leadership (see Fig. 20-3 below). Let's paint an initial map of what learning may be about by looking at each level.

---

[1] *The Knowledge-Creating Company* by Ikujiro Nonaka and Hirotaka Takeuchi, Oxford University Press, 1995, p. 239.

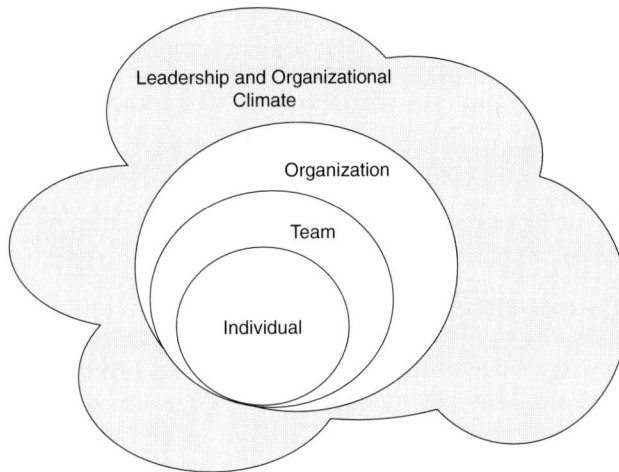

Fig. 20.3 Individuals Learn in the Context of Their Organization

20.7.4 Organizational Learning Starts with the Individual

Organizations don't learn, individuals within the organization do. An organization should not be viewed as something that has a life of its own, independent of the people who make things happen.

Yet, for many, the point of reference for learning is still bound with the association of a teacher, a classroom, or a textbook. This association often leads to a more passive view of learning and that learning is a special activity cut off from the real world and unrelated to one's work life. If it is related to work life, then it is often considered the responsibility of the organization to provide learning.

This view is changing as learning is increasingly valued as an important corporate skill and the view of taking individual responsibility for learning becomes even more valued. Taking responsibility for one's own learning begins by assessing oneself in the context of the individual learning.

How does individual learning occur? You can begin to answer this question by asking yourself:

☞ How do you prefer to learn?

☞ What is your greatest strength as a learner?

☞ What is your greatest weakness as a learner?

☞ What conditions or what kind of learning environment promote your learning?

From this exercise, you can begin to define your learning style, what contribution can be made in contributing to team learning, and suggest conditions for the learning environment.

20.7.5 The Team: Leveraging Individual Knowledge

There are certain assumptions that we can make:

☞ An organization is composed of individuals who know things.

☞ Often this knowledge is tacit and individuals have not been encouraged to make it explicit or they do not how to make it explicit.

☞ Only when knowledge is shared with others and amplified within teams does it spiral into the organization.

Knowledge is created through the interaction of tacit and explicit knowledge. Tacit knowledge is not easily visible or expressive, it is personal and context-specific. Explicit knowledge is formal and systematic, often expressed in words and numbers. The challenge is surfacing the hidden knowledge and sharing it with a team and the organization.

For example, a client recently told us: "When a critical individual recently left the company, all the knowledge went with him; we have no record of his thinking. Now we need to recreate the audit trail, which will be time-consuming and costly." This individual left with invisible tacit knowledge that was not made explicit nor visible.

Knowledge is often intended to be explicit. Many companies have final project review meetings that are intended to be explicit and visible. They intend to capture and distill the project's history and publish the results to pass knowledge to future projects.

However, our clients tell us that these learnings are very often not transferred at the end of a project. We have observed that there is significant benefit to gathering these learnings at each stage of a process so that the current project teams can learn incrementally and that their insights can be transferred to other projects as they are captured. Once project teams have disbanded and moved on to new projects, it is almost impossible to bring the group together to reflect and capture the key learnings from the project.

Teams can become more knowledgeable than the sum of their members. Through conversations and dialogue, interrelationships are developed that stimulate thought. Team learning can result from holding a meeting to outline lessons learned during a project or by solving complex problems together. It occurs when individuals, as colleagues, get beyond their assumptions and bring their collective intelligence to find new solutions to complex issues.

Leveraging individual knowledge means:

☞ developing processes to allow team members to share experiences

☞ creating opportunities to leverage knowledge beyond discreet project teams

☞ viewing existing knowledge as a platform to build upon—not "set in stone" as a final answer

☞ making sure that team members take the time to reflect on what they've learned and then share it with others

Teams often create a new language among themselves that express the new knowledge they have acquired. This new knowledge has the opportunity of becoming organizational learning by being communicated throughout the organization. How much and how fast learning can take place depends upon the culture and structure of the organization. If channels are open, flexible, networked and non-hierarchial, learning can take place faster than with rigid procedures and information systems. Groupware, when designed and implemented well, has the effect of flattening the hierarchy, and making knowledge more available to those who can use it to create benefit for the organization.

Here's the story of one consulting team that experienced the profound effect of groupware-enabled team learning first hand. The project involved a change effort in three manufacturing plants located hundreds of miles apart over two states. This 18 person team would typically have approached the assignment by establishing a sub-group for each plant, with further subdivisions by functional area. Each area and plant level team would have a leader, reporting up a ladder to the overall project manager. Most communication among the team would have been vertical, with the team leaders caucusing, and the overall team leader checking schedules and accomplishments. In this model, the leaders focus on task and schedule almost exclusively, leaving the individual consultants at the work level to figure out how best to approach the work. From the client's point of view, this leads to differing solutions at each plant, with little obvious reason why each solution emerged. There is little learning for the client and little for the consulting team. Even the individuals learn only from their own experience.

Contrast the description above with what happens when the team uses a groupware and knowledge management-enabled approach.

At the working level, the consultants are linked together by knowledge bases that contain ongoing conversations based on daily reflection—what are we observing? What are the possible approaches for solutions? What is working and not working as we begin to make changes? What good ideas are we collecting from client "experts" that should be spread to the whole organization. Having this in writing allows each consultant to stay current with the work of all the others, and to understand the effects of changes in his or her area on the other functional areas quickly. Each consultant learns from the work of all the others, and the whole is captured for use by other project teams and for distillation into the firm's Center of Excellence files.

At the management levels, status and schedule (recorded by each consultant in the system) is readily visible, allowing leaders to focus on helping to integrate the work itself across functional areas, and to help generate ideas for new approaches. In fact, the content of the work becomes so visible that the hierarchy flattens tremendously—vice presidents can add ideas to the work of junior consultants. This is not always comfortable for the project managers!

It is clear that a great deal more knowledge is created, captured, and shared in this model than in the hierarchical one. The client benefits from getting the best thinking and wisdom of a wider slice of the consulting firm, the consultants benefit because their personal knowledge bases expand more rapidly. Finally, the firm benefits in two ways:

☞ By having a constantly improving fund of knowledge on which to base their work

☞ By shrinking the time and effort required to complete client engagements, allowing them to be more profitable, more competitive, or both. In this case, the project managers estimates showed a 25 percent reduction in staff required to complete the engagement when operating with groupware-enabled knowledge management processes.

20.7.6 Organizational Learning: The Enabling Conditions of Knowledge Creation

The role of the organization in knowledge creation is to create the context or climate for enabling individual and team activities. The work of professors Takeuchi and Nonaka in their book *The Knowledge-Creating Company* (Oxford University Press, 1995), has helped us view the organization as key in creating the conditions for learning.

In order for knowledge to spiral in an organization, Nonaka and Takeuchi suggest five enabling conditions (pp. 74–84) in achieving the knowledge creation process.

☞ ***Intention*** is defined as the organization's aspiration to achieving its goals. It can be defined as the corporate guiding ideas. Intention, as it relates to the knowledge creation process involves creating a knowledge vision for the organization and developing the capability to acquire, create, and share knowledge.

☞ ***Autonomy*** refers to the individual and the freedom of the individual to act; it means giving individuals a flexible learning arena to create new knowledge.

☞ ***Creative Chaos*** is the natural or created crisis that shifts paradigms and opens possibilities. A crisis often triggers the questioning of the validity of our assumptions and attitudes. This questioning of assumptions can lead to a breakdown of certainty, which in turn can lead to dialogue, which leads to the creation of new concepts.

☞ ***Redundancy or Overlapping Knowledge*** refers to the consistent information available across the organization, which will facilitate common understanding and the ability to have equal access to all information.

☞ *Requisite Variety* means common understanding from different perspectives. It is the sharing of past and present knowledge among projects that helps to evolve the state of thinking.

20.7.7 Organizational Learning: Creating the Climate for Learning

In creating the environment for learning, there are key questions to ask:

☞ How is knowledge transferred?

☞ What can be done to leverage knowledge to better generate creativity and innovation?

☞ What tools and techniques are valuable in working to generate and narrate knowledge and creativity?

While true learning cannot be structured by the organization, it is possible for the organization to provide the tools and opportunity. The secrets that contribute to the vitality, learning, and growth of an organization seem to be found in the enthusiasm for learning, encouragement of work passions, and recognition and celebration of team success.

While a great part of the reward for learning is intrinsic, organizations can further create a climate for learning by rewarding learning, sharing, and team behaviors. Having learning goals, as well as team rewards explicitly stated in performance assessment documents, are becoming more common.

20.7.8 Leaders Create the Environment to Learn

The relationship between leadership and creating the environment to learn is key. We have found the greatest factor in fostering continuous learning is directly related to how leadership demonstrates commitment and support for collaboration. In order to manage knowledge assets, it is not enough to identify knowledge, but to understand the leader's role in designing an organization for continuous learning.

The primary tasks of the leader are to:

☞ create vision to answer the larger view for going through the learning process

☞ provide encouragement and celebrate learners

☞ be a role model and set a personal example of learning and sharing knowledge

The "leader who learns" role models for the organization the behavior he or she expects from others: open mindedness, questioning self and others, and searching for ideas and betterment.

A knowledge curriculum, intended to build the capability for continuous learning in an organization, develops learning skills in people at all levels. Some examples of the kinds of skills developed in a knowledge curriculum are:

- active listening
- creativity in finding new approaches
- accountability
- openness to new ideas
- playfulness

- dialogue
- relationship building
- experimentation
- enthusiasm
- compassion

20.8 GROUPWARE WILL AFFECT ORGANIZATIONAL STRUCTURE

The key organizational challenge is to create structures and processes that foster and support learning and the integration of work. If we believe that knowledge is the key driver in the organization, the sharing of knowledge needs to be formalized.

Everyone in a knowledge-creating company is a knowledge worker/creator. The value a person brings is not by the level in hierarchy but by information that is provided to teams. As we think of structure, we must also rethink organizational roles. Mapping an organization's knowledge into domains or providing support to projects or event-driven knowledge requires different roles. Today, new roles are emerging with titles like:

Chief Knowledge Officer (CKO)
Knowledge Integrator
Information Agent
New-Age Librarian

These roles are key in the development of a knowledge management structure to document advances of an organization's core competence, and to foster debate, experimentation, and learning from each other's experience.

A learning process that connects the day-to-day work of the company with the evolution of its core competencies must be designed. Usually, a computer support system is critical if the knowledge bases are to be easily accessible by all who need them and if capturing knowledge is to be easy enough that people will actually be able to do it.

20.9 THE "LEARNING ORGANIZATION" AND GROUPWARE

The Learning Organization, a term popularized by Peter Senge, a professor at M.I.T., has come to be the starting point for the work of many other organization theorists. In a Learning Organization, new approaches, practices, and concepts are continuously being discovered or invented and put into practice. Not only do individuals learn from their personal experiences, but there are also multiple means for storing and communicating the learning of others so that each individual benefits from the learning of all his or her colleagues. Both *personal mastery* and *team learning* are essential in this process. A *holistic* (or "systems") point of view, expressed as graphic *mental models* of a *shared vision* of the world, is a key tool in achieving a high level of ongoing learning.

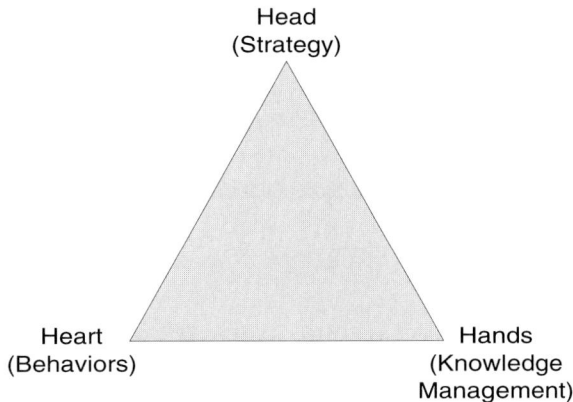

Fig. 20.4 The Biology of the Learning Organization

Each of these five central themes of Senge's work can be supported effectively with groupware. A major consulting organization identified the connections between Senge's work and the internal development of a groupware support system then being developed, as follows:

☞ ***Personal Mastery***—requires committing to lifetime learning, striving to achieve a special level of proficiency, and focusing energies on personal visions. Without individual learning, there can be no organizational learning. One way that we can support individual learning and facilitate organization-wide growth, is by providing technical capabilities, for example: desktop learning, a referencing system for mentoring on specific issues, a network of experts, access to past presentations and reports, and forums for seeking advice.

☞ ***Team Learning***—Teams are the fundamental learning units of an organization. When a team works effectively, it produces outstanding results and team members learn more as participants in the group than they could have alone.

Tapping the potential of many minds to think insightfully about complex issues is a critical dimension of team learning. Technology can facilitate team learning by helping to coordinate action and enabling an individual to play roles on many teams. When technologies such as networked PCs and video conferencing are widespread in our firm, they will enable us to work in new kinds of teams, using technology to provide forums for ongoing dialogue within topic areas, capture documents as corporate memory, and perform electronic problem-solving.

☞ ***Holistic, Systems Thinking***—Systems thinking is a conceptual framework that enables us to "see the forest *and* the trees." A shift to a more

holistic or systems way of thinking is critical if we are to transfer knowledge and continuously learn.

Technology plays a key role in creating a holistic mind set. As we use technology to identify connections, for instance by cross referencing topics or
searching documents for key ideas, we can learn to better leverage the organization's body of knowledge and tools. Through this widespread access to
information, we will be able to more powerfully respond to complexity and
change.

☞ *Shared Vision*—A powerful shared vision galvanizes the organization and
motivates individuals to grow and excel. To ensure commitment, the vision
must be developed from within the organization, not trickled down from
the top.

By identifying and communicating detailed "pictures of the future," or "To
Be" models, we can gain commitment to our vision of becoming a "Learning
Organization." Technology can support this vision by providing widespread
access to our past learning and guidelines for future action. Further, communication of the vision through technologies such as desktop learning
modules and video conferencing will reinforce team members' understanding of, and commitment to, our common direction.

☞ *Shared Mental Models*—Mental models are images of how we understand
the world and how we take action. These models are often hidden and can
be barriers to achieving growth and change. Surfacing our assumptions,
testing them through discussion, and changing our internal pictures are
cornerstones in building a Learning Organization.

The development of our capacity to work with mental models in order to
learn new skills and implement innovations will be facilitated by the high
graphics capability of the technology we will utilize. Models will be used as
information maps, with each document connected to a map in some meaningful way.

In the Learning Organization model, continuous learners are in a constant
state of change and improvement. They apply what they learn, they reflect and
understand, they are engaged, and they improve their own performance and that
of their associates. Continuous learning, supported with groupware, improves
personal and organizational performance, and its benefits are reflected in the
bottom line.

The learning process includes both knowledge transfer and behavioral
change. The key behavioral challenge we face in our distributed organizations is
finding a way to get knowledge from individuals' heads into the shared knowledge base of the organization. Even the culture of our organizations will be
affected by this shift to more collaborative models, where the knowledge of one is

the property of all. Groupware provides a way to make this knowledge capture task easy enough to be possible.

Building the groupware tools to channel this growing fund of knowledge will require substantial attention to the structure and content of the information we save and share. From its format to its naming and indexing, we must challenge our assumptions and learn new ways to capture and use knowledge.

Groupware technology can add a lot to the Learning Organization process, by adding speed and universal accessibility in ways impossible until now. Groupware also provides a mechanism for knowledge to flow and legitimizes an organization's informal network. Technology networks support the real network of knowledge workers. The real network consists of the people in the organization. The technology is less important that the organization's purpose, sociology of interaction, and management.

20.10 HOW GROUPWARE ENABLED KNOWLEDGE CREATION CONTRIBUTES TO WEALTH CREATION

20.10.1 Short Term Benefits

Groupware helps to manage knowledge by creating a *collective memory*—a way of being able to "remember" all the important things we have learned as a team or as a company.

This memory can take the form of a "Frequently Asked Questions" database where experts answer questions once, then post the answers so that the next person can begin their questioning with the benefit of the previous discussion. This benefits the questioner by providing an initial set of insights and by helping to identify the current experts in specific areas. The expert benefits from having additional time to work on advanced issues, and by making productive connections with questioners more often—fewer contacts result in "that's not entirely my field, why don't you call 'Mary,' she is the expert on this."

Another sort of collective memory is the "Why did we...?" collection of critical decisions and the rationale for each. This kind of memory captures our assumptions about the future. Having our assumptions clearly visible allows us to check them regularly, and, if they turn out to be false, to change direction quickly.

A third kind of collective memory is the record of past projects that make it possible for practitioners new to a given area of work to understand the dynamics, critical success factors, frequently encountered barriers, and the like quickly, and without having to personally experience each variation on the theme to benefit from the common store of wisdom.

Finally, many companies have a distinctive view of the world—a set of viewpoints, prejudices, and assumptions that underlay their particular marketplace positioning. These statements are not always explicit in an organization, they may have to do with uncommon understandings of cause and effect, or with assumptions about how customers and competitors will react to certain types of initiatives. ("We never have off-price sales, it would cheapen our product...") If we focus on markets that are geographically remote from our major competitor, we can share without creating an aggressive reaction.") Making these explicit in a knowledge base is useful leadership work that guides action in the firm.

Corporate memory can also be more specific and transaction-based. Relationship marketing, the idea of working with large populations of customers on an individual basis, demands a corporate knowledge of the customer that is specific, up-to-date, and readily available to anyone who might come in contact with that customer. Even such simple things as who has made the most recent contact and what was discussed can have profound implications for creating customer satisfaction.

In consumer marketing, corporate memory means knowing your customers as individuals: their history of orders; their requests for services or products which we couldn't supply; their patterns of buying "our" products or competitor's products; and changes in life stages (like having a baby) or economic circumstances (like moving to a wealthier area) which make them better prospects or which open the door to new products or services we can provide. Knowing your customer's buying habits, product preferences, and personal circumstances allows you to use computers to create highly targeted, personalized direct mail or telemarketing propositions to bring a customized offering to people who are likely to want what you have to sell.

For industrial customers, there is generally a network of people who must say "yes" before a sale is made and a network of our sales representatives and executives who must face off with the customer in a coordinated way. Corporate memory in this case takes the form of a record of the strategies we are pursuing, the contacts that each of us have had, and our evaluation of the motivation, degree of enthusiasm, and needs to satisfy for each member of the client buying network.

20.10.2 Four Rules for Making Corporate Memory Work Well

1. **Connect the building of corporate memory to "real work."**
   Make it easy, part of the core work—"Nice But Not Necessary" won't work.

2. **Corporate memory must help connect people to people.**
   Documents alone are not enough. There must be an index, a "yellow pages" that summarizes who knows what in addition to the documents that are the artifacts of past work. Encouraging these connections leads to more efficient transfer of knowledge and to the kinds of interactions that create new insights.

3. Use Groupware to increase knowledge creation by facilitating collaboration.

Especially when the collaborators cannot be in the same place at the same time, groupware provides an alternative "space" for collaboration conversations.

4. Build mental models, maps, and a common vocabulary.

Sharing the same models creates a frame of reference, a common starting point with each other that helps us work together more effortlessly, like a champion basketball team passing the ball as they move down court.

20.10.3 Knowledge in Support of "Real Work"

Imagine how water flows down a hill. It finds its own path and the water pools naturally in different locations along its journey. This is very similar to how knowledge flows through an organization. The difference is that knowledge is tied directly to the work of the organization. Work defines the paths that knowledge takes and the "pools" of knowledge are formed where groups of people have a natural need to gather and share knowledge. If you're going to change the flow of knowledge in the organization, then the path of work must be changed as well.

Many companies will try unsuccessfully to capture the learning and knowledge of the firm. They will build groupware applications to hold the knowledge but can't understand why no one is using them.

Why?

The most important task for any employee is getting their job done. If capturing knowledge is viewed as extra work or they are not explicitly rewarded for taking the time to share, they won't do it. This happens not out of spite, or lack of desire. People just don't have the time or energy to do things that are not "real work," that are not directly connected to doing their jobs.

To solve this problem, any knowledge management or learning system must also play a role in helping users to get their work done easier, faster, and more conveniently. This tradeoff allows more time to share their knowledge. If the knowledge management effort they are making is making their job (or their perception of their job) easier, it will help you change the behaviors within the organization. Remember, you must answer both "What's in it for me?" and "What's in it for our company?"

Groupware helps make processes work better and more consistently. By making the processes more visible, more tangible, and more malleable, it can create virtuous spirals of process improvement that reduce costs, improve customer satisfaction, or increase revenues.

By creating a window into the work itself, groupware allows process participation by members outside the core team—for example, executive team members who bring strategic direction and insight. This participation results in a solution to the common complaint, "They would never let us . . ." by having "them" as part of this virtual team, moving the issue out of the realm of assumption and putting it in the realm of fact. More often than you might guess, "they" would love to see innovative rather than rote responses.

This same window allows members of interdependent teams to see what is going on that might affect them. The manufacturing team can get an early look at the requirements for new products, and the customer credit and accounts receivable teams can see what is coming in terms of sales promotion that will create new customer demand.

Industry Week magazine describes one such process support effort:

> For Arian Ward, the self-appointed (and unbudgeted) leader of learning and change for Hughes Space & Communications Co. (HSC) in El Segundo, Calif., this trip is limited only by the extent of his missionary zeal. Fashioning himself as a knowledge broker and catalyst, Ward has gathered an entire constellation of projects and supporting technology for mapping, managing, and capitalizing on knowledge into a conceptual framework called the Knowledge Highway, which he deploys "like a Madison Avenue campaign."

> Through "massive amounts of networking" and the understanding that "you have to make an impact as quickly and cheaply as possible," he sniffs out nascent projects, plants new seeds, and cross-pollenates various efforts. At the same time, Ward emphasizes the importance of "focusing on the structured work," especially for an organization as entrepreneurial as Hughes' satellite business. "We need to make routine the things that are routine so that people are freed up. Part of this is getting to the point where we move stuff out of the esoteric knowledge-work arena into the structured arena. So, understanding your work in general is the first requirement. The next is to figure out what is the most powerful thing you can do with that work."

> For a business in which one loose wire can cost $5 million and a month of cycle time, the most important thing turns out to be recycling. "We create way too much knowledge," says Ward. "We have to start learning how to reuse." He calculates: If 50 percent of HSC's cost of labor is design labor and 50 percent of all designs were reused designs (assuming it takes about one-tenth the labor to recycle and, more important, that the engineers could learn to reuse) the organization could save $7 million to $25 million per spacecraft. One effective recycling initiative called "lessons learned," a closed-loop learning process for embedding organizational experience back into practices supported by Web-based technology, is on the verge of enterprise-wide implementation after four successful pilots.

20.11 GETTING TO ACTION FROM INSIGHT MORE RAPIDLY

A major computer manufacturer (Fortune 100) recognizes that the market is forcing their product's life cycle to become shorter and shorter, and that they must learn to develop each new generation of machines at lower and lower cost.

They have, over the last three years, externalized their engineers and manager's tacit knowledge of what works well in the development process into a common framework and vocabulary for describing and managing the New Product Process, and have seen some significant reductions in cycle time as a result.

However, getting the process down on paper is only the first step—now they realize that they must combine their process with some communication and database technology (groupware) to systematize their New Product Process.

The visible problems they are motivated to solve include:

☞ Decision delays due to the need to physically convene meetings of executives at the phase gate points (executives are often traveling, and always juggling multiple priorities for their time)

☞ The need to manage a great many information linkages for even the smallest project

☞ The need to assign management level people full-time on major development projects just to remain informed of the current status of other organizations with whom they have inter-dependencies

Most of all, they wish to capture and use the many insights that occur during the development of a new product and provide ways for the next project to internalize and learn from these lessons.

Based on an investigation phase, which included interviews, information flow analysis, and a technical review (among other things), we are working with them to design a Lotus Notes based system that will be like a *knowledge generation conveyor belt* for the many documents and ideas that make up the content of a product development process.

We expect that this set of backbone applications will provide an on-line environment for different time and different place meetings, that it will allow documents to be routed to those who need to work on them next—automatically—through both pre-defined and ad hoc work flows, and that it will increase, dramatically, the amount of cross-organizational collaborative knowledge generation.

The new system will also contain a set of learning points at which the developer or manager can record insight immediately. This learning loop will allow the capture of ongoing learning—supporting continuous improvement of the organization on many levels.

Based on benchmarking against peer companies and world class levels, it appears that the benefits of further sophisticating the process could be enormous. The real payoff is in the ability to put new and better products into the market faster than competitors. Since the process improvements are leveraged against the main revenue flow of the company, the financial value is very high.

20.12 A GLIMPSE OF THE FUTURE—COMPREHENSIVE GROUPWARE SUPPORT FOR KNOWLEDGE CREATION

Figure 20.5 below shows a next generation groupware support system that supports the day-to-day work process, captures and disseminates learning, and ties strategy formulation to all parts of the firms efforts.

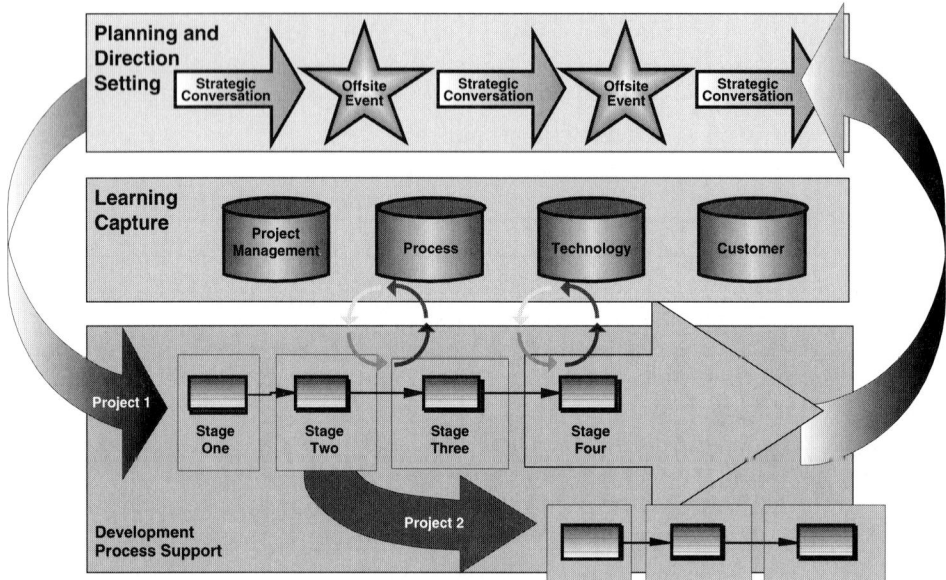

Fig. 20.5 Next Generation Groupware—Integrating the Learning Enterprise

20.12.1 Strategy Formulation and Planning

The pressures of day-to-day business operations tend to keep executives from working on strategic issues as much as they would like, or as much as the business needs. Therefore, most companies will take their executive group off-site (usually to a facility near a golf course and/or a beach) to work uninterrupted for several days on examining the business and crafting new strategic directions.

A much more current-events way to keep strategy crafting on the "front burner," without taking everyone from their jobs forever, is the on-line strategy conversation. Using knowledge management principles, supported by computer based groupware tools, executives can continue their strategy work at their convenience, all year round. The constantly emerging strategy can readily be communicated to the organization, and new insights from the "battle field" can be incorporated into the strategic discussion immediately.

20.12.2 Groupware Support for Learning Capture

A great deal of learning happens as work in the business process proceeds, as people collaborate to design new products, serve customers, or market and sell the firm's services. In most firms, this learning is either lost entirely, or at best, it is confined to the memory of one or a few people. Creating corporate memory, collaborative knowledge bases about customer behavior, market dynamics, the technologies used in the product, or even how we are managing the organization is a first step. Making it easy to contribute new thinking or discoveries is an important design consideration and "mobilizing" people by getting them to understand what's in it for them personally as well as how the company benefits, completes the cycle and results in effective knowledge management.

20.12.3 Work Process Support in Groupware

Work support is an absolutely necessary foundation for all knowledge management in the firm. Connecting the daily tasks of working in a business process and making it easy to find useful and relevant material in context provides the first level of gains for the organization—people learn how to work more consistently at the best levels so far discovered.

The second level of gains comes as those involved in the process continue to invent improvements. Improvements can take the form of incremental gains in stages of the process or result in insights that discard the process entirely and replace it with a whole new approach.

In the current stage of evolution of knowledge management, the systems and processes are often applied to individual steps or parts of processes, gaining significant, but partial, results.

It is critical at the outset of a knowledge management program to build and assess a model of the current process and the knowledge flows that surround it to serve as a starting point for designing a "whole process" approach in which the use of groupware can result in major gains.

20.13 BARRIERS TO SUCCESS

20.13.1 The "Knowledge Is Power" barrier

If all work is knowledge work, and if people are rewarded for applying their individual knowledge in competition with their peers—then of course they won't share the knowledge that they consider crucial to winning, to getting ahead. But the enterprise wins if everyone knows everything, or at least those pieces that will help them perform better.

So what do we do? We can explicitly reward more for knowledge sharing activities. We can role model and ask for corporate (or at least team) performance and incent people to help others win by, among other things, sharing knowledge.

We must usually remove barriers to sharing. Creating strong financial incentives is less important than removing the financial disincentives. People are social animals and, in most cases, are happy to share what they know with colleagues—they get the satisfaction of being "smarter" or at least better informed that their peers, and they will usually find that this is a rewarding experience all by itself. But businesses put barriers in the way of this free sharing. Reward systems that emphasize individual contributions to the successes of the firm, even to the point of demanding that project team contributions are analyzed, and "who did what" is made clear. Bonus schemes with a strong flavor of "what have you personally done..." rather than "how have you helped others win..." will create a powerful disincentive to sharing knowledge. From the individual's point of view, there is little to gain from taking the time to share, and at worst, someone else will win at his expense.

Once the disincentives are out of the way, recognition can play a powerful role. For example, in a large, general management consulting firm, we found that the practitioners had two strong reasons not to contribute knowledge to the knowledge management system. First, their managers viewed "typing on the computer" as wasted time—not spent on direct client contact. Second, the performance appraisal system valued only contributions to revenue production and to personal participation in projects.

Changing the reward system to include a section for contributions to the firm's base of knowledge—weighted equally with the revenue and project contributions—helped to level the playing field in the minds of both the consultants and their managers. The most excitement, however, was generated by a "Knowledge Base Best Sellers" contest. The reward—a 100% cotton tee shirt. It is amazing what people will do for a tee shirt!

20.13.2 The Information Overload Barrier

Overwhelming! That's the reaction that many people have to the sheer amount of information and knowledge that is available to them—in newspapers, magazines, and books; in each day's mail, where a seemingly infinite number of things to buy is presented; and over computer networks like the World Wide Web (WWW). At work, the amount of information is often worse, with reams of computer reports arriving daily, analyses and business plans, recommendations from staff, and who knows what else hitting our desks.

And the stuff we would most like to see, the pieces of knowledge that are most critical to getting our work done successfully, are often missing. The sales departments latest projections are considered confidential and are not shared with manufacturing. The most recent best thinking on customer satisfaction is being done by some guy on the other coast. The expert in retailing management is in Germany. So finding the "tree" you really need in the "forest" of available knowledge is tough.

Sometimes we don't even know what we need to know—at least until not knowing creates a crisis.

20.13.3 So What's the Answer?

First, creating mental and visual models of the most relevant and strategically important knowledge for each organization allows people throughout the firm to see the world in somewhat the same way. These models can be nested— drilling down on a section of the top level model brings up a sub-model. Or there may be separate and parallel models for various aspects of the firm's business. The important part is that people in the organization literally learn to "see" the organization in similar ways, so that it is obvious where to look for knowledge relevant to each part of the operation.

Second, new roles must be designed into the system. Each knowledge domain (large block in the mental model) will need a champion, whose job it is to assure that the knowledge contained in the system is up-to-date, and that it represents the best thinking of the firm at that time. Other roles that evolve in a knowledge intensive organization are:

☞ The knowledge manager who works with the champion and with the people involved in the business processes to assure that the process of collecting and disseminating knowledge is working smoothly

☞ The knowledge guide who can help find relevant material in the system, and answer questions even when the questions are not altogether clear.

Finally, we can build electronic support tools to reduce the amount of stuff that we get that we can't use and to increase our ability to find useful stuff quickly. To the degree that we know the kinds of knowledge that we want to see, we can create filters to allow only those kinds of materials to wind up on our screen. This assumes, however, that everything we would want to see is somehow directed at us. To find material that might well be useful to us, but which is not being sent in our direction, we use electronic agents that can go out and search our electronic world (and beyond, into the Internet potentially) and retrieve new bits of information that might be relevant to our interests as we have defined them. Over time, we can refine the criteria used by our agents so that the likelihood of a retrieved piece of information being useful to us is greater and greater.

20.13.4 The "Nice But Not Necessary" Barrier

We are all busy with our "real work." I have seldom heard anyone in an organization say "I have all this time on my hands, can you help me find ways to fill it productively?" There are any number of activities, tasks, and projects vying for our attention—so many that most of us must decline at least some of the things we could be involved in. This is normal. So when along comes yet another opportunity to do something useful, something that would contribute to the well-being of the firm and of ourselves, we weigh it against all the other commitments we already have, almost intuitively examining what connection this new task has to our core work. This comparison can easily lead to the conclusion that this would be nice to do in a perfect world... but it is not necessary to my success, happiness, or well being here and now, and it gets put aside.

Overcoming this barrier requires designing knowledge capture and reuse into the work process so that the easiest way to get the core work done is also the way that documents the decisions that are made and the lessons learned in the process. Generally, the ability of the technology to speed up the communications process and to manage commitments to closure are sufficient reasons for a well-designed knowledge management system to be attractive to those who must use it. For example, a project manager who is developing a new, high-tech product can see all the interactions that are going on in his or her project, both within the project team and in its interactions with other teams. This dramatically reduces the number of telephone calls and face-to-face status meetings, and allows time to be spent on substantive issues of the design—how to get cost out, how to design in more features, and how to design for greater manufacturability.

20.13.5 Elimination Is as Important as Creation (Peter Drucker)

Peter Drucker, in an interview by Peter Schwartz published in *Wired* magazine—1993 said:

> Thirty-odd years ago, I began to counsel that you should build organized abandonment into your system. It follows the old line that it makes more sense for you to make obsolete your own products than to wait for the competitor to do it. But this is very hard for organizations to do. The internal resistance is great. They have to be forced. Remember the Edsel? After eighteen months, the Ford Motor Company announced that it was abandoning the Edsel. I think we all roared with laughter. We had already abandoned the Edsel. The Ford Motor Company just took a hell of a long time to accept it.

> So why is it that so many organizations, even in the United States, have such a high resistance to that process of systematically abandoning their past and building a future?

> One reason is ignorance. People do not know that you cannot successfully innovate in an existing organization unless you systematically abandon. I come from a medical family. My Aunt Trudy was one of the great pediatricians of continental Europe and the first woman physician in Austro-Hungary. She invented neonatal medicine. One evening, when Aunt Trudy was at dinner at our house, the telephone rang. It was some mother calling and she said, "Doctor, my Johnny won't eat." And Aunt Trudy said, "Has he had a bowel movement?" And the mother said, "Yes, doctor, every day." And Aunt Trudy said, "Don't you worry, he'll eat soon enough."

> As long as you eliminate, you'll eat again. But if you stop eliminating, you don't last long.

20.13.6 Groupware Supports Knowledge Creation, the Raw Material of Business Success

Success in business today increasingly results from having the right knowledge in the right place at the right time. If organizations are to be successful, everyone in them must know what to do all the time, even though the marketplace, technology, and competitors are constantly changing the rules of the game. This chaotic situation requires that the best thinking, best intelligence, and best insights be at the disposal of all who need them, when they need them.

☞ To capture the wealth of knowledge in an organization requires that reflecting and capturing insights be valued as highly as "doing" whatever the most visible and heroic work is for that firm.

☞ Creating new knowledge requires making spaces in our work lives for the collaborative invention and discovery process that creates new, actionable insights.

☞ Capturing a corporate memory of the path we have taken to the knowledge we have requires the ability to warehouse that knowledge and make it available quickly and easily to wherever it can create benefit for the organization.

☞ Groupware is the platform we use to build this strategic knowledge management system. This is still emerging technology, but the power of todays PCs, coupled with the Internet and with software like Lotus Notes, is beginning to offer the ability to create seamless, worldwide systems that give the ability to capture and utilize knowledge.

Those companies who learn to manage knowledge best will win, regardless of where in the pack they started, given enough time. Therefore, some form of groupware, carefully designed around the strategic knowledge needs of the business, is becoming essential for most businesses.

REFERENCES

1. Ackoff, Russell L., *Creating the Corporate Future*. John Wiley and Sons, 1981.
2. Argyris, C., *Knowledge for Action*, Jossey-Bass, 1993.
3. Clark, K. B. and Wheelwright, S.C., *Leading Product Development: The Senior Managers Guide to Creating and Shaping the Enterprise*. New York, The Free Press, 1995.
4. Csikszentmhalyi, M., *Flow: The Psychology of Optimal Experience*. New York, Harper-Collins Publishers, 1990.
5. Davis, S. and Botkin, J., *The Monster Under the Bed: How Business is Mastering the Opportunity of Knowledge for Profit*. New York, Simon and Schuster, 1994.
6. Hamel, G. and Prahalad, C.K., *Competing for the Future: Breakthrough Strategies for Seizing Control of Your Industry and Creating the Markets of Tomorrow*. 1993.
7. Imparato, N. and Harari, O., *Jumping the Curve: Innovation and Strategic Choice in an Age of Transition*. San Francisco, Jossey-Bass, 1994.
8. Katzenbach, J. R. and Smith, D.K., *The Wisdom of Teams: Creating the High Performance Organization*. 1993.
9. Leonard-Barton, D., *Wellsprings of Knowledge*. Boston, Harvard Business School Press, 1995.

10. Lipnack, J. and Stamps, J., *The Age of the Network: Organizing Principles for the 21st Century.* 1995.

11. McGill, Michael and John W. Slocum Jr. *The Smarter Organization: How to Build a Business that Learns and Adapts to Marketplace Needs.* John Wiley and Sons. 1994.

12. Nonaka, I. and Takeuchi, H., *The Knowledge-Creating Company: How Japanese Companies Create the Dynamics of Innovation.* London, Oxford University Press. 1995

13. Schrage, M., *No More Teams! Mastering the Dynamics of Creative Collaboration.* 1994.

14. Senge, P.M., *The Fifth Discipline: The Art and Practice of the Learning Organization.* New York, Doubleday, 1990.

15. Senge, P. M., Roberts, C., Ross, R., Smith, B., and Kleiner, A., *The Fifth Discipline Fieldbook.* Currency Doubleday, 1994.

16. Wheatley, M.J., *Leadership and the New Science.* San Francisco: Berrett-Koehler Publishers, Inc., 1992.

Collaborative Resources

THE COLLABORATIVE STRATEGIES BOOKSHELF

Argyris, Chris. *Knowledge for Action: A Guide to Overcoming Barriers to Organizational Change,* Josse-Bass Publishers, San Francisco, 1993.

Argyris, Chris. *Organizational Learning II: Theory, Method, and Practice*, Addison-Wesley, Reading, MA, 1996.

Barrabba, Vincent P. *Meeting of the Minds: Creating the Market-Based Enterprise,* Harvard Business School Press, Boston, 1995.

Beck, Nuala. *Shifting Gears: Thriving in the New Economy*, HarperCollins, 1992.

Becker, Franklin and Fritz Steele. *Workplace by Design: Mapping the High-Performance Workscape,* Jossey-Bass, San Francisco, 1995.

Bleeke, Joel and David Ernst. *Collaborating to Compete: Using Strategic Alliances and Acquisitions in the Global Marketplace,* John Wiley & Sons, Inc., New York, 1993.

Bock, Geoffrey E. and Dave A. Marca. *Designing Groupware,* McGraw-Hill, New York, 1995.

Bostrom, Robert P., Richard T. Watson, and Susan T. Kinney. *Computer Augmented Teamwork: A Guided Tour*, Van Nostrand Reinhold, 1992.

Champy, James. *Reengineering Management: The Mandate for New Leadership,* Harper Business, New York, 1995.

Chawla, Sarita and John Renesch. *Learning Organizations: Developing Cultures for Tomorrow's Workplace,* Productivity Press, Portland, OR, 1995.

Cheryl Currid & Company. *Reengineering ToolKit: 15 Tools and Technologies for Reengineering Your Organization,* Prima Publishing, Rocklin, CA, 1994.

Coleman, David. *Groupware: Technology and Applications,* Prentice Hall, New York, 1995.

Csikszentmihalyi, Mihaly. *Flow: The Psychology of Optimal Experience,* Harper-Perennial, 1990.

Csikszentmihalyi, Mihaly. *The Evolving Self: A Psychology for the Third Millennium,* HarperPerennial, 1993.

Davenport, Thomas. *Process Innovation, Re-engineering Work Through Information Technology,* Harvard Business School Press, Boston, 1993.

Davidow, William H. and Michael S. Malone. *The Virtual Corporation: Structuring and Revitalizing the Corporation of the 21st Century,* Harper Business, New York, 1992.

Davis, Stan and Jim Botkin. *The Monster Under the Bed: How Business Is Mastering the Opportunity of Knowledge for Profit,* Simon & Schuster, New York, 1994.

Dekoven, Bernard. *Connected Executive: A Strategic Communication Plan*, Institute For Better Meetings, Palo Alto, 1990.

Doyle, Michael and David Straus. *How to Make Meetings Work: The New Interaction Method,* Berkeley Books, New York, 1993.

Drucker, Peter F. *Managing for the Future: The 1990s and Beyond*, Truman Talley Books/Dutton, New York, 1992.

Fraase, Michael. *Groupware For the Macintosh: A Complete Guide to Collaborative Computing*, Business One Irwin, Homewood, IL, 1991.

Frame, J. Davidson. *The New Project Management,* Josse-Bass Publishers, San Francisco, 1994.

Frame, J. Davidson. *Managing Projects in Organizations,* Josse-Bass Publishers, San Francisco, 1995.

Galegher, J., R.E. Kraut and C. Egido. *Intellectual Teamwork: Social and Technological Foundations of Cooperative Work*, Lawrence Erlbaum Associates, Hillsdale, NJ, 1990.

Gardner, Howard. *Leading Minds: An Anatomy of Leadership,* Basic Books, New York, 1995.

Goldstein, Jeremy. *Videoconferencing and Money, Money, Money,* Boca Press, Boca Raton, FL, 1995.

Gouillard, Francis J. and James N. Kelly. *Transforming the Organization,* McGraw-Hill, Inc., New York, 1995.

Grantham, Charles E. and Larry D. Nichols. *The Digital Workplace: Designing Groupware Platforms*, Van Nostrand Reinhold, 1993.

Grief, Irene. *Computer-Supported Cooperative Work: A Book of Readings*, Morgan Kaufman Publishers, San Francisco, 1988.

Hamel, Gary and C.K. Prahalad. *Competing for the Future: Breakthrough Strategies for Seizing Control of Your Industry and Crating the Markets of Tomorrow,* Harvard Business School Press, Boston, MA, 1994.

Hammer, Michael and James Champy. *Reengineering the Corporation: A Manifesto for Business Revolution,* HarperBusiness, New York, 1993.

Hammer, Michael and Steven A. Stanton. *The Reengineering Revolution: A Handbook,* HarperBusiness, New York, 1995.

Holtzman, Steven R. *Digital Mantras: The Languages of Abstract and Virtual World,* MIT Press, Cambridge, MA, 1994.

Huczynski, Andrzej. *Management Gurus,* Routledge, London, 1993.

Imparato, Nicholas and Oren Harari. *Jumping the Curve: Innovation and Strategic Choice in an Age of Transition,* Jossey-Bass, San Francisco, 1994.

Jayachandra, Y. *Re-Engineering the Networked Enterprise*, McGraw-Hill, New York, 1994.

Jessup, Leonard M. and Joseph Valacick. *Group Support Systems: New Perspectives,* Macmillan Publishing, U.S.A., 1993.

Johansen, Robert. *Groupware: Computer Support for Business Teams*, Macmillan Publishing, U.S.A., 1988.

Johansen, Robert, David Sibbet, Suzyn Benson, Alexia Martin, Robert Mittman, and Paul Saffo. *Leading Business Teams; How Teams Can Use Technology and Group Process Tools to Enhance Performance*, Addison-Wesley, Reading, MA, 1991.

Johansen, Robert and Mary O'Hara-Devereaux. *GlobalWork*, San Francisco, Jossey-Bass, 1994.

Johansen, Robert and Rob Swigart. *Upsizing the Individual in the Downsized Organization*, Addison-Wesley, Reading, MA, 1994.

Kaner, Sam with Lenny Lind, Catherine Toldi, Sarah Fisk and Duane Berger. *Facilitator's Guide to Participatory Decision-Making*, New Society, Philadelphia, 1996

Kanter, Rosabeth Moss, Barry A. Stein and Todd D. Jick. *The Challenge of Organizational Change: How Companies Experience It and Leaders Guide It*, Free Press, New York, 1992.

Katzenbach, Jon R. and Douglas K. Smith. *The Wisdom of Teams: Creating the High-Performance Organization*, Harvard Business School Press, Boston, MA, 1993.

Kaye, Anthony R. *Collaborative Learning Through Computer Conferencing, The Najaden Papers,* Institute Of Educational Technology, Open University, UK, 1992.

Keen, Peter G.W. *Every Manager's Guide to Information Technology: A Glossary of Key Terms & Concepts for Today's Business Leader*, Harvard Business School Press, Boston, 1995.

Keen, Peter G. W. and J. Michael Cummins. *Networks in Action: Business Choices and Telecommunications Decisions,* Wadsworth Publishing, Belmont, CA, 1994.

Keen, Peter G.W. and Ellen M. Knapp. Process Payoffs: *Building Value Through Business Process Investment,* Harvard Business School Press, Boston, 1995.

Keen, Peter G.W. and Ellen M. Knapp. *Every Manager's Guide to Business Processes: A Glossary of Key Terms & Concepts for Today's Business Leader.* Harvard Business School Press. Boston, 1996.

Keen, Peter G.W. *Shaping the Future: Business Design through Information Technology*, McGraw Hill, New York, 1991.

Kelly, Kevin. *Out of Control: The New Biology of Machines, Social Systems, and the Economic World,* Addison-Wesley, New York, 1994.

Kennedy, Carol. *Instant Managment: The Best Ideas from the People Who Have Made a Difference in How We Manage,* William Morrow and Company, Inc., New York, 1991.

Khoshafian, Setrag and Marek Buckiewicz. *Introduction to Groupware, Workflow, and Workgroup Computing,* John Wiley & Sons, Inc., New York, 1995.

Kostner, Jaclyn. *Knights of the Tele-Round Table,* Warner Books, New York, 1994.

Koulopoulos, Thomas M. *Workflow Imperative: Building Real World Business Solutions,* Van Nostrand Reinhold, New York, 1995.

Laborde, Genie Z. *Influencing with Integrity: Management Skills for Communication & Negotiation,* Syntony Publishing, Mountain View, 1987.

Lipnack, Jessica and Jeffrey Stamps. *The TeamNet Factor: Bringing the Power of Boundary Crossing Into the Heart of Your Business,* Oliver Wight, Wiley, Essex Junction, 1993.

Lipnack, Jessica and Jeffrey Stamps. *The Age of the Network: Organizing Principles for the 21st Century,* Wiley, New York, 1993.

Lloyd, Peter. *Groupware in the 21st Century: Computer Supported Co-operative Working Toward the Millennium,* Adamantine Press Ltd., London, 1994.

Lynch, Dudley and Paul L. Kordis, *Strategy of the Dolphin: Scoring a Win In a Chaotic World,* Fawcett Columbine, New York, 1988.

Mallach, Efrem, G. *Understanding Decision Support Systems and Expert Systems,* Dow/Irwin, 1993.

Marca, David and Geoffrey Bock. *Groupware: Software for Computer Supported Cooperative Work,* IEEE Computer Press, Los Alamitos, CA, 1992.

McGill, Michael and John W. Slocum, Jr. *The Smarter Organization: How to Build a Business that Learns and Adapts to Marketplace Needs,* John Wiley and Sons, New York, 1994.

Mohrman, Susan Albers, Susan G. Cohen and Allan M. Mohrman, Jr. *Designing Team-based Organizations. New Forms for Knowledge Work,* Jossey-Bass, San Francisco, 1995.

Moore, Geoffrey A. *Crossing the Chasm: Marketing and Selling Technology Products to Mainstream Customers,* Harper Business, New York, 1991.

Moore, Geoffrey A. *Inside the Tornado (Marketing Strategies of the Silicon Valley's Cutting Edge),* Harper Business, New York, 1995.

Moore, James F. *The Death of Competition: Leadership & Strategy in the Age of Business Ecosystems,* Harper Business, New York, 1996.

Morris, Langdon. *Managing the Evolving Corporation.* Van Nostrand Reinhold, New York, 1995.

Morton, Michael S. Scott. *The Corporation of the 1990s: Information Technology and Organizational Transformation,* Oxford University Press, New York, 1991.

Nolan, Richard L., David C. Croson. *Creative Destruction: A Six-Stage Process for Transfoming the Organization,* Harvard Business School Press, Boston, 1995.

Nonaka, Ikujiro and Hirotaka Takeuchi. *The Knowledge-Creating Company: How Japanese Companies Create the Dynamics of Innovation,* Oxford University Press, New York, 1995.

Olson, G.M., J.S. Olson, L.A. Mack, P. Cornell, and R. Luchetti. *Computer Augmented Teamwork Flexible Facilities for Electronic Meetings,* Van Nostrand Reinhold, New York, 1993.

Olson, M. H. *Technological Support for Work Group Collaboration,* Lawrence Earlbaum and Associates, Mahweh, 1989.

Opper, Susanna and Henry Fersko-Weiss. *Technology for Teams: Enhancing Productivity in Networked Organizations,* Van Nostrand Reinhold, 1992.

Penzias, Arno. *Harmony: Business, Technology & Life After Paperwork,* HarperBusiness, New York, 1995.

Peters, Tom. *The Tom Peters Seminar: Crazy Times Call for Crazy Organizations,* Vintage Books, New York, 1994.

Peters, Tom. *Liberation Management: Necessary Disorganization for the Nanosecond Nineties,* Fawcett, 1994.

Poirier, Charles and William Houser. *Business Partnering for Continuous Improvement: How to Forge Enduring Alliances Among Employees, Suppliers and Customers,* Berrett-Koehler, 1994.

Popcorn, Faith. *The Porcorn Report: Faith Popcorn on the Future of Your Company, Your World, Your Life,* HarperBusiness, New York 1991.

Prigogine, Ilya and Isabelle Stengers. *Order Out of Chaos: Man's New Dialogue with Nature,* Bantam Books, New York, 1984.

Ray, Michael and Alan Rinzler, Eds. *The New Paradigm in Business: Emerging Strategies for Leadership and Organizational Change,* Putnam Publishing Group, New York, 1994.

Robbins, Harvey and Michael Finley. *Why Teams Don't Work: What Went Wrong and How to Make It Right,* Pace-Setter Books, Princeton, NJ, 1995.

Sakiaya, Taichi. *The Knowledge Value Revolution or a History of the Future,* Kodansha International, New York, 1991.

Salvendy, Gavriel. *Handbook of Human Factors,* Wiley Modules, New York, 1987.

Schrage, Michael. *Shared Minds: The New Technologies of Collaboration,* Random House, New York, 1990.

Schrage, Michael. *No More Teams! Mastering the Dynamics of Creative Collaboration,* Doubleday, New York, 1993.

Schwartz, Peter. *The Art of the Long View: Planning for the Future in an Uncertain World,* Doubleday Currency, New York, 1991.

Semler, Ricardo. *Maverick: The Success Story Behind the World's Most Unusual Workplace,* Warner Books, New York, 1993.

Senge, Peter M. *The Fifth Discipline: The Art & Practice of The Learning,* Currency Doubleday, New York, 1990.

Senge, Peter M. *The Fifth Discipline Fieldbook: Strategies and Tooks for Building a Learning Organization,* Currency Doubleday, New York, 1994.

Shonk, James H. *Team-Based Organizations: Developing a Successful Team Environment,* Irwin Professional Publishing, Burr Ridge, 1992.

Sproull, Lee and Sara Kiesler. *Connections: New Ways of Working in the Networked Organization,* The MIT Press, Cambridge, MA, 1991.

Tapscott, Don and Art Caston. *Paradigm Shift: The New Promise of Information Technology,* McGraw-Hill, New York, 1993.

Tapscott, Don. *The Digital Economy: Promise and Peril in the Age of Networked Intelligence,* McGraw-Hill, New York, 1996.

Taylor, James, C. and David Felton. *Performance by Decision,* Prentice Hall, 1993.

Toffler, Alvin. *PowerShift: Knowledge, Wealth and Violence at the Edge of the 21st Century,* Bantam Books, New York, 1990.

Turban, E. *Decision Support Systems and Expert Systems* (3rd. Ed.), Macmillan, 1993.

Weatherall, Alan and Jay Nunamaker. *Introduction to Electronic Meetings,* Electronic Meetings Services Ltd., Hampshire, England, 1995.

Wellins, Richard S., William C. Byham and Jeanne M. Wilson. *Empowered Teams: Creating Self Directed Work Groups That Improve Quality, Productivity, and Participation,* Jossey-Bass, San Francisco, 1991.

Wheatley, Margaret J. *Leadership and the New Science,* Berrett-Koehler Publishers, Inc., San Francisco, 1994.

White, Thomas and Layna Fischer. *The Workflow Paradigm: The Impact of Information Technology on Business Process Re-engineering,* Future Strategies, Inc., Lighthouse, 1994.

Whyte, David. *The Heart Aroused,* Doubleday, New York, 1994.

Wiig, Karl M. *Knowledge Management Foundations: Thinking About Thinking— How People and Organizations Create, Represent, and Use Knowledge,* Schema Press, Arlington, TX, 1993.

Wiig, Karl M. *Knowledge Management Methods: Practical Approaches to Managing Knowledge,* Schema Press, Arlington, TX, 1995.

Wiig, Karl M. *Knowledge Management: The Central Management Focus for Intelligent-Acting Organizations,* Schema Press, Arlington, TX, 1994.

Wilson, Paul. *Computer Supported Cooperative Work,* Intellect Books, UK, 1991.

Wurman, Richard Saul. *Information Anxiety,* Bantam, New York, 1990.

CONFERENCES, SYMPOSIA AND ACADEMIC PROCEEDINGS

The Annual Conference and Exposition of the Electronic Messaging Association, Conference Proceedings Vols. I, II, and III, 1995.

Baecker and Buxton. *Readings in HCI,* 1987.

BCS-HCI: People and Computers, Cambridge, MA, 1985–1991.

Bierman, Bob. *WorkFlow'95, Business Pricess Re-engineering Conference, Proceedings,* Patricia Seybold Group, 1995.

CHI: Human Factors in Computing Systems, ACM. 1982–1992.

Coleman, David and Collaborative Strategies. *Conference Proceedings, Groupware 93, 94, & 95,* The Conference Group, 1993, 1994, 1995.

Coleman, David and Peter Huckle. *Groupware '94 Europe, Groupware '94 Boston,* The Conference Group, 1994.

Conference & Exposition Project World '95: Proceedings Volume One, A Center for Management Research Program, 1995.

CSCW: Computer-Supported Cooperative Work, ACM, 1990.

Desktop Videoconferencing Conference, Technical Seminar Proceedings, 1995.

Global Networks: Computers and International Communication, MIT Press, 1993.

Guilfoyle, Christine and Ellie Warner. *Intelligent Agents: The New Revolution in Software,* Ovum Limited, 1994.

Janca, Peter C. *Pragmatic Application of Information Agents, A Multi-Client Research Study,* BIS Strategic Decisions, May 1995.

The Knowledge Enterprise: Locating & Tapping into the Intellectual Capital in Your Organization (Two Day Conference), International Quality & Productivity Center, December 1995.

Lockwood, Rose, Mandy Lavery, and Laurent Lachal. *Groupware: Market Strategies,* Ovum Limited, 1993.

Mantei, M., *Capturing the Capture Lab Concepts: A Case Study in the Design Of Computer Supported Meeting Environments,* CSCW, 1988.

Marshak, Ronni. *Workflow '94 and Workflow '95* (Boston and San Jose), The Conference Group, (800) 247-0262, 1994.

Networld Interop '94, General Conferences Notes, 1994.

Martz, W.B., D.A. Chappell, E.E. Roberts, and J.F. Nunamaker. *Designing Integrated Information Facilities to Support Electronic Meetings,* HICSS Proceedings, 1991.

Portway, Patrick S. and Ed D. Lane. *Guide to Teleconferencing & Distance Learning, Second Edition,* Applied Business TeleCommunications, 1994.

Stark, Heather and Laurent Lachal. *Ovum Evaluates Workflow,* Ovum Limited, 1995.

TECHNICAL/TRADE PUBLICATIONS

Business Communications Review, http://www.bcr.com

Byte, www.byte.com

Communications of the ACM, http://www.acm.org/

CommunicationsWeek, http://www.techweb.cmp.com

ComputerWorld, (800)669-1002

Computer: Innovative Technology for Computer Professionals, http://www.computer.org

Connections: Journal of Macintosh Connectivity, info@mactivity.com

Datamation, http://www.datamation.com

DBMS Client-Server Computing, (800) 334-8152

Enterprise Reeengineering, http://www.reengineering.com

Fast Company, loop@fastcompany.com

Forbes, (800) 888-9896

Fortune, Fortune@cis.compuserve.com

Harvard Business Review, (800) 274-3214

Info World, http://www.infoworld.com

InformationWeek, http://www.techweb.cmp.com/iw

Inform, http://www.aiim.org

Internet World, http://www.mecklerweb.com

Knowledge Inc.: The Executive Report onKnowledge, Technology & Performance, http://www.knowledgeinc.com/britton

MacWeek, http://www.zdnet.com/~macweek/

NetGuide, http://www.netguidemag.com

Network World, (508) 875-6400

OpenComputing, http://wcmh.com/oc

PC Computing, http://www.zdnet.com/~pccomp

PC Magazine, http://www.pcmag.com

PC Week, http://www.pcweek.com

PC World, http://www.pcworld.com

Scientific American, info@sciam.com

Software Magazine, softwaremagazine@mcimail.com

Upside, http://www.upside.com

Wired, http://www.hotwired.com

World-Wide Web Week, http://www.mecklerweb.com

CONFERENCES

Comdex
Contact: (617) 449-5554
URL: www.comdex.com

ComNet Conference & Expo
Contact (800) 545-EXPO
URL: www.mha.com\comnet\

Data Warehousing & DSS/EIS Conference
Contact: (800) 874-9980

Desktop Videoconferencing Conference
Contact: (800) 227-1234
URL: www.bcr.com

DCI Data Warehousing
Contact: (508) 470-3880
URL: www.dciexpo.com

DCI's Internet Expo
Contact: (508) 470-3870
URL: www.dciexpo.com

Documation '97 Expo and Conference
Contact: 617 837-7200

Electronic Commerce Technologies Conference
Contact: (800) 888 5121

Electronic Commerce World
(800) 248-2317

EMA Solutions Summit: Mesaging and Intranet ntegration
(703) 524-5550

E-MAIL World/WEB World
Contact: (508) 470-3880
URL: www.dciexpo.com

Empower 96
Contact: (800) 575-3367

Field & Sales Force Automation Conference
Contact: (508) 470-3880
URL: www.dciexpo.com

HRMS/Expo '96
Contact: (800) 232-3976

Information Managment: The Next Generation
Contact: (312) 787-2200

Internet Expo/E-mail World/Web World
Contact: (800) 324-3976

Internet Commerce Expo
Contact (800) 667-4423

Managing Internet/intranet Issues
Contact (508) 470-0526

National Business Process Reengineering Conference & Expo 1996
Washington, DC
Contact: (703) 761-0646

Networld + Interop DotCom
Contact: (800) 488-2883
URL: interop.com

Object World
Contact: (800) 241-4600

PC Expo
Contact: (800) 829-3976
URL: www.shownet.com

Project World
Contact: (888) 943-4444

TPM: Total Productive Maintenance
Contact: (800) 966-5423

Windows Solutions: NT Intranet
Contact: (800) 488-2883
URL: www.sbexpos.com/sbexpos/windows_solutions

Workflow: Joining the Islands of Automation
Contact (617) 247-1025
URL: www.delphigroup.com

Unix Expo '96
Contact (800) 829-EXPO
URL: www.shownet.com